American Foreign Relations

VOLUME 1

A History • to 1920

SEVENTH EDITION

Thomas G. Paterson

J. Garry Clifford

Shane J. Maddock

Deborah Kisatsky

Kenneth J. Hagan

D0166061

WADSWORTH
CENGAGE Learning™

Australia • Brazil • Japan • Korea • Mexico • Singapore • Spain • United Kingdom • United States

WADSWORTH
CENGAGE Learning™

**American Foreign Relations, Volume 1:
A History • to 1920, Seventh Edition**
Thomas G. Paterson, J. Garry Clifford,
Shane J. Maddock, Deborah Kisatsky,
Kenneth J. Hagan

Editor in Chief: PJ Boardman
Senior Publisher: Suzanne Jeans
Sponsoring Acquisitions Editor: Ann West
Development Manager: Jeffrey Greene
Assistant Editor: Megan Curry
Editorial Assistant: Megan Chrisman
Senior Media Editor: Lisa Ciccolo
Senior Marketing Manager: Katherine
    Bates
Marketing Coordinator: Lorreen Pelletier
Marketing Communications Manager:
    Christine Dobberpuhl
Senior Managing Editor: Kathy Brown
Senior Content Project Manager:
    Aileen Mason
Senior Art Director: Cate Rickard Barr
Print Buyer: Linda Hsu
Senior Rights Acquisition Account
    Manager: Katie Huha
Text Researcher: Terri Hampton
Production Service: S4Carlisle Publishing
    Services
Senior Photo Editor: Jennifer Meyer Dare
Photo Researcher: Pembroke Herbert
Cover Designer: Faith Brosnan
Cover Image: United States Naval
    Academy Museum, Annapolis, MD
Compositor: S4Carlisle Publishing Services

For product information and technology assistance, contact us at
Cengage Learning Customer & Sales Support, 1-800-354-9706

For permission to use material from this text or product, submit all requests online at **www.cengage.com/permissions.** Further permissions questions can be emailed to **permissionrequest@cengage.com.**

Library of Congress Control Number: 2009922145
ISBN-13: 978-0-547-22564-7
ISBN-10: 0-547-22564-4

Wadsworth
20 Channel Center Street
Boston, MA 02210
USA

Cengage Learning products are represented in Canada by Nelson Education, Ltd.

For your course and learning solutions, visit
www.cengage.com.
Purchase any of our products at your local college store or at our preferred online store **www.ichapters.com.**

Printed in Canada
1 2 3 4 5 6 7 13 12 11 10 09

for

Suzanne Monchamp Paterson

Thomas Paterson, Jr.

Carol Davidge

Vera Low Hagan

Emily Rose Maddock

Benjamin Quinn Maddock

About the Authors

Thomas G. Paterson, professor emeritus of history at the University of Connecticut, graduated from the University of New Hampshire (B.A., 1963) and the University of California, Berkeley (Ph.D., 1968). He has written *Soviet-American Confrontation* (1973), *Meeting the Communist Threat* (1988), *On Every Front* (1992), *Contesting Castro* (1994), *America Ascendant* (with J. Garry Clifford, 1995), and *A People and a Nation* (with Mary Beth Norton et al., 2001). Tom has also edited *Cold War Critics* (1971), *Kennedy's Quest for Victory* (1989), *Imperial Surge* (with Stephen G. Rabe, 1992), *The Origins of the Cold War* (with Robert McMahon, 1999), *Explaining the History of American Foreign Relations* (with Michael J. Hogan, 2004), and *Major Problems in American Foreign Relations* (with Dennis Merrill, 2010). With Bruce Jentleson, he served as senior editor for the *Encyclopedia of American Foreign Relations* (1997). A microfilm edition of *The United States and Castro's Cuba, 1950s–1970s: The Paterson Collection* appeared in 1999. He has served on the editorial boards of the *Journal of American History* and *Diplomatic History.* Recipient of a Guggenheim fellowship, he has directed National Endowment for the Humanities Summer Seminars for College Teachers. In 2000 the New England History Teachers Association recognized his excellence in teaching and mentoring with the Kidger Award. Besides visits to many American campuses, Tom has lectured in Canada, China, Colombia, Cuba, New Zealand, Puerto Rico, Russia, and Venezuela. He is a past president of the Society for Historians of American Foreign Relations, which in 2008 honored him with the Laura and Norman Graebner Award for "lifetime achievement" in scholarship, service, and teaching. A native of Oregon, Tom is now informally associated with Southern Oregon University.

J. Garry Clifford teaches at the University of Connecticut, where he is a professor of political science and director of its graduate program. Born in Massachusetts, he earned his B.A. from Williams College (1964) and his Ph.D. in history from Indiana University (1969). He has also taught at the University of Tennessee and Dartmouth College and has participated in two National Endowment for the Humanities seminars for high school teachers at the Franklin D. Roosevelt Library. For his book *The Citizen Soldiers* (1972), he won the Frederick Jackson Turner Award of the Organization of American Historians. With Norman Cousins, he has edited *Memoirs of a Man: Grenville Clark* (1975), and with Samuel R. Spencer, Jr., he has written *The First Peacetime Draft* (1986). He also co-authored *America Ascendant* (with Thomas G. Paterson) in 1995. With Theodore A. Wilson, he edited and contributed to *Presidents, Diplomats, and Other Mortals: Essays in Honor of Robert H. Ferrell* (2007). Garry's chapters have appeared in Gordon Martel, ed., *American Foreign Relations Reconsidered* (1994), Michael J. Hogan and Thomas G. Paterson, eds., *Explaining the History of American Foreign Relations* (1991 and 2004), Arnold A. Offner and Theodore A. Wilson, eds., *Victory in Europe, 1945* (2000), and in the *Journal of American History, Review of Politics, Mid-America, American Neptune,* and *Diplomatic History.* Garry has served on the editorial board of *Diplomatic History* as well as on the editorial board of the Modern War Series of the University Press of Kansas. He is currently writing a book on FDR and American intervention in World War II.

Shane J. Maddock is professor of history at Stonehill College in Easton, Massachusetts, where he also serves on the faculty of the Martin Institute for Law and Society. Born in North Dakota, he earned his B.A. from Michigan State University (1989) and his Ph.D. from the University of Connecticut (1997). He also taught at the U.S. Coast Guard Academy. Shane edited *The Nuclear Age* (2001) and contributed a chapter to G. Kurt Piehler and Rosemary Mariner, eds., *The Atomic Bomb and American Society* (2008). He has also published in the *Journal of American History, International History Review, Pacific Historical Review, New England Journal of History, Presidential Studies Quarterly, Mid-America, Journal of Military History, American Jewish History, Canadian Journal of Latin American and Caribbean Studies, History in Dispute,* and *The Encyclopedia of U.S. Foreign Relations.* He received fellowships from the Institute for the Study of World Politics, the U.S. Arms Control and Disarmament Agency, and the Hoover, Truman, Eisenhower, Kennedy, and Johnson presidential libraries. His book, *Nuclear Apartheid: The American Quest for Atomic Supremacy* will be published by University of North Carolina Press.

Deborah Kisatsky is associate professor of history at Assumption College in Worcester, Massachusetts. Born in Pennsylvania, she earned her B.A. (1990) and her Ph.D. (2001) from the University of Connecticut. Deborah published *The United States and the European Right, 1945–1955* with Ohio State University Press in 2005. She has published as well in *The American Historical Review, Intelligence and National Security, The Historian, Presidential Studies Quarterly, The Journal of Interdisciplinary History,* and the *Encyclopedia of U.S. Foreign Relations.* Deborah has received fellowships from the Alexander von Humboldt Foundation, the Center for European Integration Studies (University of Bonn), the Society for Historians of American Foreign Relations, the Franklin D. Roosevelt Library, and the Harry S. Truman Institute. She is currently writing a book about the life, thought, and transnational legacy of the nineteenth-century communitarian and social radical Adin Ballou.

Kenneth J. Hagan is a professor of strategy and policy at the U.S. Naval War College, Monterey Program, and professor of history and museum director emeritus at the U.S. Naval Academy, Annapolis. He previously taught at Claremont McKenna College, Kansas State University, and as an adjunct at the U.S. Army Command and General Staff College. A native of California, he received his A.B. and M.A. from the University of California, Berkeley (1958, 1964) and his Ph.D. from the Claremont Graduate University (1970). Ken is the author of *This People's Navy: The Making of American Sea Power* (1991), a comprehensive history of American naval strategy and policy since the Revolution, and *American Gunboat Diplomacy and the Old Navy, 1877–1889* (1973), and co-author with Ian J. Bickerton of *Unintended Consequences: The United States at War* (2007), a critical reassessment of ten American wars from the Revolution to Iraq. His scholarship also includes two edited collections of original essays: *In Peace and War: Interpretations of American Naval History, 30th Anniversary Edition* (2008) and, with William Roberts, *Against All Enemies: Interpretations of American Military History from Colonial Times to the Present* (1986). He has lectured on the history of U.S. naval strategy at the Canadian Forces College, the Defence Academy of the United Kingdom, and the U.S. National War College. Ken has given papers on naval and diplomatic history at professional meetings in Sweden, Greece, Turkey, France, Spain, and the United Kingdom. In 2006 and 2007 he spoke on naval history at conferences hosted by the Royal Australian Navy in Sydney and Canberra. In 2007 and 2008 he discussed the unintended consequences of war at Oxford University and at Strathclyde University in Glasgow, Scotland. For thirty years he has advised the Naval ROTC college program on its naval history course. He currently is writing a biography of Admiral William S. Sims, who served as President Theodore Roosevelt's naval aide and as the commander of U.S. naval forces in Europe in World War I. A retired captain in the naval reserve, Ken served on active duty with the Pacific Fleet from 1958 to 1963.

Contents

Maps and Graphs

Preface

Much has happened to challenge and to redirect American foreign relations since the sixth edition of this text appeared in 2005. A seemingly endless war in Iraq and Afghanistan; continued confrontations with putative nuclear threats from so-called "rogue" states and terrorist networks; fluctuating relations with former Cold War adversaries China and Russia; a possible new relationship with Cuba after Fidel Castro; complaints from allies about Washington's unilateral behavior as a "hyperpower"; ongoing debates about "globalization" and its myriad effects; increased alarm over fast-spreading deadly diseases, global warming, and environmental decline; controversial new definitions of national security and "homeland defense" that include preemptive war as well as "rendition" and torture of prisoners; anguished questioning as to why our enemies "hate" us; a financial meltdown and economic recession of international proportions; and the election and inauguration of a new president promising to rectify the mistakes of his predecessor—all have riveted attention on America's global travails and how they came to be. These urgent contemporary developments, along with new scholarship and encouraging comments from instructors and students, have again prompted us to revise *American Foreign Relations*. As before, in this seventh edition we engage current perspectives on the United State's engagement with the world. We seek to explain foreign relations in the broadest manner as the many ways that peoples, organizations, states, and systems interact—economic, cultural, strategic, environmental, political, and more.

We continue to emphasize the theme of expansionism, exploring its myriad manifestations. We also show that on almost every issue in the history of American foreign relations, alternative voices unfailingly sounded among and against official policymakers. Americans have always debated their place in the world, their wars, their overseas commitments, and the status of their principles and power, and they have always debated the people of other nations about the spread of U.S. influence. We try to capture with vivid description and quotation the drama of these many debates.

A historical overview such as this one necessarily draws on the copious work of scholars in the United States and abroad. Their expertise informs this book and lends it the authority that instructors and students have come to expect. Our "Further Reading" and "Endnotes" sections provide one way to thank them for their books, articles, and conference papers. We have also appreciated their recommendations for text revisions and their suggestions for teaching the courses for which this book is intended. We thank them, too, for challenging us to consider the many different approaches and theories that have commanded attention in this field, including world systems, corporatism, dependency, culture, ideology, psychology and personality, medical biography, lessons from the past, bureaucratic politics, public opinion, executive-legislative competition, race, gender, national security and power, and the natural environment. This book also presents the findings of our own ongoing archival research and writing as we continually discover the past.

The subjects of diplomacy, war, economic intercourse, and politics remain central to our presentation of the foreign-relations story. We have made this edition more comprehensive by further extending our discussion of the cultural dimensions of foreign relations: how race-based and gendered thinking conditions the decision-making environment; how media and film reflect cultural myths and capture public perceptions of international events; how American mass culture (such as rock and roll and sports) proliferates world-wide with its innumerable effects; the relationship between travel, tourism, and expansionism; and the ways in which "public diplomacy"—the presentation of a positive image of the United States through media propaganda—reflects official U.S. efforts to employ culture in service to American foreign policy.

We have also increased our coverage of the self-conscious expansion of American "empire" from its westward displacement of Native Americans in the eighteenth and nineteenth centuries to its overseas incarnations in the twentieth and twenty-first centuries. We add new details about "makers" of American foreign relations from presidents such as John Adams, Theodore Roosevelt, and George W. Bush to diplomats such as Nicholas Trist, Sumner Welles, and Condoleeza Rice. We take note, for example, of recent scholarship that shows how the "iconography" of empire after the Spanish-American-Cuban-Filipino War of 1898 often depicted opponents of empire in gendered terms—as carping old "aunties" (a pun on "anti-imperialists") dressed in skirts and bonnets—in sharp contrast to a virile Uncle Sam who willingly took up the burdens of empire.

Amid such recent catastrophes as Hurricane Katrina, tsunamis in the Indian Ocean, earthquakes in China, and typhoons in Myanmar, we pay greater attention to issues that spring from human interaction with the natural environment and the international conferences convened to deal with damage to the environment. American relations with Middle East countries before and after World War II receive more coverage, as do linkages between the civil rights movement and American relations with the Third World in the 1940s through the 1960s. Recent scholarship prompted by such anniversaries as the Louisiana Purchase and Lewis and Clark Expeditions, the Spanish-American-Cuban-Filipino War, the cruise of the Great White Fleet, Korean War, the Cuban Missile Crisis, and the Vietnam War, among others, have brought fresh insights to these important events.

Equally important, with the Cold War International History Project providing scholars with a treasure trove of declassified documents from foreign archives (Russian, East German, Cuban, and Chinese among them), we have enriched our treatment of Joseph Stalin's goals and tactics during and after World War II, the origins of the Korean War, Nixon's opening to China in 1972, Cuban policy toward Africa, the Soviet invasion of Afghanistan, the failure of détente in the 1970s, and the end of the Cold War in 1989–1991. Similarly, recently declassified U.S. government documents made available via "electronic briefing books" from the National Security Archive have added nuance to our coverage, for example, of the attempted Hungarian Revolution (1956), U.S. reactions to secret contacts between North and South Vietnam in 1963, the India-Pakistan War of 1971, and the Indonesian invasion of East Timor in 1976, as well as new evidence regarding Washington's Cold War initiatives toward the Soviet Union, the People's Republic of China, and Castro's Cuba. The declassification, duplication, and public release of presidential audio tapes from the Kennedy, Johnson, and Nixon years help to recapture those leaders' colorful language and reveal how the assumptions, styles, and emotions of presidents have influenced decision-making. We have reorganized the final three chapters of Volume II, reflective of an emerging consensus that the terrorist attacks of September 11, 2001, commenced a new era in U.S. foreign relations history. Chapter 10 now covers the period 1969–1981, while Chapter 11 runs from 1981 to 2001. Our final chapter concentrates on events from 2001 to the present and includes expanded treatment of the Iraq War and U.S. policies toward Iran, North Korea, and Afghanistan.

In preparing this edition, we once again immersed ourselves in the memoirs, diaries, letters, speeches, recorded tapes, and oral histories of U.S. and international leaders. We often let them speak for themselves in the frankest terms, guarded and unguarded. We have sought to capture their anger and their humor, their coopera-tion and their competitiveness, their truths and their lies, their moments of doubt and times of confidence, their triumphs and setbacks. *American Foreign Relations,* in short, strives to capture the erratic pulse of international relations through peoples' struggles to plan, decide, and administer. We study not only the lead-ers who made influential decisions, but also the world's peoples who welcomed, resisted, or endured the decisions that profoundly influenced their lives. In this regard, we have drawn on the growing scholarship that studies non-state actors, including peace groups, African Americans, and international bodies such as the World Health Organization.

Each chapter opens with a significant and dramatic event—a "Diplomatic Crossroad"—that helps illustrate the chief characteristics and issues of the era. The introductory and concluding sections of each chapter set the themes. Illustrations— several of them new to this edition—from collections around the world, are closely tied to the narrative in image and caption description. Also in this seventh edition, to generate student debate, we have added a new feature called "What If" to every chapter. We intend these speculative counterfactual essays to spark the reader's imagination as to what might have happened had leaders made different decisions or if conditions or events had turned out differently. What consequences might have followed had the British recognized the Confederacy during the Civil War? What if the United States had joined the League of Nations in 1919–1920? What if John F. Kennedy had lived to make the key decisions on Vietnam after 1963? What if Bill Clinton had succeeded in capturing or killing Osama Bin Laden? We make no claim to definitive scholarly answers in these mini-essays. We hope, however, to excite appreciation for the counterfactual reasoning implicit in all historical writing and to stimulate discussion of many contingencies that together comprise the history of American foreign relations.

The maps, graphs, and "Makers of American Foreign Relations" tables in each chapter provide essential information. The updated chapter bibliographies guide further reading and serve as a starting point for term or research papers. The "General Bibliography" at the end of the book is also a place to begin research or seek more information. The "General Bibliography" consists of three parts: first, general reference works, such as biographical dictionaries, atlases, statistics, encyclopedias, and bibliographies; second, overviews of U.S. relations with countries and regions, from Afghanistan to Zimbabwe; and, third, overviews of subjects, such as Air Force and air power, CIA and covert action, Congress, cultural relations, ethnic conflict, human rights, isolationism, Manifest Destiny, Monroe Doctrine, oil, refugees, slave trade and slavery, terrorism, and United Nations.

In the late 1970s, the People's Republic of China adopted a new system for rendering Chinese phonetic characters into the Roman alphabet. Called the Pinyin method, it replaced the Wade-Giles technique, which had long been used in English. Use of the Pinyin method is now common, and we use it in *American Foreign Relations.* Many changes are minor—Shantung has become Shandong and Mao Tse-tung has become Mao Zedong, for example. But when we have a possibly confusing Pinyin spelling, we have placed the Wade-Giles spelling in parentheses—for example, Beijing (Peking) or Jiang Jieshi (Chiang Kai-shek).

Instructors and students interested in the study of foreign-relations history are invited to join the Society for Historians of American Foreign Relations (SHAFR). This organization publishes a superb journal, *Diplomatic History,* and a newsletter; offers book, article, and lecture prizes and dissertation research grants; and holds an annual conference where scholars present their views and research results. For information, contact the SHAFR Business Office, Department of History, Ohio State University, 106 Dulles Hall, 230 West 17th Avenue, Columbus, OH 43210, or email to shafr@osu.edu.

Another informative web site is H-Diplo: Diplomatic History, found at www.h-net.org/~diplo/. Besides presenting provocative online discussions on foreign-relations history, including "Round Table" reviews of important recent books, this site also provides research and bibliographic aids and an extensive list of links to other useful resources, including journals, newspapers, archives and presidential libraries, research organizations such as the National Security Archive, and government agencies such as the Central Intelligence Agency and Department of State. Readers should also note our citations to relatively new scholarly journals in foreign relations history—*Cold War History, Journal of Cold War Studies, Diplomacy & Statecraft, International History Review, Intelligence and National Security, Journal of the Gilded Age and Progressive Era, Journal of Military History,* among others. Such journals often publish fresh perspectives from younger scholars before they appear in book form.

Many colleagues, friends, students, and editors contributed to this edition of *American Foreign Relations* by providing research leads, correction of errors, reviews of the text, library searches, documents and essays, and editorial assistance. We give our heartiest thanks to Ian Bickerton, Mark Boyer, David Brown, Frank Costigliola, Carol Davidge, Robert H. Ferrell, Irwin Gellman, Robert E. Hannigan, Christine Luberto, Marc O'Reilly, Heather Perry and other members of the interlibrary loan staff of Stonehill College's MacPháiden Library, Jeremy Pressman, Larry Spongberg and Janice Wilbur of Assumption College's d'Alzon

Library, Jennifer Sterling-Folker, Mark Stoler, and Hal Wert. We also thank the following reviewers, who gave many helpful comments and suggestions for this new edition: David Fogelsong, Rutgers University; Max Friedman, American University; Barbara Keys, California State University – Sacramento; and Lorraine Lees, Old Dominion University. Wadworth/Cengage Learning's talented team merits the highest of praise: Jeff Greene, Leslie Kauffman, and Aileen Mason. Ken Hagan generously shared naval illustrations from his latest edition of *In Peace and War* (2008).

We are also eager to thank the many people who helped us in previous editions: Philip J. Avillo, Jr., Richard Baker, Ann Balcolm, Michael A. Barnhart, Robert Beisner, Michael Butler, R. Christian Berg, Kenneth J. Blume, Linda Blundell, Richard Bradford, Kinley J. Brauer, John Burns, Richard Dean Burns, Robert Buzzanco, Charles Conrad Campbell, Chen Jian, John Coogan, Alejandro Corbacho, Frank Costigliola, Carol Davidge, Mark Del Vecchio, Ralph Di Carpio, Justus Doenecke, Michael Donaghue, Xavier Franco, Frances Gay, Paul Goodwin, James Gormly, Eric Hafter, Hope M. Harrison, Alan Henrikson, Gregg Herken, George Herring, Ted Hitchcock, Joan Hoff, Kristin Hoganson, Reginald Horsman, Michael Hunt, Edythe Izard, Holly Izard, Richard Izard, Leith Johnson, Mary Kanable, Burton Kaufman, Melville T. Kennedy, Jr., Thomas Lairson, Lester Langley, Jane Lee, Thomas M. Leonard, Li Yan, Terrence J. Lindell, Florencia Luengo, Paul Manning, Martha McCoy, David McFadden, Charles McGraw, Elizabeth McKillen, Matt McMahon, Robert McMahon, James T. McMaster, Elizabeth Mahan, Herman Mast, Dennis Merrill, Jean-Donald Miller, William Mood, Jay Mullen, Carl Murdock, Brian Murphy, R. Kent Newmyer, Arnold Offner, John Offner, Marc O'Reilly, Chester Pach, Jerry Padula, Carol Petillo, David Pletcher, Salvadore Prisco, Stephen G. Rabe, Carol S. Repass, Wayne Repeta, Barney J. Rickman III, Michael Roskin, John Rourke, Evan Sarantakes, Kenneth E. Shewmaker, Kent M. Schofield, David Sheinin, Anna Lou Smethurst, Elbert B. Smith, Kevin Smith, Thomas G. Smith, Kenneth R. Stevens, Mark A. Stoler, William W. Stueck, Jr., Duane Tananbaum, Chris Thornton, George Turner, Jonathan G. Utley, Thomas Walker, Wang Li, Kathryn Weathersby, Ralph E. Weber, Edmund S. Wehrle, Immanuel Wexler, Lawrence Wittner, Sol Woolman, Jean Woy, Sherry Zane, and Thomas Zoumaras.

We welcome comments and suggestions from students and instructors.

T. G. P.
J. G. C.
S. J. M.
D. K.
K. J. H.

CHAPTER 1

Embryo of Empire: Americans and the World Before 1789

Treaty of Paris, 1783. *This famous painting by the artist Benjamin West (1738–1820) of the treaty that ended the American Revolutionary War was never completed because the British peace commissioners refused to pose. From left to right are the American commissioners John Jay, John Adams, Benjamin Franklin, Henry Laurens, and William Temple Franklin (Franklin's grandson and secretary). (Library of Congress)*

❖ *Jay, Franklin, Adams, and Negotiations for Independence, 1782*

TWO DISGRUNTLED AMERICANS rode the same carriage from Versailles on the afternoon of August 10, 1782. John Jay and Benjamin Franklin had just spent two frustrating hours with the French foreign minister, the Comte de Vergennes. These American peace commissioners, seeking to end the Revolutionary War waged since 1775, had asked for advice on two problems in their negotiations with British and Spanish representatives. Because the Continental Congress had instructed them to make no decisions without the "knowledge and concurrence" of the French, Jay and Franklin had asked Vergennes whether the United States should insist on explicit recognition of independence from England *prior* to a final peace treaty and whether the western boundary of the new American nation should be the Mississippi River.[1] On both points Vergennes seemed to deny American aspirations. Do not worry about technicalities, Vergennes advised. If the British granted independence in the final treaty, as they were proposing, Americans should not fuss about formal titles during the negotiations. On the western boundary, according to Jay, Vergennes hinted that "we [Americans] claimed more than we had a right to," and that Spain and England had valid claims to territory east of the Mississippi.[2]

Jay and Franklin wondered why their French ally seemed so pessimistic. Jay suspected that Vergennes was plotting to delay negotiations with England so that Spain, having captured West Florida, could acquire the whole Gulf Coast and additional territory to the north. Franklin agreed that Spain wanted to "coop us up within the Allegheny Mountains," but he did not think that the French were conniving with the Spanish at American expense.[3]

Franklin invited Jay inside his apartment to continue their increasingly animated discussion. "Have we any reason to doubt the good faith of the King of France?" inquired Franklin. "We can depend on the French," Jay rejoined, "only to see that we are separated from England, but it is not in their interest that we should become a great and formidable people, and therefore they will not help us to become so." Franklin asked on whom the United States should rely. "We have no rational dependence except on God and ourselves," Jay solemnly answered. The Pennsylvanian shot back: "Would you deliberately break Congress's instructions [on not negotiating separately]?" "Unless we violate these instructions the dignity of Congress will be in the dust," Jay asserted. The septuagenarian Franklin pressed further: "Then you are prepared to break our instructions if you intend to take an independence course now." Jay stood up. "*If* the instructions conflict with America's honor and dignity I would break them—like this!" The prideful New Yorker threw his clay pipe hard into Franklin's fireplace. The pipe shattered.[4]

Nothing that occurred during the next several weeks elevated John Jay's opinion of the French and Spanish. In early September, Vergennes's secretary offered Jay his "personal ideas" for expediting peace negotiations with England and a boundary settlement with Spain. Again the Frenchman cautioned not to press for the Mississippi. When that same official suddenly left on a secret mission to London, Jay immediately became suspicious. Even the usually unflappable Franklin fretted. Perhaps the French would bring the same arguments to the British that they were making to the Americans; perhaps France supported British claims north of the Ohio River and wanted Spain to have full control over the Mississippi.

Jay had seen enough. On September 11, without first informing Franklin, Jay boldly sent his own secret emissary to London with the proposal that secret and separate negotiations for peace begin at once. The British jumped at the chance to split the Franco-American alliance. When he learned what his younger colleague had done, Franklin protested. But he went along.

By late October, when the third American peace commissioner, John Adams, arrived in Paris, private talks with the British had been going on for several weeks. Adams had just successfully negotiated a commercial treaty with the Dutch. As a diplomat in Paris earlier in the war, he had come to distrust both the French and Franklin, whom he considered an "old conjurer" who seemed too cozy with Vergennes.[5] The "passionate, candid, and disputatious" New Englander immediately found a kindred spirit in Jay, who confided that the French were "endeavoring to deprive Us of the Fishery, the Western Lands, and the Navigation of the Mississippi."[6] Like Jay, Adams thought that Vergennes opposed American expansion and kept "his hand under our chin to prevent us from drowning, but not to lift our heads out of the water."[7] On meeting Franklin, Adams immediately launched into a lecture. Everything Jay had done was correct. Jay was right in his suspicions toward Vergennes. Jay was right to insist on prior independence, access to the fisheries, and extensive western boundaries. Adams praised the decision to negotiate separately with the British on these issues. To do otherwise would be leaving "the lamb to the custody of the wolf."[8]

Franklin hardly acknowledged Adams's outburst. Suffering from gout, the old philosopher listened patiently and tolerantly to the person he later described as "always an honest man, often a wise one, but sometimes, and in some things, absolutely out of his senses."[9] Franklin agreed that the United States should remain firm on both the fisheries and the Mississippi boundary. Access to the Newfoundland fishing grounds was vital to New England's economy, while the Mississippi stood as an indispensable highway for trans-Allegheny commerce; "a Neighbor might as well ask me to sell my Street Door," he said.[10] What bothered Franklin most was the failure to consult Vergennes. French loans had kept America solvent through six long years of war, and French ships and troops had contributed mightily to the decisive victory at Yorktown in 1781. If America, after taking "a French instead of an English husband … [were] to cuckold him very soon," Franklin explained, then "America could never place herself among the venerable matrons, the other republics, without blushing, as an adulteress and vile prostitute."[11] Unlike his younger colleagues, Franklin did not believe that the French were dealing with Spain and England behind American backs. Franklin nonetheless recognized the importance of a united American front in negotiations. Just prior to meeting with the British commissioners, he startled Jay: "I am of your opinion, and will go with these gentlemen in the business without consulting this [French] court."[12]

John Adams (1735–1826). Native of Braintree (Quincy), Massachusetts, graduate of Harvard, Boston lawyer, colonial rebel, and diplomat. Benjamin Franklin summarized their different attitudes toward France in 1782: Adams "thinks … that America has been too free in Expressions of Gratitude toward France; for that she is more obliged to us than we to her, and that we should shew Spirit in our Applications." Franklin believed that "an Expression of Gratitude is not only our Duty but our Interest." When Vergennes later toasted Adams as "the Washington of the Negotiation," the vain Bostonian exulted in his diary: "This is the finishing Stroke … It is impossible to exceed this." (Library of Congress)

"Blessed Are the Peacemakers." In this critical British cartoon of 1783, a Spaniard and a Frenchman lead George III by the neck while Lord Shelburne carries the "Preliminaries of Peace." The procession is commanded by an American wielding a whip and tugging a sulking, boorish Dutchman. (Library of Congress)

Franklin kept his word, and on November 30, 1782, England and the United States signed a "preliminary treaty" of peace. The terms, enumerated in a comprehensive treaty some ten months later, guaranteed American independence and provided generous boundaries. The historian Samuel Flagg Bemis has called the accord "the greatest victory in the annals of American diplomacy."[13]

The American decision to negotiate separately in 1782 was both symbolic and successful. By going to war with England, the colonies had sought to win their independence, enlarge their commerce, and expand their territorial domain. Patriot leaders hoped to attain these goals without getting entangled in European politics. One motive for independence was the desire to escape the constant wars and dynastic intrigues that characterized eighteenth-century Europe. But victory required help. France became America's ally in 1778, and within two years Spain and the Netherlands also entered the fray, transforming America's war for independence into a world war. The entanglements Americans hoped to avoid inexorably followed. At the critical point in the peace negotiations, Jay and Adams rightly suspected that their French ally, although committed to American independence, did not share the expansive American vision of that independence. The two commissioners thereupon persuaded Franklin to pursue an *independent* course, take advantage of European rivalries, and extract a generous treaty from the British. In Adams's eyes especially, American honor could best be maintained by breaking instructions that French diplomats had forced on a pliant Congress. It was an ironic moment. Americans said they pursued independence and empire not merely for selfish motives, but to effect a more civilized mode of international relations, free from the monarchical double-dealing of European power politics. "Let Us above all things avoid as much as possible Entangling ourselves with their Wars or Politicks," wrote Adams in 1780. "America has been the Sport of European Wars and Politicks long enough."[14] To gain their lofty ends, however, Franklin, Jay, and Adams employed the same Machiavellian tactics that they so despised in Europeans.

Reaching for Independence: Ideology and Commercial Power

The United States could not have won independence from England without assistance from France. Such was the inescapable fact of early American foreign relations. However much the patriots of 1776 wanted to isolate themselves from the wars and diplomatic maneuverings of Europe, European events—indeed, global trends—provided the opportunity for national liberation and the prospect of future entanglement.

From the beginnings of British settlement in the early 1600s, as the historian Michael H. Hunt has written, American colonies were a product "of forces at play in the North Atlantic world," sharing "in the wealth and ambition that increasingly defined that world and that separated European peoples from others." With European empires "mastering other regions, controlling the international economy, maintaining military [and technological] superiority," Americans sought to inherit the "mantle borne earlier by Portugal, Spain, the Netherlands, France, and England."[15] The century-old Franco-British rivalry for preeminence in Europe and North America provided the immediate backdrop for the American Revolution. Four wars fought between 1689 and 1763 originated in Europe but spread to the New World. The most recent war, called the Seven Years' War in Europe (1756–1763) and the French and Indian War in America (1754–1763), had virtually eliminated French power from North America. By the Treaty of Paris (1763) the defeated French ceded Canada and the Ohio Valley to the British and relinquished Louisiana to Spain, which in turn gave up the Floridas to England.

Most colonial leaders cheered Britain's victorious war for empire. The Reverend Jonathan Mayhew of Boston envisaged the colonies as "*a mighty empire …* mighty cities rising on every hill, and by the side of every commodious port, mighty fleets … laden with the produce of … every other country under heaven; happy fields and villages … through a vastly extended territory."[16] Benjamin Franklin, then a colonial agent in England, had urged removal of France from Canada. "The future grandeur and stability of the British empire lay in America," he wrote in 1760. "All the country from the St. Lawrence to the Mississippi will be in another century filled with British people."[17] With America's population doubling every twenty-five years, Franklin calculated that "the greatest Number of Englishmen will [soon] be on this side [of] the Water."[18] According to the historian Gordon H. Wood, "this demographic explosion, this gigantic movement of people, was the most basic and the most liberating force working on American society during the latter half of the eighteenth century."[19]

As soon as the Seven Years' War ended, however, London tightened the machinery of empire. A standing army of 10,000 men was sent to America for imperial defense. To pay for its upkeep, and to help defray the costs of the recent war with France, Parliament levied new colonial taxes. London now enforced mercantile regulations forbidding direct American trade with foreign ports in the West Indies. Even though the Treaty of Paris seemed to open the West to colonial settlement, an impressive Indian alliance under the Ottawa chief Pontiac united the western Indian nations, attacked British outposts, and raided settlements from the Great Lakes to Virginia during 1763. The British ministry ended Pontiac's uprising with a peace treaty and ineffectually sought control over the interior by issuing the Proclamation of 1763, which delineated the headwaters of rivers flowing into the Atlantic as a line beyond which settlers had "forthwith to remove themselves."[20] The Treaty of Fort Stanwix (1768) moved the line to the Ohio River, but settlers soon swarmed beyond the Ohio with "utter disregard for Indian rights," thus renewing conflict along the frontier from Pennsylvania to Kentucky by 1774.[21]

In response to London's apparent disregard for their interests, the colonials retaliated with petitions, economic boycotts, and sporadic outbreaks of violence. Parliament responded with more taxes. The Tea Act of 1773 led to the Boston Tea Party, which, in turn, triggered the Coercive Acts. When the Quebec Act of 1774 made the Ohio Valley an integral part of Canada, colonial leaders who had speculated in western lands supported revolution to obtain empire. Armed resistance exploded at Lexington and Concord in the spring of 1775, followed by battles around Boston. Then came an abortive American invasion of Quebec in December 1775. By this time John Adams and Benjamin Franklin were urging ties with the same country they had helped to defeat twenty years before.

As Americans moved cautiously toward independence, the emerging republican ideology, which embraced the "rights of Englishmen" and the principles of representative government, also contained the roots of an independent foreign policy. Historical lessons seemed to point toward independence. Benjamin Franklin asked: "Have not all Mankind in all Ages had the Right of deserting their Native Country? … Did not the Saxons desert their Native Country when they came to Britain?"[22] Americans pondered their immediate colonial past. As British mercantile restrictions tightened in the 1760s, colonial leaders began to argue that the imperial connection with England was one-sided, and that Americans became constantly embroiled in England's wars against their will. Attacks by French and Indian antagonists along the northern frontier usually had their origins in European quarrels, yet Americans nevertheless had to pay taxes, raise armies, and fight and die. Britain did not always value colonial sacrifices, most notably in 1745 when New Englanders captured the strategic French fortress of Louisbourg on Cape Breton Island, only to have the British hand it back later in exchange for French conquests in India.

Americans had no wish to be pawns in England's colonial wars. Franklin exaggerated when he told Parliament in 1766 that the Americans had enjoyed "perfect peace with both French and Indians" and that the recent conflict had been "really a British war."[23] He nonetheless expressed what one scholar has called "a deep-seated" American desire for "escape from Europe and a strong tendency, encouraged by European diplomacy, to avoid becoming entangled in European conflict, whenever it was to their interest to do so."[24]

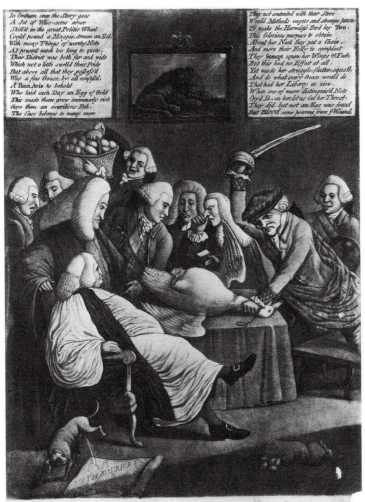

"The Wise Men of Gotham and Their Goose" (1776). This British cartoon satirized Britain's American policy as "folly." British politicians are killing the colonial goose that laid the golden eggs (in basket) while the plump king leans back in his chair and a dog urinates on a map of North America. (Library of Congress)

Americans also found lessons in recent British history. Many of the same English Whig writers quoted in defense of "no taxation without representation" had also vigorously debated British foreign policy during the first half of the eighteenth century. These Whigs had criticized British involvement in continental European wars. Since Europe's balance of power always seemed unstable, they argued that continental entanglements might improve the German territorial interests of the House of Hanover but certainly not those of England. Whigs distrusted England's German kings. "This great, this powerful, this formidable kingdom, is considered only as a province to a despicable electorate [Hanover]," William Pitt complained in 1743.[25] England's true interests lay in expanding its commerce and empire which "will turn deserts into fruitful fields, villages into great cities, cottages into palaces, beggars into princes, convert cowards into heroes, blockheads into philosophers."[26] One pamphleteer posited a general rule: "A Prince or State ought to avoid all Treaties, except such as tend towards Commerce or Manufactures. ... All other Alliances may be look'd upon as so many Incumbrances."[27] The similarity between British arguments for isolation from Europe and the later American rationale for independence is striking. In their desire to avoid British wars and British taxes, Revolutionary leaders not surprisingly appropriated British precepts.

Another source of American thinking on foreign policy lay in the writings of the French *philosophes*. As Enlightenment enthusiasts and advocates for the rising bourgeoisie, the *philosophes* launched an attack on all diplomatic and political practices that thwarted the proper rule of reason in international affairs. Traditional diplomacy had become synonymous with double-dealing, they argued, "an obscure art which hides itself in the folds of deceit, which fears to let itself be seen and believes it can succeed only in the darkness of mystery."[28] Like the English Whigs, the *philosophes* emphasized commercial expansion over standard power politics. Political barriers were artificial; commerce tied the "family of nations" together with "threads of silk."[29] Trade should be as free as possible, unfettered by mercantilism—the then-prevalent imperial practice of limiting imports and encouraging exports in order to enrich state coffers. Baron de Montesquieu, who believed that "the natural effect of commerce is to lead to peace," postulated that "everywhere there are gentle mores, there is commerce and that everywhere there is commerce, there are gentle mores."[30] Europe's wars "perpetually renew themselves," wrote Jean Jacques Rousseau, "like the waves which forever trouble the surface of the sea without altering its level."[31] More radical *philosophes* wanted to take diplomacy out of the hands of princes altogether. "Alliances," wrote the Marquis de Condorcet, "are only means by which the rulers of states precipitate the people into wars from which they benefit either by covering up their mistakes or by carrying out their plots against freedom."[32] Diplomacy should consist mainly of commercial, rather than political, interchanges.

Along with Whig writings, such continental ideas provided American Revolutionary War leaders with a missionary credo as they sought to win independence and an empire from the British Crown. Like John Winthrop's Puritans in the 1600s, they would not merely benefit themselves but also erect a model for the rest of the world. John Adams made this point when he told Vergennes in 1781 that "the dignity of North America does not consist in diplomatic ceremonials ... [It] consists solely in reason, justice, truth, the rights of mankind, and the interests of the nations of Europe."[33] The Revolutionary generation believed itself "providentially assigned ... to lead the world to new and better things," to create "an exemplary state *separate* from the corrupt and fallen world" while at the same time hoping to "push the world along by means of regenerative *intervention*."[34] Americans also shared with Europeans the belief that a single dominant power always carried forward civilization, and that historically such empires always moved, as the Reverend Thomas Brockway observed in 1784, "from east to west, and this continent is the last western state" wherein God is "erecting a stage on which to exhibit the great things of his kingdom."[35]

The movement for an independent foreign policy culminated with the convocation of the Second Continental Congress, following Lexington and Concord, in the summer of 1775. Some Americans who still wanted to remain within the British Empire held out hope that continued commercial opposition—no imports, no exports—would force Parliament and the king to negotiate. More radical delegates wanted to continue the war and declare independence. Benjamin Franklin proposed "articles of confederation" that gave Congress full power to make war and peace. John Adams urged construction of an American navy. Others called for the opening of American ports to foreign trade, arguing that only with protection from foreign navies could American merchant ships reach European ports. With their British market no longer available, the thirteen colonies needed avenues of commerce to survive. Foreign trade required foreign assistance. The argument for independence, made repeatedly behind the closed doors of Congress, became popularized on January 10, 1776, with the publication of Thomas Paine's pamphlet *Common Sense.*

Tom Paine was an English Quaker who had come to America in 1774. Once in Philadelphia he became friends with those members of Congress who urged independence. Paine's pamphlet summarized their arguments. Opposing further petitions to the king, demanding construction of a navy and the immediate formation of a confederation, emphasizing the need for international assistance, and calling for the opening of American ports to the rest of the world, Paine's celebrated call

Thomas Paine (1737–1809). This working-class Englishman found his way to Philadelphia in 1774, where he took a job as a journalist. "From shopkeepers, tradesmen, and attorneys," the Scottish philosopher Adam Smith wrote after reading Paine's *Common Sense* (1776), Americans "are become statesmen and legislators … contriving a new form of government for an extensive empire, which, they flatter themselves, will become, and which, indeed, seems very likely to become, one of the greatest and most formidable that ever was in the world." The irascible Paine joined the Continental Army and later participated in the French Revolution. This is a photographic reproduction of a ca. 1876 painting by Auguste Milliére, after an engraving by William Sharp, after a 1792 painting by George Romney. (Library of Congress)

to "begin the world over again" also spelled out the benefits of an independent foreign policy. Reconciliation with England was no longer possible, and there was no "advantage" to "being connected with Great Britain." On the contrary, "France and Spain never were … our enemies as Americans, but as Our being subjects of Great Britain." American agricultural products, he emphasized, were "the necessaries of life and will always have a market while eating is the custom of Europe." For Paine and his American friends, "Our plan is commerce, and that, well attended to, will secure us the Peace and friendship of all Europe; because it is in the interest of all Europe to have America as a free port. … As Europe is our market for trade, we ought to form no partial connection with any part of it. It is the true interest of America to steer clear of European contentions."[36] Declare independence, he predicted, and Europe would compete for America's commercial favors. America would benefit, and so would the rest of the world.

Of course, part of what Paine wrote was more nonsense than "common sense," particularly his playing down of privileges that Americans enjoyed as part of the British Empire. After independence, Americans would miss British naval protection, British credit, and easy access to the trade of British West Indies. The pamphlet nonetheless served as effective propaganda. *Common Sense* sold more than 300,000 copies, the equivalent of one copy for every ten persons living in the thirteen colonies in 1776. "With its idealism, its internationalism, and its hostility to power politics and reasons of state," one historian has written, Paine's pamphlet embedded "decidedly nontraditional—indeed, revolutionary—ideas in early American foreign relations."[37]

With the abortive invasion of Canada in the winter of 1775–1776 and the arrival of British reinforcements, it became obvious that some external help was imperative. Congress opened American ports to European ships in April 1776, but Paine's logic seemed irrefutable: "No State in Europe," Virginia's Richard Henry Lee argued in June, "will either Treat or Trade with us so long as we consider ourselves Subjects of G.B. … It is not choice … but necessity that calls for Independence, as the only means by which foreign Alliances can be obtained."[38] Thomas Jefferson wrote the Declaration of Independence, and Congress endorsed it on July 4, 1776.

To solicit overseas support, Congress designated a committee to prepare a "model treaty" to be presented to the French court of Louis XVI. Benjamin Franklin carried a final, amended version to France when he became American minister at the close of the year. The committee's Plan of 1776, which Congress debated in August, would also serve as the basis for alliances with other countries. John Adams drafted the Model Treaty. Like Paine, the lawyer from Braintree eschewed political entanglements. "I am not for soliciting any political connection, or military assistance, or indeed naval, from France," he told a friend. "I wish for nothing but commerce, a mere marine treaty with them."[39] Adams's imprint on the Model Treaty became clear, for it was almost purely a treaty of commerce and navigation, which would permit American ships free entry into French ports while French military supplies entered American ports in ever-increasing quantities. Included also were elaborate rules protecting neutral commerce in wartime. The Model Treaty suggested that the United States and France grant the nationals of each country the same "Rights, Liberties, Privileges, Immunities and Exemptions" in trade, or at least agree to a most-favored-nation clause, whereby

American merchants would receive the same commercial benefits enjoyed by other nations.[40] In effect, the treaty "intended to secure France as a de facto ally by encouraging it to violate the British monopoly of colonial trade and thereby draw it into war with Britain."[41]

Some in Congress, Adams later recalled, "thought there was not sufficient temptation to France to join us. They moved for cessions and concessions, which … I had studiously avoided."[42] Like most Americans in 1776, he feared that France, if offered political inducements, might demand Canada and the Newfoundland fisheries, both of which the new republic sought for itself. Somewhat naively, Adams and his colleagues convinced themselves that the ending of England's monopoly over North American commerce, accomplished through American independence, should be "ample Compensation to France for Acknowledging our Independence."[43] The only political obligation came in Article VIII, which stipulated that America would not aid the British in any conflict between Britain and France.

The neutral-rights provisions of the Model Treaty deserve special attention. Although these commercial articles would not apply to the war against England, in which the United States was already a belligerent, they formed the basis of what later became America's historic policy of "freedom of the seas." These commercial clauses guaranteed the principles of "free ships, free goods" (that is, the neutral flag protected noncontraband cargoes from capture), the freedom of neutrals to trade in noncontraband between ports of belligerents, and a restricted and narrowly defined list of contraband (illegal cargo) exempting naval stores and foodstuffs from seizure. Regarding the neutral flag as an extension of territorial sovereignty on the high seas, Americans claimed broad freedom to trade in wartime, except in contraband articles and with places blockaded or besieged. Such principles of neutral rights were becoming increasingly accepted in the late eighteenth century, particularly among enlightened publicists and by countries lacking large navies. Although England had adopted liberal provisions in a few treaties, British diplomats grew understandably reluctant to endorse them as international law. If Britain went to war against an inferior naval force, for example, the British enemy might very well encourage neutral shipping to carry its commercial goods to protect its own vulnerable vessels from British warships. If neutrals could also supply an enemy nation freely, especially with naval stores, they could eventually undermine Britain's maritime supremacy. Americans, looking ahead to independence, envisaged future European wars and hoped to expand their commerce at such times. France, in a naval war against the more powerful British, would benefit from American neutrality. Americans could fatten their pocketbooks and at the same time serve humanity by supporting more civilized rules of warfare.

The Model Treaty, then, introduced the main themes of early American foreign policy. It set forth the ideal of commercial expansion and political isolation. By specifically binding France against acquiring Canada, it also projected a continental domain for America beyond the thirteen coastal settlements. As the historian Peggy K. Liss has written, the Model Treaty underscored "the faith of the leaders of the new nation in the power of trade, and a concomitant desire to stay out of European struggles," politically, and a belief "that America, now liberty's home, must be maintained as 'an asylum for mankind.'"[44]

Opportunity and Necessity: Alliance with France

Patriot leaders did not err in thinking that France would aid American independence. Indeed, since 1763, when France had been stripped of its empire, the compelling motive of French foreign policy became *revanche.* "There will come in time a revolution in America," the French foreign minister in the 1760s predicted, "which will put England into a state of weakness where she will no longer be a terror in Europe. … The very extent of English possessions in America will bring about their separation from England."[45] Americans knew of this intense French preoccupation. "All Europe is attentive to the dispute," Franklin wrote from London in 1770, and "our part is taken everywhere."[46] Aside from strengthening the Bourbon Family Compact with Spain and sending secret observers to North America, France made no overt moves to intervene before 1770.

The decision to succor the Americans fell to a new foreign minister, Charles Gravier, the Comte de Vergennes. Suave, polished, outwardly unemotional, Vergennes looked every inch the epitome of a successful diplomat of the ancien régime. In actuality, he could act impetuously. When the American colonies began their armed rebellion, he adopted the motto *Aut nunc aut nunquam* ("now or never").

A perfect scheme for aiding the rebels short of war presented itself early in 1776 in the person of Pierre Augustin Caron de Beaumarchais. Confident that the Americans "must be invincible," the adventurous author of *The Barber of Seville* created a dummy trading house, Rodrigue Hortalez and Company, through which he could secretly ship military supplies to the American colonies.[47] The French court could provide secret financing. Vergennes jumped at the scheme. In a persuasive memorandum to the French king, Vergennes argued that American independence would "diminish the power of England and increase in proportion that of France." Assistance to the Americans might permit France to recover "the possessions which the English have taken from us in America, such as the fisheries of Newfoundland. … We do not speak of Canada."[48] By May 1776, before any American agent reached France and even before the publication of the Declaration of Independence, Paris took the plunge. The French Treasury quietly transferred 1 million livres (about $200,000) to Beaumarchais's "company." Charles III of Spain made a similar grant, and the first shipments of muskets, cannon, powder, tents, and clothing soon crossed the Atlantic. When Franklin arrived in December 1776, French assistance already existed. Whether this assistance would evolve into recognition and a formal treaty remained to be seen.

Franklin took Paris by storm. Plainly dressed and wearing a woodsman's fur cap, the seventy-year-old philosopher was already well known in France. *Poor Richard's Almanack,* with its catchy aphorisms, had run through several French editions, and Franklin's electrical experiments and philosophical writings had earned him honored membership in the French Academy. Disarmingly modest and soft-spoken, the rotund Franklin—he called himself "Dr. Fatsides"—won friends everywhere.[49] Because Franklin seemed "a very dangerous engine," the British ambassador reported that "we can postpone" but not "prevent" war with France.[50] Vergennes warmed to Franklin, whose kindly features soon adorned medals and snuffbox covers—so much so that "my Face is now almost as well known as that of the Moon."[51] With the elegant women of the French court adopting a *coiffure à la Franklin* in imitation of his coonskin cap, a jealous Adams grumbled that the Philadelphian's name was so ubiquitous that "there was scarcely a peasant or a citizen, a *valet de chambre,* coachman or footman, a lady's chambermaid or a scullion in a kitchen, who … did not consider him as a friend to human kind."[52] Franklin explained physics to Queen Marie Antoinette, played chess with the Duchesse de Bourbon, and even proposed marriage to the wealthy Madame Helvetius. She avoided Franklin's entangling alliance, but her "careless, jaunty air" and the fact that she kissed the "Good Doctor" in public scandalized Abigail Adams, who "never wished for an acquaintance with any ladies of this cast"[53] Helped along by a dose of "radical chic," the enthusiastic French reception completed what a recent biographer has termed the "Americanization of Benjamin Franklin," namely, his transformation into the "symbolic American."[54] Thomas Jefferson did not exaggerate when, on becoming minister to France in 1784, he said that he was merely succeeding Franklin, for no one could replace him.

Social popularity did not ensure diplomatic success, however. Vergennes might have recognized American independence prior to Franklin's arrival had not the successful British military campaign in New York in the summer of 1776 made the French court cautious. Recognition meant war with England, and the French hesitated without Spanish assistance. Spain, however, was dragging its feet. Although French loans and supplies continued through 1776 and 1777, Vergennes avoided a formal commitment until there was a sure sign of American military success. "We are now acting a play which pleases all the spectators," observed one American in Europe, "but none seem inclined to pay the performers."[55] Then came Saratoga on October 17, 1777, a battle in which 90 percent of American arms and ammunition had come from French merchants. The defeat of "Gentleman Johnny" Burgoyne's troops in the forests of northern New York helped persuade England to send out peace feelers, with terms offering less than complete independence. Franklin used the threat of reconciliation with England as a lever on Vergennes. When asked what action was necessary to prevent Congress from coming to an agreement with England short of full independence, Franklin replied: The immediate conclusion of a treaty of commerce and alliance.

On February 6, 1778, Vergennes and Franklin signed two pacts. The first, a treaty of amity and commerce, gave the United States most-favored-nation privileges (which meant that America would enjoy any commercial favors granted by France to other countries). The two nations also accepted definitions of contraband and neutral rights that followed the articles of the Model Treaty.

The second pact, a treaty of alliance, contained political commitments that departed from John Adams's original plan. Instead of the meager promise not to aid England if France entered the war for independence, Franklin agreed not to make peace with the British without first obtaining French consent. Vergennes made a parallel promise. Although Franklin managed to retain the prohibition against French territorial gains on the North American continent, the United States agreed to recognize any French conquests in the Caribbean and to guarantee "from the present time and forever" all French possessions in America and any others obtained at the peace table. France paid an equivalent price. According to Article II,

Benjamin Franklin (1706–1790) at the Court of King Louis XVI of France. The elderly philosopher-journalist-humorist-politician-diplomat fascinated the court of France. In *Benjamin Franklin* (2002), Edmund S. Morgan has written that Franklin's "style of dealing with the French was not the suspicious, secretive, aggressive assertion of American demands … but an openhanded confession of American needs and American gratitude for French help. And it had worked." A British diplomat less flatteringly called Franklin "a subtle, artful man … void of all truth." (Library of Congress)

"The essential and direct End of the present defensive alliance is to maintain effectually the liberty, Sovereignty, and independence absolute and unlimited of the said United States, as well in matters of Gouvernement as of commerce." Vergennes also guaranteed "from the present time and forever" American "Possessions, and the additions or conquests … during the war, from any of the Dominions now or heretofore possessed by Great Britain in North America."[56] In short, Vergennes seemed ready to guarantee whatever territories could be wrested from England.

The French alliance seemed to constitute the kind of political entanglement that John Adams had warned against. Certainly the stipulation prohibiting any peace without French consent, as well as the guarantee of territories, entangled American interests in the foreign policies of another nation. Congress had already retreated from the principles of 1776 when it had instructed Franklin to seek an alliance with Spain in which the United States would assist Spain in conquering Florida and declare war against Portugal in return for diplomatic recognition and outright military assistance. Such a treaty did not materialize, but the instructions indicated that Congress, after two years without a major victory, could compromise its ideals for military help against Britain. Both Paine and Adams accepted the French alliance, Paine so enthusiastically that he named his next daughter Marie Antoinette after the French queen. "No event was ever received with more heartfelt joy," commented George Washington.[57] The treaty did fulfill the most important of Adams's original predictions—that the political and economic independence of the United States from England would be too great a prize for France to pass up. The French so dreaded "the United British Empire" that they could not "let slip the opportunity of striking one pistol at least" from "an enemy who constantly threatened them with two."[58] In fact, Vergennes had no wish to replace Britain with a great American empire that might eventually chase the French and the Spanish out of the

New World. "[T]hey would not stop here," he said in 1775, "but would in process of time advance to the Southern Continent of America … and in the end not leave a foot of that Hemisphere in the possession of any European power."[59] The French made a commitment to American independence, not to American expansion.

That commitment was tested at the very beginning of the alliance. When the Elector Maximilian of Bavaria died, on December 30, 1777, Joseph II of Austria promptly occupied and annexed that German principality. Frederick the Great of Prussia went to war on behalf of Bavarian independence. Austria urged France, allied to Austria since 1756, to join the War of Bavarian Succession against Prussia. The Austrian Netherlands would be France's reward, but Vergennes resisted temptation. Toward Austria, he slyly assumed the role of benevolent mediator, hoping to keep Europe quiet in order to concentrate on the maritime war against England. This mediation of the *Kartoffelkrieg* ("Potato War"), so-called because the starving soldiers of Austria and Prussia spent the winter of 1778–1779 eating frozen potatoes, was successfully accomplished in 1779.

Ironically, Emperor Joseph resented French interference, and when the opportunity presented itself in the summer of 1781, he returned the favor and offered to mediate between Britain and France. Russia also joined in the mediation offer. Since it came at a low point in the military struggle in America, Vergennes might have felt compelled to accept Austro-Russian mediation (the terms would *not* have recognized American independence) in 1781 had not English king George III stubbornly resisted any solution short of complete submission by the American colonies. The French matched obstinacy with obduracy. Whatever the entanglements and temptations of the European continent, France was intent on defeating England by backing American independence. By 1783 France had expended some 48 million livres on the war for American independence, a struggle no longer confined to North America. In fact, French designs on the British West Indies caused London to divert forces from the American mainland to the Caribbean, a pivotal step "in the events that led to the British defeat at Yorktown."[60]

King George III (1738–1820). He ruled England from 1760 to 1820, slowly falling victim to a degenerative blood disease called porphyria, now treatable, but not at the time, that joined other health ailments in disabling him mentally. In 1787, for example, he alighted from his carriage in Windsor Park and addressed an oak tree as the King of Prussia. Although against leniency toward the rebellious Americans, the king eventually appointed Lord Shelburne prime minister, who made a generous peace settlement. (Library of Congress)

What if ... *France had not formally allied with the United States beginning in 1778?*

The American victory at Saratoga had prompted the Comte de Vergennes to conclude the alliance with Benjamin Franklin in February 1778. It also encouraged London to seek reconciliation by repealing prewar taxes and offering Americans virtual home rule within the British Empire. When both Britain's proposals and the French treaty arrived in Philadelphia in April, the Continental Congress rejected British terms and ratified the treaty immediately. In other words, when faced with the prospect of either ending the war quickly by remaining within the British Empire on terms that redressed the revolutionaries' prewar grievances, or else continuing to fight for full independence with the aid of France, U.S. leaders readily chose the latter course. Without a French alliance the embattled Americans might still have continued their rebellion, perhaps relying on covert French and Spanish subsidies and supplies. George Washington's army could have avoided set-piece battles favoring the British and instead fought a war of attrition that parlayed British war-weariness into eventual peace terms that included American independence. But without a conspicuous French role, and without Dutch and Spanish participation in the war, Britain would not have been compelled to scatter its forces globally to fight its European adversaries. Without this wider war, American diplomats would have been hard-pressed to gain the expansive Mississippi and Great Lakes boundaries achieved in 1782–1783 because London would have felt no need to "buy" a separate peace to break up the Franco-American coalition. Instead of complaining about entanglements with perfidious allies, the founders of a tiny republic east of the Alleghenies might have bemoaned the absence of allies.

Had the Americans accepted autonomy within the British Empire in 1778, history might have been quite different. Even if Americans had followed the subsequent Canadian or Australian pattern of dominion status to eventual independence, British alliances with Native Americans would likely have constrained westward expansion, just as slavery in the South would have run counter to London's growing opposition to the international slave trade and its abolition of slavery within the empire in the 1830s. Remaining within the empire would have benefited American commerce and shipping by retaining access to the West Indies and continuing the Royal Navy's protection of cargoes and crews from Barbary corsairs. If Britain had gone to war with France again after 1793, Americans would not have quarreled with London over impressment and neutral rights, and there would have been no War of 1812.

Of course, had Vergennes not allied with the Americans in 1778, France's treasury might not have experienced the profound economic crisis that helped spark the French Revolution of 1789. The so-called Age of Democratic Revolutions might have amounted to a handful of unsuccessful North American rebellions (similar to the political uprisings that flared throughout Europe in 1848), and the independence of European colonies in the Americas might not have occurred until the twentieth century. Even as part of a mighty British empire, American territorial expansion westward and southward might have been blocked by a balance of power within the Western Hemisphere. With its isolationist traditions curtailed, the United States might have joined Britain's other dominions in going to war with Germany in 1914 and 1939. As Theodore Roosevelt and Winston S. Churchill later boasted, the twentieth century would still have been dominated by countries that spoke English.

Suspicious Suitors in Europe

Franklin had argued that "a virgin state should preserve the virgin character, and not go about suitoring after alliances, but wait with decent dignity for the application of others."[61] Congress, needing money and hoping for military assistance, ruled otherwise. Thus did American diplomats scurry to Berlin, Madrid, Vienna, St. Petersburg, Amsterdam, and other capitals in quest of alliances that never quite materialized. Frederick the Great had intimated that Prussia would recognize American independence if France did, but when William Lee arrived in Berlin, Frederick told his chief minister: "Put him off with compliments."[62] Fear of revolutionary principles, the danger of British retaliation, trading opportunities, and territorial ambitions closer to home—all made the European monarchies reluctant to challenge Britain. Neutrals should identify their own interests with America and join the war, John Adams grumbled: "All may nibble and piddle and dribble and fribble, waste a long time, immense treasures, and much human blood, and they must come to it at last."[63]

The Dutch exemplified Adams's point. With representative government firmly entrenched in the Dutch Estates General, one might have expected the Netherlands to be the first to recognize American independence. Not so. The burghers of Amsterdam preferred making money. Until Britain declared war on the United Provinces in December 1780, the Dutch busied themselves by carrying naval stores from the Baltic to France, as well as using their West Indian island of St. Eustatius as an entrepôt for contraband trade with the Americans. These activities, plus a willingness to join Catherine the Great's League of Armed Neutrality in 1780, led to war with England, but the Dutch steadfastly refused any treaty with the United States until October 1782, by which time the war had all but ended. Adams, who finally concluded the treaty of amity and commerce (following the Plan of 1776), compared himself to "a man in the midst of an ocean negotiating for his life among a school of sharks."[64] Although the Dutch treaty came too late to authorize effective military assistance in the war, Adams secured a loan of 5 million guilders in June 1782 from Amsterdam bankers, the first of a series of Dutch loans, totaling some 9 million guilders ($3,600,000), that sustained American credit through the 1780s.

American efforts to join the Armed Neutrality of 1780 marked another episode in futility. Organized by Catherine II of Russia, the Armed Neutrality also included Denmark, Sweden, Austria, Prussia, Portugal, and the Kingdom of the Two Sicilies. Its purpose was ostensibly to enforce liberal provisions of neutral rights ("free ships, free goods," no paper blockades, narrow definition of contraband) in trading with belligerents. Because the Armed Neutrality's principles so closely resembled the Model Treaty, Congress immediately adopted its rules by resolution and sent a plenipotentiary to St. Petersburg to gain formal adherence to the league by treaty. It was an impossible mission. Aside from the obvious incongruity of a belligerent nation attempting to join an alliance of neutrals, Catherine would not risk war with England by granting recognition prematurely. Her real purpose was to divert British attention while preparing to seize the Crimea from Ottoman Turkey. American envoy Francis Dana of Massachusetts returned "most heartily weary of the old world" after two long years in the Russian capital without ever being received officially.[65] Formal relations with Russia did not begin until 1809, when Catherine's grandson, Tsar Alexander I, received as American minister John Quincy Adams, who as a fourteen-year-old had been Dana's secretary during the abortive wartime mission. "Nobody here but princes and slaves," young Adams described Russia in 1781.[66]

Once peace negotiations in Paris had established American independence in 1783, however, the Dutch urged the United States to join the Armed Neutrality through a formal treaty with the Netherlands. But now, with the war all but over, Congress changed its collective mind. The reason? "The true interest of these [United] states requires that they should be as little as possible entangled in the politics and controversies of European nations."[67] Thus, however much Americans desired freedom of trade for both profit and principle, they rejected political entanglements to achieve such an objective. They would face this dilemma again and again.

The most frustrating diplomacy of all involved Spain. Despite previous financial support for the embattled colonials, and notwithstanding the outwardly close alliance with France, the government of King Charles III was in no hurry to take up arms against England—especially if Spain could obtain its principal objective, the return of Gibraltar, by other means. In view of its own extensive colonial empire in the Americas, moreover, Spain was understandably less eager than France to encourage overseas revolutions. Not only might colonial rebellion prove to be a contagious disease, but a powerful American republic could threaten Spanish possessions as effectively as an expanding British Empire. Determined to "make our decisions without rushing," Spanish Foreign Minister Count Floridablanca played a double game by dickering with both France and England in the hope of regaining Gibraltar.[68] Only by the Treaty of Aranjuez, signed on April 12, 1779, did Spain agree on war against England, and even then the alliance was with France, not with the United States. One article held enormous importance for American foreign policy. Because of Madrid's obsession with Gibraltar, the French agreed to keep on fighting until they wrested that rocky symbol of Spanish pride from the British. According to the alliance of 1778, the United States and France had pledged not to make a separate peace and to continue the war until England recognized American independence. Now France was promising to fight until Gibraltar fell. In this circuitous fashion, without being a party to the treaty or even being consulted, the Americans found their independence, in the historian Samuel Flagg Bemis's notable phrase, "chained by European diplomacy to the Rock of Gibraltar."[69] And because the terms of Aranjuez remained secret, American diplomats could only guess at these new political entanglements.

Congress dispatched John Jay to Madrid in September 1779 to obtain a formal alliance. Described by the French as a "serious," "grave," "sedate young man" whose self-confidence "begat a not disagreeable vanity," the thirty-four-year-old New Yorker of Huguenot descent did not have an easy time of it.[70] Not once during his two-and-a-half-year stay did the Spanish court officially receive Jay. With Jay's mail opened and read and spies snooping everywhere, "only the lice in Spanish inns gave him a warm welcome."[71] Rarely did Count Floridablanca deign to communicate with him. Even more frustrating, Jay ran out of money and had to ask the Spanish for funds. The Spanish did give Jay some $175,000, but only to keep the American dangling while Floridablanca secretly negotiated with a British agent in the hope that Britain would accept outside mediation and cede Gibraltar. Even though the British prime minister, Lord North, privately vowed "to get rid of this d ... d war," the Spanish ploy failed because George III remained as unyielding on Gibraltar as he was about American independence.[72]

In the summer of 1781, Congress instructed Jay to give up the demand for navigation rights on the Mississippi River, if only Spain would recognize American independence and make an alliance. Such a message reflected the military dangers the colonists faced in the autumn of 1780, following the successful British invasion of the South. Although personally believing it "better for America to have no treaty with Spain than to purchase one on such servile terms," Jay obediently sought an

John Jay (1745–1829). A graduate of King's College (now Columbia University), this upper-class New Yorker became one of America's most prominent diplomats. Before helping to negotiate the peace treaty with Great Britain, Jay represented the United States in Spain (1780–1782), where he met unrelenting frustration. Under the Articles of Confederation, Jay served as secretary of foreign affairs with a minuscule staff of only one secretary, part-time translators, and a doorkeeper-messenger. He later became chief justice of the Supreme Court (1789–1795). Sent by President George Washington on a special mission to Britain in 1794, Jay negotiated the controversial treaty that bears his name. (National Portrait Gallery, Smithsonian Institution/Art Resource, NY)

interview with the Spanish foreign minister.[73] After several weeks he obtained an audience. The New Yorker made his proposal: a treaty relinquishing navigation rights on the Mississippi south of 31° north latitude, a Spanish guarantee to the United States of "all their respective territories," and an American guarantee to the Spanish king of "all his dominions in America."[74] Floridablanca refused. Had he accepted, the navigation of the "Father of Waters" and the boundary of West Florida—both destined to be troublesome issues in Spanish-American diplomacy—would have been settled to Spain's advantage. But Floridablanca preferred to gamble. Already Spanish troops from New Orleans had occupied West Florida, and possibly they could claim more territory between the Mississippi and the Alleghenies.

Rebuffed, Jay withdrew the offer on Mississippi navigation. He explained to Congress that if Spain refused to make an alliance during the war, the United States should reassert its Mississippi claims in any final peace treaty. Congress endorsed his decision. Americans would "always be deceived if we believe that any nation in this world has or will have a disinterested regard for us," Jay wrote.[75] He had also begun to suspect, from conversations with the French ambassador in Madrid, that the French were encouraging Spain in its trans-Appalachian territorial ambitions. Indeed, following his sojourn in Spain, this "almost xenophobic American" and his suspicions of European intentions helped shape the American posture at the 1782 peace negotiations.[76]

A Separate Peace: The Treaty of Paris

The surrender of Lord Cornwallis's army at Yorktown on October 19, 1781, precipitated serious peace negotiations. An embattled George III invoked an early version of the "domino theory" by suggesting that if "America [should] succeed, the West Indies must follow … Ireland would soon follow … then this poor island [Great Britain] … soon would be a poor island indeed."[77] Nonetheless, the burgeoning public debt and war weariness finally caused the ministry of Lord North to fall early in 1782. The king reluctantly accepted a new ministry under the Marquess of Rockingham, committed to a restoration of peace but undecided as to the terms.

The Rockingham ministry sent Richard Oswald to Paris in April 1782 to sound out Benjamin Franklin. The two men talked candidly as Franklin "opened his mind" about the "desirability of restoring American goodwill toward England" and how to achieve it.[78] After introducing the British envoy to Vergennes and saying that the United States would make no separate peace without French concurrence, Franklin privately intimated to Oswald the possibility of a separate peace if England granted complete independence and generous boundaries. The American did not demand Canada, but its voluntary cession would have "an excellent effect … [on] the mind of the [American] people in general."[79] Oswald promised to try to persuade his superiors in London. "We parted exceedingly good friends," Franklin wrote in his journal.[80]

Peace talks stalled as another cabinet crisis distracted the British. Not until Rockingham's death and Lord Shelburne's succession as prime minister on July 1 could the British agree on a negotiating position. During this interval, Franklin summoned his fellow peace commissioners, Jay and Adams, to Paris. Jay, delighted to escape Madrid, arrived by the end of June. Adams continued commercial negotiations in the Netherlands and did not reach the French capital until October 26.

The success of the separate negotiations, which began in October and ended on November 30, owed much to the conciliatory attitude of Shelburne. A believer in natural rights and free trade through his friendship with French *philosophes,* the prime minister wanted to break up the French–American alliance, and by encouraging the expansion of American territory and population, he now envisaged "new markets for British goods to conquer."[81] The peace terms were thus exceedingly generous; as Vergennes later put it: "The English buy peace rather than they make it."[82] Not only did the United States gain complete independence, but also extensive boundaries (the Great Lakes and St. Lawrence River to the north, Mississippi River to the west, 31° north latitude line across Florida to the south) that far surpassed what Americans had won on the battlefield. Greater territorial gains were probably thwarted by eleventh-hour British naval victories in the Caribbean and the failure of a French-Spanish siege of Gibraltar in September 1782. Canada thus remained in the British Empire. Henceforth, in one scholar's words, "American expansionism had a westward, but not a northward gaze."[83]

With independence and boundaries easily settled, much wrangling focused on the Atlantic fisheries, without which, so Thomas Paine had declared, "independence would be a bubble."[84] The British argued that access to the fishing grounds off the Grand Banks of Newfoundland, as well as the right to dry and cure fish on Canadian shores, should be limited to subjects of the British Empire. The Americans disagreed. New England, where "Tom Cod," not George III, was king, had a stubborn advocate in John Adams, who claimed that the fisheries were "indispensably necessary to the accomplishment and preservation of our independence."[85] Many coins minted during the American Revolution had embossed images of cod on them. The Americans finally won their point, although the treaty ambiguously granted the "liberty" to fish, not the "right," thus perpetuating a controversy over which generations of diplomats (and generations of Adamses) battled for more than a century.

The sharpest disagreement arose over the intertwined issues of Loyalists and pre-Revolutionary debts, The British sought generous treatment for the thousands of colonials who had fled into exile for their loyalty to the Crown, demanding restitution of confiscated property, or at least compensation. The Americans adamantly refused. Even the moderate Jay spoke of Loyalists as having "the most dishonourable of human motives" and urged that "every American must set his face and steel his heart" against them.[86] As to the 5 million pounds in credit owed by Americans (mostly southern planters) to British merchants, Americans hesitated to repay obligations contracted prior to 1775. Adams found acceptable compromise language whereby British creditors would "meet with no lawful impediment" in collecting their lawfully incurred debts.[87] This particular clause helped gain the support of the British commercial classes for what was an otherwise unpopular treaty. As Adams put it, American concession on the debts prevented the British merchants "from making common Cause with the Refugees [Loyalists]."[88] The British accepted an article that forbade all further persecution of Loyalists and "earnestly recommended" to the states that properties seized during the war be restored. Because Congress could not dictate to the states under the Articles of Confederation (see below), both the British and American commissioners understood that the "earnest recommendations" might not be followed.

Americans enthusiastically greeted the preliminary peace terms but worried that the independent negotiations might alienate France. After two weeks of silence, Vergennes wrote plaintively to Franklin: "You perfectly understand what is due to propriety; you have all your life performed your duties. I pray to you to consider how you propose to fulfill those which are due to the [French] King?"[89] Franklin thereupon delivered one of the most beguiling replies in the history of diplomacy. He admitted that the American commissioners had been indiscreet—guilty of a lack of *bienséance* (propriety)—in not keeping the French fully informed, but he hoped King Louis's generous support would not "be ruined by a single indiscretion of ours." "The English, I just now learn," he told Vergennes, "flatter themselves they have already divided us." Franklin added that he hoped the British would find themselves "totally mistaken."[90] The French foreign minister said nothing more. In fact, he even agreed to an additional loan of some 6 million livres, which Franklin had requested earlier.

Vergennes, Charles Gravier, compte de (1719–1787).
France's foreign minister respected "the integrity and wisdom" of
Benjamin Franklin and wished that "this minister should have a dominant
influence over his colleagues." Franklin, in turn, praised Vergennes as
one "who never promised anything which he did not punctually perform."
This "most conservative of men," the historian Stacy Schiff writes of
Vergennes in *A Great Improvisation* (2005), "took a rash step to maintain
a balance of power that he was inadvertently to destroy, by bankrupting
his nation." When Vergennes died in 1787, Louis XVI was so grief-
stricken that he did not hunt that day. (Library of Congress)

Why did the French respond so mildly? With Paris honeycombed with spies,
Vergennes knew all along about the "most unexpected" negotiations.[91] He did not
protest, because he understood that England was indeed trying to break up the
Franco-American alliance. The separate American peace, moreover, offered Vergennes a way out of a sticky tangle with Spain. He could now tell the stubborn
Spaniards that Gibraltar (Floridablanca's "pile of stones") was no longer a practicable
objective with the Americans effectively out of the war.[92] To Vergennes American
independence counted far more than Gibraltar, and although he would have preferred a treaty that left the United States more dependent on France, he was not
displeased with what Jay, Adams, and Franklin had accomplished.

The final Treaty of Paris was not signed until September 3, 1783. Except for some
complications regarding Florida (Britain finally ceded all of Florida to Spain, whose
military forces had captured West Florida in 1780–1781), the terms were precisely those
of the preliminary treaty between England and the United States. America's diplomats
had successfully eluded political entanglements and exploited European rivalries. "Un-
disciplined marines as we were," said John Adams, "we were better tacticians than we
imagined."[93] Even though American success "depended on a heavy dose of foreign help

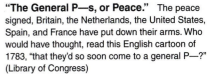

"The General P—s, or Peace." The peace signed, Britain, the Netherlands, the United States, Spain, and France have put down their arms. Who would have thought, read this English cartoon of 1783, "that they'd so soon come to a general P—?" (Library of Congress)

and abundant good luck," a Spanish diplomat sagely predicted that the United States "will grow into a giant, even a fearsome colossus in the hemisphere" and "will forget the assistance received from [us] and will think only of its own exaltation."[94]

Ill-Treated under the Articles of Confederation

Americans were in an exuberant, expansive mood in 1783. Two years earlier all thirteen states had ratified the Articles of Confederation, giving them a new, if cumbersome, government. "This ball of liberty," wrote Jefferson, "is now so well in motion that it will roll around the world."[95] Nearly half the national territory, some

220 million acres of wilderness, lay across the Appalachian chain, and the westward flood of emigrants, fleeing from heavy taxes to lower ones, from poorer to better lands, became inexorable. More than 100,000 Americans settled in Kentucky and Tennessee in the years between 1775 and 1790. As Jay put it in 1785, "a rage for emigrating to the western country prevails … and the seeds of a great people are daily planting beyond the mountains."[96] For George Washington, roads and canals would turn the trans-Allegheny region into a field almost too extensive for imagination. A Spanish official in Louisiana complained that Yankees were "advancing and multiplying … with a prodigious rapidity."[97]

The "Thunder-Gust of Peace" also meant that foreign ships could now enter American ports without fear of British retaliation.[98] Americans could regain British markets for their agricultural exports, trade directly with other European countries, and develop as extensive and free a trade as possible with the rest of the world. The geographer Thomas Hutchins boasted that Americans "have it in their power to engross the whole commerce," and "to possess, in the utmost security, the dominion of the sea throughout the world."[99]

Impressive trade expansion fueled American optimism in the 1780s. Some 72,000 tons of shipping cleared America's busiest port, Philadelphia, in the year 1789, compared with an average of 45,000 tons in 1770–1772. Boston's tonnage increased from 42,506 in 1772 to 55,000 in 1788. Clearances in Maryland and Virginia doubled in volume over the figures for 1769. Tobacco exports brought a favorable balance of more than $1 million a year in trade with France during the 1780s. By 1788 the Netherlands was importing more than $4 million annually of tobacco, rice, and naval stores from the United States.

Merchants found new markets. The *Empress of China,* the first American ship to trade with Asia, set sail from New York in February 1784 and reached Guangzhou (Canton) some six months later. The cargo was ginseng, which the Chinese believed would restore sexual potency to the aged. Another pioneering vessel, the *Columbia,* left Boston in 1787, wintered on the Pacific coast of North America near Vancouver Island, and traded metal trinkets to the Indians for otter furs. The *Columbia* then voyaged to China, exchanged the furs for tea, and returned to Boston— the first American ship to circumnavigate the globe. Other ships soon followed. Thus began a curiously complicated trade, which often included a stop at the Hawaiian Islands to pick up sandalwood for Chinese consumers. The Pacific trade thus became "Boston's high school of commerce for forty years."[100] On its second voyage, in 1792, the *Columbia* entered the mouth of the river named after it and helped establish the American claim to Oregon. In December 1785, Elias Hacket Derby of Salem sent the *Grand Turk* to the French island of Mauritius in the Indian Ocean, beginning a lucrative trade with India and other Asian ports. In their search for profitable cargoes, American captains made the first contacts in the Indian and Pacific Oceans at least a generation prior to official diplomatic attention from the U.S. government.

Spanish America also loomed as a new market in the 1780s. Shipments of wheat, flour, and some reexported manufactures went to Cuba, Venezuela, and Argentina, and in particular to Santo Domingo, which served as an entrepôt for New Orleans, where American smuggling flourished as never before. By 1785 the viceroy of Buenos Aires in Argentina was reporting numerous *bostoneses* vessels plying southern waters "on the pretext of whaling and probably with hidden intentions."[101] Although most of this trade with Latin America remained in the Gulf of Mexico and the Caribbean, by 1788 American whalers and China traders had reached the west coast of South America, where they took on pelts and specie for the Asian market.

Despite expanded trade, the instant prosperity that many Americans expected in 1783 did not materialize because the United States had to adjust from a wartime to a peacetime economy and from a favored position within the British Empire to independent status in a world dominated by mercantilist restrictions. Because of commercial habits and British credit facilities, the bulk of American trade continued to be with England. In 1790, nearly half of all American exports went to England, and 90 percent of American imports originated in England. Fully three-fourths of America's foreign trade remained with the former mother country. Contrary to Paine's *Common Sense,* however, independence brought an end to privileges that had been part of the imperial connection. New England suffered when London prohibited American ships from trading with the British West Indies. By 1786 the exports of Massachusetts totaled only one-fourth of what they had been in 1774. Because each state had its own customs service and tariff schedules, moreover, American diplomats could not threaten commercial retaliation against England. George Washington complained: "One State passes a prohibitory law respecting some article, another State opens wide the avenue for its admission. One Assembly makes a system; another Assembly unmakes it."[102] Indeed, as peacetime problems multiplied, structural weaknesses under the Articles of Confederation inhibited diplomacy. Beyond commercial policy, states' rights thwarted national power in other respects. Congress had raised a continental army and constructed a small navy during the war, but in peace these "implied" powers collapsed; all naval vessels were sold or scrapped by the mid-1780s, and the army dwindled to a mere regiment. Congress remained nominally in charge of foreign policy. Yet during the war this large body had proven so faction-ridden and irresponsible that it had given the French foreign minister veto power over American peace commissioners. The legislative body did take a forward step in 1784 by creating a Department of Foreign Affairs and selecting John Jay as secretary. Although Congress retained the right to make war and peace, to send and receive ambassadors, to make treaties and alliances, it lacked the power to enforce its diplomacy. Individual states violated the 1783 peace treaty with impunity. Instead of a world in which America would be "friends to all, and enemies to none," the reality seemed quite the opposite.[103]

Relations with England quickly deteriorated after 1783. In the first flush of peace it had looked as though the United States might actually conclude a favorable commercial treaty with the British. Lord Shelburne's grand scheme of rapprochement would have continued the benefits Americans had enjoyed under the Crown, including free access of American goods and ships to British and West Indian ports. But Shelburne was soon forced from office for having given the Americans too much, and his successors found commercial reciprocity with the United States a political impossibility. Mercantilist thinking still held sway in England. Protectionists argued that the United States, if allowed the privileges of the British Empire without any of the responsibilities, would eventually outstrip Britain in shipping, trade, and the production of manufactured goods. A restrictive policy, however, would allow England to increase its carrying trade, particularly in the West Indies, where

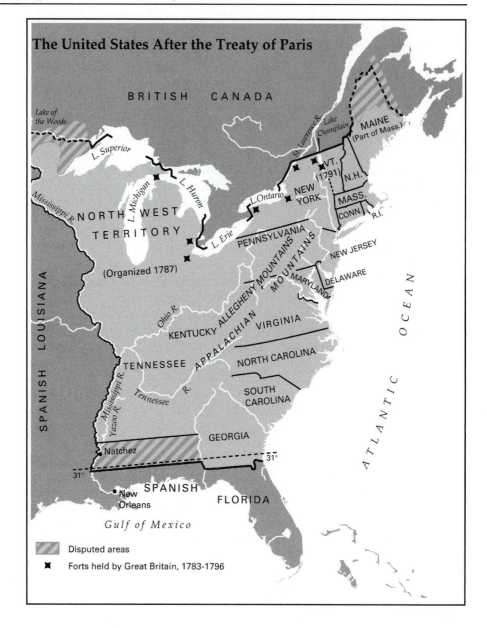

The United States After the Treaty of Paris

colonial shipping had long predominated. Canada and Ireland could offer alternative provisions for the West Indian planters.

Such mercantilist precepts were codified in a series of orders in council, according to which American raw materials and foodstuffs, but not manufactures, could enter the British home islands aboard American vessels, while Canada and the West Indies remained closed to American shipping. Such restrictions, it was believed, would not hurt British exports to America. As the Earl of Sheffield prophetically observed: "At least four-fifths of the importations from Europe into the American States were at all times made upon credit; and undoubtedly the States are in greater want of credit at this time than at former periods. It can be had only in Great Britain."[104] As for possible commercial retaliation, the British scoffed at whether "A DISUNITED PEOPLE, till the End of Time" could ever agree on uniform tariffs.[105] "Pish! … What can Americans do?" boasted one Briton. "They have neither government nor power. Great Britain could shut up all their ports."[106]

The British refusal to evacuate the northwest forts also rankled. These fortified posts, which ranged from Dutchman's Point on Lake Champlain to Michilimackinac on Lake Michigan (see map on page 26), strategically controlled the frontier, including the fur trade. Indian tribes between the Great Lakes and the Ohio River—the Six Nations of the Iroquois in the northeast, the Shawnees and Algonquins in the northwest, and the Creeks, Cherokees, and Seminoles in the southeast—resisted white encroachment. Abandoned by the Paris treaty, "we are determined to pay no attention to the Manner in which the British Negotiators have drawn out the lines," vowed the Creek leader Alexander McGillivray.[107] Indian claims to land above and below the Ohio remained valid under their previous treaties, Native Americans insisted.

Partly to placate the Indians, the British did not lower the Union Jack from the forts, despite their treaty promise to relinquish them with "all convenient speed." They later justified retention of the posts on the grounds that Americans themselves had violated the treaty by their failure to repay debts to British creditors and by the shabby treatment accorded Loyalists. The British adopted a "wait-and-see" policy in the West, holding the forts, encouraging the Indians, but refusing Indian requests to guarantee their territorial claims. American shipping was thus effectively excluded from the Great Lakes after 1783, and new settlements were confined largely to Kentucky and Tennessee. In 1786, British officials in Canada entered into secret talks with separatist leaders in Vermont, luring them with special trade privileges along the Champlain–St. Lawrence water route. If the confederation were to dissolve, Vermont could easily be attached to Canada, along with the lightly populated territories north of the Ohio.

Other issues troubled Anglo-American relations, including slaves the British had carried off during the war and a controversy over the Maine–New Brunswick boundary. With no army, no navy, no executive, no power to control the national commerce, the United States under the Articles of Confederation could do little to force British respect for the 1783 peace treaty. Indeed, British policies "may well have contributed more to the convoking and to the success of the Federal Convention of 1787 than many who sat in that august body."[108]

The thankless task of enduring humiliation fell to John Adams, who became the first American minister to the Court of St. James's in 1785. King George III scarcely concealed his contempt for the young republic. When Adams protested British failure to send a minister to the United States, he was curtly asked whether there should be one envoy or thirteen. Adams could make no dent in British policy toward trade or the forts. The author of the Model Treaty saw the impossibility of free trade. "If we cannot obtain reciprocal liberality," he wrote in 1785, "we must adopt reciprocal prohibitions, exclusions, monopolies, and imposts."[109] British smugness infuriated the New Englander. "If an angel from heaven," he noted sarcastically, "should declare to this nation [Britain] that our states will unite, retaliate, prohibit, or trade with France, they would not believe it."[110] Adams repeated one message in dispatch after dispatch during his three frustrating years in England: Congress must have the power to regulate commerce; otherwise the British would not negotiate. Thomas Jefferson also complained that "our overtures of commercial arrangement have been treated with a derision which shew their [Britain's] firm persuasion that we shall never unite to suppress their commerce or even to impede it."[111]

Diplomacy with Spain after 1783 fared little better. Just as the British refused to evacuate the Ohio Valley after the war, so did the Spanish try to retain control over the Southwest. Part of the problem stemmed from ambiguities in the peace treaty. According to Article VII of the Anglo-American treaty, the United States gained free navigation of the Mississippi "from its source to the ocean," and the northern boundary of Florida was set at 31° north latitude. Yet Spain had not agreed to either stipulation. British Florida prior to the war had extended northward to the Yazoo River, and Spain had no intention of yielding territory or encouraging American settlement by guaranteeing free navigation. Spanish troops continued to hold Natchez on the Mississippi. Like the British north of the Ohio, Spain made alliances with the Creeks and other Indian tribes and bribed some frontier leaders into becoming "Spaniards to all intents and purposes."[112] The most threatening move came in 1784 when Spain closed the mouth of the Mississippi to American commerce. Westerners exploded in violent protest, for control over the Mississippi meant the difference between a subsistence economy and one of agrarian expansion. George Washington, visiting the frontier territories that summer, reported: "The western settlers ... stand as it were upon a pivot; the touch of a feather would almost incline them any way."[113]

Unprepared for a war on the frontier, the Spanish opted to negotiate. Don Diego de Gardoqui arrived in New York in 1785. The skillful, charming envoy had instructions to obtain an American surrender on the Mississippi by dangling trade concessions with respect to Spain and the Canary Islands. He also brought a Spanish offer to intercede with the Sultan of Morocco, whose pirates were seizing American merchant ships. Since such a treaty would obviously benefit the commercial Northeast at the expense of southern expansionists and western farmers, the Spanish envoy worked hard at flattering Secretary John Jay and the other easterners. He passed out "Havanna Segars," gave splendid dinners with the finest wines, presented a Spanish donkey to George Washington, and squired Mrs. Jay to numerous festivities.[114] "This woman," Gardoqui reported, "dominates [Jay] and nothing is done without her consent."[115]

In 1786, Jay asked Congress for permission to negotiate a treaty whereby the United States would relinquish the *use* of the Mississippi River for twenty-five or thirty years while reserving the *right* to navigate until a time when American power would be sufficient to force Spanish concessions. Jay's request sparked heated debate. Dividing geographically, seven northern congressional delegations voted to make the necessary concession, while the five southern delegations stood unanimously opposed. Jay concluded that "a treaty disagreeable to one-half of the nation had better not be made, for it would be violated."[116] He told Congress that it must decide "either to wage war with Spain or settle all differences by treaty on the best terms available."[117] Congress did neither.

Spain temporarily reopened the Mississippi River to American shipping in 1788 after the payment of special duties. Although a definitive treaty did not come until 1795 (see Chapter 2), Spanish officials began in the mid-1780s to permit American immigrants ("new and vigorous people … multiplying in the silence of peace") to settle in Louisiana and Florida provided they take an oath of allegiance. The Americanization of Spanish borderlands thus commenced long before the United States acquired those territories officially, eventually providing, as Jefferson prophesied, "the means of delivering to us peaceably, what may otherwise cost us a war."[118] In the short run, the Jay-Gardoqui talks consolidated a political alliance between the South and the West and ensured a clause in the new Constitution that provided for a two-thirds majority for senatorial approval of treaties.

Relations with France also proved frustrating. Thomas Jefferson, who succeeded Franklin as minister to France in 1784, hoped that France could replace England as America's principal trading partner, and he worked to convert the French to liberal commercial theories. Except for the opening of some French West Indian ports in 1784 and the negotiation of a consular treaty four years later, he ran into the same mercantilist restrictions John Adams faced in England. Whenever Jefferson pressed for commercial concessions, he was always reminded of the outstanding Revolutionary War debt of 35 million livres. The inability of Congress to retaliate distressed Jefferson. He momentarily thought of abandoning commerce and diplomacy altogether and having the United States "stand, with respect to Europe, precisely on the footing of China."[119] Given political and economic realities in America, however, Jefferson understood that such complete isolation was impossible, so he advocated constitutional reform instead. "My primary object in the formation of treaties," he wrote in 1785, "is to take the commerce of the states out of the hands of the states, and to place it under the superintendence of Congress, so far as the imperfect provisions of our constitution will admit, and until the states by new compact make them more perfect."[120]

Another impetus to constitutional reform grew out of the dreary record of dealings with the Barbary "pirates" in the 1780s. The rulers of the North African states—Algiers, Tunis, Tripoli, and Morocco—had transformed piracy into a national industry. As a Tripoli official rationalized with some exaggeration, "it was their duty to make war" upon all *infidels* and to "make slaves of all they could take as prisoners, and every [Moslem] who was slain in battle was sure to go to paradise."[121] By capturing merchant ships, holding sailors and cargoes for ransom, and extorting protection money from nations willing to pay, the sultans nearly drove American shipping out of the Mediterranean. The United States obtained a satisfactory treaty with Morocco in 1787, at the bargain price of only $10,000, but other negotiations proved fruitless. "We have neither troops nor treasury nor government," complained Alexander Hamilton.[122] Calling the Barbary states "a pettifogging nest of robbers," Thomas Jefferson asked for a fleet of 150 guns, which he hoped could enforce "a permanent peace" in the Mediterranean, but Congress took no steps toward constructing a navy.[123] With Yankee sailors languishing in North African jails, John Jay saw a blessing in disguise: "The more we are ill-treated abroad the more we shall unite and consolidate at home."[124]

The New Constitution and the Legacy of the Founding Generation

Within this troubled international setting, fifty-five delegates attended the Federal Convention in Philadelphia from May to September 1787. Although economic woes and Shays's Rebellion provided the immediate impetus for reform, the Founders had foreign relations in mind, too. The federal Constitution, approved by the Philadelphia assembly and ratified by the states over the next two years, eliminated most of the weaknesses that had plagued diplomacy under the Articles of Confederation. A central government consisting of an executive, a bicameral legislature, and a judiciary—all designed to balance one another—replaced the weak confederation of sovereign states.

Negotiations with foreign nations rested with the president, who would make treaties "by and with the advice and consent of the Senate … provided two-thirds of the Senators present concur." The impunity with which the individual states had violated the 1783 treaty with England prompted Benjamin Franklin's proposal that treaties shall be "the Supreme Law of the land … any thing in the Constitution or laws of any State to the contrary notwithstanding."[125] Southerners, remembering the Jay–Gardoqui negotiations, hesitated to allow Congress too much power over commerce. In return for a constitutional prohibition against taxes on exports and a twenty-year moratorium on interference with the slave trade, however, southern delegates granted Congress the right to regulate imports by a simple majority. The way now seemed clear for commercial retaliation against England. The Constitution also provided for a standing army and navy, thus freeing national defense from dependence on requisitions from the various states. "We are no longer the scoff of our enemies," one delegate boasted.[126]

A heated discussion at Philadelphia erupted over the warmaking power. Early drafts of the Constitution granted Congress the power to "make" war. Delegates soon perceived, however, that both houses might lack sufficient knowledge and unity to act quickly in the event of attack. Congress might not even be in session. When someone suggested that the president should be responsible, the delegate Elbridge Gerry of Massachusetts exclaimed that he "never expected to hear in a republic a motion to empower the Executive alone to declare war."[127] Virginia's George Mason advocated "clogging rather than facilitating war; but … facilitating peace." Fearful of executive tyranny, but not wanting to leave the country defenseless, Gerry and James Madison of Virginia proposed a compromise whereby Congress retained the power to "declare" war, while the president, as commander in chief, could still "repel sudden attacks."[128] Since Congress was granted authority to raise and support armies and navies, call out the militia, make rules and regulations for all of the armed forces, and control all policy functions associated with national defense, it seems evident that the Philadelphia delegates intended to subordinate the executive to the national legislature on this issue.

The size of the federal republic also aroused debate at Philadelphia. According to classic political theory, republics stood the best chance of survival if their territory remained small. What about the obvious disparity between the thirteen coastal states and the vast trans-Allegheny expanse stretching to the Mississippi? It took the thirty-five-year-old Virginia lawyer James Madison to articulate the philosophy of a growing republican empire. Not only did Madison draft much of the handiwork at Philadelphia, he also (along with John Jay and Alexander Hamilton) wrote the *Federalist Papers,* which exerted so much influence in the campaign for ratification of the new Constitution in 1787–1788. According to Madison, the greatest threat to a republic arose when a majority faction tyrannized others. Expansionism could benefit a republic by defusing the influence of factions, especially those that formed over economic issues. As Madison argued in *Federalist 10,* once you "extend the sphere" of government, "you take in a greater variety of parties and interests; you make it less probable that a majority … will have a common motive to invade the right of other citizens." Indeed, his close friend Jefferson would later claim that American growth proved "the falsehood of Montesquieu's doctrine that a republic can be preserved only in a small territory. The reverse is the truth."[129] Thus did the two men who later presided over the huge Louisiana Purchase in 1803 welcome westward expansion from the outset. So did most delegates at Philadelphia. Still, they had not yet answered a basic question—"whether domestic liberty could flourish alongside an ambitious and strongly assertive foreign policy."[130]

Congress's last official measure under the Articles of Confederation during the same summer of 1787 dealt with this very issue of westward expansion. With a bare quorum of eight states represented, the dying Congress enacted the Northwest Ordinance of 1787, which set up guidelines for governing the territories of the Old Northwest until they became ready for statehood. Its terms called for Congress to appoint a governor, secretary, and three judges, who would govern until the population of a territory reached 5,000 free men, at which time the settlers would elect a legislature. The territorial legislature would then rule in conjunction with a council of five selected by the governor and by Congress. The governor retained veto power. As soon as the population grew to 60,000, the inhabitants could write a constitution and apply for statehood on terms of equality with the original thirteen. Slavery was forbidden. The Founders at Philadelphia took cognizance of the new law, and stipulated, according to Article IV, Section 3 of the new Constitution, that "Congress shall have Power to dispose of and make all needful Rules and Regulations respecting the territory or other property belonging to the United States." A blueprint for an American colonial system was thus established. The same process that led to statehood in the Old Northwest for Ohio, Indiana, Michigan, Illinois, and Wisconsin continued into the twentieth century, including the admission of Hawai'i and Alaska as states in 1959.

Concurrent with these plans for a territorial system, American commissioners negotiated with representatives of the Indians who still occupied these territories. At Fort Stanwix, New York, in 1784, and at Hopewell, South Carolina, in 1785–1786, officials signed treaties opening new lands for white settlement with emissaries claiming to represent the Iroquois, Choctaw, Chickasaw, and Cherokee nations. Although Native Americans later denied that those who had signed the treaties

James Madison (1751–1836). The Virginia-born politician graduated from Princeton, sat in the Continental Congress, and served in the state legislature before journeying to Philadelphia in 1787, where he earned the title "Father of the Constitution." He later served as Jefferson's secretary of state (1801–1809) and was elected the fourth U.S. president (1809–1817). Madison believed strongly that economic coercion would compel European countries to make concessions to the Americans, especially on trade principles. (Library of Congress)

ceding lands had the authority to do so, the United States regarded these treaties as confirmation of its sovereignty over the trans-Allegheny interior. The Creeks, who did not sign the Hopewell treaties, continued to resist along the Georgia frontier until 1790. Although these treaties later became mechanisms for national expansion (or "licenses for empire"), the military power to defend frontier settlements was conspicuously lacking under the Articles.[131]

When George Washington took the oath of office as president at Federal Hall in New York on April 30, 1789, he could look optimistically at the international prospects of the new republic. Not only could Washington employ the diplomatic tools fashioned at Philadelphia, but he and his compatriots could also make good use of the foreign-relations experiences of the past thirteen years. The American Revolution and its aftermath had produced a remarkable reservoir of leaders who had become sophisticated in world affairs. Diplomats such as Jefferson, Jay, and Adams soon contributed their expertise to the new administration. Washington's wartime collaboration with the French demonstrated that he understood the intricacies of alliance politics, as did his wartime aide, Alexander Hamilton, the nation's first secretary of the treasury. Because intellectual and political leaders were often the same people in this era, and because domestic, economic, and foreign policies were inextricably related, the founding generation gave rise to a foreign-policy elite of exceptional skills.

The diplomatic goals of independence and expansion were both practical and idealistic. Adams's Model Treaty of 1776 had projected a vision whereby American commerce would be open to the entire world, thus simultaneously diminishing one of the major causes of war and increasing American profits. Independence and extensive boundaries would protect a republican experiment that, in turn, could serve as a countervailing model for a world of monarchies. The Mississippi River, it seems, even had divine sanction. John Jay told the Spanish in 1780 that "Americans, almost to a man, believed that God Almighty had made that river a highway for the people of the upper country to go to the sea."[132] Even more expansive, the geographer Jedidiah Morse predicted in 1789 that America would soon become the "largest empire that ever existed," including "millions of souls, west of the Mississippi."[133] Of course, before Americans could move beyond the Mississippi, the boundaries of 1783 had to be made secure.

The Revolutionary generation that looked westward optimistically believed that "they could teach the peoples of the rest of the world to govern themselves in happiness and prosperity; they did not believe that the majority of other peoples were unteachable or expendable."[134] Yet as Americans moved across the Alleghenies, they entered "a cultural contact zone" of blurred boundaries and contested terrain, a frontier in which "no culture, group, or government can claim effective control or hegemony over others."[135] Agents of rival European empires, overlapping legal jurisdictions, alien customs and religions, and especially heterogeneous Indian populations with established linkages to European metropoles, all blocked the path of peaceful westward expansion. Over time, the Enlightenment belief in an innate general human capacity for progress gave way to the racist belief in Anglo-Saxon superiority over those whom Americans destroyed or dominated.

Americans sought independence and empire without resort to European-style power politics. But the attractions of American commerce proved insufficient to

Daniel Boone (1734–1820). The legendary "pathfinder," "trailblazer," and "Indian fighter" who came to symbolize early westward expansion and the conquest of an ever-moving frontier is here depicted in Horatio Greenough's marble statue, *The Rescue Group* (1852), defending his family against an Indian attack. The adventurer, popularized in print and art, became a mythical folk hero. Born into a Quaker family in Pennsylvania, Boone moved from there to North Carolina and then to Kentucky, exploring the region in the early 1750s and founding Boonesboro. During the American Revolution, Shawnees captured Boone, but he escaped. Because of defective titles, he lost large tracts of his Kentucky lands, and in 1799 he and his wife, Rebecca, moved to Spanish Missouri, where he received a substantial land grant. After the Louisiana Purchase of 1803, Boone again suffered legal contests over his land holdings, some of which Congress restored to him in 1814. Boone experienced the multicultural complexities of the trans-Allegheny frontier. His son Daniel Morgan Boone married a French Creole, Constantine Philibert, whose daughters, Elizabeth and Eulalie, grew up in Creole Kansas City, spoke French, and became baptized Catholics. (Library of Congress)

bring automatic aid and recognition; so Franklin in 1778 negotiated the alliance with France. The American preference for commercial treaties instead of political alliances did not diminish after 1778, however, and the commercial and neutral-rights provisions of the Model Treaty remained central to American foreign relations. Commercial treaties in the 1780s with Sweden, Prussia, and the Netherlands followed those principles. Americans believed, moreover, that the emphasis on commerce did not exalt profits over principles. As James Monroe later wrote: "People in Europe suppose us to be merchants, occupied exclusively with pepper and ginger. They are much deceived. … The immense majority of our citizens … are … controlled by principles of honor and dignity."[136]

The United States, of course, had been forced to compromise principle—to make the alliance with France to win independence. Without Comte de Rochambeau's army and Admiral de Grasse's fleet, Washington could not have forced Cornwallis's surrender in 1781. Indeed, at the decisive battles around Yorktown, more French than American soldiers fought against the British. French loans of some 35 million livres had kept an impecunious Congress solvent during the war. To be sure, Vergennes wanted to limit American boundaries; French agents in Philadelphia used their influence with Congress to hamstring American diplomats abroad; and as late as 1787 the French chargé d'affaires predicted that America would break up and urged his government to plan the seizure of New York or Rhode Island before the British could act. Still, the French alliance had helped secure American independence, and the treaty remained valid in 1789, including the provision guaranteeing French possessions in the New World.

The French alliance notwithstanding, the eschewing of foreign entanglements remained a cardinal American tenet in the 1780s. "The less we rely on others," wrote Connecticut's Roger Sherman, "the more surely shall we provide for our own honor and success and retrieve that balance between the contending European powers."[137] Americans regarded the European balance of power as a "vortex of death and destruction, not a sensitive mechanism that could be made to work for neutral rights, free trade and world peace."[138] American diplomats abroad simply did not trust European countries. Europe had its own set of interests, America another. Even a Francophile like Jefferson could write: "Our interest calls for a perfect equality in our conduct towards [England and France]; but no preferences any where."[139]

Americans, in short, sought fulfillment of their goals without war or foreign allies. The federal Constitution strengthened national authority. With an abundant federal revenue came stronger national credit. A flourishing foreign commerce and the power to regulate that commerce, it was hoped, would provide an important diplomatic lever. American military strength hardly existed. Europeans who visited America in the 1780s analyzed American speech patterns, described the flora and fauna, admired the landscape, but said little of military matters. The United States with its population of 3.5 million seemed a slight threat to the 15 million British or 25 million French nationals. The traditional Anglo-Saxon fear of standing armies, and the expense of naval construction, made Americans, even under the Constitution, slow to build a defense establishment. Even Hamilton, the most military-minded member of Washington's government, predicted that fifty years would pass before "the embryo of a great empire" could tip the balance between competing European powers or between the Old World and the New.[140] Without military power or a foreign ally, the United States might find it difficult to maintain its independence, claim and extend its boundaries, and expand its commerce.

FURTHER READING FOR THE PERIOD TO 1789

For the colonial period, see Fred Anderson, *Crucible of War* (2001); Frank W. Brecher, *Losing a Continent* (1998); T. H. Breen and Timothy Hall, *Colonial America in an Atlantic World* (2004); Marc Egnal, *A Mighty Empire* (1988); J. H. Elliott, *Empires of the Atlantic World* (2007) and *Spain, Europe, and the Wider World, 1500–1800* (2009); David H. Fischer, *Champlain's Dream* (2008); Felix Gilbert, *The Beginnings of American Diplomacy* (1965); Lawrence S. Kaplan, *Colonies into Nation* (1972); Peggy K. Liss, *Atlantic Empires* (1983); Robert Olwell and Allen Tully, eds., *Cultures and Identities in British Colonial America* (2006); Max Savelle, *The Origins of American Diplomacy* (1967); Matt Schumann and Karl W. Sweitzer, *The Seven Years War* (2008); and Robert W. Tucker and David C. Henrickson, *The Fall of the First British Empire* (1982).

Revolutionary-era issues are treated in Bernard Bailyn, *To Begin the World Anew* (2003); Samuel Flagg Bemis, *The Diplomacy of the American Revolution* (1957); Richard Buel, Jr., *In Irons* (1998); Thomas E. Chavez, *Spain and the Independence of the United States* (2002); Stephen Conway, *The British Isles and the War of American Independence* (2000); John Crowley, *The Privileges of Independence* (1993); Jonathan R. Dull, *A Diplomatic History of the American Revolution* (1985); John Ferling, *Setting the World Ablaze* (2000) and *A Leap in the Dark* (2003); Eliga H. Gould, *The Persistence of Empire* (2000); David C. Hendrickson, *Peace Pact* (2003); Ronald Hoffman and Peter J. Albert, eds.,

Diplomacy and Revolution (1981) and *Peace and the Peacemakers* (1986); Reginald Horsman, *The Diplomacy of the New Republic, 1776–1815* (1985); Francis Jennings, *The Creation of America* (2000); Lawrence S. Kaplan, ed., *The American Revolution and "A Candid World"* (1977); Richard B. Morris, *The Peacemakers* (1965); Orville T. Murphy, *Charles Gravier, Comte de Vergennes* (1982); J. W. S. Nordholt, *The Dutch Republic and American Independence* (1986); Peter Onuf and Nicholas Onuf, *Federal Union, Modern World* (1993); Andrew Jackson O'Shaughnessy, *An Empire Divided* (2000); Bradford Perkins, *The Creation of a Republican Empire, 1776–1865* (1993); Norman E. Saul, *Distant Friends* (1991) (on Russia); Stacy Schiff, *A Great Improvisation* (2005); H. M. Scott, *British Foreign Policy in the Age of the American Revolution* (1990); William Stinchcombe, *The American Revolution and the French Alliance* (1969); Reginald C. Stuart, *United States Expansionism and British North America, 1775–1871* (1988); William Earl Weeks, *Building the Continental Empire* (1996); Stanley Weintraub, *Iron Tears* (2005); Peter Whitely, *Lord North* (1996); and Gordon S. Wood, *The Creation of the American Republic* (1969).

Foreign relations under the Articles of Confederation and foreign-policy questions during the making of the Constitution are discussed in Joyce Appleby, *Inheriting the Revolution* (2000); Richard Beeman et al., eds., *Beyond Confederation* (1987); Daniel G. Lang, *Foreign Policy in the Early Republic* (1985); Charles A. Lofgren, *"Government from Reflection and Choice"* (1986); Frederick W. Marks III, *Independence on Trial* (1986); Richard B. Morris, *The Forging of the Union, 1781–1789* (1987); Peter S. Onuf, *Statehood and Union* (1987); Jack N. Rakove, *The Beginnings of National Politics* (1979); Charles R. Ritcheson, *Aftermath of Revolution* (1969); Abraham Sofaer, *War, Foreign Affairs and Constitutional Power,* vol. 1, *The Origins* (1976); and J. Leitch Wright, *Britain and the American Frontier, 1783–1815* (1975).

For the frontier and relations with Indians, see Andrew Clayton and Fredrika Teute, eds., *Contact Points* (1998); Gregory Evans Dowd, *A Spirited Resistance* (1992); Walter S. Dunn, *Opening New Markets* (2002); Eric Hinderaker, *Elusive Empires* (1997); Frederick E. Hoxie, ed., *Indians in American History* (1988); Robert Kagan, *Dangerous Nation* (2006); Dorothy Jones, *License for Empire* (1992); Jane T. Merritt, *At the Crossroads* (2003); and David M. Weber, *The Spanish Frontier in North America* (1992).

For individuals, see William H. Adams, *The Paris Years of Thomas Jefferson* (1997); Joyce Appleby, *Thomas Jefferson* (2003); Jeremy Black, *George III* (2009); H. W. Brands, *The First American* (Franklin) (2002); Noble E. Cunningham, Jr., *In Pursuit of Reason* (1988); John P. Diggins, *John Adams* (2003); Jonathan R. Dull, *Franklin the Diplomat* (1982); Joseph Ellis, *Founding Brothers* (2000) and *American Creation* (2007); Eric Foner, *Tom Paine and Revolutionary America* (1976); John Ferling, *John Adams* (1992); Don Higginbotham, *George Washington* (2002); James H. Hutson, *John Adams and the Diplomacy of the American Revolution* (1980); Walter Isaacson, *Benjamin Franklin* (2003); Lawrence S. Kaplan, *Jefferson and France* (1963); John Keane, *Tom Paine* (1995); David McCullough, *John Adams* (2001); Robert Middlekauff, *Benjamin Franklin and His Enemies* (1996); Edmund S. Morgan, *The Genius of George Washington* (1980); Mark Philip, *Thomas Paine* (2007); George B. Shackelford, *Thomas Jefferson's Travels in Europe, 1784–1789* (1995); Walter Stahr, *John Jay* (2005); Evan Thomas, *John Paul Jones* (2003); Gordon H. Wood, *The Americanization of Benjamin Franklin* (2004); and books on diplomatic leaders listed in Chapter 2.

See also the General Bibliography, the notes below, and Robert L. Beisner, ed., *Guide to American Foreign Relations Since 1600* (2003).

NOTES TO CHAPTER 1

1. Quoted in David C. Hendrickson, *Peace Pact* (Lawrence: University Press of Kansas, 2003), p. 191.
2. Quoted in Richard B. Morris, *The Peacemakers* (New York: Harper and Row, 1965), p. 307.
3. Quoted in Francis Wharton, ed., *The Revolutionary Diplomatic Correspondence of the United States* (Washington, D.C.: Government Printing Office, 1889; 6 vols.), *V,* 657.
4. Quoted in Morris, *Peacemakers,* pp. 309–310.
5. Adams quoted in Edmund S. Morgan, *Benjamin Franklin* (New Haven: Yale University Press, 2002), p. 294.
6. Gregg L. Lint, "John Adams and the 'Bolder Plan,'" in Richard Alan Ryerson, ed., *John Adams and the Founding of the Republic* (Boston: Massachusetts Historical Society, 2001), p. 112; Jay quoted in John Ferling, *Setting the World Ablaze* (New York: Oxford University Press, 2000), p. 258.

7. Quoted in Bradford Perkins, "The Peace of Paris," in Ronald Hoffman and Peter J. Albert, eds., *Peace and the Peacemakers* (Charlottesville: University of Virginia Press, 1992), p. 206.

8. Quoted in Morris, *Peacemakers,* p. 357.

9. Quoted in Bernard Bailyn, *To Begin the World Anew* (New York: Knopf, 2003), p. 65.

10. Quoted in Jonathan R. Dull, *A Diplomatic History of the American Revolution* (New Haven: Yale University Press, 1985), p. 147.

11. Quoted in Stacy Schiff, *A Great Improvisation: Franklin, France, and the Birth of America* (New York: Henry Holt, 2005), p. 312.

12. Quoted in L. H. Butterfield, ed., *Diary and Autobiography of John Adams* (Cambridge: Harvard University Press, 1961; 4 vols.), *III,* 82.

13. Samuel Flagg Bemis, *The Diplomacy of the American Revolution* (Bloomington: Indiana University Press, 1957), p. 256.

14. Quoted in John Ferling, "John Adams, Diplomat," *William and Mary Quarterly, LI* (April 1994), 252.

15. Michael H. Hunt, *The American Ascendancy* (Chapel Hill: University of North Carolina Press, 2007), p. 4.

16. Quoted in Marc Egnal, *A Mighty Empire* (Ithaca: Cornell University Press, 1988), p. 12.

17. Leonard W. Labaree, ed., *The Papers of Benjamin Franklin* (New Haven: Yale University Press, 1951—; 37 vols. to date), *IX,* 7.

18. Quoted in T. H. Breen and Timothy Hall, *Colonial America in an Atlantic World* (New York: Longman, 2004), p. 274.

19. Gordon H. Wood, *The Radicalism of the American Revolution* (New York: Knopf, 1992), pp. 133–134.

20. Quoted in Daniel K. Richter, "Native Americans, the Plan of 1764, and a British Empire That Never Was," in Robert Olwell and Allen Tully, eds., *Cultures and Identities in Colonial British America* (Baltimore: Johns Hopkins University Press, 2006), p. 276.

21. Kenneth M. Morisson, "Native Americans and the American Revolution," in Frederick E. Hoxie, ed., *Indians in American History* (Arlington Heights, Ill.: Harlan Davidson, 1988), p. 101.

22. Quoted in H. Trevor Colbourn, *The Lamp of Experience* (Chapel Hill: University of North Carolina Press, 1965), p. 129.

23. Labaree, *Franklin Papers, XIII,* 151.

24. Max Savelle, "Colonial Origins of American Diplomatic Principles," *Pacific Historical Review, III* (1934), 337.

25. Quoted in Felix Gilbert, *The Beginnings of American Diplomacy* (New York: Harper and Row, 1965), p. 25.

26. Quoted in Eliga H. Gould, *The Persistence of Empire* (Chapel Hill: University of North Carolina Press, 2000), p. 56.

27. Quoted in Gilbert, *Beginnings,* p. 28.

28. Quoted *ibid.,* p. 61.

29. Quoted *ibid.,* p. 57.

30. Quoted in David M. Fitzsimons, "Tom Paine's New World Order," *Diplomatic History, XIX* (Fall 1995), 573.

31. Quoted in Hendrickson, *Peace Pact,* p. 45.

32. Quoted in Gilbert, *Beginnings,* p. 65.

33. Quoted in Jan W. Schulte Nordholt, *The Dutch Republic and American Independence* (Chapel Hill: University of North Carolina Press, 1982), p. 190.

34. Anders Stephanson, *Manifest Destiny* (New York: Hill and Wang, 1995), p. xii.

35. Quoted *ibid.,* p. 19.

36. Thomas Paine, *Common Sense* (New York: Wiley, 1942 ed.), pp. 26–32.

37. Quoted in Fitzsimons, "Paine's New World," 575.

38. Quoted in Richard Van Alstyne, *Empire and Independence* (New York: Wiley, 1965), p. 106.

39. Edmund C. Burnett, ed., *Letters of Members of the Continental Congress* (Washington, D.C.: Carnegie Institution, 1921–1936; 8 vols.), *I,* 502.

40. Worthington C. Ford, ed., *Journals of the Continental Congress* (Washington, D.C.: Government Printing Office, 1904–1937; 34 vols.), *V,* 768–769.

41. John E. Crowley, *The Privileges of Independence* (Baltimore: Johns Hopkins University Press, 1993), p. 58.

42. Charles Francis Adams, ed., *The Works of John Adams* (Boston: Little, Brown, 1850–1865; 10 vols.), *X,* 269.

43. Quoted in Ferling, "Adams," p. 232.

44. Peggy K. Liss, *Atlantic Empires* (Baltimore: Johns Hopkins University Press, 1983), p. 106.

45. Quoted in Claude H. Van Tyne, "French Aid Before the Alliance of 1778," *American Historical Review, XXXI* (October 1925), 27.

46. Quoted in Van Alstyne, *Empire and Independence,* p. 43.

47. Quoted in Orville T. Murphy, *Charles Gravier* (Albany: State University of New York Press, 1982), p. 233.

48. Quoted in Bemis, *Diplomacy of the American Revolution,* p. 27.

49. Quoted in Schiff, *Great Improvisation,* p. 21.

50. Quoted in H. M. Scott, *British Foreign Policy in the Age of the American Revolution* (London: Oxford University Press, 1990), p. 243.

51. Franklin quoted in Morgan, *Franklin,* p. 243.

52. Quoted in Bailyn, *To Begin the World Anew,* p. 65.

53. Quoted in Claude-Anne Lopez, *Mon Cher Papa: Franklin and the Ladies of Paris* (New Haven: Yale University Press, 1966), pp. 257–258.

54. Gordon H. Wood, *The Americanization of Benjamin Franklin* (New York: Penguin, 2004), pp. 174–175.

55. Quoted in Bradford Perkins, *The Creation of a Republican Empire, 1776–1865* (New York: Cambridge University Press, 1993), p. 30.

56. Gilbert Chinard, ed., *The Treaties of 1778 and Allied Documents* (Baltimore: Johns Hopkins University Press, 1928), pp. 51–55.

57. Quoted in John S. Ferling, *A Leap in the Dark* (New York: Oxford University Press, 2003), p. 204.

58. John Adams quoted in James H. Hutson, "Early American Diplomacy," in Lawrence S. Kaplan, ed., *The American Revolution and "A Candid World"* (Kent, Ohio: Kent State University Press, 1977), pp. 56–57.

59. Quoted in Van Alstyne, *Empire and Independence,* p. 93n.

60. Andrew Jackson O'Shaughnessy, *An Empire Divided* (Philadelphia: University of Pennsylvania Press, 2000), p. 210.

61. Quoted in Elmer Bendiner, *The Virgin Diplomats* (New York: Knopf, 1976), p. 63.

62. Quoted in P. L. Haworth, "Frederick the Great and the American Revolution," *American Historical Review, IX* (April 1904), 468.

63. Wharton, ed., *Revolutionary Correspondence, V,* 415.

64. Quoted in Schiff, *Great Improvisation,* p. 293.

65. Quoted in Norman E. Saul, *Distant Friends* (Lawrence: University Press of Kansas, 1991), p. 15.

66. Quoted in Robert P. Remini, *John Quincy Adams* (New York: Times Books, 2002), pp. 11–12.

67. Ford, ed., *Journals of the Continental Congress, XXIV,* 394.

68. Quoted in Thomas E. Chavez, *Spain and the Independence of the United States* (Albuquerque: University of New Mexico Press, 2002), p. 75.

69. Samuel Flagg Bemis, *A Diplomatic History of the United States* (New York: Holt, Rinehart and Winston, 1965; 5th ed.), p. 34.

70. Quoted in Murphy, *Gravier,* p. 328.

71. Esmond Wright, "The British Objectives, 1780–1783," in Hoffman and Albert, *Peace and the Peacemakers,* p. 6.

72. Quoted in Peter Whitely, *Lord North* (London: Hambledon Press, 1996), p. 175.

73. Quoted in Frank Monaghan, *John Jay* (Indianapolis: Bobbs-Merrill, 1935), p. 136.

74. Quoted in Morris, *Peacemakers*, p. 242.

75. Quoted in Walter Stahr, *John Jay* (New York: Hambledon and London, 2005), p. 136.

76. Lawrence S. Kaplan, *Colonies into Nation* (New York: Macmillan, 1972), p 135.

77. Quoted in Fabian Hilrich, "Visions of the Asian Periphery," in Andreas W. Daum, Lloyd C. Gardner, and Wilfried Mausbach, eds., *America, Vietnam, and the World* (New York: Cambridge University Press, 2004), pp. 46–47.

78. Morgan, *Franklin*, p. 286.

79. Quoted in Morris, *Peacemakers*, p. 263.

80. Quoted in Carl Van Doren, *Benjamin Franklin* (New York: Viking Press, 1938), p. 671.

81. Scott, *British Foreign Policy*, p. 327.

82. Quoted in Stanley Weintraub, *Iron Tears* (New York: Simon & Schuster, 2005), p. 325.

83. Reginald C. Stuart, *United States Expansionism and British North America, 1775–1871* (Chapel Hill: University of North Carolina Press, 1988), p. 26.

84. Quoted in Crowley, *Privileges*, p. 64.

85. Quoted in Mark Kurlansky, *Cod* (New York: Walker and Company, 1997), p. 100.

86. H. P. Johnston, ed., *Correspondence and Public Papers of John Jay* (New York: G. P. Putnam's Sons, 1890–1893; 4 vols.), II, 344.

87. Quoted in Mary Beth Norton *The British-Americans* (Boston: Little, Brown, 1972), pp. 175–176.

88. Quoted *ibid.*, p. 176.

89. Wharton, ed., *Revolutionary Correspondence, VI,* 140.

90. Quoted in Schiff, *Great Improvisation*, p. 322.

91. Hendrickson, *Peace Pact*, p. 195.

92. Quoted in Chavez, *Spain and Independence*, p. 135.

93. Quoted in Morris, *Peacemakers*, p. 459.

94. Dull, *A Diplomatic History*, p. 163; Count Aranda quoted in James G. Cusick, *The Other War of 1812* (Gainesville: University Press of Florida, 2003), p. 17.

95. Quoted in Michael Hirsh, *At War with Ourselves* (New York: Oxford University Press, 2003), p. 77.

96. Johnston, ed., *Correspondence of John Jay, III,* 154.

97. Quoted in David M. Weber, *The Spanish Frontier in North America* (New Haven: Yale University Press, 1992), p. 274.

98. Stephen Collins quoted in Richard Buel, Jr., *In Irons* (New Haven: Yale University Press, 1998), p. 241.

99. Quoted in Laura Jensen, *Patriots, Settlers, and the Origins of American Social Policy* (New York: Cambridge University Press, 2003), p. 136n.

100. Quoted in Richard P. Tucker, *Insatiable Appetite* (Berkeley: University of California Press, 2000), p. 66.

101. Quoted in Liss, *Atlantic Empires*, p. 112.

102. 'Quoted in Samuel Flagg Bemis, *Jay's Treaty* (New Haven: Yale University Press, 1962), p. 34.

103. Hendrickson, *Peace Pact*, p. 202.

104. Quoted in Kaplan, *Colonies into Nation*, pp. 160–161.

105. Josiah Tucker quoted in Hendrickson, *Peace Pact*, p. 4.

106. Quoted in Frederick W. Marks III, *Independence on Trial* (Baton Rouge: Louisiana State University Press, 1973), p. 135.

107. Quoted in Gregory Evans Dowd, *A Spirited Resistance* (Baltimore: Johns Hopkins University Press, 1992), p. 93.

108. Julian P. Boyd, *Number 7* (Princeton: Princeton University Press, 1964), p. xi.

109. Quoted in Jerald A. Combs, *The Jay Treaty* (Berkeley: University of California Press, 1970), p. 24.

110. Quoted in Charles R. Ritcheson, *Aftermath of Revolution* (Dallas: Southern Methodist University Press, 1969), p. 44.

111. Quoted in Peter S. Onuf and Leonard J. Sadosky, *Jeffersonian America* (Malden, Mass.: Blackwell, 2002), p. 186.

112. Arthur St. Clair quoted in John Craig Hammond, *Slavery, Freedom, and Expansion in the Early American West* (Charlottesville: University of Virginia Press, 2007), p. 16.

113. Quoted in Fred Anderson and Andrew Cayton, *The Dominion of War* (New York: Viking, 2005), p. 183.

114. Quoted in Jon Kukla, *A Wilderness So Immense* (New York: Knopf, 2003), p. 54.

115. Quoted *ibid.*, p. 53.

116. Quoted in Richard B. Morris, *The Forging of the Union, 1781–1789* (New York: Harper and Row, 1987), p. 243; quoted in Marks, *Independence on Trial*, p. 31.

117. Baron de Condorolet quoted in Kagan, *Dangerous Nation* (New York: Knopf, 2006), pp. 78–79.

118. Quoted in Weber, *Spanish Frontier*, p. 281.

119. Quoted in Lawrence S. Kaplan, *Jefferson and France* (New Haven: Yale University Press, 1963), p. 23.

120. Quoted in Noble E. Cunningham, Jr., *In Pursuit of Reason* (Baton Rouge: Louisiana State University Press, 1988), p. 93.

121. Tripoli ambassador quoted in Stahr, *John Jay*, p. 218.

122. Quoted in Robert Kagan, *Dangerous Nation*, p. 58.

123. Quoted in Michael B. Oren, *Power, Faith, and Fantasy* (New York: Norton, 2007), p.32; quoted in James R. Sofka, "The Jeffersonian Idea of National Security," *Diplomatic History, XXI* (Fall 1997), 534.

124. Quoted in Marks, *Independence on Trial,* p. 48.

125. Article VI of the Constitution.

126. Lyman H. Butterfield, ed., *Letters of Benjamin Rush* (Princeton: Princeton University Press, 1951; 2 vols.), I, 475.

127. Quoted in Jacob Javits, *Who Makes War* (New York: Morrow, 1973), p. 13.

128. Quoted in Charles A. Lofgren, *"Government from Reflection and Choice"* (New York: Oxford University Press, 1986), p. 7.

129. Jacob E. Cooke, ed., *The Federalist* (Middletown, Conn.: Wesleyan University Press, 1961), p. 64; Jefferson quoted in Niall Ferguson, *Colossus* (New York: Penguin, 2004), p. 34.

130. Michael H. Hunt, *Ideology and U.S. Foreign Policy* (New Haven: Yale University Press, 1987), p. 21.

131. Dorothy Jones, *License for Empire* (Chicago: University of Chicago Press, 1982).

132. Quoted in Stahr, *John Jay*, p. 135.

133. Quoted in Ferguson, *Colossus*, p. 35.

134. Reginald Horsman, *Race and Manifest Destiny* (Cambridge: Harvard University Press, 1981), p. 299.

135. Emily S. Rosenberg, "A Call to Revolution," *Diplomatic History, XXII* (Winter 1998), 65.

136. Quoted in Ernest R. May, *The Making of the Monroe Doctrine* (Cambridge: Harvard University Press, 1975), p. 19.

137. Quoted *ibid.*, p. 205.

138. Peter Onuf and Nicholas Onuf, *Federal Union, Modern World: The Law of Nations in an Age of Revolutions, 1776–1814* (Madison, Wis.: Madison House, 1993), p. 162.

139. Julian Boyd, ed., *The Papers of Thomas Jefferson* (Princeton: Princeton University Press, 1950–1974; 19 vols.), *VIII,* 545.

140. Quoted in Hunt, *Ideology*, p. 25.

CHAPTER 2

Independence, Expansion, and War, 1789–1815

***Leopard* Versus *Chesapeake* 1807.**   *This naval encounter highlighted the impressment issue in Anglo-American relations and nearly caused war. After the incident, President Thomas Jefferson closed U.S. ports to the Royal Navy, only to find that British commanders haughtily anchored their ships in Chesapeake Bay. Preoccupied at the time by Aaron Burr's treason trial, Jefferson chose economic coercion over military retaliation. The British frigate* Shannon *later captured the ill-fated* Chesapeake *in 1813 outside Boston harbor following a battle in which the dying American captain, James Lawrence, uttered the now immortal words: "Don't give up the ship." The Royal Navy broke up and sold the vessel after the Napoleonic wars. (Watercolor by Irwin J. Bevan, courtesy of the Mariners' Museum, Newport News, Virginia)*

DIPLOMATIC CROSSROAD

❖ *The Chesapeake Affair, 1807*

AT 7:15 A.M. on June 22, 1807, the thirty-six-gun American frigate *Chesapeake* weighed anchor at Hampton Roads, Virginia. Commanded by Commodore James Barron, the *Chesapeake* was bound for the Mediterranean Sea as flagship of the small naval squadron that protected American merchant vessels from the Barbary states. The ship's crew numbered 329, several of whom had deserted the Royal Navy and enlisted on the *Chesapeake* under assumed names. Sick sailors, recovering from a drinking bout of the night before, sought relief in the sunny air on the upper deck. Loose lumber cluttered the gun deck. Four of the guns did not fit perfectly into their carriages. Only five of the powder horns used to prime the guns were actually filled, and officers had not exercised the crew at the guns during the ship's fitting out in Hampton Roads. Barron set sail anyway. Already four months behind schedule, the ship would have ample opportunity for gunnery practice during the long sea voyage.

At 9:00 the *Chesapeake* passed Lynnhaven Bay, where two seventy-four-gun British ships of the line, *Bellona* and *Melampus,* lay anchored. A rumor had circulated in Norfolk, Virginia, that the captain of the *Melampus* was threatening to seize alleged deserters from the *Chesapeake,* but Barron took no special precautions. Neither British ship stirred. Soon after midday the *Chesapeake* sighted the fifty-six-gun ship H.M.S. *Leopard.* At approximately 3:30 P.M., some ten miles southeast of Cape Henry, the *Leopard*'s captain hailed that he wanted to send dispatches to the Mediterranean through the courtesy of the American commodore. The *Chesapeake* then hailed back: "We will heave to and you can send your boat on board of us."[1] At this point Barron made a serious mistake by allowing a foreign warship to approach close alongside without first calling his crew to battle stations. But to Barron the idea of a British naval attack "was so extravagant that he might as well have expected one when at anchor in Hampton Roads."[2]

British lieutenant John Meade came aboard at 3:45 and handed Barron a copy of orders instructing him to search the *Chesapeake* for British deserters. "I know of no such men as you describe," Barron replied correctly; he could never allow his crew to be mustered "by any other but their own officers. It is my disposition to preserve harmony, and I hope this answer ... will prove satisfactory."[3] Meade returned to the *Leopard.* Barron now ordered the gun deck cleared for action.

It was nearly 4:30. To prepare the frigate for battle required a full half hour. The *Leopard* used the windward advantage to move closer. Captain S. P. Humphreys called through the hailing pipe: "Commodore Barron, you must be aware of the necessity I am under of complying with the orders of my commander-in-chief." Barron tried to gain time by shouting: "I do not hear what you say."[4] He ordered the men to stations without drumbeat. The *Leopard* fired a shot across the *Chesapeake*'s bow. Another shot followed a minute later. Then, from a distance of less than 200 feet, the helpless *Chesapeake* was pounded by a full broadside of solid shot and canister.

James Barron (1769–1851). The commander of the *Chesapeake,* according to court-martial proceedings conducted in 1808, had not prepared his ship properly for battle with the *Leopard.* Many of his fellow officers thought Barron had prematurely surrendered. The U.S. Navy suspended Barron for five years without pay. He returned to service but was given only shore duty. Years later he killed his nemesis, naval officer Stephen Decatur, in a duel. Decatur, formerly a close friend, had sat as a judge at the trial that condemned Barron in 1808. (Library of Congress)

The Americans had no time to carry lighted matches or loggerheads from below decks to their loaded guns before three broadsides pummeled them. In ten minutes the *Chesapeake* was hulled twenty-two times. Its main masts badly damaged, the ship suffered three men killed, eighteen wounded, including Commodore Barron, who stood exposed on the quarterdeck throughout the barrage. Finally, not wanting to sacrifice lives needlessly, Barron ordered the flag struck. The Americans salvaged a modicum of honor by firing a lone shot at the *Leopard.* A lieutenant had managed to discharge the gun by carrying a live coal in his fingers all the way from the galley. The eighteen-pound shot penetrated the *Leopard's* hull but fell harmlessly into the wardroom.

British officers took only four sailors from the *Chesapeake.* Of the four, three were undeniably Americans, deserters from the *Melampus* the previous March. Two of these, both African Americans, had previously deserted from an American merchant vessel and had voluntarily enlisted in the Royal Navy in 1806. The fourth deserter was a surly Londoner, Jenkin Ratford, who had openly insulted his former British officers on the streets of Norfolk. The British eventually hanged him from a Halifax yardarm; the three Americans received prison sentences.

The American people exploded in anger when they heard about the attack on the *Chesapeake.* "This event has excited a universal Ferment," a British envoy reported.[5] Heretofore the Royal Navy's practice of impressing alleged British sailors from American merchant ships had caused much diplomatic wrangling, but little else. Just a few months earlier, President Thomas Jefferson and Secretary of State James Madison had rejected a treaty with England largely because it failed to disavow "this authorized system of kidnapping upon the ocean."[6] British war-ships constantly stopped and searched merchant vessels in American waters, and the previous year H.M.S. *Leander* had killed an American when firing a shot across a merchant ship's bow. But the *Chesapeake* affair lacked precedent: The British had deliberately attacked an American *naval* vessel, a virtual act of war.

Federalists and Republicans alike expressed shock. In the historian Henry Adams's words, "the brand seethed and hissed like the glowing olive-stake of Ulysses in the Cyclops' eye, until the whole American people, like Cyclops, roared with pain and stood frantic on the shore, hurling abuse at their enemy, who taunted them from his safe ships."[7] Outraged citizens of Norfolk proposed that British officers "be stitched in buckram and pricked to death by needles" and their com-mander's "eyes be bunged up, so that he may not see to write more orders for the murders of Americans."[8] An angry British admiral urged a retaliatory attack on New York City that would "disable" Americans from going to war and "compel them to any treaty." Only "red hot [cannon] balls" can keep the British "from our Rivers & Bays," warned one American veteran of the Revolutionary War.[9]

Jefferson issued a proclamation on July 2 closing coastal waters to British war-ships. Two weeks later he told the French minister: "If the English do not give us the satisfaction we demand, we will take Canada."[10] Treasury Secretary Albert Gallatin believed that war with England might salvage "the independence and honor of the nation" and "prevent our degenerating, like the Hollanders, into a nation of mere calculators."[11]

The *Chesapeake* affair did not lead to war—at least not immediately. The pres-ident first tried military preparations and diplomatic alternatives. Even before Congress convened late in the year, he moved to strengthen U.S. defenses. Without public fanfare, the president called all naval and merchant vessels home, ordered naval gunboats to be readied, armed seven coastal fortresses, sent field guns to state militia, gave war warnings to all frontier posts, and informed state governors that he might call 100,000 militia members to federal service. In readying the ramparts, however, Jefferson discovered the inadequacy of U.S. defenses. The Navy Department could not even send a ship to the East Indies to call home American merchant vessels because that agency lacked funds for such a voyage. Even Washington, D.C. seemed vulnerable to attack. Gallatin warned prophetically that the British could "land at Annapolis, march to the city, and re-embark before the militia could be collected to repel [them]."[12] When Congress met in December 1807, Jefferson persuaded reluctant Republicans to triple the size of the regular army—not to fight the British but to enforce embargoes against them. He similarly requested inexpensive coastal gunboats in preference to oceangoing frigates.

Nor did diplomacy quiet the crisis. The British government might have settled the matter amicably if the Americans had asked only for an apology and repara-tions for the *Chesapeake* incident. Foreign Secretary George Canning told the U.S. minister James Monroe exactly that in July 1807, but Jefferson insisted that England abandon impressment altogether. Canning was willing to disavow the incident but not the practice. England did not formally apologize for the *Chesapeake* attack until 1811, by which time America's wounded sense of honor and British stubbornness made war almost unavoidable. By then, the *Chesapeake* affair had also advanced

American thoughts about invading Canada, as the British began repairing their alliances with Native Americans in the Ohio Valley. When the Shawnee chiefs Tecumseh and Tenskwatawa began forming a confederation of western Indians, the governor of Indiana territory warned of the impending "assassination and murder" of U.S. settlers.[13] In this way maritime grievances became linked to frontier friction. By 1812, most voting Americans could endorse South Carolina politician John C. Calhoun's declaration of a "second struggle for our liberty" that "will prove to the enemy and to the World, that we have not only inherited the liberty which our Fathers gave us, but also the will and power to maintain it."[14]

The French Revolution Reverberates in America

The *Chesapeake* affair came during a series of wars that engulfed Europe after 1789. These conflicts initially benefitted the United States. The economic prosperity of the young republic depended on disposing of agricultural surpluses abroad on favorable terms, and war in Europe created new trading opportunities for neutral carriers. U.S. exports amounted to $20,750,000 in 1792, the last year of peace between France and England; by 1796 exports had jumped to $67,060,000. European wars also enhanced U.S. diplomatic leverage over territorial disputes in North America. Since England and Spain battled France, and both sides desired American trade, the administration of George Washington could negotiate more forcefully with Spain over the Mississippi and Florida, and with Great Britain over the northwest forts still occupied by the hated redcoats.

Yet Europe's wars also threatened to engulf and damage the fragile new nation. France might demand American assistance under the terms of the 1778 alliance. England and Spain might fight rather than concede territorial claims in North America. Even if the United States maintained neutrality, belligerent nations might still disrupt America's neutral commerce. Americans differed over the proper response to Europe's wars, and the ensuing debate over foreign policy helped spawn national political parties. The stakes were high indeed, nothing less than the political and economic fate of the new republic itself.

Makers of American Foreign Relations, 1789–1815

Presidents	Secretaries of State
George Washington, 1789–1797	Thomas Jefferson, 1790–1794
	Edmund Randolph, 1794–1795
John Adams, 1797–1801	Timothy Pickering, 1795–1800
	John Marshall, 1800–1801
Thomas Jefferson, 1801–1809	James Madison, 1801–1809
James Madison, 1809–1817	Robert Smith, 1809–1811
	James Monroe, 1811–1817

George Washington always sought the best counsel before making decisions. Although several others offered recommendations, the making of foreign policy during Washington's first administration often resembled an essay contest between Secretary of State Thomas Jefferson and Secretary of the Treasury Alexander Hamilton. Hamilton usually won, sometimes by unscrupulous tactics. Around his policies coalesced the first national political party in the United States, the Federalists, while Jefferson eventually inspired a counterpart grouping, the Republicans. Washington tried to remain above partisanship and usually accepted Hamilton's advice because he thought it in the national interest. With close working and personal ties forged during wartime service as a chief aide to Washington, Hamilton admitted that the popular Founding Father "was an *Aegis very essential to me.*"[15]

Hamilton dominated diplomacy because early in Washington's administration he had, as Treasury secretary, won congressional approval for a fiscal program with major foreign-policy implications. By funding the national debt at par, assuming the Revolutionary debts of several states, and paying the arrears on the national debt owed abroad, Hamilton sought to attract financial support for the federal experiment from wealthy commercial interests. Such a program required revenue. Hamilton provided the necessary monies through a tariff on imports and a tax on shipping tonnage. The revenue laws, passed in July 1789, levied a tax of fifty cents per ton on foreign vessels in American ports and attached a 10 percent higher tariff on imports arriving in foreign bottoms. Such navigation laws served to stimulate U.S. shipping by discriminating moderately against foreigners, but not enough to curtail trade. Hamilton particularly opposed stiff tariffs against England, implicit in a bill sponsored by James Madison in 1791 that would have prohibited imports from countries that forbade imports in American ships, as England did with respect to Canada and the British West Indies. In Hamilton's view, any interference with Anglo-American commerce spelled disaster. Fully 90 percent of American imports came from England, more than half in British ships; nearly 50 percent of American exports went to British ports. Revenue would dry up if trade were curtailed. National credit, said Hamilton, would be "cut up … by the roots."[16] This brilliant, illegitimate son of a West Indian planter spent most of his tenure at the Treasury Department defending the sanctity of Anglo-American trade and hence Anglo-American diplomatic cooperation.

Hostility to Hamilton's definition of the national interest quickly developed, particularly among southern agrarian interests seeking new markets for grain, cotton, and tobacco on the European continent. Echoing Jefferson, who resented Hamilton's encroachment on his prerogatives, Madison raised questions in Congress. Unlike the Federalists, Madison wanted to use commercial discrimination as a lever to obtain trade and territorial concessions from England. As spokesmen for southern planters whose crops had long been shackled to British markets and British credit, Madison and Jefferson wanted to loosen Anglo-American patterns through favorable commercial treaties with other European states and by legislation favoring non-British shipping. Britain might retaliate, but, as Madison bragged: "The produce of this country is more necessary to the rest of the world than that of other countries is to America. … [England's] interests can be wounded almost mortally, while ours are invulnerable."[17] In particular, he calculated that the British West Indies, in the event of a European war, would starve without vital U.S. supplies. Even though Hamilton's supporters blocked Madison's navigation bill in the Senate, the mere threat of commercial reprisals induced the British to send their first formal minister, George Hammond, to the United States in October 1791.

The French Revolution of 1789 exacerbated what Jefferson called the "heats and turmoils of conflicting parties" over trade policy.[18] The initial phase of the French upheaval, with familiar figures such as Thomas Paine and the Marquis de Lafayette in positions of leadership, elicited almost universal approbation in America. Then came the spring of 1793 and news that King Louis XVI had been guillotined and France had declared war on England and Spain. While Federalists feared that the terror in France would "disturb the repose of mankind," as Hamilton put it, an enthusiastic Jefferson cheered the revolutionaries, claiming that the "liberty of the whole earth depended on their victory.[19] France and England became "symbols of two alternative futures or fates for the United States: England as the model of sober, ordered constitutional government … and France, presenting a vision of what a society of free men might be."[20]

Federalists feared that the "murderous orgies of Paris" would spread to America via the French alliance.[21] Hamilton sneered that Jefferson and his friends harbored "*a womanish attachment to France and a womanish resentment against Great Britain.*"[22] The Jeffersonians, in turn, advocated a "manly neutrality" that would tilt toward France and accused Federalists (or "Monocrats") of subverting "human liberty."[23] Rising political passions in 1793 obscured the reality that neither party placed the interests of France or England above those of the United States. Although Hamilton sometimes talked indiscreetly to British diplomats, he did so in the belief that the twin American goals of commercial and territorial expansion could be best achieved in close relationship with Great Britain. As for Jefferson's celebrated Francophilism, the French minister Pierre Adet commented in 1796: "Jefferson … cannot be sincerely our friend. An American is the born enemy of all the European peoples."[24] Nonetheless, most Americans favored one side or the other in the symbolic struggle between "Jacobin and Angloman," between "revolutionary France and conservative England."[25]

President Washington did proclaim neutrality on April 22, 1793, with the unanimous backing of his cabinet advisers. How to reconcile neutrality with the French alliance was another matter. Hamilton argued that the 1778 treaties had lapsed with the death of Louis XVI. But in receiving the new minister of the French Republic, Citizen Edmond Charles Genet, Jefferson set two important diplomatic precedents: American respect for the sanctity of treaties and quick diplomatic recognition of regimes that had de facto control over a country. The thirty-year-old Genet did not ask the United States to become a belligerent; he even proposed that American merchants should take over France's colonial trade with the West Indies. "He offers everything and asks nothing," noted Jefferson.[26]

Complications soon followed, however. Genet outfitted some fourteen privateers—privately owned American ships, equipped in American ports for war under French commission. Before long they had captured more than eighty British merchant ships. Such activities openly violated neutrality regulations announced in August. British minister Hammond protested and Jefferson warned Genet, but

George Washington (1732–1799). The esteemed Virginia gentleman farmer and first president always maintained a regal, if not cold, countenance. Thomas Jefferson subsequently became so angry over Jay's Treaty that he labeled Washington one of "the apostates who have gone over to the heresies, men who were Samsons in the field and Solomons in the council, but who have had their heads shorn by the harlot England." (Library of Congress)

pro-French juries often acquitted those Americans who were arrested. Genet in-furiated Jefferson by promising that he would not send a captured British prize, *Little Sarah,* to sea as a privateer only a few hours before the vessel slipped down the Delaware River to embark on a career of destroying commerce. "Mr. Jeff" did wink at Genet's scheme to "excite insurrections" in Spanish Louisiana through an expedition comprised mostly of American volunteers.[27] Although the plan fizzled, the French envoy dramatically informed Paris: "I am arming the Canadians to throw off the yoke of England; I am arming the Kentuckians, and I am preparing an ex-pedition by sea to support the descent on New Orleans."[28] Genet also encouraged pro-French editorials in the press of the nation's capital, and at one point appealed to the American people to disobey the president's neutrality proclamation. As President Washington grew apoplectic, Jefferson did "everything in [his] power to moderate the impetuosity" of the French envoy.[29]

The furor over Genet abated somewhat by late summer 1793. By now Genet had made himself so obnoxious that the Washington administration agreed unani-mously to ask the French government to recall its envoy. Even Jefferson considered Genet "hot headed, all imagination, no judgment, passionate, disrespectful & even indecent toward the P[resident]."[30] Meanwhile, Washington replaced Gouverneur Morris, the American minister in Paris. Morris had proven himself a shrewd judge of the French Revolution but had alienated his hosts by befriending French aristo-crats, at one point even aiding an abortive attempt to spirit the king and queen out of France. Washington's nomination of James Monroe, a firm Virginia Republican, to replace Morris patched up quarrels temporarily, as did the arrival of Genet's successor, Joseph Fauchet, in February 1794.

Commerce, Politics, and Diplomacy: Jay's Treaty

No sooner had the crisis with France eased than the country found itself on the edge of war with England in early 1794. Indignation raged in Congress when it learned in late February that British cruisers, under a secret order in council (Admiralty decree) declaring foodstuffs contraband, had seized more than 250 American mer-chant ships trading with the French West Indies. These maritime actions, coupled with an inflammatory speech to the western Indians by the governor-general of Canada, directly menaced the young republic. Congress responded on March 26, 1794, by imposing a thirty-day embargo (later extended to sixty days) on all U.S. shipping bound for foreign destinations. Although ostensibly impartial, the legisla-tion clearly targeted England.

Cool heads sought to prevent a rupture. Fearful that permanent embargoes might cause war with England, Federalists suggested a special mission to London. By a vote of 18 to 8, the Senate on April 18 confirmed the appointment of Supreme Court Chief Justice John Jay. Treasury Secretary Hamilton conceived the special mission and drafted instructions for Jay, whose concern for maintaining peace with Great Britain stood almost as high as Hamilton's. Only after strenuous argument from Edmund Randolph, who had replaced Jefferson as secretary of state, was a reference inserted to sounding out Russia, Sweden, or Denmark about an alliance of neutrals. The Anglophilic Hamilton defused this threat when he leaked to British minister

Hammond the information that Washington's cabinet, ever wary of entanglements, had actually decided not to join a neutral alliance. "If ever appeasement was called for," one Hamilton biographer has gushed, "this was the time."[31] Except for forbidding any agreement that contradicted the 1778 alliance with France, and prohibiting any commercial treaty that failed to open the British West Indies to American shipping, the special minister's instructions afforded him wide discretion.

Amid much wining, dining, and expressions of sincere friendship from the British foreign secretary, Lord Grenville, Jay negotiated the Treaty of Amity, Commerce, and Navigation, signed on November 19, 1794. England, locked in deadly combat with France, found it prudent to conciliate the United States on North American issues but did not yield on the vital questions involving its maritime supremacy. Jay did gain the British surrender of the northwest forts, which London had promised to relinquish in the 1783 peace treaty. This time the redcoats actually left.

London's military evacuation of the Northwest also aborted efforts to unite the Indians north and south of the Ohio River against American encroachment. When General Anthony Wayne defeated the Miami confederacy in the Battle of Fallen Timbers in August 1794, the British commander at nearby Fort Miami closed his gates to the retreating Indians. In the Treaty of Greenville (1795), the Indians ceded much of what soon became the state of Ohio. The towns of Dayton, Youngstown, and Cleveland sprang into existence within months. In return, the U.S. government formally recognized Indian sovereignty over unceded lands thereby slowing white settlement and preventing "lawless emigrants" from grabbing "the whole of it," as one Federalist put it.[32] The agreement brought peace to the Ohio Valley for a decade.

Another British concession, opening the British East Indies to American commerce, held promise for future trade with Asia. Jay also secured trade with Great Britain on a most-favored-nation basis. As for the British West Indies, however, the treaty limited U.S. shipping to vessels of less than seventy tons and also forbade the American export of certain staples, such as cotton and sugar, to those islands. Other controversial matters, including compensation for recent maritime seizures, pre-Revolutionary debts still owed by Americans, and the disputed northeast boundary of Maine, were deferred to future arbitration. In regard to neutral rights, Jay made concessions that violated the spirit, if not the letter, of treaty obligations to France. Under certain circumstances American foodstuffs bound for France might be seized and compensation offered, while French property on American ships constituted a fair prize. In short, "free ships" no longer meant "free goods," at least not where France was concerned. The commercial clauses were to remain in effect for twelve years, thus ensuring a "twelve year moratorium" on Republican efforts to discriminate against British trade.[33] Jefferson angrily denounced Jay's "treaty of alliance between England and the Anglomen of this country against the people of the United States."[34]

Despite Republican opposition, Jay's Treaty bolstered the nation's sovereignty. Faced with the loss of American trade, England had compromised on territorial issues in North America. By avoiding war, the treaty also sparked a short-term trading boom with both England and Europe, "a golden shower," as one merchant called it.[35] In the long run, it also linked American security and development to the

The Treaty of Greenville, 1795. Measuring seventeen by twenty-three feet, this mural has graced the capitol building in Columbus, Ohio, since 1945. Chief Little Turtle of the Miami stands on the left, offering his peace pipe to Major General Anthony Wayne. At the center, on a small table, is the treaty that ceded lands north of the Ohio River to the new republic. Lieutenants William Clark and William Henry Harrison stand to the right of General Wayne. (Courtesy of Ohio Historical Society, Columbus, Ohio)

British fleet, which provided "a protective shield of incalculable value throughout the nineteenth century." In effect, Jay's Treaty bet on England rather than France as "the hegemonic European power of the future."[36] In view of the contempt England had shown American diplomacy since 1783, any concession by treaty constituted real proof that the United States could maintain its independence in a hostile world. By inaugurating a critical period of relatively amicable relations between England and the United States, Jay's Treaty gave the United States time in which to grow in territory, population, and national consciousness. By the time war with Britain came in 1812, the United States had fought both France and the Barbary states and had doubled in territorial size.

The signed treaty arrived in Philadelphia on March 7, 1795. The Senate had just dispersed, so Washington did not actually submit the document for approval until early June. The senators debated in executive session, and only by eliminating Article XII (the West Indian trade restrictions) could the Federalists secure a bare two-thirds vote of 20 to 10 on June 24. While Washington pondered whether he needed to resubmit the accord to England (without Article XII) before formally ratifying it, a Republican senator leaked Jay's Treaty to the press, which spread it "like an electric velocity to every part of the Union."[37] Critics quickly charged that Jay had surrendered American maritime rights for minor British concessions and betrayed the French alliance. "Foes of order," as Washington put it, "working like bees, to distill their poison," staged protests in many cities.[38] Struck by a protester's rock while defending the treaty in New York, Hamilton vowed "to fight the Whole '*Detestable faction*' one by one."[39] In Philadelphia a mob hanged John Jay in effigy and

Edmund Randolph (1753–1813). Attorney, governor of Virginia, and first attorney general of the United States, Randolph succeeded Thomas Jefferson as secretary of state in 1794. Randolph resigned in August 1795 when false charges of treason against him prompted President George Washington to reject his advice and to ratify Jay's Treaty. Randolph later acted as chief defense attorney at Aaron Burr's treason trial in 1807. (Library of Congress)

stoned the residence of the British minister. A Massachusetts farmer called the treaty "the worst instrument that ever was signed in America"—a "monster … reprobated from one end of the continent to the other."[40]

Federalist leaders quailed at the "mad-dog" onslaught.[41] "Who gave the common farmers, blacksmiths, and tailors sufficient knowledge to prove that two-thirds of the Senate are knaves or fools?" asked the president of Bowdoin College.[42] The "one step that can arrest this mania," another Federalist wrote, was a presidential announcement "that he had ratified the treaty."[43] Yet Washington hesitated. Irked that the British had resumed seizures of American vessels carrying foodstuffs to France, he followed Randolph's advice to wait for British explanations.

Always a deliberate man, Washington might have put off ratification indefinitely had not suspicions of treason intervened and thereby removed Edmund Randolph, the chief obstacle to normalizing relations with England. In March 1795, a British man-of-war had captured a French corvette carrying dispatches from Minister Joseph Fauchet to Paris. Dispatch Number Ten recounted conversations in which Randolph had allegedly sought from Fauchet money for Republican leaders in Pennsylvania during the Whiskey Rebellion of 1794. Foreign Minister William Grenville sensed his chance and sent Dispatch Number Ten to Minister Hammond suggesting that "the communication of some of [the information] to well disposed persons in America may possibly be helpful to the King's service."[44] Hammond showed the dispatch to Secretary of War Timothy Pickering, a tall, pinch-faced

New Englander and diehard Federalist. Convinced of Randolph's treason, he deliberately mistranslated certain French passages in Number Ten to make the evidence against Randolph look more incriminating. Then he wrote to Mount Vernon asking for a special meeting with Washington.

Washington arrived in Philadelphia in August, read Pickering's translation of Number Ten, and was told that his secretary of state "is a traitor."[45] On August 18, 1795, the president put his official signature on Jay's Treaty. The next day he confronted Randolph. Washington handed him Fauchet's dispatch, pronouncing coldly, "Mr. Randolph! Here is a letter which I desire you to read, and make such explanations as you choose."[46] The young Virginia Republican defended himself to no avail. Even though most scholars accept Randolph's innocence, he made the mistake of quarreling openly with Washington, and in the heated political atmosphere of 1795–1796 neither the Republicans nor the Federalists would take up his cause. Randolph resigned.

The Republicans made one last effort in the House of Representatives to negate Jay's Treaty by trying to block appropriations for its implementation. During the House debates in March 1796, Republican leaders asked to see all official documents and correspondence relating to the treaty. Citing the need for secrecy, Washington rejected the request as "a dangerous precedent" that violated the doctrine of separation of powers.[47] The debate raged on in 1796. Federalist Fisher Ames of Massachusetts evoked the fear of Indian warfare in the Northwest if Congress rejected appropriations. Another Federalist warned his congressman: "If you do not give us your vote, your son shall not have my Polly."[48] A bare majority (51 to 48) of the House voted the necessary funds on April 30.

Pinckney's Treaty, France, and Washington's Farewell

One reason why the House, despite a Republican majority, voted appropriations for Jay's Treaty was the fear that its negation might jeopardize the more popular Pinckney's Treaty with Spain. This treaty delighted the South and West by obtaining everything that the United States had sought from Spain since the Revolution. Signed by Thomas Pinckney in Madrid on October 27, 1795, the agreement secured for American farmers free navigation of the Mississippi River and the right to deposit goods at New Orleans for transshipment. This privilege of deposit was stipulated to last for three years, renewable at either New Orleans or some other suitable place on the Mississippi (see map on page 60). Spain also set the northern boundary of Florida at 31° north latitude. The Senate approved the accord unanimously on March 3, 1796. With America's southeastern frontier now settled with "quiet neighbours," some Republicans did not want to risk losing a similarly favorable settlement in the Northwest by voting against Jay's Treaty.[49] In the sense that they redeemed America's borderlands from foreign control, Jay's Treaty and Pinckney's Treaty stood together.

The popular treaty with Spain followed logically from Jay's handiwork in England. When Thomas Pinckney arrived in Spain in June 1795, the Spanish knew of Jay's Treaty, but no one had seen the actual text. The Spanish prime minister, Don Manuel de Godoy, feared that "the greatest evil that could happen to Spain was that the new power [the United States] should succeed in uniting with England."[50] Godoy extricated Spain from war with France in July 1795, and he hoped to renew the old Franco-Spanish alliance. Fearing England's wrath after Madrid switched sides, Godoy sought to appease the grasping Americans before they could align with the British and seize Louisiana. Concessions on the Mississippi River and Florida boundary offered a temporary stopgap. "You can't put doors on an open country [the United States]," Godoy lamented.[51] With the seemingly perpetual war in Europe diverting Spain's attention from North America and facilitating U.S. expansion, Pinckney's Treaty epitomized, in the historian Samuel Flagg Bemis's famous phrase, "America's advantage from Europe's distress."[52]

Nevertheless, the pact generated only trouble with France. James Monroe, who had assured the French that Jay's instructions precluded any violation of American obligations to the 1778 alliance, had to bear the brunt of French outrage over the surrender of "free ships, free goods." The only foreign diplomat to remain in Paris during the Reign of Terror, Monroe had ingratiated himself by hailing France's contributions to human liberty in a speech before the National Convention. When news of Jay's Treaty reached Paris, however, Monroe erred by publicly predicting the treaty's defeat. In July 1796, the angry French government announced that American ships would no longer be protected under the neutral-rights provisions of the 1778 treaty. A disgruntled Washington ordered Monroe home in late August. French agents in America, meanwhile, stepped up their efforts to wean American policy from its pro-British orientation. Minister Pierre Adet did his best to bring about "the right kind of revolution" by lobbying unsuccessfully in the House of Representatives against Jay's Treaty and openly backing Thomas Jefferson for the presidency.[53] Adet's electioneering could not prevent John Adams's victory over Jefferson by an electoral vote of 71 to 68.

The well-timed publication of Washington's Farewell Address on September 19, 1796, contributed to Adams's election. Washington, ever conscious of history's verdict, bequeathed a nonpartisan document that would leave "the field clear for *all*."[54] At the same time, the first president and Hamilton, who revised Washington's draft of the speech, had French intrigues very much in mind in making the famous warning: "Against the insidious wiles of foreign influence ... the jealousy of a free people ought to be *constantly* awake."

Washington's valedictory stands as an eloquent statement of American diplomatic principles. It reiterated the "Great Rule" that "in extending our commercial relations" the United States should have "as little *political* connection as possible" with foreign nations. Like Thomas Paine, he posited American uniqueness. "Europe," said Washington, "has a set of primary interests which to us have none or a very remote relation. ... Our detached and distant situation invites and enables us to pursue a different course." Then came perhaps his most memorable words: "'Tis our true policy to steer clear of permanent alliances, with any portion of the foreign world. ... Taking care always to keep ourselves ... on a respectable defensive posture, we may safely trust to temporary alliances for extraordinary emergencies."[55] Washington did not preclude westward expansion. Even though he feared a French connection more than a British linkage in 1796, the evenhandedness of his phraseology gave the Farewell Address an enduring quality. "Our countrymen," Jefferson commented in agreement, "have divided themselves by such strong affections to the French and the English that nothing will secure us internally but a divorce from both nations."[56]

Skillful Fencing: The XYZ Affair and the Quasi-War with France

"My entrance into office," the newly elected President John Adams wrote, "is marked by a misunderstanding with France, which I shall endeavor to reconcile, provided that no violation of faith, no stain upon honor, is exacted."[57] In July 1796, the French decreed that they would treat neutral vessels the way neutrals permitted England to treat them—that is, "free ships" would not guarantee "free goods." Shortly thereafter, French privateers and warships began seizing American merchant vessels in the West Indies. By June 1797 the French had seized 316 ships. In addition, the five-man Directory that ruled France had refused to receive Charles C. Pinckney, the South Carolina Federalist whom Washington had sent to replace Monroe. Threatened with arrest, Pinckney fled to the Netherlands, thus presenting Adams with a complete diplomatic rupture. Rejecting suggestions of war made by bellicose Federalists, the new president dispatched a special commission to negotiate outstanding differences with the French. To accomplish this delicate task, Adams named Pinckney, Federalist John Marshall of Virginia, and Massachusetts Republican Elbridge Gerry. Adams displayed his nonpartisanship by selecting Gerry, an old friend, only after Jefferson and Madison had emphatically declined to serve.

The three U.S. envoys arrived in Paris in October 1797, whereupon they encountered perhaps the most fascinating, most unscrupulous diplomat of all time. The wily Charles Maurice de Talleyrand-Périgord, formerly a bishop in the ancien régime, recently an exile for two years in the United States, had become French foreign minister that summer. Despite his firsthand acquaintance with Americans, Talleyrand evinced little affection for the United States, a nation of mere "fishermen and woodcutters" that deserved not "greater respect than [the city-states] Geneva or Genoa."[58]

Talleyrand sought a convenient way to persuade the Americans to acknowledge their commercial obligations under the treaty of 1778. The French still wanted Yankee ships to take over their carrying trade with the French West Indies, an impossible undertaking if the Americans refused to defend such commerce against the British. Talleyrand did not want open war, but as one of his diplomatic agents put it: "A little clandestine war, like England made on America for three years, would produce a constructive effect."[59] The prolonged massive military conflict in Europe had begun tilting toward France under the young Corsican general Napoleon Bonaparte. American questions were not deemed urgent. If Talleyrand could string out negotiations with the U.S. commission, party divisions would reappear in the United States, and France could easily make a favorable settlement. Or so Talleyrand hoped.

Three French agents, later identified in the American dispatches as X, Y, and Z, soon approached the commissioners on behalf of Talleyrand. The message, although indirect, seemed unmistakable. If the Americans expected serious and favorable

Talleyrand (1754–1838). The crafty French statesman majored in survival during the stormy years of the French Revolution. He hoped that bribes from U.S. envoys in the XYZ Affair might compensate for financial losses suffered while living in exile in Pennsylvania in the 1790s. Among other complaints Talleyrand disdained American cuisine. "Thirty-two religions and only one dish to eat," he sniffed. Napoleon, whom he served with questionable loyalty, later described the slippery diplomat as "*merde* in a silk stocking." (Library of Congress)

negotiations, they should pay a bribe of 50,000 pounds sterling ("*beaucoup d'argent*") to the French foreign minister and arrange for a large loan to the French government.[60] To the first request, Pinckney made his celebrated reply: "No; no; not a sixpence."[61] This initial attempt at bribery did not terminate negotiations. Conversations continued throughout the autumn and into the new year. Talleyrand apparently employed a beautiful woman to work her charms on Gerry and Marshall. "Why will you not lend us money?" she asked at one point. "If you were to make us a loan, all matters will be adjusted. When you were contending your Revolution we lent you money."[62]

Talleyrand's methods were common enough in Europe. The Americans refused to pay because they had no instructions, not solely because they were indignant. Gradually, however, they lost patience. Marshall correctly observed that "this haughty, ambitious government is not willing to come to an absolute rupture with America during the present state of the war with England but will not condescend to act with justice or to treat us as a free and independent nation."[63] In January 1798, Marshall drew up a memorial, signed by Gerry and Pinckney, which recounted all American grievances against France, including the personal indignities that French agents had gratuitously inflicted on the American commissioners. Talleyrand made no reply. The French issued new and harsher decrees that made a neutral cargo liable to capture if any part of it—even a jug of rum—had British origins. Marshall and Pinckney asked for their passports, although Gerry did linger another three months in a futile attempt to negotiate.

Rumors of French insolence filtered back to the United States in early 1798. After receiving the first dispatches from his three emissaries, Adams went before Congress on March 19. Announcing that his peace overtures had been refused, the president asked for authority to arm U.S. merchant ships and to take other defensive measures. Jeffersonian Republicans smelled a Federalist trap. The House of Representatives demanded all relevant diplomatic correspondence. Adams, ignoring the precedent of Washington's refusal in the case of Jay's Treaty, sent all dispatches to the House, substituting the letters X, Y, and Z for the real names of Talleyrand's highwaymen. The country was soon aflame. Alexander Hamilton denounced France as "the most flagitious, despotic and vindictive government that ever disgraced the annals of mankind," and crowds hailed John Marshall as a triumphant hero on his return to New York.[64] Even the dour Adams aroused cheers when he promised Congress in June that he would never "send another minister to France without assurance that he will be received, respected, and honored as the representative of a great, free, powerful, and independent nation."[65] According to Jefferson, the president's "insane message" produced "such a shock on the republican mind, as has never been since independence."[66]

In the summer of 1798, Congress passed measures that amounted to "quasi-war." It declared all French treaties null and void, created a Navy Department, funded the construction of new warships, and increased the regular army. George Washington came out of retirement to lead the new forces, although effective command, at Washington's request, rested in the hands of Inspector General Alexander Hamilton. Jeffersonians saw the army, in conjunction with the new Alien and Sedition Laws directed against pro-French radicals, as suppression of political opposition. One

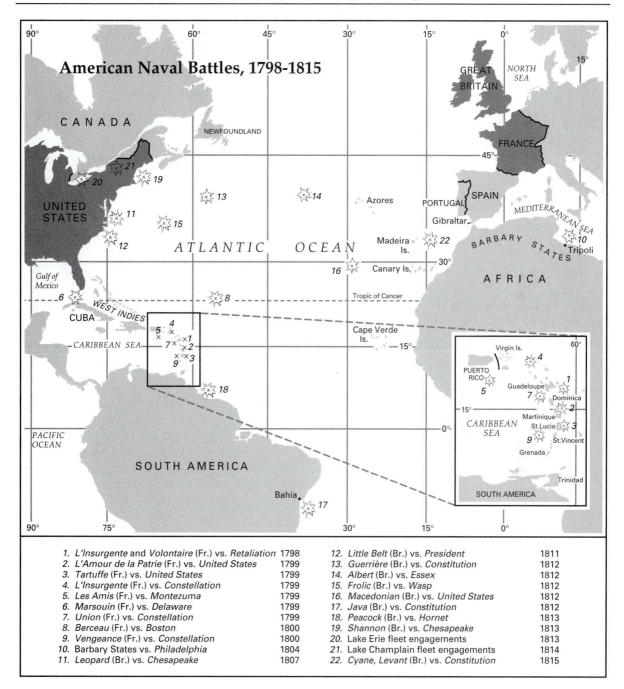

American Naval Battles, 1798-1815

1. *L'Insurgente* and *Volontaire* (Fr.) vs. *Retaliation* 1798
2. *L'Amour de la Patrie* (Fr.) vs. *United States* 1799
3. *Tartuffe* (Fr.) vs. *United States* 1799
4. *L'Insurgente* (Fr.) vs. *Constellation* 1799
5. *Les Amis* (Fr.) vs. *Montezuma* 1799
6. *Marsouin* (Fr.) vs. *Delaware* 1799
7. *Union* (Fr.) vs. *Constellation* 1799
8. *Berceau* (Fr.) vs. *Boston* 1800
9. *Vengeance* (Fr.) vs. *Constellation* 1800
10. Barbary States vs. *Philadelphia* 1804
11. *Leopard* (Br.) vs. *Chesapeake* 1807
12. *Little Belt* (Br.) vs. *President* 1811
13. *Guerrière* (Br.) vs. *Constitution* 1812
14. *Albert* (Br.) vs. *Essex* 1812
15. *Frolic* (Br.) vs. *Wasp* 1812
16. *Macedonian* (Br.) vs. *United States* 1812
17. *Java* (Br.) vs. *Constitution* 1812
18. *Peacock* (Br.) vs. *Hornet* 1813
19. *Shannon* (Br.) vs. *Chesapeake* 1813
20. Lake Erie fleet engagements 1813
21. Lake Champlain fleet engagements 1814
22. *Cyane, Levant* (Br.) vs. *Constitution* 1815

Alexander Hamilton (1755–1804). Hamilton served as General Washington's aide-de-camp during the Revolution and as the first secretary of the treasury. In the late 1790s, the pro-British Hamilton favored a muscular policy toward France. The fact that Hamilton would assume command of a wartime army helped restrain Adams from a military solution to the XYZ Affair. Hamilton died after he was shot in a duel with Aaron Burr. (Library of Congress)

Connecticut Federalist denounced Republicans for their "intimate acquaintance with treason" because they "vomited" falsehood "on everything sacred, human, and divine."[67] Nonetheless, Adams did not request, nor did Congress authorize, a declaration of war. The American navy received orders only to retaliate against attacking French warships and privateers. The quasi-war lasted more than two years, during which the U.S. Navy captured some eighty-five French vessels. The new frigates performed brilliantly, and such spectacular victories as that of the *Constellation* over *L'Insurgent* in February 1799 helped to deter the French from widening hostilities. Content with naval retaliation only, Adams correctly perceived that France, bogged down in campaigns in Europe and Egypt, would not respond with full-scale war or invasion. Adams lost interest in the army because "there is no more prospect of seeing a French army here, than there is in Heaven."[68]

Federalist partisans, including a majority of Adams's cabinet, were more bellicose. "The cannon ball that smashes John Bull's brains out will lay us on our backs," warned one Federalist.[69] Unaware that a French army under Napoleon Bonaparte was headed toward Egypt, not the Americas, Secretary of War James McHenry voiced exaggerated fears that the French might "convoy an army of ten thousand blacks and people of colour in vessels seized from our own citizens."[70] This force might spark a slave insurrection in Virginia or the Carolinas, he predicted. Hamilton became particularly fascinated by a strategic scenario promoted by the Venezuelan revolutionary Francisco de Miranda, whereby "a fleet of Great Britain and an army of the u[nited]states" would launch a preemptive war against both Spain and France in the Americas, thus securing the liberation of all Latin America, the acquisition of the Floridas and Louisiana for the United States, and military glory for Hamilton.[71] The idea of a British alliance intrigued Secretary Pickering, Treasury Secretary Oliver Wolcott, and U.S. minister to England Rufus King who prophesied that "the destinies of the new world" would be determined by a "lasting concord" between the "rising [Anglo-American] empires."[72]

The design collapsed. Adams, suspicious of any scheme connected with Hamilton, rejected the plan as "far less innocent than … an excursion to the moon in a cart drawn by geese."[73] The British, too, balked at aiding a new revolution, even one aimed at reducing French and Spanish power in the New World. Still, enough Anglo-American cooperation did occur during the quasi-war for the scholar Bradford Perkins to label this period the "first rapprochement."[74]

The individual most responsible for stopping full-scale war, ironically enough, was the same Talleyrand who had initiated the crisis. Once he learned about the American outrage over his bribery attempt, Talleyrand made it known throughout the summer and fall of 1798 that France wanted peace. He promised that any new American envoy sent to make peace would "undoubtedly be received with the respect due to the representative of a free, independent, and powerful nation."[75] Adams had spoken those words before Congress in June 1798. To emphasize such assurances, the French repealed their decrees against American shipping and reined in their privateers.

Adams seized the chance to end hostilities. He had received reports from his son John Quincy Adams, now U.S. minister to Prussia, assuring him that France was not bluffing and "a negotiation might be risked."[76] Always a solitary person, President Adams deliberated in private, shunning his cabinet, and, on February 18, 1799, "dropped his bombshell on an unsuspecting cabinet and Congress" by nominating William Vans Murray as minister plenipotentiary to France.[77] Abigail Adams wrote from Massachusetts: "It comes so sudden, was a measure so unexpected, that the whole community were like a flock of frightened pigeons." She correctly ranked it as "a master stroke of policy."[78]

Federalist partisans, their appetites whetted for war with France, threatened to block Murray's confirmation unless Adams also nominated Chief Justice Oliver Ellsworth and William R. Davie of North Carolina, both Federalists, as additional plenipotentiaries. Secretary of State Pickering managed to delay departure of the three negotiators for several months. Adams eventually fired him. In what one historian has called "enlightened perversity," the president understood that his decision meant political suicide, but he persisted nonetheless.[79] Abigail wrote of her husband: "He has sustained the whole force of an unpopular measure which he knew would excite the passions of many, thwart the views of some, and shower down upon his head a torrent of invective."[80] Years later Adams himself declared: "I desire no other inscription over my gravestone than: 'Here lies John Adams, who took upon himself the responsibility of the peace with France in the year 1800.'"[81]

The American commissioners arrived in Paris in March 1800, and negotiations continued into autumn. Politics had again shifted in France. Napoleon Bonaparte had returned from Egypt, seized power, and become first consul. Joseph Bonaparte, the future king of Spain, took charge of talks with the Americans. Although the war in Europe still raged, the new leadership had begun to think seriously of reconstituting France's empire in North America; Talleyrand envisioned "a wall of brass forever impenetrable to the combined efforts of England and America."[82] Rebuilding the French empire required peace with Europe, and especially reconciliation with the United States. The Americans, according to Talleyrand, "will achieve a destiny we can no longer prevent, and the nation that hangs onto their friendship will be the last to retain colonies in the New World."[83] Napoleon's great victory at Marengo in June 1800 made a European settlement possible by assuring French control of territory in Italy, which Spain might accept in exchange for Louisiana. Only one day after the Franco-American Treaty of Mortefontaine, the French and Spanish, on October 1, 1800, concluded secret arrangements whereby Napoleon promised Spain the Italian Kingdom of Tuscany in return for Louisiana. Although the American negotiators did not know about this Treaty of San Ildefonso, the French desire for Louisiana played a vital, if silent, role in the Franco-American accord.

The Treaty of Mortefontaine amounted to a horse trade. The American negotiators had presented two basic demands: The French must nullify the 1778 treaties and pay some $20 million in compensation for illegal seizures of American cargoes. America, the French retorted, had itself invalidated the 1778 treaties by conceding maritime rights to the British in Jay's Treaty; thus French prizes taken after 1795 were not illegal. The impasse broke when the Americans agreed to assume the claims of their own citizens, whereupon the French abrogated all previous treaties. Napoleon then suggested the insertion of a statement reaffirming neutral rights as enumerated in the Model Treaty and in the 1778 alliance. The Americans, seeing no entangling commitments, agreed. The formal signing of the treaty, on September 30, 1800, came after a deer hunt and huge banquet echoing with toasts to Franco-American harmony. Napoleon, that "most skillful self possest Fencing master," was trying to lull the Americans until his plans for Louisiana solidified.[84]

The peace of Mortefontaine, followed by Thomas Jefferson's victory in the election of 1800, ended the Federalist era in American diplomacy. The administrations of Washington and Adams, despite internal debate and external pressures, pursued a consistent foreign policy. Seeking to maintain independence and honor while expanding trade and territorial boundaries, the young republic at times seemed to veer in a pro-French direction and on other occasions tilted toward the British. At every juncture, however, Washington and Adams escaped being pulled into the European maelstrom by allying with "neither John Bull nor Louis Baboon."[85] Like Jay's Treaty, the peace of Mortefontaine avoided a full-scale war advocated by hotheaded partisans. Jefferson's Inaugural Address seemed to promise continuity. "We are all Federalists; we are all Republicans," he memorably uttered. Echoing Washington's advice, the former Francophile pledged "peace, commerce, and honest friendship with all nations, entangling alliances with none."[86]

Jefferson's Empire for Liberty

The new president showed an immense interest in American westward expansion. A few months after his inauguration, Jefferson told fellow Virginian James Monroe: "However our present interests may restrain us within our limits, it is impossible not to look forward to distant times when our rapid multiplication will expand beyond those limits, & cover the whole northern if not the southern continent."[87] Jefferson primarily eyed the Mississippi Valley, but his vision also embraced the Pacific coast, the Floridas, Cuba, and a Central American canal. So long as Spain occupied America's borderlands, standing like a "huge, helpless, and profitable whale," Jefferson advised patience.[88] When Spain encouraged trans-Appalachian pioneers to settle in Louisiana as Spanish citizens, Jefferson hoped that "a hundred thousand of our inhabitants would accept the invitation," thereby acquiring Spanish lands peacefully, "peice by peice."[89]

Then came rumors in the summer of 1801 about Spain's retrocession of Louisiana to France, along with news that England and France had made peace. Soon French ships were carrying an army to the New World, commanded by Napoleon's brother-in-law, Victor Emmanuel Leclerc, with orders to put down the black rebellion led by Toussaint L'Ouverture on Hispaniola (the island shared by Haiti and Santo Domingo in the Caribbean) and then, presumably, to occupy New Orleans, Louisiana, and perhaps the Floridas as well. Revealing the race-based limits of his own revolutionary vision, Jefferson at first regarded Toussaint and his followers as "cannibals" and encouraged the French "to reduce Toussaint to starvation," but the president grew alarmed at the size of the French forces and belatedly realized that "St. Domingo delays their taking possession of Louisiana."[90] Instead of a "surrender of Toussaint to Leclerc," Jefferson now hoped for a "surrender of Leclerc to Toussaint."[91] Napoleonic control of New Orleans and the Mississippi might provoke western farmers to wage war or secede from the union. Rumors circulated that frontier settlers were like "a large combustible mass[:] they want only a spark to set them on fire."[92] Indeed, the "jealousies and apprehensions" arising from a possible "French neighborhood" prompted Jefferson to consider a complete about-face in foreign policy.[93] In a letter of April 1802 to Minister Robert Livingston in Paris, the president warned that the day France took possession of New Orleans "we must marry ourselves to the British fleet and nation."[94] Although Jefferson made sure that the warning became public knowledge in France, he did not directly approach the British.

The implied Anglo-American alliance made little impact on France during 1802. Talleyrand baldly denied the existence of a retrocession treaty for several months (the Spanish king did not actually sign the order of transfer until October 1802), and then he refused to consider Livingston's offer to purchase New Orleans and West Florida. Napoleon, bent on reviving a grand French empire in America, redoubled his efforts to acquire the Floridas from Spain.

On October 16, 1802, the Spanish suddenly withdrew the American right of deposit at New Orleans, in direct violation of Pinckney's Treaty. Most Americans suspected Napoleon's hand in the plot. The riflemen of Kentucky and Tennessee "already *talk of war*" and "*kick up a dust*" to seize New Orleans.[95] Some Federalists proposed war to embarrass Jefferson. "We should annex … all the territory east of the Mississippia [*sic*], New Orleans included," urged Hamilton.[96] To calm the growing clamor and buy time for diplomacy, Jefferson, in January 1803, nominated James Monroe as special envoy to France and Spain, empowered to assist Livingston in purchasing New Orleans and Florida for $10 million. The former governor of

Thomas Jefferson (1743–1826). A Republican who in the heat of partisan politics saw his once close friendship with Federalist John Adams shattered, Jefferson became the third president, claiming that the United States was "the world's best hope." Jefferson's expansionist achievement in the Louisiana Purchase won favor with the American people, who reelected him in 1804. (Library of Congress)

Virginia reportedly had "*carte blanche*" to go to London if "badly received in Paris."[97] Congress provided additional diplomatic muscle by authorizing the president to call some 80,000 militia members into federal service. "If Mr. Monroe … should fail, we shall have noise, bustle, & Bloodshed," predicted army general James Wilkinson.[98] Monroe finally arrived in Paris on April 12, 1803. The previous day Talleyrand had astonished Livingston by asking how much the United States "would give for the whole" of Louisiana.[99]

The "fortuitous concurrence of unforeseen and unexpected circumstances" caused Napoleon to sell Louisiana.[100] The French failure in Haiti loomed large, as Leclerc's 30,000-man army disintegrated from guerrilla attacks and yellow fever. When Bonaparte learned in January that his brother-in-law had also succumbed to fever, he cursed the "Damn sugar, damn coffee, damn colonies" that had foiled his imperial design.[101] Napoleon had envisioned Louisiana as the source of food supplies for the sugar and coffee plantations of Haiti, but without Haiti, Louisiana became a liability. In the event of war, England could easily overrun Louisiana, and the First Consul already contemplated war. Selling Louisiana, a project "conceived by me, negotiated by me, shall be ratified and executed by me, alone," Napoleon instructed his subordinates.[102] The sale price would fill French coffers in preparation for the next campaigns and at the same time eliminate American hostility.

The negotiations did not take long. "They ask of me a town … and I give them an empire," said Bonaparte.[103] Instead of paying $10 million for New Orleans, Monroe and Livingston pledged $15 million for New Orleans and an empire "of so great an extent" that stretched to the west of the Mississippi and included 50,000

New Orleans, 1803. The American eagle spreads its wings over the port of New Orleans at the mouth of the Mississippi River—a prize acquisition of the Louisiana Purchase. (Chicago History Museum)

UNDER MY WINGS EVERY THING PROSPERS

new citizens of French-Spanish descent and 150,000 Indians.[104] The treaty, signed on April 30, 1803, stipulated that the United States received Louisiana on the same terms that Spain had retroceded the territory to France. Livingston, wondering if any of West Florida came with the purchase, asked what the precise boundaries were. Talleyrand replied vaguely: "You have made a noble bargain for yourselves, and I suppose you will make the most of it."[105] This enigmatic remark provided the basis for future American claims to Spanish territory in Florida and Texas. In fact, acquiring some 828,000 square miles of a "new, immense, unbounded world" at three cents an acre marked an enormous achievement for a nation just two decades removed from colonial status itself.[106] Bonaparte remarked: "This accession of territory affirms forever the power of the United States, and I have just given England a maritime rival that sooner or later will lay low her pride."[107]

The Senate still had to approve the treaty. Some Federalists waxed skeptical. Why spend money for so great "a wilderness unpeopled with any beings except wolves and wandering Indians," protested one Bostonian.[108] "Let those who wish for the increase in slaves," wrote a former diplomat, "rejoice in this new nursery for them."[109] Because the purchase arbitrarily incorporated tens of thousands of Indians, Spaniards, and Frenchmen without their consent, another Federalist complained that "the powers that be concern themselves little about the Constitution."[110] The president, however, deemed Louisiana's multiracial inhabitants "as incapable of self-government as children." When Livingston reported that Napoleon was having second thoughts and that any delays might sabotage the treaty, Jefferson decided that "the less we say about constitutional difficulties respecting Louisiana the better, and that what is necessary for surmounting them must be done sub silentio."[111] The purchase quickly passed the Senate 24 to 7 in October. The formal transfer of territory came at noon on December 20, 1803, in the Place d'Armée in New Orleans. As the French flag fluttered down and the Stars and Stripes climbed upward, the United States officially doubled its territorial domain.

The Spanish borderlands continued to attract American diplomatic interest for the next several years. Claiming that Louisiana included West Florida, Jefferson sent troops in 1804 to the border area where American residents greatly outnumbered Spaniards and French. Only when persuaded that military action would offend "the opinion of mankind and even of America" did the president back away from forceful seizure.[112] Jefferson's failed attempt in 1806 to bribe Napoleon into forcing Spain to sell Florida prompted one critic to charge "base prostration of the national character to excite one nation by money to bully another nation out of its property."[113]

Other Americans probed the Spanish empire to the west. In 1806–1807 an American military officer, Lieutenant Zebulon M. Pike, led a cartographic expedition up the Arkansas River into Spanish territory, failed to climb the mountain peak that bears his name, and was temporarily detained by Spanish troops for violating Spanish sovereignty. Praising the New Mexicans' "heaven-like … hospitality and kindness," Pike published an account of his travels that extolled the furs, precious minerals, and commercial attractions of Spanish territory, thus anticipating what became the Santa Fe Trail of the 1820s.[114] Aaron Burr and sixty followers meanwhile cruised down the Mississippi on flatboats, ostensibly to capture Texas from the Spanish, but more likely to install Burr as the emperor of a secessionist Louisiana.

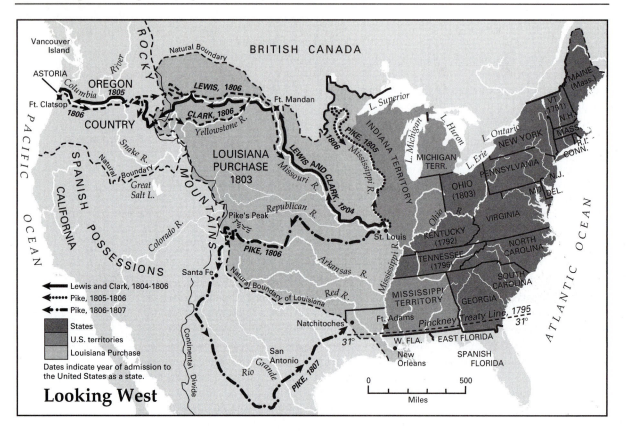

Looking West

Legend:
- Lewis and Clark, 1804-1806
- Pike, 1805-1806
- Pike, 1806-1807
- States
- U.S. territories
- Louisiana Purchase

Dates indicate year of admission to the United States as a state.

Whatever the purpose of Burr's conspiracy, Jefferson had his former vice president arrested and took special care to keep the peace with Spain.

The most enduring example of Jefferson's "happy ability to combine an intense and lively scientific curiosity with political and national economic purposes" was his sponsorship of the Lewis and Clark Expedition (May 14, 1804–September 23, 1806).[115] Conceived by Jefferson even before he bought Louisiana, the trek was intended to find "direct water communication from sea to sea formed by the bed of the Missouri and perhaps the Oregon," to map the region, and to develop fur trade with the Indians.[116] Leaving St. Louis, the "Corps of Discovery" went up the Missouri, crossed the Continental Divide, and followed the Snake and Columbia rivers to the Pacific. Lewis and Clark returned along the same route, reaching St. Louis in September 1806. This epic exploration, which Jefferson painstakingly publicized, strengthened subsequent U.S. territorial claims, stimulated interest in the rich furs and abundant fauna of the Rocky Mountains, and suggested wrongly that the Missouri-Columbia route formed a convenient waterway for trade with China. Meriwether Lewis and William Clark became "the vanguard for an expanding intellectual frontier … engaged in a momentous contest for empires of the mind and flag, trading post and lodge."[117] John Jacob Astor chartered his American Fur Company in 1808, and with Jefferson encouraging him to "oust foreign traders," Astor

Destruction of the Frigate USS *Philadelphia* in Tripoli Harbor, February 16, 1804. Many Americans made their living from the sea. When foreign warships threatened their lucrative commerce, as in the 1790s and early 1800s, they prepared themselves for naval warfare. The citizens of Philadelphia raised the funds for the building of this American warship, launched in 1799. In a fall 1803 action against Tripoli on the Barbary coast, the ship fell into enemy hands. Led by Lt. Stephen Decatur in the ketch *Intrepid* (in the left foreground), a U.S. raiding party burned the vessel in Tripoli harbor. Other "gifts from seaport cities," as the historian G. Terry Sharrer has put it, went on to battle the British in the War of 1812. (Naval Historical Foundation)

projected a line of fortified posts from St. Louis to the Pacific.[118] Only Astoria, at the mouth of the Columbia River, was completed when war broke out in 1812.

The acquisition of continental empire also planted "the seeds of extinction" for Indian culture. As Jefferson put it, if Native Americans did not "willingly abandon traditional ways, take up the plough, and eventually melt into the larger white population," he would banish them to the trans-Mississippi region.[119] Jefferson's imperial vision anticipated a loose confederation of possibly two republics, divided at the Mississippi, sharing a common language and tradition, shutting out Britain, Spain, and Native Americans. "The future inhabitants of the Atlantic and Mississippi States will be our sons," he wrote.[120] As one biographer puts it, Jefferson viewed western empire as "a self-renewing engine that drove the American republic forward." He conceived of the West much as "modern optimists think of technology, as almost endlessly renewable and boundlessly prolific," a "fountain of youth" that made "republicanism immune to the national aging process."[121] Yet Jefferson's vaunted "empire for liberty" meant freedom for "whites only." It not only necessitated Indian removal to advance white settlement; it also made possible "the vast expansion and entrenchment of a brutal regime of plantation slavery" in much of the Louisiana territory.[122]

The expansionist president also wanted to protect American commerce on the high seas, and he repudiated any "Quaker" notion that "our government ... will turn the left cheek when the right has been smitten."[123] Jefferson eagerly employed the U.S. Navy in the Mediterranean to resist the depredations of the Barbary pirates from Algiers, Tripoli, Tunis, and Morocco. The war with Tripoli lasted for years. A squadron consisting of the flagship *Constitution,* the frigate *Philadelphia,* and smaller vessels performed erratically but creditably under the command of the feisty

Stephen Decatur (1779–1820) Battles Muslims. This popular engraving shows two American heroes and two Muslim enemies during the Barbary War of 1804. Stephen Decatur aims his pistol at a Tripolitan while an American sailor shields the lieutenant from a Muslim sailor about to slash Decatur with his sword. According to the historian Robert J. Allison, this engraving reflects the negative cultural images Americans had of the Muslim world in the eighteenth and nineteenth centuries—"where honest commerce was perverted into piracy by avaricious deys and pashas" and "women were debased in harems and seraglios, the victims of unrestrained sexual power." (U.S. Naval History Center)

Commodore Edward Preble and his successor in the Mediterranean, Commodore Samuel Barron, brother of the inept commander of the *Chesapeake.* In October 1803 the *Philadelphia* ran aground while chasing marauders outside the harbor of Tripoli. The captain of the ill-fated ship surrendered. A few months later, in what Lord Horatio Nelson called "the most bold and daring act of the age," Lieutenant Stephen Decatur heroically slipped into Tripoli harbor and burned the American frigate, rendering her useless to the Tripolitans.[124] In summer 1804 Preble's guns bombarded the walled city, and in early 1805 a contingent of seven U.S. marines and 400 soldiers of fortune of various nationalities, led by Consul William Eaton, marched from Egypt across the Libyan desert and captured the port of Derna on the shores of Tripoli. The pasha of Tripoli cut a deal in June 1805, freeing the American captives for $60,000 in ransom. The extended encounter with the Barbary states disgusted Eaton, who expressed astonishment that the sultan of Tunis, despite his harem of beautiful wives, preferred a "lusty Turk of thirty-three" as his lover, behavior which made "the most *depraved* of nature's children blush."[125] While Americans were themselves no strangers to duplicity, infidelity, or double-dealing, the prevailing American picture of the Muslim world, as conveyed by captivity narratives, poems, and other contemporary writings, contrasted Oriental despotism and depravity with presumably more enlightened and civilized American behavior.

Americans had to wait until after the War of 1812 when three navy squadrons— two American and one British—put an end to Barbary piracy, finally permitting the American flag to "pass through the Mediterranean unmolested, without tribute."[126] Jefferson's vigorous defense of American rights nonetheless set the United States on a course of projecting its naval presence throughout the world.

European Madhouse: Blockades, Neutral Trade, and Impressment, 1803–1807

Some two weeks after selling Louisiana to the Americans in the spring of 1803, Napoleon picked a quarrel with England over the island of Malta. War raged for twelve years, spreading over much of the world and ending only with the Congress of Vienna (September 1814–June 1815) and Bonaparte's lonely exile to St. Helena in the south Atlantic. The war transformed the United States into the world's largest neutral carrier. American shipping expanded at a rate of 70,000 tons annually, particularly between French and Spanish ports in the West Indies and French and Spanish ports on the European continent. Because such direct trade violated Britain's arbitrary Rule of 1756 (which decreed that trade not open to a nation in time of peace could not be opened in time of war), American merchants usually "broke" the voyage by stopping at a U.S. port and paying duties on the cargo, thus converting it to "free goods." The voyage would then continue until the "neutralized cargo" reached France or Spain. While direct American exports amounted to a steady $42 million annually in 1803–1805, the lucrative reexport trade soared from $13 million in 1803 to $36 million in 1804 to $53 million in 1805. A British diplomat angrily denounced the Americans, complaining that "there is not, thanks to our Tars, a single French or Spanish merchantman that now navigates these seas— & these Jews want to navigate for them."[127]

For more than two years neither the British nor the French interfered seriously with American commerce. Indeed, British Admiralty courts, in the case of the American ship *Polly* (1800), had not disputed the legality of the "broken voyage." But on October 21, 1805, Lord Horatio Nelson's rapidly firing line-of-battle ships smashed the combined French and Spanish fleets off Trafalgar, thus establishing England's overwhelming control of the seas. Some two months later Napoleon crushed the Russian and Austrian armies at Austerlitz, rendering him master of Europe. A commercial struggle ensued, as Jefferson noted, between "one nation bestriding the continent of Europe like a Colossus, and another roaming unbridled on the ocean."[128] In the ensuing web of blockades and counterblockades, America's neutral trade became inextricably ensnared.

The British decision in the *Essex* case, in May 1805, spelled trouble. British warships had captured the American merchant brig *Essex,* en route to Havana, Cuba, from Barcelona, after it had stopped (the "break" in the voyage) in Salem, Massachusetts. The British Admiralty judge reversed the *Polly* decision, claiming that the *Essex* had not paid bona fide duties on its cargo. Thereafter American shippers had to prove that importation of enemy goods into the United States was not merely a legal subterfuge to bypass the Rule of 1756. Under the new doctrine of the "continuous" voyage, trade carried by a neutral between a belligerent colonial port and home port violated British maritime regulations, regardless of any stopover in the United States. Soon British cruisers lurked outside American harbors, practically blockading the coastline.

The British followed with an order in council of May 1806 calling for a complete blockade of Napoleonic Europe, from Brest to the Elbe River. Americans

"John Bull Taking a Lunch." The Englishman enjoys a French warship for lunch. In a study of Republican rhetoric in 1811–1812, the scholars Ronald L. Hatzenbuehler and Robert L. Ivie have shown that congressional "war hawks" projected a diabolic image of John Bull, depicting the covetous British "trampling on America's rights and wresting independence from its citizens in order to sate a bestial appetite for control of world commerce." (Library of Congress)

angrily denounced this "paper blockade" because British cruisers were often not physically present to deny access to enemy ports. Napoleon retaliated in November with his Berlin Decree, which declared that any ship that had previously touched at a British port was a lawful prize and its cargo forfeit. The London government struck back with two more orders in council (January and November 1807), barring all trade with ports under French jurisdiction unless that shipping first passed through a system of British controls and taxes. England in essence told neutrals that they could trade with the continent of Europe only if they paid tribute first. Napoleon's Milan Decree of December countered that any ship that paid British taxes to the British, submitted to visit and search by British cruisers, or stopped at a British port, would be treated, ipso facto, as a British ship.

The French emperor was erecting his "Continental System," a gigantic attempt to ruin England's export trade by closing off all European outlets. The Continental System never became fully effective, as Spain, Sweden, and Russia opened their ports to British goods at various intervals after 1807. John Quincy Adams likened it to excluding "air from a bottle, by sealing up hermetically the mouth, while there was a great hole in the side."[129] Caught between French decrees and British orders in council, Yankee traders ran the risk of British seizure if they traded directly with French-controlled ports, whereas they incurred Napoleonic displeasure if they first submitted to British trade regulations.

"I consider Europe as a great mad-house," Jefferson lamented, "& in the present deranged state of their moral faculties to be pitied & avoided."[130] In the diplomatic protests that followed, American efforts aimed more at England than at France, because British warships operating in U.S. waters more directly jeopardized American commerce. The British, so absorbed in the life-or-death struggle against Napoleon, hardly acted humbly or apologetically toward Washington. By contrast, French seizures usually occurred in French ports and in the Caribbean and were often shrouded in official verbiage that smacked of misunderstanding and promised rectification. With the Americans, Napoleon was evasive but seldom arrogant.

Impressment, which exploded as an issue in the *Chesapeake* affair, helped focus resentment on England rather than France. With American shipping expanding rapidly, and with service on a British naval vessel resembling prison life, English seamen in increasing numbers jumped ship, took advantage of liberal American naturalization laws, and then enlisted in the American merchant marine. For example, the vessel carrying the new British minister Anthony Merry to America in the autumn of 1803 lost fourteen men to desertion when the ship touched port. By 1812, according to official British claims, some 20,000 English sailors were manning American vessels, so many that Jefferson decided to let any "negotiation take a friendly nap."[131] Since the Royal Navy required 10,000 new recruits annually to maintain full strength, the need to impress British deserters from American service grew urgent. In carrying out impressment, however, British captains "resorted to the scoop rather than the tweezers," and soon naturalized Americans by the hundreds were manning Royal Navy yardarms.[132] According to U.S. figures, some 6,257 Americans suffered impressment after 1803.

The British could not accept any abridgment of a practice that they saw as vital to their maritime supremacy. Americans admitted the British right to search for contraband or enemy personnel, but denied that this right justified the impressment of American citizens. "That an officer from a foreign ship," wrote Secretary of State James Madison in 1807, "should pronounce any person he pleased, on board an American ship on the high seas, not to be an American Citizen, but a British subject, & carry his interested decision … into execution on the spot … is anomalous in principle, … grievous in practice, and … abominable in abuse."[133]

Jefferson and Madison missed a possible solution when they rejected the Monroe-Pinkney Treaty of December 1806. Jefferson had sent William Pinkney, an able Maryland lawyer, to join James Monroe in London in an attempt, similar to the Jay mission of 1794, to settle outstanding differences with England. The British would make concessions on broken voyages and the reexport trade, but withheld explicit disavowal of impressment itself. The most London would concede was a separate note, attached to the final treaty, promising "the greatest caution in the impressing of British seamen; … the strictest care … to preserve the citizens of the United States from any molestation or injury; and … immediate and prompt redress … of injury sustained by them."[134] Because the British promised to mitigate in practice what they would not surrender in principle, Pinkney and Monroe signed an accord that offered greater commercial benefits than the United States had enjoyed under the expiring Jay's Treaty.

The new treaty, signed on December 31, 1806, probably amounted to the best bargain that the United States could have extracted from England during the Napoleonic wars. Still, Jefferson refused to submit it to the Senate. He and Madison believed that the passage of time, plus the threat of American economic retaliation, would force the British to reconsider. Like John Adams in the Model Treaty of 1776, Jefferson and Madison thought that the attractions of American commerce, not to mention the rightness of American principles, would cause England to mend its ways. In one historian's phrase, they were "old-fashioned men still dreaming that Hobbes was wrong and Locke was right."[135]

"Peaceable Coercion" and the Path to the War of 1812

Anglo-American relations deteriorated following the abortive Monroe-Pinkney Treaty. The *Chesapeake* episode of June 1807 underscored the volatility of the impressment issue. "Never since the battle of Lexington," Jefferson wrote in July, "have I seen this country in such a state of exasperation as at present."[136] The president contemplated a declaration of war, but, owing partly to the country's military and naval weakness, he sought another alternative. As he had written in 1801, the United States could employ "peaceable coercion" to achieve its goals because American commerce was "so valuable" to European nations "that they will be glad to purchase it when the only price we ask is to do us justice."[137] Congress passed the Embargo Act on December 22—"the greatest of all efforts to capitalize on the value of the American economy and to bend the Europeans by the policy of giving or withholding favor."[138]

Evenhanded in principle, the embargo, combined with a nonimportation measure against England, primarily targeted the British. The embargo banned the export of American goods anywhere, by sea or land, although coastal American trade continued with increasingly elaborate controls. Recorded American exports dropped 80 percent in 1808. American imports from Britain, not strictly enforced under the nonimportation act, decreased by 56 percent. The embargo effectively "stimulated manufactures, injured agriculture, and prostrated commerce."[139]

Domestic protest erupted. John Randolph, citing the loss of shipping and declining agricultural prices, charged his fellow Virginians with attempting to "cure the corns by cutting off the toes."[140] Numerous vituperative epistles reached the White House, including one of August 1808: "Thomas Jefferson/You are the damdest/dog that God put life into/God Dam you."[141] Such dissent, when combined with widespread resistance to enforcement, caused Jeffersonians to despair. The law's unpopularity was "Federalizing all the eastern States," fretted a Republican matron from Philadelphia.[142]

In New England, where Yankee merchants and sailors had long depended on commerce for their livelihood, the economy slumped. Ships rotted in harbor and weeds grew on once busy wharves. Federalists accused Jefferson of conspiring with Napoleon in initiating the embargo, and during the winter of 1808–1809 rumors flourished of secessionist conversations between New Englanders and British agents. "I did not expect a crop of so sudden and rank growth of fraud," wrote Jefferson, urging Congress to "legalize *all* means which may be necessary to obtain *its end*."[143] On March 1, 1809, three days before Jefferson left the presidency, Congress replaced the embargo with the Non-Intercourse Act, thus permitting American exports to go to all ports except those controlled by England and France, and promising renewed trade with either belligerent if it respected American neutral rights.

Jefferson's embargo failed to deliver the desired diplomatic effect. London at first welcomed the measure, which gave British shippers a virtual monopoly over trade with continental Europe. Alternative markets for British goods conveniently appeared in Spain (which resisted Napoleonic rule in 1808) and Spain's Latin American colonies. The French continued to seize American ships, even those that evaded the British blockade, claiming that such ships must be British in disguise because U.S. law prohibited their presence on the high seas. Rising food prices in England, plus the decline of manufacturing sales, might have tempted the British to appease their best trading partner if the embargo had lasted longer. Actually, the rising prices had attracted the most American violators in the last months of the embargo. The historian Burton Spivak has concluded that "it was the winter evasions and not the March repeal that spoiled [Jefferson's] dream."[144]

The embargo also exacerbated sectional and party differences over foreign policy. New England Federalists argued that, absent the embargo, they could freely trade with other parts of the world where British restrictions did not apply. The embargo, not London, cut commercial ties with India, the East Indies, South America, and the Mediterranean. Southern planters, however, saw their prosperity dependent on selling their produce primarily in England and on the European continent. The British closing of continental markets hurt the South, and the British market itself became glutted. Tobacco and cotton prices fell below what it cost southerners to raise their crops.

Thus Republicans grew more willing to support all "peaceable coercions" to force British concessions, while Federalists increasingly opposed to all restrictions on trade.

A face-saving substitute, nonintercourse actually favored the British more than the French. American ships could clear port ostensibly for a neutral destination such as Sweden but illegally take their cargo to Halifax in British Canada; vessels heading for French-controlled ports still had to face British blockade ships. The new president, James Madison, nonetheless hoped nonintercourse would modify British policy. He found a willing collaborator in British minister David M. Erskine. Married to an American, Erskine was the only British envoy in the early national period who developed cordial personal relations with his American hosts. When he came to Washington in 1806, he wanted very much to avoid war with America and, at Madison's urging, Erskine recommended repeal of the orders in council, provided that the United States retain its policy of nonintercourse against France. In April, Madison lifted nonintercourse against Britain, effective June 10, the date that England, according to the Erskine agreement, would repeal its orders in council. More than 600 American vessels laden with two years' accumulation of goods promptly set sail for British ports. Huzzas echoed from Maine to Georgia.

The whoops soon turned into whimpers as Foreign Secretary Canning repudiated the agreement and the "damned Scotch flunkey" who had negotiated it.[145] Erskine had circumvented Canning's instruction to demand U.S. approval of continued Royal Navy seizures of ships that violated the Rule of 1756. Canning, of course, conveniently allowed American ships still at sea to bring supplies to England. News of the repudiation stunned Americans and angered Madison, who termed it a "mixture of fraud and folly."[146] The president quickly renewed nonintercourse, but the damage had been done. "We are not so well prepared for resistance as we were one year ago," Treasury Secretary Gallatin reported. "We have wasted our resources without any national unity."[147]

Canning aggravated matters further by replacing Erskine with Francis James ("Copenhagen") Jackson, whose notorious diplomatic mission to Denmark in 1807 had consisted of issuing a brutal ultimatum followed by the British fleet's bombardment of the Danish capital.[148] The bumptious Briton managed to offend almost everyone in Washington, and diplomacy went nowhere. "God damn Mr. Jackson," shouted one Kentuckian, "the President ought to … have him kicked from town to town until he is kicked out of the country. God damn him."[149] Madison finally declared Jackson persona non grata, and London did not send a replacement for nearly two years.

When the Non-Intercourse Act expired in the spring of 1810, legislation known as Macon's Bill Number Two replaced it. Derided by opponents as a "miserable feeble puff," the new law ostensibly removed all restrictions on American commerce, including trade with England and France; it also empowered the president to renew nonintercourse against one belligerent if the other gave up its punitive decrees.[150] This "weird form of reverse blackmail," as the historian Garry Wills calls it, seemed to say: "We will be nice to you both until one is nice in return, upon which we will turn nasty to the other."[151] Now came an opportunity for Napoleon who promised to repeal the Berlin and Milan decrees against American commerce, provided only that the United States "shall cause their rights to be respected by the English."[152]

The French pledged to lift their decrees on November 1, 1810. Madison naively assumed that the French promises were genuine. On November 2, 1810, without adequate proof that Napoleon had released captured American vessels (he had not), the president proclaimed nonintercourse against Britain.

London, however, refused to be coerced. Not only did the British not rescind their orders in council, they enforced them even more vigorously. (Altogether the French confiscated 558 American vessels in the period 1803–1812, compared with 917 British seizures. In the years 1811–1812, however, French confiscations dwindled to a mere 34.) "The United States," wrote the new secretary of state, James Monroe, "cannot allow Great Britain to regulate their trade, nor can they be content with a trade to Great Britain only. … The United States are, therefore, reduced to the dilemma either of abandoning their commerce, or of resorting to other means more likely to obtain a respect for their rights."[153]

Disputes with Native Americans on the frontier also deepened Anglo-American acrimony. Beginning in 1806 two remarkable Shawnees, Tecumseh and Tenskwatawa, took advantage of a nativist religious revival to organize a Pan-Indian movement against further white expansion. When the U.S. government purchased 2.5 million acres of Indian land in the Treaty of Fort Wayne in 1809, Tecumseh claimed the sale invalid. "Sell a country!" he told Governor William Henry Harrison. "Why not sell the air, the clouds, and the great sea as well as the earth."[154] Frontier leaders quickly attributed conspiratorial designs to the British in Canada, where Tecumseh's followers received food and shelter (but not guns and ammunition, as Americans alleged).

On November 7, 1811, an armed clash occurred at Tippecanoe Creek in what is now Indiana. U.S. forces under Harrison barely defeated a superior Indian concentration. Americans simply and inaccurately assumed that the British were stirring up the tribes. In Congress and in the West people talked of taking Canada. Congressman Henry Clay of Kentucky asked rhetorically: "Is it nothing to us to extinguish the torch that lights up savage warfare?"[155]

The United States thus moved inexorably, if haltingly, toward war in the winter and spring of 1812, not knowing that economic distress was finally causing Britannia to alter course. Beginning in autumn 1810, a depression hit the British, accompanied by poor harvests, unemployment, higher taxes, higher prices, and bread riots. British exports to the continent of Europe dropped by one-third from 1809 to 1811, and exports to the United States diminished by seven-eighths. Manufacturing interests put pressure on Parliament. On June 16, 1812, Britain scrapped the orders in council. Two days later, an unknowing Congress declared war against England.

In All the Tenses: Why War Came

The close vote for war (79 to 49 in the House, 19 to 13 in the Senate) prompted one agitated representative to exclaim: "The suspense we are in is worse than hell!!!"[156] Only 61 percent of voting senators and representatives supported war, with most members from Pennsylvania and the South and West voting aye and most from the North and East voting nay. The vote followed partisan lines—81 percent of Republicans in both houses voted for war (98 to 23), and all Federalists voted nay (39 to 0).

Tecumseh (1768–1813). The Shawnee chief and his brother Tenskwatawa sought but failed to block white expansion into Indian territory by forming a confederacy. During the War of 1812, Tecumseh joined the British army along the Canadian border. He died at the Battle of the Thames. (Library of Congress)

Had speedier transatlantic communications existed in 1812, war might have been prevented. But it does not follow that Americans went to war for frivolous reasons. The causes of the War of 1812 were numerous, and Madison gave a reasonably accurate listing in his war message of June 1. The president placed impressment first, spotlighting those hundreds of Americans "dragged on board ships of war of a foreign nation and exposed, under the severities of their discipline, to be exiled to the most distant and deadly climes, to risk their lives in the battles of their oppressors." Second, Madison mentioned British depredations against American commerce within sight of U.S. harbors, as well as "pretended blockades" that disregarded international law. Third, he charged that Britain's orders in council waged war on American trade in order to maintain "the monopoly which she covets for her own commerce and navigation." And last, Madison blamed the English for igniting "the warfare just renewed by the savages on one of our extensive frontiers."[157] Privately, Madison noted that the United States had "no choice but between that [war] & the greater evil of a surrender of our sovereignty."[158]

Historians have speculated about the seeming contradiction between Madison's emphasis on maritime causes and the fact that a majority of war votes came from the agrarian South and West, not from the commercially minded Northeast. Part of the apparent paradox can be unraveled with an eye towards economic self-interest: the West and South were wracked by depression in 1812, while eastern merchants, even with British and French depredations, still made profits. Jeffersonian farmers and frontier settlers, many dependent on the export trade, blamed falling agricultural prices on the British blockade. As John C. Calhoun of South Carolina argued: "They are not prepared for the colonial state to which again that Power is endeavoring to reduce us."[159]

Some scholars have echoed John Randolph's depiction of the war as "a scuffle and scramble for plunder," listing land hunger and expansionist urges as major causes of the war.[160] "War hawks" did talk of adding Canada to the American union, but James Monroe urged an invasion northward "not as an object of the war but as a means to bring it to a satisfactory conclusion."[161] Westerners focused on Canada in part because of their belief that England was stirring up the Indians north of the Ohio River and because Canada was the only place to retaliate against British maritime practices. Matthew Clay of Virginia proclaimed: "We have the Canadas as much under our command as she [Great Britain] has the ocean; and the way to conquer her on the ocean is to drive her from our land."[162] Others urged an invasion of Canada because it had developed as an alternative source of supplies for the West Indies and as a mecca for American smugglers. Indeed, Canadian exports undermined Madison's assumption that the British empire depended on the United States for "necessaries."[163]

National honor seemed at stake. Commercial coercion had not worked. "To have shrunk under such circumstances from manly resistance," explained Madison, "would have been a degradation blasting our best and proudest hopes."[164] The real issue, wrote another Virginian in 1812, "went beyond" certain rights of commerce: "it is now clearly, positively, and directly *a question of* ... whether the U. States are an independent nation."[165] When Federalists impugned the "weak and wavering" Madison administration for its "tame and humiliating submission," younger, "energized"

Republicans "ceased worrying whether war would corrupt the republic. Rather, they grew convinced that it *must* absorb the shock of violent conflict to prove its worth."[166]

England realized too late that the unprepared United States might actually fight. Federalists such as Josiah Quincy contributed to London's misjudgment when he jeered: "No insult, however gross, offered either by France or Great Britain, could force this majority into a declaration of war."[167] British minister Augustus Foster also misled his superiors by fraternizing too much with Federalists and ignoring Madison's bellicose threats. Preoccupied by the war against Napoleon and by economic dislocation and unrest at home, British politicians became even more inward-looking at the close of 1810, when the aged George III finally went incurably insane. Several months were consumed by political debate over a regency. Seeing themselves "contending against France, in defense not only of the liberties of Great Britain, but of the World," the British felt betrayed that the United States would become "a willing Instrument and abettor of French Tyranny."[168] Irritation had turned into "hatred of America" by 1812, according to one British pamphleteer.[169] Despite these emotions and distractions, perceptive reporting by U.S. diplomats in

Henry Clay (1777–1852). The powerful Kentucky politician and presidential aspirant served several terms in the House of Representatives and Senate. A "war hawk" in 1812, Clay helped negotiate the Treaty of Ghent that ended the war. As President John Quincy Adams's secretary of state (1825–1829), Clay negotiated twelve treaties to facilitate U.S. foreign trade. As expansionism and the issue of slavery in the territories threatened the Union, Clay helped compose the Compromise of 1850, which allowed California statehood without slavery and a territorial government in New Mexico without a ban on slavery. (Library of Congress)

England might have noticed the signs that pointed to eventual repeal. Nonetheless, chargé d'affaires Jonathan Russell instead discounted the effect of public protests and petitions on Parliament. Russell's last dispatches, which reached the United States on May 22, 1812, offered no indication that England would repeal its decrees. Unaware that Britain had repealed the orders in council, Madison chose war to defend American commerce, honor, and independence.

Why not declare war against France as well? In a preliminary vote on June 12, a Federalist proposal to place France and England on the same belligerent footing just failed to pass, 17 to 15. The suspicious Federalists, citing Madison's false claim that France had repealed the Berlin and Milan Decrees, subsequently charged that the declaration of war against England was made in collusion with Napoleon. Not so. Madison and his Republican colleagues nourished no love for the French emperor. "The Devil himself could not tell [whether] England or France is the most wicked," declared one North Carolinian.[170] Yet a triangular war seemed out of the question. "We resist the enterprises of England first," Jefferson observed, "because they first come vitally home to us."[171] French outrages occurred in European waters. British press gangs roamed just off American shores, and British officers—not French— were allegedly stirring up the Indians. The United States could deal with Napoleon *after* it captured Canada. "As to France," the hawkish Henry Clay explained, "we have no complaint … but of the past. Of England we have to complain in all the tenses."[172]

Madison welcomed the potential advantages of cobelligerency with France. Napoleon's forces could keep the British bogged down in Spain. The French invasion of Russia, which began a week after the U.S. declaration of war, might bring about the full application of the Continental System, thus putting added pressure on Britain. American cruisers and privateers, meanwhile, could use French ports to refit and sell their prizes. But Madison shunned any formal alliance with France. Even in going to war with England, he tried to make the most of an independent foreign policy.

What if ... *President Madison had not asked Congress for war in 1812?*

With his own Republican Party divided geographically over economic coercion against England, and with Federalist partisans taunting him as Bonaparte's lackey, it may seem surprising that the usually cautious and circumspect president acted so precipitously. This is especially true with the benefit of hindsight: At the very moment Madison was signing the declaration of war, a British vessel carrying documents that repealed the Orders in Council was scudding across the Atlantic, promising an end to the British seizures of American neutral commerce that had ostensibly sparked the U.S. declaration of war. In any case, Madison might have awaited news of Napoleon's unsuccessful invasion of Russia instead of committing inexperienced forces to a futile attack on Canada. Taking advantage of England's continental distractions, Madison could have sent James

Monroe or John Quincy Adams to London to negotiate the best deal possible without risking war. Trade with Britain would have expanded accordingly, to the benefit of the still economically vulnerable new nation. Military campaigns against Spanish Florida and against British-allied Indians in the Northwest and Southeast might have satisfied "war hawks" at home. Andrew Jackson would have been deprived of his legendary defense of New Orleans, but his victory over the Creeks might have led to his incursion into East Florida as early as 1814. Britain, still preoccupied with Napoleonic Europe, probably would not have retaliated. With Florida thus secured, subsequent U.S. negotiations with Spain over Louisiana might have gained Texas as well as a boundary to the Pacific. "Masterly inactivity," as John C. Calhoun later phrased it, might have become enshrined as the preferred U.S. diplomatic tactic.

Would avoiding war in 1812 have altered Anglo-American relations over time? Madison would not have needed to paint the presidential mansion white to cover parts burned by the British. Benevolent neutrality during the Napoleonic wars—a policy of officially allying with neither belligerent in the conflict while conducting trade in such a way as to benefit England—might have eased the way for a joint Anglo-American warning against possible European intervention in Latin America in the 1820s. A more conciliatory London might also have opened the West Indies to U.S. trade after Napoleon's defeat instead of waiting until the 1830s. Without a North American war, however, the Duke of Wellington might not have postulated the enduring lesson that it was better to conciliate the Americans than to risk losing Canada by fighting two wars simultaneously. Less chastened, the British might subsequently have strengthened their alliances with Native Americans, engaged in a naval race on the Great Lakes, and overreacted to border skirmishes in the 1830s. British diplomats might have applied balance-of-power tactics more vigorously on behalf of Texas, Mexico, California, and Oregon in the 1840s. British suppression of the international slave trade and other antislavery policies might have proceeded with less concern for alienating Washington.

The home front might also have fared differently without war in 1812. No Hartford Convention of disgruntled New England states would have met to discuss secession; its sensible proposal to require a two-thirds vote for war might not have elicited ridicule. The Federalists could have remained a viable political party through the 1840s. Their disappearance after 1815, amid charges of treason, would not have deterred opponents from voting against later unpopular wars. Because many scholars view the War of 1812 as a war that probably should never have occurred, we can at very least imagine that, without it, some 3,860 American and British regulars, combined with untold civilians, militia fighters, Indians, and slaves, would not needlessly have died in the fighting of it.

Wartime Diplomacy and the Peace of Ghent

"At the moment of the declaration of war, the President regretted the necessity which produced it, looked to its termination, and provided for it."[173] Thus did Secretary Monroe write to chargé d'affaires Russell, with instructions to seek an armistice, provided that England agreed to end impressment and revoke its orders in council. Several weeks after Congress declared war, news reached Washington that Parliament had repealed its decrees. Hopes for a quick peace evaporated, however, when the British clung stubbornly to impressment. "The Government could not consent to suspend the exercise of a right," Foreign Secretary Castlereagh told Russell, "upon which the naval strength of the empire mainly depends."[174] The Americans also stood firm. Two more years of war followed.

The next hint of peace came from St. Petersburg in the winter of 1812–1813. The Russian foreign minister offered mediation to U.S. envoy John Quincy Adams, an offer that President Madison grasped eagerly. Without waiting for formal British agreement, Madison appointed Federalist James Bayard and Treasury Secretary Albert Gallatin to join Adams as peace commissioners in the Russian capital. British Prime Minister Lord Liverpool complained that "the Emperor of Russia is half an American."[175] In fact, Tsar Alexander's potential friendliness to the United States gained impetus from many "extremely affable chats" with Louisa Catherine Adams, whose personal popularity at the Russian court greatly facilitated her husband's formal diplomacy.[176] Not wanting to offend their powerful continental ally and alert to the mutual interest of Russia and the United States in defending neutral rights, the British avoided mediation by "prevarication."[177] The British had no objection to treating directly with the Americans, but no one bothered to tell the three plenipotentiaries in St. Petersburg. Not until January 1814 did Castlereagh formally propose direct negotiations to the United States, and even then he remained vague as to time and place.

In North America neither England nor the United States could deliver a knockout blow in the war. Master Commandant Oliver Hazard Perry's decisive victory on Lake Erie, the recapture of Detroit, and the death of Tecumseh in 1813 effectively thwarted British and Indian efforts to roll back American expansion in the Old Northwest. Elsewhere U.S. forces found themselves constantly on the defensive. The conquest of Canada was not accomplished with a single "rapier thrust" or by any other means.[178] American generals displayed incompetence, New England governors refused to release state militia for federal service, 12.7 percent of wartime recruits deserted "at least once," and the Canadians fought loyally under British command.[179] The Madison administration shuddered at the prospect of British reinforcements after the defeat of Napoleon in the spring of 1814. At sea the Americans fared better, with swift Yankee frigates winning several duels with British men-of-war, and numerous American privateers savaging British maritime trade. All told, the Americans captured 1,408 British prizes. But even on the oceans British supremacy began to assert itself against the puny American navy. The Royal Navy showed in 1814 that it could land troops almost anywhere on American shores, and the burning of Washington in August prompted one Federalist to call the fleeing president "a faint-hearted, lily-livered runaway."[180] Little wonder, then, that Madison welcomed Castlereagh's offer to negotiate. The president shrewdly added Jonathan Russell and Henry Clay to the three peace commissioners already in Europe. The appointment of Clay, the loudest "war hawk" of all, would provide insurance with Congress if the peace treaty did not obtain the war goals of 1812.

A diplomatic retreat seemed unavoidable. On June 27, 1814, a few weeks before peace negotiations began in Belgium, Secretary Monroe instructed the plenipotentiaries to "omit any stipulation on the subject of impressment," if such action would facilitate a peace settlement.[181] The American peacemakers waited anxiously for six weeks in the picturesque Flemish village of Ghent in Belgium before the British delegation finally arrived in early August. Castlereagh had stalled sending his commissioners. Preoccupied by European negotiations at the "Great Congress" in Vienna (which Castlereagh attended in person), the foreign secretary thought that news of British military successes in North America would simplify diplomacy at the "little Congress" in Ghent.[182] Meanwhile, like penned thoroughbreds, the American delegates chafed and snapped at each other. The acerbic John Quincy Adams often found fault with his colleagues. Clay's predilection for poker, brandy, and cigars irritated the doughty New Englander, whose stoic regimen commenced each dawn with an hour of Bible study. Gradually, however, Clay's affability, Gallatin's tactful urbanity, and Bayard's good-humored patriotism persuaded Adams to "be animated by the same desire of *harmonizing* together."[183]

The British nearly ended negotiations at the start by asking for a separate Indian buffer state in the Old Northwest, some adjustment in the Canadian-American boundary south of the Great Lakes, and a quid pro quo for renewing American fishing rights. Only Clay, a self-proclaimed expert at "outbragging" an opponent, thought the British were bluffing.[184] His insight proved prescient. After a few weeks the Indian issue gradually faded away. The British still insisted on boundary changes, direct access to the Mississippi, and compensation for fishing privileges. John Quincy Adams experienced a sense of déjà vu. Similar to "that in which you were situated in 1782," he wrote to his father in Massachusetts, "I am called upon to support … the same identical points … [regarding] the boundary, the fisheries and the Indian savages."[185] He told the British that any attempt to stop white encroachment on Indian lands would be like "opposing a feather to a torrent."[186]

Next came a British demand for *uti possidetis,* or peace based on the war map of the moment, meaning that the English would continue to hold eastern Maine and some territory south of the Great Lakes. The Americans insisted on the 1783 boundary. News finally reached Ghent in late October that the British invasion of the Hudson Valley had been stopped dead at Plattsburgh, New York, and an amphibious attack on Baltimore repelled. Worse yet for Britain, President Madison had rallied support by violating diplomatic etiquette and publishing the initial British peace demands. "Mr. Madison has acted most scandalously," sniffed Lord Liverpool.[187]

Great Britain had a choice—continue the war or accept a peace without territorial gain. Facing complicated negotiations in Vienna, Castlereagh hoped to make a European peace "without the millstone of an American war," as he put it.[188] The British cabinet thereupon sought advice to the Duke of Wellington, then in command of occupied and unruly Paris. The Iron Duke said that he would lead His Majesty's troops in America, if ordered, but would prefer, after the defeat at Plattsburgh, to negotiate peace on the terms *status quo ante bellum.* Lord Liverpool agreed, advising Castlereagh on November 18, 1814, to "settle without securing any acquisition of territory."[189] European trouble once again had served the American cause.

Another month of speedy negotiations settled all remaining questions. During this last phase the one serious disagreement arose among the American delegates. The British, still hoping for a quid pro quo in return for American fishing rights, sought access to the Mississippi River. When Adams, ever the protector of Yankee fishermen, seemed favorably disposed, Russell accused him of trying to "barter the patriotic blood of the West for blubber, and exchange ultra-Allegheny scalps for codfish."[190] Gallatin then suggested that any reference to the Mississippi and the fisheries be omitted from the final treaty. The British delegation agreed. And so, on the night before Christmas 1814, the treaty of peace was signed, reaffirming the *status quo ante bellum*. "I hope," said Adams, "it will be the last treaty of peace between Great Britain and the United States."[191] And so it proved to be.

The pact elicited great rejoicing when it reached Washington. On February 11, 1815, the Senate voted its approval 35 to 0, even though the war's goals had been "abandoned, given up, surrendered," as one critic noted.[192] Partly responsible for the euphoria was the *previous* arrival of news concerning Andrew Jackson's smashing victory over the British at New Orleans on January 8. Many Americans believed erroneously that Jackson's achievement influenced the Ghent treaty, and Madison grandiloquently proclaimed that God had endowed the United States with "the resources which have enabled them to assert their national rights and enhance their national character."[193] News of Ghent and New Orleans also undermined any impact that delegates from the Hartford Convention might have had on American diplomacy. Composed of New England Federalists who opposed Madison's war against England, the Hartford Convention had sent a delegation to Washington with proposals to amend the Constitution (the suggestions included a sixty-day limit on embargoes and a two-thirds vote of Congress for war). Madison snubbed the New Englanders, who slunk home in disgrace.

The Legacy of a War Neither Won Nor Lost

The Peace of Ghent, coinciding with the end of the Napoleonic wars in Europe, marked the culmination of an important phase of American foreign relations. The United States, after 1793, had reacted to Europe's wars by trying to expand its commerce as a neutral carrier and enlarge its territory by playing on European rivalries. American diplomats sought these goals without war or European entanglements until 1812, when the accumulation of grievances against America's neutral rights and a traditional interest in territorial gains catapulted an unprepared country into a second war of independence against Great Britain. The end of that Anglo-American conflict, combined with peace in Europe, made questions of maritime rights academic. For the next thirty years or so, American relations with Europe focused mainly on the matter of territorial expansion in the Western Hemisphere. A biographer of Madison has written: "The red sea of British dead created by the fire of Jackson's men [at New Orleans] dramatically and finally underscored American possession of the Western empire."[194]

By twentieth-century standards the War of 1812 seems inexpensive—2,260 American battle deaths, 1,600 British fighters dead, and $158 million in direct costs, including U.S. veterans' benefits. Yet its consequences were large. James Monroe thought that "we had acquired a character and rank among other nations which we did not enjoy before. ... We cannot go back."[195] Albert Gallatin offered a more balanced accounting: "The War has been productive of evil & good," he wrote, "but I think the good preponderates. ... Under our former system we were become too selfish. ... The people ... are more Americans: they feel & act more as a Nation."[196] The French minister in Washington concluded that "the war has given the Americans what they so essentially lacked, a national character founded on a glory common to all."[197]

This sense of national confidence and glory rested partly on illusion. Jackson's heroics at New Orleans caused people to forget the burning of Washington, to forget that the war was a draw at best, hardly a spectacular success. The view arose, not easily dispelled, that "citizen soldiers" could defend against European professionals, and that frontier captains outperformed West Point graduates. Many forgot the lack of preparedness. John Quincy Adams spoke only for himself in hoping that the United States would learn "caution against commencing War without a fair prospect of attaining its objects."[198] Jefferson regarded "the complete suppression of party" as the war's "best effect," but the revulsion against the Federalists for their apparent lack of patriotic fervor provided an ominous precedent for future opponents of American wars.[199] Forgotten, too, was the probability that, with more patience on the part of the Madison administration, and less haughtiness and more attentiveness to American issues on the part of the British, the War of 1812 need never have been fought.

The naval successes of the war, if limited, had a more enduring effect, as Americans hailed a growing navy as "the most safe, most effectual, and the cheapest mode of defense."[200] In the ensuing decades naval officers gained fame as advance agents of American empire. But even in naval matters Americans remembered the limits of power less than the superpatriotism of Captain Stephen Decatur's famous toast: "Our country! In her intercourse with foreign nations may she always be in the right; but our country, right or wrong."[201]

Even if the peace settled no major issues by treaty, the United States, with its population doubling every twenty-three years, profited. In Henry Adams's words, "they gained their greatest triumph in referring all their disputes to be settled by time, the final negotiator, whose decision they could safely trust."[202] However much the United States risked by going to war in 1812, the paradoxical effect of that war was to increase American self-confidence and to ensure European respect. The young republic still had not reached the rank of a great power by Europe's standards, but the war with England had shown that in North America the United States could not be treated like Geneva or Genoa.

Native Americans in the trans-Allegheny west came to know U.S. power only too well. The unity that Tenskwatawa and Tecumseh had worked to build collapsed when General William Henry Harrison's forces killed Tecumseh at the Battle of the Thames in 1813. In an even bloodier campaign against Pan-Indian opposition in the South in 1814, Andrew Jackson's troops turned "much of Upper Creek country into a charnel house, destroying towns, killing men, sparing some women and children but forcibly relocating them." It all culminated in the "dreadful victory" at Horseshoe Bend in present-day Alabama, where some 800 Indians perished.[203] After Castlereagh's diplomats failed to obtain an Indian buffer state at the Ghent negotiations, Native Americans could no longer rely on British protection against white encroachment. By 1817 the U.S. War Department reported that the Indians had "ceased to be an object of terror, and have become that of commiseration."[204]

The legacy of 1812 significantly altered Anglo-American relations. Even if the British refused to revoke impressment in theory, the end of the war brought the release of hundreds of U.S. citizens from British ships and prisons. Never again would the forceful abduction of U.S. citizens on the high seas disrupt Anglo-American relations. Engaged in a life-or-death struggle with Napoleon, Britain had found the United States a tough adversary. As the Duke of Wellington recognized, Canada was useless as an offensive base and could be defended only with the greatest difficulty. Postwar British exports to America rose substantially, thus presaging a commercial interdependence that served to promote peaceful Anglo-American relations. Rivalry between the two English-speaking nations did not end in 1815, of course, and Great Britain and Canada still stood as a barrier to U.S. expansion. So did Canada. As the British historian John Latimer notes, "the one really decisive and lasting result" of the war was "the complete British victory in Canada that secured Canadian independence," thereafter causing American expansion to move south and west rather than north.[205] In the West, the United States would again collide with British interests. Still, after 1815, Britain chose to settle differences with the United States at the negotiating table, not on the battlefield. When the British West Indies finally opened to American trade in 1830, an aging James Madison predicted that England could "no longer … continue mistress of the seas" and the "Trident must pass to this hemisphere."[206] Eventually it did.

FURTHER READING FOR THE PERIOD 1789–1815

General histories include Catherine Allgor, *Parlor Politics* (2000); Don E. Fehrenbacher, *The Slaveholding Republic* (2001); Joseph J. Ellis, *American Creation* (2007); Joanne Freeman, *Affairs of Honor* (2001); Michael H. Hunt, *Ideology and U.S. Foreign Policy* (1987); Robert Kagan, *Dangerous Nation* (2006); Peggy Liss, *Atlantic Empires* (1983); William N. Parker, *Europe, America, and the Wider World,* vol. 2 (1991); Bradford Perkins, *The Creation of a Republican Empire, 1776–1865* (1993); Marie-Jeanne Rossignol, *The Nationalist Ferment* (2004); and Paul A. Varg, *New England and Foreign Relations, 1784–1850* (1983).

For George Washington and 1790s issues, see William H. Adams, *The Paris Years of Thomas Jefferson* (1997); John R. Alden, *George Washington* (1984); Harry Ammon, *The Genet Mission* (1973); Joyce Appleby, *Capitalism and a New Social Order* (1984); Samuel Flagg Bemis, *Jay's Treaty* (1962) and *Pinckney's Treaty* (1960); James M. Burns and Susan Dunn, *George Washington* (2004); Ron Chernow, *Alexander Hamilton* (2005); Jerald A. Combs, *The Jay Treaty* (1970); Stanley Elkins and Eric McKitrick, *The Age of Federalism* (1993); Joseph Ellis, *His Excellency* (2005) (Washington); Todd Estes, *The Jay Treaty Debate, Public Opinion, and the Evolution of Early American Political Culture* (2006); Don Higginbotham, *George Washington* (2002); Conor Cruise O'Brien, *The Long Affair* (1996) (Jefferson and the French Revolution); Glenn A. Phelps, *George Washington and American Constitutionalism* (1993); James Roger Sharp, *American Politics in the Early Republic* (1993); Matthew Spalding and Patrick J. Garrity, *A Sacred Union of Citizens* (1996) (Farewell Address); and Arthur P. Whitaker, *The Spanish-American Frontier, 1783–1795* (1927).

For the Adams presidency, see Ralph A. Brown, *The Presidency of John Adams* (1979); Matthew Dawson, *Partisanship and the Birth of America's Second Party, 1796–1800* (2000); Alexander DeConde, *The Quasi-War* (1966); John P. Diggins, *John Adams* (2003); Joseph J. Ellis, *Passionate Sage* (1993); Lawrence S. Kaplan, *Entangling Alliances with None* (1987); and William Stinchombe, *The XYZ Affair* (1981).

Jefferson and his vision of empire are studied in Joyce Appleby, *Thomas Jefferson* (2003); Lance Banning, *The Jeffersonian Persuasion* (1978); R. B. Bernstein, *Thomas Jefferson* (2003); Andrew Burstein, *Jefferson's Secrets* (2005); Alexander DeConde, *This Affair of Louisiana* (1976); Susan Dunn, *Jefferson's Second Revolution* (2004);

Joseph J. Ellis, *American Sphinx* (1997); Annette Gordon-Reed, *The Hemingses of Monticello* (2008); John Craig Hammond, *Slavery, Freedom, and Expansion in the Early American West* (2007); Christopher Hitchens, *Thomas Jefferson* (2005); James Horn et al., eds., *The Revolution of 1800* (2002); Lawrence S. Kaplan, *Thomas Jefferson* (2002); Peter J. Kastor, ed., *The Louisiana Purchase* (2002); Roger Kennedy, *Mr. Jefferson's Lost Cause* (2003); John Kukla, *A Wilderness So Immense* (2003); Sanford Levinson and Bartholomew H. Sparrow, eds., *The Louisiana Purchase and American Expansion, 1803–1898* (2005); Dumas Malone, *Jefferson the President* (1970); Drew R. McCoy, *The Elusive Republic* (1980); Peter Onuf, *Jefferson's Empire* (2000); Peter Onuf, *The Mind of Thomas Jefferson* (2007); Peter Onuf and Leonard Sadosky, *Jeffersonian America* (2002); Norman K. Risjord, *Thomas Jefferson* (1994); Robert W. Tucker and David C. Henrickson, *Empire of Liberty* (1990); and Patrick C. Williams et al., eds., *A Whole Country in Commotionest* (2005).

Studies of the Lewis and Clark Expedition include John L. Allen, *Passage Through the Garden* (1975); Stephen E. Ambrose, *Undaunted Courage* (1996); Gunther Barth, ed., *The Lewis and Clark Expedition* (1998); Albert Furchtwanger, *Acts of Discovery* (1999); David Lavender, *The Way to the Western Sea* (1988); James P. Ronda, *Jefferson's West* (2002); and Douglas Seefeldt et al., eds., *Across the Continent* (2005).

The foreign-policy ideas and record of James Madison are treated in Jack Rakove, *James Madison and the Creation of the American Republic* (2002); Robert A. Rutland, *James Madison* (1987) and *The Presidency of James Madison* (1990); J. C. A. Stagg, *Borderlines in Borderlands* (2009); and Garry Wills, *James Madison* (2002).

Issues leading to the War of 1812 are traced in Richard Buel, Jr., *America on the Brink* (2007); James C. Cusick, *The Other War of 1812* (2003); Clifford L. Egan, *Neither Peace nor War* (1983); Richard J. Ellings, *Embargoes and World Power* (1985); Julie Flavell and Stephen Conway, eds., *Britain and America Go to War* (2004); Ronald L. Hatzenbuehler and Robert L. Ivie, *Congress Declares War* (1983); Reginald Horsman, *The Causes of the War of 1812* (1962); Bradford Perkins, *The First Rapprochement* (1955) and *Prologue to War* (1961); Scott A. Silverstone, *Divided Union* (2005); Joshua M. Smith, *Borderland Smuggling* (2006); Burton Spivak, *Jefferson's English Crisis* (1979); J. C. A. Stagg, *Mr. Madison's War* (1983); Spencer C. Tucker and Frank T. Reuter, *Injured Honor* (1996) (*Chesapeake-Leopard*); and Steven Watts, *The Republic Reborn* (1987).

For wartime questions and Ghent peacemaking, see James Banner, *To the Hartford Convention* (1970); Richard J. Barbuto, *Niagara 1814* (2000); Pierre Berton, *The Invasion of Canada, 1812–1813* (1980); Harrison Bird, *War for the West, 1790–1813* (1971); Kenneth J. Hagan, *This People's Navy* (1991); Donald R. Hickey, *The War of 1812* (1989); John Latimer, *1812* (2007); Robert Malcomson, *Capital in Flames* (2009); Bradford Perkins, *Castlereagh and Adams* (1964); C. Edward Skeen, *1816* (2003); and Richard J. Skeen, *Citizen Soldiers and the War of 1812* (1999).

For aspects of expansionism, see Robert J. Allison, *The Crescent Obscured* (1995); Gordon S. Brown, *Toussaint's Clause* (2005); Evan Cornog, *The Birth of Empire* (1998); Jacques M. Downs, *The Golden Ghetto* (1997); Jonathan Goldstein, *Philadelphia and the China Trade, 1682–1846* (1978); Frank Lambert, *The Barbary Wars* (2005); Frederick Leiner, *The End of Barbary Terror* (2006); Tim Mathewson, *A Proslavery Foreign Policy* (2002); Frank L. Owsley, Jr., and Gene A. Smith, *Filibusters and Expansionists* (1997); Richard B. Parker, *Uncle Sam in Barbary* (2004); James P. Ronda, *Astoria and Empire* (1990); and Reginald C. Stuart, *United States Expansionism and British North America, 1775–1871* (1988).

Borderlands issues and relations with Native Americans are discussed in John F. Bannon, *The Spanish Borderlands Frontier* (1970); James F. Brooks, *Captives and Cousins* (2003); Gregory Evans Dowd, *A Spirited Resistance* (1992); Stephen G. Hyslop, *Bound for Santa Fe* (2002); Dorothy V. Jones, *License for Empire* (1982); James E. Lewis, Jr., *The American Union and the Problem of Neighborhood* (1998) (U.S.–Spain); John Sugden, *Tecumseh* (1998); Anthony F. C. Wallace, *Jefferson and the Indians* (2001); and David J. Weber, *The Spanish Frontier in North America* (1992) and ed., *New Spain's Far Northern Frontier* (1988).

To the biographical studies listed above and in Chapter 1, add Robert J. Allison, *Stephen Decatur* (2005); Harry Ammon, *James Monroe* (1971); Samuel Flagg Bemis, *John Quincy Adams and the Foundations of American Foreign Policy* (1949); George A. Billias, *Elbridge Gerry* (1979); Joseph Ellis, *Founding Brothers* (2001); John Lamberton Harper, *American Machiavelli* (2004) (Hamilton); Robert Hendrickson, *The Rise and Fall of Alexander Hamilton* (1981); Peter P. Hill, *William Vans Murray* (1971); Lawrence S. Kaplan, *Alexander Hamilton* (2002); Stuart Leiberger, *Founding Friendship* (1999); Jonn C. Niven, *John C. Calhoun and the Price of Union*

(1988); Robert M. Owens, *Mr. Jefferson's Hammer* (2008) (William Henry Harrison); Robert W. Remini, *Andrew Jackson and the Course of American Empire, 1767–1821* (1977) and *Henry Clay* (1991); and Martin R. Zahniser, *Charles Cotesworth Pinckney* (1967).

See also the General Bibliography, the notes below, and Robert L. Beisner, ed., *Guide to American Foreign Relations Since 1600* (2003).

NOTES TO CHAPTER 2

1. Quoted in Henry Adams, *History of the United States During the Administrations of Jefferson and Madison* (New York: Charles Scribner's Sons, 1889–1891; 9 vols.), *IV*, 11.
2. Barron quoted in Robert J. Allison, *Stephen Decatur* (Amherst: University of Massachusetts Press, 2005), p. 87.
3. Quoted in Robert E. Cray, "Remembering the USS *Chesapeake*," *Journal of the Early Republic, XXV* (Fall 2005), 434; and quoted in Adams, *History*, p. 14.
4. Quoted *ibid.*, pp. 15–16.
5. Quoted in Spencer C. Tucker and Frank T. Reuter, *Injured Honor* (Annapolis: Naval Institute Press, 1996), p. 124.
6. Quoted in Dumas Malone, *Jefferson and His Time* (Boston: Little, Brown, 1948–1974; 5 vols.), *V*, 401.
7. Adams, *History, IV*, 27.
8. Cray, "*Chesapeake*," 459.
9. Quoted in Tucker and Reuter, *Injured Honor*, pp. 105, 108.
10. Quoted in Reginald Horsman, *The Causes of the War of 1812* (Philadelphia: University of Pennsylvania Press, 1962), p. 169.
11. Quoted in Adams, *History, IV*, 33.
12. Quoted in Paul A. Varg, *Foreign Policies of the Founding Fathers* (Baltimore: Penguin Books, 1970), p. 192.
13. William Henry Harrison quoted in Robert M. Owens, *Mr. Jefferson's Hammer: William Henry Harrison and the Origins of American Indian Policy* (Norman: University of Oklahoma Press, 2008), p. xiv.
14. Quoted in John C. Niven, *John C. Calhoun and the Price of Union* (Baton Rouge: Louisiana State University Press, 1988), p. 42.
15. Henry Cabot Lodge, ed., *The Works of Alexander Hamilton* (New York: G. P. Putnam's Sons, 1904; 12 vols.), *X*, 357.
16. Quoted in Samuel Flagg Bemis, *Jay's Treaty* (New Haven: Yale University Press, 1962; rev. ed.), p. 372.
17. Quoted in Jerald A. Combs, *The Jay Treaty* (Berkeley: University of California Press, 1970), p. 76.
18. Quoted in Noble E. Cunningham, Jr., *In Pursuit of Reason* (Baton Rouge: Louisiana State University Press, 1987), p. 172.
19. Hamilton quoted in James MacGrego Burns and Susan Dunn, *George Washington* (New York: Times Books, 2004), p. 109; Jefferson quoted in Robert Kagan, *Dangerous Nation* (New York: Knopf, 2006), p.110.
20. Joyce Appleby, *Capitalism and a New Social Order* (New York: New York University Press, 1984), p. 57.
21. Hamilton quoted in John M. Owen IV, *Liberal Peace, Liberal War* (Ithaca: Cornell University Press, 1997), p. 73.
22. Jefferson quoted in John Lamberton Harper, *American Machiavelli* (New York: Cambridge University Press, 2004), p. 117.
23. Jefferson quoted in Jack N. Rakove, *James Madison and the Creation of the American Republic* (Boston: Little, Brown, 2002), p. 125.
24. Quoted in Conor Cruise O'Brien, *The Long Affair: Thomas Jefferson and the French Revolution* (Chicago: University of Chicago Press, 1996), p. 241.
25. Appleby, *Capitalism*, p. 203.
26. Quoted in Marie-Jeanne Rossignol, *The Nationalist Ferment* (Columbus: The Ohio State University Press, 2004), p. 42.
27. Genet quoted in Jon Kukla, *A Wilderness So Immense* (New York: Knopf, 2003), p. 62.
28. Quoted in Harry Ammon, *The Genet Mission* (New York: Norton, 1973), p. 86.
29. Quoted in Claude G. Bowers, *Jefferson and Hamilton* (Boston: Houghton Mifflin, 1925), p. 229.
30. Quoted in Stanley Elkins and Eric McKitrick, *The Age of Federalism* (New York: Oxford University Press, 1993), p. 351.
31. Harper, *American Machiavelli*, p. 129.
32. Timothy Pickering quoted in James E. Lewis, *The American Union and the Problem of Neighborhood, 1783–1829* (Chapel Hill: University of North Carolina Press, 1998), p. 21.
33. John E. Crowley, *The Privileges of Independence* (Baltimore: Johns Hopkins University Press, 1993), p. 168.
34. Quoted in Christopher Hitchens, *Thomas Jefferson* (New York: Times Books, 2005), p. 106.
35. Quoted in Elkins and McKittrick, *Federalism*, p. 441.
36. Joseph J. Ellis, *American Sphinx* (New York: Knopf, 1997), p. 159.
37. Madison quoted in Joseph J. Ellis, *Founding Brothers* (New York: Knopf, 2000), p. 137
38. Quoted in Todd Estes, "Federalists and the Jay Treaty Debate," *Journal of the Early Republic, XX* (Fall 2000), 405.
39. Quoted in Joanne B. Freeman, *Affairs of Honor* (New Haven: Yale University Press, 2001), p. xiv.
40. Quoted in Todd Estes, *The Jay Treaty Debate and the Evolution of Early American Political Culture* (Amherst: University of Massachusetts Press, 2006), p. 21.
41. Washington quoted in Joseph J. Ellis, *His Excellency* (New York: Knopf, 2004), p. 228.
42. Jesse Appleton quoted in Estes, *Jay Treaty Debate,* p. 235.
43. Christopher Gore quoted in Estes, "Jay Treaty Debate," p. 410.
44. Bernard Mayo, ed., "Instructions to the British Ministers to the United States, 1791–1812," *Annual Report of the American Historical Association for 1936* (Washington, D.C.: Government Printing Office, 1941; 3 vols.), *III*, 83.
45. Pickering quoted in Burns and Dunn, *George Washington*, p. 112.
46. Quoted in John A. Carroll and Mary W. Ashworth, *George Washington* (New York: Charles Scribner's Sons, 1957), p. 294.
47. Quoted in Ellis, *Excellency*, p. 229.
48. Quoted in Owen, *Liberal War, Liberal Peace*, p. 81; quoted in Sean Wilentz, *The Rise of American Democracy* (New York: Norton, 2005), p. 68.
49. Rufus King quoted in Lewis, *American Union*, p. 25.
50. Quoted in Kukla, *Wilderness*, p. 183.
51. Quoted in David J. Weber, *The Spanish Frontier in North America* (New Haven: Yale University Press, 1992), p. 290.

52. Samuel Flagg Bemis, *Pinckney's Treaty* (New Haven: Yale University Press, 1960; rev. ed.), p. vii.

53. Quoted in Henry Blumenthal, *France and the United States: Their Diplomatic Relations, 1789–1914* (Chapel Hill: University of North Carolina Press, 1970), p. 14.

54. Quoted in Stuart Leibiger, *Founding Friendship* (Charlottesville: University of Virginia Press, 1999), p. 213.

55. James D. Richardson, ed., *A Compilation of the Messages and Papers of the Presidents, 1789–1901* (Washington, D.C.: Government Printing Office, 1896–1914; 10 vols.), I, 221–223.

56. Quoted in A. H. Bowman, *The Struggle for Neutrality* (Knoxville: University of Tennessee Press, 1974), pp. 268–269.

57. Quoted in Alexander DeConde, *The Quasi-War* (New York: Charles Scribner's Sons, 1966), p. 3.

58. Quoted in Roger G. Kennedy, *Orders from France* (New York: Knopf, 1989), p. 102; and in William Stinchombe, "Talleyrand and the American Negotiations of 1797–1798," *Journal of American History, LXII* (December 1975), 578.

59. Quoted in Bowman, *Struggle for Neutrality,* p. 277.

60. Pickering quoted in Harper, *American Machiavelli,* p. 207.

61. Walter Lowrie and Matthew St. Clair Clarke, eds., *American State Papers, Foreign Relations* (Washington, D.C.: Gales and Seaton, 1832–1859; 6 vols.), II, 161.

62. Quoted in DeConde, *Quasi-War,* p. 52.

63. Quoted in Lawrence S. Kaplan, *Colonies into Nation* (New York: Macmillan, 1972), p. 276.

64. Quoted in Lawrence S. Kaplan, *Alexander Hamilton* (Wilmington, Del.: Scholarly Resources, 2002), p. 143.

65. Richardson, *Messages of the President,* I, 256.

66. Quoted in John P. Diggins, *John Adams* (New York: Times Books, 2003), p. 99; quoted in O'Brien, *Long Affair,* p. 246.

67. John Allen quoted in Susan Dunn, *Jefferson's Second Revolution* (Boston: Houghton Mifflin, 2004), p. 99.

68. Quoted in Elkins and McKitrick, *Federalism,* p. 606.

69. Fisher Ames quoted in Kagan, *Dangerous Nation,* p. 117.

70. Quoted in Elkins and McKitrick, *Federalism,* pp. 645–646.

71. Quoted in Harper, *American Machiavelli,* p. 222.

72. King quoted in Rossignol, *Nationalist Ferment,* p. 88.

73. Quoted in Ron Chernow, *Alexander Hamilton* (New York: Penguin, 2004), p. 568.

74. Bradford Perkins, *The First Rapprochement* (Philadelphia: University of Pennsylvania Press, 1955).

75. Lowrie and Clarke, *Foreign Relations,* II, 242.

76. Quoted in Page Smith, *John Adams* (Garden City, N.Y.: Doubleday, 1962; 2 vols.), II, 995.

77. Gordon S. Brown, *Toussaint's Clause* (Jackson: University Press of Mississippi, 2005), p. 150.

78. Quoted in Smith, *Adams. II,* 1000.

79. Ellis, *Founding Brothers,* p. 58.

80. Quoted in Phyllis Lee Levin, *Abigail Adams* (New York: St. Martin's Press, 1987), p. 371.

81. Quoted in Bradford Perkins, *The Creation of a Republican Empire, 1776–1865* (New York: Cambridge University Press, 1993), p. 109.

82. Quoted in Kennedy, *Orders from France,* p. 305.

83. Quoted in Elkins and McKitrick, *Federalism,* p. 680.

84. William Vans Murray quoted in Alan Schom, *Napoleon Bonaparte* (New York: HarperCollins, 1997), p. 225.

85. Quoted in Ralph Ketchum, *Presidents Above Party* (Chapel Hill: University of North Carolina Press, 1984), p. 94.

86. Richardson, *Messages of the Presidents, I,* 323.

87. A. A. Lipscomb, ed., *The Writings of Thomas Jefferson* (Washington, D.C: Jefferson Memorial Association, 1903; 19 vols.), X, 296.

88. Adams, *History, I,* 340.

89. Quoted in Jeremy Adelman and Stephen Aron, "From Borderlands to Borders," *American Historical Review, CIV* (June 1999), 827; quoted in Marshall Smelser, *The Democratic Republic, 1801–1815* (New York: Harper & Row, 1968), p. 87.

90. Jefferson quoted in Robin Blackburn, "Haiti, Slavery, and the Age of the Democratic Revolution," *William and Mary Quarterly, LXIII* (October 2006), 11; also quoted in Tim Matthewson, "Jefferson and Haiti," *Journal of Southern History, LXI* (May 1995), 215, 229.

91. Quoted in Joseph Ellis, *American Creation* (New York: Knopf, 2007), p. 217.

92. James Barbour quoted in Lewis, *American Union,* p. 26.

93. Madison quoted *ibid.,* p. 27.

94. Quoted in Rossignol, *Nationalist Ferment,* p. 145.

95. Quoted in Kukla, *Wilderness,* p. 248.

96. Quoted in Kaplan, *Hamilton,* p. 172.

97. Quoted in Albert H. Bowman, "Pichon, the United States, and Louisiana," *Diplomatic History, I* (Summer 1977), 266.

98. Quoted in Theodore J. Crackel, *Mr. Jefferson's Army* (New York: New York University Press, 1987), p. 102.

99. Talleyrand quoted in Dunn, *Jefferson's Second Revolution,* p. 240.

100. Hamilton quoted in Kaplan, *Hamilton,* p. 173.

101. Quoted in E. W. Lyon, *Louisiana in French Diplomacy* (Norman: University of Oklahoma Press, 1934), p. 194.

102. Quoted in Ellis, *American Creation,* p. 221.

103. Quoted in Eugene V. Rostow, *A Breakfast for Bonaparte* (Washington, D.C.: National Defense University Press, 1991), p. 119.

104. Quoted in Peter J. Kastor, "Local Diplomacy in Louisiana, 1803–1821," *William and Mary Quarterly, LVIII* (October 2001), 819.

105. Quoted in Alexander DeConde, *This Affair of Louisiana* (New York: Charles Scribner's Sons, 1976), p. 174.

106. Samuel White quoted in James P. Ronda, "Race, Geography and the Invention of Indian Territory," *Journal of the Early Republic, XIX* (Winter 1999), 741.

107. Quoted in Lyon, *Louisiana in French Diplomacy,* p. 206.

108. Quoted in Ellis, *American Creation,* p. 227.

109. David Humphreys quoted in Dunn, *Jefferson's Second Revolution,* p. 241.

110. Fisher Ames quoted in David Mayers, *Dissenting Voices in America's Rise to World Power* (New York: Cambridge University Press, 2007), p. 22.

111. Quoted in Malone, *Jefferson and His Time, IV,* p. 316; quoted in Walter LaFeber, "The American View of Decolonization, 1776–1920," in David Ryan and Victor Pungong, eds., *The United States and Decolonization* (New York: St. Martin's, 2000), p. 25.

112. Albert Gallatin quoted in Weber, *Spanish Frontier,* p. 292.

113. Quoted in James R. Sofka, "Thomas Jefferson and the Problem of World Politics," in Kastor, *Louisiana Purchase,* p. 61.

114. Quoted in Stephen G. Hyslop, *Bound for Santa Fe* (Norman: University of Oklahoma Press, 2002), p. 18.

115. Peggy K. Liss, *Atlantic Empires* (Baltimore: Johns Hopkins University Press, 1983), p. 122

116. Jefferson quoted in James P. Ronda, "'So Vast an Enterprise,'" in James P. Ronda, ed., *Voyages of Discovery* (Helena: Montana Historical Society Press, 1998), p. 13.

117. James P. Ronda, "Dreams and Discoveries: Exploring the American West, 1760–1815," *William and Mary Quarterly, XLVI* (January 1989), 145–146.

118. Jefferson quoted in Alan Taylor, "Jefferson's Pacific," in Douglas Seefeldt et al., eds., *Across the Continent* (Charlottesville: University of Virginia Press, 2005), p. 40.
119. Ronda, "Indian Country," p. 740; quoted in Ellis, *American Sphinx*, pp. 201–202.
120. Quoted in Peter S. Onuf, *Jefferson's Empire* (Charlottesville: University of Virginia Press, 2000), p. 119.
121. Ellis, *American Sphinx*, p. 212.
122. James Horn, Jan Ellen Lewis, and Peter S. Onuf, eds., *The Revolution of 1800* (Charlottesville: University of Virginia Press, 2002), p. xiv.
123. Quoted in James R. Sofka, "The Jeffersonian Idea of National Security," *Diplomatic History, XXI* (Fall 1997), 538.
124. Quoted in Frank Lambert, *The Barbary Wars* (New York: Hill & Wang, 2005), p. 144.
125. Quoted in Robert J. Allison, *The Crescent Obscured* (New York: Oxford University Press, 1995), p. 65.
126. *New York Evening Post* quoted in Lambert, *Barbary Wars*, p. 194.
127. Quoted in Clifford L. Egan, *Neither Peace nor War* (Baton Rouge: Louisiana State University Press, 1983), p. 27.
128. Quoted in Joyce Appleby, *Thomas Jefferson* (New York: Times Books, 2003), p. 121.
129. Charles F. Adams, ed., *Memoirs of John Quincy Adams* (Philadelphia: Lippincott, 1874–1877; 12 vols.), *II*, 92.
130. Quoted in Bradford Perkins, *Prologue to War* (Berkeley: University of California Press, 1961), p. 41.
131. Jefferson quoted in R. B. Bernstein, *Thomas Jefferson* (New York: Oxford University Press, 2003), p. 166.
132. Varg, *Foreign Policies*, p. 173.
133. Quoted in Perkins, *Prologue to War*, p. 89.
134. Quoted in Varg, *Foreign Policies*, p. 182.
135. Robert A. Rutland, *Madison's Alternatives* (Philadelphia: Lippincott, 1975), p. 5.
136. Lipscomb, *Writings of Jefferson, XI*, 274.
137. Quoted in Robert David Johnson, *The Peace Progressives and American Foreign Relations* (Cambridge: Harvard University Press, 1995), p. 12.
138. James A. Field, Jr., "1778–1820: All Economists, All Diplomats," in William H. Becker and Samuel F. Wells, Jr., eds., *Economics and World Power* (New York: Columbia University Press, 1984), p. 32.
139. Walter W. Jennings, *The American Embargo, 1807–1809* (Iowa City: University of Iowa, 1921), p. 231.
140. Quoted in Perkins, *Prologue to War*, p. 163.
141. Robert H. Ferrell, ed., *Foundations of American Diplomacy, 1775–1872* (New York: Harper and Row, 1968), p. 6.
142. Maria Beckley quoted in Rosemarie Zagarri, "Women and Party Conflict in the Early Republic," in Jeffrey L. Pasley et al., eds., *Beyond the Founders* (Chapel Hill: University of North Carolina Press, 2004), p. 114.
143. Quoted in Richard Mannix, "Gallatin, Jefferson, and the Embargo of 1808," *Diplomatic History, III* (Spring 1979), 168.
144. Burton Spivak, *Jefferson's English Crisis* (Charlottesville: University Press of Virginia, 1979), p. 203.
145. Quoted in Perkins, *Prologue to War*, p. 220.
146. Quoted in Smelser, *Democratic Republic*, p. 194.
147. Quoted in Ralph Ketcham, *James Madison* (New York: Macmillan, 1971), p. 496.
148. Adams, *History, V*, 103.
149. Quoted in Horsman, *Causes of the War of 1812*, p. 155.
150. Quoted in Ralph Ketcham, *James Madison* (Charlottesville: University Press of Virginia, 1990), p. 499.
151. Garry Wills, *James Madison* (New York: Times Books, 2002), p. 87.
152. Quoted in Richard Buel, Jr., *America on the Brink* (New York: Palgrave, 2005), p. 110.
153. Quoted in Varg, *Foreign Policies*, p. 286.
154. Quoted in Patrice Higonnet, *Attendant Cruelties* (New York: Other Press, 2007), p. 68.
155. Quoted in Perkins, *Prologue to War*, p. 283.
156. Quoted in Donald R. Hickey, *The War of 1812* (Urbana: University of Illinois Press, 1989), p. 46.
157. Richardson, *Messages of the Presidents, II*, 484–490.
158. Quoted in Varg, *Foreign Policies*, p. 292.
159. Quoted in Scott A. Silverstone, *Divided Union* (Ithaca: Cornell University Press, 2004), p. 86.
160. Randolph quoted in John Latimer, *1812* (Cambridge: Harvard University Press, 2007), p. 31.
161. Quoted in Silverstone, *Divided Union*, p. 95.
162. Quoted in Horsman, *Causes of the War of 1812*, p. 182.
163. J. C. A. Stagg, *Mr. Madison's War* (Princeton: Princeton University Press, 1983), p. 46.
164. Quoted in Kagan, *Dangerous Nation*, p. 144.
165. Quoted in Norman K. Risjord, "1812: Conservatives, War Hawks, and the Nation's Honor," *William and Mary Quarterly, XVII* (April 1961), 205.
166. Thomas Pleasants and James Milner quoted in Albrecht Koschnik, "Young Federalists, Masculinity, and Partisanship during the War of 1812," in Pasley et al., *Beyond the Founders*, pp. 172–173; Steven Watts, *The Republic Reborn* (Baltimore: Johns Hopkins University Press, 1987), p. 242.
167. Quoted in Buel, *America on the Brink*, p. 70.
168. Lord Liverpool quoted in Eliga Gould, "The Making of an Atlantic State System," in Julie Flavell and Stephen Conway, eds., *Britain and America Go to War* (Gainesville: University Press of Florida, 2004), p. 257.
169. Quoted in Latimer, *1812*, p. 6.
170. Nathaniel Macon quoted in Mayers, *Dissenting Voices*, p. 35.
171. Quoted in Lawrence S. Kaplan, "France and Madison's Decision for War," *Mississippi Valley Historical Review, L* (March 1964), 658.
172. J. F. Hopkins, ed., *The Papers of Henry Clay* (Lexington: University of Kentucky Press, 1959–1973; 5 vols.), *I*, 674.
173. Lowrie and Clarke, *Foreign Relations, III*, 585–586.
174. *Ibid.*, *III*, 589–590.
175. Quoted in Bradford Perkins, *Castlereagh and Adams* (Berkeley: University of California Press, 1965), p. 14.
176. Quoted in Catherine Allgor, "'A Republican in a Monarchy': Louisa Catherine Adams in Russia," *Diplomatic History, XXI* (Winter 1997), 26.
177. Normal E. Saul, *Distant Friends* (Lawrence: University Press of Kansas, 1991), p. 72.
178. Madison quoted in Robert A. Rutland, *The Presidency of James Madison* (Lawrence: University Press of Kansas, 1990), p. 108.
179. J. C. A. Stagg, "Comparative Perspectives on the Recruitment of the United States Army, 1802–1815," *William and Mary Quarterly, LVII* (January 2000), 113.
180. Daniel Webster quoted in Mayers, *Dissenting Voices*, p. 39.
181. Lowrie and Clarke, *Foreign Relations, III*, 704.
182. Quoted in Latimer, *1812*, p. 361.
183. Quoted in Bradford Perkins, *Castlereagh and Adams*, (Berkeley: University of California Press, 1965), p. 49.
184. Quoted in Robert V. Remini, *Henry Clay* (New York: Norton, 1991), p. 117.

185. Quoted in Samuel Flagg Bemis, *John Quincy Adams and the Foundations of American Foreign Policy* (New York: Knopf, 1949), p. 196.
186. Quoted in James E. Lewis, Jr., *John Quincy Adams* (Wilmington, Del.: Scholarly Resources, 2001), p. 29.
187. Quoted in Perkins, *Castlereagh and Adams*, p. 113.
188. Quoted in Wills, *Madison*, p. 144.
189. Quoted in Latimer, *1812*, p. 390.
190. Quoted in Wills, *Madison*, p. 124.
191. Quoted in Bemis, *John Quincy Adams*, p. 218.
192. Cyrus King quoted in C. Edward Skeen, *1816* (Lexington: University Press of Kentucky, 2003), p. 26.
193. Quoted in Kenneth J. Hagan and Ian Bickerton, *Unintended Consequences* (London: Reaktion Books, 2007), p. 47.
194. Ketcham, *James Madison*, p. 596.
195. Quoted in Richard V. Barbuto, *Niagara 1814* (Lawrence: University Press of Kansas, 2000), pp. 321–322.
196. Quoted in Raymond Walters, Jr., *Albert Gallatin* (New York: Macmillan, 1957), p. 288.
197. Quoted in Ketcham, *James Madison*, pp. 597–598.
198. Quoted in Perkins, *Castlereagh and Adams*, p. 151.
199. Quoted in Lewis, *American Union*, p. 61.
200. John C. Calhoun quoted in Skeen, *1816*, p. 148.
201. Quoted in Charles J. Peterson, *The American Navy* (Philadelphia: James B. Smith, 1858), p. 287.
202. Adams, *History, IX*, 53.
203. Dowd, *Spirited Resistance*, p. 187.
204. Quoted in Hickey, *War of 1812*, p. 304.
205. Latimer, *1812*, p. 408.
206. Quoted in Stagg, *Mr. Madison's War*, p. 517.

CHAPTER 3

Extending and Preserving the Sphere, 1815–1848

A NEW RULE IN ALGEBRA.

Five from Three and One remains!!

or

"The Three Mexican Prisoners, having but one leg between them all."

Series Nº 2.

"A New Rule in Algebra."   *In this political cartoon from 1846, Edwin Jones and George Newman portray three Mexican prisoners of war with their legs amputated. The caption reads: "Five from three and one remains!!" Such medical treatment to prevent gangrene was common practice during the War with Mexico. The alarmed expression of the Mexicans at their severed limbs also anticipates the loss of more than half of their national territory to the United States at the end of the war. (Library of Congress)*

◈ *Mexican-American War on the Rio Grande, 1846*

THE MOMENTOUS ORDER to march to the Rio Grande reached "Old Rough and Ready" General Zachary Taylor on February 3, 1846. Planning took several weeks, so the first infantry brigades did not tramp out from Corpus Christi until March 9. The army averaged ten miles a day, through suffocating dust, across sunbaked soil, through ankle-deep sands, past holes of brackish water, into grasslands capable of supporting vegetation. Near a marshy stream called the Arroyo Colorado, U.S. troops nearly tangled with a Mexican cavalry unit, but the numerically superior U.S. forces managed to cross unmolested. Late in the morning of March 28, Taylor's army reached the north bank of the Rio Grande in disputed Texas territory. Across the 200 yards of mud-colored river stood the Mexican town of Matamoros with its garrison of 3,000 men. Taylor encamped, set up earthworks (Fort Texas), and waited. "The attitude of the Mexicans is so far decidedly hostile," Taylor informed his superiors.[1]

The next three weeks passed nervously but peacefully. The "government" had sent Taylor's army "on purpose to bring on a war, so as to have a pretext for taking California and as much of this country as it chooses," so one officer wrote incisively in his diary.[2] Taylor had to conduct his initial parley with the Mexicans in French because no American officer could speak Spanish and none of the Mexicans present had mastered English. Taylor assured them that his advance to the Rio Grande was neither an invasion of Mexican soil nor a hostile act. The suspicious Mexicans reinforced their garrison with 2,000 additional troops. Then, on April 24, Major General Mariano Arista notified Taylor that hostilities had begun. Mexican cavalry, 1,600 strong, crossed the river at La Palangana, fourteen miles upstream from Matamoros. Taylor sent dragoons to investigate, but they returned having seen nothing. That same evening, April 24, Taylor ordered out another cavalry force under Captain Seth B. Thornton. This time the Americans rode into an ambush. Thornton tried to fight his way free but lost eleven men. The Mexicans took the rest of his sixty-three-man contingent captive. "We have vengeance to take on Mexico for more than one man's blood, and our boys … feel so indignant at the rascality of the brutes," one U.S. officer wrote home.[3] News of the fight reached Taylor at reveille on April 26. "Hostilities may now be considered as commenced," he immediately alerted Washington, D.C.[4] His dispatch took two weeks to reach the capital.

A stiff, angular man, with sharp gray eyes set in a sad, thin face, President James K. Polk met with his cabinet on the morning of May 9. The Democratic chief executive was looking for an excuse to declare war on Mexico. Reviewing the diplomacy of the past year, which included U.S. annexation of Texas, suspension of relations with Mexico, and abortive attempts to solve boundary disputes and to purchase California and New Mexico, Polk self-righteously told his cabinet that "in my opinion we had ample cause of war, and that it was impossible that we could stand in *statu quo,* or that I could remain silent much longer."[5] He hoped that the Mexicans would commit an act of aggression against Taylor's army, but as yet nothing had happened. Polk polled the cabinet. All agreed that he should soon

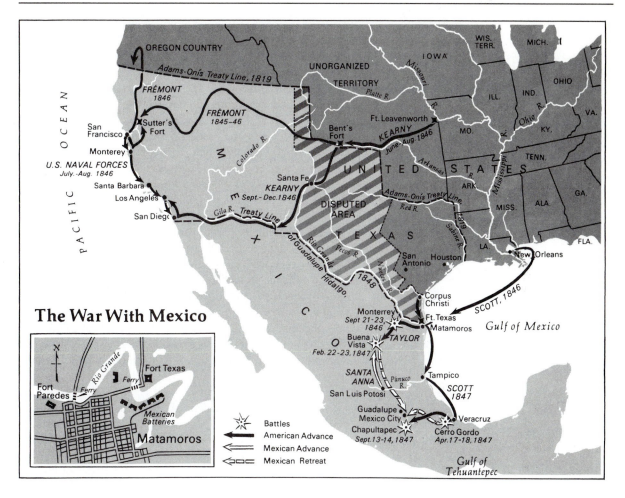

The War With Mexico

send a request for war to Congress, although one adviser thought it would be better if some hostile act on the border occurred first. The meeting adjourned, and Polk began to compose the war message.

At six o'clock that evening news of the Rio Grande skirmish reached the White House. The cabinet hastily reconvened and reached a unanimous decision: Submit a war message to Congress as quickly as possible. All day May 10, Polk anxiously labored over his statement, conferring with cabinet colleagues, military advisers, and congressional leaders. At noon the next day he sent his recommendation to Congress. "The cup of forbearance has been exhausted," Polk wrote. "After reiterated menaces, Mexico has passed the boundary of the United States, has invaded our territory and shed American blood upon American soil." War existed, and "notwithstanding all our efforts to avoid it, exists by the act of Mexico herself." A bill accompanied the war message authorizing the president to accept militia and volunteers for military duty. The bill asked Congress to recognize that "by the act of … Mexico, a state of war exists between the [Mexican] government and the United States."[6]

A disciplined Democratic majority responded swiftly. Debate in the House was limited to two hours. Angry Whigs asked for time to examine 144 pages of documents that Polk sent with his request. Denied. The Speaker of the House repeatedly failed to recognize members who wanted to ask detailed questions about how the war started. Only by demanding permission to explain why they should be excused from voting did two dissenters gain the floor and denounce Polk's war rationale as falsehood. The House vote of 174 to 14 represented a victory for stampede tactics. In the Senate the following day, the vote was 40 to 2. Whigs and antiwar Democrats, remembering the political fate of Federalists who had opposed the War of 1812, either voted aye or did not vote. Democratic senator John C. Calhoun of South Carolina, who "opposed the conquest of a people who were alien to American culture and whose ruling classes opposed slavery," later insisted that fewer than 10 percent of his colleagues would have voted for war if Polk had presented the issue fairly.[7] Nonetheless, Calhoun abstained when his name was called.

Thus began the War with Mexico, a conflict that lasted nearly two years and added to the United States a vast domain, which included the present-day states of New Mexico, Arizona, California, Nevada, and Utah. Contemporaries called it "Mr. Polk's War," a most appropriate appellation. With backing from a unanimous cabinet and congressional fire-eaters pledging "money to any amount, and men to any numbers," the Tennessean made the crucial decisions for war.[8] It was Polk who unilaterally defined the geographic limits of Texas as including disputed land between the Nueces River and the Rio Grande. Polk, as commander in chief, ordered General Taylor to the Rio Grande. Polk decided that Mexico had fired the first shot. Polk presented Congress with an accomplished fact.

The presidential war did not go unchallenged. Declaring Polk's claim of Mexican aggression "in direct and notorious violation of the truth," Representative John Quincy Adams, long an advocate of expansion, stood with thirteen northern Whigs to vote against an "unrighteous" war to extend slavery.[9] Calling Polk "the Father of Lies," the Whig editor Horace Greeley claimed that "the laws of Heaven are suspended and those of Hell installed" with the satanic Commandments saying "Thou *shalt* kill Mexicans; Thou *shalt* steal from them, hate them."[10] Because of their own aggressive behavior in the acquisition of Florida a generation earlier, of course, both Calhoun and Adams, as one historian has noted, "knew well how easy it was to stampede the Congress into supporting executive actions of dubious legitimacy."[11] If the president can "invade a neighboring nation, whenever he shall deem it necessary to repel an invasion," Illinois Representative Abraham Lincoln warned, "you allow him to make war at pleasure."[12] Nonetheless, as the historian Piero Gliejeses has put it, "Polk marched to war against Mexico, the country knew it, and did nothing to stop it. Not because it thought it was moral but because it thought it would be easy."[13]

Expanding the Sphere: Manifest Destiny

The war on the Rio Grande came at a critical juncture and dramatized the expansionist themes that dominated American foreign relations after the War of 1812. At the very time Taylor's troops were fighting Mexicans in the Southwest, Polk was quietly settling a dispute with England over the Pacific Northwest. By dividing Oregon at 49° north latitude in June 1846, Polk temporarily abated the rivalry with England over the territory and commerce of North America. The anti-British fervor of the Revolutionary era remained strong in the 1830s and 1840s, and the fear of British encroachment in Texas and California contributed to the outbreak of war against Mexico. That the United States fought Mexico and not Britain in 1846 illustrated another theme: American expansionists behaved more aggressively against weaker Spaniards, Mexicans, and Indians than against the stronger British. According to the expansionist ideology, those peoples who neither improved the land they held nor developed effective political institutions had to make way for those who could. The lands Polk wanted from Mexico had sparse populations that could easily assimilate American institutions, or so he assumed. England, with greater power and traditions similar to the United States, could be a rival but not a victim. Indeed, as Polk moved toward war in winter 1845–1846, he invoked the Monroe Doctrine in warning England against further expansion in North America, thus making explicit what had been implicit in 1823—that Europeans could not seize territory in the Western Hemisphere, but the United States could. The cause, moreover, seemed just. Polk sincerely believed that Mexico fired the first shot on the Rio Grande, just as many sincerely believed that God had destined the United States to control the entire continent. The sincerity of such beliefs in American exceptionalism did not stop expansionism from being both racist and imperialistic.

Continental expansion became the catchphrase in the three decades after 1815. Having defended their territorial integrity during the second war with Great Britain, American nationalists proceeded to acquire Florida, Texas, Oregon, and the Mexican cession, some 1,263,301 square miles. The population nearly trebled, from 8,419,000 in 1815 to 22,018,000 in 1848. American commerce expanded into new channels,

Makers of American Foreign Relations, 1815–1848

Presidents	Secretaries of State
James Madison, 1809–1817	James Monroe, 1811–1817
James Monroe, 1817–1825	John Quincy Adams, 1817–1825
John Quincy Adams, 1825–1829	Henry Clay, 1825–1829
Andrew Jackson, 1829–1837	Martin Van Buren, 1829–1831
	Edward Livingston, 1831–1833
	Louis McLane, 1833–1834
Martin Van Buren, 1837–1841	John Forsyth, 1834–1841
William H. Harrison, 1841	Daniel Webster, 1841–1843
John Tyler, 1841–1845	Abel P. Upshur, 1843–1844
	John C. Calhoun, 1844–1845
James K. Polk, 1845–1849	James Buchanan, 1845–1849

"The Way They Go to California."   Nathaniel Currier's lithograph captures the American expansionist frenzy—in this case for California after the War with Mexico. (Library of Congress)

notably Latin America and Asia, with total exports climbing from $53 million in 1815 to $159 million in 1847. The gross output of farm production increased from $338 million in 1820 to $904 million thirty years later. Cotton production, a vital ingredient in Anglo-American relations, rose from 209,000 bales in 1815 to 2,615,000 bales in 1847. Construction of canals and railroads created a transportation and market revolution that quickened U.S. growth. It became the purpose of U.S. diplomacy during these years to facilitate this expansion. "Everyone always grows a little in this world," said Tsar Alexander I of Russia after John Quincy Adams told him of the American acquisition of West Florida.[14]

The roots of expansion were many—historical, economic, demographic, intellectual, strategic. To be sure, "extending the sphere" (in Madison's phrase) was nothing new, and much that occurred after 1815 derived from earlier decisions.[15] One rationale for acquiring East Florida in 1819 followed the example of Louisiana: Florida, just like New Orleans, might be ceded by Spain to a more dangerous power; hence the argument for peremptorily possessing it before England or France could grab it. Popular support for Latin American revolutions, combined with opportunities for Latin American markets, helped prompt the Monroe Doctrine of 1823.

By stipulating that Europe and the Americas had distinctly different political systems, Monroe's message recalled the isolationist principles of Paine's *Common Sense* and Washington's Farewell Address.

Echoes of the past reverberated in the Anglo-American trade rivalry in Latin America and in the attempts to gain equal access to the British West Indian trade in the 1820s. A more explicit reference to earlier concerns about neutral rights came in 1831 when President Andrew Jackson negotiated an agreement whereby France promised to pay an indemnity of 25 million francs for illegal seizures of American shipping in the years 1805–1812. When the French defaulted on an installment in 1834, Jackson reportedly shouted: "I know them French. They won't pay unless they are made to."[16] France paid the debt. Jackson's pugnacity undoubtedly reflected sound electioneering instincts, but it also served notice that the United States would insist on the right to expand its carrying trade in the event of another European conflagration. Jackson's diplomatic agents also negotiated a Treaty of Navigation and Commerce with Ottoman Turkey in 1830, sparking a trade boom in which "Yankee clocks and glass windows" were exchanged for "dates, figs, and carpets" throughout the Middle East.[17]

An important element in expansion after 1815 derived from the growing vision of what was possible. Despite treaties with England and Spain in 1818 and 1819 that established a firm claim to the Pacific coast, most Americans still thought of the Rocky Mountains as a "natural" boundary. Oregon seemed far away. It had taken Lewis and Clark eighteen months to travel to the Pacific from St. Louis. A sea voyage from Boston to the Pacific coast lasted six to eight months. Even Senator Thomas Hart Benton of Missouri, who would catch Oregon "fever" with a vengeance in the 1840s, went on record in 1825 in favor of the Rockies as the stopping point. "Along the back of this ridge," he intoned, "the Western limit of the republic should be drawn, and the statue of the fabled god, Terminus, should be raised upon its highest peak, never to be thrown down."[18] Within a generation the Rocky Mountains became "less terminus than pivot to empire."[19]

Technology shrank geography and expanded horizons. Steamboats, canals, and railroads stimulated imaginations as well as commerce. Just as the Erie Canal signaled "the birth of empire" by linking the Great Lakes to New York City in 1825, so could publicists boast in the 1840s that "railroad iron is a magician's road, in its power to evoke the energies of land and water."[20] The development of high-speed printing presses gave rise in the early 1840s to mass-circulation newspapers, which in turn trumpeted expansionist rhetoric to a larger foreign-policy public. Samuel F. B. Morse's invention of the telegraph in 1844 created "the world's first Internet."[21] "The magnetic telegraph," boasted the editor John L. O'Sullivan in 1845, "will enable the editors of the 'San Francisco Union …' to set up in type the first half of the President's Inaugural before the echoes of the latter half shall have died away."[22] Steamboats and railroads would open the western frontiers and "bind them fast in one web," proclaimed the essayist Ralph Waldo Emerson.[23]

The same John L. O'Sullivan, as editor of the *Democratic Review,* nurtured such writers as Herman Melville, Nathaniel Hawthorne, and Walt Whitman in creating an expansive national literature—"another ligament to the ties which bind a people together."[24] One of his contributors, Jane McManus Storm, gave the expansionist

"Manifest Destiny."   John Gast's painting captures the ebullient spirit of the trek westward. Pioneers relentlessly move on, attracting railroads and driving out Native Americans, as "Columbia" majestically pulls telegraph wires across America. The gendered image of "Columbia" also underscores the historian Amy Kaplan's contention that the "rhetoric of Manifest Destiny and that of [female] domesticity share a vocabulary that turns imperial conquest into spiritual regeneration." (Collection of Harry T. Peters, Jr.)

process a name in 1845 when she proclaimed it was America's "manifest destiny to overspread the continent allotted by Providence for the free development of our yearly multiplying millions."[25] Although the geographical limits of the Temple of Freedom were not always clear—the Pacific? the continent? the hemisphere?— most believers in Manifest Destiny agreed with John Quincy Adams's claim that the United States and North America were identical. Manifest Destiny meant republicanism, religious freedom, states' rights, free trade, inexpensive land. It appealed to the individualistic ideology of Jacksonianism—"opportunity and expansion for everyone amid minimal or no government regulation, a rhetoric of republican equality that actually masked a profoundly unequal society."[26]

Manifest Destiny in its purest form did not envisage taking territory by force. "The manifest course of events guarantee an early and reasonable acquisition," wrote Madison regarding Florida as early as 1803.[27] Peaceful occupation of uninhabited wilderness, followed by self-government on the American model and eventual annexation by mutual consent—this was the ideal. Neighboring peoples of Spanish and Indian heritage, given time and the American example, might qualify for peaceful incorporation. The process seemed almost automatic. "Go to the West," shouted an Indiana member of Congress in 1846, "and see a young man with his mate of eighteen; and [after] a lapse of thirty years, visit him again, and instead of two, you will find twenty-two. … How long, under this process of multiplication, will it take to cover the continent with our posterity?"[28]

Reality did not match the ideal, as "Polk's War" on the Rio Grande sadly attested. Racism inevitably corroded Manifest Destiny. One diplomat compared a typical South American to "an obedient animal that fawns when chastised," thereby reflecting the dominant racist thinking that posited Anglo-Saxon superiority as a proven scientific fact and denigrated peoples who resisted the inexorable march of democratic institutions.[29] Protestant missionaries who sought to assimilate Indians into white society firmly believed that "any right-thinking savage should be able to recognize the superiority of Christian society." Thus any failures in the acculturation process were attributed to the victims.[30] Just as the negative stereotypes of African Americans in the nineteenth century justified slavery and the unequal treatment of freedmen, while the prevailing image of the Indians as savages was used to rationalize their subjugation, so too did expansionists project their notions of racial superiority against Mexicans ("scarce more than apes" in the prevailing depiction) who were allegedly too cowardly to fight or too treacherous to win if they did fight.[31] In the historian Thomas Hietala's words, "manifest destiny" offered nothing to nonwhite peoples but the prospect of "decline, expulsion, or final extinction."[32] According to such logic, there was no imagined place in God's America for non-white races, other than on the lowest rungs of the social order, serving or making way for God's chosen people—Christian white settlers of Northern European descent.

Indian relocation became official policy under President Andrew Jackson. Once native people lived apart from whites, Jackson believed, Indians would be "free to pursue happiness in their own way and under their rude institutions."[33] In the Removal Act of 1830 Congress gave Jackson the money and authority to impose new treaties and forcibly resettle 85,000 Indians of the five "civilized nations" from the southeastern states—Cherokee, Choctaw, Creek, Chickasaw, and Seminole—across the Mississippi. The French visitor Alexis de Tocqueville, stopping in Memphis during the winter of 1831–1832, described Choctaws crossing the great river: "The wounded, the sick, newborn babies, and the old men on the point of death … the sight will never fade from my memory."[34] Even the assimilated, self-governing, literate, and agriculturally flourishing Cherokees suffered nearly 8,000 deaths as they trekked to "the barren plains of the West" where they awaited "degradation, dispersion," and virtual extinction.[35] According to Secretary of War Lewis Cass, removal offered the only hope for Indians to survive because "a barbarous people … cannot live in contact with a civilized community."[36]

In a larger context, the government's treatment of Native Americans became "part of a global pattern of intensified conflict" during the nineteenth century wherein European-style imperialism expanded at the expense of indigenous populations, including the British subjugations of the Aborigines in Australia, the Maori in New Zealand, and the Xhosa in South Africa.[37] Despite the fact that colonized subjects always resisted such conquests, most Americans viewed their own westward

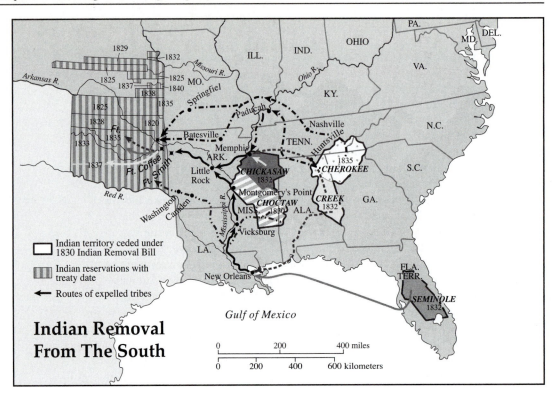

Indian Removal From The South

Indian territory ceded under 1830 Indian Removal Bill

Indian reservations with treaty date

Routes of expelled tribes

expansion as natural and organic. They always sought greater productivity through the cultivation of new lands. Problems generated by increased population, inadequate transportation, depressed agricultural prices, and general hard times also caused periodic migrations into new areas. Whether emigrants moved into American territory beyond the Alleghenies or into fertile North American lands under the sovereignty of other nations, they retained their distinctly Yankee customs and sometimes established their own virtual American "colonies." Friends, relatives, and politicians at home directed U.S. foreign policy toward the "protection" of their compatriots. Thus arose the spread-eagle appeals to national prestige, the glittering description of natural resources and arable lands. As the American enclaves grew in size, fears grew that some European power, probably perfidious England, would snatch the potential prize. Politicians exaggerated the extent to which England meddled in California, Oregon, and Texas, but the multifaceted rivalry with the British did accelerate the expansionist momentum.

Population movements tended to come on the heels of economic downturns. The Panic of 1819, combined with Mexico's generous land policies, encouraged the first flood of immigration into Texas in the 1820s. Similarly, the severe economic depression in 1837–1842 stimulated more western farmers and southern planters to migrate westward. The population of Texas ballooned to 100,000 by 1845, and some 5,000 Americans had crossed the Rockies to far-off Oregon. As one resident of California put it: "Once let the tide of emigration flow toward California, and the American population will soon be sufficiently numerous to play the Texas game."[38] This seemingly unstoppable process of agrarian migration prompted John C. Calhoun in 1843 to advocate "masterly inactivity" on the part of the U.S. government.[39] Whigs especially believed that "whenever and wherever expansion came, it must be peaceful, [and] must proceed gradually with the consent of the governed."[40] Force did not seem necessary—at least not in theory. God, fate, and nature all conspired on behalf of American power.

Commercial Ambitions in the Pacific

Growing global "intercourse in every direction, [and the] universal interdependence of nations" also fueled U.S. expansion.[41] Trade with Latin America increased, and merchants plying the west coast of South America made profits that could be used to purchase the products of East Asia. "The North American road to India" was Senator Benton's description of the Columbia River during the 1840s.[42] Whaling, salmon fisheries, furs, the fabled China trade, commercial rivalry with Britain and Russia—all were stressed from the 1820s onward by publicists seeking to colonize Oregon as a means to commercial expansion throughout the Pacific.

Just as the first wave of settlers reached Oregon in 1843, the British, victorious in the Opium War (1839–1842), were breaking down Chinese trade barriers. By the Treaty of Nanjing in 1842, Britain forced China to open five new coastal ports (Guangzhou, Xianen, Ningbo, Fuzhou, and Shanghai) and grant broad rights of extraterritoriality (legal trials for foreigners in special courts of their own nationality). This British success prompted Americans to seek their own treaty for trade purposes. Already American clipper ships carried cotton to China and returned with tea. Already U.S. merchants used Cantonese middlemen to trade Turkish opium for tea—without which the Chinese believed that the "barbarians" would go "blind and contract intestinal diseases."[43] "His eye fixed upon China," President John Tyler entrusted Massachusetts Whig Caleb Cushing with the mission to negotiate with the Chinese.[44] Determined to counter British "rapacity, illiberality, and gross disregard of our just rights," Cushing bought a special uniform of white pantaloons with gold stripes, white vest, blue coat with gilt buttons, and plumed headpiece, all presumably calculated to overawe the Chinese.[45] His Treaty of Wangxia (1844) gained for the United States the same rights, on an unconditional most-favored nation basis, that England had won in the Opium War. The ensuing influx of Yankee traders, missionaries, and diplomats created an "open door constituency" committed to "penetrating China and propagating at home a paternalistic vision … of defending and reforming China."[46] Nonetheless, reflecting one U.S. diplomat's comment that the "China-man" was "surely the most grotesque animal," Cushing's treaty also created "a mechanism that was to humiliate China and threaten her sovereignty for a century to come."[47]

The U.S. Navy's Asiatic Squadron sometimes used force to protect the China trade in the 1840s—as "the Society for the Diffusion of Cannon Balls," in one missionary's quaint phrase.[48] One sailor wrote prophetically: "how much better it would be to let them [native peoples] go their own way, but No, No! We must have the whole world like us, if we can."[49] The navy's chief contribution to enhancing familiarity with China came indirectly in the exploratory expeditions, especially the one led by Lieutenant Charles Wilkes from 1838 to 1842. Charting coastlines, publicizing points of commercial and strategic interest, enlightening Washington about the Pacific, Wilkes and other naval explorers became "'maritime frontiersmen,' mirror images of the thousands of mountain men, traders, pioneers, adventurers, and army surveyors who trekked westward to the Pacific."[50] A key stimulus for expansion appeared with the publication in 1844 of Wilkes's *Narrative of the United States Exploring Expedition,* which provided accurate data about the Pacific coast from Vancouver Island to Baja California. Wilkes's unqualified praise for San Francisco and the Strait of Juan de Fuca contrasted sharply with his dismissal of the Columbia River, with its shifting sandbars, as a viable entrepôt. American statesmen, particularly Daniel Webster, stepped up efforts thereafter to acquire one or both of these harbors. The main reason Americans pressed so hard for the triangle of Oregon between the Columbia and the strait was the desire for a deepwater port. Only seven Americans lived north of the Columbia River in 1845.

Commercial empire became even more the object in Mexico's California. When a British naval officer entered San Francisco Bay in 1845, he exclaimed: "D——n it! is there nothing but Yankees here?"[51] The Americans were connected primarily with the Boston trading company of Bryant & Sturgis. Having pioneered the otter trade in the Pacific and opened an office in Portuguese Macao, Bryant & Sturgis began in the 1820s to shift from furs to hides ("California bank notes"), which it bought cheaply from Catholic missions and rancheros.[52] The firm established offices in Santa Barbara and Monterey. Thomas O. Larkin, later appointed the first American consul to California and a crucial figure in the diplomacy of 1845–1846, worked for Bryant & Sturgis, as did Richard Henry Dana, author of the epic narrative *Two Years Before the Mast* (1840), depicting a voyage to California around Cape Horn. Altogether, some 25,000 people lived in California in 1845, including 800 Americans. Its link with Mexico City, more than 1,500 miles away, was weak. Overland communications were extremely difficult, and courts, police, schools, and newspapers scarcely existed. American merchants, whalers, and sailors competed ardently with their British counterparts.

Commercial opportunities also beckoned in Hawai'i, which by the 1840s resembled New England in the mid-Pacific. After white settlers ("*haoles,*" or "men without souls") had stripped Hawai'i of its abundant sandalwood for the China trade in the 1820s, others came to save pagan souls for Christ, to plant "large fields of [sugar] cane and some mulberry orchards" for silk production, and to kill whales.[53] By the 1840s, Protestant missionaries had established seventy-nine mission stations, six schools, and two printing houses to spread the gospel. In 1842 President Tyler informed Congress that U.S. stakes in Hawai'i had become so extensive that any attempt by another nation "to take possession of the islands, colonize them, and subvert the native Government" would meet U.S. opposition.[54] Although this Tyler Doctrine endorsed Hawai'i's independence, the United States in declaring its special interest in the archipelago was clearly warning other powers to stay away.

The Pacific and beyond yielded more than profits, as mariners and missionaries brought back by the 1820s enough artifacts to start museums such as the East India

Marine Society of Salem, Massachusetts. Straight-laced Yankee merchants left diaries that described lightly-clothed "Manila girls" as the "handsomest in the world," noting that just "a small puff of wind would discover their nakedness." A catalogue similarly noted that a "Sash" constituted "the entire dress of females in the Fegee [Fiji] Islands."[55] Although apparently less interested in erotica than New Englanders, Midwest entrepreneurs sought to link maritime trade to agrarian migration. Farmers moving to Oregon had in mind an expanded market for their products in Asia, as did some southerners, who viewed the Chinese as potential buyers of cotton and tobacco. Stephen Douglas and other agrarians saw Oregon "not merely as territory for settlement, but as the shortest road to China, and as the source of immense commercial interest."[56] They were reinforced by powerful Eastern entrepreneurs. In January 1845, Asa Whitney, a prosperous New York merchant engaged in the China trade, first proposed government land grants to build a railroad from the Great Lakes to Oregon. Such schemes did not reach fruition until after the Civil War, but their existence in the era of Manifest Destiny testifies to the dual maritime and agrarian nature of continental expansion.

John Quincy Adams, the Floridas, and the Transcontinental Treaty

Following the Louisiana Purchase of 1803, American diplomats had tried to obtain Florida by arguing that it had always been a part of Louisiana. The Spanish rejected such a claim. The first U.S. bite out of the territory came in September 1810, when a group of American settlers revolted against Spanish rule, captured the fortress at Baton Rouge, and proclaimed the "Republic of West Florida." A blue woolen flag with a single silver star replaced the Bourbon banner. Prophesying that all of Florida would eventually be absorbed "either by purchase or conquest," Madison annexed West Florida by proclamation and sent troops to the Pearl River in October.[57] During the War of 1812, American soldiers occupied Mobile and all of West Florida to the Perdido River—the only tangible addition of territory resulting from that war.

It fell to the Monroe administration (1817–1825) and Secretary of State John Quincy Adams to complete the absorption. Spanish minister Don Luis de Onís proved himself a dogged, skillful advocate of his own nation's imperial cause. Adams took the diplomatic offensive, arguing that Spain should cede East Florida to the United States because Spanish authorities had not prevented Indians from raiding American territory (as required by Pinckney's Treaty of 1795). Adams also blamed the Spanish for not returning thousands of escaped slaves and for allegedly assisting British forces during the War of 1812. In addition, a continuing alliance between fugitive blacks and Seminoles, as well as a "Negro fort" on the Apalachicola River, made the acquisition of Florida imperative for those Americans who could not "tolerate a southern sanctuary from slavery."[58] Faced with revolts in its South American empire, Spain wanted a promise from the United States neither to assist the revolutionaries nor to recognize their declared independence. Madrid also instructed Onís to settle the disputed western boundary of Louisiana, and only to cede Florida in exchange for the best frontier he could get. Adams urged that the boundary be set well southwest at the Rio Grande, or at least the Colorado River of Texas. After first insisting on the Mississippi, Onís moved grudgingly to the Mermentau and Calcasieu rivers in the middle of present-day Louisiana. The negotiators stood far apart. "There had never been a negotiation," Adams wrote gloomily, with "so little prospect that the parties would ever come to an understanding."[59]

The man who would break the impasse bivouacked with 4,800 troops at Big Creek, near the Georgia-Florida boundary in early 1818. General Andrew Jackson, the hero of New Orleans, embodied a volatile mixture of frontier passion and calculating ambition. Ostensibly under orders to pursue and punish Seminole Indians and runaway slaves who had been using Spanish Florida as a base from which to raid American settlements, Jackson had suggested secretly to Monroe that "the whole of East Florida [be] seized and held as indemnity for the outrages of Spain upon the property of our Citizens."[60] Whether or not Monroe or Secretary of War John C. Calhoun explicitly approved Jackson's proposal, neither man ever told Jackson *not* to cross the border. To the pugnacious Tennessean, this silence from Washington constituted tacit agreement that the Spanish were every bit as much the enemy as were the Seminoles and "Black Indians."[61]

"Old Hickory" burst across the border in late March 1818. On April 6 the Spanish garrison at St. Marks surrendered, and inside Jackson found "the noted Scotch villain Arbuthnot."[62] Alexander Arbuthnot, in actuality, was a kindly, seventy-year-old Scots trader from Nassau whose scrupulously honest commercial dealings with the Indians had annoyed his profit-minded superiors in England. Convinced that Arbuthnot was in cahoots with the Seminoles, Jackson plunged into the jungle swamps looking for the main Indian camp. He found the camp but not the Indians. He seized another Englishman, Robert C. Ambrister, formerly of the British Royal Colonial Marines. Returning to St. Marks, Jackson convened a court-martial, hanged Arbuthnot, and shot Ambrister, thereby administering American "justice" on Spanish soil to two British subjects. Pensacola capitulated on May 28, whereupon "Old Hickory" promptly replaced the Spanish governor with one of his own colonels and declared in force the revenue laws of the United States. In two short months, although he had killed or captured very few Indians, Jackson had occupied every important Spanish post in Florida except St. Augustine. With more troops and a frigate, he informed Monroe, "I will insure you Cuba" and thus add to "the growing greatness of our nation."[63]

Upon learning of Jackson's deeds, Onís roused Secretary Adams from his morning Bible study and demanded an indemnity, as well as punishment of Jackson. Calhoun and other cabinet members suggested a court-martial for the rambunctious general. Monroe, fearful that Spain wanted war to "unite Europe against us," quietly agreed to return the captured posts to Spain.[64] But he did not censure Jackson and even offered to falsify some of the general's dispatches so that the invasion would appear in a more favorable light. Congress launched an investigation. Only Adams stoutly defended Jackson, saying that "everything" he did "was *defensive.*"[65]

When the British did not protest the deaths of Arbuthnot and Ambrister, Monroe gave his secretary of state full backing. Avoiding any "appearance of truckling to Spain," Adams drew up a memorable reply to Onís's demands for censure and indemnity.[66] If Spain could not restrain its Indians, the United States would do so in

Andrew Jackson (1767–1845).   Sculptor Clark Mills's colossal equestrian statue of the famous victor in the Battle of New Orleans (1815) was completed in 1853. Although Jackson's presidency (1829–1837) did not involve the country in any foreign wars, his aggressive military intervention into Spanish Florida in 1818 personified what the scholar Walter Russell Mead has called the "Jacksonian School" in American foreign policy. Still relevant nearly two centuries later, the Jacksonian school represents "a deeply embedded, widely spread populist and popular culture of honor, independence, courage, and military pride among the American people." It can also lead to "crude cowboy diplomacy," writes Mead in *Special Providence* (2001). (Library of Congress)

self-defense. Adams boldly claimed that the right of defensive invasion was "engraved in adamant on the common sense of mankind." Charging the Spanish with "impotence" rather than perfidy, the secretary demanded that Spain must either "place a force in Florida adequate at once to the protection of her territory and to the fulfillment of her engagements, or cede to the United States a province, of which she retains nothing but the nominal possession, but which is, in fact, a derelict, open to the occupancy of every enemy, civilized or savage, of the United States."[67] Onís's superiors in Madrid reacted to Jackson's forays and Adams's demands with instructions to cede Florida quickly and retreat to the best possible boundary between Louisiana and Mexico.

More negotiations completed the Adams-Onís Treaty (or Transcontinental Treaty), signed in Washington on February 22, 1819. The United States acquired East Florida and a new boundary line that began at the mouth of the Sabine River, moved stairstep fashion along various rivers in a northwesterly direction to the forty-second parallel, and then plunged straight west to the Pacific. The secretary of state pushed the boundary to the Pacific entirely on his own. "I closed the day with ejaculations of fervent gratitude," Adams noted in his diary, because "a definite line of boundary to the South Sea forms a great *epocha* in our history."[68] (See map on page 117.)

In return for these gains, Adams surrendered vague U.S. claims to Texas arising from the Louisiana Purchase. In fact, Onís had instructions to retreat even on the Sabine boundary, but Monroe thought Florida more important than Texas and did not press the matter. The United States also agreed to assume the claims of its own citizens against Spain, some $5 million resulting from Franco-Spanish seizures of American shipping during the undeclared war of 1798–1800. The Transcontinental Treaty said nothing about U.S. recognition of Spain's rebellious colonies, as Adams staunchly resisted any hand-tying nonrecognition pledge. Minor disputes delayed ratifications until 1821.

The importance of the Adams-Onís Treaty lay in what it foreshadowed. Just as in his diplomacy with England in the Convention of 1818 (see p. 117), Adams projected a continental vision—one which encompassed all of the as-yet unconquered Western expanses and that anticipated the railroad and other future technologies. It did not matter if he and Onís were drawing lines across deserts that did not exist or around mountains that were not where maps said they should be. "Americans," Onís wrote prophetically, "believe that their dominion is destined to extend, now to the Isthmus of Panama, and hereafter over all the regions of the New World." They "consider themselves superior to the rest of mankind."[69]

John Quincy Adams (1767–1848). This 1846 portrait of the famed diplomat, secretary of state, president, and congressman from Massachusetts demonstrates well his dour countenance. "My natural disposition," Adams once wrote, "is of an over-anxious cast, and my struggles to accommodate myself to circumstances … have given my constitution in less than fifty years the wear and tear of seventy." Ralph Waldo Emerson wrote that Adams "must have sulphuric acid in his tea." (Library of Congress)

More ominous was the way in which Jackson's invasion of Florida had buttressed diplomacy. Spain's willingness to yield Florida, combined with Britain's refusal to question the executions of Ambrister and Arbuthnot, minimized diplomatic repercussions. Nevertheless, as the congressional investigation revealed, Monroe and Jackson had virtually waged war without the approval of Congress. "If it not be war," one legislator jeered, "let it be called a man-killing expedition which the President has a right to direct whenever he pleases."[70] Because Monroe had apparently pledged that Jackson would not seize any Spanish forts if he crossed the border in pursuit of Seminoles, Henry Clay urged Congress to "assert our constitutional powers, and vindicate the instrument from military violation."[71] Nonetheless, on February 8, 1819, after a twenty-seven-day debate, the four congressional resolutions condemning Jackson went down to defeat by comfortable margins. Appreciative that the headstrong general had facilitated expansion of the national domain, Congress accepted a precedent of unilateral executive military action that would repeat itself often in American history. By endorsing the administration's undeclared war, Congress voted to abdicate its own constitutional purview to check and balance the executive branch on issues of war and peace.

The Monroe Doctrine Sets the Compass

The next notable milestone for expansion came with the Monroe Doctrine of 1823. At first glance, that statement of American diplomatic principles appears entirely anti-imperialist in intent—a stern warning to reactionary Europe not to interfere with revolutions in the New World, a gesture of solidarity and sympathy with the newly independent republics to the south. Monroe's declaration was indeed a warning and a gesture, but its motives were hardly selfless. In saying "Thou Shalt Not" to Europe, James Monroe and John Quincy Adams carefully exempted the United States. By facilitating commercial expansion into Latin America and landed expansion across the North American continent, the Monroe Doctrine became "an official declaration fencing in the 'western hemisphere' as a United States sphere of influence."[72]

The Latin American revolutions (1808–1822) had exerted a magnetic effect on the United States. The exploits of such Latin American leaders as Simón Bolívar, José San Martín, and Bernardo O'Higgins, who liberated their continent from Spanish rule, rekindled memories of 1776. Henry Clay eloquently proposed a new inter-American system as a "counterpoise" to monarchical Europe, "a rallying point" of freedom that would inspire "the friends of Liberty throughout the world."[73]

That the United States did not immediately recognize the Latin American republics was mainly due to the calculating diplomacy of John Quincy Adams. Cynical and cautious, Adams "wished well" to the new nations but doubted that they could "establish free or liberal institutions of government. ... Arbitrary power, military and ecclesiastical, was stamped upon their education, upon their habits, and upon all their institutions."[74] Adams carefully avoided de jure recognition, thereby easing negotiations with Spain over the Transcontinental Treaty. After signing, he worried that Madrid would jettison the treaty if the United States recognized the new Latin American states. Adams also warned that meddling in independence struggles might arouse such aggressive ambitions that the United States "would no longer be the ruler of her own spirit." So the secretary of state proclaimed on July 4, 1821: "Wherever the standard of freedom and independence has or shall be unfurled, there will her [the U.S.] heart, her benedictions, and her prayers be. But she goes not abroad in search of monsters to destroy."[75] Not until the spring of 1822, after the expulsion of Spanish armies from the New World, and following a sharp rise in U.S. trade with Latin America, did President Monroe extend formal recognition to the new governments of La Plata, Peru, Colombia, and Mexico. Both Monroe and Adams feared the continued "intrigues of foreign powers" and "subserviency to *European* interests."[76]

European threats did loom. Following Napoleon's final defeat, European statesmen had endeavored to restore order and legitimacy to an international system thrown out of kilter by the French Revolution and the conquests of Bonaparte. Conservatism became the watchword, and by the Treaty of Paris of 1815 the members of the Quadruple Alliance (Austria, Prussia, Russia, and Britain) bound themselves to future diplomatic congresses for the maintenance of peace and the status quo. A penitent France formally joined the "Concert of Europe" in 1818, and the Quadruple Alliance turned into the Quintuple Alliance. The allies also organized in 1815 the new Holy Alliance. By 1819–1820 the Austrian foreign minister, Prince Klemens von Metternich, enthusiastically supported by Tsar Alexander I of Russia, had transformed both alliances into instruments for suppressing revolutions. At the Congress of Troppau in 1820 the Allies agreed that if internal revolutions posed threats to neighboring states, "the powers bind themselves, by peaceful means, or if need be by arms, to bring back the guilty State into the bosom of the Great Alliance."[77]

In 1821, Austrian armies put down uprisings in Naples and Piedmont. The following year a French army marched across the Pyrenees in support of Spain's unstable Ferdinand VII, who was then resisting a liberal constitutionalist government. The Allies also gave diplomatic support to Ottoman Turkey in its attempt to snuff out a national revolution in Greece. With Americans particularly incensed at the betrayal of freedom in Greece, Adams worried that any gesture to the Greeks would get the United States "encumbered with a quarrel with all of Europe."[78] He and Monroe also feared that the zeal of the Allies "to crush every vestige of liberty" in Europe might also "approach our [American] shores."[79]

British diplomacy during these years waffled. Foreign Secretary Castlereagh wanted very much to support the system he had helped devise at the Congress of Vienna and to preserve the grand coalition that had defeated Napoleon, but London would not condone counter-revolutionary military adventures. Confident of the stability of their own political institutions, and guarded by the English Channel and the Royal Navy, many Britons regarded the use of French and Austrian troops to suppress foreign revolts as upsetting the balance of power. When the Congress of Verona (1822) sanctioned the deployment of French military forces in Spain, something the British had fought to prevent in the bitter Peninsular War (1809–1814), England's withdrawal from the Holy Alliance became inevitable. Castlereagh's successor, George Canning, promised a return to isolation from continental entanglements.

Also influencing Canning was Great Britain's position "at the top of the wheel of fortune."[80] Enjoying global economic hegemony and naval supremacy, the British eyed ever-expanding commercial opportunities—and threats to them. British merchants had captured the lion's share of trade with rebellious Spanish ports in the New World. These lucrative commercial dealings, however, had not overcome London's antipathy to revolution so as to bring about formal recognition, although the British did fear that Spanish reconquest might curtail British trade. As Canning later boasted, "I resolved that if France had Spain, it should not be Spain 'with the Indies.' I called the New World into existence to redress the balance of the old."[81]

Canning's determination to prevent any restoration in Latin America led, in August 1823, to a remarkable conversation with U.S. minister Richard Rush. In discussing French armies in Spain, Rush casually mentioned that the British should never permit France to interfere with the independence of Latin America or to gain territory there by conquest or cession. Canning listened intently. What, he asked Rush, would the U.S. government say to going hand in hand with England in such a policy? No concerted action would be necessary; if they simply told the French that the United States and Britain held the same opinions, would that not deter them? Both nations would also disavow any intention of obtaining territories for themselves. Four days later, Canning wrote Rush: "There has seldom, in the history of the world, occurred an opportunity, when so small an effort of two friendly Governments, might produce so unequivocal a good and prevent such extensive calamities."[82] Intrigued but cautious, Rush referred the matter to Washington, D.C.

Rush's dispatch arrived in early October, and it sparked one of the most momentous discussions in American history. Monroe sought the advice of Thomas Jefferson and James Madison. These two elder Virginians urged the president to accept the British proposal. "Great Britain," Jefferson wrote, "is the nation which can do us the most harm of any one, or all on earth; and with her on our side we need not fear the whole world."[83] Madison also counseled that "with British cooperation we have nothing to fear from the rest of Europe."[84] Madison even suggested a joint statement on behalf of Greek independence. Armed with these opinions, Monroe called a cabinet meeting on November 7, fully prepared to embrace British cooperation.

Adams, however, fought vigorously for a unilateral course. He did not trust the British. Hoping to compete successfully for Latin American markets, and not wanting to tie U.S. hands in some future acquisition of, say, Texas or Cuba, the secretary of state argued that it would be more dignified and candid to make an independent declaration to the Holy Alliance than "to come in as a cockboat in the wake of the British man-of-war."[85] In this and subsequent meetings Adams gradually persuaded Monroe. U.S. leaders did not know that Canning, on October 9, had made an agreement with the French, the so-called Polignac Memorandum, whereby the French disclaimed "any intention or desire" to act against the former Spanish colonies in Latin America.[86] The Americans did learn, however, of the French capture of Cadiz, Spain, along with rumors that a French fleet might soon embark for the New World. Monroe said he had no doubt that if "the allied powers … succeeded with the colonies[,] they would … invade us."[87] Adams remained stubbornly optimistic. Citing competing national interests within the Holy Alliance, especially England's stake in Latin America, he no more believed "that the Holy Allies will restore the Spanish dominion on the American continent than that the Chimborazo [a mountain in

James Monroe (1758–1831). Before becoming president in 1817, the distinguished Virginian served as secretary of state (1811–1817). Sharing John Quincy Adams's nationalist perspective, Monroe helped shape his namesake doctrine barring European intrusions into Latin America. Apprehensive "that the greatest danger to the United States lay in the expansion of European influence, institutions, or principles in its expanded neighborhood," according to the historian James E. Lewis, Monroe and Adams sought "to foster a North American model of national independence, republican government, and liberal commerce in the new states" of Latin America "without incurring excessive risks in Europe." (Library of Congress)

Ecuador] will sink beneath the ocean."[88] Adams won his point, and Monroe followed his advice.

Next came the official declaration. Monroe's original draft followed Adams's previous arguments in the cabinet, but it also included a ringing indictment of the French intervention in Spain and a statement favoring the independence of revolutionary Greece. Adams opposed both points. However much he deplored events in Spain and Greece, the secretary advocated isolation from European embroilments. He urged the president "to make an American cause and adhere inflexibly to that."[89] Monroe excised the offending passages. The Monroe Doctrine then became part of the president's message to Congress of December 2, 1823. It contained three essential points: noncolonization, "hands off" the New World, and American noninvolvement in European quarrels.

Noncolonization focused specifically on Russia and responded to the tsar's announcement in 1821 that Russian dominion extended southward from Alaska along the Pacific to the fifty-first parallel. Adams had protested to the Russian minister in the summer of 1823, so Monroe simply reiterated the axiom that "the American continents, by the free and independent condition which they have assumed and maintain, are henceforth not to be considered as subjects for future colonization by any European powers." By implication, the noncolonization principle also applied to England and the Holy Alliance.

Monroe's second principle, "hands off," posited the notion of two different worlds. He observed that the monarchical system of the Old World "is essentially different from that of America" and warned that "any attempt" by the European powers to "extend their system to any portion of this hemisphere" would be regarded as "dangerous to our peace and safety" and "unfriendly" to the United States. As for the final principle, abstention, Monroe echoed Washington's Farewell Address: "In the wars of the European powers in matters relating to themselves we have never taken any part, nor does it comport with our policy to do so."[90]

An implicit corollary to the Monroe Doctrine, although not mentioned in the address, was the principle of "no transfer." Earlier that same year, in response to reports that Britain might try to negotiate the cession of Cuba from Spain, Adams had informed both the Spaniards and the Cubans that the United States opposed British annexation. "Cuba," Adams wrote in April 1823, "forcibly disjoined from its own unnatural connection with Spain, and incapable of self-support, can only gravitate towards the North American Union, which by the same law of nature cannot cast her off from its bosom."[91] Thus, when read in the context of Adams's concern over Cuba, the noncolonization principle in the Monroe Doctrine also warned Spain against transferring its colony to England or to any other European power.

The immediate effect of Monroe's message was hardly earthshaking. Brave words, after all, would not prevent the European dismemberment of Latin America. The Polignac Memorandum and the British navy actually took care of such a contingency. Metternich called Monroe's message "fully as audacious, and as no less dangerous" than the American Revolution.[92] Realizing that Monroe and Adams might steal his thunder and turn Latin gratitude into Yankee trade opportunities, Canning rushed copies of the Polignac Memorandum to Latin American capitals to show that England, not Washington, had thwarted "any project" of possible intervention.[93] When the United States refused to negotiate military alliances with Colombia and Brazil, a wary Simón Bolívar sought military cooperation with Mexico and Guatemala—"those states that fear an attack from the North."[94] He saw London, not Washington, as the protector of Latin America. At home, most U.S. public opinion applauded Monroe's message for its "explicit and manly tone," which "has evidently found in every bosom a chord which vibrates in strict unison."[95] As Jefferson prognosticated: "This sets our compass and points the course which we are to steer through the ocean of time."[96]

Adams knew that the United States lacked the power to back up the words with deeds. Later generations talked less about matching commitment and power and more about Monroe's words as justifying U.S. expansion in the name of hemispheric solidarity. Indeed, from the beginning, Monroe's message—"a vague statement of policy, a lecture, a doctrine, an ideal"—pledged the United States "only to its own self-interest."[97]

Measuring John Bull: Trade, Canada, and Other Intersections

For years after the Monroe Doctrine, because of commercial rivalry in Latin America, squabbles over West Indian trade, politics in Canada, boundary disputes, and British attempts to suppress the international slave trade, most Americans continued to regard Britain as *the* principal threat to the national interest. As co-occupant of the North American continent, supreme naval power in the world, and commercial giant, only England could block U.S. expansion.

Still, just as in the 1790s, the intertwining of the two economies lessened the likelihood that "some tempest may suddenly arise."[98] In 1825, for example, the United States exported $37 million in goods to England, out of total exports valued at $91 million; by 1839 the figures stood at $57 million and $112 million. The burgeoning British textile industry came to depend on American cotton. Imports from Britain during the 1820s and 1830s fluctuated between one-half and one-third of total U.S. imports. In 1825, 18 percent of all British exports went to the United States; in 1840, 10 percent. In those same years England received 13 percent and 27 percent of its total imports from America. "John Bull is becoming rapidly Americanized," boasted Polk's treasury secretary in 1847, "how can he help it poor fellow when we furnish him food & raiment—cotton & corn?"[99]

These figures, combined with the British decision in 1830 to open the West Indies to direct trade with the United States, reflected a growing British trend toward free trade, which in the 1840s meant dismantling imperial "preferences," repealing protective tariffs, and concentrating on manufactured exports. Anglo-American economic interdependence, although hardly a guarantee against war, acted as a brake against military hostilities. "England's hungry cities," writes the historian Eliga Gould, "supplied the markets that enabled Jefferson's yeoman farmers to open western Pennsylvania, upstate New York, and the Midwest to commercial agriculture."[100] Increased trade brought cooperation as well as competition. In far distant ports such as Singapore and Hong Kong, American merchants relied on British bills of exchange and letters of credit and on the services of British agents. "Wherever English enterprise goes, ours is quickly alongside it," remarked an American diplomat.[101] In effect, the "two English-speaking empires" were erecting a nascent Atlantic state system "animated by mutually beneficial trade and respect for the rule of law."[102]

The years immediately following the War of 1812 marked a high point in Anglo-American relations, thanks largely to the conciliatory diplomacy of John Quincy Adams and Lord Castlereagh. After signing the Treaty of Ghent, Adams, Albert Gallatin, and Henry Clay went directly to London and negotiated a commercial treaty with the British Board of Trade in 1815. A reciprocal trade agreement, it repeated the trade terms of Jay's Treaty. The accord also forbade discriminatory duties by either country against the other, thus tacitly conceding the failure of Jefferson's "peaceable coercions." The accord said nothing about impressment or neutral rights. The two nations renewed this commercial convention in 1818 for ten more years.

War's end also found the British and Americans engaged in feverish warship construction on the Great Lakes. Confident that the United States could build vessels quickly in a crisis, the Monroe administration proposed a standstill agreement to the British. Much to the dismay of the Canadians, Castlereagh agreed. By the Rush-Bagot agreement, negotiated in Washington in April 1817, each country pledged to maintain not more than one armed ship on Lake Champlain, another on Lake Ontario, and two on all the other Great Lakes. The Rush-Bagot accord applied only to warships and left land fortifications intact. Although the "unguarded frontier" between Canada and the United States did not become reality until the Treaty of Washington in 1871 (see page 180), the Rush-Bagot agreement ranks as one of the world's first successful disarmament treaties.

The Convention of 1818, negotiated in London by Richard Rush and Albert Gallatin, dealt with the fisheries and the northwestern boundary. In an effort to settle the vaguely defined limits of the Louisiana Purchase, the Americans initially proposed to extend the Canadian-American boundary westward from Lake of the Woods to the Pacific Ocean along the line of 49° north latitude. Because Britain refused to abandon its claims to the Columbia River Basin, the convention stipulated that the boundary should run from Lake of the Woods to the "Stony Mountains" along the forty-ninth parallel. Beyond the Rockies, for a period of ten years, subject to renewal, the Oregon territory should remain "free and open" to both British and American citizens. "Keep what is yours, but leave the rest of the continent to us," as Adams later put it.[103]

As for the vexatious matter of the Atlantic fisheries, the 1818 agreement won confirmation of the "liberty" to fish "for ever" along specific stretches of the Newfoundland and Labrador coasts, as well as to dry and cure fish along other areas of the same coastline.[104] Adams accepted the agreement as vindication of his family's honor. Not for nothing was the motto on the Adams family seal *Piscemur, venemur ut olim* ("We will fish and hunt as heretofore").

After the Monroe Doctrine, Canning hoped to minimize friction with Washington. "Let us hasten settlement, if we can," he wrote, "but let us postpone the day of difference, if it must come."[105] Yet a series of crises disrupted relations. Most important was the Canadian rebellion of 1837, led by William Lyon Mackenzie. Some Americans cheered the Canadian quest for self-government and volunteered to fight. Coming a year after the Texas war for independence from Mexico, the Canadian rebellion also revived expansionist visions of 1812. Rensselaer Van Rensselaer, son of an American general, tried to become a Canadian version of Sam Houston, leading Canadian rebels and American sympathizers on raids into Canada from New York.

In December 1837 pro-British Canadians struck Van Rensselaer's stronghold on Navy Island in the Niagara River, hoping to capture the rebel supply ship *Caroline*. The troops crossed to the American shore, found the forty-five-ton *Caroline,* set it afire, and cast it adrift to sink a short distance above the great falls. During the fracas an American, Amos Durfee, died. Outrage gripped Americans along the border. Durfee's body was displayed before 3,000 mourners at Buffalo city hall. Demonstrators in Lewiston, New York, made a bonfire of books by British authors. In May 1838 some Americans boarded the Canadian steamboat *Sir Robert Peel,* plying the St. Lawrence River. They burned and looted the vessel, all the while shouting "Remember the *Caroline!*" Raids and counterraids continued through 1838. President Martin Van Buren sent General Winfield Scott to the New York–Ontario border to restore quiet. The War of 1812 veteran brooked no nonsense. "Except if it be over my body," he shouted to an unruly crowd, "you shall not pass this line."[106] When Mackenzie and Van Rensselaer fled to the American border, local U.S. authorities quickly arrested them, and the rebellion petered out.

Agitation spread to northern Maine in February 1839. The vast timberlands spanning the Maine–New Brunswick border had long provoked diplomatic dispute because of cartographic "doubts" in the 1783 peace treaty.[107] In the mid-1830s, settlers moved to the fertile Aroostook Valley and occasional brawls ensued. Soon axe-wielding lumberjacks became embroiled in the "Aroostook War." Maine mobilized its militia, as did New Brunswick, and Congress appropriated some $10 million for defense. It seemed an opportunity to whip the "Warriors of Waterloo."[108] As the "Maine Battle Song" had it: "Britannia shall not rule the Maine, / Nor shall she rule the water; / They've sung that song full long enough, / Much longer than they oughter."[109] The "war" did not last long. General Scott again rushed to the scene, diffused the "bad temper prevailing," and after a few tense weeks the British minister in Washington and Secretary of State John Forsyth negotiated a temporary armistice pending a final boundary settlement.[110] The only American death came at the very end when a Maine militiaman, firing his musket in celebration of the peace, accidentally killed a farmer working his field.

Any possibility that Americans would forget the *Caroline* affair disappeared in November 1840, when a Canadian grocer named Alexander McLeod allegedly bragged in a Niagara, New York, saloon that he personally had killed Amos Durfee. New York State authorities quickly arrested McLeod and charged him with murder and arson. British foreign secretary Lord Palmerston fulminated that McLeod's execution "would produce … a war of retaliation and vengeance."[111] Anglo-American amity fortunately survived this crisis. McLeod produced credible witnesses who swore that the Canadian grocer had not participated in the *Caroline* raid. The jurors believed the witnesses, and McLeod went free.

Within a month of McLeod's acquittal, another crisis erupted. In November 1841, a cargo of slaves being transported from Hampton Roads to New Orleans mutinied and took control of the American vessel *Creole,* killing one white man. The slaves sought refuge at Nassau in the Bahamas, where British authorities liberated all but the actual murderers. Southerners demanded retribution. The Supreme Court recently had passed judgment on the similar case of the Spanish slaver *Amistad,* in which fifty-three African captives, led by Joseph Cinque, killed the captain and crew in Cuban waters in 1839 and then attempted unsuccessfully to sail to Africa. U.S. authorities seized the *Amistad* off Long Island and jailed the Africans in New Haven, Connecticut. Despite Spain's demand for the return of "property" under existing treaties, John Quincy Adams, acting as a private attorney with strong backing from northern abolitionists, won freedom for the *Amistad* blacks on the basis of their natural rights as kidnapped Africans since Spain had outlawed the African slave trade in 1820. Nonetheless, the *Creole* affair seemed more explosive because it involved legal American slaves freed by the British, whose efforts to suppress the international slave trade often collided with America's refusal to permit its vessels to be searched. Southern outrage forced Secretary Webster to demand, as a matter of "comity and discretion," the return of the *Creole* mutineers to stand trial.[112] Yet the U.S. minister to France pointedly asked: Who made John Bull the "great Prefect of police on the ocean?"[113]

Thus did a long list of troubles beset Anglo-American relations in 1842. The northeastern boundary remained in contest. Britain had not apologized for the *Caroline* affair. British interest in Oregon and Texas worried Americans, who

Daniel Webster (1782–1852).
A famed constitutional lawyer from Massachusetts,
Webster served as a member of Congress
(1823–1827), a U.S. senator (1827–1841), and secretary
of state (1841–1843). He helped settle the northeastern
boundary dispute. As a senator again in 1845–1850, he
opposed the acquisition of Texas and the War with Mexico.
From 1850 until his death, this imposing political figure sat
once more as secretary of state. (Library of Congress)

disliked British snobbery—exemplified by the art critic John Ruskin's refusal to
visit or reside in such a country "with no castles."[114] But the time seemed ripe
for the settlement of many of these issues. A new Tory government took office in
September 1841, and Lord Aberdeen, a conciliatory protégé of Castlereagh, replaced
the cantankerous Palmerston at the Foreign Office. Aberdeen appointed as a special envoy to Washington the accommodating Lord Ashburton, who had opposed
British maritime restrictions before the War of 1812. Beetle-browed Daniel Webster
reciprocated Ashburton's amicability. Indeed, Webster had long acted as the American
legal agent for Ashburton's bank, often earning a good salary through British commissions. Three years earlier the erudite and eloquent orator, then at the peak of
his political career, had toured England, dined with Queen Victoria, and won wide
acclaim. The two diplomats met leisurely in the summer of 1842, feasting for several
weeks on Maine salmon, Virginia terrapin, Maryland crabs, and Chesapeake duck,
before producing the Webster-Ashburton Treaty, signed and approved in August.

The Anglo-American agreement drew a new Maine boundary. Far enough south to permit a British military road between New Brunswick and Quebec, the border was still considerably north of Britain's maximum demand. The United States received approximately 7,000 of the 12,000 square miles under dispute. Farther west Webster won most of the disputed territory near the headwaters of the Connecticut River, as well as a favorable boundary from Lake Superior to Lake of the Woods. Included in the latter acquisition was the valuable iron ore of the Mesabi Range in Minnesota. Although not part of the treaty per se, notes expressing mutual regrets over the *Caroline* and *Creole* affairs were exchanged by the diplomats, and in 1853 a joint claims commission awarded $110,330 to owners of the freed slaves.

Webster's discussions with Ashburton seemed simple compared with his diplomacy with Maine and Massachusetts. The Bay State had retained half ownership in Maine's public domain after the latter had become a separate state in 1820, and so Webster enticed both states to approve the new boundary through some dubious cartographic persuasion. One of Webster's friends was Jared Sparks, a historian who later became president of Harvard. Sparks had been researching the diplomacy of the American Revolution in the British archives, and he told Webster he had seen the original map on which Benjamin Franklin had drawn a strong red line delineating the northeast boundary. From memory Sparks reproduced the line on a nineteenth-century map, and it corresponded closely to British claims. A second map turned up, older but still not genuine, also supporting the British position. Accepting both spurious maps as authentic, Webster sent Sparks to Augusta and Boston with this new "evidence" to persuade local officials to accept the treaty before the British backed out of the agreement. Webster also offered each state $150,000. Maine and Massachusetts then endorsed the treaty.

The original maps used in the 1782 peace negotiations actually did have lines that supported American boundary claims. Palmerston had found one such authentic map in 1839 but said nothing. A second map showed up in the Jay family papers in 1843. But the lines on these maps seemed preliminary rather than definitive, as Webster later recognized, not at all "drawn for the purpose of shewing [*sic*] on the map, a boundary which had been agreed on."[115] Thus, by reasonable compromise, "a good and wise measure," in Ashburton's words, did 32,207,680 acres of Maine woodland become part of Canada.[116]

Contest over the Oregon Country

The Webster-Ashburton negotiations did not settle the question of the "Oregon country"—that great expanse west of the Rocky Mountains lying between the forty-second parallel in the south and 54°40' in the north. Webster proposed yielding territory north of the Columbia River if the British would, first, offer a quadrilateral tract of land adjoining the Strait of Juan de Fuca, which Webster believed had the best deepwater ports in the disputed territory, and, second, persuade Mexico to sell Upper California. Ashburton declined.

That same year, 1842, saw the beginning of "Oregon fever," as large numbers of farmers began to arrive in the lush Willamette Valley. Oregon suddenly became controversial. In 1843 the Senate called for forts along the Oregon route, but the House demurred. When rumors leaked of Webster's offer to surrender some of

Oregon, numerous "Oregon conventions" met, especially in the Midwest, to reassert America's claim to 54°40'. "Thirty thousand rifles in Oregon will annihilate the Hudson's Bay Company, drive them off our continent," bellowed Senator Thomas Hart Benton.[117] The Democratic party platform of 1844 called for the "reoccupation" of Oregon, and the party's candidate, James K. Polk, vowed to effect it. At stake was not only the fate of Native Americans and U.S. citizens living in the contested lands but also ports for ships plying waters to Asian markets, especially after the Treaty of Wangxia opened more of China to American vessels.

In actuality, war over Oregon lacked urgency. The American population in Oregon, increasing every year, still numbered only 5,000 people in 1845, and all but a handful lived south of the Columbia River. In contrast, the 700-odd trappers and traders associated with the Hudson's Bay Company all lived north of the river. Four times, in 1818, 1824, 1826, and 1844, the British had proposed the Columbia as the boundary. Each time the United States had countered with 49°. The dispute centered on the triangle northwest of the Columbia, including the deepwater Strait of Juan de Fuca. Notwithstanding shouts of "Fifty-four forty or fight," only a minority of the Democratic party, mainly midwesterners, seemed eager to challenge England. Southern Democrats cared more for Texas than for Oregon, which one Senator claimed was not worth "a pinch of snuff."[118] A few Whigs, such as Webster, wanted Pacific ports, but not at the risk of war. Even though Polk had won his election on an expansionist platform, the new president had ample opportunity to settle the Oregon boundary through diplomacy.

Polk began his Oregon gambit badly. Bound by the Democratic platform to assert full U.S. claims, he announced in his inaugural address of March 4, 1845, that the American title to the whole of Oregon was clear and unquestionable. This claim raised British hackles. Polk, it seems, was talking more for domestic consumption, for in July Secretary of State James Buchanan proposed the forty-ninth parallel (including the southern tip of Vancouver Island) as a fair compromise. Buchanan explained that the president "found himself embarrassed, if not committed, by the acts of his predecessors."[119] Buchanan's offer, however, did not include free navigation of the Columbia River, and this omission, coupled with Polk's earlier blustering about 54°40' caused British minister Richard Pakenham to reject the proposal. Polk waited several weeks. Then, on August 30, despite tensions with Mexico over Texas, the president withdrew his offer and reasserted American claims to 54°40'.

Polk increased the pressure further in his annual message to Congress of December 1845. Again claiming all of Oregon, he urged giving Britain the necessary year's notice for ending joint occupation and hinted at military measures to protect Americans in Oregon. Polk also cited the Monroe Doctrine: "The United States cannot in silence permit any European interference on the North American continent, and should any such interference be attempted [the United States] will be ready to resist it at any and all hazards."[120] Polk had Texas and California in mind, in addition to Oregon, and he was pointedly warning Britain.

For the next five months, while Congress debated ending joint occupation, Polk remained publicly adamant for 54°40'. Twice London offered to arbitrate; each time Washington refused. Although Lord Aberdeen believed "we have no alternative but to leave the field open to the U. States," he could not afford to retreat in the face of

Thomas Hart Benton (1782–1858). Rugged and rambunctious, a Missouri senator from 1821–1851, this splashy orator championed westward expansion. But he accepted the forty-ninth-parallel compromise boundary for Oregon and only reluctantly voted for war with Mexico because he considered the Nueces the true boundary. Some expansionists opposed a field command for Benton during the war because they believed, correctly, that he would oppose a large territorial grab from Mexico. (Library of Congress)

Yankee braggadocio.[121] Moving carefully, the foreign secretary already had begun a propaganda campaign in the London *Times* to prepare public opinion for the loss of the Columbia River triangle. It helped when the Hudson's Bay Company, faced with the flood of American settlers into the Willamette Valley, decided in 1845 to abandon the "trapped-out" southern part of Oregon and move its main depot from the Columbia River north to Vancouver Island. Still, the British statesman warned of offensive military preparations in Canada, including the immediate dispatch of "thirty sail of the line." In late February 1846, Polk replied that if the British proposed "extending the boundary to the Pacific by the forty-ninth parallel and the Strait of Fuca," he would send the proposition to the Senate, "though with reluctance."[122]

The British proposed treaty to extend the forty-ninth parallel dutifully arrived in early June. Before signing the accord, however, Polk decided on an unusual ploy: He submitted it to the Senate for *previous* advice. This procedure placed responsibility for the settlement squarely on the Senate and absolved Polk of responsibility for his retreat from 54°40'. The Senate advised Polk, by a vote of 38 to 12, to accept the British offer. On June 15, 1846, the president formally signed the treaty, which the Senate then approved, 41 to 14. Polk and the Senate accepted this "capacious compromise" so willingly, of course, because war with Mexico had begun some six weeks earlier.[123]

The Texas Bombshell

The acquisition of Texas pushed the United States and Mexico toward war. The United States had confirmed Spanish claims to this northernmost province of Mexico in the Adams-Onís Treaty of 1819, but the self-denial was only temporary. After Mexico won independence from Spain in 1821, two American envoys attempted to purchase the area. The first, South Carolinian Joel Poinsett, tried to work through friendly liberals in the Mexican congress. His successor, Anthony Butler, an unscrupulous crony of Andrew Jackson, tried bribery. Both efforts came to naught. As in the case of Oregon and Florida, migration became the chief engine of U.S. expansion.

Large-scale American settlement did not begin until the 1820s. Spanish authorities, hoping to build up Texas as a buffer against U.S. expansion, had encouraged immigration through generous grants of land. Moses Austin, a Connecticut Yankee from Missouri, and his son Stephen became the first *empresarios* (colonizing agents) by pledging to bring in 300 families, who, in return, would swear allegiance to Spain and the Catholic faith. In 1821, the new Mexican government confirmed these grants and issued others. Within a decade, more than 20,000 Americans had crossed into Texas—"nominally" recognizing the Mexican Government's "authority" but soon ready "to set at defiance any attempt to enforce it," as the British minister to Mexico reported.[124] "A gentle breeze shakes off a ripe peach," wrote Stephen Austin. "The more the American population is increased," the more "the peach will be ripe."[125] Despite Mexico's formal abolition of slavery in 1829, most emigrants were slaveholders seeking the fertile delta soil along the Gulf Coast to grow cotton. In addition, the "de facto economic integration of Mexico's Far North" with American commercial markets encouraged "interethnic alliances" between Anglos and Tejanos and accelerated Texas's growing autonomy.[126]

Friction soon developed. The newcomers, required by law to become Roman Catholics and Mexican citizens, remained predominantly Protestant and never ceased to think of themselves as Americans. Sporadic trouble erupted over immigration, tariffs, slavery, and Mexican army garrisons. Finally, General Antonio López de Santa Anna seized dictatorial power in 1834 and attempted to establish a strong centralized government in Mexico City. Regarding this change as a violation of their rights under the Mexican Constitution of 1824, Texans submitted a "Declaration of Causes" that resembled the "Declaration of Rights and Grievances" of 1775. By autumn 1835, Texans had skirmished with local Mexican soldiers, set up a provisional government, and begun raising a rebel army under Sam Houston. Stephen Austin urged Americans outside Texas to join in "a *national war* in defense of nationalist rights interests and principles and of Americans" against an invasion "by the mongrel Spanish-Indian and Negro race."[127]

Calling the rebels "pirates" and vowing to treat them "as such," Santa Anna responded by leading a large force north across the Rio Grande.[128] At the old Alamo mission in San Antonio, some 200 Texans stood off 1,800 Mexicans for nearly two weeks. Then, on March 6, 1836, with Mexican bugles sounding "no quarter," Santa Anna's forces broke through the Alamo's defenses and killed every resister, including the legendary Davy Crockett and James Bowie. Three weeks later another Texan force, swelled by recent volunteers from the United States, surrendered at Goliad. The Mexicans promptly executed more than three hundred. These atrocities enraged North Americans, hundreds of whom joined Sam Houston's army, which retreated eastward. The showdown came on April 21, 1836, when Houston's force, now numbering 800, turned and attacked the Mexican military near the San Jacinto River, not far from present-day Houston, Texas. Yelling "Remember the Alamo," the Texans charged across an open field, and routed the Mexicans, killing about 630. Taken by surprise when the Texans attacked during afternoon siesta, Santa Anna was captured. Instead of hanging Santa Anna from the nearest tree, Houston extracted a treaty from the Mexican leader that recognized Texas's independence and set a southern and western boundary at the Rio Grande. Mexico repudiated this agreement after Santa Anna's release, but the Battle of San Jacinto ensured Texas's independence.

Texas sought immediate annexation to the United States—"as a bride adorned for her espousals," in Houston's words.[129] Houston's good friend President Andrew Jackson certainly desired Texas, but by 1836 annexation had become a political taboo. The problem was slavery. Fervent continentalists such as John Quincy Adams saw as never before that expansion westward also meant the expansion of slavery. The balance in 1836 stood at thirteen slave states and thirteen free states. With critics shouting that Texas would become "*a vast and profitable* SLAVE MARKET," Jackson tiptoed.[130] Not until eleven months after San Jacinto did "Old Hickory" even recognize Texas's independence. His chosen successor, Martin Van Buren, also spurned annexation "out of deference to the [anti-slavery] prejudices of the North."[131] The annexation issue languished until 1843, when the unpopular Whig President John Tyler seized on Texas as a vehicle for lifting his political fortunes. He successfully negotiated an annexation treaty with the Texans and submitted it to the Senate in April 1844, just prior to the presidential nominating conventions.

Stephen F. Austin (1793–1836).
Born in Virginia, educated in Connecticut and Kentucky, Austin grew up in Missouri, with its polyglot population of Indians, French, Spaniards, Anglo Americans, and African Americans. Taking over from his father in 1821 as *empresario,* Austin began his self-defined mission to "redeem Texas from its wilderness state." As the founder of Anglo-American Texas, he speculated in land, displaced Native Americans, introduced slavery, learned Spanish, became a loyal Mexican citizen, and rebelled only when Santa Anna drastically limited Texas's self-government. His biographer, Gregg Cantrell, has depicted this "consummate manager and exhorter, politician and diplomat, statesman and manipulator" as the antithesis of the "rugged, self-reliant, innocent, democratically inclined frontier leader. He was neither Davy Crockett nor John Wayne." (Courtesy, Center for American History, University of Texas at Austin. Prints and Photographs Collection CN01436.)

Tyler, and later Polk, urged support for the absorption of Texas by playing on fears of British intrusion. To block American expansion, the British had extended diplomatic recognition in 1840 to what they disdainfully called "the Band of outlaws who occupy Texas."[132] Further, Texas could offer an alternative supply of cotton for England's textile factories. A low-tariff Lone Star Republic might grow into a large British market and, by example, stimulate southern states to push harder in Washington for tariff reduction. Certain Britons also tried to persuade Texas to abolish slavery, a prospect that Texan leaders manipulated to gain British support against Mexico. England did arrange a truce between Mexico and Texas in 1842, and two years later Lord Aberdeen toyed with the idea of an international agreement whereby Mexico would extend diplomatic recognition to Texas, whereupon England, France, and possibly the United States would guarantee the independence and existing borders of both Texas and Mexico. Mexico stubbornly refused any dealings with Texas. Not until May 1845, after a resolution for annexation had already passed the U.S. Congress, did Mexico agree to recognize Texas. Too late.

Such maneuvers alarmed U.S. expansionists. By arousing the "jealousy of British interest in Texas," the Tyler administration might have achieved annexation in 1844.[133] If Texas were lost, according to proponents, southern slavery could not "exist surrounded on all sides by free States."[134] Then Secretary of State John C. Calhoun injudiciously boasted that annexation would guard against the danger of abolition of slavery under British tutelage. In what was called the "Texas bombshell," Calhoun publicly defended slavery as "essential to the peace, safety, and prosperity" of the South, using pseudoscientific arguments that offended the British far less than they antagonized abolitionists and free soilers in the North.[135] When the Senate took its final vote on June 8, 1844, the tally was 35 to 16, a two-thirds majority *against* annexation.

Texas became central to the 1844 presidential campaign. Nominating James K. Polk of Tennessee, the Democrats fervently embraced expansion. The party platform promised the "reoccupation of Oregon and the re-annexation of Texas," implying that somehow the United States once owned Texas. The Whigs nominated Henry Clay, who warned: "Annexation and war with Mexico are identical."[136] After a fierce campaign, Polk won by a close margin: 1,337,000 to 1,299,000 in the popular vote and 170 to 105 in the Electoral College. Although people at the time considered the Democratic victory a mandate for expansion, other factors, including an abolitionist third-party candidate who took votes from Clay in the decisive state of New York, help explain Polk's victory. Thus, in one of the rare presidential elections in which foreign-policy issues predominated, voters had elected the candidate who would bring war. If Clay had won in 1844, he almost certainly would have kept peace with Mexico.

Even before Polk took office, the expansionists acted. The lame-duck Tyler suggested annexation by joint resolution (simple majorities of both houses). Opponents howled, demanding a two-thirds vote for a treaty in the Senate. Albert Gallatin called it "an undisguised usurpation of power," and John Quincy Adams growled that the Constitution had become a "monstrous trap."[137] But the annexationists had the votes—120 to 98 in the House, 27 to 25 in the Senate—and on March 1, 1845,

Tyler signed the fateful measure. Five days later the Mexican envoy in Washington asked for his passport and went home.

Polk did not inherit an inevitable conflict with Mexico. Rather, the president made decisions and carried them out in ways that exacerbated already existing tension and made war difficult to avoid. Mexico had promised that it would sever diplomatic relations if the United States annexed Texas, but Polk compounded the problem by supporting Texas's flimsy claim to the Rio Grande as its boundary. Except for Santa Anna's treaty in 1836, the Nueces River had always stood as the accepted boundary, and Texas made no subsequent move to occupy the disputed territory south of Corpus Christi (see page 85). During the negotiations to complete annexation in the summer of 1845, however, Polk's emissaries apparently urged Texas president Anson Jones to seize all territory to the Rio Grande. Polk's orders to U.S. military and naval forces, although couched in defensive terms, were intended to prevent any Mexican retaliation. At this time, too, the president sent secret orders to Commodore John D. Sloat of the Pacific Squadron to capture the main ports of California in the event that Mexico attacked Texas. Whether Polk actively sought to provoke war or merely used force to buttress diplomacy, he was making unilateral decisions that disregarded Mexican sensibilities and ignored congressional prerogatives.

When Mexico failed to retaliate, Polk again tried diplomacy. He had received word from the U.S. consul in Mexico City that the government, although furious at annexation, did not want war and would receive a special emissary to discuss Texas. Polk sent John Slidell, a Louisiana Democrat, as a full minister plenipotentiary empowered to reestablish formal relations and to negotiate issues other than Texas. California now loomed large in Polk's mind, even larger than Texas. No sooner had the president instructed Slidell to purchase New Mexico and California for $25 million than a report arrived from Consul Thomas Larkin in Monterey describing in lurid terms British machinations to turn California into a protectorate. This misinformation prompted Polk to conclude that "Texas must immediately become American or [it] will soon be British."[138] He thus instructed Larkin to inspire Californians "with a jealousy of European dominion and to arouse in their bosoms that love of liberty and independence so natural to the American Continent."[139] These same orders also reached Lieutenant John C. Frémont, head of a U.S. Army exploring party in eastern California, who interpreted the instructions as a command to foment insurrection among American settlers. This he proceeded to do in the summer of 1846, vowing that "we must be first."[140]

Despite Polk's buoyancy, the Slidell mission failed. When the envoy reached Mexico City in early December 1845, officials refused to receive him because his title of minister plenipotentiary suggested prior acceptance of Texas's annexation. Even if Slidell had made the monetary offer for California, no Mexican leader could sell territory to the United States without inviting charges of treason. Any offer to purchase California, coming so closely on the heels of Texas's annexation, seemed out of the question. War was deemed preferable. While some Mexicans thought their large professional army could defeat the corrupt, land-grabbing Yankees, others dreaded that the "triumph of the Anglo-Saxon race" would bring enslavement since Mexican "color was not as white as that of the conquerors."[141] "Nothing is to be done with these people," Slidell arrogantly reported, "until they have been chastised."[142]

Polk responded on January 13, 1846, by ordering General Taylor to move south from Corpus Christi and occupy the left bank of the Rio Grande. Even though Polk initially regarded this action as added pressure on Mexico to negotiate, Mexicans interpreted it as heralding a war of aggression. Taylor blockaded Matamoros, itself an act of war under international law. The Mexicans retaliated. The first clash occurred on April 24, and Polk presented Congress with a fait accompli.

The War with Mexico and the Treaty of Guadalupe Hidalgo

Polk gambled on a short war. California and the Rio Grande boundary were his principal objectives, and he was willing to explore diplomatic alternatives. Shortly after hostilities broke out, the president conferred with an emissary of Santa Anna, then in exile in Cuba. Santa Anna promised that if the United States helped him return to Mexico he would help Polk get the territory he desired. The president ordered the U.S. fleet to "allow him to pass freely," and Santa Anna landed at Veracruz.[143] A revolution propitiously occurred in Mexico City and Santa Anna became president. Instead of making peace, however, the self-proclaimed Napoleon of the West marched his army north to fight General Taylor. Only belatedly did Polk understand that Santa Anna had conned him.

Another diplomatic opportunity presented itself in November 1846 in the persons of Moses Y. Beach and Jane McManus Storm. Beach, the Democratic editor of the *New York Sun* and a chief drumbeater for Manifest Destiny, had contacts in the Mexican army and the Mexican Catholic hierarchy. He persuaded Polk to appoint him a confidential agent to Mexico, empowered to negotiate a peace that would include, in addition to Texas and California, the right to build a canal across the Isthmus of Tehuantepec. Beach then journeyed to Veracruz and Mexico City, accompanied by Storm, the Manifest Destiny advocate whose friendships with prominent Texans, fluency in Spanish, and personal contacts with the Polk administration made her "the author of the entire episode."[144] Storm gained fame as publicist, lobbyist, political fixer, and participant in various expansionist projects from the 1830s to the 1860s. Once in Mexico City, however, she and Beach rashly joined a clerical uprising against Santa Anna. The rebellion collapsed, along with hopes for a quick peace. The two Americans fled to the cover of U.S. forces in Tampico.

President Polk finally decided in early 1847 to send an accredited State Department representative along with General Winfield Scott's army, which landed at Vera Cruz in preparation for an assault on Mexico City. He selected Nicholas P. Trist, chief clerk of the department, an apparently loyal Democrat who could also keep a watchful eye on the politically ambitious Scott, a Whig. The president immediately regretted his choice. In May Trist reached the U.S. Army, then marching toward the plain of central Mexico. He soon quarreled furiously with the "utterly incompetent" Scott, who resented Trist's power to decide when hostilities should cease.[145] The two men did not speak to one another for six weeks, communicating only through vituperative

James K. Polk (1795–1849). Tennessean, graduate of the University of North Carolina, and Democratic expansionist, Polk cast his eyes on Mexican lands and sparked war with Mexico to obtain them. One member of Polk's administration noted a presidential "trait of sly cunning which he [Polk] thought shrewdness, but which was really disingenuousness and duplicity." (Whole plate daguerreotype, 1949.) (Library of Congress)

letters. Then Trist fell ill, and Scott chivalrously sent a "box of Guava marmalade" to speed his recovery.[146] The diplomat whom Scott had called "the personification of Danton, Marat, and St. Just" suddenly became "able, discreet, courteous, and amiable," as the two prickly prima donnas resolved to work together.[147]

By this time, September 1847, Scott's troops had battered their way into Mexico City, and the diplomat and warrior were trying to conclude peace with any Mexican faction that would negotiate. Polk, suspicious at the political implications of the Scott-Trist entente and angry that Trist had forwarded to Washington a Mexican peace proposal that still insisted on the Nueces as the Texas boundary, summarily recalled his unruly representative. Military successes had made it possible to obtain more territory than Polk had originally sought—perhaps Lower as well as Upper California, the Isthmus of Tehuantepec, and Mexico's northern provinces. Polk even contemplated absorbing all Mexico. Some expansionists depicted the "spoils of war" in gendered terms, arguing that soldiers could intermarry with Mexican women and thus "regenerate" Mexico by "gradually infusing vigor into the race." Texan Sam Houston similarly claimed that "annexation" of the "beautiful señoritas" would produce the "most powerful and delightful evidence of civilization."[148]

Nicholas P. Trist (1800–1874). Married to Thomas Jefferson's granddaughter and formerly private secretary to Andrew Jackson, the man who defied President Polk and made peace with Mexico in 1848 had impeccable Democratic credentials. On Trist's return to Washington, however, Polk fired him for insubordination and refused to pay his salary. Not until the administration of President Ulysses S. Grant, who had regretted his own participation in the conquest of Mexico as a young officer, did Trist receive his salary and expenses, plus twenty-three years of interest: $14,600. (Library of Congress)

Trist now took an extraordinary step. He refused his own recall. Trist believed deeply in the promise of Manifest Destiny, "confident that Mexico, left to herself, would someday enter the temple of freedom."[149] But such a process could not be forced. Reconciliation had to come first. Any peace that demanded too much would violate this canon. Even before he received his recall notice, Trist had begun negotiations with a moderate faction that he deemed "perfectly and absolutely *constitutional* in all respects."[150] These Mexicans urged him to remain. Scott facilitated "regime change" by promising to protect the new Mexican government from revolution if it made peace.[151] "My object," Trist later explained, "was … to make the treaty as little exacting as possible from Mexico, as was compatible with its being accepted at home."[152] He thereupon informed Polk, in a bristling sixty-five-page letter, that he was continuing peace talks under his original instructions. Polk seethed. The envoy had been "arrogant, impudent, and very insulting to his Government, and personally offensive," he told his diary.[153]

Trist negotiated his peace treaty, signed on February 2, 1848, at Guadalupe Hidalgo, near Mexico City at a site sacred to Mexicans due to a reported appearance of the Virgin Mary in 1531. Mexico ceded California and New Mexico to the United States and confirmed the annexation of Texas with the Rio Grande as the boundary. In return, the United States paid $15 million and assumed the claims of U.S. citizens totaling another $3.25 million. When the treaty arrived in Washington, the president reluctantly submitted it to the Senate, notwithstanding that Trist "has acted worse than any man in the public employ whom I have ever known."[154] The territorial gains comprised all he had empowered Slidell to obtain in his 1845–1846 mission. "If I were now to reject a treaty," Polk explained, "made upon my own terms … the probability is that Congress would not grant either men or money to prosecute the war."[155] The Whig-dominated Senate had just passed a resolution praising Taylor's victories in "a war unnecessarily and unconstitutionally begun by the President of the United States." Despite their distaste for territory by conquest, as one Whig noted, the choice was "between the continuance of an expensive & unfortunate war & a *bad* treaty—the people want peace."[156] The treaty thereupon passed the Senate, 38 to 14, on March 10, 1848. One Whig justified his favorable vote because "it is less evil, to have … a most sparsely settled part of Mexico, than the whole with its mixed breed of Spaniards, Indians, and negroes."[157]

War with Mexico swelled the membership of pacifist organizations such as the American Peace Society, which offered a $500 prize for the best essay analyzing the war. Yet the antiwar forces in Congress, consisting largely of Whigs and Calhoun Democrats, made little impact. Opponents at first criticized the questionable way in which Polk had begun the war, and after Scott's victorious march to the Halls of Montezuma, they rallied against any administration effort to take "All Mexico." "They jes want this Californy/So's to lug new slave states in," jeered the abolitionist poet James Russell Lowell, "To abuse ye, an' to scorn ye,/An' to plunder ye like sin."[158] Polk struck back at his critics by suggesting that they were aiding the enemy, a stinging charge using the Constitution's definition of treason. Few opponents chose to risk voting against military supplies. As one Whig phrased it: "We support the war, though we condemn those who have brought us into it."[159] A war, right or wrong, which Congress had voted for, had to be upheld. Polk's attacks on his opponents as traitors set a deplorable precedent that would be repeated in the twentieth and twenty-first centuries.

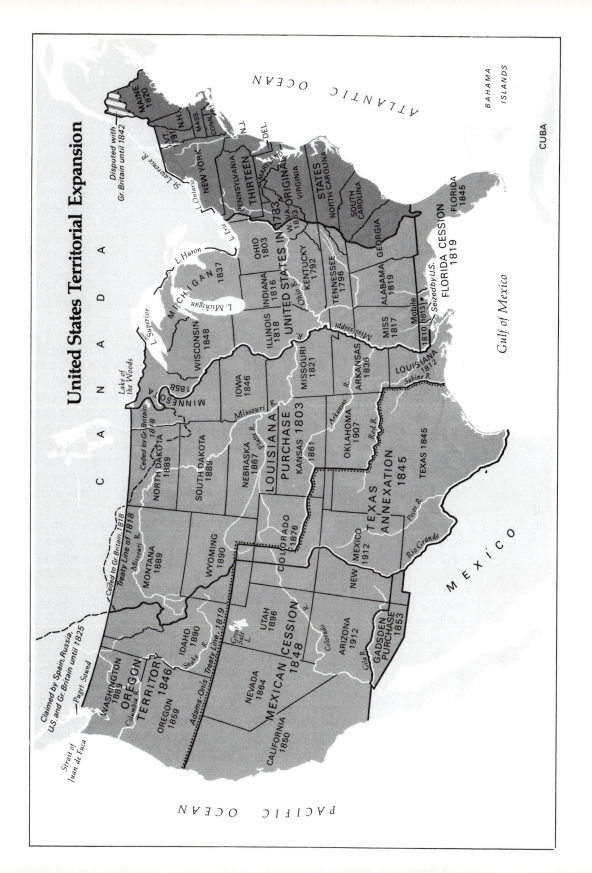

United States Territorial Expansion

CANADA

St. Lawrence R.

Disputed with
Gr. Britain until 1842

MAINE
1820

VT. N.H.
1791
MASS.
CONN. R.I.

NEW YORK

N.J.

PENNSYLVANIA
DEL.
MARYLAND

THIRTEEN

W. VA. ORIGINAL
1863 VIRGINIA

STATES

NORTH CAROLINA

SOUTH
CAROLINA

GEORGIA

FLORIDA
1845

FLORIDA CESSION
1819

L. Ontario

L. Erie

OHIO
1803

L. Huron

MICHIGAN
1837

L. Michigan

INDIANA
1816

ILLINOIS
1818

UNITED STATES IN 1783

Ohio R.

KENTUCKY
1792

TENNESSEE
1796

ALABAMA
1819

Mobile

MISS.
1817

Seized by U.S.
1810 1813

L. Superior

WISCONSIN
1848

Lake of
the Woods

Ceded by Gr. Britain 1818

MINNESOTA
1858

IOWA
1846

Missouri R.

MISSOURI
1821

Mississippi R.

ARKANSAS
1836

Arkansas R.

LOUISIANA
1812

Sabine R.

LOUISIANA
PURCHASE 1803

NORTH DAKOTA
1889

SOUTH DAKOTA
1889

NEBRASKA
1867

Platte R.

KANSAS
1861

OKLAHOMA
1907

Red R.

TEXAS 1845

Ceded to Gr. Britain, 1818

Treaty Line of 1818

Missouri R.

MONTANA
1889

WYOMING
1890

COLORADO
1876

TEXAS ANNEXATION 1845

NEW MEXICO
1912

Pecos R.

Rio Grande

MEXICO

Claimed by Spain, Russia,
U.S. and Gr. Britain until 1825

Puget Sound

Strait of
Juan de Fuca

Adams-Onis Treaty Line, 1819

WASHINGTON
1889

OREGON
TERRITORY
1846

Columbia R.

IDAHO
1890

Snake R.

UTAH
1896

Great
Salt
L.

Colorado R.

MEXICAN CESSION
1848

ARIZONA
1912

Gila R.

GADSDEN
PURCHASE
1853

NEVADA
1864

OREGON
1859

CALIFORNIA
1850

PACIFIC OCEAN

ATLANTIC OCEAN

BAHAMA
ISLANDS

CUBA

Gulf of Mexico

117

The Wilmot Proviso sparked the most ominous debates of the war. Attached as a rider to the war appropriation bill of August 1846 by Democrat David Wilmot of Pennsylvania, the proviso held that no territory acquired from Mexico should be open to slavery. Keep slavery "within given limits," Wilmot promised, "and in time it will wear itself out."[160] Supporters consisted almost exclusively of northerners, and a coalition of southern Whigs and administration Democrats sufficed to defeat it. Nonetheless, the Wilmot Proviso was introduced again and again, never passing but arousing increasingly partisan emotions. When an Indiana representative bitterly complained that this nation claiming "to be the freeest on earth" wanted to "extend the area of freedom by enlarging the boundaries of slavery," southerners such as Calhoun began to despair for the Union.[161]

What if ...   *Nicholas P. Trist had not negotiated a peace treaty with Mexico in 1848?*

Had President James K. Polk's unaccredited agent, Nicholas P. Trist, not signed the Treaty of Guadalupe Hidalgo in February 1848, a longer war and ill fortune might well have afflicted both the United States and Mexico. Even though the president had fired Trist for not following his instructions, the defiant diplomat concluded a treaty that obtained the original goals of California, Texas (with the Rio Grande boundary), and the territories in between for half the price that Polk had authorized. Trist disobeyed Polk and made peace because he feared a resumption of hostilities and a protracted conflict could result in the annexation of all Mexico. In Trist's eyes, such a war of conquest would violate American ideals and expose his Anglo-Protestant republic to contamination from multi-racial Spanish-speaking Catholics.

Trist had ample reason to dread renewed war and the further dismemberment of Mexico. Certainly the rhetoric on behalf of "All Mexico" was reaching a crescendo in Congress and in the penny press in the fall and winter of 1847–1848. Polk himself had thought of demanding Lower California, the isthmus of Tehuantepec, and other northern provinces as a war indemnity. Invoking the specter of Mexicans turning to a European monarch to protect and govern them, the president promised Congress in December 1847 not to withdraw American troops until Mexico agreed to a territorial cession. Even after Polk approved the Treaty of Guadalupe Hidalgo, in the spring of 1848 he seriously contemplated the military occupation of Yucatán—a secessionist Mexican province whose white governing class faced rebellion by its Indian population. Without Trist's treaty, Polk's recall of General Winfield Scott, whose scrupulous dealings with Mexican authorities had won respect, might also have spelled disaster. Under the less than benevolent command of Benjamin Butler, a long-term U.S. occupation could well have exacerbated racial and cultural prejudices on both sides and possibly ignited guerrilla warfare. The aged Duke of Wellington might have proved correct when he prophesied that the 10,000-strong U.S. army in Central Mexico would be doomed if separated from its base of supplies. Instead of the easy conquest of all Mexico, a lengthy war against *Yanqui* invaders might have united Mexicans and thwarted U.S. expansionists for at least a generation.

Ironically, the same considerations that persuaded Polk to accept the moderate territorial gains in Trist's treaty would probably have encouraged him to approve a similar diplomatic compromise. Because of opposition by Whigs and Northern Democrats to the expansion of slavery into any conquered territories, as indicated by growing support for the Wilmot Proviso, the president worried that Congress might not vote appropriations for a wider war. A few Southern Democrats, led by John C. Calhoun, also opposed annexation because they believed that no part of Mexico was suitable to slavery. Of course, another diplomatic agent sent to replace Trist might have lacked the latter's skill to negotiate successfully with a Mexican government divided between *Moderados* and *Puros* (war party).

Nonetheless, Polk had little desire to continue a war that would heighten sectional tensions and enable the Whigs to win the White House, as they actually did. The discovery of gold in California and outbreak of revolutions in Europe in the spring of 1848 might also have reinforced the president's desire to end a divisive and distractive war. A longer war with Mexico would likely have constrained U.S. initiatives elsewhere, such as the opening of Japan. U.S. soldiers still fighting in Mexico could not have joined filibuster expeditions to Central America and Cuba. It was lucky for Polk that his disavowed diplomat made peace when he did. As the French would learn when they occupied Mexico City in 1863, decisive military victories do not always translate into lasting peaceful settlements.

The Lessons and Costs of Expansion, 1815–1848

By adding 500,000 square miles of land from Mexico, the United States stood "three times as large as the whole of France, Britain, Austria, Prussia, Spain, Portugal, Belgium, Holland, and Denmark together," boasted the head of the Census Bureau.[162] Polk did not obtain "All Mexico," but he had taken what he wanted: Texas and California. The casualties: 1,548 Americans killed in battle and 10,970 died from other causes, mainly disease. At least 50,000 Mexicans died.

The war brought other ugly consequences not so easily quantified. The arrogant rationalizations for expansion appalled the old Jeffersonian Albert Gallatin, who noted: "All these allegations of superiority of race and destiny neither require nor deserve any answer; they are pretences [sic] … to disguise ambitions, cupidity, or silly vanity."[163] John C. Calhoun had warned in 1847 that "Mexico is to us the forbidden fruit" because "eating it" would "subject our institutions … to political death."[164] Indeed, debates over the Wilmot Proviso raised the all-important question whether the new territories would become free or slave. It took two more decades and a bloody civil war to answer the question. In fact, the issue of race in the 1850s blocked any possibility that the United States might acquire additional territories in the Caribbean or Pacific. Such potential prizes as

Cuba or Hawai'i had racially mixed populations and thus seemed less adaptable to American settlers and institutions than did the more lightly populated prairies of North America.

The American Indian became a casualty of westward expansion. "Land enough—Land enough! Make way, I say, for the young American Buffalo!" boomed one fervent orator for Manifest Destiny in 1844.[165] It was the Native American who had to give way. While white Americans in the 1820s and 1830s sought fertile lands in Texas and Oregon, other farmers were encroaching on Indian lands east of the Mississippi. Despite treaties that one governor called "expedients by which ignorant, intractable, and savage people were induced without bloodshed to yield up what civilized peoples had a right to possess," the federal government removed most Native Americans in the Old Northwest and Southwest to new reservations in Oklahoma and Missouri.[166] It became a brutal process, a national disgrace—a "trail of tears." Forced to march thousands of miles, robbed by federal and state officials, ravaged by disease, some tribes resisted, as evidenced by the Black Hawk War of 1832 and the guerrilla warfare waged by the Seminoles in the Everglades for nearly a decade. The Seminole War finally ended in 1842 with the order: "Find the enemy, capture, or exterminate."[167] In the case of the Creeks, the population in 1860 comprised only 40 percent of what it had been thirty years earlier. Other Indians suffered similar losses. The roughly 486,000 Native Americans beyond the Mississippi would feel the crunch of empire after 1848—"a dress rehearsal for the acquisition of overseas empire" at the end of the century.[168]

Defeated Mexico relinquished more than half of its national territory and saw large amounts of real estate, foodstuffs, art treasures, and livestock destroyed by the invading armies. One Mexican statesman blamed defeat on the absence of a cohesive "national spirit," for there was at that time no "nation" of Mexico, just as no unified

"The Trail of Tears." Robert Lindneux's poignant painting of Indian removal illustrates a tragic consequence of U.S. expansion. Of the 100,000 Indians transported beyond the Mississippi between 1824 and 1845, perhaps one-fourth to one-third died during or shortly after the forced marches. Why did not white Americans strip Indians of their names? asked one foreign visitor to the United States during this period. "They have robbed the Indians of everything else." (Woolaroc Museum, Bartlesville, Oklahoma)

Germany or Italy yet existed.[169] A Mexican scholar, Jorge Castañeda, has conversely discerned unity and strength at work in his country's effort to resist U.S. imperialism. Mexico, by waging war rather than ceding half the national patrimony to John Slidell, ultimately kept Sonora, Chihuahua, and Baja California from becoming American, and thus "fighting and losing proved to be a better deal than selling and perhaps losing far more."[170]

The Yankee invaders treated Mexicans as they did the Indians—as racial inferiors. General John Quitman called Mexico's 8 million inhabitants "beasts of burden, with as little intellect as the asses whose burdens they share."[171] The multiracial, multicultural Hispanic "frontier of inclusion" that had welcomed American settlers gave way to an Anglo-American "frontier of exclusion."[172] Mexicans who had lived in Texas lost most of their lands through fraud and outright confiscation, as did the Comanches, Kiowas, and other native tribes in what the historian Gary Clayton Anderson has called an official Texas "policy of ethnic cleansing" aimed at "the forced removal of certain culturally identified groups from their lands."[173] Tumultuous Mexico had to endure another twenty-five years of rebellion, civil war, and European intervention before attaining a degree of national unity under the authoritarian regime of Porfirio Díaz. The war increased the disparity in size, power, and population between the United States and Mexico, creating longstanding attitudes of suspicion, distrust, and prejudice on both sides of the border.

The success of continental expansion left one obvious imprint on the United States—that of increased power. No country had grown so fast as the United States, "the *wunderkind* nation of the nineteenth century."[174] At the height of the Oregon crisis Senator Lewis Cass of Michigan could brag that "we can neither be overrun nor conquered. England may as well attempt to blow up Gibraltar with a squib [small firecracker], as to attempt to subdue us."[175] No longer "a low-rung power with little international clout," the United States had become dominant within the hemisphere, as evidenced by the growth of the Monroe Doctrine.[176] President Monroe had hurled his defiant message in 1823 without the power to enforce it. When Britain seized the Falkland (Malvinas) Islands in 1833 and the French bombarded Mexican ports in 1838, U.S. leaders did nothing. In 1842, however, President Tyler virtually extended the geographic scope of the Monroe Doctrine when he warned England and France not "to take possession of" Hawai'i.[177] Three years later Polk arrogantly invoked the doctrine in proclaiming U.S. rights to Texas, California, and Oregon. As U.S. power continued to increase after 1848, as economic interests began to focus on the Caribbean and the possibility of an isthmian canal, U.S. diplomats would repeatedly invoke the Monroe Doctrine. The same mixture of motives that operated in the 1820s would continue—namely, a resolute desire to forestall European interference, combined with a wish to extend U.S. influence throughout the hemisphere.

Polk told one member of Congress in 1846 that "the only way to treat John Bull was to look him straight in the eye."[178] The president's confrontational style seemed successful with both Britain and Mexico. Polk himself thought the war had boosted national prestige abroad by demonstrating that a democracy could prosecute a foreign war "with all the vigor" usually associated with "more arbitrary forms of government."[179] The Tennessean's "lessons" for later generations take on added importance when one considers his high reputation in the twentieth century. Theodore Roosevelt saw in Polk a model for reasserting strong executive leadership in foreign policy. So did Harry S. Truman. Polls of historians continue to rank Polk among the top ten presidents.

In fact, Polk was lucky. Unlike John Quincy Adams, whose forceful diplomacy against Spain and the Holy Alliance rested on a shrewd understanding of international power realities, Polk moved inexpertly against Mexico and Britain. Regarding Oregon, his initial call for 54°40' unnecessarily heightened jingo fevers on both sides of the Atlantic and postponed any settlement until the spring of 1846. In view of the concurrent crisis with Mexico, such a delay invited the disastrous possibility of a war on two fronts. British conciliation owed more to troubles at home—potato famine in Ireland, tensions with France, political turmoil over repeal of the Corn Laws—than to U.S. bravado. Aberdeen's sobering presence also helped. Had Palmerston become foreign secretary, Polk's "eyeball" tactics might have meant war. Given the influx of American immigration into the Pacific Northwest in 1844–1846, Calhoun's policy of "masterly inactivity" almost certainly would have produced a favorable settlement without risking war. Polk apparently had not heard what Castlereagh said a generation earlier: "You need not trouble yourselves about Oregon, you will conquer Oregon in your bedchambers."[180]

"Masterly inactivity" might have worked with Mexico as well. Polk did not want war so much as he desired the fruits of war. He wanted California, New Mexico, and the Rio Grande boundary; and he hurried because he suspected British intrigues. Keeping Taylor's army at Corpus Christi would have protected Texas with little provocation to Mexico. Negotiations could resume when tempers cooled. As for California, Polk should have understood, after a careful reading of all the diplomatic correspondence, that England had no serious intention of seizing that lucrative prize.

The president might have waited to see if the influx of American settlers would make California another Texas or Oregon. Annexation might have come peacefully—perhaps during some subsequent European crisis such as the Crimean War. As it turned out, Polk's decision for war in the spring of 1846 was reckless, coming as it did while tensions with England remained so acute. War risked all the expansionist goals. A major Mexican victory (in February 1847 Santa Anna nearly defeated Zachary Taylor in the battle of Buena Vista) might have brought a European loan to Mexico, military stalemate, and possible British mediation. Polk might have lost California. He was also lucky that his repudiated agent, Trist, made a treaty of peace when he did. Scott's capture of Mexico City and the successful negotiations that quickly followed obscured the fact that insistence on "All Mexico" might have led to the kind of protracted guerrilla war against U.S. occupation forces that Mexicans waged against French armies twenty years later (see Chapter 4). If Polk truly believed in Manifest Destiny, he should not have risked what Americans had long deemed inevitable. But because Polk could boast of annexing "a country large enough for a great empire and second only to that of Louisiana in 1803," the blemishes in his diplomatic record will probably continue to be covered with the cosmetic cream of national celebration.[181]

FURTHER READING FOR THE PERIOD 1815–1848

For Manifest Destiny and expansionism, see Evan Cornog, *The Birth of Empire* (1998); Richard Drinnon, *Facing West* (1980); Yonatan Eyal, *The Young America Movement and the Transformation of the Democratic Party, 1828–1861* (2007); Laura E. Gomez, *Manifest Destinies* (2007); Amy S. Greenberg, *Manifest Manhood and the Ante Bellum American Empire* (2005); John Craig Hammond, *Slavery, Freedom, and Expansion in the Early American West* (2007); Thomas R. Hietala, *Manifest Design* (2003); Reginald Horsman, *Race and Manifest Destiny* (1981); Daniel Walker Howe, *What Hath God Wrought* (2007); Nancy Isenberg, *Sex and Citizenship in Antebellum America* (1998); Howard Jones, *Mutiny on the* Amistad (1987); Robert Kagan, *Dangerous Nation* (2006); Robert F. May, *Manifest Destiny's Underworld* (2002); Frederick Merk, *Manifest Destiny and Mission in American History* (1963); Christopher Morris and Sam W. Haynes, eds., *Manifest Destiny and Empire* (1997); Michael A. Morrison, *Slavery and the American West* (1997); Gregory H. Nobles, *American Frontiers* (1997); Walter Nugent, *Habits of Empire* (2008); Paul Pappas, *The United States and the Greek War for Independence, 1821–1828* (1985); David Reynolds, *Waking Giant* (2008); Charles Sellers, *The Market Revolution* (1991); Joel H. Silbey, *Martin Van Buren and the Emergence of American Popular Politics* (2002); Richard Slotkin, *Regeneration Through Violence* (1996); Anders Stephanson, *Manifest Destiny* (1995); William Earl Weeks, *Building the Continental Empire* (1996); Edward L. Widmer, *Young America* (1999); Sean Wilentz, *The Rise of American Democracy* (2005); and Valarie H. Ziegler, *The Advocates of Peace in Antebellum America* (1992).

Leaders in this period are featured in K. Jack Bauer, *Zachary Taylor* (1985); John Buchanan, *Jackson's Way* (2001); Andrew Burstein, *The Passions of Andrew Jackson* (2003); Greg Cantrell, *Stephen F. Austin* (1999); Edward P. Crapol, *John Tyler* (2007); Noble E. Cunningham, *The Presidency of James Monroe* (1996); John Eisenhower, *Agent of Destiny* (1997) (Scott); William Dusinberre, *Slavemaster President* (2003) (Polk); Will Fowler, *Santa Anna of Mexico* (2007); Sam W. Haynes, *James K. Polk and the Expansionist Impulse* (2002); Linda S. Hudson, *Mistress of Manifest Destiny* (2001) (Storm); Timothy D. Johnson, *Winfield Scott* (1998); Thomas Leonard, *James K. Polk* (2000); Willard C. Lunder, *Lewis Cass and the Politics of Moderation* (1996); Jon Meacham, *American Lion* (2008) (Jackson); John Niven, *John C. Calhoun and the Price of Union* (1988); Norma Lois Peterson, *The Presidencies of William Henry Harrison and John Tyler* (1989); Robert Remini, *Andrew Jackson and the Course of American Freedom* (1981) and *Henry Clay* (1991); Ilene Stone and Suzanna M. Grenz, *Jesse Benton Fremont* (2005); Sean Wilentz, *Andrew Jackson* (2005); and Major L. Wilson, *The Presidency of Martin Van Buren* (1984). For John Quincy Adams and Daniel Webster, see below.

For the U.S. Navy and explorations, see Kenneth J. Hagan, *This People's Navy* (1991); Henry Savage, Jr., *Discovering America, 1700–1875* (1978); John H. Schroeder, *Shaping a Maritime Empire* (1985); Gene A. Smith, *Thomas ap Catesby Jones* (2000); William Stanton, *The Great United States Exploring Expedition of 1838–1842* (1975); and Herman Viola and Carolyn Margolis, eds., *Magnificent Voyages* (1985).

John Quincy Adams is treated in Samuel Flagg Bemis, *John Quincy Adams and the Foundations of American Foreign Policy* (1949); Mary Hargreaves, *The Presidency of John Quincy Adams* (1985); James E. Lewis, *John Quincy Adams* (2001); Paul C. Nagel, *John Quincy Adams* (1997); Lynn Hudson Parsons, *John Quincy Adams* (1998); Robert P. Remini, *John Quincy Adams* (2003); Leonard Richards, *The Life and Times of Congressman John Quincy Adams* (1986); Greg Russell, *John Quincy Adams and the Public Virtues of Diplomacy* (1995); and William E. Weeks, *John Quincy Adams and American Global Empire* (1992).

For the Floridas, the Adams-Onís Treaty, Latin America, and the Monroe Doctrine, see Philip C. Brooks, *Diplomacy and the Borderlands* (1939) (Adams-Onís); David S. Hendler and Jeane T. Hendler, *Old Hickory's War* (2003); Paul E. Hoffman, *Florida's Frontiers* (2002); John J. Johnson, *A Hemisphere Apart* (1990); Lester D. Langley, *The Americas in the Age of Revolution* (1996); James E. Lewis, *American Union and the Problem of Neighborhood* (1998); Ernest R. May, *The Making of the Monroe Doctrine* (1975); Gretchen Murphy, *Hemispheric Imaginings* (2004); and Bradford Perkins, *Castlereagh and Adams* (1964).

Daniel Webster is studied in Maurice G. Baxter, *One and Inseparable* (1984); Robert Remini, *Daniel Webster* (1997); and Kenneth Shewmaker, ed., *Daniel Webster* (1990). Shewmaker and his coeditors provide analysis with documents in *The Papers of Daniel Webster: Diplomatic Papers* (1983, 1987).

Anglo-American issues, including Oregon and Canada, appear in Charles C. Campbell, *From Revolution to Rapprochement* (1974); Francis A. Carroll, *A Good and Wise Measure* (2001); Howard Jones, *To the Webster-Ashburton Treaty* (1977); Howard Jones and Donald Rakestraw, *Prologue to Manifest Destiny* (1997); Kenneth R. Stevens, *Border Diplomacy* (1989); and Reginald C. Stuart, *United States Expansionism and British North America, 1775–1871* (1988).

Texas, California, the War with Mexico, and President Polk are explored in Gary Clayton Anderson, *The Conquest of Texas* (2005); Paul H. Bergeron, *The Presidency of James K. Polk* (1987); John P. Bloom, ed., *The Treaty of Guadalupe Hidalgo, 1848* (1999); Gene Brack, *Mexico Views Manifest Destiny* (1975); William C. Davis, *Lone Star Rising* (2004) and *Three Roads to the Alamo* (1998); William A. DePalo, Jr., *The Mexican National Army, 1822–1852* (1997); Janice T. Driesbach et al., *Art of the Gold Rush* (1998); John D. Eisenhower, *So Far from God* (1989) (War with Mexico); Paul Foos, *A Short, Offhand, Killing Affair* (2002); Richard Francaviglia and Douglas W. Richmond, eds., *Dueling Eagles* (2000); Donald S. Frazier, ed., *The United States and Mexico at War* (1999); Neal Harlow, *California Conquered* (1982); Robert W. Johannsen, *To the Halls of Montezuma* (1985); Timothy Johnson, *A Gallant Little Army* (2007); Paul D. Lack, *The Texas Revolutionary Experience* (1992); Ernest M. Lander, Jr., *Reluctant Imperialists: Calhoun, the South Carolinians, and the Mexican War* (1980); Kristyna M. Libura et al., *Echoes of the Mexican American War* (2004); Dean Mahin, *Olive Branch and Sword* (1997); Timothy M. Matouina, *The Alamo Remembered* (1995); James F. McCaffrey, *Army of Manifest Destiny* (1992); Aims McGuiness, *The Path of Empire* (2007); Anna K. Nelson, *Secret Agents* (1988); Wallace Ohrt, *Defiant Peacemaker* (1998) (Trist); David M. Pletcher, *The Diplomacy of Annexation* (1973); Stuart Reid, *The Secret War for Texas* (2007); Andres Resendez, *Changing National Identities at the Frontier* (2005); Cecil Robinson, *The View from Chapultepec* (1981); Malcolm J. Rohrbough, *Days of Gold* (1997) (California gold rush); Pedro Santoni, *Mexicans at Arms* (1996); John H. Schroeder, *Mr. Polk's War* (1973); Scott Silverstone, *Divided Union* (2005); David J. Weber, *The Mexican Frontier, 1821–1846* (1982); Joseph Richard Werne, *The Imaginary Line* (2007); and Richard Bruce Winders, *Mr. Polk's Army* (1997) and *Crisis in the Southwest* (2002).

For encounters with Asia—especially China—see Warren I. Cohen, *America's Response to China* (2000); Jacques M. Downs, *The Golden Ghetto* (1997) (U.S.–China); Jonathan Goldstein, *Philadelphia and the China Trade, 1682–1846* (1978); Jonathan Goldstein et al., eds., *America Views China* (1991); Edward V. Gulick, *Peter Parker and the Opening of China* (1973); John Rogers Haddad, *The Romance of China* (2008); Curtis Henson, Jr., *Commissioners and Commodores* (1982); Michael Hunt, *The Making of a Special Relationship* (1983); Thomas N. Layton, *The Voyage of the "Frolic"* (1997); Gary Okihiro, *Island World* (2008) (Hawai'i); John C. Perry, *Facing West* (1994); and James Thomson et al., *Sentimental Imperialists* (1981).

See also the General Bibliography, the following notes, and Robert L. Beisner, ed., *Guide to American Foreign Relations Since 1600* (2003).

NOTES TO CHAPTER 3

1. Quoted in K. Jack Bauer, *Zachary Taylor* (Baton Rouge: Louisiana State University Press, 1985), p. 145.
2. Ethan Hitchcock quoted in Josefina Zoraida Vazquez, "Causes of the War with the United States," in Richard V. Francaviglia and Douglas W. Richmond, eds., *Dueling Eagles* (Ft. Worth: Texas Christian University Press, 2000), p. 58.
3. Quoted in Robert H. Ferrell, ed., *Monterrey Is Ours!* (Lexington: University Press of Kentucky, 1990), p. 48.
4. Quoted in David M. Pletcher, *The Diplomacy of Annexation* (Columbia: University of Missouri Press, 1973), p. 377.
5. Milo M. Quaife, ed., *The Diary of James K. Polk, 1845–1849* (Chicago: McClurg, 1919; 4 vols.), I, 384.
6. James D. Richardson, ed., *A Compilation of the Messages and Papers of the Presidents, 1789–1897* (Washington, D.C.: Government Printing Office, 1897–1900; 9 vols.), *IV*, 442.
7. John Niven, *John C. Calhoun and the Price of Union* (Baton Rouge: Louisiana State University Press, 1988), p. 304.
8. Robert B. Rhett, quoted in Willam C. Davis, *Rhett* (Columbia: University of South Carolina Press, 2001), p. 230.
9. Quoted in James E. Lewis, Jr., *John Quincy Adams* (Wilmington, Del.: Scholarly Resources, 2001), pp. 135–136.
10. Quoted in John Byrne Cooke, *Reporting the War* (New York: Palgrave, 2007), p. 27.
11. William Earl Weeks, *John Quincy Adams and American Global Empire* (Lexington: University Press of Kentucky, 1992), p. 196.
12. Quoted in Arthur M. Schlesinger, Jr., *War and the American Presidency* (New York: W. W. Norton, 2004), p. 43.
13. Piero Gliejeses, "A Brush with Mexico," *Diplomatic History*, XXIX (April 2005), 254.

14. Quoted in Charles F. Adams, ed., *Memoirs of John Quincy Adams* (Philadelphia: Lippincott, 1874–1877; 12 vols.), *II*, 261.

15. Jacob E. Cooke, ed., *The Federalist* (Middletown, Conn.: Wesleyan University Press, 1984), p. 64.

16. Quoted in John M. Belohlavek, *"Let the Eagle Soar!"* (Lincoln: University of Nebraska Press, 1985), p. 115.

17. Missionary quoted in Michael B. Oren, *Power, Faith, and Fantasy* (New York: Norton, 2007), p. 115.

18. Quoted in Frederick Merk, *Albert Gallatin and the Oregon Problem* (Cambridge: Harvard University Press, 1950), p. 13.

19. John Seelye, *Beautiful Machine* (New York: Oxford University Press, 1991), p. 224.

20. Evan Cornog, *The Birth of Empire* (New York: Oxford University Press, 1998), p. 156; Ralph Waldo Emerson quoted in Robert W. Johannsen, "Young America and the War with Mexico," in Francaviglia and Richmond, *Dueling Eagles*, p. 157.

21. Walter La Feber, "Technology and U.S. Foreign Relations," *Diplomatic History, XXIV* (Winter 2000), 5.

22. *Democratic Review, XVII* (July–August 1845), 9.

23. Quoted in Michael Adas, *Dominance by Design* (Cambridge: Harvard University Press, 2006), p. 72.

24. O'Sullivan quoted in Edward L. Widmer, *Young America* (New York: Oxford University Press, 1999), p. 22.

25. Quoted in Linda S. Hudson, *Mistress of Manifest Destiny* (Austin: Texas State Historical Association, 2001), p. 61.

26. Anders Stephanson, *Manifest Destiny* (New York: Hill & Wang, 1995), p. 30.

27. Quoted in Marie-Jeanne Rossignol, *The Nationalist Ferment* (Columbus: Ohio State University Press, 2004), p. 161.

28. *Congressional Globe*, January 10, 1846, p. 180.

29. Beaufort Watts quoted in Lars Schoultz, *Beneath the United States* (Cambridge: Harvard University Press, 1998), p. 13.

30. Robert F. Berkhofer, Jr., *Salvation and the Savage* (New York: Knopf, 1976), p. 14.

31. Noah Smithwick, quoted in David J. Weber, " 'Scarce More Than Apes,'" in Michael Krenn, ed., *Race and U.S. Foreign Policy from the Colonial Period to the Present* (New York: Garland, 1998), p. 304.

32. Thomas R. Hietala, *Manifest Design* (Ithaca: Cornell University Press, 1985), p. 172.

33. Quoted in James P. Ronda, "Race, Geography, and the Invention of Indian Territory," *Journal of the Early Republic, XIX* (Winter 1999), 745.

34. J. P. Mayer and Max Lerner, eds., Alexis de Tocqueville, *Democracy in America* (New York: Harper and Row, 1966), pp. 298–299.

35. John Ross quoted in Ronda, "Race," p. 751.

36. Quoted in Willard Carl Lunder, *Lewis Cass and the Politics of Moderation* (Kent, Ohio: Kent State University Press, 1996), p. 51.

37. James O. Gump, "A Spirit of Resistance," *Pacific Historical Review, LXVI* (February 1997), 25.

38. Quoted in Norman A. Graebner, ed., *Manifest Destiny* (Indianapolis: Bobbs-Merrill, 1968), p. xxxvii.

39. *Congressional Globe*, January 4, 1843, p. 139.

40. Michael A. Morrison, *Slavery and the American West* (Chapel Hill: University of North Carolina Press, 1997), p. 73.

41. *Communist Manifesto* quoted in Joseph S. Nye, Jr., *The Paradox of American Power* (New York: Oxford University Press, 2002), p. 78.

42. Quoted in William H. Goetzmann, *When the Eagle Screamed* (New York: Wiley, 1966), pp. xvii, 43.

43. Yen P'ing Hao quoted in Kristin Hoganson, "Stuff it: Domestic Consumption and the Americanization of the World," *Diplomatic History, XXX* (September 2006), 591.

44. Quoted in Macabe Keliher, "Anglo-American Rivalry and the Origins of U.S. China Policy," *Diplomatic History, XXXI* (April 2007), 247.

45. Cushing quoted *ibid.*, 251.

46. Quoted in Michael A. Morrison, "Partisan Politics of Texas Annexation," *Journal of Southern History, LXI* (November 1995), 608.

47. Quoted in George C. Herring, *From Colony to Superpower* (New York: Oxford University Press, 2008), p. 212; Jacques M. Downs, *The Golden Ghetto* (Bethlehem, Penn.: Lehigh University Press, 1997), p. 320.

48. Quoted in Michael H. Hunt, *The Making of a Special Relationship* (New York: Columbia University Press, 1983), p. 36.

49. William Reynolds quoted in Thomas Schoonover, *Uncle Sam's War of 1898 and the Origins of Globalism* (Lexington: University Press of Kentucky, 2003), p. 15.

50. Geoffrey S. Smith, "Charles Wilkes and the Growth of American Naval Diplomacy," in Frank J. Merli and Theodore A. Wilson, eds., *Makers of American Diplomacy* (New York: Charles Scribner's Sons, 1974), p. 143.

51. Quoted in Norman A. Graebner, *Empire on the Pacific* (New York: Ronald Press, 1955), p. 79.

52. Quoted in Walter A. McDougall, *Let the Sea Make a Noise* (New York: Basic Books, 1993), p. 198.

53. Richard P. Tucker, *Insatiable Appetite* (Berkeley: University of California Press, 2000), p. 74; missionaries quoted in Jennifer Fish Kashay, "Agents of Imperialism: Missionaries and Merchants in Early-Nineteenth-Century Hawaii," *New England Quarterly, LXXX* (June 2007), 295.

54. Quoted in Kenneth E. Shewmaker, "Forging the 'Great Chain,' " *Proceedings of the American Philosophical Society, CXXIX* (September 1985), 232.

55. Quoted in James M. Lindgren, "'That Every Mariner May Possess the History of the World,'" *New England Quarterly, LXVIII* (June 1995), 196.

56. W. King quoted in Yonatan Eyal, *The Young America Movement and the Transformation of the Democratic Party, 1828–1861* (New York: Cambridge University Press, 2007), p. 125.

57. Madison quoted in James C. Cusick, *The Other War of 1812* (Gainesville: University Press of Florida, 2003), p. 20.

58. Gregory Evans Dowd, *A Spirited Resistance* (Baltimore: Johns Hopkins University Press, 1992), p. 188.

59. Quoted in Lewis, *John Quincy Adams*, p. 60.

60. John S. Bassett, ed., *Correspondence of Andrew Jackson* (Washington, D.C.: Carnegie Institution, 1926–1935; 6 vols.), *II*, 346.

61. Quoted in Paul E. Hoffman, *Florida's Frontiers* (Bloomington: Indiana University Press, 2002), p. 277.

62. Quoted in Marquis James, *The Life of Andrew Jackson* (Indianapolis: Bobbs-Merrill, 1938) p. 288.

63. Quoted in Sean Wilentz, *Andrew Jackson* (New York: Times Books, 2005), p. 38.

64. Quoted in James E. Lewis, *American Union and the Problem of Neighborhood* (Chapel Hill: University of North Carolina Press, 1998), p. 113.

65. Quoted in Andrew L. Burstein, *The Passions of Andrew Jackson* (New York: Knopf, 2003), p. 132.

66. Adams quoted in Lewis, *John Quincy Adams*, p. 57.

67. Quoted in Samuel Flagg Bemis, *John Quincy Adams and the Foundations of American Foreign Policy* (New York: Knopf, 1949), p. 327.

68. Quoted in Daniel Walker Howe, *What Hath God Wrought* (New York: Oxford University Press, 2007), p. 109.

69. Quoted in Lester D. Langley, *The Americas in the Age of Revolution, 1750–1850* (New Haven: Yale University Press, 1996), p. 226.

70. James Cobb quoted in Alexander DeConde, *Presidential Machismo* (Boston: Northeastern University Press, 2000), p. 35

71. Quoted in Robert V. Remini, *Henry Clay* (New York: Norton, 1991), p. 165.

72. Richard Van Alstyne, *The Rising American Empire* (Chicago: Quadrangle, 1965), p. 99.

73. Quoted in Lewis, *American Union*, pp. 158–59.

74. Adams, *Memoirs of John Quincy Adams, V*, 325.

75. Quoted in William H. Seward, *Life and Public Services of John Quincy Adams* (Auburn, N.Y.: Derby, Miller, 1849), p. 132.

76. Quoted in Lewis, *American Union*, p. 175.

77. Quoted in Charles K. Webster, *The Foreign Policy of Castlereagh* (London: G. Bell and Sons, 1963), p. 295.

78. Quoted in Lawrence S. Kaplan, "The Monroe Doctrine and the Truman Doctrine," *Journal of the Early Republic, XIII* (Spring 1993), 13.

79. Monroe quoted in Lewis, *American Union*, p. 173.

80. Paul Kennedy, *The Rise and Fall of the Great Powers* (New York: Random House, 1987), p. 158.

81. Quoted in Harold Temperley, *The Foreign Policy of Canning* (London: G. Bell and Sons, 1925), pp. 380–381.

82. Quoted in Dangerfield, *Awakening*, p. 177.

83. Paul L. Ford, ed., *The Works of Thomas Jefferson* (New York: G. P. Putnam's Sons, 1904–1905; 12 vols.), XII, 319.

84. *Letters and Other Writings of James Madison* (Philadelphia: Lippincott, 1865; 4 vols.), III, 339.

85. Quoted in Mark T. Gilderhus, "The Monroe Doctrine," *Presidential Studies Quarterly, XXXVI* (March 2006), 7.

86. Quoted in Wendy Hindle, *George Canning* (New York: St. Martin's Press, 1974), p. 351.

87. Quoted in Lewis, *American Union*, p. 179.

88. Adams, *Memoirs of John Quincy Adams, VI*, 186.

89. *Ibid., VI*, 198.

90. Quoted in Andrew Preston, "The Congressional Debate over U.S. Participation in the Congress of Panama, 1825–1826," *Diplomatic History, XXX* (November 2006), 817.

91. Ford, *Writings of John Quincy Adams, VI*, 371–372.

92. Quoted in Gary Hart, *James Monroe* (New York: Times Books, 2005), p. 102.

93. Quoted in Hindle, *Canning*, p. 355.

94. Quoted in Piero Gleijeses, "The Limits of Sympathy," *Journal of Latin American Studies, XXIV* (October 1992), 489.

95. Quoted in Noble E. Cunningham, Jr., *The Presidency of James Monroe* (Lawrence: University Press of Kansas, 1996), p. 161.

96. Quoted in Daniel Feller, *The Jacksonian Promise* (Baltimore: Johns Hopkins University Press, 1995), p. 9.

97. John J. Johnson, *A Hemisphere Apart* (Baltimore: Johns Hopkins University Press, 1990), p. 86.

98. Henry Clay quoted in Lewis, *American Union*, p. 71.

99. Robert Walker quoted in Eyal, *Young America*, p. 144.

100. Eliga H. Gould, "The Making of an Atlantic State System," in Julie Flavell and Jack Conway, eds., *Britain and America Go to War* (Gainesville: University Press of Florida, 2004), p. 259.

101. Quoted in Kinley J. Brauer, "1820–1860," in William H. Becker and Samuel F. Wells, Jr., eds., *Economics and World Power* (New York: Columbia University Press, 1984), p. 68.

102. Gould, "Atlantic State System," p. 242.

103. Quoted in Robert P. Remini, *John Quincy Adams* (New York: Times Books, 2002), p. 58.

104. Quoted in Bemis, *John Quincy Adams*, p. 291.

105. Quoted in Bradford Perkins, *Castlereagh and Adams* (Berkeley: University of California Press, 1964), p. 346.

106. Quoted in Scott Kaufman and John A. Soares, Jr., "'Sagacious Beyond Praise?" *Diplomatic History, XXX* (January 2006), 63.

107. Quoted in David Demeritt, "Representing the 'True' St. Croix," *William and Mary Quarterly, LIV* (July 1997), 515.

108. Quoted in Howard Jones, "Anglophobia and the Aroostook War," *New England Quarterly, XLVII* (December 1975), 527.

109. Quoted in John F. Sprague, *The Northeastern Boundary Controversy and the Aroostook War* (Dover, Maine: Observer Press, 1910), pp. 110–111.

110. Scott quoted in Kaufman and Soares, "Sagacious," p. 69.

111. Quoted in Charles Campbell, *From Revolution to Rapprochement* (New York: Wiley, 1974), pp. 56–57.

112. Webster quoted in Robert Remini, *Daniel Webster* (New York: Norton, 1997), p. 542.

113. Lewis Cass quoted in Howard A. Jones and Donald A. Rakestraw, *Prologue to Manifest Destiny* (Wilmington, Del.: Scholarly Resources, 1997), p. 70.

114. Jessica C. E. Gienow-Hecht, "Always Blame the Americans," *American Historical Review, CXI* (October 2006), 1073.

115. Quoted in Jones and Rakestraw, *Prologue*, pp. 104, 107.

116. Quoted in Francis A. Carroll, *A Good and Wise Measure* (Toronto: University of Toronto Press, 2001), p. 305.

117. Quoted in McDougall, *Let the Sea*, p. 224.

118. George McDuffie quoted in Scott A. Silverstone, *Divided Union* (Ithaca: Cornell University Press, 2004), p. 127.

119. Quoted in Campbell, *From Revolution*, p. 66.

120. Richardson, *Messages of the Presidents, IV*, 398.

121. Quoted in Michael Lind, *The American Way of Strategy* (New York: Oxford University Press, 2006), p. 70.

122. Quoted in Campbell, *From Revolution*, p. 70.

123. Charles S. Maier, *Among Empires* (Cambridge: Harvard University Press, 2006), p. 29.

124. Henry Ward quoted in Stuart Reid, *The Secret War for Texas* (College Station: Texas A & M University Press, 2007), p. 17.

125. Quoted in David J. Weber, *The Mexican Frontier, 1821–1846* (Albuquerque: University of New Mexico Press, 1982), p. 178.

126. Andrés Reséndez, *Changing National Identities at the Frontier* (New York: Cambridge University Press, 2005), p. 6.

127. Quoted in Andrew R. L. Cayton, "Continental Politics," in Jeffrey L. Pasley et al., eds., *Beyond the Founders* (Chapel Hill: University of North Carolina Press, 2004), p. 323.

128. Quoted in Richard Bruce Winders, *Crisis in the Southwest* (Wilmington, Del.: Scholarly Resources, 2002), p. 62.

129. Quoted in Amy Kaplan, *The Anarchy of Empire in the Making of U.S. Culture* (Cambridge: Harvard University Press, 2002), p. 27.

130. Benjamin Lundy quoted in Sean Wilentz, *Andrew Jackson*, p. 147.

131. Quoted in Major L. Wilson, *The Presidency of Martin Van Buren* (Lawrence: University Press of Kansas, 1984), p. 151.

132. Palmerston quoted in Leila M. Roeckell, "British Opposition to the Annexation of Texas," *Journal of the Early Republic, XIX* (Summer 1999), 257.

133. Quoted *ibid.*, p. 277.

134. Abel Upshur quoted in Donald Kagan, *Dangerous Nation* (New York: Knopf, 2006), p. 221.

135. Quoted in Sean Wilentz, *The Rise of American Democracy* (New York: Norton, 2005), p. 567; quoted in Michael F. Holt, *Political Parties and American Political Development* (Baton Rouge: Louisiana State University Press, 1992), p. 62.

136. Quoted in David P. Currie, "Texas," in Sanford Levinson and Bartholomew H. Sparrow, eds., *The Louisiana Purchase and American Expansion, 1803–1898* (New York: Rowman & Littlefield, 2005), p. 115.

137. Quoted in Greg Russell, *John Quincy Adams* (Columbia: University of Missouri Press, 1995), p. 63.

138. Quoted in Silbey, *Van Buren*, p. 173.

139. Quoted in Harlan Hague and David J. Langum, *Thomas O. Larkin* (Norman: University of Oklahoma Press, 1990), p. 114.

140. Quoted in Sam W. Haynes, "Great Britain, the United States, and the War with Mexico," in Francaviglia and Richmond, *Dueling Eagles*, p. 34.

141. Quoted in Gene Brack, "Mexican Opinion, American Racism, and the War of 1846," in Krenn, *Race and U.S. Foreign Policy*, pp. 171, 174.

142. Quoted in Dean Mahin, *Olive Branch and Sword* (McFarland, Jefferson, N.C.: 1997), p. 61.

143. Polk quoted in William A. DePalo, Jr., *The Mexican National Army, 1822–1852* (College Station: Texas A & M University Press, 1997), p. 103.

144. Anna Kasten Nelson, "Mission to Mexico," *New York State Historical Quarterly, LIX* (July 1975), 230.

145. Trist quoted in Wallace Ohrt, *Defiant Peacemaker* (College Station: Texas A&M University Press, 1997), p. 113.

146. Scott quoted in Timothy D. Johnson, *A Gallant Little Army* (Lawrence: University Press of Kansas, 2007), p. 143.

147. Quoted in John Eisenhower, *Agent of Destiny* (New York: Free Press, 1997), p. 267.

148. Polk quoted in Silverstone, *Divided Union*, p. 182; *Democratic Review* and Houston quoted in Nancy Isenberg, *Sex and Citizenship in Antebellum America* (Chapel Hill: University of North Carolina Press, 1998), p. 140.

149. Frederick Merk, *Manifest Destiny and Mission* (New York: Vintage, 1963), p. 181.

150. Quoted in Joseph Richard Werne, *The Imaginary Line* (Fort Worth: Texas Christian University Press, 2007), p. 12.

151. Kenneth J. Hagan and Ian J. Bickerton, *Unintended Consequences* (London: Reaktion Press, 2007), p. 61.

152. Quoted in Josefina Zaraida Vasquez, "The Significance in Mexican History of the Treaty of Guadalupe Hidalgo," in John Porter Bloom, ed., *The Treaty of Guadalupe Hidalgo* (Las Cruces, New Mexico: Yucca Tree Press, 1999), p. 91.

153. Quaife, *Diary of James K. Polk, III*, p. 201.

154. Quoted in Johnson, *Gallant Little Army*, p. 267.

155. Quaife, *Diary of James K. Polk, III*, pp. 346–351.

156. Daniel Berringer quoted in Morrison, *Slavery*, p. 83.

157. David Outlaw quoted in Holt, *Rise and Fall*, p. 311.

158. Quoted in Wilentz, *Rise of American Democracy*, 605.

159. Daniel Bernard quoted in Morrison, *Slavery*, p. 71.

160. Quoted in Kagan, *Dangerous Nation*, p. 229.

161. Samuel Sample quoted in Don E. Fehrenbacher, *The Slaveholding Republic* (New York: Oxford University Press, 2001), p. 91.

162. Quoted in D. W. Menig, *The Shaping of America*, vol. 2 (New Haven: Yale University Press, 1993), p. 159.

163. Quoted in Reginald Horsman, "Scientific Racism and the American Indian in the Mid-Nineteenth Century," *American Quarterly, XXVII* (May 1975), 168.

164. Quoted in Schoultz, *Beneath the United States*, p. 30.

165. Quoted in Albert K. Weinberg, *Manifest Destiny* (Baltimore: Johns Hopkins University Press, 1935), p. 119.

166. Quoted in Joseph A. Fry, "Late Nineteenth Century U.S. Foreign Relations," in Charles W. Calhoun, ed., *The Gilded Age* (New York: Rowman & Littlefield, 2007), p. 313.

167. Quoted in William B. Skelton, *An American Profession of Arms* (Lawrence: University Press of Kansas, 1992), p. 321.

168. Nathan J. Citino, "The Global Frontier," *Diplomatic History, XXV* (Fall 2001), 681.

169. Mariano Otero quoted in Pedro Santoni, *Mexicans at Arms* (Fort Worth: Texas Christian University Press, 1996), p. 232.

170. Robert A. Pastor and Jorge G. Castañeda, *Limits to Friendship* (New York: Knopf, 1988), p. 35.

171. Quoted in Blanche Wiesen Cook, "American Justification for Military Massacres from the Pequot War to Mylai," *Peace and Change, III* (Summer–Fall 1975), 9.

172. Weber, *Mexican Frontier*, p. 278.

173. Quoted in W. Dirk Raat, *Mexico and the United States* (Athens: University of Georgia Press, 1992), p. 74; Gary Clayton Anderson, *The Conquest of Texas* (Norman: University of Oklahoma Press, 2005), p. 11.

174. James McPherson, *The Battle Cry of Freedom* (New York: Ballantine Books, 1989), p. 6.

175. Quoted in Silverstone, *Divided Union*, p. 147.

176. Mary Ann Heiss, "The Evolution of the Imperial Idea and U.S. National Identity," *Diplomatic History, XVII* (Fall 2002), 520.

177. Quoted in Eric Love, "White is the Color of Empire," in James T. Campbell et al., eds., *Race, Nation, and Empire in American History* (Chapel Hill: University of North Carolina Press, 2007), p. 77.

178. Quoted in Howe, *What God Hath Wrought*, p. 721.

179. Quoted in Robert W. Johannsen, *To the Halls of Montezuma* (New York: Oxford University Press, 1985), p. 309.

180. Quoted in Pletcher, *Diplomacy of Annexation*, p. 103.

181. Quoted in Paul Kens, "A Promise of Expansion," in Levinson and Sparrow, eds., *Louisiana Purchase*, p. 141.

CHAPTER 4

Expansionism, Sectionalism, and Civil War, 1848–1865

"William Walker (1824–1860)." The most infamous of American filibusters terrorized Latin American nations, ruled Nicaragua for a short time, and flouted U.S. law—all by the age of thirty-six. He fell before a firing squad and remains buried in an unmarked grave in Honduras. The journalist Horace Greeley called him the "Don Quixote of Central America." (Matthew Brady daguerreotype, Library of Congress)

❖ *William Walker and Manifest Manhood in Central America, 1855–1860*

"THERE ARE BUT a few men now living who occupy so much of the public mind as Gen. William Walker," a Kentucky newspaper proclaimed in 1858. "[He] is, indeed, the hero of the time."[1] In the decade before the Civil War, this unprepossessing adventurer from Tennessee, "standing barely five feet four in his boots" and weighing only 115 pounds, gained notoriety as the most successful of American filibusters (a derivative of the Dutch *vrijbuiter,* meaning "pirate" or "freebooter"), those soldiers of fortune who attempted to grab territories through unauthorized and illegal attacks on sovereign nations.[2] Walker won renown as the "grey-eyed man of destiny" because he allegedly fulfilled the prophesy that a "grey-eyed" man of the Anglo-Saxon race would rescue the indigenous peoples of Nicaragua from Spanish oppression.[3]

An exemplar of what the historian Amy S. Greenberg has called "martial manhood," this self-styled "regenerator of Central America" earned a physician's degree from the University of Pennsylvania, studied medicine in Paris, practiced law in Louisiana, and edited a New Orleans newspaper before embarking on imperial schemes in Mexico and Nicaragua.[4] Lured to California in 1850 by the gold rush, Walker hatched plans for an invasion of Baja California. Barely thirty years old in 1853, he marched forty-five companions into Mexican lands, captured the capital of La Paz, and declared himself president of a new republic. In little time, however, the invasion collapsed from faulty organization and discontent among Walker's followers. Arrested for violating U.S. neutrality laws, Walker won acquittal from an admiring San Francisco jury. (Another filibuster into Sonora in 1857 ended when the local authorities executed its leader Harry Cobb and preserved his head in a jar of alcohol.)

Walker next eyed Nicaragua, a country often mentioned as a route for an Isthmian canal. Hardly the agent of benevolent democratic Manifest Destiny that his admirers attempted to portray, he became a "freckle-faced despot" who sought to subjugate Nicaragua in 1855, 1857, 1858, and 1860.[5] In contrast to travel writers who extolled Nicaragua's fertile lands and scantily clad "señoritas" with "big lustrous eyes," Walker plundered and killed.[6] In the first expedition, leading fifty-seven men (the "American Phalanx") whom he described as "tired of the humdrum of common life," Walker joined one side in a civil war, won promotion to commander in chief, and seized the presidency for himself.[7] Some local elites at first supported the filibuster as a leader who would establish "liberty and order" and help Nicaragua "develop its resources by industry."[8] Apparently influenced by a visit from Louisiana's proslavery politician Pierre Soulé, Walker decreed the legal reestablishment of slavery. The U.S. minister in Nicaragua, North Carolina slaveholder John Hill Wheeler, abetted Walker because he believed that the "rich soil so well adapted to the culture of cotton, sugar, rice, corn, cocoa, indigo, etc., can never be developed without

The Filibuster Polka.   This sheet music from 1852 is one example of how filibustering became part of popular culture in the decade before the Civil War. (Courtesy of the Music Division, Library of Congress)

slave labor."[9] Walker dreamed beyond Nicaragua: He wanted to build a Central American federation and then construct an interoceanic canal that would turn Nicaragua into a "grand emporium."[10] Wheeler urged diplomatic recognition from Washington, hailing Walker as the vanguard of a superior white race that would "purify and elevate" the supposedly degenerate Nicaraguans, who would become "Americanized by the industrious and interprizing from the North."[11] Reluctant at first to approve "a violent occupation of power, brought about by an irregular self-organized military force, as yet unsanctioned by … the people of Nicaragua," President Franklin Pierce officially recognized Walker's regime in 1856.[12]

But Walker soon wobbled. He alienated Nicaraguans through pillaging and dictatorial orders, and his soldiers fell victim to frequent drunkenness and disease. When he brutally sacked the city of Granada in November 1856, he discouraged such potential recruits as future Confederate general P. G. T. Beauregard, who recoiled at such "ferocity, & Vandalism, unworthy of the American character."[13] Walker then antagonized the railroad magnate Cornelius Vanderbilt, whose Accessory Transit Company carried 2,000 Americans per month across the waist of Nicaragua and then, by steamship, to California. The powerful Vanderbilt "declared war by proxy" in backing Honduras, Guatemala, El Salvador, and Costa Rica when they took up arms against the intruding adventurer.[14] As the tide turned, proslavery sympathizers such as Jefferson Davis blamed "black republicanism" of "the North" for the flow of arms and gold to Walker's opponents.[15] In May 1857 the filibuster

William Walker: Matinee Idol. Playbill for theatrical production in New York City celebrating William Walker's conquests in Nicaragua. (Courtesy of the Tennessee Historical Society, War Memorial Building, Nashville)

fled to the United States, claiming that he had been betrayed "for the paltry profits of a railroad company."[16]

Walker returned to Nicaragua in November 1857, but marines from the U.S.S. *Wabash* forced his surrender. The "lion-hearted devil," when captured, "wept like a child" and eventually escaped prosecution.[17] Walker's third effort, in 1858, ended ingloriously near British Honduras, where his ship ran aground on a coral reef. A British naval vessel captured the filibusters and returned them to the United States. Still claiming to be president of Nicaragua, the irrepressible Walker headed for his adopted country once again in spring 1860. This time he invaded Honduras first. Honduran troops inflicted heavy casualties, and Walker soon surrendered. "Will the South stand by and permit him to be shot down like a dog?" exhorted one southern woman. "If so, let her renounce her reputation for chivalry, valor, policy, or pride!"[18] Such appeals went unheeded, and Walker died before a Honduran firing squad on September 12, 1860.

During his heyday Walker became "an iconic figure of male determination, a private warrior whose quest redeemed all American males," as evidenced by the hit musical, *Nicaragua, or General Walker's Victories* at New York's Pardy's National Theater in 1856.[19] Newspapers across the country reported his exploits. He became the subject of poems, novels, and songs. More than a century later, in the Hollywood film *Walker* (1988), actor Ed Harris's performance in the title role reminded viewers of Lieutenant Colonel Oliver North, a Reagan-era American who also meddled in Nicaragua. In the end Walker symbolized for many the survival of slavery and the southern way of life. In his quest for glory and adventure, Walker mastered the rhetoric of southern expansion, especially in his presidential decree reinstituting slavery in Nicaragua in 1856, which he called an act of "benevolence and philanthropy" for "inferior" blacks, "half-castes," and Indians.[20] Southern "fire-eaters" took heart, thinking it easier to implant slavery in the tropics than in contested Kansas. Hindered by northern opponents from making territorial gains through diplomacy or war, the ardent defenders of the "peculiar institution" turned to the illegal machinations of the filibusters. They would opt for secession and civil war in 1861. As for Walker's victims, "the violent impulse of U.S. filibusterism has remained etched in Nicaraguans' consciousness," along with their "bitter memories ... refreshed by future U.S. interventions."[21]

Sectionalism and Sputtering Expansionism

As Walker's fate indicated, the momentum of American expansionism had slackened in the aftermath of the War with Mexico, and Manifest Destiny became markedly less manifest in the 1850s. Tough talk about annexing Canada subsided. Even in Latin America, an area of prime focus, expansionist schemes fizzled. Attempts to grab Cuba collapsed, and cries for acquiring more Mexican territory became muffled. Notions of planting an American colony in slaveholding Brazil enjoyed some currency after an exploration inspired by Lieutenant Matthew F. Maury, but nothing came of the scheme. Washington did persuade Mexico to negotiate the Gadsden Purchase of 1853, which added 29,640 square miles to the United States at a cost of $10 million for a potential railroad route to the Pacific—the only land acquired in the period from 1848 to the end of the Civil War. Expansionists nonetheless clamored for more. "Let England pursue her march of conquest and annex India ... or Russia subjugate her barbarous neighbors in Asia," argued Senator John Slidell of Louisiana. "We claim in this hemisphere the same privilege that they exercise in the other."[22] New York's William H. Seward wanted American borders "to greet the sun when he touches the tropics, and when he sends his gleaming rays toward the polar circle, and [they] shall include even distant islands in either ocean."[23]

Yet such ambition faltered because of the heated sectional debates over chattel slavery that drew the nation into the Civil War. Northern appetites soured for ventures into Latin America, where black servitude might flourish and newly arisen slave states might vote with the South. After defeating such restrictions as the

Wilmot Proviso, many southerners continued the cry for empire, hoping to enhance their declining political status and defend slavery, the cornerstone of their way of life. In 1856 Secretary of War Jefferson Davis even imported seventy-nine camels from Middle East countries in a futile attempt to domesticate the deserts of the Southwest. In contrast, northerners such as the Illinois attorney Abraham Lincoln claimed that slavery "deprives our republican example of its just influence in the world—enables the enemies of free institutions to taunt us as hypocrites."[24] Divided at home by insistent northern abolitionists and southern "fire-eaters," the United States lacked a consensus to undertake further bold ventures in international affairs. Intensely preoccupied by domestic disputes over slavery, Americans gave only sporadic attention to foreign-policy questions.

Some leaders tried to harmonize sectional discord by trumpeting the nationalistic "Young America" movement. They hailed the revolutions of 1848 in Europe as evidence of New World, republican influence on the Old, and applauded Camillo Bensi di Cavour, Giuseppe Mazzini, and Giuseppe Garibaldi, all of Italy, and Lajos Kossuth of Hungary, whose short-lived rebellions against entrenched monarchies kindled American sympathies. Orators proclaimed the "young Giant of the West," standing in the "full flush of exulting manhood," whose "onward progress" the "worn-out Powers of the Old World may not hope either to restrain or impede."[25] The novelist Herman Melville even boasted in 1850: "The political Messiah ... has come in us."[26]

In 1850 the Whig Secretary of State Daniel Webster lectured the Hapsburg government, claiming that, compared to the mighty United States, Austria was "but a patch on the earth's surface."[27] Webster wanted his rebuke to those who crushed the Hungarian revolution to "touch the national pride, and make a man feel *sheepish* and look *silly* who would speak of disunion."[28] When Lajos Kossuth, the leader of the failed Hungarian Revolution, excited the United States in 1851–1852 during a rousing visit, Webster once again stirred nationalist sentiment by publicly rejoicing "to see our American model upon the lower Danube."[29] Nonetheless, the secretary privately vowed to "have ears more deaf than adders" if Kossuth asked for U.S. intervention on behalf of Hungary.[30] In the 1852 Democratic party platform, the rallying cry was "Young America." The following year, "Young America" advocate and Democratic Secretary of State William Marcy ordered a new dress code for U.S. diplomats—the "simple dress of an American citizen" to reflect "republican institutions."[31]

"Young America" tried, in effect, to pour "the old wine of Jefferson and Jackson—a broad, nationally based republicanism of slavery and territorial aggrandizement—into new bottles."[32] Claiming that "the more degrees of latitude and longitude embraced beneath our Constitution, the better," enthusiasts such as Democratic Senator Stephen A. Douglas urged Young Americans to "come together upon the basis of *entire silence on the slavery question*."[33] Yet the hope that expansion would subsume sectional differences over slavery proved illusory. Popular sovereignty, wherein settlers themselves voted whether territories should be free or slave, as in the Kansas–Nebraska Act of 1854, seemed a contradiction in terms—in Abraham Lincoln's view, a "deceitful pretense for the benefit of slavery."[34] In the opinion of many opponents, "Young America" expansionists were hypocrites who claimed to champion liberty abroad but permitted slavery "like a slimy reptile ... to defile a second Eden."[35]

James Buchanan (1791–1868). Member of Congress, senator, minister to Russia and England, secretary of state, and fifteenth president of the United States, the Pennsylvania-born Buchanan brought diplomatic experience and expansionist zeal to the White House. Called a "dough-face" because of his desire to appease southern slaveholders, Buchanan preferred expansion into what he called the "vacant lands" of Oregon, California, northern Mexico, and Alaska; he also sought to acquire more populous regions of mixed races in the belief that American settlers would bring the blessings of democracy and economic growth to the inhabitants. He tried to purchase Cuba to prevent its "Africanization" because he feared that the South could not survive with another black-ruled Haiti so near. Although he disdained Mexicans as an "inferior, indolent, mongrel" race, Buchanan sought unsuccessfully to buy Baja California and territories north of the Sierra Madre that would have brought a substantial Mexican population into the Union as free citizens. Buchanan's failed presidency helped bring on the Civil War. (Library of Congress)

Makers of American Foreign Relations, 1848–1865

Presidents	Secretaries of State
James K. Polk, 1845–1849	James Buchanan, 1845–1849
Zachary Taylor, 1849–1850	John M. Clayton, 1849–1850
Millard Fillmore, 1850–1853	Daniel Webster, 1850–1852
	Edward Everett, 1852–1853
Franklin Pierce, 1853–1857	William L. Marcy, 1853–1857
James Buchanan, 1857–1861	Lewis Cass, 1857–1860
	Jeremiah S. Black, 1860–1861
Abraham Lincoln, 1861–1865	William H. Seward, 1861–1869
Andrew Johnson, 1865–1869	

Most scholars rate American political leaders between the war with Mexico and the Civil War as mediocre. The presidents and secretaries of state conducted a blustering foreign policy, often playing to domestic political currents through bombastic rhetoric. Although both James Buchanan and Lewis Cass had extensive service as diplomats in Europe, neither had acquired much finesse. An opponent mocked Stephen Douglas for thinking "he can bestride the continent with one foot on the shore of the Atlantic, the other on the Pacific. But he can't do it—he can't do it. His legs are too short."[36] Inept leaders muddled relations, crudely grasped at an elusive Cuba, permitted filibusters to alienate Latin America, squabbled clumsily with Britain in Central America, meddled with emotion but without power in European revolutions, followed the British in humiliating the Chinese, and gave only sporadic attention to Japan after "opening" it. President Lincoln and his imperial-minded secretary of state, William H. Seward, certainly raised the level of competence in Washington, managing to win the Civil War, contain it as a "localized" conflict, and avoid the world war it might have become. In so doing they preserved American power, which permitted the United States to resume its expansionist trajectory after the fratricidal conflict.

The South's Dream of Empire

Many southern leaders tried to exploit Manifest Destiny for territorial conquest in the Caribbean. They failed largely because they provoked domestic opposition by insisting that slavery be permitted in new lands. In the 1850s most northern expansionists parted company with southern sectionalists and steadfastly opposed ventures into Latin America that might add slave territories to the Union. At the same time, some northern expansionists, such as Seward—then senator from New York—hoped that the abolition of slavery would eliminate northern opposition to expansion into the Caribbean and Mexico. Paradoxically, southern expansionists sought a larger empire for the United States while they denigrated the supremacy of the federal government itself. "You are looking toward Mexico, Nicaragua, and Brazil," member of Congress Thomas Corwin of Ohio lectured his southern colleagues, "while you are not sure you will have a government to which these could be ceded."[37]

For southerners, expansion seemed essential. Since the Missouri Compromise of 1820, they had witnessed a profound shift in the political and economic balance to the North, the free states. Under the Compromise of 1850, the territories seized from Mexico received instructions: California would enter the Union as a free state, and the rest of the Mexican cession could determine whether it wished to be slave or free (according to the dictates of "popular sovereignty"). A strong majority of southern Congressmen voted against the compromise bill because they viewed popular sovereignty as "moonshine"—that "there will never be slavery in any new territory."[38]

Fearing that slavery could not adapt to the arid regions of the West, southern expansionists looked elsewhere to redress the balance. Tropical states where black slaves could toil under white mastery had long piqued the southern imagination, but intensifying sectionalism during the 1850s gave the matter more urgency. Such belligerent voices as those of James D. E. B. DeBow, in his widely read *DeBow's Review,* and the Knights of the Golden Circle, a secret society of several thousand members that included prominent politicians, loudly demanded tropical expansion. The Gulf of Mexico, DeBow contended, comprised the "great *Southern sea.*"[39] Even after the Kansas–Nebraska Act in 1854 opened the territories to slavery through popular sovereignty, expansionists preferred Central America, Mexico, and Cuba, which, one southerner pronounced, would accord to the South "more power & influence than would a dozen wild deserts" in the American West.[40] "I want them all for the same reason—for the planting or spreading of slavery," a Mississippi senator declared.[41]

Diplomacy could not satisfy southern desires quickly enough, so many southerners supported the filibusters. Although often backed by New York financial interests and cheered by the penny press, most filibuster bands originated in New Orleans, featured thoroughly "southern" goals and personnel, and employed the rhetoric of Manifest Destiny for sectional purposes. Narciso López, John A. Quitman, and William Walker led the ill-fated ventures.

Venezuelan by birth, General Narciso López had careers as a Spanish military officer and Cuban businessman before he attempted to invade Cuba in 1849. Married into an aristocratic proslavery Cuban family, he came to see himself as the island's savior from the perfidies of imperial Spain. He wished to decolonize Cuba and annex it to the United States. Using New York City and New Orleans as bases, López enlisted veterans from the War with Mexico, promising them "plunder, women, drink, and tobacco"; each soldier would receive a $1,000 bonus and 160 acres of Cuban land if the expedition succeeded—indeed, a perfect way for men to "show their manhood."[42] López gathered his several hundred mercenaries at Round Island, off the Louisiana coast, but in September 1849 the U.S. Navy foiled his plans with a blockade.

López sought support elsewhere in the South. He won over southern expansionists such as John A. Quitman, a wealthy sugar and cotton planter, former

General López the Cuban Patriot Getting His Cash. In this satiric portrait, the Venezuelan-born filibuster Narciso López (1797–1851) is shown fleeing to Key West, Florida, in May 1850, chased by Spanish troops. He is holding a bag marked $50,000 stolen from the Cardenas customhouse. The artist John Magee quotes him as saying: "We have got what we came for, my Comrades came for Glory, I came for Cash ... & I suppose we're all satisfied." (Library of Congress)

general in the War with Mexico, and governor of Mississippi (1850–1851); Laurence J. Sigur, the editor of the *New Orleans Delta*; John Henderson, a former senator and cotton planter from Mississippi; and John L. O'Sullivan, editor of Manifest Destiny fame. In May 1850, disguised as emigrants to California, the

The Southern Perspective on Expansion

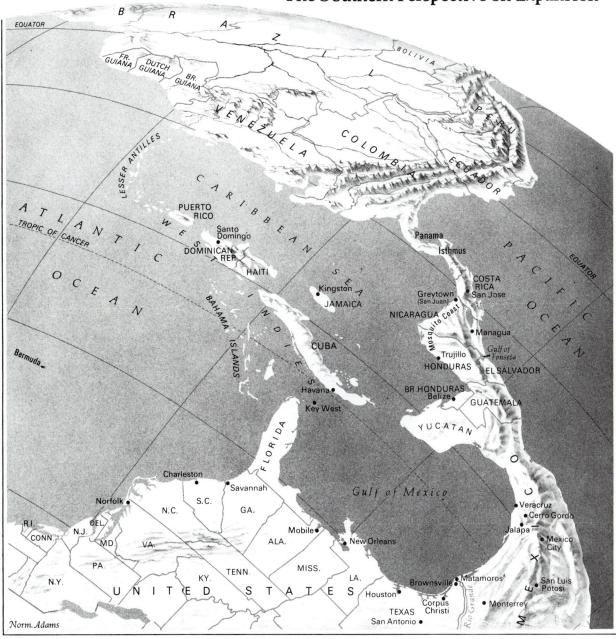

Norm. Adams

filibusters of the López expedition departed New Orleans for Cuba. Upon landing, they suffered sixty-six casualties to superior Spanish forces and attracted little Cuban support. López and most of his followers fled to Key West with a Spanish warship in hot pursuit. López, Quitman, Henderson, Sigur, and O'Sullivan, among others, stood trial in New Orleans for violating the Neutrality Act of 1818, which forbade military operations from American soil against countries at peace with the United States. Sympathetic southern juries soon acquitted them.

López launched another attack against Cuba in August 1851 with 500 "freebooters, pirates, and plunderers."[43] Federal officials in New Orleans obligingly looked the other way. The mustachioed López invoked American icons, telling his followers: "We are sons of Washington … come to free a people" and "to add another glorious star to the banner which already waves … over 'The land of the Free.'"[44] This time López met his doom, as Spanish authorities captured most of his ragtag army. Tried by a military court, López and fifty of his mercenaries, including William Crittenden, nephew of the U.S. attorney general, were executed.

Undeterred by the López debacle, DeBow proclaimed that the American "lust for dominion" over Cuba remained undiminished.[45] An angry mob broke into the Spanish consulate in New Orleans, defaced portraits of the Spanish queen, and shredded the Spanish flag. Secretary of State Daniel Webster apologized in early 1852 and paid Spain $25,000 in damages. Quitman, who had resigned his governorship in 1851 because of the filibustering flap, grew apoplectic. He detested the Compromise of 1850 and feared that Spain might free the slaves in Cuba. Only filibustering offered a quick means to avert "Africanization" and the arming of "black against white."[46] The filibusters could conquer Cuba, proclaim an independent republic on the Texas model, prevent emancipation, and insist on slave status as a condition of annexation to the United States. When a group calling itself the Cuban Junta offered Quitman "all of the powers and attributes of dictatorship," he organized an expedition of 3,000 men, but financial shortages, lack of support in Cuba, and warnings that President Franklin Pierce had "determined to prevent any expedition" forced Quitman to abandon the filibuster in April 1855.[47]

Among those who supported Walker, Lopez, and other filibusters were the redoubtable journalist Jane McManus Storm and her new husband, the Texas entrepreneur William Cazneau. Motivated less by proslavery sentiment than by a "Young America" vision of liberating Caribbean countries, the Cazneaus hoped to mix profits with patriotism. Land deals in Mexico, silver mines in Nicaragua, propaganda tracts for the New York Cuban Council—all were a prelude to their special plans for the Dominican Republic, a country that occupied the eastern two-thirds of the island of Hispaniola, which it shared with Haiti. Through his wife's contacts with Secretary of State Marcy, William Cazneau wangled an appointment in 1854 as a commissioner to investigate trade opportunities. The Cazneaus described the country's resources in glowing terms, recommending immediate diplomatic recognition and acquisition of the strategic harbor of Samaná Bay. As with Cuba, racism influenced U.S. policy, for expansionists stressed the lighter complexions of Dominicans in contrast to their black Haitian neighbors—"the more ardently expansionist the report, the lighter the portrayal of the Dominican people."[48] The Cazneaus also saw the Dominican Republic as a potential haven for emancipated slaves. When the British and French consuls tried to block Cazneau's negotiations, he protested their interference with President Monroe's "principles of 1823."[49] Nonetheless, the Dominicans, following British advice, attached amendments to Cazneau's treaty that made it unacceptable to Washington.

Recalled in late 1854, the Cazneaus embarked on a second Dominican mission in 1859–1860. Because of Washington's preoccupation with the sectional crisis, however, their pleas for a "free commercial entrepôt at the gates of the Gulf of Mexico and the Caribbean Sea" and their warnings that the debt-ridden Dominican government might seek reannexation to Spain brought no official response.[50]

Cuban Allure

The Caribbean island of Cuba lay too close to the United States to escape expansionist urges. "You might as well try to stop the progress of the Mississippi with a bundle of hay" as to prevent the acquisition of Cuba, shouted one South Carolinian.[51] Another southerner waxed erotic: "The Queen of the Antilles [Cuba] … sits on her throne, upon the silver waves, breathing her spicy, tropic breath, and pouting her rosy, sugared lips. Who can object? None. She is of age— take her, Uncle Sam."[52]

Spain once called Cuba the "Ever Faithful Isle" because Cuba did not revolt against Madrid in the stormy decades of the early nineteenth century. After 1818, with the opening of the island to world trade, a Cuba–U.S. commercial nexus began to replace the connection with Spain. "Havana will soon become as much American as New Orleans," the British novelist Anthony Trollope wrote from Cuba in 1859.[53] Cuba's rich sugar production attracted North American entrepreneurs, slaveholders, engineers, and machinists. The new order also included the growth of Protestantism in the predominantly Catholic island.

Slave revolts in the 1830s and 1840s and anticolonial rebellions in the following decade, aroused North Americans, especially southerners who feared the abolition of slavery (45 percent of the island's population of 1 million were slaves). Slaveholders in Cuba had a reputation as cruel masters who participated in an illicit slave trade. A corrupt and inept Spanish administration exacerbated Cuba's plight and tugged at North American sympathies. Expansionists believed that by "natural growth," Cuba would be taken under their eagle's outstretched wings. Or, to use a metaphor of the times: "The fruit will ripen, and fall from the parent stem."[54] In Cuba itself, members of the Creole elite (Spaniards born in Cuba) increasingly made the case for annexation because, as part of the United States, "their sugar would be given preferential treatment and their slave property would be secure."[55]

In 1848 President Polk, seeking to gather other fruits to match Oregon and the Mexican cession, contemplated purchasing Cuba from Spain for $100 million. But Spanish refusal joined the fervent opposition of France and Britain to block him. President Zachary Taylor and his successor Millard Fillmore had little interest in purchasing Cuba and worked to prevent filibustering. In 1852 Britain and France asked the United States to sign a three-power statement to disavow "all intention of obtaining possession" of the island.[56] Unwilling to sign such a self-denying

Pierre Soulé (1801–1870). This revolutionary exile from France and one-term senator from Louisiana proved an incompetent diplomat as the U.S. minister to Spain in 1853–1855. He resigned his post when the Pierce administration blamed him for the negative public reaction to the Ostend Manifesto. Matthew Brady's daguerreotype catches Soulé in a rare placid pose. (Library of Congress)

agreement, Fillmore replied that "this question would fall like a bomb in the midst of the electoral agitation for the presidency" and divide North from South.[57] Secretary of State Edward Everett informed London and Paris that the United States did not "covet" Cuba, but the status of the island was nonetheless "mainly an American question."[58] By quoting Washington's Farewell Address and Jefferson's aversion to "entangling alliances," Everett shunned a pact with European nations. Nor would the United States permit the transfer of Cuba to any other power.

Unlike his two predecessors, President Pierce did covet Cuba. Backed by such expansionists as Secretary of State William L. Marcy, minister to Britain James Buchanan, minister to Spain Pierre Soulé, and minister to France John Y. Mason, Pierce played to the Cuban fancies of southern Democrats. Born in France, schooled as a lawyer, and elected U.S. senator from Louisiana, the impetuous Soulé became a central figure in the North American quest for Cuba. Soon after his arrival in Madrid, Soulé wounded the French ambassador in a duel. Fearful that "the fruit [Cuba] might become spoiled" through slave rebellion if the United States waited too long to pick it, this mercurial "diplomat" constantly irritated Spanish court officials.[59] Marcy believed that Spain would perceive the wisdom of selling its troublesome colony, so he instructed Soulé to inquire discreetly about sale. "Discreetly," however, did not exist in Soulé's vocabulary.

In February 1854, Havana authorities seized the American merchant ship *Black Warrior* for allegedly violating port regulations. President Pierce demanded a $100,000 indemnity and stoked American fervor for revenge by sending a belligerent anti-Spanish message to Congress. Pierce thus fed Soulé's intemperance. The haughty envoy demanded an apology from the Spanish government for an affront to the U.S. flag. The Spanish agreed to restore the ship to its owner and pay a smaller indemnity which Marcy accepted, even though he found the Spanish reply full of "evasions."[60]

The *Black Warrior* affair soon became overshadowed by a new, rash attempt to annex Cuba. Because Spanish authorities had ended the slave trade and were arming free blacks to defend against filibusters, panicky U.S. consuls in Cuba predicted "a fearful revolution" and "a disastrous bloody war of the races."[61] Marcy thereupon instructed Soulé in April 1854 to try to buy Cuba for $130 million or less. Failing that, "you will then direct your efforts to the next desirable object which is to detach that island from the Spanish dominion and from all dependence on any European power."[62] Then, in August, the secretary told Soulé to meet with ministers Buchanan and Mason to discuss annexation. The three expansionists relished the chance; they met in October at Ostend, Belgium, and then at Aix-la-Chapelle in Prussia, where they created the confidential document known as the Ostend Manifesto. The three emissaries recommended the purchase of Cuba for no more than $120 million. Should Madrid refuse to sell, "we shall be justified in wresting it from Spain" to prevent Cuba from becoming a "second St. Domingo, with all its attendant horrors to the white race."[63]

The manifesto arrived in Washington on election day, November 1854, and was leaked to the press. Democrats had just suffered losses in midterm congressional elections, which they blamed on fierce opposition to the Kansas-Nebraska Act, thereby depriving the Pierce administration of "that strength which was needed & could have been much more profitably used for the acquisition of Cuba."[64] Critics now accused Pierce of propagating a slave conspiracy to annex Cuba, characterizing the manifesto as "the highwayman's plea, that might makes right."[65] Grasping for a scapegoat, Pierce and Marcy reprimanded Soulé, who resigned in indignation. The indefatigable Marcy then instructed Soulé's successor to encourage Spain to grant independence to Cuba. Madrid refused.

One author of the Ostend Manifesto, James Buchanan, became president in 1857. "If I can be instrumental in settling the slavery question ... and then add Cuba to the Union, I shall be willing to give up the ghost," he remarked.[66] In December 1858, "Old Buck" praised the commercial and strategic virtues of Cuba, urged its purchase, and asked Congress to appropriate a large sum for this purpose. The Senate Foreign Relations Committee then issued a favorable report that declared the "law of our national existence is growth. We cannot, if we would, disobey it."[67] If the United States did not act, a European power might. The report also recommended $30 million—some of it no doubt for bribes of Spanish public officials. But antislavery Republicans who opposed annexation blocked action on what one Ohioan called a bill to add 750,000 "niggers" to the United States.[68] A slow learner, Buchanan in his annual messages of 1859 and 1860 futilely appealed to Congress to pass the "Thirty Million Dollar Bill." The ardent southerner Jefferson Davis pointed to the "indispensable" importance of Cuba to a South "formed into a separate confederacy."[69] Abraham Lincoln's election as president in 1860 definitively frustrated any further attempts to embrace Cuba.

Openings to East Asia

As southerners dreamed of Caribbean empires to the south, so did other Americans gaze westward across the Pacific. With California firmly a part of the Union in 1850 and with a long Pacific coastline, the strengthening of links with Asia seemed a logical and likely progression. American interest in Asia flamed anew after 1848 for a variety of reasons: new and faster steamships, the valuable ports of San Diego and San Francisco, already existing commercial and missionary ties, prospects of a canal across Central America and a transcontinental railroad to reduce travel time between New York and San Francisco, and the population of California ballooning because of the gold rush of 1849. Lieutenant John Rodgers, who headed a U.S. surveying expedition to the northern Pacific Ocean in 1853–1856, predicted lucrative trade with the Chinese: The prospects "are so vast as to dazzle sober calculation."[70]

This interest in Asia was nothing new. The first American ship to China sailed in the 1780s, and U.S. merchants and missionaries had been active for decades. Caleb Cushing, the first American commissioner to China, had secured trading privileges in five Chinese ports in 1844. John Quincy Adams regarded Cushing's treaty as a "nest egg" for much greater trade with Asia, including Japan.[71] By the early 1850s, Americans carried about one-third of Chinese trade with the West. The United States did not yet play a major role in Asian politics. As junior partners, Americans usually trailed behind the British, who readily used military force to build up imperial privileges, as in the Opium War. The Americans, complained a Chinese official, "do no more than follow in England's wake and utilize her strength."[72] Although the United States did not

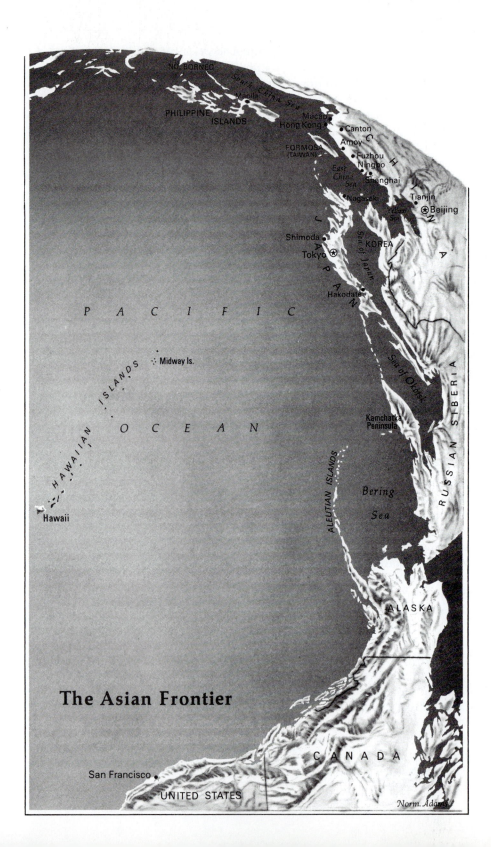

The Asian Frontier

gobble up Asian territory as did Britain (India), the Netherlands (East Indies), and Portugal (Macao), Asians could only view Americans as another nation of grasping foreigners who denied them their sovereignty and dignity.

The most important American initiative came with the "opening" of Japan in 1853–1854. Except for a single port, Nagasaki, where the Dutch traded, few westerners were welcome in a Japan governed by feudal lords bent on maintaining their isolation from "barbarian" whites. American commodore James Biddle, commanding two warships, had tried to open negotiations with this "double-bolted" land in 1846, only to have Japanese officials treat him rudely and warn him "never again to appear on the Japanese coast."[73] Seven years later, in July 1853, Commodore Matthew C. Perry sailed into Tokyo Bay with an armada of "black ships" that included two coal-powered, steam-driven side-wheelers, the *Susquehanna* and the *Mississippi*. Confronted by smoke-belching warships, the Japanese seemed puzzled by these "barbarians … in floating volcanoes."[74]

President Millard Fillmore had given Perry the specific task of "opening" Japan to westerners. Instructed to obtain a treaty that granted the United States trading and coaling stations and promised safe treatment of shipwrecked American sailors, Perry handed Japanese officials a document from President Fillmore. "Our steamships can go from California to Japan in eighteen days," Fillmore's letter boasted. "I am desirous that our two countries should trade with each other." The Japanese grudgingly accepted the impertinent letter "in opposition to Japanese law" and asked Perry to "depart." The commodore agreed to leave but promised to return the next year with all of his ships "and probably more."[75] During Perry's next visit in March 1854, the Japanese appeared more welcoming. Banquets, sumo wrestlers, and an American minstrel entertained guests and hosts. The Americans set up a quarter-scale railroad train and a telegraph system. The Shogun's commissioners were "enthralled" by telegraph sets, Colt revolvers, farm machines, 100 gallons of Kentucky bourbon whiskey, and four volumes of John James Audubon's *Birds of America*.[76]

The resulting Treaty of Kanagawa, signed on March 31, 1854, guaranteed protection for shipwrecked seamen, opened two ports for obtaining coal and other supplies, and established consular privileges at those ports. Yet the two ports, Shimoda and Hakodate, were relatively inaccessible and unimportant. Although Japan granted the United States most-favored-nation treatment, the treaty contained no binding commitment for trade. Perry had "opened" Japan only slightly. When Perry returned to the United States in April 1855, the New York Chamber of Commerce nonetheless presented him with a 381-piece silver dinner service, Boston merchants pinned a medal on him, and Congress voted him a bonus of $20,000. The Senate approved the treaty unanimously.

Perry saw his Japan expedition as but one step toward a U.S. empire in the Pacific. He wished to seize Okinawa and the Bonin Islands as coaling stations for a projected Pacific steamship line. He envisioned American settlement on the "magnificent island" of Formosa (Taiwan), and he urged U.S. military intervention in the internal affairs of Asian states to meet the "responsibilities with which our growing wealth and power must inevitably fasten upon us."[77] He wanted to "extend the advantages of our national friendship and protection" to Siam (Thailand), Indochina,

"Black Ship." In 1853 and 1854 Commodore Matthew C. Perry entered Tokyo Bay with a fleet that included two coal-powered, steam-driven side-wheelers, the *Susquehanna* and the *Mississippi*. Both ships later served in the Civil War blockade against the Confederacy. Here one of the ships is sketched as an alarming dragonlike vessel billowing black smoke. (Courtesy of the Mariners' Museum, Newport News, Virginia)

and the East Indies. Eventually, Perry prophesied, the American people would "extend their dominion and their power, until they shall have brought within their mighty embrace the Islands of the great Pacific, and place the Saxon race upon the eastern shores of Asia."[78]

For the moment, Perry's grandiose vision fell short. In Japan, where Townsend Harris went as consul to capitalize on the commodore's treaty, the gains were modest. Isolated at the post of Shimoda, Harris patiently waited for an opportunity to negotiate a genuine commercial treaty. Lacking the naval power exerted by the westerners in China and displayed by Perry in 1854, Harris could not threaten Japanese leaders, who resented his very presence; but he tenaciously pressed his case in another classic example of "personal diplomacy." In 1858 he secured a treaty whereby Japan opened other ports, provided for freedom of trade, and created a tariff schedule. The next year Harris became minister to

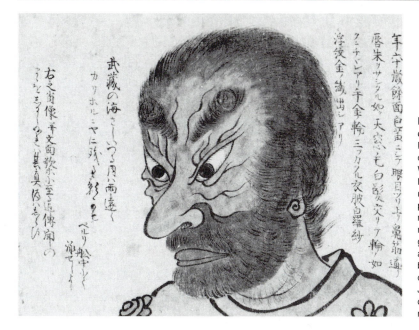

武蔵の海さいつゝ月両遠く
右之貨像ヲ打文彩ゥ小図至近傳聞の
うくヲミつゝ其真似ぬ

カリおルニ月に残す影色と
ペリ船中のユエコ

年六十歳餘面白畵ニテ眼目ツリより亀節遍リ
唇朱ヲサシクル如ク天窓ノ毛白髮交リテ輪ノ如
クニテンアリ千金輪三ツカ化衣波白羅紗

浮後金ノ織出シテアリ

Matthew C. Perry (1794–1858). This career naval officer was born in Newport, Rhode Island, designed steam-driven warships, and directed the siege of Vera Cruz during the War with Mexico. According to the historian Peter Booth Wiley, Perry's mission to Japan represented part of "the offensive projection of power into the Western Pacific on behalf of the masters of a political economy who judged the markets and resources of Asia to be crucial to its growth." One U.S. sailor noticed that Japanese artists always began their portraits of Americans by drawing a large nose and then sketching other features around it, as suggested by this Japanese rendition of Perry. (Honolulu Academy of Arts, Gift of Mrs. Walter F. Dillingham in memory of Alice Perry Grew, 1960)

Japan and established an American legation in Tokyo. The intrepid diplomat did not gain lasting fame until a century later when John Wayne portrayed him in the motion picture *The Barbarian and the Geisha* (1958).

Despite these evidences of U.S. engagement in the 1850s, "Asia remained an abstract idea, a distant area that was only one part of a worldwide commercial empire."[79] In language that suggested a presumed differential of civility and power, admiring American visitors enthused about Japan's "dwarfed" shrubs, "pygmy" lawns, and "liliputian streams," an exotic miniature "fairyland" viewed "through a reversed opera glass"—all implying a conception of the Japanese as something other than completely human or real.[80] The euphoria following Perry's drama soon evaporated. The State Department gave little guidance to its representatives in Asia, who often acted on their own. In 1856, for example, Commodore James Armstrong's warships destroyed five Chinese forts near Guangzhou (Canton) after a Chinese cannon fired on an American vessel. President Franklin Pierce subsequently reprimanded the naval officer. As another example of America's secondary interest in Asia, John Rodgers of the North Pacific Surveying Expedition found on returning to San Francisco in 1856 that he could not complete his survey of trade routes because his funds had run out. Two years later, following a civil war called the Taiping Rebellion, France and Britain further gouged China by opening ten new treaty ports, whereupon the United States, via "hitchhiking imperialism," gained access to these ports and low tariffs in the dictated treaty of Tianjin (Tientsin)—a momentary reversal of the downward trend in U.S. interest and activity in East Asia. Thereafter the U.S. Civil War stalled further commercial expansion.

Anglo-American Détente, an Isthmian Canal, and Central America

After the War with Mexico, Anglo-American relations seemed tranquil, but Great Britain kept a worried eye on U.S. attempts, official and unofficial, to expand in the Caribbean and Central America. In 1842 Webster and Ashburton had drawn the Maine boundary and a line of demarcation from Lake Superior to Lake of the Woods, and in 1846 President Polk had compromised on Oregon. The danger of war over the Canadian-American border declined, while the "Atlantic economy" revived. In the mid-1840s the growth of trade between the United States and Britain had resumed after a decade of sluggishness; by the 1850s the United States supplied Great Britain with 50 percent of its imports and 80 percent of its raw cotton, the basis of England's largest export industry. Forty percent of all U.S. imports originated in Great Britain, and America's expanding economy attracted British capital, especially during the railroad building boom of the 1840s. "Increased Commercial Intercourse may add to the Links of mutual Interest," observed Lord Palmerston, who also warned that "commercial Interest is a Link that snaps under the Pressure of National Passions."[81]

A treaty negotiated with New Granada (later Colombia) in 1846 and ratified in 1848 granted the United States transit rights across the Isthmus of Panama, a promising railroad and canal route. Within a year the California gold rush had turned Panama City into "half American" where "native boys whistled 'Yankee Doodle.'"[82] Alarmed by this intrusion on their maritime supremacy in the Caribbean, the British struck back. In January 1848 they seized a Nicaraguan town, which they renamed Greytown. This port controlled the most feasible transisthmian canal route, given the technology of the time. When added to the British protectorate over the Mosquito Indians inhabiting Nicaragua's eastern coast, possession of Belize (later British Honduras) and the Bay Islands, and the Royal naval base at Jamaica, Greytown accorded Great Britain a potentially dominant position in Central America.

That same month John Marshall discovered gold at Sutter's Mill in California. The great gold rush soon swelled California's population by 100,000 and led to admission of the Golden State to the Union in 1850. Most of the "forty-niners" reached San Francisco by steamship. The trip included arduous overland travel through Nicaragua or Panama. Some adventurers made their long way to the West Coast by taking clipper ships from the eastern seaboard around the southern tip of the hemisphere at treacherous Cape Horn. Construction of an isthmian canal or railway became a matter of urgency, although the conspicuous British presence in Central America precluded unilateral U.S. action. Whig Secretary of State John M. Clayton therefore proposed "a great highway" across the isthmus, "to be dedicated especially by Great Britain and the United States, to the equal benefit and advantage of all nations of the world."[83] Foreign Secretary Palmerston replied that Britain had "no selfish or exclusive views" about the isthmus. Like Clayton, he hoped "that any undertaking of this sort ... should be generally open to and available to all the nations of the world."[84] To confirm this understanding, he sent Sir Henry Bulwer to Washington in 1849. The amicably negotiated Clayton-Bulwer Treaty of April 19, 1850, stipulated that neither Great Britain nor the United States alone would ever monopolize or fortify a canal in

Lord Palmerston (1784–1865). Henry John Temple, 3d Viscount Palmerston, dominated English politics as foreign secretary (1830–1834, 1835–1841, 1846–1851) and prime minister (1855–1858, 1859–1865). "His dominance," the biographer Donald Southgate has written, "coincided with Britannia ruling the waves and London ruling the exchanges." "Old Pam" viewed Americans as "ingenious Rogues" who might take over Central America through the "indirect agency" of filibusters like William Walker — "Texas all over again." (Mansell/Getty Imahes)

Central America, and that neither would "colonize, or assume, or exercise any dominion over … any part of Central America."[85]

The isthmian canal would have to await the twentieth century, but American enterprise soon began to saturate Central America. Cornelius Vanderbilt organized an interoceanic steamship and railroad connection through Nicaragua, and other entrepreneurs completed a railroad across Panama in 1855. But the flag did not follow investors into Central America. The deepening domestic crisis over slavery prevented Presidents Pierce and Buchanan from doing much more than nipping verbally at the heels of the gradually retreating British, even as Palmerston continued to berate the "vulgar minded Bullies" of North America.[86] When a Greytown mob assaulted an American diplomat in 1854, Pierce ordered the U.S.S. *Cyane* to bombard the "pretended community" of "outlaws" and "savages."[87] Despite their initial determination to "stick there till doomsday sooner than be evicted by the Yankees," the British quietly let the matter drop.[88]

The costly Crimean War (1854–1856), which pitted England and France against Russia, also dampened prospects for a showdown with the United States over Central America. When the British government dispatched agents to the United States to recruit soldiers, Secretary Marcy sent them packing for violating U.S. neutrality laws. Palmerston thereupon recommended "some little Flourish" addressed to the "free, enlightened and Generous Race … of the great North American Union" as a means of dampening Marcy's "Bunkum vapouring."[89]

Marcy responded by offering to negotiate a long-desired reciprocity treaty in 1854. A crisis over American fishing rights and navigation of the St. Lawrence River also prompted London to send the governor-general of Canada, Lord Elgin, to negotiate with Marcy. "Lord Elgin pretends to drink immensely," his secretary recorded, "but I watched him [at a party], and I don't believe he drank a glass between two and twelve. He is the most thorough *diplomat* possible."[90] In the ensuing Marcy-Elgin Treaty of June 5, 1854, Americans gained navigation of the St. Lawrence without restriction and fishing rights within three miles of British North America, while Canadians could send duty-free a wide variety of agricultural products into the United States. U.S. consul Israel Andrews thought reciprocity might lead to a U.S.-Canadian "convergence" wherein "under different governments we shall be one people, laboring hand in hand to accomplish the high destiny of the North American continent."[91] The Marcy-Elgin Treaty, like the Webster-Ashburton Treaty and the Oregon settlement, fostered tranquility along the northern border of the United States.

American pursuits once again benefitted from European distance and weakness. Always the bellwether of official British opinion, Palmerston wrote in 1857, in regard to Central America, that the Americans "are on the Spot, strong, deeply interested in the matter, totally unscrupulous and dishonest and determined … to carry their Point. We are far away, weak from Distance, controlled by the Indifference of the Nation … and by its Strong commercial Interest in maintaining Peace with the United States."[92] When he became prime minister in June 1859, Palmerston relinquished the Bay Islands to Honduras and the Mosquito Coast to Nicaragua. The new foreign secretary, Lord Malmesbury, allowed that "all the Southern part of North America must come under this Government of the United States; that he had no objection to what seemed the inevitable course of things."[93]

The American Civil War and International Relations

On April 12, 1861, at Charleston, South Carolina, Confederate forces opened fire on the federal garrison barricaded in Fort Sumter. With this defiant act the rebellious South forced Abraham Lincoln to choose between secession and civil war. Sworn to defend the Constitution, the new Republican president called for 75,000 militiamen to suppress the insurrection.

For support, Lincoln leaned on a fractious cabinet of politically ambitious men, headed by a secretary of state who thought himself far abler than his chief. Willing to act as prime minister to a hesitant president, William Henry Seward concocted plans to "wrap the world in flames" in order to melt domestic disunity in the furnace of foreign war.[94] On April 1 he sent Lincoln "Some Thoughts for the President's Consideration," which proposed hostility or war against Britain, France, Russia, and Spain. The next day Seward responded to Spain's reannexation of the Dominican Republic with a threat of war. Spain ignored him, and Lincoln said he would formulate policy with the "advice of all the Cabinet."[95]

Scarcely deterred, Seward challenged Britain's interpretation of international maritime law. He persuaded Lincoln to proclaim a blockade of the southern ports as a matter of domestic policy. Britain quite properly interpreted the Union block-ade as the act of a nation at war and recognized the belligerent status of the Con-federacy. With equal logic, Confederate president Jefferson Davis met Lincoln's blockade by calling for privateers, a historic mode of American naval warfare.

In the 1856 Declaration of Paris following the Crimean War, Britain and France had codified the rules of maritime warfare and outlawed privateering. The United States had refused to sign away a favorite naval strategy, but the Confederacy's resort to privateering impelled Seward to inform the British min-ister, Lord Richard Lyons, that he wished belatedly to initial the covenant. Lyons welcomed U.S. adherence but noted Washington's inability to obligate the South. To Seward's claim that the South had no independent status, Lyons cooly replied: "Very well. If they are not independent then the President's proclamation of blockade is not binding. A blockade … applies only to two nations at war." Seward retorted: "Europe must interpret the law our way or we'll declare war."[96] The secretary's truculence caused Palmerston to see him as a "vapouring, blustering, ignorant Man" who "may drive us into a quarrel without intending it."[97]

Seward spoke from weakness, and the British knew it. The Union had twice the population of the South and produced 92 percent of all goods manufactured in the United States. But the North faced the difficult military task of subdu-ing 9 million hostile people and sealing off innumerable harbors strung along a 3,500-mile coastline. To blockade this coast, the U.S. Navy could muster only forty-two operational warships. To win, "Confederate armies did not have to invade and conquer the North; they needed only to hold out long enough to force the North to the conclusion that the price of conquering the South and annihilating its armies was too high, as Britain had concluded in 1781 and as the United States concluded with respect to Vietnam in 1972."[98] British officials, especially Lyons, thought it unlikely that Lincoln could preserve the Union against such odds.

William H. Seward (1801–1872). Union College graduate, U.S. senator (1849–1861), and secretary of state (1861–1869), Seward spent the Civil War years by decreasing his bellicosity toward the European Powers and increasing his attempts to keep them neutral. A British journalist described Seward as a "subtle, quick man not quite indifferent to kudos." (Library of Congress)

The economic balance sheet also seemed to favor the South. Prior to the Civil War, British subjects invested widely in American securities, sent at least 25 percent of their annual exports to the United States, and depended on America for 55 percent of all foodstuffs imported each year. But these economic ties favoring the industrial North and farming West paled beside the South's share of three quarters of the British market for raw cotton, the staple undergirding an industrial and commercial empire employing between 4 and 5 million people. Stop the cotton trade and England's economy would allegedly collapse. Palmerston summed up British policy: "we do not like slavery, but we want cotton."[99] Nonetheless, Lord Lyons astutely predicted that the South's "very exaggerated and very false ideas … about cotton will lead to very foolish conduct."[100]

President Jefferson Davis moved quickly. In March he dispatched three ministers to Europe to seek full diplomatic recognition, or even intervention, in exchange for an uninterrupted supply of cotton, free trade with the Confederacy, and expansion of European power throughout the Western Hemisphere.

To parry this diplomatic thrust, Seward whisked Charles Francis Adams to the Court of St. James's. The son of the author of the Monroe Doctrine and grandson of the diplomat who had negotiated the 1783 peace with England, the poised Adams softened Seward's bombastic language without deviating from the secretary's goals. Especially effective with British foreign secretary Lord John Russell, Adams came across as "equally cold: formal, diplomatic, and almost equally British. A diamond come to cut a diamond."[101]

Adams arrived in London on May 14, 1861, dismayed to learn that England had recognized Confederate belligerency. Although the British government had forbidden its subjects to supply ammunition or privateers to either side, Russell had received but not officially met with Confederate commissioners. Adams thought of severing diplomatic relations but rejected such action as the "extreme of shallowness and folly," because a war with England, added to the Civil War, "would grind us all into rags in America."[102]

Seward nonetheless drafted a hostile dispatch for Adams, threatening to declare war if Britain recognized Confederate independence, only to have Lincoln pencil out the most bellicose phrases and send it for Adams's guidance rather than as an ultimatum. As Adams quietly pocketed the diplomatic bombshell, reverses at the front rendered the secretary's threats of war with Europe ridiculous. On July 21, 1861, at Manassas Junction, Virginia, Confederate troops stampeded a Union army into full retreat north.

The summer and fall of 1861 brought more bad news. In England James D. Bulloch, head of the Confederacy's overseas secret service, contracted for the construction of two sloops. Disguised as merchant ships until their departure from British waters in order to circumvent neutrality laws, the *Florida* and *Alabama* soon played havoc with northern commerce. In August the *Bermuda*, a blockade runner laden with war matériel for Savannah, dashed from the Thames. Russell deflected Adams's protest with an invitation to sign the Declaration of Paris. To exploit these favorable events, President Davis sent two fresh and aggressive ministers to Europe, the aristocratic James M. Mason of Virginia and John Slidell, formerly

"King Cotton Bound; or, the Modern Prometheus." In Greek mythology, Prometheus was the creator and savior of humankind whom Zeus chained to a mountain peak. In this rendition by the British humor magazine *Punch,* the northern eagle picks at the Confederate "King Cotton," manacled by the naval blockade. Although the mythical character was later freed, in this cartoon the monarch appears doomed. In the end, northern exports of wheat ("King Corn") to Britain proved more important than southern cotton. (*Punch,* 1861) (Punch, November 2, 1861)

Charleston, South Carolina. Its wharves piled with cotton for export, this southern city governed by wealthy planters relied heavily on the cotton trade for prosperity. In 1860 Charleston ranked third behind New Orleans and Mobile as a cotton-exporting port. (Library of Congress)

Polk's emissary to Mexico in 1845. On October 11, they boarded the Confederate steamer *Nashville* at Charleston to begin their journey.

Hoping to avoid capture by crossing the Atlantic under a neutral flag, Mason and Slidell transferred to the British mail steamer *Trent* in Havana. Captain Charles Wilkes, one of the U.S. Navy's most audacious officers, intercepted the *Trent* as it left Cuban waters on November 8, 1861. Since the British vessel carried Confederate mail, Wilkes could have seized it as a prize. Instead, he hauled Mason and Slidell aboard the U.S.S. *San Jacinto* and allowed the *Trent* to continue its voyage, an act reminiscent of British impressment before the War of 1812. Ecstatic Americans cheered Wilkes, and Congress voted him a gold medal. Lincoln himself feared Mason and Slidell might become "white elephants" but doubted he could free the prisoners without a public backlash.[103]

News of Wilkes's deed reached London on November 27, igniting a panic on the stock exchange. One London editor blustered that Lincoln could not be "so utterly blind as to provoke a collision with a power which with little difficulty could blow to the four winds their dwarf fleet and shapeless mass of incoherent squads."[104] The British government instructed Lyons to demand the release of Mason and Slidell and a formal apology "for the insult offered to the British flag." Queen Victoria's husband, Prince Albert, a staunch advocate of Anglo-American peace, devised a loophole allowing the U.S. government, if it wished, to deny that Wilkes had acted under instructions, "or, if he did, that he misapprehended them." Russell then directed Lyons "to abstain from anything like menace" and "to be rather easy about the apology."[105]

As the watered-down ultimatum crossed the Atlantic, British officials tempered their enthusiasm for war because of the vulnerability of Canada. They also feared marauding Yankee cruisers that might prey on British shipping. Albert's death on December 14 further sobered the national mood. Two days later, Russell advised restraint: "I do not think the country [Britain] would approve an immediate declaration of war."[106] Lyons made "the pill as easy to swallow as possible" when he delivered the message on December 19.[107] Pressure mounted for U.S. capitulation. From London, Charles Francis Adams warned of implacable British determination to see Mason and Slidell set free. Seeing the folly of "two wars ... at a time," Lincoln and Seward opted to defuse the crisis.[108] Seward's reply to Lord Lyons defended Wilkes's right to stop, search, and seize the *Trent* but admitted that the American naval officer had erred in not taking the vessel into port for hearings before a legal tribunal. The secretary thus disavowed Wilkes, congratulated the British for accepting American views on impressment, and "cheerfully liberated" the two Confederates.[109] Clever or not, Seward's settlement of the *Trent* affair "further embittered the opinion of this people toward Great Britain," the Mexican envoy Matías Romero reported from Washington.[110]

Just prior to the *Trent* crisis, Britain, France, and Spain had landed troops at Veracruz, Mexico, ostensibly to compel payment on a $65 million foreign debt. Lord Russell had cautiously invited U.S. participation in this intervention. Seward declined, but he acknowledged the right of the powers to collect debts forcibly, provided they did not harbor political or territorial ambitions in Mexico. U.S. fears of European plots against Latin America were realistic. In early 1862, Prime Minister Palmerston thought a European monarch in Mexico City "would be a great blessing for Mexico. ... It would also stop the North Americans ... in their absorption of Mexico."[111] In April 1862, Britain and Spain settled their Mexican debts and withdrew from the joint venture. French troops continued their march westward toward Mexico City, where Napoleon III hoped to pose "an insuperable barrier to the encroachments of the United States" by installing a puppet government under Archduke Ferdinand Maximilian, brother of the Austrian emperor.[112] Fierce Mexican resistance delayed French occupation of the capital city until June 1863. This entrapment forced Napoleon to follow Britain's lead in Civil War diplomacy, despite his own bias in favor of the South. Seward and Lincoln watched these machinations without protest. "Why should we gasconade about Mexico," Seward explained, "when we are engaged in a struggle for our own life?"[113]

British "Lookers On" Across the Atlantic

In 1862, along the southern coast, the Union's tightening blockade locked up Confederate privateers and harassed neutral shipping. In Tennessee an unknown general, Ulysses S. Grant, chased the rebels from Forts Donelson and Henry. Admiral David G. Farragut captured New Orleans in April, opening the Mississippi River to a campaign that would finally sever Texas, Arkansas, and Louisiana from the Confederacy. Neither North nor South, however, could secure a decisive victory in the critical eastern theater. Union general George B. McClellan faltered outside Richmond in July 1862, just as Virginia's Robert E. Lee pulled back after the bloodletting at Antietam two months later. The British government watched the strategic stalemate and waited. London prudently acquiesced in the Union blockade, accumulating precedents useful for future conflicts when once again England would be a belligerent and the United States neutral.

Cotton did not drive British policy—at least not at first. England did not initially crave raw cotton. The bumper American crop of 1861 provided 1.6 million bales for the saturated Lancashire mills. Anticipating an early end to the Civil War, British cotton manufacturers complacently counted on their stockpiled raw cotton to carry them through a short-term crisis. As the military deadlock deepened in 1862, the textile producers developed alternative sources, notably in Egypt and India. These new fields began to yield amply by 1863. In France, Napoleon's insistence on following British policy toward the Civil War prevented the Confederacy from capitalizing on discontent in the French cotton industry. As the historian Thomas Schoonover has concluded: "The Confederacy exaggerated the power of cotton in the world system and misunderstood its own subordinate role in it. Cotton was not king, and it never had been."[114]

The South fared better in maritime Liverpool. Contemptuous of Queen Victoria's neutrality proclamation of May 13, 1861, Liverpool shipping interests sought to recoup from the costly disruption of trade with the South by building blockade runners, commerce raiders, and rams for the Confederate naval agent James D. Bulloch. The blockade runners returned high profits to builders, skippers, and crews. Of 2,742 runs attempted during the war, steam-driven runners completed 2,525, or 92 percent, mainly during the ineffective first year of the blockade. Greed for profits, moreover, induced many southern shippers to import luxury items rather than military matériel, thus wasting precious cargo space and scarce southern capital.

Commerce raiders presented a greater threat. Bulloch contracted for these vessels and disguised them as cargo ships during construction in order to circumvent the queen's neutrality proclamation, which forbade outfitting warships for either belligerent. In March 1862 the *Oreto,* renamed *Florida* once at sea, slipped from Liverpool. Adams protested vainly and pleaded with Lord Russell to detain a larger second vessel, "Number 290," then nearing completion. On July 31, Russell grudgingly concluded that the new rover was intended to be a Confederate commerce raider, but his order to seize it conveniently arrived a day after the *Alabama* had sailed. In the Azores, the ship was armed with eight guns and outfitted as a maritime predator. Under the command of the South's most gifted naval officer, Raphael Semmes, the raider sank nineteen Union merchant vessels in its first three months at sea. Together with the *Florida* and lesser raiders, it preyed on Union commerce worldwide, driving northern merchants to flags of foreign registry.

Two months after the *Alabama*'s escape, awed by the Confederate victory at the Second Battle of Bull Run (Second Manasses) and the endless rivers of blood irrigating America, Russell proposed to Palmerston an Anglo-French mediation "with a view to the recognition of the independence of the Confederates."[115] Cotton shortages added impetus to Russell's proposal, and William E. Gladstone, a member of the cabinet, declared publicly that Jefferson Davis had "made a nation."[116] Caught in a cabinet crisis over Mexico, however, the French hesitated, and from St. Petersburg came a resounding endorsement of "the maintenance of the American Union as one indivisible nation," which the tsar favored as a check on

British supremacy in the Atlantic.[117] News of Lee's reversal at the battle of Antietam (Sharpsburg) in September finally inclined Palmerston to "continue to be lookers on till the war shall have taken a more decided turn."[118] This repudiation on October 22, 1862, of both mediation and recognition of Confederate independence remained British policy until the end of the war.

Lincoln did all he could to ensure continued European neutrality. Emboldened by the victory at Antietem and convinced that no "European Power would dare to recognize and aid the Southern Confederacy if it became clear that the Confederacy stands for slavery and the Union for freedom," he issued the Emancipation Proclamation on September 22.[119] This historic gesture set January 1, 1863, as the date for freedom of slaves in areas not controlled by the Union—in short, only in districts still in rebellion. The British chargé in Washington dismissed Lincoln's words as having "no pretext for humanity … cold, vindictive, and entirely political."[120] Within a few months, however, the British liberal activist Richard Cobden reported that the proclamation "has closed the mouths of those who have been advocating the side of the South."[121] Even pro-Confederate Britons denounced slavery as a "gross anachronism" and "foul blot."[122]

As 1863 opened, a Polish uprising against Russian rule threatened to disrupt the critical European balance of power. Charles Francis Adams welcomed such continental distractions and waited impatiently for Union victories to give him diplomatic clout. Then in July came the double-barreled good news: The northern armies held at Gettysburg, and Grant won control of the Mississippi River at Vicksburg.

As Confederate bonds plummeted on the London market, Minister Adams pressed Lord Russell to seize two ironclad, steam-driven vessels nearing completion at the Laird yards in Liverpool. These shallow-draft warships mounted seven-foot iron rams, theoretically an ideal weapon for piercing the wooden hulls of the Union's blockaders. Bulloch had ordered the Laird rams but covered his tracks so thoroughly that the Pasha of Egypt seemed their legal owner. Since the rams lacked guns and the Crown lacked proof of Confederate ownership, Russell's law officers could not find them in violation of British neutrality. Russell, however, dared not disregard Adams's increasingly shrill warnings, nor the Union's midsummer military victories. Nor was it in Britain's national interest to encourage the precedent of weak naval powers constructing warships in neutral shipyards during wartime. On September 3, 1863, he prudently detained the rams, telling Palmerston that "neutral hostility should not be allowed to go on without some attempt to stop it."[123]

Unaware of the foreign secretary's concession, Adams on September 5 penned a scathing note warning that if the rams were not halted, "it would be superfluous in me to point out to your lordship that this is war!"[124] Palmerston bridled at Adams's "insolent threats of war" and thought Russell should "say to him in civil terms, 'You be damned.'"[125] Such pique stayed private.

Northern morale received a boost from the visit of the Russian Baltic and Pacific squadrons to New York and San Francisco in September and October of 1863. Fearful of war with England and France over Poland, Russia sent its ships in the hope that they could operate against the Royal Navy from ice-free American ports. One Russian officer predicted that if France recognized the Confederacy and Polish belligerency, "the Russian eagle might extend its talon to the American eagle

Charles Francis Adams (1807–1886). Son of John Quincy Adams, graduate of Harvard, and Republican member of Congress from Massachusetts before Lincoln appointed him minister to Great Britain (1861–1868), the suave diplomat labored diligently to keep London neutral during the Civil War. (National Portrait Gallery, Smithsonian Institution/Art Resource, N.Y.)

to give a joint shake to the Gallic cock not only in words."[126] As Russian sailors marched down Broadway, northerners wishfully interpreted the visit as a sign of support for the Union cause. Secretary of the Navy Gideon Welles thought "our Russian friends are rendering us a great service."[127]

In 1863, too, the troops of Napoleon III finally fought their way into Mexico City. In July, the victorious French emperor proclaimed a Mexican monarchy under Austrian archduke Maximilian. Seward denied recognition to Maximilian when the aspiring royal arrived in Mexico in July 1864. By then General William T. Sherman was marching through Georgia and Grant crept bloodily toward Richmond. The apparently inevitable Union triumph would place a huge army and one of the world's largest navies along the border of Napoleon's puppet state. Napoleon began to scale down his commitment, intending to remove all but 20,000 French troops from Mexico by 1867. He also curried favor with Washington by directing Maximilian not to receive Confederate ministers, and he seized two Confederate rams under construction at Nantes in May 1864. A month later the U.S.S. *Kearsarge* sank the C.S.S. *Alabama* within sight of Cherbourg.

The diplomatic and naval isolation of the Confederacy became complete. "King Cotton" had failed. Confederate diplomacy, lacking decisive support from the battlefield, did not win European capitals to its cause. The "War Between the States" had remained just that.

What if ...   *Great Britain had recognized the Confederacy during the Civil War?*

Suppose that General Robert E. Lee's army had won the battle of Antietam in September 1862. The British government of Prime Minister Lord Palmerston was prepared, in cooperation with the French under Napoleon III, to offer mediation to end the fratricidal war between North and South. Implicit in such a proposal was the expectation that Great Britain would extend formal recognition to the Confederate government if Abraham Lincoln's administration refused mediation. If the British had intervened diplomatically, the North might have declared war on England and tried to invade Canada, though such a move would have violated Lincoln's preferred strategy of one war at a time.

With victorious Confederate armies on the offensive in both eastern and western theaters, as well as the prospect of British military reinforcement of the South, a mediated peace that guaranteed Confederate independence would have been a likely outcome. The French occupation of Mexico would probably have succeeded more quickly and Emperor Maximilian's puppet regime would have lasted longer. The Monroe Doctrine would have become an anachronism, and a Balkanized North America, with England and France as balancers, might have emerged. Britain's antislavery policies could have blocked southern ambitions to annex more potential slave territory in the Caribbean or Central America. The South's "peculiar institution" would have survived temporarily, but humanitarian norms, economic concerns, and international politics would have exerted continued pressure on the South, forcing an eventual choice between the maintenance of an aristocratic, slave-based order that was becoming increasingly antiquated in the western world and the embrace of a democratizing, market-based industrialized political and economic order on the rise in the North. As for the truncated, industrialized North, British mediation in 1862 probably would have inflamed Anglophobia, nurtured revenge against the South, and curtailed any imperial or global ambitions until scores could be settled within North America. So long as two disunited republics coexisted, no American superpower could arise to exert dominating global influence.

In another possible scenario, however, Abraham Lincoln could have issued his Emancipation Proclamation even if the British had recognized the Confederacy after Antietam. By a stroke of his pen the president still could have transformed northern war aims from suppressing rebellion to that of a crusade to end slavery. Once emancipation became the goal, no European power could easily take sides against a government committed to the destruction of slavery. Because of the Palmerston government's own antislavery policies and its unwillingness to alienate the staunch pro-Union sentiments of British Liberals and working classes, it would likely have stopped short of outright intervention. Just as the British later reversed their unneutral behavior in permitting Confederate agents to purchase warships built in British shipyards, so too could Palmerston and Foreign Secretary Lord Russell have repudiated premature recognition. Poland's uprising against Russia in 1863 and Britain's need for northern wheat imports in 1864 would have reinforced such prudence. Lincoln's government would have been free to wage the kind of total war that led to unconditional surrender at Appomattox in 1865. Of course, northern resentment at Britain's abortive mediation would have added more emotional fuel to the *Alabama* claims and other demands made after the war in reaction to London's unneutral wartime practices. The Andrew Johnson and Ulysses S. Grant administrations might have pursued Senator Charles Sumner's strategy of demanding Canada as compensation for such alleged transgressions. Britain might then have faced two stark and unpalatable alternatives: either yield its remaining North American possessions or go to war against a well-armed, military seasoned, and highly Anglophobic United States.

War as Catalyst

When the Civil War finally ended at Appomattox in April 1865, more than 600,000 Americans lay dead, and hundreds of thousands nursed disfiguring wounds. The war cost at least $20 billion in destroyed property and expenditures. The American merchant marine lay in shambles. U.S. commerce was badly disrupted. The eleven Confederate states suffered heavy economic losses, as a dislocated population and labor force, including 4 million former slaves, worked in denuded agricultural fields and burned-out cities. Although the Union became whole once again, regional bitterness persisted. The wrenching Civil War experience and the reconstruction and military occupation of the South suggested that sectionalism might yet impede U.S. expansion abroad.

Countervailing evidence, however, indicated that the expansionism that had flourished in the 1840s and slowed in the 1850s would enjoy a rebirth. The United States, after all, had become an economic power before the Civil War. Although overall trade had stalled, northern commerce in grain with England expanded greatly during the war, and prospects for a renewal of the cotton trade were good. Even during the French occupation of Mexico (1862–1867), U.S. investors expanded into mining, petroleum, and agriculture south of the border.

During the war northern politicians established high protectionist tariffs to protect their own manufacturers, stabilized the banking system, passed the Homestead Act to settle western lands and the Morrill Act to build land-grant colleges, and provided for the construction of a transcontinental railroad. Large federal expenditures of about $2 million a day generated capital accumulation and stimulated some industries. The Civil War thus helped spur the American "industrial revolution" of the late nineteenth century, which increasingly shifted the character of the nation's foreign trade from agricultural to industrial goods and necessitated the sale of surplus production overseas. An economic and political "colossus ... has been created on the other side of the Atlantic," a French observer noted in 1866, so that "within thirty years North America will be a rival to Europe, competing with her in everything."[128]

The victory of Republican principles elevated America's international status. Despite taunts and gibes about the American "smashup" from foreign critics, the Lincoln administration had won the war, freed the slaves, and preserved federal institutions. The Italian patriot Giuseppe Mazzini blessed the victorious people "who have done more for us in four years than fifty years of teaching, preaching, and writing from all your European brothers."[129] None other than the European socialist Karl Marx congratulated Lincoln on delivering "the Union from this curse and shame" of slavery.[130] Indeed, as one historian has noted: "Before 1861 the two words 'United States' were generally regarded as a plural noun: 'The United States *are* a republic.' The war marked the transition of the United States to a singular noun."[131] Simply put, "the vision of a voluntary union of the states" had given way to "the imperatives of nation and empire, from which there could be no withdrawal."[132]

Once freed from the constraints of war, Secretary Seward envisioned a larger U.S. empire. An avid expansionist before the Civil War, Seward in 1865 turned his attention southward, intent on driving the French and Maximilian from Mexico, annexing territories, expanding trade, and building naval bases in the Caribbean. Santo Domingo, which Spain ruled from 1861 to mid-1865, became one of Seward's first targets. Moreover, Lincoln's diplomatic recognition of the free black countries of Haiti and Liberia in 1861, heretofore blocked by southern opposition, suggested that racism might prove less inhibiting to American expansion after the war.

The British in particular had good reason to be wary. Northerners angrily remembered the depredations of the *Alabama* and the seeming British tolerance of southern secession. Also, Anglo-American competition in Central

America and the Caribbean joined competition in the Pacific and Asia to propel London and Washington along a contentious course. Reciprocity with Canada was breaking down (Congress abrogated the Agreement of 1854 in 1866). A new generation of American Anglophobes vowed to twist the British lion's tail, with some insisting that London cede Canada to atone for its sins. Indeed, to blunt U.S. advances, the formation of the Dominion of Canada, accomplished in 1867, proved to be the "most tangible international repercussion of the American Civil War."[133]

The British nonetheless carried away from the contest some welcome precedents in international law. The seafaring nation acquiesced in the tortuous U.S. rendering of maritime rights during the Civil War. While the Confederacy relied futilely on such honored American policies as embargoes and the destruction of commerce, the Lincoln administration reversed the traditional U.S. view of neutral rights and adopted what had been the British position. Seward insisted that the war was a *domestic* conflict, yet the United States declared a paper-thin blockade under *international* law. Not only did this behavior constitute a glaring contradiction; it also violated international law, for blockades must be effective (as the Union blockade was not in the first two years of the war). Seward even reversed the hallowed American doctrine that neutral shipping was immune to capture when moving between neutral ports, regardless of the ultimate destination of the cargo. In 1863 he approved the capture of the *Peterhoff,* a British steamer loaded with Confederate goods en route to Matamoros, Mexico, suggesting that the cargo's ultimate destination made the voyage "continuous." During the period of American neutrality in the First World War (1914–1917), the British dusted off their history tomes and reminded Washington of Seward's Civil War policies. The legacy of the Civil War had a long reach indeed.

FURTHER READING FOR THE PERIOD 1848–1865

For the 1850s, Latin America, and the coming of the Civil War, see Frederick M. Binder, *James Buchanan and the American Empire* (1994); James C. Bradford, ed., *Captains of the Old Steam Navy* (1986) (U.S. Navy); H. W. Brands, *The Age of Gold* (2002); Charles H. Brown, *Agents of Manifest Destiny* (1980) (filibusters); E. Bradford Burns, *Patriarch and Folk* (1991) (Nicaragua); Tom Chaffin, *Fatal Glory* (1996) (López); James Dunkerley, *Americana* (2000); Yonatan Eyal, *The Young America Movement* (2007); Don E. Fehrenbacher, *The Slaveholding Republic* (2001); John E. Findling, *Close Neighbors, Distant Friends* (1987) (Central America); William H. Freehling, *The Road to Disunion* (1990); Larry Gara, *The Presidency of Franklin Pierce* (1991); Michel Gobat, *Confronting the American Dream* (2005) (Nicaragua); Amy S. Greenberg, *Manifest Manhood and the Antebellum American Empire* (2005); Kenneth J. Hagan, *This People's Navy* (1991); Michael F. Holt, *The Rise and Fall of the Whig Party* (1999) and *The Fate of Their Country* (2004); Robert W. Johannsen, *The Frontier, the Union, and Stephen A. Douglas* (1989) and *Lincoln, the South, and Slavery* (1991); Robert Kagan, *Dangerous Nation* (2006); Lester D. Langley, *Struggle for the American Mediterranean,* (1976); Luis Martínez-Fernández, *Torn Between Empires* (1994) (Spanish Caribbean); Robert E. May, *The Southern Dream of a Caribbean Empire, 1854–1861* (2002), *John A. Quitman* (1985), and *Manifest Destiny's Underworld* (2002); Aims McGuinness, *Path of Empire* (2008); Michael A. Morrison, *Slavery and the American West* (1997); Gretchen Murphy, *Hemispheric Imaginings* (2004); Louis A. Pérez, Jr., *Cuba and the United States* (2003); Bradford Perkins cited in Chapter 2; Thomas D. Schoonover, *The United States in Central America* (1991); John Schroeder, *Shaping a Maritime Empire* (1985) (U.S. Navy); Joel H. Silbey, *The Partisan Imperative* (1985); Scott A. Silverstone, *Divided Union* (2004); Elbert Smith, *The Presidencies of Zachary Taylor and Millard Fillmore* (1988) and *The Presidency of James Buchanan* (1975); Joseph A. Stout, *Schemers and Dreamers* (2002) (filibusters); James T. Wall, *Manifest Destiny Denied* (1982); and Sean Wilentz, *The Rise of American Democracy* (2005).

For key characters, see Jean H. Baker, *James Buchanan* (2004); K. Jack Bauer, *Zachary Taylor* (1985); Michael Burlingame, *Abraham Lincoln* (2008); William C. Davis, *Rhett* (2001); David Donald, *Charles Sumner and the Rights of Man* (1970); Linda S. Hudson, *Mistress of Manifest Destiny* (2001) (Jane Storm Cazneau); Robert W. Johannsen, *Stephen A. Douglas* (1973); William C. Klunder, *Lewis Cass and the Politics of Moderation* (1996); and Ernest N. Paolino, *The Foundations of the American Empire* (1973) (Seward). See Chapter 3 for studies of Daniel Webster.

For Japan and Asian issues, see Warren I. Cohen, *America's Response to China* (2000); Peter Duus, *The Japanese Discovery of America* (1996); Fumiko Fujita, *American Pioneers and the Japanese Frontier* (1994); Arrell M. Gibson, *Yankees in Paradise* (1993); Gerald S. Graham, *The China Station* (1978); Joseph Henning, *Outposts of Civilization* (2000); Curtis T. Henson, Jr., *Commissioners and Commodores* (1982); Michael Hunt, *The Making of a Special Relationship* (1983) (China); Walter LaFeber, *The Clash* (1997); Walter A. McDougall, *Let the Sea Make a Noise* (1993); Samuel E. Morison, "*Old Bruin*" (1967); Robert A. Rosenstone, *Mirror in the Shrine* (1988) (Japan); John Schroeder, *Matthew Calbraith Perry* (2001); and Peter Booth Wiley, *Yankees in the Land of the Gods* (1991) (Perry).

Anglo-Canadian-American relations are examined in Charles S. Campbell, *From Revolution to Rapprochement* (1974); Martin Crawford, *The Anglo-American Crisis of the Mid-Nineteenth Century* (1987); Wilbur D. Jones, *The American Problem in British Diplomacy* (1974); H. G. Nicholas, *The United States and Britain* (1975); and Reginald C. Stuart, *United States Expansionism and British North America, 1775–1871* (1988).

For European questions, see Henry Blumenthal, *France and the United States* (1970); Alan Dowty, *The Limits of American Isolation* (1971) (Crimean War); James A. Field, Jr., *America and the Mediterranean World, 1776–1882* (1969); David Foglesong, *The American Mission and the "Evil Empire"* (2007); Paola Gemme, *Domesticating Foreign Struggles* (2005) (Italy); Normal Saul, *Distant Friends* (1991) (Russia); and Donald M. Spencer, *Louis Kossuth and Young America* (1977).

For Union and Confederate foreign policies, especially naval issues and maritime rights, see works cited above and Eugene H. Berwanger, *The British Foreign Service and the American Civil War* (1994); R. J. M. Blackett, *Divided Hearts* (2001); David W. Blight, *Race and Reunion* (2001) and *Beyond the Battlefield* (2002); Gabor S. Boritt, ed., *Why the Confederacy Lost* (1992); Lynn M. Case and Warren F. Spencer, *The United States and France* (1970); Adrian Cook, *The Alabama Claims* (1975); David P. Crook, *Diplomacy During the American Civil War* (1975) and *The North, the South, and the Powers, 1861–1865* (1974); David H. Donald, *Lincoln* (1995) and ed., *Why the North Won the Civil War* (1996); Norman B. Ferris, *The Trent Affair* (1977) and *Desperate Diplomacy: William H. Seward's Foreign Policy, 1861* (1975); Gary Gallagher, *The Confederate War* (1997); Doris Kearns Goodwin, *Team of Rivals* (2005); Matthew Pratt Guterl, *American Mediterranean* (2008); Charles M. Hubbard, *The Burden of Confederate Diplomacy* (1998); Brian Jenkins, *Britain and the War for the Union* (1974–1980); Howard Jones, *Union in Peril* (1992) and *Abraham Lincoln and a New Birth of Freedom* (1999); Dean B. Mahin, *One War at a Time* (1999); Robert E. May, ed., *The Union, the Confederacy, and the Atlantic Rim* (1995); James M. McPherson, *Battle Cry of Freedom* (1989), *Ordeal by Fire* (1982), and *Tried by War* (2008); Frank J. Merli, *Great Britain and the Confederate Navy* (1970); Philip E. Meyers, *Caution and Cooperation* (2008); Philip S. Paludan, *"A People's Contest"* (1988) and *The Presidency of Abraham Lincoln* (1994); Charles M. Robinson III, *Shark of the Confederacy* (1995) (*Alabama*); Warren F. Spencer, *The Confederate Navy in Europe* (1983); David G. Surdam, *Northern Naval Superiority and the Economics of the American Civil War* (2001); Craig Symonds, *Lincoln and His Admirals* (2008); Philip Thomas Tucker, ed., *Cubans in the Confederacy* (2002); Gordon H. Warren, *Fountain of Discontent* (1981) (*Trent*); and Robert W. Young, *Senator James Murray Mason* (1998).

For Mexico and the French intervention, see Alfred J. Hanna and Kathryn A. Hanna, *Napoleon III and Mexico* (1971); John M. Hart, *Empire and Revolution* (2002); Donathon C. Olliff, *Reforma Mexico and the United States* (1981); W. Dirk Raat, *Mexico and the United States* (1992); and Thomas D. Schoonover, *Dollars over Dominion* (1978).

See also the General Bibliography, the following notes, and Robert L. Beisner, ed., *Guide to American Foreign Relations Since 1600* (2003).

NOTES TO CHAPTER 4

1. Quoted in Robert E. May, "Filibustering in the Age of Manifest Destiny," *Journal of American History, LXXVII* (December 1991), 861.

2. Quoted in Amy S. Greenberg, "A Grey-Eyed Man," *Journal of the Early Republic, XX* (Winter 2000), 680.

3. Quoted *ibid.*, p. 699.

4. Amy S. Greenberg, *Manifest Manhood and the Antebellum American Empire* (New York: Cambridge University Press, 2005), p. 11; quoted in Greenberg, "Grey-Eyed Man," p. 694.

5. Quoted in Roy F. Nichols, *Franklin Pierce* (Philadelphia: University of Pennsylvania Press, 1931), p. 459; quoted in William Earl Weeks, *Building the Continental Empire* (Chicago: Ivan R. Dee, 1996), p. 159.

6. Quoted in Greenberg, "Grey-Eyed Man," p. 684.

7. Walker quoted in Michel Gobat, *Confronting the American Dream* (Durham: Duke University Press, 2005), p. 29; also quoted in Robert E. May, *The Southern Dream of a Caribbean Empire, 1854–1861* (Gainesville: University Press of Florida, 2002), p. 91.

8. Quoted in Gobat, *American Dream*, p. 28.

9. Quoted in Randall O. Hudson, "The Filibuster Minister," *North Carolina Historical Review, XLIX* (July 1972), 295.

10. Quoted in Gobat, *American Dream*, p. 33.

11. Quoted in May, *Southern Dream*, p. 91.

12. William Marcy quoted *ibid.*, p. 96.

13. Quoted in May, "Filibustering," p. 894.

14. Quoted in E. Bradford Burns, *Patriarch and Folk* (Cambridge: Harvard University Press, 1991), p. 202.

15. Davis quoted in Robert E. May, *Manifest Destiny's Underworld* (Chapel Hill: University of North Carolina Press, 2002), p. 277.

16. Quoted in Linda S. Hudson, *Mistress of Manifest Destiny* (Austin: Texas State Historical Association, 2001), p. 163.

17. Quoted in Kenneth Stampp, *America in 1857* (New York: Oxford University Press, 1990), p. 296.

18. Quoted in May, *Southern Dream*, pp. 131–132.

19. Nancy Isenberg, review of *Manifest Manhood*, *Civil War History, LII* (March 2006), 95.

20. Quoted in Burns, *Patriarch*, p. 208.

21. Gobat, *American Dream*, pp. 40–41.

22. Quoted in Scott A. Silverstone, *Divided Union* (Ithaca: Cornell University Press, 2004), p. 203.

23. Quoted in Ernest N. Paolino, *The Foundations of the American Empire* (Ithaca, NY: Cornell University Press, 1973), pp. 7–9.

24. Quoted in George C. Herring, *From Colony to Superpower* (New York: Oxford University Press), p. 223.

25. Quoted in Robert W. Johannsen, "Young America and the War with Mexico," in Richard F. Francaviglia and Douglas W. Richmond, eds., *Dueling Eagles* (Fort Worth: Texas Christian University Press, 2000), p. 161.

26. Quoted in Alan Brinkley, "Messiah Complex," *The Atlantic, CCC* (November 2007), 34.

27. Quoted in Michael F. Holt, *The Rise and Fall of the American Whig Party* (New York: Oxford University Press, 1999), p. 601.

28. Quoted in George T. Curtis, *Life of Daniel Webster* (New York: Appleton, 1870; 2 vols.), *II*, 537.

29. Quoted in Elbert B. Smith, *The Presidencies of Zachary Taylor and Millard Fillmore* (Lawrence: University Press of Kansas, 1988), p. 232.

30. Quoted in Robert V. Remini, *Daniel Webster* (New York: Norton, 1997), p. 702.

31. Quoted in Robert R. Davis, Jr., "Diplomatic Plumage," *American Quarterly, XX* (Summer 1968), 173.

32. Tom Chaffin, *Fatal Glory* (Charlottesville: University Press of Virginia, 1996), p. 10.

33. Quoted in Edward L. Widmer, *Young America* (New York: Oxford University Press, 1999), p. 194; quoted in Robert W. Johannsen, *Stephen A. Douglas* (New York: Oxford University Press, 1973), p. 347.

34. Quoted in Robert W. Johannsen, *Lincoln, the South, and Slavery* (Baton Rouge: Louisiana State University Press, 1991), p. 89.

35. Quoted in Robert E. Bonner, "Empire of Liberty, Empire of Slavery," in Peter J. Kastor, ed., *The Louisiana Purchase* (Washington: CQ Press, 2002), p. 136.

36. Quoted in Robert W. Johannsen, *The Frontier, the Union, and Stephen A. Douglas* (Urbana: University of Illinois Press, 1989), p. 87.

37. Quoted in David Potter, *The Impending Crisis, 1848–1861* (New York: Harper and Row, 1976), p. 198.

38. Member of Congress quoted in Michael F. Holt, *The Fate of Their Country* (New York: Hill & Wang, 2004), p. 30.

39. Quoted in Robert F. Durden, "J. D. B. DeBow," *Journal of Southern History, XVII* (November 1951), 450.

40. Quoted in Robert E. May, *John A. Quitman* (Baton Rouge: Louisiana State University Press, 1985), p. 278.

41. Quoted in Luis Martínez-Fernández, *Torn Between Empires* (Athens: University of Georgia Press, 1994), p. 37.

42. Quoted in Philip S. Foner, *A History of Cuba and Its Relations with the United States* (New York: International Publishers, 1962–1963; 2 vols.), *II*, 43; quoted in Greenberg, *Manifest Manhood*, p. 14.

43. Frederick Douglass quoted in Foner, *History of Cuba, II*, 64.

44. Quoted in Tom Chaffin, "Sons of Washington," *Journal of the Early Republic, XV* (Spring 1995), 89.

45. Quoted in Durden, "DeBow," p. 451.

46. Quoted in Yonatan Eyal, *The Young America Movement and the Transformation of the Democratic Party, 1828–1861* (New York: Cambridge University Press, 2007), p. 137.

47. Quoted in Robert E. May, "The Slave Power Conspiracy Revisited," in David W. Blight and Brooks Simpson, eds., *Union and Emancipation* (Kent, Ohio: Kent State University Press, 1997), p. 17.

48. Luis Martínez-Fernández, "Caudillos, Annexationism, and the Rivalry Between Empires," *Diplomatic History, XVII* (Fall 1993), 579.

49. Quoted in Hudson, *Mistress*, p. 154.

50. Quoted in Robert E. May, "Plenipotentiary in Petticoats," in Edward E. Crapol, ed., *Women and American Foreign Policy* (Westport, Conn.: Greenwood, 1992, 2nd ed.), p. 33.

51. Andrew Pickens quoted in Gretchen Murphy, *Hemispheric Imaginings* (Durham: Duke University Press, 2004), p. 94.

52. Quoted in May, *Southern Dream*, p. 7.

53. Quoted in Louis A. Pérez, Jr., *Cuba and the United States* (Athens: University of Georgia Press, 1991), p. 14.

54. Quoted in Robert W. Young, *Senator James Murray Mason* (Knoxville: University of Tennessee Press, 1998), p. 69.

55. Anton L. Allahar, "Sugar, Slaves, and the Politics of Annexation," *Colonial Latin American Historical Review, III* (Summer 1994), 285.

56. Quoted in John A. Logan, Jr., *No Transfer* (New Haven: Yale University Press, 1961), p. 227.

57. Quoted in Basil Rauch, *American Interest in Cuba, 1848–1855* (New York: Columbia University Press, 1948), p. 176.

58. John Bassett Moore, *A Digest of International Law* (Washington, D.C.: Government Printing Office, 1906; 8 vols.), VI, 462.

59. Quoted in Martínez-Fernández, *Torn Between Empires*, p. 38.

60. Quoted in Amos A. Ettinger, *The Mission to Spain of Pierre Soulé* (New Haven: Yale University Press, 1932), p. 378.

61. Quoted in Martínez-Fernández, *Torn Between Empires*, p. 37

62. Quoted in Henry B. Learned, "William Learned Marcy," in Samuel Flagg Bemis, ed., *American Secretaries of State and Their Diplomacy* (New York: Cooper Square Publishers, 1963; 18 vols.), VI, 193.

63. Quoted in Jean H. Baker, *James Buchanan* (New York: Times Books, 2004), p. 65; quoted in Don E. Fehrenbacher, *The Slaveholding Republic* (New York: Oxford University Press, 2001), p. 129.

64. William Marcy quoted in Sean Wilentz, *The Rise of American Democracy* (New York: Norton, 2005), p. 671.

65. G. B. Henderson, "Southern Designs on Cuba, 1854–1857," *Journal of Southern History, V* (Aug. 1939), 374.

66. Quoted in Philip S. Klein, *President James Buchanan* (University Park: Penn State University Press, 1962), p. 324.

67. Quoted in Graebner, *Manifest Destiny*, p. 298.

68. Quoted in Robert David Johnson, *The Peace Progressives and American Foreign Relations* (Cambridge: Harvard University Press, 1995), p. 23.

69. Quoted in Donald Kagan, *Dangerous Nation* (New York: Knopf, 2006), p. 244.

70. Quoted in Richard Van Alstyne, *The Rising American Empire* (New York: Norton, 1974 [1960]), p. 175.

71. Quoted in Michael A. Morrison, *Slavery and the American West* (Chapel Hill: University of North Carolina Press, 1997), p. 15.

72. Quoted in Warren I. Cohen, *America's Response to China* (New York: Wiley, 1990; 3rd ed.), p. 19.

73. Quoted in Shunsuke Kamei, "The Sacred Land of Liberty," in Akira Iriye, ed., *Mutual Images* (Cambridge: Harvard University Press, 1975), p. 55; quoted in Arrell M. Gibson, *Yankees in Paradise* (Albuquerque: University of New Mexico Press, 1993), p. 33.

74. Quoted in Arthur Walworth, *Black Ships off Japan* (New York: Knopf, 1946), p. 71.

75. Francis L. Hawks, ed., *Narrative of the Expedition of an American Squadron to the China Seas and Japan* (Washington, D.C.: Senate Printer, 1856; 3 vols.), I, 256–257, 261, 263.

76. Michael Adas, *Dominance by Design* (Cambridge: Harvard University Press, 2006), p. 15.

77. Quoted in John Schroeder, *Shaping a Maritime Empire* (Westport, Conn.: Greenwood, 1985), pp. 158–159.

78. Quoted in Kenneth J. Hagan, *This People's Navy* (New York: Free Press, 1991), p. 149.

79. Charles E. Neu, *The Troubled Encounter* (New York: Wiley, 1975), p. 9.

80. Quoted in Joseph M. Henning, *Outposts of Civilization* (New York: New York University Press, 2000), p. 22.

81. Quoted in Philip Guedalla, ed., *Gladstone and Palmerston* (New York: Kraus Reprint, 1971 [1928]), p. 208.

82. Bayard Taylor quoted in Greenberg, *Manifest Manhood*, p. 85

83. U.S. Senate, Executive Doc. 27 (1853), 32 Cong., 2 Sess., p. 30.

84. Quoted in Wilbur D. Jones, *The American Problem in British Diplomacy, 1841–1861* (Athens: University of Georgia Press, 1974), p. 75.

85. Hunter Miller, ed., *Treaties and Other International Acts of the United States of America* (Washington D.C.: Government Printing Office, 1931–1948; 8 vols.), V, 672.

86. Quoted in Kenneth Bourne, *Britain and the Balance of Power in North America, 1815–1908* (London: Longmans, Green, 1967), p. 182.

87. Quoted in Alexander DeConde, *Presidential Machismo* (Boston: Northeastern University Press, 2000), p. 56.

88. Quoted in F. M. Binder, "James Buchanan and the Earl of Clarendon," *Diplomacy & Statecraft, VI* (July 1995), 333.

89. Quoted *ibid.*, p. 189.

90. Quoted in Margaret O. W. Oliphant, *Memoir of the Life of Laurence Oliphant and of Alice Oliphant, His Wife* (Edinburgh: Blackwood, 1891; 2 vols.), I, 120.

91. Quoted in Reginald C. Stuart, *United States Expansionism and British North America, 1775–1871* (Chapel Hill: University of North Carolina Press, 1988), p. 209.

92. Quoted in Michael H. Hunt, *The American Ascendancy* (Chapel Hill: University of North Carolina Press. 2007), p. 19.

93. Quoted in Paul A. Varg, *United States Foreign Relations 1820–1860* (East Lansing: Michigan State University Press, 1979), p. 233.

94. Jay Monaghan, *Diplomat in Carpet Slippers* (Indianapolis: Charter, 1945), p. 58.

95. Quoted in John G. Nicolay and John Hay, *Abraham Lincoln* (New York: Century, 1890; 10 vols.), III, 445–449.

96. Quoted in Monaghan, *Diplomat in Carpet Slippers*, p. 82.

97. Quoted in Jones, *American Problem*, pp. 199–200.

98. James M. McPherson, "American Victory, American Defeat," in Gabor S. Boritt, ed., *Why the Confederacy Lost* (New York: Oxford University Press, 1992), p. 21.

99. Quoted in Loch K. Johnson, *Seven Sins of American Foreign Policy* (New York: Pearson Longman, 2007), p. 18.

100. Quoted in David G. Surdam, *Northern Naval Superiority and the Economics of the American Civil War* (Columbia: University of South Carolina Press, 2000), p. 198.

101. *Ibid.*, p. 100.

102. Worthington C. Ford, ed., *Letters of Henry Adams* (Boston: Houghton Mifflin, 1930–1938; 2 vols.), I, 92.

103. Quoted in Allan Nevins, *The War for the Union* (New York: Charles Scribner's Sons, 1959–1971; 4 vols.), I, 392.

104. Quoted in R. J. M. Blackett, *Divided Hearts* (Baton Rouge: Louisiana State University Press, 2001), pp. 21–22.

105. Quoted in David P. Crook, *The North, the South, and the Powers* (New York: Wiley, 1974), pp. 133–134.

106. Quoted *ibid.*, pp. 147, 140.

107. James J. Barnes and Patience Barnes, eds., *Private and Confidential* (Selinsgrove, Pa: Susquehanna University Press, 1993), p. 274.

108. Quoted in David H. Donald, *Lincoln* (New York: Simon & Schuster, 1995), p. 323.

109. Gordon H. Warren, *Fountain of Discontent* (Boston: Northeastern University Press, 1981), p. 184.

110. Quoted in Thomas Schoonover, ed., *A Mexican View of America in the 1860s* (Rutherford, N. J.: Fairleigh Dickinson University Press, 1991), p. 91.

111. Quoted in Crook, *North, South, and Powers*, pp. 93, 184.

112. Napoleon III quoted in Thomas Schoonover, *Uncle Sam's War of 1898 and the Origins of Globalism* (Lexington: University Press of Kentucky, 2003), p. 27.

113. Quoted in Philip S. Paludan, *"A People's Contest"* (New York: Harper and Row, 1988), p. 275.

114. Thomas D. Schoonover, *The United States in Central America* (Durham, N.C.: Duke University Press, 1991), p. 26.

115. Quoted in Emory M. Thomas, *The Confederate Nation, 1861–1865* (New York: Harper and Row, 1979), p. 179.

116. Quoted in Howard Jones, *Abraham Lincoln and a New Birth of Freedom* (Lincoln: University of Nebraska Press, 1999), p. 122.

117. Quoted in Normal Saul, *Distant Friends* (Lawrence: University Press of Kansas, 1991), p. 333.

118. Quoted in Norman A. Graebner, "European Interventionism and the Crisis of 1862," *Journal of the Illinois State Historical Society, LXIX* (February 1976), 43.

119. Quoted in Jones, *Lincoln*, p. 56.

120. William Stuart quoted in Howard Jones, "Lincoln and the Death of Slavery," in J. Garry Clifford and Theodore A. Wilson, eds., *Presidents, Diplomats, and Other Mortals* (Columbia: University Press of Missouri, 2007), p. 24.

121. Quoted in David Mayers, *Dissenting Voices in America's Rise to Power* (New York: Cambridge University Press, 2007), p. 141.

122. James Spence quoted in Robert E. Bonner, "Slavery, Confederate Diplomacy, and the Racialist Mission of Henry Hotze," *Civil War Diplomacy, LI* (September 2005), 296.

123. Quoted in Monaghan, *Diplomat in Carpet Slippers*, p. 328.

124. Quoted in Frank J. Merli, *Great Britain and the Confederate Navy* (Bloomington: Indiana University Press, 1970), p. 201.

125. Quoted in Frank L. Owsley and Harriet C. Owsley, *King Cotton Diplomacy*, rev. ed. (Chicago: University of Chicago Press, 1959), p. 402.

126. Quoted in Robert Ivanov, "Russian Warships in North America," *International Affairs*, August 1988, p. 138.

127. Quoted in Howard K. Beale, ed., *Diary of Gideon Welles* (New York: Norton, 1960; 3 vols.), *I*, 484.

128. Quoted in David Reynolds, *Britannia Overruled* (New York: Longman, 2000), p. 19.

129. Quoted in James M. McPherson, "The Whole Family of Man," in Robert E. May, ed., *The Union, the Confederacy, and the Atlantic Rim* (West Lafayette, Ind.: Purdue University Press, 1996), p. 46.

130. Quoted in Azza Salama Layton, *International Politics and Civil Rights in the United States, 1941–1960* (New York: Cambridge University Press, 2000), p. 33.

131. James M. McPherson, *The Battle Cry of Freedom* (New York: Ballantine, 1989), p. 859.

132. William Earl Weeks, "American Nationalism, American Imperialism," *Journal of the Early Republic, XIV* (Winter 1994), 493.

133. Robert E. May, "Introduction," in May, *The Union*, p. 10.

CHAPTER 5

Establishing Regional Hegemony and Global Power, 1865–1895

RED HOT REPUBLICANS ON THE DEMOCRATIC GRIDIRON.

'THE SAN DOMINGO WAR DANCE'

"The San Domingo War Dance." This political cartoon by the artist John Cameron attacks several Republicans critics who opposed a U.S. treaty to annex the Dominican Republic in 1869–1870. At the left the Devil (only his horns, tail, and cloven hoof appear) roasts six Republicans on a gridiron as two black men watch from a ledge at right. Missouri senator Carl Schurz chortles: "I am loud on San Domingo; And I can't be stopped by jingo!" In the middle Senator Charles Sumner invites the two blacks to "jump right on the Gridiron … while it's hot and lively," implying that the Dominican Republic might become a hellish refuge for freed slaves. On the right, the editor Horace Greeley, who ran for president in 1872 as an independent Liberal Republican with Democratic support, claps his hands and sings: "Anything to get office." Such caricatures exposed the racism that accompanied both the Grant administration's failed effort to acquire this strategically important Caribbean country and much opposition to U.S. imperialism itself. (Library of Congress)

◆ *The Foiled Grab of the Dominican Republic, 1869–1870*

PRESIDENT ULYSSES S. GRANT enthused over his pet project as he visited the elegant brick home of the chair of the Senate Foreign Relations Committee, Charles Sumner. The flattery of senatorial egos sometimes brought fruitful results, and in this case Grant sought a two-thirds vote. On that evening of January 2, 1870, in Washington, Sumner was entertaining two politicos when Grant appeared, uninvited and unexpected. Awkward moments passed before the president revealed his mission. Would the Massachusetts senator support an annexation treaty for the Dominican Republic? Grant only briefly sketched his case for this imperialistic scheme. "Mr. President," said Sumner, "I am an Administration man, and whatever you will do will always find in me the most careful and candid consideration."[1] The president left, satisfied that this polite remark signaled senatorial backing for the project. A Dominican land grab seemed imminent—or so Grant thought.

The Dominican Republic, which shared the island of Hispaniola with Haiti, had a stormy history. Formerly part of both the French and the Spanish empires, the Dominicans declared independence from Spain in 1821 only to be occupied by Haiti from 1822 to 1844. *República Dominicana* then won its independence, but from 1861 to 1865 Spain reestablished rule over the strife-torn nation. Often known at the time by the name of its capital, Santo Domingo, the Dominican Republic suffered from misrule. Dominican president Buenaventura Báez, "an active intriguer of sinister talents," seemed eager to sell his country.[2]

Described by Grant as "one of the richest territories under the sun," the Dominican Republic had long held the eye of U.S. expansionists.[3] The U.S. Navy coveted the harbor at Samaná Bay, a choice strategic site in the Caribbean. The country's raw materials, especially timber and minerals, attracted foreign entrepreneurs; others thought of Santo Domingo as a potential sanitarium for isthmian canal workers stricken with yellow fever. Yet, as expansionists warned, Europeans might try to thwart the "inevitable destiny" that "territorial fruits" would gravitate to the United States.[4]

In July 1869, Grant's personal secretary, General Orville Babcock, had visited this "Gibraltar of the New World." Later exposed as a member of the Whiskey Ring, which defrauded the U.S. Treasury of millions of dollars, Babcock was also seeking personal profit. He befriended William and Jane Storm Cazneau and Joseph Fabens, American speculators and sometime diplomatic agents who owned key Dominican mines, banks, and port facilities, including the frontage to Samaná Bay. The trio also represented a steamship company that sought traffic between New York and the island. With the Cazneaus and Fabens in the wings, and warning that any attack "upon Dominicans ... will be considered an act of hostility to the Flag of the United States," Babcock and Báez struck a deal in two treaties signed on November 29, 1869.[5] In the first, the United States agreed to annex the Dominican Republic and assume its national debt of $1.5 million. The second treaty promised that if the U.S. Senate refused to take all of the country, Washington could buy Samaná Bay for $2 million.

Ulysses S. Grant (1822–1885). Graduate of the U.S. Military Academy, soldier in the War with Mexico, and Civil War general before becoming president, Grant failed to annex the Dominican Republic. The historian William J. Nelson calls Grant "a North American *caudillo* trapped in a political system that demanded alternative forms of persuasion." (Library of Congress)

Extolling the Dominican Republic as an asylum "to sustain the entire colored population of the United States, should it choose to emigrate," Grant lobbied hard for annexation.[6] His visit to Sumner's house was a calculated step to build support. Yet the independent-minded Sumner remained noncommittal for months. The more Sumner and his colleagues learned, the more they recoiled from the untidy affair. When the U.S. Navy intervened to prevent rebels from toppling Báez, Republican Senator Carl Schurz of Missouri claimed that Grant had usurped "the warmaking power of Congress."[7] Annexation, Schurz argued, "would put us on the high road to military rule" and result in "rapacity, extortion, plunder, oppression, and tyranny ... most destructive of republican" principles.[8] Babcock, moreover, had acted as a presidential agent, not as an accredited diplomat. Along with Fabens and the Cazneaus, he saw a lucrative opportunity and had enthralled the gullible Grant with a best-case Dominican scenario. Moreover, Haiti seemed poised to join Báez's opponents and invade Santo Domingo, especially when Grant talked loosely about purchasing "that island."[9] Sumner grumbled about these unsavory facts. Other skeptics sniffed another scandal like that which had tarnished the Alaska purchase in 1867.

Grant redoubled his efforts. "Can anyone who voted $7,200,000 for the icebergs of [Alaska]" reject "so valuable a gift," he asked?[10] The secretary of state, Hamilton Fish, threatened to quit, but a sense of loyalty and Grant's personal appeal kept him at his post. Fish opposed annexation but favored some form of a "protectorate." He could not persuade the stubborn president, who seemed bent on total victory or total defeat. On March 15, 1870, the Foreign Relations Committee, by a 5 to 2 vote, with Sumner in the lead, disapproved the treaty. Days later, Sumner disparaged annexation but favored a "free confederacy" in the West Indies where the "black race should predominate" under U.S. protection.[11]

Annexationists countered that the absorption of Baez's domain would ensure a steady flow of raw materials to the United States. Displaying pieces of Dominican hemp, two senators performed an impromptu tug-of-war to demonstrate the fiber's strength. Another predicted that the spindles of New England textile mills would whirl once the Dominicans began to buy American cotton goods. Anti-imperialists retorted that the Dominican populace consisted of two-thirds "native African" and one-third "Spanish Creole," a mixture "still more barbaric and savage than the pure African"; that annexation would spur the building of a larger navy, which would in turn entangle the United States in foreign troubles; that Americans were acting too much like colonizing Europeans; and that Congress had a constitutional duty to check such overweening presidential schemes.[12]

To regain the offensive, Grant on May 31 sent a special message to Congress extolling the virtues of the tiny island nation. It read like an expansionist's shopping list: raw materials, excellent harbors, a naval base, national security, a market for American products, and a site from which to help settle the anti-Spanish revolution raging in Cuba. Without evidence, the president claimed that "a first class European power stands ready now to offer $2,000,000 for Samaná Bay," thus violating the Monroe Doctrine.[13] He even reported the result of a farcical plebiscite in which the Dominicans registered their support for selling themselves to the United States by the rigged vote of 15,169 to 11.

Personal feuding complicated this issue. The plainspoken Grant nurtured an almost visceral loathing for the urbane Sumner. Unenthusiastic about Grant's nomination in 1868, Sumner had opposed some of the president's appointees and belonged to the radical wing of the Republican party—a faction to which Grant never warmed. Grant also felt betrayed, remembering that night in January when "puffed up" Sumner had apparently given his pledge of support.[14] Stung by Sumner's charges of corruption within the administration, Babcock denounced the senator as a "liar and coward" and "poor *sexless* fool."[15] Sumner, for his part, had little respect for the intellectually and culturally inferior Grant and probably felt pique at not having been named secretary of state. Sumner's explosive temper, florid rhetoric, and intellectual certitude sparked obstinacy, anger, and contempt in Grant. The editor E. L. Godkin of *The Nation* remarked that Sumner "works his adjectives so hard that if they ever catch him alone, they will murder him."[16] The Dominican treaty brought these personal antagonisms and different styles to the forefront.

In June, the Senate voted 28 to 28 on the treaty, well short of the two-thirds vote required for approval. "I will not allow Mr. Sumner to ride over me," Grant fumed.[17] The president and loyal Republicans vowed to strip Sumner of his leadership of the Foreign Relations Committee. Sumner lost support among his colleagues when he refused even to approve a commission to study Dominican annexation. The senator denounced it as a trick, a "dance of blood," in his dramatic "Naboth's Vineyard" speech (referring to the biblical story of King Ahab, who coveted his neighbor's vineyard). Sumner scorned the Cazneaus and Fabens as "political jockeys" who had "seduced" Babcock. Santo Domingo, he insisted, belonged to the "colored" Dominicans and "our duty is as plain as the Ten Commandments. … [T]heir independence is as sacred to them as ours is to us."[18]

The Senate nonetheless voted 32 to 9 to establish the commission (it issued a favorable report in early 1871). Many senators voted aye not because they supported annexation but because the commission provided a face-saving device for Grant and a rebuke to the carping Sumner. In March 1871, the Republican caucus voted 26 to 21 to remove Sumner altogether from the Foreign Relations Committee. Sumner, ill and irascible, still savored his victory over the Dominican land-grab scheme.

Charles Sumner (1811–1874). Harvard graduate, lawyer, abolitionist, critic of the War with Mexico, senator from Massachusetts, and chair of the Foreign Relations Committee (1861–1871), the strong-willed Sumner blocked attempts to annex the Dominican Republic and harassed England over the *Alabama* claims. In opposing annexation, Sumner complained that President Grant should have spent half "the time, money, zeal, will," and personal effort in protecting southern blacks from the Ku Klux Klan as he did in seeking to "obtain half an island in the Caribbean." (Library of Congress)

The Culture of Expansionism and Imperialism

The foiled grab at Santo Domingo, coming so soon after the Civil War, suggests that the sectional conflict only briefly interrupted the continuity of expansion. To be sure, most Americans in the late 1860s were not thinking about the Caribbean or other foreign-policy issues, preoccupied as they were with healing the wounds of war, reconstructing a fractured nation, and settling the trans-Mississippi West. And, although the soaring oratory of Manifest Destiny sounded again through the late nineteenth century, the United States lacked well-defined, sustained foreign "policies" and "seemed strangely quiescent" about overseas expansion in an era of alleged "imperial understretch."[19] As the Dominican episode illustrates, domestic politics, personal whims and antagonisms, and tensions between the executive and legislative branches could wreck plans. Congressional dominance over the executive branch resulted in a "strong nation, weak state" until the 1880s.[20] Fierce anti-imperialist sentiment also warned that overseas empire would undermine institutions at home, invite perpetual war, and violate such honored traditions as self-determination. Unable to work its will in some parts of the world, U.S. power largely confined itself to the Western Hemisphere and parts of the Pacific.

Still, the direction of U.S. foreign policy after the Civil War quickly became unmistakable: Americans intended to exert their influence beyond the continental United States. The more concerted, less restrained, and less erratic foreign policy that emerged in the 1890s consummated an imperial trend evident intermittently but persistently since the 1860s—"an accumulation of calculated decisions."[21] Before the Civil War, American expansion had both commercial and territorial goals. The commercial expansion became global and largely maritime; the territorial expansion was regional and limited to areas contiguous to the United States (see Chapters 3 and 4). After the Civil War, as Secretary of State James G. Blaine put it, the United States showed more interest in the annexation of trade than in the annexation of territory. Americans did seek and take a few territories in the 1865–1895 period, of course—Alaska and Midway. Unlike the pre–Civil War additions, these annexed territories were noncontiguous to the United States, and they remained in a long-term colonial status.

Most Americans applauded economic expansion and they supported westward territorial grabs that displaced and subjugated Native Americans. Yet many felt uneasy with imperialism—the imposition of control over other peoples, denying them the freedom to make their own choices, undermining their sovereignty—when it was directed overseas rather than contiguously. The critical factor in empire-building was power—the power to make others move the way the imperial state dictated. Imperialism took several forms, both formal (annexation, colonialism, or military occupation) and informal (the threat of intervention or economic or political manipulation). Economic domination of a country through trade and investment constituted informal imperialism, even though the United States did not officially annex the territory and make it a colony. The United States never formally acquired the Dominican Republic but by the early twentieth century, after years of private American economic expansion into the island, it had become subservient to the United States and hence part of the informal U.S. empire. Expansionism always held imperialism latent within it, insofar as the outward movement of goods, dollars, ships, people, and ideas always had the potential to shape and condition attitudes and practices of faraway peoples and cultures.

An intertwined set of ideas infused post–Civil War expansion: nationalism, capitalism, exceptionalism, Social Darwinism, paternalism, and the categorization of overseas peoples in dismissive age-, race-, and gender-based language. Fear and prejudice also influenced American attitudes toward the world and "the Other"—fear of revolutionary disorder, fear of economic depression, fear of racial and ethnic mixing, fear of women's emancipation, fear of a closed frontier, fear of declining international stature. To assuage these fears and promote American values, it seemed necessary to remake other societies in the image of the United States.

A reinvigorated nationalism fueled the expansionist impulse. After the Civil War, national leaders sought to narrow sectional divisions. The 1876 centennial celebration emphasized national unity. Confederate and Union soldiers met on former battlefields to exchange flags. New patriotic associations emerged to champion nationalism: Colonial Dames of America (1890), Daughters of the American Revolution (1890), and Society of Colonial Wars (1893). World's fairs such as Chicago's Columbian Exposition of 1893 aimed to "teach ... to the world, what a young republic ... has done in its brief past, is doing in the present, and hopes to do in the greater future for its people and for mankind."[22] Americans thought themselves a special people, even God-favored, whose industrial power would soon surpass Great Britain's. As emissaries of Christ, representatives of the Young Women's Christian Association helped indigenous women in China and India, for example, by trying to end such practices as the crippling binding of feet, child marriage, and suttee (widow immolation). Reformers in the Women's Christian Temperance Union (WCTU) spread the gospel in "heathen" lands and competed against other Anglo-Saxons who exported another "kind of American dream"—alcoholic beverages.[23]

The prevalence of Social Darwinist thought—that by the natural order of things some people were meant to survive and dominate and others to fail—encouraged notions of racial and national superiority. In their sense of racial hierarchy, Americans placed "uncivilized" people of black color and Indians at the bottom. As the Reverend Josiah Strong put it, "to be a Christian and an Anglo-Saxon and an American ... is to stand at the very mountaintop of privilege."[24] Americans ranked European peoples slightly lower on the ladder—"aggressive" Germans followed by "peasant" Slavs, "sentimental" French and Italians, and "Shylock" Jews. Once viewed as civilized, Russia allegedly regressed into a land of "dark people" as it expanded eastward, persecuted Jews, and turned Siberia into "a vast prison."[25] The middle rank comprised Latinos, the Spanish-speaking peoples of Latin America. Often disparaging Latinos as "dagoes" and "half-castes" unable to govern themselves, North American imperialists also portrayed Latin Americans as distressed damsels in need of manly rescue, as sister republics amenable to avuncular advice, and as squabbling children requiring paternalistic supervision. After a visit to Honduras, the future playwright Eugene O'Neil maligned Central Americans as "the lowest ignorant bunch of brainless bipeds that ever polluted a land or retarded its future."[26] Also in middle rank stood the peoples of East Asia, the "Orientals" or "Mongolians" whom Americans perceived as crafty, inscrutable, somnolent, and immoral, albeit in the case of the Japanese ("the most un-Mongolian people in Asia") sometimes capable of regeneration with outside tutelage.[27]

A masculine ethos also shaped American conceptions of foreigners. Words such as "manliness" and "weakling" coursed through the language of American leaders. The naval historian Theodore Roosevelt often described other nations as weak and effeminate—unable, in contrast to a virile Uncle Sam, to cope with the imperatives of world politics. Roosevelt also denounced "prattlers who sit home in peace," and he railed against "over-sentimentality, over-softness, ... wishiness and mushiness."[28] The gendered imagery prevalent in U.S. foreign relations joined racist thinking to place women, people of color, and impoverished nations lowest in the power hierarchy, rationalizing their dependent status and offering a tautological justification for U.S. efforts to exert control.

The magazine *National Geographic,* which first appeared in 1888, chronicled with photographs America's growing overseas interests. The editors chose pictures that

"The Stride of a Century."   This Currier & Ives print captured the centennial spirit of 1876, which regenerated American nationalism and a celebration of the "progress" of the United States. (Library of Congress)

underscored American ethnocentric notions about foreigners. Even when smiling faces predominated, the images reflected were those of presumably strange, exotic, premodern people who had not yet become "Western." Emphasizing this perspective, *National Geographic* regularly carried photographs of bare-breasted women. Fairs, too, stereotyped other peoples as falling short of "civilized." Not only did fair managers tout the technological wonders of "Western civilization," but they also put people of color on display in the "freaks" or "midway" sections. Anthropologists at the New Orleans fair of 1884 displayed the smaller skulls of "primitive races" next to larger skulls of "more advanced races," thus reinforcing the need for "nurturing and protection" by Anglo-Saxon civilization.[29] At the 1895 Atlanta and 1897 Nashville fairs, exhibits of Cubans and Mexicans in native village settings stood next to bearded women and the world's fattest man.

Religious zeal added impetus to imperialist attitudes. "A hundred thousand heathen a day are dying without hope because we are not there teaching the Gospel to them," exhorted the traveling secretary of the Student Volunteer Movement, founded by college students in the 1880s.[30] However benevolent their intentions, missionaries often carried chauvinistic prejudices abroad, as indicated by one missionary "Mother Goose" rhyme: "Ten little heathen standing in a line;/One went to mission school, then there were but nine. … /Three little heathen didn't know what to do;/One learned our language, then there were two./Two little heathen couldn't have any fun/One gave up idols, then there was but one./One little heathen standing all alone;/He learned to love our flag, then there were none."[31] American tourists,

"The Mexican Wild Man."   Among the exhibits at American fairs were "freak shows," where people of color from abroad were displayed in exaggerated ways to suggest exotic, untamed, and uncivilized characteristics. Sometimes whites dressed up in animal skins as "wild men" and "wild women." Here, George Stall does so in the early 1890s. Such images reflected pejorative American views of foreign peoples of color and helped condition the environment in which U.S. leaders made imperial decisions. In his book on U.S. relations with Latin America, *Beneath the United States* (1998), the scholar Lars Schoultz argues that North American perceptions of Latin Americans as fundamentally inferior and underdeveloped consistently drove U.S. policy towards a "civilizing mission." (Photo by Charles Eisenmann, Becker Collection, Syracuse University Library)

including Ulysses S. Grant, George B. McClellan, and William H. Seward visited the Holy Land and other Middle East countries in unprecedented numbers after the Civil War. By the 1870s Bedouin guides at the Great Pyramids were reportedly speaking English with American accents and calling their donkeys "Yankee Doodle."[32]

The multiple arguments for expansion and empire seemed all the more urgent when Americans anticipated the closing of the frontier at home. In 1893 Professor Frederick Jackson Turner postulated his thesis that an ever-expanding continental frontier had shaped the American character. With its democratic safety-valve gone, Turner thought Americans needed a new frontier marked by "an interoceanic canal, … a revival of our power upon the seas, and … the extension of American influence to outlying islands and adjoining countries."[33] Similarly, the novelist Frank Norris likened America without a frontier to "the boy shut indoors who finds his scope circumscribed and fills the whole place with the racket of his activity."[34]

The dying frontier did regenerate itself, figuratively speaking, in Europe when Colonel William F. ("Buffalo Bill") Cody toured for five money-making years with his famed Wild West Show to England, France, Germany, Spain, Italy, and Austria-Hungary, beginning in 1887. Replete with bronco-riding, steer-roping, trick shooting, and a reenactment of General Custer's Last Stand, the stylized pageant celebrated the defeat of the primitives and "glorified the march of civilization across the American landscape" wherein the dignified, buckskin-clad Cody comported himself like "a knight of the plains" with "a chivalric past."[35] The Wild West Show also became a popular fixture in the United States.

Of course, the "Anglo-centered" Turner thesis that American distinctiveness derived from exploiting "virgin soil" in "unoccupied territory" rhetorically relegated Native Americans "to the edge of significance."[36] So too did official policy work to remove Indians in the post–Civil War era, pushing tribes into smaller reservations, taking lands for the railroad, killing buffalo, fighting military campaigns against the Sioux, Nez Percé, and Utes in the 1870s and against the Apache a decade later, culminating in the massacre of the Lakota Sioux at Wounded Knee, South Dakota, in January 1890, when U.S. Army units killed 146 men, women, and children. The Oglala Sioux's defeat of General George A. Custer at the Little Big Horn in Montana in 1876, like temporary Zulu success against British forces in South Africa in 1879, proved to be minor reverses in the inexorable contest between "western powers and less technologically developed peoples."[37] "The white man makes our young men drunk," said one Navaho chief. "He steals away our daughters. ... He is a wolf."[38]

By 1868 the Supreme Court ruled that Congress could override old treaties by passing new statutes without the consent of the Indians. The Dawes Severalty Act of 1887 ended communal ownership of Indian lands and granted land allotments to individual Native American families, promising citizenship to those who accepted allotments. Federal commissions soon forced the sale of unallotted lands at "unconscionable" low prices.[39] Thus did the government pursue a "clear pattern of colonialism toward Native Americans" by the 1890s that set a "precedent for imperialist domination" of Filipinos and other peoples after the Spanish-American-Cuban-Filipino War.[40]

Economic Expansion and Imperial Rivalry

The dynamics of the international system favored the United States. Victorian England, heretofore the dominant power with advantages over its rivals in wealth, production, colonies, and naval strength, started to suffer relative decline. In the 1870s, European imperialists began to carve up Asia and Africa into colonies and exclusive spheres of influence. As one of "the great nations of the world," a senator warned, "the United States must not fall out of the line of march."[41] When the U.S. economy, unburdened by large defense expenditures, surged after the Civil War and passed Britain as the world's foremost industrial power in the early 1890s, it seemed imperative that Washington should compete in what Secretary of State James G. Blaine called "the race for development and empire," or be left behind.[42]

When nationalistic Americans boasted about their country, they especially celebrated its economic achievements. After the Civil War, railroads knit the nation together, creating a coast-to-coast marketplace. Bold entrepreneurs such as John D. Rockefeller and Andrew Carnegie built huge corporations whose assets and incomes dwarfed those of many of the world's nations. In the process of industrialization, inventors such as Thomas Edison and George Westinghouse pioneered whole new enterprises—in their case, electricity. The spread of the telegraph and telephone linked Americans together in a national communications network. Sprawling, busy cities became the centers of rapidly expanding manufacturing production. The federal government, through subsidies, land grants, loans, tariffs, and tax relief, stimulated the growth of American business. Not all went well, of course. Major depressions in 1873–1878 and 1893–1897, the financial insolvency of railroads, farm indebtedness, inhumane working conditions, child labor, political corruption, business abuses necessitating antitrust and regulatory measures, discriminatory wages favoring men over women, and the failure of consumption to keep pace with production in the age of the "robber barons" tarnished the American record. Still, the United States by 1900 had become an economic giant surpassing Great Britain and Germany. Steel production increased from 77,000 tons per year in 1870 to 11,227,000 tons in 1900; wheat and corn output more than doubled in the same period. From the early 1870s to 1900 the gross national product more than doubled.

Foreign trade helped to spur this growth. The United States "feeds and clothes Europe," a French writer observed in 1876: "It feeds us grain and salt and dresses us in cotton; it gives us half the tobacco we need."[43] Exports expanded from $281 million in 1865 to $1.2 billion in 1898. Although exports of manufactured items increased, becoming predominant for the first time in 1913, agricultural goods (cereals, cotton, meat, and dairy products) accounted for about three-quarters of the total in 1870 and about two-thirds in 1900. From 1874 until 1934, with the one exception of 1888, the United States enjoyed a favorable balance of trade (exports exceeded imports).

Growing American production efficiency, a decline in prices that made American goods less expensive in the world market, the high quality of American products, and improvements in transportation (steamships and the Suez Canal) help explain this impressive upturn in foreign trade. In 1866, through the persevering efforts of Cyrus Field, an underwater transatlantic cable linked European and American telegraph networks. James A. Scrymser, backed by J. P. Morgan's capital, connected the U.S. telegraph system with Latin America, first wiring Florida to Havana, Cuba, and then, in 1881, Galveston, Texas, to Mexico City. By 1883 Americans could communicate directly with Brazil; in 1890 Scrymser's lines reached Chile. By hooking into

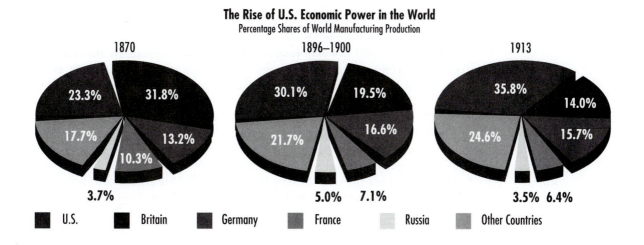

The Rise of U.S. Economic Power in the World
Percentage Shares of World Manufacturing Production

1870 · 1896–1900 · 1913

U.S. · Britain · Germany · France · Russia · Other Countries

British cables, Americans could "talk" with Asian cities as well. Whereas the transfer of information had once taken days and weeks, it could now flow around the world more cheaply and securely in hours. Business leaders, diplomats, naval officers, and journalists worked the new communications system to seize opportunities. Nellie Bly, a reporter for the *New York World,* completed a trip around the world in seventy-two days in early 1890 and showed how much technology had shrunk the globe.

Although exports represented a very small percentage (between 6 and 7 percent) of the gross national product, American prosperity and key segments of the economy came to rely on foreign sales. It became popular to think that surplus production, or the "glut," had to be exported to avert economic calamity at home. "What is to become of this surplus?" asked one member of Congress in the 1880s. Such products "are now far beyond the requirements of our home consumption" so that "we must have foreign markets or none."[44] Otherwise, the economist David A. Wells warned, "we are certain to be smothered in our own grease."[45]

The glut thesis appealed particularly to farmers, for the domestic marketplace could not absorb their bounty. Producers of cotton, tobacco, and wheat counted on foreign markets. Over half of the cotton crop was exported each year, and wheat growers in the period 1873–1882 received about a third of their gross annual income from exports. Wisconsin cheesemakers shipped to Britain; the Swift and Armour meat companies sold refrigerated beef in Europe; and Quaker Oats became an international food. To sell American grain in Asia, James J. Hill of the Great Northern Railroad distributed cookbooks translated into several languages. Even Frank Norris's muckraking novel *The Octopus* (1901) celebrated the American wheat harvests that would "roll like a flood from the Sierras to the Himalayas to feed thousands of scarecrows on the barren plains of India."[46]

John D. Rockefeller's Standard Oil also sold abroad, notably in Germany, England, Cuba, and Mexico. "Even the sacred lamps over the Prophet's tomb at Mecca," one U.S. diplomat bragged in 1879, "are fed with oil from Pennsylvania."[47] Cyrus McCormick of International Harvester sent his "reaper kings" into Russian fields, and by the turn of the century his company's foreign sales accounted for about 20 percent of its business. The same company established "an informal empire" over the henequen fiber market of Yucatan after 1880, controlling 99.8 percent of all production by 1910.[48] Metal-products firms such as National Cash Register and Remington became active globally. Alexander Graham Bell and Thomas Edison collaborated in 1880 to install England's first telephone system. By the turn of the century, 50 percent of America's copper and 15 percent of its iron and steel were sold abroad. U.S. entrepreneurs also planted a huge banana industry—an "empire in green and gold"—in the Caribbean and Central America after the Civil War, culminating in the creation of the United Fruit Company in 1899, whose steamships and railroads soon controlled 90 percent of the banana market in the United States.[49] As the trademark "Made in America" came to signify superior products at affordable prices, Europeans prophesied the "Americanization of the world."[50] French voices complained about inferior "American Bordeaux."[51] One British journalist griped that the average Briton "rises in the morning from his New England sheets," shaves with a "Yankee safety razor, pulls on his Boston boots over his socks from North Carolina, slips his Waltham or Waterbury watch in his pocket," sits at his office on "a Nebraska swivel chair, before a Michigan roll-top desk," and writes letters on a "Syracuse typewriter, signing them with a New York fountain pen."[52] Even Albert G. Spalding's much ballyhooed professional baseball tour of Hawai'i, Australia, Ceylon, Egypt, Italy, France, Britain, and Holland in 1888–1889 was designed to create "a market" for his "sporting goods business [in] that quarter of the globe."[53]

Official Washington subsidized exhibitions in foreign trade fairs and assisted business in other ways to expand abroad. Consular service officers prepared reports on commercial prospects, and naval officers scouted markets and protected merchants. The government provided help in expanding the telegraph, negotiated reciprocity treaties to open trade doors, and kept up the drumbeat of patriotic rhetoric about the wonders of the export market.

Until the 1890s, however, economic expansion derived primarily from the activities of private companies and individuals, not from governmental policies. Washington neglected the merchant marine, letting it decline so that by 1900 American ships carried only 10 percent of U.S. trade. The diplomatic corps and consular service were stained by the spoils system; too many political hacks rather than professionals filled their ranks. The writer Ambrose Bierce quipped that "American diplomats were failed politicians who were finally chosen for office, on condition that they leave the country."[54] Washington also maintained a high-tariff policy, with rates reaching a peak in the 1890 McKinley Tariff (average duties of 49 percent). This exclusionist policy may have slowed the pace of economic expansion by stimulating foreign retaliatory tariffs against American products. The United States could nonetheless successfully pursue protection at home and commercial expansion abroad because England, still the world's leading economic power (or "hegemon"), maintained a liberal trade strategy and welcomed American exports. In effect, Washington was "free riding on free trade."[55]

How significant were foreign commerce and investments (American capital invested abroad equaled $700 million in 1897) to the U.S. economy? The aforementioned statistics tell only part of the story. The rest lies in perception. Prominent Americans *believed* that the economic health of the nation depended on selling their surplus production in foreign markets. During depressions especially, goods stacked up at home could be peddled abroad, thus stimulating the American economy and perhaps even heading off the social and political unrest that feeds on economic crisis. Hypothetically, even if only 1 percent of American goods sold abroad and exports represented only 1 percent of the gross national product, foreign trade would be inescapably intertwined with foreign policy and thus a factor of importance. Anticipating conflicts and wars, the navy's policy board in 1890 concluded: "In the adjustment of our trade with a neighbor we are certain to reach out and obstruct the interest of foreign nations."[56] And even if all the efforts to expand trade delivered minimal results, the quest itself would necessitate naval and diplomatic activity.

Why did American leaders believe foreign trade to be so important? First, exports meant profits. Second, exports might relieve social unrest at home caused by overproduction and unemployment. Third, economic ties could facilitate political influence (as in Hawai'i and Mexico) without the formal necessity of military occupation and management. Fourth, foreign trade, hand in hand with religious missionary work, could promote "civilization" and human uplift. Fifth, economic

Singer Sewing Machine in Zululand.   The Singer Manufacturing Company distributed this promotional postcard at the 1893 Columbian Exposition in Chicago. Three-quarters of all sewing machines sold in world markets were Singers. This machine was sold in South Africa, where, the company advised, the "Zulus are a fine warlike people" moving toward "civilization" with Singer's help. (Wisconsin Historical Society WHi (x3) 48814)

expansion helped spread the American way of life, creating a world more hospitable to Americans. Sixth, foreign trade, if it conquered new markets abroad and helped bring prosperity to the United States, enhanced national pride at a time of intense international rivalry. Foreign trade, then, held an importance beyond what the statistics suggest. It became an intricate part of American "greatness" because leaders believed it vital to the national interest.

Toward Command of the Seas: The New Navy

In the late nineteenth century, a popular doctrine gradually took hold: To protect overseas commerce, deemed vital to America's well-being, the nation had to build a larger navy because the navy acted as "the pioneer of commerce."[57] To fuel and repair ships in distant waters, naval stations and colonies had to be added. To ensure that foreigners did not endanger American merchants, property, investments, and trade, U.S. warships had to go on patrol, ready to use force to protect U.S. interests and prestige in an era of deepening international rivalry. As one naval officer put it bluntly, "The man-of-war precedes the merchantman and impresses rude people."[58] Since the War of 1812, the United States had been stationing warships in Latin America, Africa, and Asia to protect the American merchant marine and merchants. New to the 1880s and 1890s was the shrinking theater of free operations, as European imperialists hastened to seize colonies and close out other foreigners. For the U.S. Navy, then, the next enemy might be an imperial European navy rather than a truculent "mob" in an Asian port. New strategies and technologies became imperative.

By European standards, the American military before the 1890s was small. The army demobilized after the Civil War, shrinking in size to fewer than 30,000 troops, which it then employed against frontier Indians in a strategy of "annihilation."[59]

The navy concentrated on defending the long American coastline from hypothetical enemies and protecting American lives and property abroad. For these tasks, the U.S. military seemed adequate. The European powers, feuding in the Old World, did not threaten America. Even the most bellicose European militarist would have been deterred by the difficulties of transporting forces across the Atlantic and supplying them in the United States. On distant station the navy's archaic sailing vessels could punish unarmed peoples, chase pirates, protect missionaries and traders, and chart unexplored regions. Without faraway fueling stations for taking on coal, a navy of long-range, steam-driven, blue-water vessels did not make much sense. The brown-water ships designed for coastal defense and riverine operations seemed adequate.

In the 1880s and 1890s, as U.S. expansionism and imperialism accelerated and overseas commitments increased, young naval officers joined politicians, shipbuilders, armaments manufacturers, and commercial expansionists to lobby for a new fleet to replace the "alphabet of floating wash tubs," as one reformer sarcastically called them.[60] The U.S. Navy had not kept pace with European technological advances in hulls, engines, and guns. Dominated by the political spoils system, government-operated shipyards had become corrupt and inefficient. Naval leaders lobbied for higher appropriations to launch significant naval improvements. As the Europeans built fast, heavily armed, well-armored battleships, America's slower, wooden cruisers and gunboats became obsolete—mere floating museums, snickered European officers. Because foreign-born sailors comprised more than half of the navy's enlisted personnel in the 1870s, recruiters increasingly sought "boys who … have no old world allegiance or affiliations. We want the brawn of Montana, the fire of the South and the daring of the Pacific slope."[61]

Rear Admiral Stephen B. Luce, the so-called father of the modern U.S. Navy, became an effective naval politician. He founded the Naval War College in 1884, instilled greater professionalism, and encouraged officers such as Captain Alfred T. Mahan to disseminate their ideas. Mahan earned an international reputation for popularizing the relationship between a navy and expansion. An instructor at the Naval War College, Mahan published his lectures in 1890 as *The Influence of Sea Power upon History.* British, German, and Japanese leaders read the book, but, most importantly, it became a treasured volume in the libraries of American imperialists such as Henry Cabot Lodge and Theodore Roosevelt. A nation's greatness depended on its sea power, Mahan argued. Victory in war and a vigorous foreign trade, two measurements of greatness, depended on an efficient and strong navy. Ships of war, in turn, required fueling stations or "resting places" and colonies, which would further enhance foreign commerce and national power.[62]

During the 1880s, the navy evolved from sail-driven and wooden-hull ships to steam-powered and steel-clad vessels. Its mission decidedly shifted from coastal defense to command of the seas. In 1883 Congress funded the *Atlanta, Boston,* and *Chicago*—steel-hull, steam-powered cruisers. Between 1884 and 1889, money was appropriated for thirty more vessels, including the battleship *Maine*. With Secretary of the Navy Benjamin F. Tracy (1889–1893) urging seagoing battleships for this "New Navy," the fast armor-plated *Oregon, Indiana, Massachusetts,* and *Iowa* soon joined the fleet bearing the names of states to rally public support for naval expansion. The sleek battleship designs featuring modern armored turrets and jutting guns so

Alfred Thayer Mahan (1840–1914). A graduate of the U.S. Naval Academy, this bookish officer, historian, and strategist articulated the necessity for overseas expansion and a large navy. He became world famous for his writings. Oxford and Cambridge universities gave him honorary degrees, and German and Japanese leaders read his many books and articles. Mahan believed that Americans could defend against foreign dangers by honing their "masculine combative virtues." (*American Review of Reviews,* 1894)

impressed the editors of *Scientific American* that they reproduced them in seventeen cover engravings in 1887, prompting widespread fits of "battleship envy."[63] In the process, the government, military, and industry forged a partnership that would grow through the twentieth century.

By 1893 the U.S. Navy ranked seventh in the world. Anti-imperialists presciently warned that this large fleet would propel Americans into a larger empire. "New Navy" ships in fact did figure in the imperialist ventures of the 1890s: the *Boston* and its crew helped attach Hawai'i to the United States; the destruction of the *Maine* in the harbor of Havana accelerated the United States toward war with Spain; the 14,000-mile race of the battleship *Oregon* from the Pacific coast to Cuba in 1898 fired a national desire for a canal across Central America; and the cruiser *Olympia* carried Commodore George Dewey into Manila Bay to help seize the Philippines from Spain. According to one French observer, now that Americans had "an imposing and costly fleet," they would not likely use the new armada "for simple pleasure cruises."[64]

Secretary William H. Seward Projects the Future

As secretary of state from 1861 to 1869, William Henry Seward personally connected prewar and postwar expansionism. Until 1865 he had to prevent European powers from interfering in the Civil War (see Chapter 4). But after the war, this exuberant, confident Republican leader avidly redirected foreign policy toward his vision of a coordinated empire tied together by superior U.S. institutions and commerce. Latin America, the Pacific islands, Asia, and Canada, Seward prophesied, would eventually gravitate toward the United States because of the contagion of American greatness and because of some immeasurable will of God. He believed that "commerce has largely taken the place of war" and that trade would produce "influence" and bind distant areas together.[65] Surplus American meats, cereals, and cotton goods would flow to overseas markets, accompanied by "the Bible, the Printing Press, the Ballot Box, and the Steam Engine," Seward boasted.[66] His blueprint for empire stressed improved foreign trade, immigration to provide cheap labor for productive American factories, high tariffs for the protection of American industry, liberal federal land policies to open the American West to economic development, globe-circling telegraph systems, transcontinental railroads, a Central American canal, and the annexation of noncontiguous territories.

In 1865 Seward began negotiations with Denmark to purchase the Danish West Indies (Virgin Islands), whose excellent harbors offered potential naval stations for defending the Caribbean and Gulf of Mexico. Two years later the islanders voted for American annexation. Seward raised his offer to $7.5 million for two of the islands, St. Thomas and St. John, but a combination of bad weather and heated politics undercut the treaty Seward signed with Copenhagen in October 1867. When a hurricane and tidal wave wracked St. Thomas, critics resurrected a concise formula: "No annexation in the tropics."[67] The accord also reached the Senate at the very time that President Andrew Johnson was facing impeachment. Incoming President Grant shelved the treaty, and the Virgin Islanders had to wait until 1917 for American overlordship.

Seward also wanted a piece of the Dominican Republic. In 1866 he offered $2 million for Samaná Bay, but the proposed deal remained open when he left office in 1869. Seward's vision encompassed Haiti (which he thought of annexing outright), some small Spanish, French, and Dutch islands in the Caribbean, revolution-torn Cuba, Iceland and Greenland (both of which he hoped to buy), Honduras's Tigre Island, and Hawai'i, fast becoming Americanized as more sugar was planted and more churches were built. Seward's imperialist ambitions went unfulfilled in his day, except for two real estate transactions. One minor acquisition occurred in August 1867 when Captain William Reynolds of the U.S.S. *Lackawanna* formally claimed the Midway Islands, some 1,000 miles northwest of the main islands of Hawai'i. Most Americans never heard again about these tiny imperial outposts until the great American-Japanese naval battle there in 1942.

More significant and controversial was Seward's purchase of Alaska. Russia had put Alaska up for sale because it no longer remained profitable as colonial property, and because the tsar feared that Britain would seize the undefended territory in a future war. Russia also seemed resigned to the inevitable. "The ultimate rule of the United States over the whole of America is so natural," the governor of eastern Siberia told the tsar, "that we must ourselves sooner or later recede."[68] Edouard de Stoeckl, the Russian minister to the United States who negotiated the transfer, later agreed: "In American eyes this continent is their patrimony. Their destiny (manifest destiny as they call it) is to always expand."[69] American fur traders, whalers, and fishermen had been exploiting the area's natural resources for decades. It seemed opportune to cultivate a "friend" and sell the 591,000 square miles (twice the size of Texas) to the United States. Seward moved quickly. "Why wait until tomorrow, Mr. Stoeckl? Let us make the treaty tonight."[70]

Makers of American Foreign Relations, 1865–1895

Presidents	Secretaries of State
Andrew Johnson, 1865–1869	William H. Seward, 1861–1869
Ulysses S. Grant, 1869–1877	Elihu B. Washburne, 1869
	Hamilton Fish, 1869–1877
Rutherford B. Hayes, 1877–1881	William M. Evarts, 1877–1881
James A. Garfield, 1881	James G. Blaine, 1881
Chester A. Arthur, 1881–1885	Frederick T. Freylinghuysen, 1881–1885
Grover Cleveland, 1885–1889	Thomas F. Bayard, 1885–1889
Benjamin Harrison, 1889–1893	James G. Blaine, 1889–1892
	John W. Foster, 1892–1893
Grover Cleveland, 1893–1897	Walter Q. Gresham, 1893–1895
	Richard Olney, 1895–1897

William H. Seward (1801–1872). Once freed from the restraints of the Civil War, Secretary of State Seward vigorously pursued a larger U.S. empire. Asked in 1870 about his greatest achievement, Seward answered: "The purchase of Alaska! But it will take people a generation to find that out." (National Archives)

The cabinet and president remained largely ignorant of the talks until Seward presented them and the Congress with a hastily drawn treaty and a bill for $7.2 million—no small sum in March 1867. One Treasury official estimated that the United States actually paid $43.4 million: $7.2 million in principal, $12.5 million in army and navy expenses, and $23.7 million in lost interest on the principal had the money remained in the Treasury for twenty-five years. Alaska, like Louisiana a half-century before, nevertheless, constituted a substantial bargain.

Although the editor Horace Greeley joked about "Walrussia" as a worthless acquisition, Seward astutely won over Charles Sumner, who applauded Alaska's commercial potential and natural resources.[71] Sumner's influence; a vigorous propaganda program, in which Seward compared Alaska to the Louisiana Purchase; the Russian minister's hiring of lobbyists and distributing $100,000 in bribes to key members of Congress; and the exhilaration over expanding American boundaries— all combined to carry the treaty through the Senate only ten days after it was signed. The House stalled, delaying fifteen months before voting the funds, but by then Seward had already raised the Stars and Stripes over his imperial catch.

Seward acquired fewer territories than he desired, largely because of domestic obstacles. A Republican supporter of Democratic President Andrew Johnson, Seward outraged the Radical Republicans who loathed Johnson's moderate form of Reconstruction for the South. They turned against Seward, called for Seward's ouster from the cabinet, and helped block his imperialistic schemes. Some critics soured on expansion because of the corruption attending the annexation of Alaska. Reconstruction, railroad growth, an inflated economy, landless freedmen, a recalcitrant South—such issues compelled many Americans to look inward and to skimp on foreign adventures that cost money. A nation that had just freed its slaves had little interest in acquiring Cuba, in which slavery flourished. Seward could only lament "how sadly domestic disturbances of ours demoralize the National ambition."[72]

The secretary's ambition misfired, too, because articulate anti-imperialists such as Senator Justin Morrill of Vermont, the author Mark Twain, and the editor E. L. Godkin spoke out. They called for the development of America's existing lands and for an American showcase of domestic social, political, and economic improvements as the best way to persuade other people to adopt U.S. institutions. Just as some imperialists used racist arguments to justify the subjugation of "inferior" people, some anti-imperialists opposed adding more nonwhites to the American population. Godkin opposed the annexation of the Dominican Republic because of his fear that thousands of Catholic, Spanish-speaking blacks might seek U.S. citizenship. Charles Sumner urged the purchase of Alaska but warned that "our first care should be to improve and elevate the Republic [and] … keep it constant in the support of Human Rights."[73] Such critics and ideas, joined to the partisan struggle over Reconstruction, helped thwart Seward's efforts to create a larger empire. He moved too fast for most Americans.

Great Britain, Canada, and North American Disputes

Anglo-American competition and Canadian-American tensions, so evident before and during the Civil War, persisted in the 1865–1895 period. Union leaders remained irate over Britain's favoritism shown toward the South during the Civil War, especially the outfitting of Confederate vessels in British ports. At the end of the war, Seward filed damage claims against the British, even proposing at one point that Britain cede to the United States British Columbia or the Bahama Islands in lieu of a cash settlement. The secretary also grew annoyed that British officials would not permit American soldiers to pursue destitute Sioux Indians into Canadian territory. Canadians and Americans squabbled over the Irish-American terrorists, tariffs, boundaries, fishing rights in the North Atlantic, and seal hunting. The neighbors to the north bristled at arrogant predictions that the United States would one day absorb Canada.

Although annexationist rhetoric echoed throughout the United States, only the hottest heads urged the forceful attachment of Canada to the Union. Pure Manifest Destiny doctrine, after all, predicted the inevitable "Americanization" of Canadians. And while Americans were busy settling their own West, there seemed no hurry. A military attack would no doubt have precipitated war with Great Britain, and even though "twisting the Lion's tail" proved popular politics in the United States, few politicians wanted British naval assaults on the Gulf and East coasts.

Nascent Canadian nationalism also foiled northward expansion. Canadian nationalists such as John A. Macdonald actually thought of themselves as British North Americans, who disapproved of the political scandals, racial and ethnic prejudices, and flashy materialism of Gilded Age America. Macdonald became his nation's first prime minister when the Dominion of Canada came into being as a confederation of provinces on July 1, 1867. Free homesteads under the Dominion Lands Act of 1872 and construction of the Canadian Pacific Railway facilitated settlement of Canada's prairie provinces and ensured that the dominant culture would remain "Protestant, conservative, and very British."[74] Hard times in the 1880s revived discussions about commercial union, or a common market, but higher U.S. tariffs caused such ideas to "blaze, crackle, and go out with a stink," as Macdonald put it.[75] By century's end, Americans had come to see Canada less as "a northern enemy base" and more as "a brother government soon to adopt the republican principles America held dear."[76]

Despite these longer trends, Anglo-Canadian-American relations seesawed from crisis to crisis. In 1866 armed forces of the Fenian Brotherhood, an Irish-American society of some 10,000 members organized to promote Irish independence from Britain, attacked Canada from Vermont. Seward wanted Canada, but not through such methods. He sent troops to the border to squelch further skirmishes, but both London and Ottawa believed he had acted too slowly. Anglo-American "ill-feeling" flared anew in the early 1880s when the Fenians and other Irish nationalists used "devilish inventions [dynamite bombs]" against British public buildings. U.S. officials condemned such terrorist acts as "uncivilized, cruel, and barbarous," but Congress failed to strengthen laws against the trafficking of explosives.[77]

Canada became entangled in another Anglo-American dispute: the question of the English-built Confederate ships (especially the *Alabama*) that had disrupted Union shipping during the Civil War. The irrepressible Charles Sumner added the naval damages to indirect damages caused by England's "flagrant, unnatural departure from [its] antislavery rule" and its recognition of southern belligerency that "opened the gates of war."[78] He thus totaled up a bill of $2.125 billion. One British diplomat shamelessly explained that Sumner "was fool enough some year or so ago to marry a young and pretty widow. She found that he was not gifted with 'full powers' and has left him. ... He therefore makes up by vigour of tongue for his want of capacity in other organs."[79] Some Americans thought the transfer of Canada to the United States would erase the debt. After years of diplomatic wrangling, a Joint High Commission convened in Washington from February to May 1871; it produced the Washington Treaty dated May 8. The British expressed regret for the actions of British-built Confederate raiders, and the signatories agreed to establish a tribunal in Geneva, Switzerland, to determine damages and claims. That judicial body's decision in December 1872: Britain must pay the United States $15.5 million. "As the price of conciliating the United States, and protecting British naval interests," one historian has written, "it was a bargain."[80]

Another longstanding dispute proved more rancorous—the rights of American fishermen in North Atlantic waters. The Washington Treaty gave permission to Yankee fishermen to cast their nets in Canadian waters and allowed Canadians to fish the coastal regions of the United States above 39° north latitude. Macdonald grumbled that the British were conceding too much to the Americans. But the prime minister recognized Canadian weakness—the federation had not yet "hardened from gristle into bone."[81] In 1877 a fisheries commission ruled that the United States should pay $5.5 million for the privilege of fishing in Canadian waters. The United States paid, but in 1885, in protest against the award, it reactivated the fish war by unilaterally abrogating that part of the Washington Treaty dealing with fishing rights. The Canadians thereupon began seizing American vessels. A British diplomat denounced Americans as "a bunch of dishonest tricksters."[82] An Anglo-American fisheries treaty of 1888 failed to gain Senate approval.

Then British minister Sir Lionel Sackville-West committed a sin of the first order for a diplomat. When in 1888 a Republican pretending to be a former Englishman asked Sackville-West whether he should vote for the Republican candidate Benjamin Harrison or the Democrat Grover Cleveland, the reckless diplomat recommended Cleveland as the politician more friendly to Britain. Gleeful Republicans printed and distributed copies of Sackville-West's indiscreet letter. Cleveland withdrew Sackville-West's accreditation just before the president lost his reelection bid. The prime minister, Lord Salisbury, pointedly did not send a new envoy until March of the next year—after the inauguration of Republican Benjamin Harrison.

Anglo-American rivalry next flared over seals in the Bering Sea near Alaska. "Amphibious is the fur seal, ubiquitous and carnivorous, uniparous, gregarious and withal polygamous," the historian Samuel Flagg Bemis has versified.[83] Most of the seal herds lived in the Pribilof Islands near the Aleutians. American law forbade the killing of female or young seals and limited the slaughter of males. Yet foreign hunters slaughtered at will when the animals wandered on the high seas in search of food. In 1889 President Harrison warned Canadians against "pelagic" sealing (killing animals in ocean waters). When U.S. cutters seized several Canadian sealing boats in international waters, London and Ottawa protested. In mid-1890 the British sent four warships to the disputed region as Canadian sealers shot seals to death. American captains made no arrests this time. In 1891 diplomats struck a temporary agreement halting pelagic sealing for a year, and eventually placed these matters before an arbitral tribunal. In 1893 the arbiters handed Americans a defeat, for it permitted pelagic sealing for furs and skins within certain limits. Seals continued their numerical decline until 1911, when the United States, Britain, Russia, and Japan finally banned pelagic sealing altogether and limited land kills. The seal population soon rejuvenated, thus marking an early example of U.S. and international environmental regulation.

Americans in Asia: China, Japan, and Korea

With its vast territory, huge population, and tributary states, China attracted foreigners eager to sell, buy, invest, convert, and dominate. Although some Chinese leaders considered Americans less bullying than British gunboat diplomatists, the Chinese viewed all westerners as "barbarians." One diplomat regretted having to meet with his western counterparts, for it was like "associating with dog and swine—a misfortune in a man's life."[84] Indeed, the United States demanded the same privileges China granted to other nations: open ports, low tariffs, protection for missionaries, and extraterritoriality (the exemption of foreigners from the legal jurisdiction of the country in which they resided). Before the 1890s the United States largely followed the British lead by practicing coat-tail diplomacy; Americans seized opportunities created by the guns of other westerners to expand trade and missionary work. They were not passive. The Asiatic Squadron, for example, cruised the seas and visited ports to protect American lives and commerce, and U.S. naval gunboats had patrolled the Yangtze River since the 1840s.

In 1870, fifty American companies operated in China, but that number dropped to thirty-one a decade later. U.S. exports to China slumped to $1 million in 1880; and although they rose to $3 million in 1890 and $15 million in 1900, trade with China claimed a minuscule part of American overseas commerce. Cotton goods and kerosene constituted the largest exports. "It is my dream," vowed the governor of Georgia in 1878, to see "in every valley … a cotton factory to convert the raw material of the neighborhood into fabrics which shall warm the limbs of Japanese and Chinese."[85] Cheap, coarse cloth from U.S. mills soon undercut finer British textiles and came to dominate the Chinese market and to account for about half of the American industry's foreign sales. Kerosene also became big business in China; Standard Oil of New York advertised widely and, to improve sales, introduced small, inexpensive lamps. American investments in China remained modest, growing to less than $20 million by 1900.

Protestant missionaries, another American presence in China, steadily expanded their work, moving from treaty ports to the interior. They first visited China in the 1830s; by 1900 their number, mostly women, had grown to more than 1,000, and they spread the Gospel wherever they went in China. They not only gained converts; they also helped promote American products simply by using them in front of curious Chinese. In some cases, religious missionaries and economic expansionists joined hands, as when Singer executives and missionaries championed the "civilizing medium" of the sewing machine.[86] "Fancy what would happen to the cotton trade if every Chinese wore a shirt!" remarked Charles Denby, who represented the State Department in China in 1885–1898. "Well, the missionaries are teaching them to wear shirts."[87]

"Pacific Chivalry." How Californians handled the Chinese. The historian David M. Pletcher has written that increased contact with Chinese immigrants after the 1840s created a stereotype in which the "heathen Chinee" were seen as "backward, unreliable, deceitful, and immoral, perhaps not even human." (*Harper's Weekly,* 1869)

Between 1850 and 1900 about half a million Chinese, mostly males, emigrated to the United States. Many returned home after several years, and most sent money home after first paying travel debts. They mined, built railroads, farmed, and laundered the white men's clothes. By the mid-1870s about 150,000 Chinese resided in the United States, with the largest number in the San Francisco area. Wherever they settled, the Chinese formed close-knit communities, or "Chinatowns," and maintained their cultural identity. Sinophobia on the West Coast wreaked hatred and violence on the expatriate Chinese and created laws to exclude Asian immigrants. White Americans in California spawned myths about filthy, rat-eating, opium-drunk "Mongolians" who threatened American culture by refusing to assimilate. White laborers, especially Irish Americans, complained that Chinese workers ate little and depressed wages. Anti-Chinese violence flared throughout the 1860s and 1870s; riots rocked Los Angeles in 1870 and San Francisco seven years later. "Dead, my reverend friends, dead," wrote Bret Harte of one murdered immigrant, "Stoned to death in the streets of San Francisco ... by a mob of half-grown boys and Christian school children."[88] In October 1880, 3,000 white men attacked the Chinese district in Denver, killing one resident, beating others, destroying property.

Five years later at Rock Springs, in the Wyoming Territory, white miners invaded Chinatown during labor and ethnic unrest. The Chinese workers fled, but many were shot; others burned to death in fires set to raze the Chinese community. At least twenty-eight mutilated Chinese bodies lay in the debris. China's consul in San Francisco protested the massacre, calling the local judicial proceedings, in which all rioters won acquittal, a "burlesque."[89] President Cleveland, who dispatched federal troops to restore order, deemed the result a "ghastly mockery of justice."[90] Congress eventually paid an indemnity of $424,367 to the Chinese government for "losses sustained by Chinese subjects [from] mob violence."[91]

Washington strongly lectured the western states against violence, while simultaneously informing Chinese diplomats that the federal government had no legal jurisdiction. At the same time, U.S. officials petitioned Beijing to protect Americans in China against multiplying antiforeign acts. As symbols of outside assaults on China's integrity, missionaries received the brunt of nativist hostility and violence. By undermining the authority of local elites and by seeking Christian converts who fractured the local society, missionaries became subversive "foreign devils" around whom circled myths about exotic sexual and medical practices. Antimissionary riots erupted in the 1880s and 1890s, prompting more appeals for official U.S. protection.

Washington and Beijing at first tried to reduce friction. Anson Burlingame, U.S. minister to China (1861–1867), went to work for the Chinese government after his retirement with an assignment to regulate western intrusions. With Secretary Seward he negotiated the 1868 Burlingame Treaty, providing for free immigration between the two nations and the stationing of Chinese consuls in the United States (to look after Chinese subjects). Seward welcomed the pact as a step toward improved trade.

Sinophobic politicians from the West lobbied hard to restrict Chinese immigration. In 1879 Congress legislated that only fifteen Chinese could arrive on any one ship in the United States. President Rutherford B. Hayes vetoed the measure as a violation of the Burlingame Treaty. A new treaty negotiated with China in 1880 permitted the United States to suspend, but not prohibit, Chinese immigration. Two years later Congress suspended Chinese immigration for ten years and denied Chinese immigrants U.S. citizenship. Congress renewed these provisions again and again. China could neither protect its people in the United States nor challenge American immigration policy.

In 1863–1864, despite the Civil War, the U.S. Navy deployed one armed warship alongside British, French, and Dutch vessels to punish the Japanese for their antiforeign riots and harassment of merchant ships. At Shimonoseki this Western firepower destroyed forts and boats, opening the strait to trade once again. Internally divided and militarily weak, the Japanese could not resist the $3 million indemnity forced on them by the Western powers. Then, in the Convention of 1866, Japan reluctantly bestowed low tariffs on Western imports. By the late 1890s, America's trade with Japan surpassed its trade with China but still constituted only about 2 percent of total U.S. foreign commerce. Soon the Japanese consciously adopted a policy of "westernization" (which included learning American baseball), persuading some Americans that the Japanese, unlike the Chinese, had become "civilized."

Korea became one of Japan's victims. This kingdom, called the "hermit nation" because of its self-imposed isolation, remained technically a dependency of China—a tributary state that relied on Beijing to handle its external relations. But China's weakness denied Korea any protection from the predatory Japanese and Westerners, including the French, who used gunboats in the 1860s to punish the Koreans' mistreatment of missionaries. Secretary Seward hoped to trade with the kingdom, but the fate of the merchant ship *General Sherman* revealed obstacles. In 1866, without Korean permission, the trading schooner pushed up the Taedong River toward Pyongyang. Its captain became embroiled in a dispute with local villagers and officials, who burned the ship and killed all aboard. The following year, Commodore Robert W. Shufeldt recommended a punitive force to teach Korea the lesson "taught to other Eastern nations, that it can no longer maintain that contemptuous exclusiveness."[92] Not until 1871 did the United States retaliate. That year a mission, headed by the

American Sailor and Geisha. Although official Japanese-American relations remained cool for much of the nineteenth century, U.S. ships increasingly traded with the once isolated island-nation. The inevitable intermingling of cultures occurred. This woodblock print by Yoshitora Utagawa depicts an American sailor in the company of a geisha, a Japanese hostess hired to entertain. (Library of Congress)

American minister to China and buttressed by five warships, sought not only to deal with the *General Sherman* incident but also to establish commercial relations and to guarantee the protection of shipwrecked Americans. When the fleet sailed up the Han River toward Seoul, Koreans fired on the advance party, whereupon American guns bombarded their forts, killing at least 300 defenders. "Every urchin in our kingdom [will] spit at and curse you," and the whole world "will indignantly sympathize with us," said the Koreans as they again rejected any treaty with Washington.[93]

Japan battered Korea's gates open by imposing a treaty in 1876 that recognized Korean independence from China. The Chinese then encouraged Western contacts with Korea to thwart the Japanese—"to play off the foreign enemies one against the other."[94] In 1882 a Korean-American treaty negotiated by Commodore Shufeldt provided for American diplomatic representation, a legation in Seoul, and trade relations; the Treaty of Chemulpo passed the Senate the following year. Throughout the 1880s American entrepreneurs built trade links; even Thomas Edison signed a contract for the installation of electric lights in the royal residence. For the United States, however, Korea constituted a peripheral interest, and Washington could not prevent it from moving into Japan's orbit. In the Sino-Japanese War of 1894–1895 Japanese forces crushed the Chinese. Despite President Cleveland's regret that Japan should "visit upon her feeble and defenseless neighbor the horrors of an unjust war," the United States remained neutral.[95] Most Americans, including missionaries, seemed to favor a Japanese triumph to force China into the modern age. Victorious Japan soon dominated Korea, and China became all the more vulnerable to Western and Japanese imperialists. In the late 1890s, to protect their interests in China, Americans turned to the Open Door policy (see Chapter 6).

Pacific Prizes: Hawai'i and Samoa

Hawai'i, that commercial and naval jewel of eight major islands in the Pacific, was linked with Asia in the American mind. Imagined as a paradise where beautiful native women danced "the lascivious hula-hula," the islands beckoned as exotic stations on the way to Asian markets.[96] The undeveloped port of Pearl Harbor was an admiral's dream, and sugar had become big business. "Almost all the sugar-plantations are owned by Americans," noted one visitor in 1874.[97] Although not yet ready to annex the islands, Washington repeatedly warned others not to do so. In 1875 a reciprocity treaty transformed Hawai'i into "an economic and eventually a political satellite."[98] With Hawaiian sugar now entering the United States duty free, Claus Spreckels of California became "His Royal Saccharinity" as he bought up plantations, imported Chinese and Japanese labor, and disfigured the landscape through massive hydraulic projects. After Secretary Blaine told the British in 1881 to stay out of Hawai'i because it was "essentially a part of the American system of states," American residents organized secret clubs and military units to contest the government of King Kalakaua.[99] In 1887 the conspirators forced Hawai'i's monarch to accept the so-called Bayonet Constitution, which granted foreigners the right to vote and shifted authority from the throne to the legislature. That same year, the United States gained naval rights to Pearl Harbor.

Reflecting the longstanding American interest in Hawai'i, Secretary Blaine noted that "Hawaii may come up for decision at any unexpected hour, and I hope we shall be prepared to decide it in the affirmative."[100] Like the expansionists of the 1840s, Americans hurried the hour. The McKinley Tariff of 1890 eliminated Hawaiian sugar's favored status in the United States by admitting all foreign sugar duty free. The measure also provided a bounty of two cents a pound to domestic U.S. growers, making it possible for them to sell their sugar at a price lower than that charged for foreign sugar. Sugar shipments to the United States soon declined. Hawaiian producers screamed in economic pain and plotted revolution against Queen Lili'uokalani, who became the ruling monarch in 1891. Organized into the subversive Annexation Club, the revolutionaries came from the ranks of influential white American lawyers, merchants, and sugar planters, many of them the sons of Protestant missionaries. They composed a distinct minority of the population (2,000 of a total of 90,000), but they owned a major part of the islands' wealth. One of them, Sanford B. Dole, who became Hawai'i's first president, called the queen inept and corrupt because he feared that as a Hawaiian nationalist she would roll back the political power of the *haole* (foreigners). At the root of the conspiracy, of course, lay the desire to annex Hawai'i to the United States so that Hawaiian sugar would be classified as domestic rather than foreign.

On January 16, 1893, the conspirators bloodlessly toppled the queen and proclaimed a provisional government. Surrendering in protest to what she acknowledged as the "superior force" of the United States, Queen Lili'uokalani endured confinement for several months.[101] After gaining her freedom, she continued to speak out, making the Hawaiian nationalist case against annexation in *Hawaii's Story by Hawaii's Queen* (1898). The revolution could not have succeeded without the assistance of American minister John L. Stevens and the men of the U.S.S. *Boston*. An active partisan for annexation, Stevens sent 162 armed bluejackets from the U.S. cruiser into Honolulu. They did not bivouac near American property to protect it, the announced pretext for landing, but quickly deployed near the monarch's palace. Brandishing Gatling guns and cannon, the troops by their very presence forced the queen to give up. Stevens recognized the provisional government, declared a U.S. protectorate, and alerted Washington that the "Hawaiian pear is now fully ripe, and this is the golden hour for the United States to pluck it."[102] Native Hawaiians, making up some 53 percent of the population, never voted on whether they wished to be absorbed by the United States.

Claiming that the "overthrow of the monarchy was not in any way promoted by the [U.S.] Government," President Harrison quickly signed a treaty of annexation with a "Hawaiian" commission (four Americans and one Englishman).[103] "Give a child a razor and he will hurt himself," one annexationist argued, "Give the African or Polynesian unlimited political power, and … political death will follow."[104] A popular jingle went: "Liliuokalani, / Give us your little brown hanni."[105] Before the Senate could act, however, Democrat Grover Cleveland had replaced Harrison in the White House, and the treaty became a political football. Cleveland soon withdrew the treaty and ordered an investigator, former member of Congress James H. Blount, to the islands. Blount's report confirmed that most native Hawaiians opposed the coup and that "the American Minister [Stevens] and the revolutionary leaders had determined

Queen Lili'uokalani of Hawai'i (1838–1917).
This Hawaiian nationalist sought to stem the growing economic and political power of foreigners. When her brother leased Pearl Harbor to the Americans in 1887, she wrote that it was "a day of infamy in Hawaiian history." Eager to take Hawai'i back for her people when she inherited the throne in 1891, she could not prevent the white Annexation Club's conspiracy to overthrow her in 1893. (Library of Congress)

on annexation to the United States, and agreed on the part each was to act to the very end."[106] Although a commercial expansionist, Cleveland worried about the implications of a Hawaiian annexation. What would southern Democrats think of incorporating a multiracial population in the Union? Could Hawai'i, an overseas territory, ever become a state? What if native Hawaiians revolted against their white rulers? Why stir up another heated issue when the United States was already beset at home by Chinese immigration, agricultural depression, and labor protests? Cleveland killed the treaty, but he did not restore the queen, who was falsely accused of wanting to behead the usurpers and confiscate their property. After piously rejecting President Cleveland's "right to interfere in our domestic affairs," the white leaders in Hawai'i had to await more propitious world events for the United States to annex the islands (see Chapter 6).[107]

What if ...   *there had been no McKinley Tariff in 1890?*

Had the McKinley Tariff not severely curtailed Hawai'i's sugar exports to the United States by giving bounties to U.S. domestic sugar producers, the white oligarchy might not have plotted to overthrow Queen Lili'uokalani in early 1893 and sought annexation to the United States. Without tariff alterations, members of the subversive Annexationist Club might have bided their time, content to dominate Hawaiian politics through their control of the legislature under the Bayonet Constitution of 1887. Unchanged U.S. sugar tariffs might also have prevented economic turmoil leading to rebellion in Cuba in 1895, thereby making it unlikely that a U.S.-Spanish war over Cuba would have prompted calls for annexing Hawai'i in order to supply American expeditionary forces in the Philippines. Given the vital U.S. naval base at Pearl Harbor and the interlocking of the two economies, in which U.S. citizens owned $30 million worth of property in Hawai'i and controlled 93 percent of the islands' commerce in 1897, the archipelago could have remained an American protectorate indefinitely. Any possible threat posed by growing Japanese immigration into the islands could have been resolved through an agreement, perhaps after the Russo-Japanese War of 1904–1905, in which Tokyo and Washington recognized each other's imperial spheres.

It is more probable, however, that the *haole* annexationists, led by Hollis Thurston and Sanford Dole, would have eventually tried to topple Lili'uokalani regardless of sugar trade woes. When the queen drafted a replacement to the Bayonet Constitution that would have restored veto power to the monarchy and voting rights to the disenfranchised Polynesian and Asian populations, she posed a direct threat to Anglo-Saxon supremacy on the islands. As children of the missionaries who had settled in Hawai'i earlier in the century, the white elites believed themselves destined to bring the rules of civilization to "dark-skinned savages." When the queen tried to raise revenue through a lottery and taxes on opium, the annexationists pronounced her lewd and immoral. Invoking the racial and gendered stereotypes of the day, cartoonists caricatured Lili'uokalani as a frizzy-haired prostitute in high heels and a grass skirt. Without the intervention of marines from the U.S.S. *Boston* in January 1893, the conspirators, who represented less than 3 percent of the population, might not have succeeded, as U.S. Gatling guns prevented the queen from rallying her loyal indigenous supporters.

If the annexationists had waited until the anti-imperialist Grover Cleveland occupied the White House, they could not have acted with official American complicity. Even after the white Provisional Government had proclaimed its independence, a rebellion in January 1895 headed by the native Hawaiian Robert Wilcox nearly restored Lili'uokalani to her throne. She endured two years of house arrest instead. Anti-imperialists in the U.S. Congress pointed often to this nationalist opposition to white rule when they debated Hawaiian annexation in the summer of 1898. Although President William McKinley proclaimed the annexation of Hawai'i as the inevitable consummation of a new Manifest Destiny, a bare two-thirds vote (42 to 21 in the Senate) amid patriotic exuberance over a "splendid little war" suggests that different outcomes might well have been possible.

After Hawai'i became a state in August 1959, efforts flourished to revive and maintain the Hawaiian language and culture (including the spelling of Hawai'i with a reverse apostrophe or *okina* between the final two vowels). In 1993 the U.S. Congress passed an "Apology Resolution" and expressed formal regrets to native Hawaiians "on behalf of the United States for the overthrow of the Kingdom of Hawai'i" one hundred years earlier. The resolution neither offered monetary restitution nor mentioned the McKinley Tariff.

International rivalry was increasing throughout the Pacific. Germany, Britain, and the United States collided in Samoa, a group of fourteen volcanic islands lying 4,000 miles from San Francisco. American whalers had long been stopping there, and in 1839 Charles Wilkes of the U.S. Navy had surveyed the islands. After the American Civil War, nationals of the three great powers scrambled for privileges and exploited the chaotic and often violent tribal politics of the islets. At stake were coconut plantations, national pride stimulated by the three-cornered rivalry, and coaling stations. In 1872 a tribal chief granted the United States naval rights at Pago Pago, the "most perfect land-locked harbor ... in the Pacific."[108] This pact died because the Senate took no action. In 1878 American agents for the Central Polynesian Land and Commercial Company accompanied the Samoan chief Le Mamea to Washington and negotiated a new treaty. It gave Americans privileges at Pago Pago and provided for U.S. good offices in disputes between Samoa and outside nations.

In 1885–1886, after years of "calculated hostility" from Germany, Secretary of State Thomas F. Bayard launched a more active American diplomacy toward Samoa.[109] He protested that Germany aimed at "the virtual displacement of the United States" from its "preferred status."[110] As "benevolent protector" of Samoa, Bayard convened a three-power Washington Conference in 1887, but it could not reach agreement. When Germany landed marines on Samoa, Washington dispatched a warship. The British and Americans refused to pay taxes to the German-dominated government. German chancellor Otto von Bismarck vowed to "show sharp teeth."[111] Eager for a "bit of a spar with Germany," Theodore Roosevelt admitted that the Germans might burn New York City.[112] In early 1889, Congress authorized half a million dollars to protect Americans and their Samoan property and another $100,000 to build a naval station at Pago Pago.

"Two Good Old Friends."
In this German cartoon, John Bull (Britain) and Uncle Sam try to balance their Pacific interests in Samoa and Hawai'i while native inhabitants feel the imperial weight. (*Kladderadatsch* in *Review of Reviews,* 1893)

Whether boldness or bluff, this American action prodded Bismarck to settle. A typhoon that devastated Samoa and sank or wrecked all German and American warships also facilitated peace. After that disaster, nobody had the weapons or will to fight "on account of some black people thousands and thousands of miles away in the Pacific," as one journalist wrote.[113]

At the Berlin Conference of 1889, the three powers carved Samoa into a tripartite protectorate (the United States got Pago Pago) and forced an unpopular king on the Samoans. The writer Robert Louis Stevenson, a prominent resident of the islands, protested this violation of native sovereignty by the "Triple-Headed Ass" of imperial greed.[114] Ten years later, in the aftermath of the Spanish-American-Cuban-Filipino War, the United States and Germany formally partitioned Samoa into colonies, with Britain compensated by other Pacific acquisitions.

Eyeing Africa

Before the Civil War, American ships and merchant traders frequented Africa's coasts. But the internecine conflict disrupted old trading patterns, lower transportation costs made European goods less expensive in African markets, and discriminatory trade practices undermined Yankee competition. Although some U.S. activity in Africa was kept alive by American adventurers, explorers, mining engineers, traders, and a few naval officers sent to identify prospects for commercial penetration, official Washington took few steps to advance U.S. interests in the vast land that the European powers were rushing to carve up.

American tobacco, kerosene, and rum nevertheless continued to claim a good share of African markets. Zanzibar preferred American cotton goods; in exchange, East African gum copal and ivory were shipped to New England factories. When, in the early 1880s, tribal warfare in Tanganyika (present-day Tanzania) interrupted the ivory trade, Connecticut plants had to shut down. In West Africa, where Americans had once participated in the slave trade and where many consular agents had long handled American commercial interests, British tariffs hurt American trade—for example, tobacco and rum on the Gold Coast and Sierra Leone. Higher tariffs in French West Africa also diminished American commerce. By 1900 American trade with the continent had become inconsequential.

Such a decline might not have occurred had Washington heeded the ubiquitous Commodore Shufeldt's recommendations. In 1878 the State and Navy departments ordered him to sail the U.S.S. *Ticonderoga* to Africa and Asia for "the encouragement and extension of American commerce."[115] Shufeldt wrote detailed reports on economic opportunities, port facilities, and laws. He negotiated trade treaties. For American surplus goods, especially cotton cloth, he advised, "Africa with its teeming population presents a tempting field."[116] He warned that the British and other imperialists were working to drive Americans from the continent. Washington officials took no action.

Americans nonetheless became fascinated with black Africa because individuals bent on adventure, fame, and wealth popularized it. Foremost among them was Henry M. Stanley, an immigrant from Wales who claimed U.S. citizenship. While working for the *New York Herald,* after stints in both the Confederate and the Union armies, Stanley was directed by the newspaper's owner to depart for Africa and find Dr. David Livingstone, the Scottish missionary-explorer who in 1866 had disappeared into central Africa while searching for the Nile's source. Stanley arrived in Zanzibar in 1871 and cabled dramatic stories about Africa. With an American flag at the head of his large expedition, he cut across Tanganyika and found Livingstone, who appreciated Stanley's supplies and medicine but insisted on continuing his quest for the great river's headwaters. Three years later Stanley led another venture into the African interior; in his 999-day trek through the wilderness, facilitated by dozens of African forced laborers, he battled hostile Africans, mapped the territory, disparaged natives as "wooly-headed rabble ... unchecked and uncurbed by the hand of law," cut off the tail of his hungry dog and fed it to him for supper, and made the Congo Basin and himself internationally famous.[117] Congress even voted him a resolution of thanks.

King Leopold II of Belgium saw in Stanley an instrument to bring his small nation a large empire. Unable to compete with the more powerful European imperialists, Leopold formed an organization whose announced philanthropic purpose was ending the slave trade and protecting legitimate commerce, but whose real objective was obtaining an imperial foothold for Belgium in the Congo. The king hired Stanley, who negotiated with African leaders in the mineral-rich region to gain their allegiance to the international organization. Leopold also employed Henry S. Sanford, a former American minister to Belgium who sought personal gain from

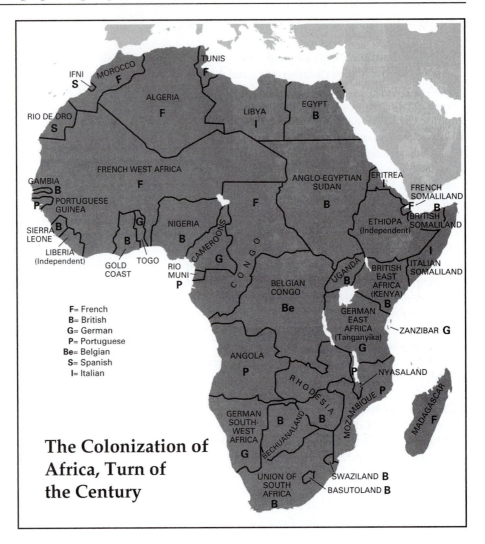

The Colonization of Africa, Turn of the Century

F= French
B= British
G= German
P= Portuguese
Be= Belgian
S= Spanish
I= Italian

enlarged U.S. trade and investments in the region. Working to thwart the encroaching Europeans, Sanford lobbied in Washington until the United States in 1884 recognized King Leopold's *Association Internationale du Congo* as sovereign over the area.

Washington then found itself in the midst of an international dispute, for other European nations claimed parts of the Congo. To head off a clash, the European rivals convened a conference in Berlin in fall 1884. The United States sent two delegates, one of them Sanford; Stanley advised the American diplomats. The conferees signed an agreement that recognized the international association's (and hence Leopold's) authority over the Congo and ensured an open door for trade. The new president, Grover Cleveland, shunning entanglements with Europeans, withdrew the accord from the Senate. Still, the United States abided by its terms and in 1890 sent representatives to another Congo conference. This time, the conferees in

Brussels closed the commercial door by permitting Leopold to levy import duties in the Congo ostensibly to eradicate the slave trade. Having inadvertently helped the Belgian monarch take over a million and a half square miles of African territory (today's Democratic Republic on the Congo) and create "a gigantic trading monopoly behind a smokescreen of philanthropy and altruism," the United States ratified the accord two years later.[118]

American Christian missionaries also entered Africa. By the end of the century, the American Board of Commissioners for Foreign Missions had built schools, hospitals, and a seminary for training an African clergy. Its missionaries established stations in South Africa, Mozambique, and Angola, and translated the Bible into Zulu. Baptists sought converts in Nigeria, and Lutherans opened missions in Madagascar. The African Methodist Episcopal Church, a major black church in the United States, sought converts in Liberia, Sierra Leone, and South Africa. In the 1890s, one of its bishops, the black nationalist Henry Turner, urged segregated and disenfranchised American blacks to emigrate to Africa—"a place of refuge ... from the horrors of American prejudice."[119] Hundreds of African Americans heeded his call. Most white Americans, ignorant of African diversity, viewed the continent through a racist prism: Big-game hunter Theodore Roosevelt denigrated Africans as "ape-like naked savages, who dwell in the woods and prey on creatures not much wilder or lower than themselves."[120]

American prospectors and mining engineers flocked to the gold and diamond regions of South Africa. One fortune seeker, Jerome L. Babe, arrived in 1870 and invented a screening apparatus for diamond mining. A self-taught engineer from Kentucky, Hamilton Smith wrote glowing reports on gold that attracted large investments from the European bank of Rothschild. More than eighty Americans became Egyptian mercenaries in the 1870s. With no connection to the U.S. government, these Civil War veterans "infused American democratic attitudes into the Egyptian army" at the military academy and around bivouac campfires.[121] On the eve of the "Egypt for Egyptians" revolt against foreign control in 1882, the leader of the rebellion attended a reception at the U.S. consulate in Cairo celebrating George Washington's birthday. To prevent the loss of the Suez Canal, however, Britain quelled the nationalist revolt and militarily occupied Egypt.

Americans knew more about Liberia than about any other African area. Settled in 1821 and governed by American blacks under the auspices of the American Colonization Society, Liberia suffered internal strife and French and British nibbling at its territory. The United States, in 1875 and again in 1879, deployed its warships to help the Americo-Liberians suppress rebellions by indigenous Africans. In the 1880s and 1890s, British and French forces coerced Liberia into ceding land. Calling it "an offshoot of our own system," President Cleveland declared that the United States had a "moral right and duty" to protect Liberia.[122] Although Washington refused to employ its meager power in the area to halt imperial ambitions, its patronage, however minimal, may have forestalled full-scale European domination of that African nation.

With the United States as an interested observer, whites carved up Africa—the British took Egypt, Sierra Leone, and the Gold Coast; the Germans feasted on Tanganyika (East Africa) and Southwest Africa; the French grabbed Tunisia and

West Africa; the Portuguese absorbed Angola and Mozambique; and the Belgians gained the Congo (see map on page 190). By 1895 imperialists had partitioned most of Africa. Washington worried, as always, that the colonial enclaves would close their doors to American trade. As at the Berlin conference more than a decade earlier, U.S. officials constantly reminded the European imperialists to keep the doors open to honor the principle of equal trade opportunity.

Latin America Moves into the Yankee Vortex

During this period the United States was more active in Latin America than in any other part of the world. Americans challenged European interests, expanded trade and investment links, intervened in inter-American disputes and revolutions, deployed warships in troubled waters to "show the flag," tried to annex territories, sought canal routes across Central America, lectured everybody about the supremacy of the Monroe Doctrine, and organized the Pan American movement.

When the French in 1861 intervened militarily in Mexico and placed the young Archduke Ferdinand Maximilian of Austria on a Mexican throne, the intrusion seemed to hurl a blatant challenge at the Monroe Doctrine. Seward first sent arms to the forces of former Mexican president Benito Juárez. After the Civil War, President Johnson ordered 52,000 American soldiers to Texas, where they staged military maneuvers along the Mexican border to buttress Washington's diplomatic demands for a French exit. In early 1866, Seward firmly asked Napoleon III when the French military would withdraw. Facing opposition at home and Prussia's competition in Europe, harassed by guerrillas in Mexico, and confronted by a noisy, well-armed, and victorious United States, the emperor recalled his troops. The hapless and abandoned "archdupe" Maximilian fell in 1867 before a Mexican firing squad. Americans believed, much too simply, that they had forced France out and that the Monroe Doctrine had gained new vigor.

A quite different challenge sprang from Cuba, the Spanish colony that many North Americans believed would one day become part of the U.S. empire. From 1868 to 1878, a Creole-led rebellion bloodied the island. With annexationist sentiment strong among the Creoles, they petitioned Washington for admission to the Union. During the Ten Years' War, U.S. officials rejected Cuban independence, urged Spain to introduce reforms, and explored possibilities of buying the island. With Secretary Hamilton Fish disparaging the rebels, President Grant denounced any recognition of Cuban independence as impractical and indefensible. The Creoles' defense of slavery posed a major obstacle to U.S. alignment in any form with Cuba. Anti-imperialists claimed it was impossible to "make citizens" of "ignorant Catholic Spanish Negroes."[123] Someday, Fish remarked in 1869, Spanish rule would collapse and "civilized nations" would "all be glad that we should interpose and regulate the control of the Island."[124]

Despite the Americans' caution, the *Virginius* affair of 1873 nearly entangled the United States in the rebellion. The Cuban-owned, gun-running vessel was captured by the Spanish, who shot as "pirates" fifty-three of the passengers and crewmen, some of them U.S. citizens. As Americans shouted for revenge, the levelheaded Fish demanded and received an apology and indemnity from Madrid of $80,000. In view of the "hundreds of thousands of children who might have been made

Hamilton Fish (1808–1893). A graduate of Columbia University and lawyer, Fish served as a U.S. senator from New York (1851–1857) and opposed the expansion of slavery in the 1850s. More sophisticated, patient, and tactful than President Grant, he served as secretary of state, 1869–1877. (*Harper's Weekly*, 1869)

orphans, in an *unnecessary* war undertaken for a dishonest vessel," Fish worked "to avoid the terrible evil." Two years later the secretary unsuccessfully proposed joint mediation with Britain to "end a disastrous and destructive conflict."[125] Cuba continued to bleed until 1878, when the rebellion ended and slavery was abolished. With islanders and exiles still shouting for *Cuba Libre,* a U.S. diplomat prophesied: "The question of Cuba still remains, palpitating, to be settled, no one knows how, perhaps by some unforeseen accident."[126]

Cubans turned more and more toward the United States. Cuban dependence on U.S. markets and capital grew when beet-sugar growers in Europe cut into Cuban sales and threw the island economy into chaos. North American investors seized opportunities to obtain plantations across Cuba. Boston banker Edwin Atkins became one of the island's largest landowners, displacing planters of the Creole elite. Cubans played the American game of baseball, forming their first professional league in 1878. Expatriates in Tampa and Key West donated baseball gate receipts to the cause of Cuban independence. *Béisbol* became "an expression of change and an agent of change," as Cubans "celebrated the modernity and progress implied in baseball, associated with the United States, and denounced the inhumanity and backwardness suggested by bullfighting, associated with Spain."[127] Further evidence of cultural fusion became evident in the flow of people back and forth between Cuba and the United States. Wealthy Creoles sent their children to American colleges, married North American spouses, took North American names, and jettisoned Catholicism for Protestant denominations.

Growing economic interests in the hemisphere seemed to promise what James G. Blaine called "a commercial empire that legitimately belongs to us."[128] American investments in and trade with Latin American countries expanded dramatically—in Cuba (sugar and mines), Guatemala (the United States handled 64 percent of the country's trade by 1885), and Mexico (railroads and mines). In Mexico, in what the historian John Mason Hart has called the beginnings of "globalization," North American elites "tested a variety of approaches they have since used to extend their power and influence around the globe."[129] Much of Mexico was "pulled into the Yankee vortex," as U.S. industrialists and financiers formed partnerships with local notables, pioneered cooperative arrangements with multinational firms, constructed railroads, mined copper ore, bought large tracts of land, developed ports, and meddled in Mexican politics.[130] Helped to power by U.S. arms and dollars, the long and stable regime of Mexican dictator Porfirio Díaz (1876–1910) invited American capital and technology in the belief that it would "modernize and transform their country."[131] By the 1890s, the United States was buying 75 percent of Mexico's exports and supplying about 50 percent of its imports. U.S. citizens had invested some $250 million in all of Latin America by 1890. Still, the region took just 5 percent of total American exports that year. Most U.S. trade remained with Europe. Although these economic ties with Latin America comprised a small part of the total worldwide U.S. economic relationships, for countries like Cuba and Mexico such links became vital and brought the United States into the internal affairs of these countries. American economic interests also drew the United States into a Brazilian civil war in 1893–1894, where Washington sent the South Atlantic Squadron to break a rebel blockade of Rio de Janeiro.

Central America attracted considerable U.S. interest because of prospects for an isthmian canal linking the Pacific Ocean and the Gulf of Mexico. The gala opening of

**James G. Blaine
(1830–1893).** Republican
representative and senator from
Maine and secretary of state
(1881, 1889–1892), Blaine
expanded U.S. interests in Latin
America. Blaine regarded Latin
Americans as Washington's
"younger sisters ... a race ...
of hot temper, quick to take
affront, ready to avenge a wrong
whether real or fancied." (Library of
Congress)

the Suez Canal in 1869 spurred American canal enthusiasts, most notably the irascible Senator John Tyler Morgan of Alabama, an ardent expansionist who hoped to convert "the Gulf of Mexico into an American Mediterranean and Mobile into a flourishing international port."[132] Panama and Nicaragua seemed possible sites. The problem was the Clayton-Bulwer Treaty (1850), which held that a Central American canal had to be jointly controlled by Britain and the United States. Washington resented this limitation on American hegemonic expansion, and when President Rutherford Hayes learned in 1880 that Ferdinand de Lesseps, builder of the Suez Canal, would attempt to construct a canal through Panama, he sent two warships to demonstrate U.S. concern. "A canal under American control, or no canal," exclaimed Hayes, who called a completed canal "virtually a part of the coastline of the United States."[133]

In 1881 Secretary Blaine denounced the Clayton-Bulwer Treaty, claiming that the United States "with respect to European states, will not consent to perpetuate any treaty that impeaches our right and long-established claim to priority on the American continent."[134] Three years later, in overt violation of the treaty, the United States signed a canal treaty with Nicaragua, although President Cleveland withdrew the offending pact when he took office. An inexorable movement led by naval officers, business leaders, and diplomats for an exclusive U.S. canal had begun nonetheless. In Panama in 1873 and 1885, U.S. troops went ashore to protect American property threatened by civil war. In the latter year an obsolescent American warship under the command of Alfred Thayer Mahan displayed U.S. power to Guatemala, whose invasion of El Salvador threatened James A. Scrymser's Central and South American Telegraph Company.

The convocation of the first Pan American Conference in Washington in 1889 bore further witness to the growing U.S. influence in Latin America. The glittering event attracted representatives from seventeen countries. After a tour of industrial sites in forty-one cities, the conferees assembled in Washington to hear Blaine's appeal for "enlightened and enlarged intercourse."[135] Unlike similar conferences in the twentieth century, the United States could not dictate the results. Opposed to hemispheric union because the "Yankees consider the Americas their own and view the remaining nations as children under their tutelage," Argentina saw Pan Americanism as a U.S. ruse to gain commercial domination.[136] Although the conferees rejected Blaine's proposals for a low-tariff zone and for compulsory arbitration of political disputes, they did organize the International Bureau of American Republics (later called the Pan American Union) and encouraged reciprocity treaties to expand hemispheric trade. The conference also promoted inter-American steamship lines and railroads and established machinery to discuss commercial questions.

The Pan American Union amounted to little in its early days. It had its most conspicuous impact on the Washington landscape, where, with major financial help from the steel baron Andrew Carnegie, the Pan American Union put up an impressive building in the nation's capital. Pan Americanism did not mean hemispheric unity; rather it represented growing U.S. influence among neighbors to the south. For that reason European powers eyed the new organization with suspicion.

Crises with Chile in 1891 and with Venezuela in 1895 (see Chapter 6) demonstrated U.S. determination to dominate the Western Hemisphere. Chilean-American relations steadily deteriorated, in part because the United States had clumsily attempted to end the War of the Pacific (1879–1883), in which Chile battled Bolivia and Peru to win nitrate-rich territory. When civil war ripped through Chile in early 1891, the United States backed the sitting government, which had tried to assume dictatorial powers. The U.S. Navy seized arms purchased in the United States and destined for the rebels. When the victorious revolutionary Congressionalists took office, President Benjamin Harrison at first withheld recognition, muttering that "sometime it may be necessary to instruct them" on "how to use victory with dignity and moderation."[137] To make matters worse, Washington suspected that Britain, ever the competitor in Latin America, was cementing close ties with the new Chilean regime.

An incident in October 1891, after the end of the civil war, nearly exploded into a Chilean-American war. At Valparaiso, a major port for North American traders, one of the ships of the Pacific Squadron, the heavily armed cruiser *Baltimore,* anchored in the harbor. Commanded by Captain Winfield S. Schley, the ship had orders to protect American interests during the civil war. On October 16 its crew went ashore on liberty. The exuberant sailors gave local taverns and brothels considerable business. Outside the True Blue Saloon, rum-drunk Americans and anti-Yankee Chileans quarreled, fists flew, and knives slashed. Two Americans died, others suffered wounds, and some were arrested.

President Harrison reacted angrily to this affront to the American uniform, especially when the Chilean government did not hurry to apologize. Captain Robley D. ("Fighting Bob") Evans of the *Yorktown* replaced Schley and warned Chileans that "if they could not control their people," he would "shoot any and every man

Punishment for Chile, 1891. An angry Uncle Sam is about to administer U.S. retribution to Chile after the *Baltimore* affair. The historian Joyce Goldberg has written that "the narrow-minded nationalism and diplomatic bullying demonstrated in the *Baltimore* affair annoyed the very powers the United States wanted to impress. They interpreted it as rude, unnecessarily belligerent, and undignified behavior." (*Harper's Weekly,* 1891)

who insulted me or my men or my flag in any way."[138] A British diplomat observed: "The President and the Secretary of the Navy wish for war; one to get re-elected, the other to see his new ships fight and get votes for more."[139] After a change in the Chilean cabinet in early 1892, the cautious South Americans expressed regret ("*sentimiento muy sincero*") and paid an indemnity of $75,000 in gold.[140] The Yankee Goliath had taught "the snarling whelps of the Pacific that we cannot be snapped at with impunity," and Latin Americans had to wonder what Pan Americanism really meant.[141] Advocates of the expanding U.S. Navy cheered the "victory" over Chile, but a British official thought the incident created a "passionate sense of hatred toward the United States, which will take a long time to remove."[142] Senator George Shoup of Iowa drew a different lesson from the Chilean episode: "The American Republic will stand no more nonsense from any power, big or little."[143]

Going Global

Indeed, by the mid-1890s, the United States had become far more self-confident and demonstrably more arrogant than it had been in 1865, and far more willing to exert its growing power, especially in Latin America. The anti-imperialist sentiments that had spoiled earlier imperial ventures had weakened by the 1890s, undercut by chauvinistic nationalism, international rivalry, the glut thesis, the depression of the 1890s, and the relentless U.S. expansion that had put Iowa farmers' cereals in England, missionaries in China, Wild West shows in Europe, cans of Armour corned beef in India, Singer sewing machines in the Caroline Islands, McCormick reapers in Russia, warships in Korea and Brazil, explorers in Africa, sugar growers in Hawai'i, baseball in Cuba, mining companies in Mexico, rollicking sailors in Chile, and Nellie Bly girdling the globe. Thus could a French observer in 1888 predict that "an American expedition to conquer Europe in the twentieth or twenty-first century is no more extraordinary or impossible than the European expeditions [to America] of the sixteenth, seventeenth, and eighteenth centuries."[144] All these tumultuous phenomena demonstrated how dramatic was the transformation of the United States from a regional to a global power in a short span of thirty years.

FURTHER READING FOR THE PERIOD 1865–1895

General and presidential studies include Robert L. Beisner, *From the Old Diplomacy to the New* (1986); Josiah Bunting, *Ulysses S. Grant* (2004); Charles W. Calhoun, ed., *The Gilded Age* (1995 and 2007); Justus D. Doenecke, *The Presidencies of James A. Garfield and Chester A. Arthur* (1981); Henry Graff, *Grover Cleveland* (2002); David Healy, *U.S. Expansionism* (1970); Ari Hoogenboom, *The Presidency of Rutherford B. Hayes* (1988) and *Rutherford B. Hayes* (1995); Robert Kagan, *Dangerous Nation* (2006); Paul A. Koistinen, *Mobilizing for Modern War: The Political Economy of American Warfare, 1865–1916* (1997); Walter LaFeber, *The American Search for Opportunity, 1865–1913* (1993) and *The New Empire,* new ed. (1998); Henry E. Mattox, *The Twilight of Amateur Diplomacy* (1989) (foreign service); Tennant S. McWilliams, *The New South Faces the World* (1988); David M. Pletcher, *The Diplomacy of Involvement* (2001) and *The Diplomacy of Trade and Investment* (1998); Serge Ricard, ed., *La république impérialiste* (1987); Homer E. Socolofsky and Allan B. Spetter, *The Presidency of Benjamin Harrison* (1987); Richard E. Welch, *The Presidencies of Grover Cleveland* (1988); Robert Wiebe, *The Search for Order* (1967); William A. Williams, *The Roots of the Modern American Empire* (1969) and *The Tragedy of American Diplomacy* (1962); Fareed Zakaria, *From Wealth to Power* (1998); and Warren Zimmermann, *First Great Triumph* (2002).

For explanations of shifting power in the international system of the late nineteenth century and for comparative studies, see Philip Darby, *Three Faces of Imperialism* (1987); Aaron L. Friedberg, *The Weary Titan* (1988); Daniel R. Headrick, *The Invisible Weapon* (1991); Paul Kennedy, *The Rise and Fall of the Great Powers* (1987); and Anne Orde, *The Eclipse of Great Britain* (1996). See also works cited in Chapters 6 and 7.

Biographical studies include Charles W. Calhoun, *Gilded Age Cato* (1988) (Gresham) and *Benjamin Harrison* (2005); Edward P. Crapol, *James G. Blaine* (2000); Michael Devine, *John W. Foster* (1980); David Donald, *Charles Sumner and the Rights of Man* (1970); Joseph A. Fry, *Henry S. Sanford* (1982) and *John Tyler Morgan and the Search for Southern Automony* (1992); David Healy, *James G. Blaine and Latin America* (2001); Tim Jeal, *Stanley* (2008); William S. McFeely, *Grant* (1981); Ernest N. Paolino, *The Foundations of the American Empire* (1973) (Seward); Ira Rutkow, *James A. Garfield* (2006); Gene E. Smith, *Grant* (2001); and Hans L. Trefousse, *Carl Schurz* (1982).

For cultural and ideological influences, including American images of foreign peoples, see Nancy Boyd, *Emissaries* (1996) (YWCA); James T. Campbell et al, eds., *Race, Nation, and Empire in American History* (2007); Holly Edwards, *Noble Dreams, Wicked Plans* (2000) (Orientalism); Patricia Hill, *The World Their Household* (1985) (women missionaries); Michael H. Hunt, *Ideology and U.S. Foreign Policy* (1987); Matthew Frye Jacobson, *Barbarian Virtues* (2000); Amy Kaplan, *The Anarchy of Empire in the Making of U.S. Culture* (2002); R. Kroes et al., eds., *Cultural Transformations and Receptions* (1993); Eric L. Love, *Race over Empire* (2004); Catherine A. Lutz and Jane L. Collins, *Reading National Geographic* (1993); Clifford Putney, *Muscular Christianity* (2001); Emily S. Rosenberg, *Spreading the American Dream* (1982); David Spurr, *The Rhetoric of Empire* (1993); Robert W. Rydell, *All the World's a Fair* (1985), ed., *Fair Representations* (1994), and *World of Fairs* (1993); Robert Rydell et al., *Fair America* (2000); Robert Rydell and Rob Kroes, *Buffalo Bill in Bologna* (2005); Anders Stephanson, *Manifest Destiny* (1995); Kim Townsend, *Manhood at Harvard* (1996); Ian Tyrrell, *Women's World/Women's Empire* (1991) (WTCU); and Thomas Zeiler, *Ambassadors in Pinstripes* (2007) (baseball). See also works cited in Chapters 6 and 7.

Economic questions are treated in William H. Becker, *The Dynamics of Business-Government Relations* (1982); Vincent P. Carosso, *The Morgans* (1987); Robert B. Davies, *Peacefully Working to Conquer the World* (1976); David A. Lake, *Power, Protection, and Free Trade* (1988); Tom Terrill, *The Tariff, Politics, and American Foreign Policy, 1874–1901* (1973); and Mira Wilkins, *The Emergence of the Multinational Enterprise* (1970).

The transformation of the U.S. Navy is discussed in John Alden, *The American Steel Navy* (2005); Benjamin F. Cooling, *Benjamin Franklin Tracy* (1973) and *Gray Steel and Blue Water Navy* (1979); Frederick C. Drake, *The Empire of the Seas* (1984) (Shufeldt); Kenneth J. Hagan, *American Gunboat Diplomacy and the Old Navy, 1877–1889* (1973), ed., *In Peace and War* (1984), and *This People's Navy* (1991); Walter R. Herrick, *The American Naval Revolution* (1966); Peter Karsten, *The Naval Aristocracy* (1972); David F. Long, *Gold Braid and Foreign Relations* (1988); Robert Seager, *Alfred Thayer Mahan* (1977); Mark R. Shulman, *Navalism and the Emergence of American Sea Power* (1995); and Peter Trubowitz et al., eds., *The Politics of Strategic Adjustment* (1999).

For the Great Britain–Canada–U.S. relationship, see Charles S. Campbell, *From Revolution to Rapprochement* (1974); Adrian Cook, *The Alabama Claims* (1975); Edward P. Crapol, *America for Americans: Economic Nationalism and Anglophobia* (1973); John M. Findlay and Ken S. Coates, eds., *Parallel Destinies* (2002); Brian Jenkins, *Fenians and Anglo-American Relations During Reconstruction* (1969); Lawrence Martin, *The Presidents and the Prime Ministers* (1982); W. S. Neidhardt, *Fenianism in North America* (1975); Richard A. Preston, *The Defense of the Undefended Border* (1977); and Reginald C. Stuart, *United States Expansionism and British North America, 1775–1871* (1988).

U.S. relations with Latin America are discussed in Richard H. Bradford, *The Virginius Affair* (1980); Jules Davids, *American Political and Economic Penetration of Mexico, 1877–1920* (1976); Joyce S. Goldberg, *The Baltimore Affair* (1986); John Mason Hart, *Empire and Revolution* (2002) (Mexico); José M. Hernández, *Cuba and the United States* (1993); Virginia Scott Jenkins, *Bananas* (2000); Luis Martínez-Fernández, *Torn Between Empires* (1994) (Spanish Caribbean); Louis A. Pérez, Jr., *Cuba and the United States* (2003) and *Cuba Between Empires* (1982); W. Dirk Raat, *Mexico and the United States* (1992); Ramón E. Ruíz, *The People of Sonora and Yankee Capitalists* (1988); Karl M. Schmitt, *Mexico and the United States, 1821–1973* (1974); Thomas D. Schoonover, *Dollars over Dominion* (1978) (Mexico) and *The United States in Central America, 1860–1911* (1991); Lars Schoultz, *Beneath the United States* (1998); Joseph Smith, *Illusions of Conflict* (1979); and Steven C. Topik, *Trade and Gunboats* (1996) (Brazil).

For Hawai'i, see Helena G. Allen, *Sanford Ballard Dole* (1988) and *The Betrayal of Queen Liliuokalani* (1982); Stuart Banner, *Possessing the Pacific* (2007); Ralph S. Kuykendall, *The Hawaiian Kingdom, 1874–1893* (1967); W. A. Russ, Jr., *The Hawaiian Revolution, 1893–94* (1959); Noenoe K. Silva, *Aloha Betrayed* (2004); Merze Tate, *The United States and the Hawaiian Kingdom* (1965); and John E. Van Sant, *Pacific Pioneers* (2000).

For Asian-American relations, see David L. Anderson, *Imperialism and Idealism* (1985); W. G. Beasley, *Japan Encounters the Barbarians* (1995); Jerome Ch'en, *China and the West* (1979); Warren I. Cohen, *America's Response to China* (2000); Wayne Flynt and Gerald W. Berkeley, *Taking Christianity to China* (1997); Gael Graham, *Gender, Culture, and Christianity* (1995) (missionaries in China); Jack L. Hammersmith, *Spoilsman in a "Flowery Fairyland"* (1998); Fred Harvey Harrington, *God, Mammon, and the Japanese* (1944) (Korea); Joseph Henning, *Outposts of Civilization* (2000) (Japan); James Huffman, *A Yankee in Meiji Japan* (2003); Michael H. Hunt, *The Making of a Special Relationship* (1983) (China); Akira Iriye, *Across the Pacific* (1967); Paul M. Kennedy, *The Samoan Tangle* (1974); Walter LaFeber, *The Clash* (1997); Yun-Bok Lee, *Diplomatic Relations Between the United States and Korea, 1866–1887* (1970); Charles J. McClain, *In Search of Equality* (1994) (Chinese in United States); Robert McClellan, *The Heathen Chinee* (1971) (Chinese); Gary Okihiro, *Island World* (2008) (Hawai'i); Jean Pfaelzer, *Driven Out* (2007) (Chinese Americans); Craig Storti, *Incident at Bitter Creek* (1991); Shih-shan Henry Tsai, *China and the Overseas Chinese in the United States, 1868–1911* (1983); and Thomas A. Tweed, *The American Encounter with Buddhism, 1844–1912* (1992).

Alaska and Russian-American relations are discussed in David S. Foglesong, *The United States Mission and the "Evil Empire"* (2007); James T. Gay, *American Fur Seal Diplomacy* (1987); Paul S. Holbo, *Tarnished Expansion* (1983); Ronald J. Jensen, *The Alaska Purchase and Russian-American Relations* (1975); Howard I. Kushner, *Conflict on the Northwest Coast* (1975); Norman E. Saul, *Concord & Conflict* (1996); and Frederick F. Travis, *George Kennan and the American-Russian Relationship, 1865–1924* (1990).

U.S. interest in Africa is studied in Edward W. Chester, *Clash of Titans* (1974); Clarence Clendenden, Robert Collins, and Peter Duignan, *Americans in Africa, 1865–1900* (1966); Sybil E. Crowe, *The Berlin West African Conference, 1884–1885* (1942); Peter Duignan and L. H. Gann, *The United States and Africa* (1987); Tim Jeal, *Stanley* (2007); Thomas Pakenham, *The Scramble for Africa* (1991); Lamin Sanneh, *Abolitionists Abroad* (1999); Elliott P. Skinner, *African Americans and U.S. Policy Toward Africa, 1850–1924* (1992); and Walter L. Williams, *Black Americans and the Evangelization of Africa, 1877–1900* (1982).

See also the General Bibliography, the following notes, and Robert L. Beisner, ed., *Guide to American Foreign Relations Since 1600* (2003).

NOTES TO CHAPTER 5

1. Quoted in Eric T. Love, *Race over Empire* (Chapel Hill: University of North Carolina Press, 2004), p. 50.

2. Charles C. Tansill, *The United States and Santo Domingo* (Baltimore: Johns Hopkins Press, 1938), p. 134.

3. Quoted in Richard F. Hamilton, *President McKinley, War, and Empire* (New Brunswick, N.J.: Transaction Publishers, 2006), p. 13.

4. William Cazneau quoted in Linda S. Hudson, *Mistress of Manifest Destiny* (Austin: Texas Historical Society, 2001), p. 188.

5. Admiral Charles Poor quoted in David Long, *Gold Braid and Foreign Relations* (Annapolis: Naval Institute Press, 1988), p. 348.

6. Quoted in Josiah Bunting III, *Ulysses S. Grant* (New York: Times Books, 2004), p. 104.

7. Quoted in Hans L. Trefousse, *Carl Schurz* (Knoxville: University of Tennessee Press, 1982), p. 195.

8. Quoted in Andrew L. Slap, *The Doom of Reconstruction* (New York: Fordham University Press, 2006), p. 118.

9. Quoted in William J. Nelson, *Almost a Territory* (Newark: University of Delaware Press, 1990), p. 102.

10. Quoted in Love, *Race over Empire,* p. 44.

11. Quoted in David Donald, *Charles Sumner and the Rights of Man* (New York: Knopf, 1970), p. 443.

12. Fernando Wood quoted in Luis Martínez-Fernández, *Torn Between Empires* (Athens: University of Georgia Press, 1994), p. 166.

13. John Y. Simon, ed., *The Papers of Ulysses S. Grant* (Carbondale: Southern Illinois University Press, 1967), *XX,* 155.

14. Grant quoted in Love, *Race over Empire,* p. 64.

15. Simon, *Grant Papers, XX,* 164n.

16. Rollo Ogden, ed., *Life and Letters of Edwin Lawrence Godkin* (New York: Macmillan, 1907; 2 vols.), *I,* 304–305.

17. Quoted in Allan Nevins, *Hamilton Fish* (New York: Dodd, Mead, 1937), p. 372.

18. *The Works of Charles Sumner* (Boston: Lee and Shepard, 1870–1883; 15 vols.), *XIV,* 94–124.

19. Mary Ann Heiss, "The Evolution of the Imperial Idea and U.S. National Identity," *Diplomatic History, XXVI* (Fall 2002), 524; Fareed Zakaria, *From Wealth to Power* (Princeton: Princeton University Press, 1998), p. 44.

20. Zakaria, *From Wealth to Power,* p. 181.

21. Edward P. Crapol, "Coming to Terms with Empire," *Diplomatic History, XVI* (Fall 1992), 593–594.

22. Quoted in Robert W. Rydell, *All the World's a Fair* (Chicago: University of Chicago Press, 1984), p. 7.

23. Ian Tyrrell, *Woman's World/Woman's Empire* (Chapel Hill: University of North Carolina Press, 1991), p. 4.

24. Quoted in Alexander DeConde, *Ethnicity, Race, and American Foreign Policy* (Boston: Northeastern University Press, 1992), p. 54.

25. Quoted in David S. Foglesong, *The American Mission and the "Evil Empire"* (New York: Cambridge University Press, 2007), pp. 7, 17.

26. Quoted in Mary Renda, *Taking Haiti* (Chapel Hill: University of North Carolina Press, 2001), p. 196.

27. William Griffis quoted in Joseph M. Henning, *Outposts of Civilization* (New York: New York University Press, 2000), p. 160.

28. Quoted in Kim Townsend, *Manhood at Harvard* (Cambridge: Harvard University Press, 1996), p. 243; quoted in Matthew Frye Jacobson, *Barbarian Virtues* (New York: Hill and Wang, 2000), p. 3.

29. Robert W. Rydell, John E. Findling, and Kimberly D. Pelle, *Fair America* (Washington, D.C.: Smithsonian Institution Press, 2000), p. 29.

30. Quoted in Emily S. Rosenberg, *Spreading the American Dream* (New York: Hill & Wang, 1982), p. 29.

31. Quoted in William R. Hutchinson, *Errand to the World* (Chicago: University of Chicago Press, 1987), p. 123.

32. Michael B. Oren, *Power, Faith, and Fantasy* (New York: Norton, 2007), p. 228.

33. Quoted in Joseph A. Fry, "Late Nineteenth Century U.S. Foreign Relations," in Charles W. Calhoun, ed., *The Gilded Age* (New York: Rowman & Littlefield, 2007), p. 318.

34. Quoted in Amy Kaplan, *The Anarchy of Empire in the Making of U.S. Culture* (Cambridge: Harvard University Press, 2002), p. 102.

35. John F. Sears, "Bierstadt, Buffalo Bill, and the Wild West in Europe," in R. Kroes et al., eds., *Cultural Transformations and Receptions* (Amsterdam: Vu University Press, 1993), pp. 11, 19.

36. Patricia Nelson Limerick, "A Panel of Appraisal," *Western Historical Quarterly, XX* (August 1989), 317.

37. James O. Gump, *The Dust Rose Like Smoke* (Lincoln: University of Nebraska Press, 1994), p. 137.

38. Quoted in Edmund J. Danziger Jr., "Native American Resistance and Accommodation," in Calhoun, ed., *Gilded Age*, p. 177.

39. Quoted in William T. Hagan, *Taking Indian Lands* (Norman: University of Oklahoma Press, 2003), p. 240.

40. Walter L. Williams, "United States Indian Policy and the Debate over Philippine Annexation," *Journal of American History, LXVI* (March 1980), 810–812.

41. Henry Cabot Lodge quoted in Henry F. Graff, *Grover Cleveland* (New York: Times Books, 2002), p. 122.

42. Quoted in Edward P. Crapol, *James G. Blaine* (Wilmington, Del.: Scholarly Resources, 2000), p. 138.

43. Louis Simon quoted in Jacques Portes, *Fascination and Misgivings* (New York: Cambridge University Press, 2002), p. 369.

44. Rep. Roger Mills quoted in Fry, "Late Nineteenth Century," p. 309.

45. Quoted in David M. Pletcher, "Rhetoric and Results," *Diplomatic History, V* (Spring 1981), 95.

46. Quoted in Michael Adas, *Dominance by Design* (Cambridge: Harvard University Press, 2006), p. 107

47. Quoted in Douglas Little, *American Orientalism* (Chapel Hill: University of North Carolina Press, 2002), p. 14.

48. Gilbert M. Joseph, *Revolution from Without* (Cambridge, Eng.: Cambridge University Press, 1982), p. 43.

49. Thomas Leonard, "Central America," in Leonard, ed., *United States–Latin American Relations, 1850–1903* (Tuscaloosa: University of Alabama Press, 1999), p. 97.

50. Quoted in Thomas Zeiler, "Globalization for Diplomatic Historians," *Diplomatic History, XXV* (Fall 2001), 538.

51. Emile Barbier quoted in Philippe Roger, *The American Enemy* (Chicago: University of Chicago Press, 2005), p. 137.

52. W. T. Stead quoted in Robert W. Rydell and Rob Kroes, *Buffalo Bill in Bologna* (Chicago: University of Chicago Press, 2005), pp. 97–98.

53. Spalding quoted in Sayuri Guthrie-Shimizu, "For the Love of the Game," *Diplomatic History, XXVIII* (November 2004), 650.

54. Quoted in Henry E. Mattox, *The Twilight of Amateur Diplomacy* (Kent, Ohio: Kent State University Press, 1989), p. x.

55. David A. Lake, *Power, Protection, and Free Trade* (Ithaca: Cornell University Press, 1988), p. 117.

56. Quoted in David Healy, *U.S. Expansionism* (Madison: University of Wisconsin Press, 1970), p. 44.

57. Quoted in Lance C. Buhl, "Maintaining 'An American Navy,' 1865–1889," in Kenneth J. Hagan, ed., *In Peace and War* (Westport, Conn.: Greenwood, 2008; 3rd ed.), p. 167.

58. Quoted in Kenneth J. Hagan, *American Gunboat Diplomacy and the Old Navy* (Westport, Conn.: Greenwood, 1973), p. 37.

59. Russell F. Weigley, *The American Way of War* (New York: Macmillan, 1973), p. 153.

60. Quoted in Michael H. Hunt, *The American Ascendancy* (Chapel Hill: University of North Carolina Press, 2007), p. 74.

61. Quoted in Mark Shulman, *Navalism and the Emergence of American Sea Power, 1882–1893* (Annapolis: Naval Institute Press, 1995), p. 41.

62. Quoted in Kenneth J. Hagan, "Alfred Thayer Mahan," in Frank Merli and Theodore A. Wilson, eds., *Makers of American Diplomacy* (New York: Charles Scribner's Sons, 1974), p. 290.

63. Shulman, *Navalism*, p. 38.

64. Jules Heret quoted in Roger, *American Enemy*, p. 134.

65. Quoted in Anders Stephanson, *Manifest Destiny* (New York: Hill & Wang, 1995), p. 62.

66. Quoted in David M. Pletcher, *The Diplomacy of Involvement* (Columbia: University of Missouri Press, 2001), p. 1.

67. Henry Adams quoted in Love, *Race over Empire*, p. 28.

68. Quoted in Oleh W. Gerus, "The Russian Withdrawal from Alaska," *Revista de historia de America, LXXV–LXXVI* (December 1973), 162.

69. Quoted in Ronald J. Jensen, *The Alaska Purchase and Russian-American Relations* (Seattle: University of Washington Press, 1975), p. 55.

70. Quoted in Milton O. Gustafson, "Seward's Bargain," *Prologue, XXVI* (Winter 1994), 263.

71. Quoted in Norman E. Saul, *Concord & Conflict* (Lawrence: University Press of Kansas, 1996), p. 3.

72. Quoted in Ernest N. Paolino, *The Foundations of the American Empire* (Ithaca: Cornell University Press, 1973), p. 207.

73. Quoted in David Mayers, *Dissenting Voices in America's Rise to Power* (New York: Cambridge University Press, 2007), p. 152.

74. Walter Nugent, *Crossings* (Bloomington: Indiana University Press, 1992), p. 144.

75. Quoted in David M. Pletcher, *The Diplomacy of Trade and Investment* (Columbia: University of Missouri Press, 1998), p. 226.

76. Reginald C. Stuart, *United States Expansionism and British North America, 1775–1871* (Chapel Hill: University of North Carolina Press, 1988), p. 261.

77. Quoted in Jonathan W. Gantt, "Irish-American Terrorism and Anglo-American Relations, 1881-1885," *Journal of the Gilded Age and Progressive Era, V* (October 2006), 14, 18.

78. Quoted in Robert Kagan, *Dangerous Nation* (New York: Knopf, 2006), p. 276.

79. Quoted in Adrian Cook, *The Alabama Claims* (Ithaca: Cornell University Press, 1975), p. 89.

80. Quoted in David P. Crook, *Diplomacy During the American Civil War* (New York: Wiley, 1975), p. 131.

81. Quoted in Gerald M. Craig, *The United States and Canada* (Cambridge: Harvard University Press, 1968), p. 149.

82. Quoted in Lawrence Martin, *The Presidents and the Prime Ministers* (Toronto: Doubleday Canada, 1982), p. 42.

83. Samuel Flagg Bemis, *A Diplomatic History of the United States* (New York: Holt, Rinehart and Winston, 1965; 5th ed.), p. 413.

84. Quoted in Michael H. Hunt, *The Making of a Special Relationship* (New York: Columbia University Press, 1983), p. 115.

85. Quoted in William A. Williams, *The Roots of the Modern American Empire* (New York: Random House, 1969), p. 219.

86. Quoted in Robert B. Davies, "Peacefully Working to Conquer the World," *Business History Review, XLIII* (Autumn 1969), 323.

87. Quoted in David L. Anderson, *Imperialism and Idealism* (Bloomington: Indiana University Press, 1985), pp. 3–4.

88. Quoted in Kagan, *Dangerous Nation*, p. 299.

89. Quoted in Jean Pfaelzer, *Driven Out* (New York: Oxford University Press, 2007), p. 211.

90. Quoted in Craig Storti, *Incident at Bitter Creek* (Ames: Iowa State University Press, 1991), p. 156.

91. Quoted in Pfaelzer, *Driven Out*, p. 215.

92. Quoted in Frederick C. Drake, *The Empire of the Seas* (Honolulu: University of Hawaii Press, 1984), p. 105.

93. Quoted in Long, *Gold Braid*, p. 379.

94. Quoted in Hunt, *Making of a Special Relationship*, p. 128.

95. Quoted in Kagan, *Dangerous Nation*, p. 334.

96. Mark Twain quoted in Kaplan, *Anarchy*, p. 67.

97. Charles Nordhoff quoted in Stuart Banner, *Possessing the Pacific* (Cambridge: Harvard University Press, 2007), p. 158.

98. Pletcher, *Diplomacy of Involvement*, p. 57.

99. Quoted in Spencer Tucker, *Insatiable Appetite* (Berkeley: University of California Press, 2000), p. 82; quoted in David M. Pletcher, *The Awkward Years* (Columbia: University of Missouri Press, 1962), p. 70.

100. Quoted in Julius W. Pratt, *Expansionists of 1898* (Chicago: Quadrangle, [1936], 1964), p. 25.

101. Quoted in Stephen Kinzer, *Overthrow* (New York: Times Books, 2006), p. 30.

102. Quoted in Merze Tate, *The United States and the Hawaiian Kingdom* (New Haven: Yale University Press, 1965), p. 210.

103. Quoted in Charles W. Calhoun, *Benjamin Harrison* (New York: Times Books, 2005), p. 152.

104. Samuel Armstrong quoted in Love, *Race over Empire*, p. 110.

105. Quoted in Henry F. Graff, *Grover Cleveland* (New York: Times Books, 2002), p. 121.

106. Quoted in Tennant S. McWilliams, *The New South Faces the World* (Baton Rouge: Louisiana State University Press, 1988), p. 34.

107. Sanford Dole quoted in Noenoe K. Silva, *Aloha Betrayed* (Durham: Duke University Press, 2004), p. 170.

108. Quoted in Long, *Gold Braid*, p. 391.

109. John Kasson quoted in Pletcher, *Diplomacy of Involvement*, p. 85.

110. Quoted in Paul M. Kennedy, *The Samoan Tangle* (New York: Barnes & Noble, 1974), p. 53.

111. Quoted *ibid.*, p. 76.

112. Quoted in Healy, *U.S. Expansionism*, p. 118.

113. *Public Opinion* quoted in Pletcher, *Diplomacy of Involvement*, pp. 88–89.

114. Quoted in Jon D. Holstine, "Vermonter in Paradise," *Vermont History, XLIII* (Spring 1975), 140.

115. Quoted in Drake, *Empire of the Seas*, p. 177.

116. Quoted *ibid.*, p. 185.

117. Quoted in David Spurr, *The Rhetoric of Empire* (Durham, N.C.: Duke University Press, 1993), p. 80.

118. Quoted in Thomas Pakenham, *The Scramble for Africa, 1876–1912* (New York: Random House, 1991), pp. 246–248.

119. Quoted in Elliott P. Skinner, *African Americans and U.S. Policy Toward Africa, 1850–1924* (Washington, D.C.: Howard University Press, 1992), p. 134.

120. Matthew Frye Jaconson, *Barbarian Virtues* (New York: Hill & Wang, 2000), p. 118.

121. Jay Mullen, "Chaillé-Long: Yankee on the Nile" (Unpub. manuscript, 2003).

122. Quoted in Thomas Borstlemann, *Apartheid's Reluctant Uncle* (New York: Oxford University Press, 1993), p. 117.

123. E. L. Godkin quoted in Frank Ninkovich, "Anti-imperialism in U.S. Foreign Relations," in Randall B. Woods, ed., *Vietnam and the American Political Tradition* (New York: Cambridge University Press, 2003), p. 17.

124. Quoted in Louis A. Pérez, Jr., *Cuba and the United States* (Athens: University Press of Georgia, 1997; 2nd ed.), p. 59.

125. Fish quoted in Richard H. Bradford, *The Virginius Affair* (Boulder: Colorado Associated University Press, 1980), p. 134 and in Jay Sexton, "The United States, the Cuban Rebellion, and the Multilateral Initiative of 1875," *Diplomatic History, XXX* (June 2006), 357.

126. Caleb Cushing quoted in Bradford, *Virginius Affair*, p. 120.

127. Louis A. Pérez, Jr., "Between Baseball and Bullfighting," *Journal of American History, LXXX* (September 1994), 505.

128. Quoted in Robert E. Hannigan, *The New World Empire* (Philadelphia: University of Pennsylvania Press, 2002), p. 54.

129. John Mason Hart, *Empire and Revolution* (Berkeley: University of California Press, 2002), p. 5.

130. Ramón Eduardo Ruíz, *The People of Sonora and Yankee Capitalists* (Tucson: University of Arizona Press, 1988), p. 1.

131. Hart, *Empire*, p. 61.

132. Joseph A. Fry, *John Tyler Morgan and the Search for Southern Autonomy* (Knoxville: University of Tennessee Press, 1992), p. xii.

133. Quoted in David Healy, *James G. Blaine and Latin America* (Columbia: University of Missouri Press, 2001), p. 40; quoted in Ari Hoogenboom, *Rutherford B. Hayes* (Lawrence: University Press of Kansas, 1995), p. 419.

134. Quoted in Richard Van Alstyne, *The Rising American Empire* (New York: Norton [1960], 1974), p. 163.

135. Quoted in Alice Felt Tyler, *The Foreign Policy of James G. Blaine* (Minneapolis: University of Minnesota Press, 1927), p. 178.

136. Vicente Quesada quoted in David Sheinin, *Searching for Authority* (New Orleans: University Press of the South, 1998), p. 2.

137. Quoted in Robert L. Beisner, *From the Old Diplomacy to the New, 1865–1900* (Arlington Heights, Ill.: Harlan Davidson, 1986; 2nd ed.), p. 102.

138. Quoted in Shulman, *Navalism*, p. 92.

139. Quoted in Kenneth J. Hagan, *This People's Navy* (New York: Free Press, 1991), p. 199.

140. *New York Sun* quoted in Healy, *Blaine and Latin America*, p. 232.

141. Quoted in William F. Sater, *Chile and the United States* (Athens: University of Georgia Press, 1990), p. 67.

142. Quoted in Ernest R. May, *Imperial Democracy* (New York: Harper and Row [1961], 1973), p. 10.

143. Quoted in Calhoun, *Harrison*, p. 128.

144. H. de Beaumont quoted in Portes, *Fascinations and Misgivings*, p. 389.

CHAPTER 6

Imperialist Leap, 1895–1900

The Battleship Maine **Explodes.**   *This imaginative contemporary artwork depicts the U.S. battleship blowing up in the early morning of February 15, 1898, in the harbor of Havana, Cuba. The warship had arrived three weeks earlier to protect American citizens caught up in the Cuban rebellion against Spanish rule. The deaths of 266 U.S. sailors in the explosions helped feed popular passions for war with Spain. (Naval Historical Foundation)*

◈   *The* Maine, *McKinley, and War, 1898*

THE BURLY U.S. battleship *Maine* steamed into Havana harbor on January 25, 1898. "A beautiful sight," reported the American consul-general Fitzhugh Lee, who had requested the visit ostensibly to protect the lives of Americans living in war-torn Cuba.[1] President William McKinley had sent the vessel to Havana hoping to calm tensions with Spain, then in its third year of battling Cuban rebels fighting for national independence. The *Maine* was to stay three weeks and then depart for New Orleans in time for Mardi Gras. But at 9:40 P.M. on February 15, a "dull sullen" roar followed by massive explosions ripped through the 6,700-ton ship, killing 266 Americans.[2] McKinley, who had been taking sedatives to sleep, awoke an hour before dawn to take a phone call from Secretary of the Navy John D. Long reporting the event. "The *Maine* blown up! The *Maine* blown up!" the stunned president kept muttering to himself.[3] Even though "the country was not ready" for it, the war with Spain would begin three months later.[4]

McKinley ordered an official investigation of the *Maine* disaster and tried to gain time. With no evidence but with considerable emotion, many Americans assumed that the *Maine* had been "sunk by an act of dirty treachery on the part of the Spaniards."[5] In early March, U.S. Minister Stewart L. Woodford protested strongly to the Spanish about the *Maine*. "End it at once—*end it at once—end it at once,*" he exhorted Madrid regarding the war in Cuba.[6] On March 6 the president met with Joe Cannon, chair of the House Appropriations Committee, and asked for $50 million for war preparedness. "It seemed as though a hundred Fourths of July had been let loose in the House," a clerk noted, as Congress enthusiastically obliged three days later.[7]

In mid-March Senator Redfield Proctor of Vermont, a friend of McKinley reportedly opposed to war, graphically told his colleagues about his recent visit to Cuba. He recounted ugly stories about Spain's notorious reconcentration policy (the forced settlement of Cubans into fortified camps): "Torn from their homes, with foul earth, foul air, foul water, and foul food or none, what wonder that one-half died and one-quarter of the living are so diseased that they cannot be saved?"[8] Shortly after this moving speech, which convinced many members of Congress and business leaders that Spain could not restore order to Cuba, the American court of inquiry on the *Maine* concluded that an external mine of unknown origin had destroyed the vessel. A Spanish commission at about the same time attributed the disaster to an internal explosion. More than a century later, after several more investigations, experts still disagree whether the *Maine* blew up because of "a coal bunker fire" or from an "undership mine."[9] In 1898 vocal Americans pinned "the crime" squarely on Spain. "Remember the *Maine*, to hell with Spain" became a popular slogan.

A decorated veteran of the Civil War, President McKinley once asserted: "I have been through one war; I have seen the dead piled up, and I do not want to see another."[10] He quietly explored the possibility of purchasing Cuba for $300 million— or some other means "by which Spain can part with Cuba without loss of respect and with certainty of American control."[11] But a jingo frenzy had seized Congress. Interventionist critics increasingly questioned the president's manhood, claiming, as did Teddy Roosevelt, that he "had no more backbone than a chocolate eclair."[12] One member of Congress called the president's policies on Cuba "lame, halting, and impotent," while another said of McKinley: "He wobbles, he waits, he hesitates. He changes his mind."[13] Following one stormy Senate session, Vice President Garrett Hobart warned McKinley: "They will act without you if you do not act at once." "Say no more," McKinley responded.[14]

On March 27, Washington cabled the president's demands to Madrid: an armistice, Cuban–Spanish negotiations to secure a peace, McKinley's arbitration of the conflict if there was no peace by October, termination of the reconcentration policy, and relief aid to the Cubans. Implicit was the demand that Spain grant Cuba its independence under U.S. supervision. As a last-ditch effort to avoid American military intervention, the scheme had little chance of success. Spain's national pride and interest precluded surrender. The Cubans had already said they would accept "nothing short of absolute independence."[15] Madrid's answer nonetheless held some promise: Spain had already terminated reconcentration, would launch reforms, and would accept an armistice if the rebels did so first. Yet by refusing McKinley's mediation and Cuban independence, the Spanish reply did not satisfy the president or Congress. McKinley began to compose a war message in early April. On April 9, Spain made a new concession, declaring a unilateral suspension of hostilities "for such a length of time" as the Spanish commander "may think prudent."[16] Too qualified, the declaration still sidestepped Cuban independence and U.S. mediation. Any chance of European support for Spain faded when the British told Washington that they would "be guided [on Cuban issues] by the wishes of the president."[17]

On April 11, McKinley asked Congress for authority to use armed force to end the Cuban war. Since neither Cubans nor Spaniards could stem the flow of blood, Americans would do so to serve the "cause of humanity" and prevent "very serious injury to the commerce, trade, and business of our people, and the wanton destruction of property." Citing the *Maine,* he described the conflict as "a constant menace to our peace." He conspicuously made no mention of Cuban independence, defining the U.S. purpose as "forcible intervention … as a neutral to stop the war." At the very end of the message, McKinley asked Congress to give "your just and careful attention" to news of Spain's recently offered armistice.[18]

As Congress debated, McKinley beat back a Senate attempt to recognize the rebels. He strongly believed that Cuba needed American tutelage to prepare for self-government. And he wanted a Cuba subservient to the United States. Indeed, as the historian Louis A. Pérez, Jr., has argued, McKinley's decision for war seemed directed "as much against Cuban independence as it was against Spanish sovereignty."[19] Congress did endorse the Teller Amendment, which disclaimed any U.S. intent to annex the island. Even Teddy Roosevelt supported the amendment lest "it seem that we are merely engaged in a land-grabbing war."[20] On April 19 Congress proclaimed Cuba's independence (without recognizing the Cuban junta), demanded Spain's evacuation from the island, and directed the president to use force to secure these goals. Spain broke diplomatic relations on April 21. The next day U.S. warships began to blockade Cuba; Spain declared war on April 24. Congress issued its own declaration the next day.

William McKinley (1843–1901). In one of his last speeches before his death in 1901, McKinley peered into the next century: "How near one to the other is every part of the world. Modern inventions have brought into close relations widely separated peoples … distances have been effaced. … The world's products are being exchanged as never before … isolation is no longer possible or desirable." (Library of Congress)

Because of the Teller Amendment, the choice for war seemed selfless and humane, and for many Americans it undoubtedly was. But the decision had more complex motives. McKinley cited humanitarian concern, property, commerce, and the removal of a regional disturbance. Senator Henry Cabot Lodge invoked politics, telling the White House that "if the war in Cuba drags on through the summer … we [Republicans] shall go down to the greatest defeat ever known."[21] Important business leaders, initially hesitant, shifted in March and April to demand an end to Cuban disorder. Farmers and entrepreneurs ogling Asian and Latin American markets thought a U.S. victory over Spain might open new trade doors by eliminating a colonial power. Republican Senator George F. Hoar of Massachusetts, later an anti-imperialist, could not "look idly on while hundreds of thousands of innocent human beings … die of hunger close to our doors. If there is ever to be a war it should be to prevent such things."[22] Another senator claimed that "any sort of war is better than a rotting peace that eats out the core and heart of the manhood of this country."[23] Christian missionaries dreamed of new opportunities to convert the "uncivilized." Imperialists hoped that war would add new territories to the United States and encourage the growth of a larger navy. "Warriors" differed from "imperialists" in that some people opposed empire and sincerely thought war would halt the protracted conflict in Cuba, whereas imperialists seized on war as an opportunity to expand the American empire.

Emotional nationalism also made an impact. The *Maine* and de Lôme (see page 216) incidents ignited what one educator called the "formidable inflammability of our multitudinous population."[24] Imperialist senator Albert Beveridge waxed ebullient: "At last, God's hour has struck. The American people go forth in a warfare holier than liberty—holy as humanity."[25] Excited statements by people such as Roosevelt, who regarded war as a sport, aroused martial fevers. War would surely redeem national honor and repudiate those "old women of both sexes, shrieking cockatoos" who made virile men "wonder whether" they lived "in a free country or not."[26] Newspapers of the "yellow press" variety, such as William Randolph Hearst's *New York Journal* and Joseph Pulitzer's *New York World,* sensationalized stories of Spanish lust and atrocities. Others proudly compared the Cuban and American revolutions. The American public, already steeped in a brash nationalism and prepared by earlier diplomatic triumphs, reacted favorably to the hyperbole.

Both Washington and Madrid had tried diplomacy without success. McKinley wanted "peace" and independence for Cuba under U.S. tutelage. The first Spain could not deliver because the Cuban rebels sensed victory and complete independence, while Spanish forces remained weak. The second Spain could not grant immediately because ultranationalists might overthrow the constitutional Bourbon monarchy. Spain promised to fight the war more humanely and grant autonomy, but McKinley and Congress wanted more. They believed they had the right and duty to judge the affairs of Spain and Cuba. "To save Cuba, we must hold it," noted one reporter.[27]

Well-meaning or not, American meddling prevented Cubans and Spaniards from settling their own affairs. Sending the *Maine* and asking Congress for $50 million probably encouraged the Cuban rebels to resist any compromise. McKinley could have given Spain more breathing space. Spain, after all, did grant partial autonomy, which ultimately might have led to Cuban independence. Some critics said the president should have recognized the Cuban insurgents and covertly aided them. American matériel, not men, might have liberated Cuba from Spanish rule. By April 1898, one U.S. official concluded that Spain had become "absolutely hopeless, … exhausted financially and physically, while the Cubans are stronger."[28] McKinley wanted to avoid war and chose it reluctantly only after trying other options. That he adamantly refused to recognize the insurgency or the republic indicates also that he did not endorse outright Cuban independence. He probably had two goals in 1898: to remove Spain from Cuba and to control Cuba in some manner yet ill defined. When the Spanish balked at a sale and both belligerents rejected compromise, McKinley chose war—the only means to oust Spain *and* to control Cuba. A new and enlarged American empire shimmered on the horizon.

The Venezuela Crisis of 1895

Three years earlier, during the administration of an avowedly anti-imperialist president, a seemingly insignificant cartographic controversy in South America had served as a catalyst for empire. In July 1895, Secretary of State Richard Olney personally delivered a 12,000-word draft document to President Grover Cleveland on the Venezuelan boundary dispute. The president, thinking it "the best thing of its kind I ever read," suggested some "softened verbiage here and there" and directed that Olney send the document to London, which he did on July 20.[29]

What became known as Olney's "twenty-inch gun" pointed directly at Great Britain, which had long haggled with Venezuela over the boundary separating that country from British Guiana. The British drew a line in the 1840s, but nobody liked it. In the 1880s, the discovery of gold in the disputed region raised the stakes. At issue, too, was control of the mouth of the Orinoco River, gateway to the potential trade of northern South America. Since the 1870s, Venezuela had appealed to the United States over Britain's alleged violation of the Monroe Doctrine. Washington repeatedly asked the British to submit the issue to arbitration but met constant rebuff. London's latest refusal in December 1894 led to Olney's "twenty-inch gun" rejoinder.

The Venezuelans had hired William L. Scruggs, a former U.S. minister to Caracas, to propagandize their case before the American public. His widely circulated pamphlet *British Aggression in Venezuela, or the Monroe Doctrine on Trial* (1895) stirred considerable sympathy for the South American nation. Stereotypes soon replaced reasoned analysis: The land-grabbing British were robbing a poor hemispheric friend of the United States. A unanimous congressional resolution of February 1894 called for arbitration, underscoring U.S. concern. Cleveland's Democratic party had lost badly in the 1894 elections, and Republicans were attacking his administration as cowardly for not annexing Hawai'i. Bold action might deflect criticism and recoup Democratic losses. One Democrat advised Cleveland: "Turn this Venezuelan question up or down, North, South, East or West, and it is a 'winner.'"[30]

The global imperial competition of the 1890s also pushed the president toward action. The British, already holding large stakes in Latin America, seemed intent on enlarging their share. Like the French intervention in Mexico a generation earlier, London's claim against Venezuela became a symbol of European intrusion

"The Real British Lion."   This is a popular American depiction of the British global presence during the crisis over Venezuela. A few years later, President Cleveland himself recalled British behavior as "mean and hoggish." (*New York Evening World,* 1895)

into the hemisphere. The economic depression of the 1890s also caused concern. Many Americans, including Cleveland, thought that overproduction had caused the slump and that expanding foreign trade could cure it. The National Association of Manufacturers, organized in 1895 to encourage exports, chose Caracas as the site of its first overseas display of American products. Might the British close this potential new market?

Nor did Cleveland like bullies. He had already rejected Hawaiian annexation in part because he thought Americans had bullied the Hawaiians. Now the British were arrogantly slapping the Venezuelans. Defense of the Monroe Doctrine became his and Olney's maxim. In unvarnished language, the "twenty-inch gun" of July 20, 1895, warned that European partition of Africa should not repeat itself in Latin America. The "safety," "honor," and "welfare" of the United States were at stake, and the Monroe Doctrine stipulated that "any permanent political union between a European and an American state [was] unnatural and inexpedient." The Cleveland–Olney message stressed that "the states of America, South as well as North, by geographical proximity, by natural sympathy, by similarity of government constitutions, are friends and allies, commercially and politically, of the United States. To allow the subjugation of any one of them by a European power … signifies the loss of all the advantages incident to their natural relations with us." The forceful overriding theme of the note boldly addressed an international audience. "To-day the United States is practically sovereign on this continent, and its fiat is law upon the subjects to which it confines its interposition." And more: The United States's "infinite resources combined with its isolated position render it master of the situation and practically invulnerable as against any or all other powers."[31] Finally, the message

"If There Must Be War." Lord Salisbury and President Grover Cleveland slug it out during the Venezuelan crisis of 1895. Britain's ambassador, Sir Julian Pauncefote, simplistically blamed the war scare on sensationalist U.S. newspapers whose "stream of mendacity and audacity and ignorance and malice and general blackguardism … is swallowed by millions and does infinite mischief." (*Life,* 1896)

demanded arbitration, threatened U.S. intervention, and requested a British answer before Cleveland's annual message to Congress in December.

British Prime Minister Lord Salisbury received the missive with some surprise and sent it to the Foreign Office for study. Distracted by crises in South Africa, Salisbury saw no urgency. In the late nineteenth century, American Anglophobic bombast was not unusual, especially before elections. Thus, by ignoring the problem in the hope that the "conflagration will fizzle away," Salisbury did not reply until after Cleveland's annual message, which was actually quite tame on Venezuela.[32] The British note, which smacked of the "peremptory schoolmaster trying—with faded patience—to correct the ignorance of dullards in Washington," denied the applicability of the Monroe Doctrine and dismissed any U.S. interest in the controversy.[33]

On reading the note, Cleveland became "mad clean through."[34] His special message to Congress on December 17 rang the alarm bell: England must arbitrate; the United States would create an investigating commission to set the true boundary line; unless London acquiesced, the United States would intervene by "every means in its power."[35] Congress quickly voted funds for the commission. Republicans and Democrats rallied behind the president, and New York City police commissioner Theodore Roosevelt boomed: "Let the fight come if it must; I don't care whether our sea coast cities are bombarded or not; we would take Canada."[36] With Irish Americans volunteering to fight their ancient foe, the British ambassador reported: "Nothing is heard but the voice of the Jingo bellowing defiance to England."[37]

War fevers cooled rapidly in early 1896. Many bankers and business leaders grew alarmed when the stock market plummeted, in part because British investors were pulling out. The *New York World* put out a special Christmas issue with portraits of the Prince of Wales and Lord Salisbury under the headline "PEACE AND GOOD WILL," suggesting the irrationality of war with Britain, a country so close in race, language, and culture.[38] Even the U.S. ambassador in London feared the president had been "too *precipitate*" in joining "the camp of aggressiveness."[39] But Cleveland never wanted war. He wanted peace on his terms.

What followed seemed anticlimactic. The British cabinet in early January 1896 decided to seek an "honourable settlement" with the United States.[40] Facing a new dispute with Germany over South Africa, England needed friends, not enemies. Formal talks continued until November 1896, when the United States and Britain agreed to set up a five-person arbitration board to define the boundary. Finally, in October 1899, the tribunal reached a decision that rejected the extreme claims of either party and generally followed the original line from the 1840s. The mouth of the Orinoco went to Venezuela, which came out of the dispute rather well, considering that neither the United States nor Britain cared much about Venezuela's national interest. In fact, both parties excluded Venezuela's duly accredited minister in Washington from the talks. Lobbyist William Scruggs complained that the United States sought to "*bull-doze*" Venezuela."[41] He had it right, but Washington's "sledgehammer subtlety" targeted others besides that South American nation.[42] The overweening theme of the "twenty-inch gun" merits repeating: "To-day the United States is practically sovereign on this continent, and its fiat is law upon the subjects to which it confines its interposition."[43]

Men of Empire

The Venezuelan crisis and the war with Spain punctuated an era of imperialist competition when, as one senator grandiosely put it: "The great nations are rapidly absorbing … all the waste areas of the earth. It is a moment which makes for civilization and the advancement of the race."[44] Cleveland and McKinley helped move the United States toward world-power status. As examples of forceful, even aggressive, diplomacy, both events accelerated important trends. Besides ignoring the rights and sensibilities of small countries, both episodes revealed a United States more certain about the components of its "policy" and more willing to confront rivals. Both events stimulated what critics at the time called "jingoism." The Monroe Doctrine gained new status as a warning to curb European meddling in the Western Hemisphere. Just as Cleveland went to the brink of war over Venezuela without consulting Congress, so too did McKinley, despite a jingoist Congress and inflamed public opinion, reinforce presidential control over foreign policy.

In both crises Latin Americans learned again that the United States sought supremacy in the Western Hemisphere and would intervene when it saw fit. The Venezuela crisis and the outbreak of revolution in Cuba in 1895 intensified North American interest in the Caribbean, a significant dimension of which was economic. Coinciding with a severe economic depression at home, the potential loss of markets

Makers of American Foreign Relations, 1895–1900

Presidents	Secretaries of State
Grover Cleveland, 1893–1897	Walter Q. Gresham, 1893–1895
	Richard Olney, 1895–1897
William McKinley, 1897–1901	John Sherman, 1897–1898
	William R. Day, 1898
	John Hay, 1898–1905

in Venezuela and Cuba brought more attention to the theory of overproduction as a cause of depression, which increased exports could allegedly cure. Commercial expansion, always a trend in American history, received another boost.

The discord with Britain over Venezuela ironically helped foster Anglo-American rapprochement. Cooperation and mutual interest increasingly characterized relations between Washington and London. British diplomats cultivated U.S. friendship as a possible counterweight to growing German power, and Britain's support over Cuba and its subsequent deference to the United States regarding the Caribbean facilitated the emerging entente.

The chief mechanism by which the United States sought to manage events in that area was through naval power. The Venezuelan crisis, joined by crises in Asia and the belief that naval construction would employ those idled by the depression, stimulated additional naval expansion. The Navy Act of 1896, for example, provided for three new battleships and ten new torpedo boats, several of which contributed to naval victories over Spain two years later.

By the end of the decade the United States had gained new U.S. colonies in the Pacific, Asia, and the Caribbean, a protectorate over Cuba, and Europe's recognition of U.S. hegemony in the Caribbean. By 1900, too, the United States had pledged itself to preserve the "Open Door" in China; it had built a naval armada that had just annihilated the Spanish navy and ranked second in the world only to Great Britain's "mammoth imperial fleet"; and it had developed an export trade amounting to $1.5 billion.[45] Steel and iron production exemplified its industrial might, which almost equaled that of Britain and Germany combined. U.S. acquisition of new colonies after the Spanish-American-Cuban-Filipino War suggests that *only then,* about 1898, did the United States become an imperialist world power. But what actually happened, one scholar writes, was a "culmination" not an "aberration."[46] Having taken halting steps toward empire before the depression of the 1890s, the United States now took a giant imperialist leap.

Assistant Secretary of the Navy Theodore Roosevelt described the anti-imperialists in 1897 as "men of a by-gone age" and "provincials."[47] Indeed, anti-imperialism waned in the late nineteenth century. Increasing numbers of educated, economically comfortable Americans made the case for formal empire (colonies or protectorates) or informal empire (commercial domination). Naval officers, diplomats, politicians,

Grover Cleveland (1837–1908). This portrait of the two-term president, overweight from frequenting saloons as a young man, exhibits the gruff American attitude toward Britain during the Venezuelan crisis. The historian Dexter Perkins has written that Cleveland was "so honest, so brave, so independent ..., but also so rigid and inflexible in his thinking, so unimaginative, so dogmatic." (Library of Congress)

farmers, skilled artisans, business leaders, and clergy made up what political scientists call the "foreign-policy public," who influenced mass opinion through their management of the printing press and the public lectern. This "elite," aided by the hawkish clamoring of the "yellow press," helped the McKinley administration maneuver America towards war and empire.

Analysis of the phrase "public opinion" helps explain the *hows* as distinct from the *whys* of decision making. One often hears that "public opinion" or "the man in the street" influenced a leader to follow a certain course of action. But "public opinion" did not comprise a unified, identifiable group speaking with one voice. Political leaders and other articulate, knowledgeable people often shaped the "public opinion" they wanted to hear by their very handling of events and their control over information. In trying to determine who the "people" are and what "public opinion" is, social scientists have demonstrated that in the 1890s the people who counted, who expressed their opinion publicly in order to influence policy, numbered no more than 1.5 million to 3 million, or between 10 and 20 percent of the voting public. This percentage—upper- and middle-income groups, highly educated, active politically—constituted the "foreign-policy public." Secretary of State Walter Q. Gresham observed in 1893: "After all, public opinion is made and controlled by the thoughtful men of the country."[48] The public opinion the president heard in the 1890s did not come from the "people," but rather from a small, articulate segment of the American population alert to foreign-policy issues. Although these educated elites included anti-imperialists, the foreign-policy public leaned heavily toward the side of imperialism.

The president ultimately dominates policymaking and may even disregard advice from the foreign-policy public itself. President Cleveland, for example, successfully resisted pressure to annex Hawai'i and withdrew the treaty from the Senate, and he never let Congress or influential public opinion set the terms of his policy toward the Venezuelan crisis. But while the initiative in foreign affairs finally rests in executive hands—with Cleveland and McKinley appearing "unabashed in their resistance" to public pressure (unlike their seemingly more pliant predecessors of the 1860s and 1870s)—no president formulates policy in a vacuum.[49] Explanations of the 1898 war are inadequate that specifically designate the yellow press or public vengeance towards Spain as *the* reason the United States fought. So, too, are explanations that stress executive leadership absent other factors. Emotional nationalism, sensationalist journalism, and a visible, active foreign policy elite did not force McKinley into war. But they did help create an environment that helped condition McKinley's perceived range of options and that enabled him, once he chose war, to disperse responsibility—and blame—for the outcomes.

Cleveland and McKinley Confront *Cuba Libre*, 1895–1898

The year 1895 brought momentous events. The Venezuelan crisis, Japan's defeat of China in the Sino-Japanese War, and the outbreak of revolution in Cuba—all carried profound meaning for U.S. foreign relations. The sugar-rich island of Cuba, since the close of its unsuccessful war for independence (1868–1878), suffered political repression and poverty. After that war Cuban nationalists prepared for a new assault on their Spanish overlords. From 1880 to 1895, the Cuban national hero José Martí plotted from exile in the United States. In 1892 he organized the Cuban Revolutionary party, using U.S. territory to recruit men and money. Martí's opportunity came when Cuba's economy fell victim in 1894 to a new U.S. tariff, which raised duties on imported sugar and hence reduced Cuban sugar shipments to the United States. On February 24, 1895, with cries of *"Cuba Libre,"* the rebels reopened their drive for independence.

Cuban revolutionaries kept a cautious eye on the United States, well known for its relentless interest in the island, and they feared an ultimate U.S. attempt to control their nation's destiny. José Martí's fifteen-year stay in the United States had turned him into a critic of what he called "the monster"—an "aggressive" and "avaricious" nation "full of hate" and "widespread spiritual coarseness." If the North Americans intervened, they might not leave. "To change masters is not to be free," he warned.[50] On May 19 Martí died in battle.

Cuban and Spanish military strategies wreaked destruction and death. Led by General Máximo Gómez, a veteran of the 1868–1878 war, the *insurrectos* burned cane fields, blew up mills, and disrupted railroads, with the goal of rendering Cuba an economic liability to Spain. "The chains of Cuba have been forged by her own richness," Gómez proclaimed, "and it is precisely this which I propose to do away with soon."[51] Spain, in turn, vowed to "use up the last peseta in her treasury and sacrifice the last of her sons" to retain Cuba.[52] Although outnumbered (about 30,000 Cuban troops fought 200,000 Spanish) and lacking adequate supplies, the insurgents, with the sympathy of the populace, wore the Spanish down through guerrilla tactics. By late 1896, rebels controlled about two-thirds of the island, with the Spanish concentrated in coastal and urban regions. That year, to break the rebel stronghold in the rural areas, Governor-General Valeriano y Nicolau Weyler instituted the brutal reconcentration program. He divided the island into districts and then herded a half-million Cubans into fortified camps, where frightful sanitation conditions, poor food, and disease contributed to the death of perhaps 200,000 people. Weyler's soldiers regarded any Cubans outside the camps as rebels and hence targets for death; they also killed livestock, destroyed crops, and polluted water sources. This effort to starve the insurgents and deprive them of physical and moral support, combined with the rebels' destructive behavior, made a shambles of Cuba's society and economy. "Blood on the roadsides, blood in the fields, blood on the doorsteps, blood, blood, blood," wrote a *New York World* reporter in 1896.[53]

The Cleveland administration could have recognized Cuban belligerency. But such an act, Olney noted, would relieve Spain of any responsibility for paying claims filed by Americans for properties destroyed in Cuba. Cleveland and Olney found recognition of Cuban independence even less appetizing, for they believed the Cubans ("the most inhumane and barbarous cutthroats in the world") incapable of self-government and feared anarchy and even racial war.[54] That course might also arouse a Spanish declaration of war or force U.S. belligerency because, legalistically, a Spanish attempt to conquer an "independent" Cuba would constitute a violation of the Monroe Doctrine. Olney toyed with buying the island at one point.

The Cleveland administration settled on a dual policy of hostility to the revolution and pressure on Spain to grant some autonomy. Diplomacy and lecturing to a foreign government seemed to work in the Venezuelan crisis; perhaps it would work with Cuba.

Prodded by a Republican Congress and by Spanish obstinacy in refusing reforms and adhering to force, Olney sent a note to Spain in April 1896. He urged a political solution that would leave "Spain her rights of sovereignty" while securing to the Cubans "all such rights and powers of local self-government as they [could] ask."[55] Spain should initiate reforms short of independence. Olney showed particular concern for the interests of Americans, not Cubans. With American property estimated at $50 million, the decline in sugar production wrought disaster to Cuban-American trade relations. In 1892 Cuba had shipped to the United States goods worth $79 million; by 1898 that figure had slumped to $15 million.

When Spain rejected Olney's advice, the Cleveland administration seemed flummoxed. It did not desire war, but it meant to protect U.S. interests. Congress kept asking for firm action. And in Havana, hotheaded Consul-General Fitzhugh Lee clamored for U.S. annexation. Cleveland did not fire Lee, nephew of General Robert E. Lee, because the incumbent president needed political friends at a time when Democrats were dumping him in favor of William Jennings Bryan. Consul-General Lee also warned that "there may be a revolution within a revolution," noting that Cuban insurgents vowed to redistribute property, which U.S. officials (and Creole elites) would not tolerate.[56] It further nettled Cleveland and Olney that Spain had approached the courts of Europe for diplomatic support, with the argument that the Monroe Doctrine threatened all European powers.

British ambassador to Spain H. Drummond Wolff accurately claimed that for Cuba the United States wanted "peace with commerce."[57] In December 1896, Cleveland reported that neither the Spanish nor the Cuban rebels had established their authority over the island. Americans felt a humanitarian concern, he said, and their trade and investments ("pecuniary interest") faced destruction. Further, to maintain its neutrality, the United States had to police the coastline to intercept unlawful expeditions. Spain must grant autonomy or "home rule," but not independence, to "fertile and rich" Cuba in order to end the bloodshed and devastation. Otherwise, the United States, having thus far acted with "restraint," might abandon its "expectant attitude."[58]

But Cleveland had more bark than bite. Through Olney he successfully buried a Senate resolution urging recognition of Cuban independence and contented himself with some limited Spanish reforms of February 1897. Thereafter he let the Cuban issue fester, bequeathing it to the incoming McKinley administration.

William McKinley had defeated William Jennings Bryan in the election of 1896. The teetotaling Ohioan seemed a stable, dignified figure in a time of crisis. He projected deep religious conviction, personal warmth, sincerity, commitment to economic development and the revival of business, party loyalty, and support for expansion abroad. Yet McKinley often gave the appearance of being a pliant follower, a mindless flunky of the political bosses. Cartoonists depicted him in women's dress and called him a "goody-goody" man.[59] Such an image was created in large part by bellicose imperialists who believed that McKinley was not moving fast

Uncle Sam—"All That You Need Is Backbone." This cartoon depicts a tall, erect Uncle Sam shoving a rifle down President McKinley's coat to provide him with a backbone. As the historian Kristin Hoganson points out in *Fighting for American Manhood* (1998), expansionist critics of McKinley often accused the president of being weak, flabby, and vacillating because he did not immediately leap into war with Spain. (*Chicago Chronicle,* in *Cartoons of the War of 1898 with Spain,* Chicago, 1898)

enough. Certainly a party regular and friend of large corporations, the president was no lackey. A manager of diplomacy who wanted expansion and empire without war and a settlement of the Cuban question without U.S. military intervention, McKinley acted as "his own man."[60]

McKinley shared America's image of itself as an expanding, virile nation of superior institutions and as a major power in Latin America. He agreed that the United States must have a large navy, overseas commerce, and foreign bases. He believed strongly that America must export its surplus goods. As a tariff specialist, he favored high tariffs on manufactured goods, low tariffs on raw materials, and reciprocity agreements. The Republican party platform of 1896 overflowed with expansionist rhetoric. It urged American control of Hawai'i, a Nicaraguan canal run by the United States, an enlarged navy, purchase of the Virgin Islands, and Cuban independence. Between election and inauguration, however, McKinley quietly joined Cleveland and Olney in sidetracking a Senate resolution for recognition of Cuba. He wanted a free hand, and he did not believe that Cubans could govern themselves. His inaugural address vacuously urged peace, never mentioning the Cuban crisis.

Beginning in March 1897, congressional resolutions on Cuba sprang up repeatedly, but the new president managed to kill them. McKinley did satisfy imperialists by sending a Hawaiian annexation treaty to the Senate. In June Madrid received an American reprimand for Weyler's uncivilized warfare and for his disruption of the Cuban economy. Spain, however, showed no signs of tempering its military response to the insurrection. American citizens languished in Spanish jails; American property continued to be razed. In July McKinley instructed Minister Woodford to demand that the Spanish stop the fighting. Increasingly convinced that the Cuban *insurrectos* would not compromise, the president implored Spain to grant autonomy. A new Spanish government soon moderated policy by offering Cuba a substantial degree of self-government. Even more significantly, it removed the hated Weyler and promised to end reconcentration. Such reforms actually encouraged intransigence, as Cuban leaders saw them as "a sign of Spain's weakening power and an indication that the end is not far off."[61]

McKinley's December 6, 1897, annual message to Congress discussed the Cuban insurrection at great length. Voicing the "gravest apprehension," McKinley rejected annexation of the island as "criminal aggression." He argued against recognition of belligerency, because the rebels hardly constituted a government worthy of recognition. And he ruled out intervention as premature at a time when the Spanish were traveling the "honorable paths" of reform. He asked for patience to see if Spanish changes would work, but he hinted that the United States would keep open all policy options, including intervention "with force."[62]

By mid-January 1898, it became evident that Spanish reforms had not moderated the crisis; in fact, insurgents, conservatives, and the Spanish army all denounced them. After antireform Spaniards rioted in Havana, McKinley sent the *Maine* to the Cuban city to protect American lives and property. On February 9, the State Department received a copy of a private letter written in late 1897 by the Spanish minister to the United States, Enrique Dupuy de Lôme, and sent to a senior Spanish politician touring Cuba. Intercepted in Cuba by a rebel sympathizer who forwarded it to the Cuban junta in New York City, the letter not only reached the State Department, but William Randolph Hearst's flamboyant *New York Journal* published it that day with the banner headline: "Worst Insult to the United States in its History." De Lôme labeled McKinley "weak," a "bidder for the admiration of the crowd," and a "would-be politician."[63] McKinley particularly resented another statement that suggested that Spain did not take its reform proposals seriously and would persist in fighting to defeat the rebels. Spain, it appeared, could not be trusted. De Lôme's hasty recall hardly salved the hurt. Less than a week later the *Maine* blew up, setting in motion events and decisions that led to war and overseas empire for the United States.

What if ...   *Spain had granted independence to Cuba in 1898?*

Had Madrid offered full independence instead of autonomy to Cuban insurgents in 1898, subsequent history might have been different. Even if full Cuban independence had come after the *Maine* explosion, the ostensible reason for U.S. military intervention would have been removed. Although President William McKinley might have preferred a U.S. protectorate rather than complete independence for Cuba, it would have been difficult, if not impossible, to justify a military occupation without war with Spain. The Cuban revolutionaries could have built their own democratic, multiracial republic and pursued social and economic reforms without having to accommodate the class and racial biases of a North American overlord. Cubans would not have perceived their apparent victory over the Spanish snatched from them by Washington, and Cuban nationalism might not have developed the strong strain of anti-Americanism that leaders such as Fidel Castro later exploited.

Of course, given the devastation of Cuba's infrastructure after three years of war, the influx of entrepreneurs and investments from the United States might have been inevitable while perhaps resulting in less overt dominance over the island's economy. Even without a Platt Amendment mandating U.S. intervention under certain circumstances, marines and "money doctors" might still have temporarily occupied Cuba, as they actually did in 1906, 1912, and 1917, whenever revolutionary disorder seemed to threaten American lives and investments. One other outcome would certainly have been different, for without the perpetual lease agreement included in the Platt Amendment of 1903, the U.S. government could not have set up an internment camp a century later at the Guantánamo Bay naval base where Afghani and other prisoners of war were tortured in the name of a U.S. "war on terror."

Cuban independence without U.S. intervention in 1898 might also have affected American policies elsewhere. Theodore Roosevelt's celebrated order to Commodore George Dewey's Far Eastern Squadron to attack the Spanish fleet in Manila Bay would not have been carried out. Nor would Puerto Rico have become a war prize. Unburdened by the conflict in Cuba, Spanish forces might have defeated Filipino insurgents, but Emilio Aguinaldo's guerrillas would likely have emerged victorious. A Philippines Republic proclaimed in 1899 might not have survived surrounded by imperial predators. The Germans, Americans, British, French, and perhaps the Japanese might have partitioned Spain's Pacific possessions among themselves, just as the Germans and Americans divided Samoa that same year. The United States might still have annexed Guam and parts of the Philippines. Such imperial arrangements might have prompted Washington to seek its own leasehold in China, similar to Hong Kong or Port Arthur, instead of promulgating the Open Door Notes to preserve America's share of the China trade. In such a context, the rationale for annexing Hawai'i to reinforce Dewey would have been less compelling, but U.S. commercial and strategic interests in the Pacific would have kept those islands within a growing informal empire.

An unfought war over Cuba would also have meant less prominence for such would-be war heroes as Teddy Roosevelt. Someone other than the Rough Rider in the White House would surely have negotiated with England, Colombia, Panama, and Nicaragua with less flamboyance and pugnacity on behalf of an isthmian canal. Nonetheless, the same arguments about commercial and strategic needs and benefits to civilization from such a canal would likely have prevailed. An American-built canal would still symbolize U.S. hemispheric preeminence. Similarly, a Roosevelt Corollary by another name (and possibly with less imperial language) would still have articulated the economic, strategic, and legal arguments to justify U.S. intervention under the Monroe Doctrine. In short, the year 1898 would likely have remained a springboard for American imperial expansion even without an American-Spanish war over Cuba.

The Spanish-American-Cuban-Filipino War

Americans enlisted in what they trumpeted as a glorious expedition to demonstrate U.S. right and might. They were cocky. Theodore Roosevelt, who resigned as assistant secretary of the navy to lead the flashy but overrated Rough Riders, said that it was not much of a war but it was the best Americans had. It was a short war, April to August 12, but 5,462 Americans died in it—only 379 of them in combat. Most expired from malaria and yellow fever. Camera operators for Thomas Edison and Biograph shot "moving pictures" of the war, and crowds flocked to see flickering images of battleships at sea, the wreck of the *Maine,* and triumphant victory parades.[64] Led by officers seasoned in the Civil War and in campaigns against Native Americans, the new imperial fighters embarked from Florida in mid-June. Seventeen thousand men, clutching their Krag-Jörgensen rifles, landed on Cuban soil unopposed because Cuban insurgents had driven Spanish troops into the cities. Cubans cooperated warily with their new American allies.

Commodore George Dewey (1837–1917) at the Battle of Manila Bay, May 1, 1898. From the bridge of his 5,386-ton flagship, U.S.S. *Olympia,* Dewey directs the battle that destroyed Spanish naval power in the Pacific. This dramatic action turned the modest sailor from Vermont into a national hero and soon led to the American acquisition of the Philippines. This print is from the original painting that is on display at the Vermont State House in Montpelier. The *Olympia* is now a floating museum in Philadelphia. (Naval Historical Foundation)

"Cuba Reconciling the North and South." Captain Fritz W. Guerin's 1898 photograph depicted nationalism in the Spanish-American-Cuban-Filipino War. Golden-haired Cuba, liberated from her chains by her North American heroes, oversees the reconciliation of the Union and Confederacy in a splashy display of patriotism. Nevertheless, as the historian David W. Blight has written in *Race and Reunion* (2001), "national unity in foreign policy … gave the promoters of Jim Crow in the South a freer hand than ever in fashioning a segregated social system." (Library of Congress)

Yet the big news had already arrived from the Philippine Islands, Spain's major colony in Asia. Only days after the American declaration of war, Commodore George Dewey sailed his Asiatic Squadron from Hong Kong into Manila Bay, where he smashed the Spanish fleet with the loss of one U.S. sailor. Slipping by the Spanish guns at Corregidor, Dewey entered the bay at night. Early in the morning of May 1, with the laconic order, "You may fire when ready, Gridley," his flagship *Olympia* began to demolish the ten incompetently handled Spanish ships. "PHILIPPINES OURS, WHAT WILL WE DO WITH THEM?" ran the headline of the *New York Journal*.[65] Some people, ignorant of U.S. interests in the Pacific, wondered how a war to liberate Cuba saw its first action in Asia. Naval officials had pinpointed the Philippines in contingency plans as early as 1896. Often credited alone with ordering Dewey on February 25, 1898, to attack Manila if war broke out, Assistant Secretary of the Navy Theodore Roosevelt actually set in motion preexisting war plans already known and approved by the president. After the war, when the Navy Department balked at revealing its advance preparations, Roosevelt was "naturally delighted at shouldering the responsibility."[66]

By late June, U.S. troops in Cuba had advanced toward Santiago, where dispirited Spanish soldiers manned antique guns. Joined by experienced Cuban rebels, the North Americans on July 1 battled for San Juan Hill. American forces, spearheaded by the Rough Riders and the black soldiers of the Ninth Cavalry, finally captured the strategic promontory overlooking Santiago after suffering heavy casualties. Two days later the Spanish squadron, penned in Santiago harbor for weeks by U.S. warships, made a desperate daylight break for open sea. Some U.S. vessels nearly collided as they hurried to sink the helpless Spanish craft, which went down with 323 dead. Its fleet destroyed, Spain surrendered—but only to the Americans. Cubans were forbidden from entering towns and cities to celebrate. Historians still debate whether Cubans could have won their independence without U.S. intervention. Louis A. Pérez, Jr., has argued that McKinley intervened because he was "alarmed at the prospect of a Cuban victory," whereas a recent multi-archival account by John Lawrence Tone suggests that "the Cuban insurgency was in a nearly terminal condition by 1897 and had no chance of victory without outside help" and therefore only "the rather small American expeditionary army … could have destroyed the Spanish army at Santiago."[67] With victory, however, came U.S. occupation and U.S. hegemony.

"Porto Rico is not forgotten and we mean to have it," wrote Senator Lodge in May 1898.[68] Thus did U.S. troops also invade another Spanish colony, Puerto Rico, which expansionists coveted as the "Malta of the Caribbean"—an ideal base for a proper navy and a strategic outpost to protect a Central American canal. In nineteen days General Nelson A. Miles, in what was described as "a picnic" and a *"fete des fleurs,"* captured the sugar- and coffee-exporting island.[69] At least at first, the Puerto Rican elite welcomed their new North American masters as an improvement over their Spanish rulers.

Manila capitulated in mid-August, after the Spanish put up token resistance in a deal that salvaged Spanish pride by surrendering to Americans and not to the "niggers," thereby keeping Filipino nationalist Emilio Aguinaldo from the walled city.[70] Washington soon ordered Aguinaldo and other Filipino rebels, who had fought against the Spanish for independence since 1896 and had surrounded Manila for weeks, to remain outside the capital and to recognize the authority of the United States.

In July, ostensibly to ensure uninterrupted reinforcement of Dewey, the United States officially absorbed Hawai'i, where troop transports took on coal en route to Manila. From 1893 to 1897, while Cleveland refused annexation, politics in Hawai'i had changed little. Despite a 556-page antiannexation petition from native Hawaiians, the white revolutionaries clung to power. Once elected, McKinley proclaimed: "We need Hawai'i … a good deal more than we did California. It is manifest destiny."[71] After negotiating a new treaty with the white-led Hawaiian government, he sidestepped the constitutional requirement of a two-thirds vote in the Senate in favor of a joint resolution. On July 7, 1898, Congress passed the resolution for annexation by a majority vote (290 to 91 in the House and 42 to 21 in the Senate), thereby formally attaching the strategically and commercially important islands to the United States. Annexation was "not a change" but "a consummation," said McKinley.[72]

Men Versus "Aunties": The Debate over Empire in the United States

Spain sued for peace, and on August 12 the belligerents proclaimed an armistice. To negotiate with the Spanish in Paris, McKinley appointed a "peace commission" loaded with imperialists and headed by Secretary of State William R. Day, friend and

"The Fools Are Not All Dead Yet" *Los Angeles Times*, May 14, 1899

"The Fools Are Not All Dead Yet." This cartoon from the *Los Angeles Sunday Times* lampoons anti-imperialists by drawing them as fussy old women, often called "aunties" (a pun on "anti"). Here they are worshipping a statue of Emilio Aguinaldo, whom some anti-imperialists hailed as the George Washington of Philippine Independence. (*Los Angeles Sunday Times,* May 14, 1899)

follower of the president's wishes. As negotiations continued into autumn, and after McKinley tested public opinion by touring the Midwest (his ear "so close to the ground that it was full of grasshoppers"), he demanded all of the Philippines ("the whole Archipelago or none"), plus the island of Guam in the Marianas, and Puerto Rico, as well independence for Cuba.[73] Articulate Filipinos pleaded for their country's freedom but met a stern U.S. rebuff. Spanish diplomats accepted this American land grab after the United States offered $20 million as compensation. In early December, U.S. delegates signed the treaty and walked out of the elegant French conference room clutching the Philippines, Puerto Rico, and Guam.

Opponents protested vigorously. They had organized the Anti-Imperialist League in Boston in November 1898, but they never acted in unison. They counted among their number such unlikely bedfellows as the steel magnate Andrew Carnegie, the labor leader Samuel Gompers, the agrarian spokesman William Jennings Bryan, the Massachusetts Senator George Hoar, Harvard president Charles W. Eliot, and the humorist Mark Twain—people who had often disagreed among themselves on domestic issues. Some anti-imperialists took inconsistent positions. Hoar, the most outspoken senator opposed to the treaty, had voted for war and annexation of

Carl Schurz (1829–1906).
Born in Germany, Schurz
emigrated to the United States
after the failed revolutions of 1948.
Journalist, diplomat, reformer,
Union General during the Civil
War, the first German-American
U.S. senator, and Secretary
of the Interior under President
Rutherford B. Hayes, he became
an outspoken leader of the
American Anti-Imperialist League
during the debates over Philippine
annexation in 1899–1900. "Our
country right or wrong," Schurz
once said. "When right, to be kept
right. When wrong, to be put right."
(Library of Congress)

Hawai'i. An expansionist, Carnegie apparently would accept colonies if they could be taken without force. He even offered to write a personal check for $20 million to buy the independence of the Philippines. And the anti-imperialists could not overcome the *fait accompli,* possession and occupation of territory, handed them by McKinley. After all, argued the president, could America really relinquish this valuable real estate so nobly taken in battle?

Imperialists ridiculed anti-imperialists as "unmanly aunties," often caricaturing their opponents as "carping old ladies" or pygmies in skirts and bonnets.[74] Many opponents did want trade, but not at the cost of subjugating other peoples or of formally absorbing non-white races into the United States. The anti-imperialist David Starr Jordan, president of Stanford University, spoke of "peaceful conquest" by trade rather than by annexation.[75] Some anti-imperialists insisted that serious domestic problems demanded attention and resources first. Labor leader Samuel Gompers feared that annexation would bring "hordes" of "semi-savage races" with "coolie" labor standards "swarming into the United States."[76] Representative Champ Clark of Missouri could not stomach the prospect of "almond eyed, brown skinned United States Senators" from the Philippines: "No matter whether they are fit to govern themselves or not, they are not fit to govern us."[77] Mark Twain referred to the $20 million payment for the Philippines as the U.S. "entrance fee into the Society of the Sceptered Thieves."[78]

Prominent women also participated in the debate, hoping to build a distinct foreign-policy constituency out of existing networks of women's clubs and organizations. The New Hampshire pacifist Lucia True Ames Mead pronounced it immoral for "any nation … which buys or takes by conquest another people, and dominates them without promise of granting them independence."[79] The social reformer Jane Addams saw children playing war games in the streets of Chicago. The kids were *not freeing Cubans,* she protested, but rather *slaying Spaniards* in their not-so-innocent play. Although unsuccessful in preventing U.S. colonization of former Spanish territories in Asia and the Caribbean, peace activists raised public consciousness about the moral quandaries of imperialism. Due to their efforts, tens of thousands of women and men were inspired to become activists, and a discourse of peace and reform became articulated that persisted into the next century.

The imperialists, led by Roosevelt, Lodge, and McKinley, and backed strongly by business leaders, engaged their opponents in vigorous debate in early 1899. These empire builders stressed geostrategic considerations, although they communicated common ideas of racial superiority and national destiny to civilize the savage world. "For a thousand years," boasted Senator Albert Beveridge, "God had prepared Americans to be the "master organizers of the world," possessors of what he called "the blood of government," which could be transfused into "their Malay [Filipino] veins."[80] The Philippines provided stepping-stones to the rich China market and strategic ports for the expanding navy that protected American commerce and demonstrated U.S. prestige. International competition also dictated that the United States keep the fruits of victory, argued the imperialists; otherwise, a menacing Germany or expansionist Japan might pick up what America discarded. Few believed that the United States should relinquish territory acquired through blood. To the charge that no one had asked the Filipinos if they desired annexation to the United States, Roosevelt delighted in telling Democratic anti-imperialists that President Thomas Jefferson took Louisiana without a vote by its inhabitants. McKinley put it simply: "Duty determines destiny."[81]

Pro-imperialist Senator Lodge described the treaty fight in the Senate as the "closest, most bitter, and most exciting struggle."[82] Shortly before the vote, word reached Washington that Filipino insurrectionists and American soldiers had begun to fight. The news apparently stimulated support for the Treaty of Paris. Democrats tended to be anti-imperialists and Republicans imperialists, yet enough of the former endorsed the treaty on February 6, 1899, to pass it, just barely, by the necessary two-thirds vote, 57 to 27. William Jennings Bryan, believing that rejection of the treaty would prolong the war and that the Philippines could be freed after terminating the hostilities with Spain, urged an aye vote on his anti-imperialist friends. The Republicans probably had enough votes in reserve to pass the treaty even if Bryan had opposed it.

Imperial Collisions in Asia: The Philippine Insurrection and the Open Door in China

Controlling, protecting, and expanding the enlarged U.S. empire became a major chore. The Filipinos resisted most forcefully. By the end of the war, Aguinaldo and rebel forces controlled most of the islands, having routed the Spanish and driven them into Manila. Aguinaldo had arrived from exile in a U.S. warship and believed that American leaders, including Dewey, had promised his country independence

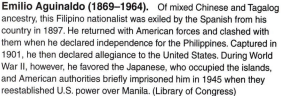

Emilio Aguinaldo (1869–1964). Of mixed Chinese and Tagalog ancestry, this Filipino nationalist was exiled by the Spanish from his country in 1897. He returned with American forces and clashed with them when he declared independence for the Philippines. Captured in 1901, he then declared allegiance to the United States. During World War II, however, he favored the Japanese, who occupied the islands, and American authorities briefly imprisoned him in 1945 when they reestablished U.S. power over Manila. (Library of Congress)

if he joined U.S. forces in defeating the Spanish. Ordered out of Manila by U.S. authorities after the Spanish-American armistice, he and his cohorts had to endure racial insults, including "nigger" and "gu gu" (the linguistic ancestor of "gook").[83] American soldiers considered the Filipinos inferior, the equivalent of Indians and blacks at home. Although one Methodist missionary boasted that the Americans had found Manila "a pesthole, and made it a health resort," critics claimed that imperialism exported the worst in American life.[84] The Treaty of Paris angered the Filipinos, as did McKinley's decree asserting the supreme authority of the United States in the Philippines. In open defiance of Washington, Aguinaldo and other prominent Filipinos organized a government at Malolos, wrote a constitution, and proclaimed the Philippine Republic in late January 1899.

McKinley deemed his new subjects unfit for self-government and proposed "benevolent assimilation" instead.[85] In February 1899 the Filipinos began fighting better armed American troops. After bloody struggles in which "the boys go for the enemy as if they were chasing jack-rabbits," U.S. forces captured Aguinaldo in March 1901.[86] Before the insurrection collapsed in 1902, some 4,165 Americans and more than 200,000 Filipinos died. One hundred twenty-five thousand American troops quelled the insurrection, which cost the United States at least $160 million. In Batangas province south of Manila, General J. Franklin Bell drove insurrectionists into the hills and killed their livestock. Thus malaria-transmitting mosquitoes "were forced to get their meals from people" instead of cattle. The result: an "epidemiological catastrophe" wherein the Batangas population declined by 90,000 (one-quarter of the people) over a six-year period.[87] Andrew Carnegie caustically deplored the pacification of the Filipinos: "About 8,000 of them have been completely civilized and sent to heaven. I hope you like it."[88] The Harvard philosopher William James similarly mocked "Civilization" as "the big, hollow, resounding, corrupting, sophisticating, confusing torrent of brutal momentum and irrationality that brings forth fruits like this!"[89]

What one U.S. general called the "most legitimate and humane war ever conducted" was hardly that.[90] After Filipinos massacred an American regiment on Samar and stuffed molasses into disemboweled corpses to attract ants, General Jacob Smith told his officers: "I want no prisoners. I wish you to kill and burn, the more you kill and burn the better you will please me."[91] With "the judicious application of the torch," U.S. soldiers burned *barrios* to the ground, placing villagers in reconcentration camps like those that had defaced Cuba.[92] To get information, Americans administered the "water cure," by which "men are pumped so full of water as to nearly drown him [sic], and then are brought back to life by thumping them over the stomach with the butts of muskets."[93] Senator Lodge defended such practices as legitimate responses to the alleged "torture and castration of [U.S.] prisoners" by Filipinos.[94] Racist notions of white superiority proliferated. "Civilize 'em with a Krag" went a popular army song, as one officer urged the same "remedial measures that proved successful with the Apaches."[95] The civil governor of the Philippines from 1901 to 1904, William Howard Taft used loftier language to make the same point. It was the American mission, he said, to "teach those people individual liberty, which shall lift them up to a point of civilization …, and which shall make them rise to call the name of the United States blessed."[96] Taft simultaneously administered a sedition act to suppress

William Howard Taft (1857–1930) Astride a Water Buffalo. The first U.S. civil governor of the Philippines, Taft weighed more than 300 pounds. He once proudly reported to Washington that he had ridden twenty-five miles to a high mountain spot. Secretary of War Elihu Root cabled back: "HOW IS HORSE?" Regarding Filipino self-rule, Taft wrote in 1907: "The principles of the Declaration of Independence do not require the immediate surrender of a country to a people like this. If they did, then it would be utterly impossible to defend the rules which exclude women, … minors, … [and] ignorant and irresponsible male adults from the ballot." (U.S. Army Military History Institute)

criticism of the United States. American colonial authorities censored newspapers and jailed dissenters in the name of bringing freedom to the Philippines.

For years, the Moros would not submit to American rule. One military expert predicted that "the Moro question will eventually be settled in the same manner as the Indian question, that is by gradual extermination."[97] In a June 1913 battle on the island of Jolo, U.S. forces killed 500 Moros. The army's premier "guerrilla warrior," General John J. Pershing, called that bloody encounter "the fiercest [fighting] I have ever seen."[98] Until 1914, moreover, the followers of Artemio Ricarte harassed the U.S. military with their hit-and-run tactics. Imprisoned from 1904 to 1910 and then deported to Japan, Ricarte himself refused allegiance to the United States, set up a government-in-exile, and "was continually imagined to be plotting an invasion with Japanese financial and military aid."[99]

The carrot joined with the stick to repress the Philippine insurrections. Local self-government, social reforms, and American schools, where American educators (called "Thomasites") taught Filipinos of all social classes English and arithmetic, helped win over elites ("*ilustrados*") and key minorities.[100] A general amnesty proclaimed by President Theodore Roosevelt on July 4, 1902, also encouraged accommodation. By restricting suffrage at the outset to Filipinos with wealth, education,

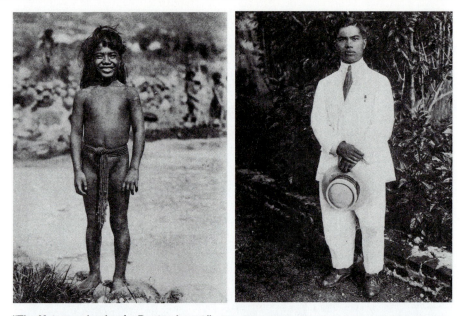

"The Metamorphosis of a Bontoc Igorot."   Dean Worcester, an American zoology professor who served as the U.S. assistant secretary of the interior for the Philippines from 1900 to 1913, included these two photographs of "Pit-a-pit," a Bontoc Igorot, in his 1914 book to illustrate his conclusion that U.S. policies and programs had a civilizing effect on Filipinos. The two pictures were taken nine years apart. Worcester classified the islands' population of 8 million into eighty-four tribes, including the Bontoc Igorot. As the historian Paul A. Kramer has noted, by "tribalizing" the Filipinos, Americans "rhetorically eradicate[d] the Philippine Republic as a legitimate state whose rights the United States might have to recognize under international law." (Dean Worcester, *The Philippines Past and Present* [New York: Macmillan Company, 1914], vol. 2, frontispiece)

and previous government service, U.S. administrators successfully wooed Filipino elites, including former revolutionaries. American roads, bridges, port improvements, and sanitation projects soon followed. Rebellion was gradually confined to the "boondocks," a Tagalog term for remote areas.[101] At the St. Louis World's Fair in 1904, a thousand Filipinos were put on display as "living exhibits," and photographs and dioramas depicted their "rapid social, educational and sanitary development" under "the kindly tutelage of the United States."[102] By 1911, Cebu City could boast an electric railway, telephone service, English-language newspapers, Fords and Buicks, movie houses, and a baseball park, but "I would prefer a government run like hell by Filipinos to one run like heaven by Americans," commented future president Manuel Quezon.[103] By the 1920s, a journalist described America's colonial project as an attempt to turn the Philippines into "a sort of glorified Iowa."[104] The Jones Act of 1916 promised eventual Philippine independence. It did not arrive until 1946.

The proximity of the Philippines to China whetted commercial appetites. In early 1898 business leaders organized the American Asiatic Association to stimulate public and governmental protection and enlargement of U.S. interests in China. Treasury official Frank Vanderlip typically lauded the Philippines as the "pickets of the Pacific, standing guard at the entrances to trade with the millions of China."[105]

American Cigarettes in China.   An American soldier in China peddles cigarettes. After the invention of the cigarette machine in 1881, the tobacco tycoon James B. Duke asked to see an atlas. Leafing through the pages, he noticed China's large population of 430 million. "That," he said, "is where we are going to sell cigarettes." Nine years later came the first exports; by 1916 Duke and other American entrepreneurs were selling 12 billion cigarettes per year in China. (Edward J. Parrish Papers, Duke University Library)

Although China attracted only 2 percent of U.S. foreign commerce, American traders had long dreamed of an unbounded China market, and missionaries romanticized a Christian kingdom. These ambitions remained dreams more than reality. Yet dreams spurred action, and during the 1890s the United States, despite limited power, sought to defend its Asian interests, real and imagined.

During that decade the European powers and Japan divided China, rendered helpless in 1895 after the Sino-Japanese War, into spheres of influence (zones) that established discriminatory trading privileges. The McKinley administration in early 1898 watched anxiously as Germany grabbed Jiaozhou (Kiaochow) and Russia gained a lease at Port Arthur on the Liaodong Peninsula. "Partition would destroy our markets," the U.S. minister to China cabled apprehensively.[106] France, already ensconced in Indochina, leased Guangzhou Bay in southern China in April of that year. Japan already had footholds in Formosa (Taiwan) and Korea. The British in March 1898 suggested a joint Anglo-American declaration on behalf of equal commercial opportunity in China. In the midst of the Cuban crisis, Washington ignored the request. Britain, which already had Hong Kong, then forced China to give up part of the Shandong Peninsula.

American interests in China seemed threatened. The American Asiatic Association and missionary groups appealed to Washington for help. Drawing on

John M. Hay (1838–1905).
The author of the Open Door notes graduated from Brown University and served as one of President Abraham Lincoln's secretaries. He became a newspaper editor and diplomat and, in 1897, ambassador to Great Britain. The following year McKinley named him secretary of state, a post he held until his death. Hay's support of the Open Door policy underscored the confidence Americans had in their ability to compete in the globalizing economy. Hay presciently told Congress in 1902 that "the financial center of the world, which required thousands of years to journey from the Euphrates to the Thames and Seine, seems [to be] passing to the Hudson between daybreak and dark." (Library of Congress)

recommendations from William W. Rockhill, an adviser on Asian policy, who in turn consulted his British friend and officer of the Chinese customs service, Alfred Hippisley, Secretary of State John Hay tried words. He sent an "Open Door" note on September 6, 1899, to Japan, Germany, Russia, Britain, France, and Italy, asking them to respect equal trade opportunity for all nations in their spheres. It was, of course, a traditional American principle, born of the nation's comparative military and economic weakness during much of its history. Lacking world economic or military status before the 1890s, the United States could pry back international trade barriers neither through force nor sheer economic might—particularly in Asia, where America's reach remained short. Hay nonetheless read into the non-committal replies what he wanted and proclaimed definitive acceptance of the Open Door proposal.

Although frail, the Open Door policy carried meaning. Americans discerned a delicate balance of power in East Asia. Excluding American commerce altogether from China might cause Washington to tip that balance by joining one of the powers against the others. A world war might even erupt from competition in Asia. Americans hoped the Open Door policy would serve their goals in an area where they had little military power. The United States wanted the commercial advantages without having to employ military force, as it did in Latin America. This policy of playing others off to U.S. advantage did not always work, but it fixed itself in the American mind as a guiding approach to Chinese affairs.

The Open Door note of 1899 notwithstanding, the Manchu dynasty (1644–1912) was nearing death, unable to cope with the foreign intruders. Resentful nationalistic Chinese, led by a secret society called *Yihequan* ("Boxers"), undertook in 1900 to throw out the imperialist aggressors. The Boxers murdered hundreds of Christian missionaries and their Chinese converts and laid siege to the foreign legations in Beijing (Peking). The foreigner "often treats the Chinese as though they were dogs," wrote the wife of the U.S. minister in Peking. "No wonder that they growl and sometimes bite."[107] To head off a complete gouging of China by vengeful Europeans and Japanese, McKinley, without consulting Congress, sent 2,500 American troops to Beijing from the Philippines to join 15,500 soldiers from other nations to lift the siege. Hay then issued another Open Door note on July 3, 1900. He defined U.S. policy as the protection of American life and property, the safeguarding of "equal and impartial trade," and the preservation of China's "territorial and administrative entity."[108] In short, keep the trade door open for the United States by keeping China intact.

Certainly these actions did not save China, which had to pay foreign governments more than $300 million for the Boxers' damages. The United States itself even asked for a territorial concession in late 1900 at Sansha Bay, Fujian Province, but then shelved the request. Thereafter Washington buttressed its support for the Open Door by increasing the Asiatic Squadron to forty-eight warships, some of which routinely patrolled the Yangtze River, and earmarking army forces in the Philippines for future emergency deployment in China. Even Buffalo Bill Cody extended America's frontier to China by reenacting the suppression of the Boxer Rebellion in his Wild West Show to depict the "triumph of Christian civilization over paganism."[109]

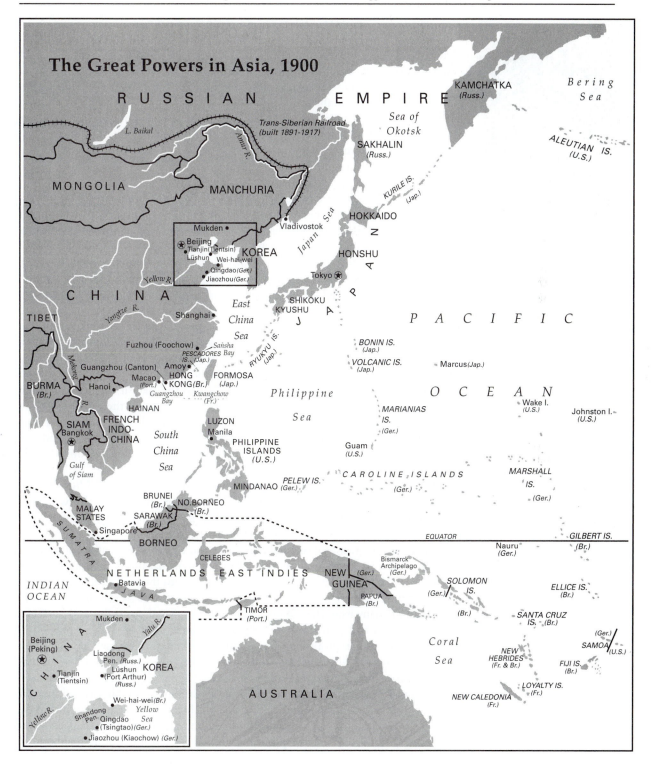

The Great Powers in Asia, 1900

RUSSIAN EMPIRE

KAMCHATKA (Russ.)

Bering Sea

L. Baikal

Trans-Siberian Railroad (built 1891-1917)

Sea of Okotsk

SAKHALIN (Russ.)

ALEUTIAN IS. (U.S.)

MONGOLIA

MANCHURIA

Amur R.

KURILE IS. (Jap.)

HOKKAIDO

Vladivostok

Japan Sea

Mukden

Beijing
Tianjin (Tientsin)
Lüshun Wei-hai-wei
Qingdao (Ger.)
Jiaozhou (Ger.)

KOREA

HONSHU

Tokyo

CHINA

TIBET

Yellow R.

Yangtze R.

Shanghai

East China Sea

SHIKOKU
KYUSHU

J A P A N

P A C I F I C

BONIN IS. (Jap.)

VOLCANIC IS. (Jap.)

Marcus (Jap.)

Fuzhou (Foochow)

Sansha Bay
PESCADORES IS. (Jap.)

RYUKYU IS. (Jap.)

Guangzhou (Canton)
Macao (Port.)
HONG KONG (Br.)

Amoy

FORMOSA (Jap.)

Philippine Sea

O C E A N

Wake I. (U.S.)

Johnston I. (U.S.)

BURMA (Br.)

Hanoi

Mekong R.

HAINAN

Guangzhou Bay

Kwangchow (Fr.)

MARIANIAS IS. (Ger.)

FRENCH INDO-CHINA

SIAM
Bangkok

South China Sea

LUZON
Manila

PHILIPPINE ISLANDS (U.S.)

Guam (U.S.)

Gulf of Siam

MINDANAO

PELEW IS. (Ger.)

C A R O L I N E   I S L A N D S (Ger.)

MARSHALL IS. (Ger.)

MALAY STATES

SUMATRA

Singapore

BRUNEI (Br.)
SARAWAK (Br.)

NO. BORNEO (Br.)

BORNEO

EQUATOR

Nauru (Ger.)

GILBERT IS. (Br.)

CELEBES

NETHERLANDS   EAST   INDIES

INDIAN OCEAN

Batavia

JAVA

NEW GUINEA (Ger.)

Bismarck Archipelago (Ger.)

SOLOMON IS. (Ger.)

ELLICE IS. (Br.)

PAPUA (Br.)

(Br.)

SANTA CRUZ IS. (Br.)

(Ger.)
SAMOA (U.S.)

TIMOR (Port.)

Coral Sea

NEW HEBRIDES (Fr. & Br.)

FIJI IS. (Br.)

AUSTRALIA

NEW CALEDONIA (Fr.)

LOYALTY IS. (Fr.)

(Inset map)

Mukden

Yalu R.

C H I N A

Beijing (Peking)

Liaodong Pen. (Russ.)

KOREA

Tianjin (Tientsin)

Lüshun (Port Arthur) (Russ.)

Wei-hai-wei (Br.)

Yellow R.

Shandong Pen.

Qingdao (Tsingtao) (Ger.)

Yellow Sea

Jiaozhou (Kiaochow) (Ger.)

Pears Soap advertisement.
This telling mixture of commercial and diplomatic advertising salutes Anglo-American rapprochement. (*Life*, 1898)

The Elbows of a World Power, 1895–1900

Venezuela, Cuba, Hawai'i, the Philippines, Open Door notes—an unprecedented set of commitments brought new responsibilities for the United States. Symbolic of this thrust to world-power status was the ascendancy of the imperialists' imperialist, Theodore Roosevelt, to the presidency in 1901. Peering into the twentieth century, Roosevelt warned Americans to avoid "slothful ease and ignoble peace." Never "shrink from the hard contests"; "let us therefore boldly face the life of strife."[110] Indeed, many diplomats looked back on the 1890s as a time of testing when the United States met the international challenge and rightfully asserted its place as a major world power. Europeans watched anxiously. Some, especially Germans, warned of a new "American peril."[111] Russia, however, supported U.S. annexation of Hawai'i because it kept the islands from becoming Japanese. Acquisition of Hawai'i and the Philippines also meant, in TR's words, that "we would have the Japs on our back."[112] With the United States becoming key factor in the global "balance of power," other states wondered: With whom would the United States ally itself?

The odds seemed to favor Great Britain, although the Anglo-American courtship would be prolonged and marriage something for the future. Ever since the eye-opening Venezuelan crisis, the British had applauded Washington for "entering the lists and sharing the task which might have proved too heavy for us alone."[113] Seeking support against an expansionist Germany, John Bull thought Uncle Sam a fit partner and counterweight. During the War of 1898 the British conspicuously tilted toward the American side and encouraged the subsequent U.S. absorption of Spanish colonies. U.S. leaders, in turn, compared the British suppression of the Boers in South Africa (1899–1902) with their own war against the Filipinos, saying that both peoples were equally "incapable of statehood."[114] Articulate Americans welcomed Britain's implicit acceptance of their imperialism. "Germany, and not England, is the power with whom we are apt to have trouble over the Monroe Doctrine," wrote Roosevelt in 1898.[115]

Britain still ranked first in naval power, but in the late 1890s the United States was growing, standing sixth by 1900. In 1898 alone, spurred by the war with Spain, the United States added 128 vessels to its navy, at a cost of $18 million. As one contemporary scholar put it: "Barriers of national seclusion are everywhere tumbling like the great wall of China. Every nation elbows other nations to-day."[116] The steel baron Andrew Carnegie boasted that "the old nations of the earth creep at a snail's pace," but the United States "thunders past with the rush of the express."[117] Many commentators reported that the United States, although still divided North and South on many issues, had united as never before. Southern racists and northern imperialists now had something in common: the need to keep inferior peoples in their place. Befitting their new imperial status, U.S. leaders often used gendered and age-based language that presumed superiority over peoples deemed "emotional, irrational, irresponsible, unbusinesslike, unstable, childlike."[118] If Americans played "the part of China, and [were] content to rot by inches in ignoble ease within our borders," warned Roosevelt, they will "go down before other nations which have not lost the manly and adventurous qualities."[119] Imperial annexation, bragged Senator Beveridge in 1900, "means opportunity for all the glorious young manhood of the republic, the most virile, ambitious, impatient, militant manhood the world has ever seen."[120]

The events of the 1895–1900 period further altered the process of decision making. Both Cleveland and McKinley conducted their own foreign policies to an extent not seen since the presidency of Abraham Lincoln, and they often thwarted or manipulated Congress. "Expansion and disorder abroad equaled centralization at home," one historian has written.[121] Woodrow Wilson, as president of Princeton University, later noted that 1898 had "changed the balance of powers. Foreign questions became leading questions again … Our President must always, henceforth, be one of the great powers of the world."[122] Wilson also welcomed the "primeval" Philippines as a new "frontier on which to turn loose the colts of the race."[123] From "a provincial huddle of petty sovereignties held together by a rope of sand," one editor boasted, "we rise to the dignity and prowess of an imperial republic incomparably greater than Rome."[124]

Indeed, the allure of empire seemed to offer the "most merciful of the world's great race of administrators" an exceptionalist mission—that of "teaching the world how to govern dependent peoples through uplift, assimilation, and eventual self-government."[125] Thus did the optimistic leaders of the "new world power" after 1900 see themselves as reforming an international system that they believed to be "working in their favor."[126] After 1900 the task of managing the expansive empire and the global responsibilities that came with it consumed U.S. foreign policy. The United States, having completed its project of contiguous imperialism, commenced the business of informal and formal global empire that would preoccupy it for much of its remaining history.

FURTHER READING FOR THE PERIOD 1895–1900

For the 1890's push for empire and the coming and waging of the Spanish-American-Cuban-Filipino War, see Ronald J. Barr, *The Progressive Army* (1998); Edward J. Berbusse, *The United States and Puerto Rico, 1898–1900* (1966); H. W. Brands, *The Reckless Decade* (1985); Cesar J. Ayala and Rafael Bernabe, *Puerto Rico in the American Century* (2007); Ada Ferrer, *Insurgent Cuba* (1999); Lillian Guerra, *The Myths of José Martí* (2005); Richard F. Hamilton, *President McKinley, War, and Empire* (2006); Robert E. Hannigan, *The New World Power* (2002); Kenneth E. Hendrickson, Jr., *The Spanish-American War* (2003); Sylvia Hilton and S. J. Ickringell, eds., *European Perceptions of the Spanish-American War* (1999); Kristin L. Hoganson, *Fighting for American Manhood* (1998); Robert Kagan, *Dangerous Nation* (2006); John M. Kirk, *José Martí* (1983); Gerald F. Linderman, *The Mirror of War* (1974); Paul T. McCartney, *Power and Progress* (2006); Ivan Musicant, *Empire by Default* (1998); John L. Offner, *An Unwanted War* (1992); Louis A. Pérez, Jr., *The War of 1898* (1998), *Cuba and the United States* (2003), and *Cuba Between Empires, 1878–1902* (1983); Hyman G. Rickover, *How the Battleship* Maine *Was Destroyed* (1976); Emily Rosenberg, *Spreading the American Dream* (1982); Peggy Samuels and Harold Samuels, *Remembering the* Maine (1995); Thomas Schoonover, *Uncle Sam's War and the Origins of Globalization* (2003); David J. Silbey, *A War of Frontier and Empire* (2007); Noenoe K. Silva, *Aloha Betrayed* (2004); Angel Smith and Emma Davila-Cox, eds., *The Crisis of 1898* (1999); James Lawrence Tone, *War and Genocide in Cuba, 1895–1898* (2006); David F. Trask, *The War with Spain in 1898* (1981); David Traxel, *1898* (1998); and Warren Zimmermann, *First Great Triumph* (2002).

For U.S. leaders, see John Braeman, *Albert J. Beveridge* (1971); H. W. Brands, *T.R.* (1997); Charles W. Calhoun, *Gilded Age Cato* (1988) (Gresham); Kathleen Dalton, *Theodore Roosevelt* (2002); Gerald Eggert, *Richard Olney* (1973); Lewis L. Gould, *The Presidency of William McKinley* (1981); Nathan Miller, *Theodore Roosevelt* (1992); H. Wayne Morgan, *William McKinley and His America* (1963); Ronald Spector, *Admiral of the*

New Empire (1974) (Dewey); Richard E. Welch, Jr., *The Presidencies of Grover Cleveland* (1988); and William C. Widenor, *Henry Cabot Lodge and the Search for an American Foreign Policy* (1980).

Anti-imperialism is treated in Kendrick A. Clements, *William Jennings Bryan* (1983); Amy Kaplan, *The Anarchy of Empire in the Making of U.S. Culture* (2002); Frank Ninkovich, *The United States and Imperialism* (2001); Thomas J. Osborne, *"Empire Can Wait": American Opposition to Hawaiian Annexation, 1893–1898* (1981); Hans L. Trefousse, *Carl Schurz* (1982); and Joseph F. Wall, *Andrew Carnegie* (1970).

The Open Door policy and Asia are discussed in Thomas A. Breslin, *China, American Catholicism, and the Missionary* (1980); Sherman Cochran, *Big Business in China* (1980) (cigarette industry); Paul A. Cohen, *History in Three Keys* (1997) (Boxers); Michael Hunt, *Frontier Defense and the Open Door* (1973) and *The Making of a Special Relationship* (1983); Thomas McCormick, *China Market* (1967); Valentin H. Rabe, *The Home Base of American China Missions, 1880–1920* (1978); and Marilyn Blatt Young, *The Rhetoric of Empire* (1968).

The Philippine rebellion and the American debate receive scrutiny in Teodoro Agoncillo, *Malolos* (1960); A. J. Bacevich, *Diplomat in Khaki* (1989) (General Frank McCoy); Vincent Cirillo, *Bullets and Bacillus* (2004); Kenton J. Clymer, *Protestant Missionaries in the Philippines, 1898–1916* (1986); John M. Gates, *Schoolbooks and Krags* (1973); Servando D. Halili Jr., *Iconography of the New Empire* (2006); Paul A. Kramer, *The Blood of Government* (2007); Brian M. Linn, *Guardians of Empire* (1997), *The U.S. Army and Counterinsurgency in the Philippine War, 1899–1902* (1989), and *The Philippine War* (2000); Glenn A. May, *Battle for Batangas* (1991) and *Social Engineering in the Philippines* (1980); Stuart C. Miller, *"Benevolent Assimilation"* (1982); Resil B. Mojares, *The War Against the Americans* (1999); Alfredo Rocas, *Adios, Patria Adorada* (2006); Angel Velasco Shaw and Luis Francia, eds., *Vestiges of War* (1999); Peter Stanley, *A Nation in the Making* (1974) and ed., *Reappraising an Empire* (1984); and Richard E. Welch, *Response to Imperialism* (1979).

For the Venezuelan crisis and Anglo-American relations, see Stuart Anderson, *Race and Rapprochement* (1981); Charles S. Campbell, *From Revolution to Rapprochement* (1974); Judith Ewell, *Venezuela and the United States* (1996); Richard B. Mulanax, *The Boer War in American Politics and Diplomacy* (1994); R. G. Neale, *Great Britain and United States Expansion, 1800–1900* (1966); Thomas J. Noer, *Briton, Boer, and Yankee* (1978); Bradford Perkins, *The Great Rapprochement* (1968); Serge Ricard and Hélène Christol, eds., *Anglo-Saxonism in U.S. Foreign Policy* (1991); and Joseph Smith, *Illusions of Conflict* (1979).

See also the General Bibliography, the following notes, and Robert L. Beisner, ed., *Guide to American Foreign Relations Since 1600* (2003).

NOTES TO CHAPTER 6

1. Quoted in H. Wayne Morgan, *William McKinley and His America* (Syracuse: Syracuse University Press, 1963), p. 359.
2. Lt. Blandin quoted in David Traxel, *1898* (New York: Knopf, 1998), p. 102.
3. Quoted in Walter Millis, *The Martial Spirit* (Boston: Houghton Mifflin, 1931), p. 102.
4. McKinley quoted in Morgan, *McKinley,* p. 361.
5. Quoted in John L. Offner, *An Unwanted War* (Chapel Hill: University of North Carolina Press, 1992), p. 123.
6. Quoted in Louis A. Pérez, Jr., *The War of 1898* (Chapel Hill: University of North Carolina Press, 1998), p. 15.
7. Quoted in Offner, *Unwanted War,* p. 129.
8. *Congressional Record, XXXI* (March 17, 1898), 2916–2919.
9. Thomas B. Allen, ed., "What Really Sank the Maine?" *Naval History, XII* (March/April 1998), 38.
10. McKinley quoted in Warren Zimmermann, *First Great Triumph* (New York: Farrar, Straus and Giroux, 2002), p. 252.
11. Quoted in Louis A. Pérez, Jr., *Cuba Between Empires, 1878–1902* (Pittsburgh: University of Pittsburgh Press, 1983), p. 172.
12. Quoted in Edmund Morris, *The Rise of Theodore Roosevelt* (New York: Coward, McCann, & Geoghegan, 1979), p. 610.
13. Sen. George Turner and Rep. William Sulzer quoted in Kristin L. Hoganson, *Fighting for American Manhood* (New Haven: Yale University Press, 1998), p. 91.
14. Quoted in Pérez, *Cuba Between Empires,* p. 174.
15. Tomás Estrada Palma quoted in Pérez, *War of 1898,* p. 9.
16. *Foreign Relations, 1898,* p. 746.
17. Quoted in Walter LaFeber, *The American Search for Opportunity, 1865–1913* (New York: Cambridge University Press, 1993), p. 143.
18. *Congressional Record, XXXI* (April 11, 1898), 3699–3702.
19. Pérez, *Cuba Between Empires,* p. 178.
20. Roosevelt quoted in H. W. Brands, *The Reckless Decade* (New York: St. Martin's, 1995), p. 336.
21. Quoted *ibid.,* p. 174.

22. Quoted in H. Wayne Morgan, *America's Road to Empire* (New York: Wiley, 1965), p. 63.

23. Senator Hernando de Soto Money quoted in Hoganson, *Fighting for Manhood*, p. 73.

24. Charles W. Eliot quoted in Frank Ninkovich, *The United States and Imperialism* (Malden, Mass.: Blackwell, 2001), p. 14.

25. Quoted in John Braeman, *Albert J. Beveridge* (Chicago: University of Chicago Press, 1971), p. 23.

26. Max O'Rell quoted in Hoganson, *Fighting for Manhood*, p. 35.

27. Quoted in Joseph A. Fry, "Late Nineteenth Century U.S. Foreign Relations," in Charles W. Calhoun, ed., *The Gilded Age* (New York: Rowman & Littlefield, 2007), p. 323.

28. William Day quoted in Pérez, *War of 1898*, p. 12.

29. Quoted in Gerald G. Eggert, *Richard Olney* (College Park: Penn State University Press, 1974), p. 208.

30. Quoted in Ernest R. May, *Imperial Democracy* (New York: Harper and Row, [1961], 1973), p. 33.

31. *Foreign Relations, 1895,* Part I (Washington, D.C.: Government Printing Office, 1896), pp. 545–562.

32. Quoted in Paul Gibb, "Unmasterly Inactivity?" *Diplomacy & Statecraft, XVI* (January 2005), 29.

33. Richard E. Welch, Jr., *The Presidencies of Grover Cleveland* (Lawrence: University Press of Kansas, 1988), p. 184.

34. Quoted in Robert L. Beisner, *From the Old Diplomacy to the New, 1865–1900* (Arlington Heights, Ill.: Harlan Davidson, 1986; 2nd ed.), p. 111.

35. Quoted in Gibb, "Unmasterly Inactivity?", 35.

36. Quoted in H. W. Brands, *T.R.* (New York: BasicBooks, 1997), p. 289.

37. Quoted in Stuart Anderson, *Race and Rapprochement* (Rutherford, N.J.: Fairleigh Dickinson University Press, 1981), p. 97.

38. Quoted in Joyce Milton, *The Yellow Kids* (New York: Harper and Row, 1989), p. 27.

39. Quoted in Allan Nevins, *Grover Cleveland* (New York: Dodd, Mead, 1932), p. 644.

40. Quoted in Joseph Smith, *Illusions of Conflict* (Pittsburgh: University of Pittsburgh Press, 1979), p. 207.

41. Quoted in George Young, "Intervention Under the Monroe Doctrine," *Political Science Quarterly, LVII* (June 1942), 277.

42. Lars Schoultz, *Beneath the United States* (Cambridge: Harvard University Press, 1998), p. 115.

43. Quoted in Mark T. Gilderhus, "The Monroe Doctrine," *Presidential Studies Quarterly, XXXVI* (March 2006), 10.

44. Henry Cabot Lodge quoted in Fredrick B. Pike, *The United States and Latin America* (Austin: University of Texas Press, 1992), pp. 158–159.

45. Lisle A. Rose, *Power at Sea: The Age of Navalism, 1890–1918* (Columbia: University of Missouri Press, 2007), p. 14.

46. Joseph A. Fry, "From Open Door to World Systems," *Pacific Historical Review, LX* (May 1996), 282.

47. Quoted in Richard E. Welch, Jr., *George Frisbie Hoar and the Half-Breed Republicans* (Cambridge: Harvard University Press, 1971), p. 209.

48. Walter Q. Gresham to Carl Schurz, October 6, 1893, Walter Q. Gresham Papers, Library of Congress, Washington, D.C.

49. Pérez, *War of 1898,* p. 74.

50. Quoted in Louis A. Pérez, Jr., *Cuba and the United States,* 2nd ed. (Athens: University of Georgia Press, 1997), p. 80; quoted in Pérez, *War of 1898,* p. 20; John M. Kirk, *José Martí* (Gainesville: University of Florida Press, 1983), pp. 52, 56, 58, 90, 118; and George C. Herring, *From Colony to Superpower* (New York: Oxford University Press, 2008), p. 310.

51. Quoted in Philip S. Foner, *The Spanish-Cuban-American War and the Birth of American Imperialism* (New York: Monthly Review Press, 1972; 2 vols.), *I,* 21.

52. P. M. Sagasta quoted in Angel Smith, "The People and the Nation," in Angel Smith and Emma Davila-Cox, eds., *The Crisis of 1898* (New York: St. Martin's, 1999), p. 165.

53. Quoted in McCartney, *Power and Progress,* p. 92.

54. Olney quoted in Schoultz, *Beneath the United States,* p. 128.

55. Quoted in Offner, *Unwanted War,* p. 26.

56. Quoted in LaFeber, *American Search,* p. 132.

57. Quoted in Eggert, *Olney,* p. 265.

58. James D. Richardson, ed., *A Compilation of the Messages and Papers of the Presidents, 1789–1897* (Washington, D.C.: Government Printing Office, 1896–1899; 10 vols.), *IX,* 716–722.

59. *Atlanta Constitution* quoted in Hoganson, *Fighting for Manhood,* p. 90.

60. Eric Rauchway, "William McKinley and Us," *Journal of the Gilded Age and Progressive Era, IV* (July 2005), 15.

61. General Calixto García quoted in Pérez, *War of 1898,* p. 9.

62. *Congressional Record, XXXI* (December 6, 1897), 3–5.

63. *Foreign Relations, 1898* (Washington D.C.: Government Printing Office, 1901), pp. 1007–1008.

64. Amy Kaplan, *The Anarchy of Empire in the Making of U.S. Culture* (Cambridge: Harvard University Press, 2002), p. 147.

65. Quoted in John Byrne Cooke, *Reporting the War* (New York: Palgrave Macmillan, 2007), p. 70.

66. Quoted in John A. S. Grenville and George B. Young, *Politics, Strategy, and American Diplomacy* (New Haven: Yale University Press, 1966), p. 278.

67. Louis A.Pérez, Jr., *Cuba and the United States,* 3d ed. (Athens: University of Georgia Press, 2003), p. 94; and John Lawrence Tone, *War and Genocide in Cuba, 1895–1898* (Chapel Hill: University of North Carolina Press, 2006), pp. xii, 280.

68. Quoted in César J. Ayala and Rafael Bernabe, *Puerto Rico in the American Century* (Chapel Hill: University of North Carolina Press, 2007), p. 15.

69. Richard Harding Davis quoted in Stephen Kinzer, *Overthrow* (New York: Times Books, 2006), p. 46.

70. Quoted in Kenneth J. Hagan and Ian J. Bickerton, *Unintended Consequences* (London: Reaktion Press, 2007), p. 93.

71. Quoted in Walter A. McDougall, *Promised Land, Crusader State* (Boston: Houghton Mifflin, 1997), pp. 111–112.

72. Quoted in Ninkovich, *United States and Imperialism,* p. 29.

73. Quoted in McCartney, *Power and Progress,* p. 217; quoted in Hagan and Bickerton, *Unintended Consequences,* p. 95.

74. Quoted in Amy S. Greenberg, *Manifest Manhood and the Antebellum American Empire* (New York: Cambridge University Press, 2005), p. 280; quoted in Servando D. Halili, Jr., *Iconography of the New Empire* (Manila: University of the Philippines Press, 2006), p. 127.

75. Quoted in Robert L. Beisner, "1898 and 1968," *Political Science Quarterly, LXXV* (June 1970), 200.

76. Quoted in Kramer, *Blood of Government,* p. 119.

77. Clark quoted in David Mayers, *Dissenting Voices in America's Rise to Power* (New York: Cambridge University Press, 2007), pp. 200–201.

78. Quoted in Jose D. Fermin, *1904 World's Fair* (Manila: University of the Philippines Press, 2004), p. 23.

79. Quoted in John M. Craig, "Lucia True Ames Mead," in Edward P. Crapol, ed., *Women and American Foreign Policy* (Westport, Conn.: Greenwood, 1992; 2nd ed.), p. 72.

80. Quoted in Paul A. Kramer, *The Blood of Government* (Chapel Hill: University of North Carolina Press, 2007), p. 2.

81. Quoted in Anders Stephanson, *Manifest Destiny* (New York: Hill & Wang, 1995), p. 87.

82. Quoted in Morgan, *McKinley*, p. 322.

83. Quoted in Paul A. Kramer, "Race-Making and Colonial Violence in the U.S. Empire: The Philippine-American War as Race War," *Diplomatic History, XXX* (April 2006), 181.

84. Quoted in Kenton J. Clymer, *Protestant Missionaries in the Philippines, 1898–1916* (Urbana: University of Illinois Press, 1986), p. 159.

85. Quoted in Kramer, *Blood of Government*, pp. 127–128.

86. Gen. Frederick Funston quoted in Brian Daizen Victoria, "When God[s] and Buddha Go to War," in Mark Selden and Alvin Y. So, eds., *War & State Terrorism* (New York: Rowman & Littlefield, 2004), p. 97.

87. Glenn A. May, *Battle for Batangas* (New Haven: Yale University Press, 1991), pp. 267, 291.

88. Quoted in Ronald J. Barr, *The Progressive Army* (New York: St. Martin's, 1998), p. 56.

89. *Boston Evening Transcript*, March 1, 1899.

90. Arthur MacArthur quoted in Patrice Higonnet, *Attendant Cruelties* (New York: Other Press, 2007), p. 186.

91. Quoted in James Chace, "Tomorrow the World," *New York Review of Books*, November 21, 2002, p. 36.

92. General S. B. M. Young quoted in Brian McAllister Linn, *The Philippine War, 1899–1902* (Lawrence: University Press of Kansas, 2000), p. 220.

93. Quoted in Cooke, *Reporting the War*, p. 83.

94. Lodge quoted in Kathleen Dalton, *Theodore Roosevelt* (New York: Knopf, 2002), p. 228.

95. S. B. M. Young quoted in Linn, *Philippine War*, p. 211; quoted in John M. Gates, *Schoolboys and Krags* (Westport, Conn.: Greenwood, 1979), p. vii.

96. Henry F. Graff, ed., *American Imperialism and the Philippine Insurrection* (Boston: Little, Brown, 1969), p. 36.

97. Benjamin Foulois quoted in Brian Linn, *Guardians of Empire* (Chapel Hill: University of North Carolina Press, 1997), p. 36.

98. Quoted in Donald Smythe, *Guerrilla Warrior* (New York: Charles Scribner's Sons, 1973), p. 198.

99. Kramer, *Blood of Government*, p. 297.

100. Fermin, *1904 World's Fair*, p. 172.

101. Kramer, "Race-Making," 197.

102. Robert W. Rydell, *World of Fairs* (Chicago: University of Chicago Press, 1993), pp. 75–76.

103. Quoted in Mayers, *Dissenting Voices*, p. 196.

104. Nicholas Roosevelt quoted in Michael Adas, "Improving on the Civilization Mission?" in Lloyd C. Gardner and Marilyn B. Young, eds., *The New American Empire* (New York: The New Press, 2005), p. 173.

105. Quoted in Thomas J. McCormick, *China Market* (Chicago: Quadrangle, 1967), p. 119.

106. Charles Denby quoted in Thomas Schoonover, *Uncle Sam's War of 1898 and the Origins of Globalism* (Lexington: University Press of Kentucky, 2003), p. 69.

107. Sarah Pike Conger quoted in Carol C. Chin, "American Women Missionaries in China at the Turn of the Twentieth Century," *Diplomatic History, XXVII* (June 2003), 350.

108. *Foreign Relations, 1901* (Washington, D.C.: Government Printing Office, 1902), Appendix, p. 12.

109. J. G. Blair, "First Steps Toward Globalization," in Reinhold Wagnleitner and Elaine Tyler May, eds., *"Here, There and Everywhere": The Foreign Politics of American Popular Culture* (Hanover, N.H.: University Press of New England, 2000), p. 25.

110. Quoted in Beale, *Theodore Roosevelt*, p. 84.

111. Quoted in Fareed Zakaria, *From Wealth to Power* (Princeton: Princeton University Press, 1998), p. 133.

112. Quoted in Serge Ricard, "The Roosevelt Corollary," *Presidential Studies Quarterly, XXXVI* (March 2006), 21–22.

113. Quoted in Anderson, *Race and Rapprochement*, p. 127.

114. A. T. Mahan quoted in Paul A. Kramer, "Empires, Exceptions, and Anglo-Saxons," *Journal of American History, LXXXVIII* (March 2002), 1335.

115. Quoted in Edward P. Crapol, "From Anglophobia to Fragile Rapprochement," in Hans-Jürgen Schröder, ed., *Confrontation and Cooperation* (Providence, R.I.: Berg, 1993), p. 21.

116. American Historical Association, *Annual Report, 1898* (Washington, D.C.: Government Printing Office, 1899), p. 288.

117. Quoted in Smith, *Illusions of Conflict*, p. 40.

118. Emily S. Rosenberg, "Walking the Borders," in Michael J. Hogan and Thomas G. Paterson, eds., *Explaining the History of American Foreign Relations* (New York: Cambridge University Press, 1991), p. 33.

119. Quoted in Gail Bederman, *Manliness & Civilization* (Chicago: University of Chicago Press, 1995), p. 193.

120. Quoted in Cecilia Elizabeth O'Leary, *To Die For* (Princeton: Princeton University Press, 1999), p. 142.

121. LaFeber, *American Search*, p. 117.

122. Quoted in Arthur Link's essay in *Wilson's Diplomacy* (Cambridge: Schenkman, 1973), p. 6.

123. Quoted in Robert Hannigan, *The New World Power* (University Park: Pennsylvania State University Press, 2002), p. 282.

124. Henry Watterson quoted in Alan Brinkley, "The Concept of an American Century," in R. Laurence Moore and Maurizio Vaudagna, eds., *The American Century in Europe* (Ithaca: Cornell University Press, 2003), p. 8.

125. A. J. Beveridge quoted in Kramer, "Empires," p. 1351.

126. Hannigan, *New World Power*, p. xii.

CHAPTER 7

Managing, Policing, and Extending the Empire, 1900–1914

"The Thirteenth Labor of Hercules." With this official poster by Perham Nahl, the Panama-Pacific Exposition in San Francisco in 1915 celebrated the opening of the Panama Canal. The artist commemorates the ten-year construction project using symbols that reflect the era's themes of empire-building and male hegemony: A powerful, muscular Hercules (the United States) forcibly parts the land (a yielding Panama) to make space for the canal. (Library of Congress)

DIPLOMATIC CROSSROAD

❖ *Severing Panama from Colombia for the Canal, 1903*

"REVOLUTION IMMINENT" WARNED the cable from the American consul at Colón, a normally quiet Colombian seaport on the Atlantic side of Panama. Acting Secretary of State Francis B. Loomis fired off an inquiry to the U.S. consul at Panama City, on the Pacific slope: "Uprising on Isthmus reported. Keep Department promptly and fully informed." The response came back in four hours: "No uprising yet. Reported will be in the night. Situation is critical." Loomis's anxiety soon increased when he learned that troops of the Colombian government had landed in Colón.

In Washington, D.C., it was now 8:20 P.M., November 3, 1903. As far as Loomis knew, a revolution had not yet broken out on the isthmus. Nonetheless, he hurriedly drafted instructions for the consuls at Panama and Colón. "Act promptly" to convey to the commanding officer of the U.S.S. *Nashville* this order: "In the interests of peace make every effort to prevent [Colombian] Government troops at Colón from proceeding to Panama [City]." Loomis agonized for another hour. Finally, a new cable arrived: "Uprising occurred to-night … no bloodshed. … Government will be organized to-night." Loomis had done his part to ensure success in the scheme to acquire a canal controlled by the United States.

November 3 was far more hectic for the conspirators in Panama. A tiny band of Panamanians and Americans living on the isthmus had actively plotted revolution since August, when the Colombian congress rejected the treaty that would have permitted the United States to construct an isthmian canal. By late October, they had become convinced that the North American colossus, frustrated in its overtures to Colombia, would lend them moral and physical support. Confident that U.S. naval vessels would be at hand, they selected November 4 as the date of their coup d'état. To their dismay, however, the Colombian steamer *Cartagena* disembarked about 400 troops at Colón early on November 3. Because the "important message" directing him to prevent the "landing of any armed force … at Colón" had not reached him, Commander John Hubbard of the *Nashville* did not interfere with the landing.

Forced to improvise, the conspirators deviously separated the Colombian commanding general from his troops, lured him aboard a train, and sped him across the isthmus to Panama City, where they arrested their guest, formed a provisional government, and paraded before a cheering crowd at the Cathedral Plaza. But the revolution would remain perilously unfinished so long as armed Colombian soldiers occupied Colón. Too weak to expel the soldiers by force, the insurgents gave the colonel in charge $8,000 in gold, whereupon he ordered his troops aboard a departing steamer. The U.S. consul at Panama City cabled: "Quiet prevails." At noon the next day, Secretary of State John Hay recognized the sovereign Republic of Panama.

The new Panamanian government appointed as its minister plenipotentiary a Frenchman, Philippe Bunau-Varilla, an engineer of an earlier failed Panama canal project. With Gallic flourish, Bunau-Varilla congratulated Secretary Hay for rescuing Panama "from the barbarism of unnecessary and wasteful civil wars to consecrate it to the destiny assigned to it by Providence, the service of humanity, and the progress of civilization."[1] On November 18, 1903, less than two weeks after U.S. recognition of Panama, Hay and Bunau-Varilla signed a new treaty by which the United States would build, fortify, and operate a canal linking the Atlantic and Pacific oceans. Washington also guaranteed the "independence of the Republic in Panama," thereby ensuring against any threat from Colombia.[2]

Hay had at last achieved a goal set by his chief, President Theodore Roosevelt, several years earlier. If an unfortified, neutral canal had existed in Central America during the recent war with Spain, Roosevelt had argued, the United States would have spent the war in "wild panic," fearful that the Spanish fleet would slip through the waterway and rush to the Philippines to attack Commodore Dewey. "Better to have no canal at all, than not give us the power to control it in time of war," Roosevelt decided.[3]

"No other arm may go around this waist."   This artistic rendering by W. A. Rogers of a lascivious Uncle Sam abducting a female Panama appeared on the cover of *Harper's Weekly* on December 29, 1900. The gendered imagery actually anticipated President Theodore Roosevelt's forceful intervention in 1903 to gain U.S. control of a canal to be built across the Isthmus of Panama. When TR subsequently tried to justify his actions in support of Panamanian independence, Secretary of War Elihu Root observed: "You have shown that you have been accused of seduction and you have conclusively proved that you were guilty of rape." (Library of Congress)

The Clayton-Bulwer Treaty of 1850, stipulating joint Anglo-American control of any isthmian canal, seemed to block the way. In December 1898, flushed with victory over Spain, President William McKinley had directed Secretary Hay to seek a modification of that agreement with the British ambassador, Sir Julian Pauncefote. The Hay-Pauncefote Treaty of February 1900 permitted the United States to build a canal but forbade its fortification, much to the dismay of Roosevelt who spearheaded an attack that defeated the treaty in the Senate. On November 18, 1901, with Roosevelt now president, Hay and Pauncefote signed a satisfactory new pact.

Then began the complex process of determining the route. In November 1901, after a two-year investigation, the Walker Isthmian Canal Commission reported in favor of Nicaragua. The decisive criterion—cost—seemed exorbitant for Panama because of the obduracy of the New Panama Canal Company, a French-chartered firm that held the Colombian concession for canal rights. The company estimated its assets on the isthmus at $109 million—machinery, property, and excavated soil left by the defunct de Lesseps organization in 1888. Purchase of the company's rights and holdings would make construction of a Panama canal prohibitively expensive if technologically easier. For these reasons, plus travelers' depiction of Panama as "a hideous dung heap of physical and moral degradation," the House passed the Hepburn Bill in January 1902 authorizing a canal through Nicaragua.[4]

The New Panama Canal Company's American lawyer, William Nelson Cromwell, schemed to sell the assets of his French client for the highest possible price. Lobbying hard, Bunau-Varilla even exposed the unsuitability of Nicaraguan terrain by deluging Congress with Nicaraguan postage stamps that depicted a belching volcano. On January 18, 1902, the Walker Commission reversed itself and decided for the technologically preferable Panama passage, citing the company's willingness to sell out for the reduced sum of $40 million. Guided by Roosevelt and Cromwell, Congress five months later chose the Panama route. The State Department soon opened negotiations with Colombia. The annual rent became a stumbling block, which Hay removed only by delivering an ultimatum to the Colombian chargé d'affaires, Tomás Herrán, in January 1903. On January 22 he and Hay signed a treaty granting Colombia an initial payment of $10 million and $250,000 annually. The United States would control the six-mile-wide Canal Zone for one hundred years, renewable at the "sole and absolute option" of the North American republic.[5]

The U.S. Senate approved the Hay-Herrán Treaty on March 17, 1903, but the Colombian government attempted to extract a $10 million payment from the New Panama Canal Company for permitting the transfer of its assets to the U.S. government. Cromwell promptly cried foul, whereupon Hay bluntly announced that any payment to Colombia was "not permissible."[6] The Colombians next tried to raise the initial American cash payment from $10 million to $15 million. Roosevelt exploded against "those contemptible little creatures in Bogotá."[7] The president believed that "you could no more make an agreement with the Colombian rulers than you could nail currant jelly to the wall."[8] TR's intransigence and Hay's extraordinary intercession on behalf of a privately owned foreign corporation increased the Colombians' resentment against U.S. infringement on their sovereignty over Panama. The Colombian congress unanimously rejected the treaty on August 12, 1903.

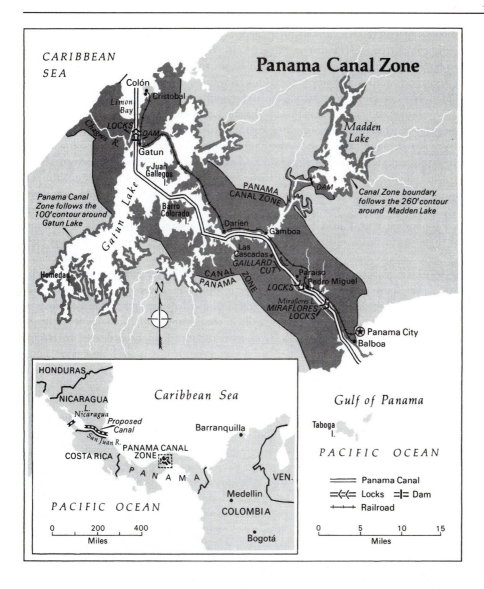

Roosevelt was already pondering undiplomatic alternatives. In June the frenetic Cromwell had met with Roosevelt and then planted a story in the *New York World* reporting that, if Colombia rejected the treaty, Panama would secede and grant to the United States "the equivalent of absolute sovereignty over the Canal Zone," and that "President Roosevelt is said to strongly favor this plan."[9] By now the president was privately castigating Colombia for its "squalid savagery," combined with "the worst forms of despotism and of anarchy, of violence and of fatuous weakness, of dismal ignorance, cruelty, treachery, greed, and utter vanity."[10]

Roosevelt now considered two options: seizure of Panama by force, or instant recognition and support for any revolutionary regime in Panama. The president inclined sharply toward the latter course after a meeting with Bunau-Varilla on October 10, during which the Frenchman predicted an uprising. When Bunau-Varilla asked what the United States would do, TR replied: "Colombia by her action has forfeited any claim upon the U.S. and I have no use for a government that would do what that government has done."[11] One week later, on October 16, Secretary Hay informed Bunau-Varilla that American naval vessels were heading toward the isthmus. Calculating the steaming time, Bunau-Varilla cabled the revolutionaries on the isthmus that warships would arrive by November 2. Early that evening the U.S.S. *Nashville* dropped anchor at Colón as predicted. Although the *Nashville* landed troops to keep order *after* the Panamanian junta had gained control, a Colombian diplomat rightfully complained: "The Americans are against us. What can we do against the American Navy?"[12]

Roosevelt urged swift ratification of the Hay–Bunau-Varilla Treaty, claiming that Colombia had forced the United States to take "decisive steps" for the benefit of "civilized mankind."[13] When critics complained about his "Bowery-boy" behavior toward Colombia, Roosevelt denounced the "small body of shrill eunuchs who consistently oppose" his "righteous" policies.[14] On February 23, 1904, the Senate approved the treaty by a vote of 66 to 14. The treaty granted the United States "power and authority" within the zone "in perpetuity" as "if it were the sovereign of the territory."[15] Later, in 1911, TR reportedly boasted that "I took the Canal Zone and let Congress debate; and while the debate goes on the Canal does also."[16]

Panama Canal. The U.S.S. *Ohio* passes through the Culebra Cut (now called the Gaillard Cut) of the Panama Canal about a year after the canal opened to traffic—both warships and commercial vessels. "For the next seven decades," the scholar Lars Schoultz has noted, "the Panama Canal Zone stands as the most obvious legacy of the age of imperialism in United States policy toward Latin America." (Library of Congress)

In what has been called "the greatest liberty Man has taken with nature," construction of the fifty-mile-long canal began in 1904, and the locks were formally opened on August 15, 1914.[17] During the first year of operation alone, 1,058 merchant vessels slid through the locks, while the Atlantic and Pacific fleets of the U.S. Navy freely exchanged ships. San Francisco in 1915 hosted the extravagant Panama-Pacific International Exposition with the theme "The Land Divided—The World United."[18] In 1922 the United States paid "conscience money" or "canalimony" of $25 million to Colombia but did not formally apologize for having taken the Canal Zone. Most Americans have applauded Roosevelt's bold venture against Colombia. TR ranked it alongside the Louisiana Purchase and the acquisition of Texas. The canal, Woodrow Wilson later asserted, shifted "the center of gravity of the world."[19]

Architects of Empire

The taking of Panama symbolized the new activism characteristic of American foreign policy after the Spanish-American-Cuban-Filipino War, and construction of the canal intensified U.S. influence over Latin America. It also accelerated Washington's participation in the global contest for empire among the great powers. "The United States will be attacked as soon as you are about to complete the canal," Germany's Kaiser Wilhelm II predicted in 1907, identifying Japan as the most likely culprit.[20] Britain, which had the power to challenge U.S. preeminence in the hemisphere, acquiesced in the hope of gaining a Yankee ally to deter a growing political and naval threat from Germany. In turn, the vigorous German Empire, having expanded its markets and investments in Central and South America to more than 2 billion marks by 1900, seemed "desirous of obtaining a foothold in the Western Hemisphere," noted the General Board of the U.S. Navy.[21] Revolutionary upheavals in Russia, China, and Mexico further shifted the international balance of power. In an era of tumultuous transformation, as European alliances consolidated and lurched toward a world war, President Roosevelt and his successors thought it imperative to defend, develop, and enlarge the new U.S. empire.

In the late nineteenth century, Roosevelt had associated closely with the most vocal pressure group agitating for an American canal, the uniformed "professors of war" at the Naval War College.[22] He corresponded regularly with Admiral Alfred

Makers of American Foreign Relations, 1900–1914

Presidents	Secretaries of State
Theodore Roosevelt, 1901–1909	John Hay, 1898–1905
	Elihu Root, 1905–1909
	Robert Bacon, 1909
William Howard Taft, 1909–1913	Philander C. Knox, 1909–1913
Woodrow Wilson, 1913–1921	William Jennings Bryan, 1913–1915

Thayer Mahan, who tirelessly touted the strategic advantages of a canal. During the war of 1898, the warship *Oregon* dashed at full speed from San Francisco around South America to Cuba in time to help destroy the Spanish fleet off Santiago. The race of more than 14,000 miles fired American imaginations, but it also consumed sixty-eight days and underscored the need for an interoceanic canal across Central America.

Roosevelt's sense of isthmian strategic necessity reflected a broad worldview he shared with many "progressives" in the early twentieth century. A patrician reformer, he "feared that unrest caused by social and economic inequities would impair the nation's strength and efficiency."[23] With similar danger lurking in disorder abroad, he sought influence to create a U.S.-friendly order on a global scale through "proper policing."[24] Roosevelt talked about doing the "rough work of the world" and the need to "speak softly and carry a big stick."[25] Imbibing Darwinist doctrines of "natural selection," he proclaimed "our duty toward the people living in barbarism [is] to see that they are freed from their chains, and we can free them only by destroying barbarism itself."[26] Anglo-Saxon superiority was best expressed in war. "All the great masterful races have been fighting races," TR lectured.[27] Not all Progressive-era reformers joined Roosevelt in advocating a vigorous activism abroad. Wisconsin's Senator Robert M. La Follette, for example, opposed imperialism and contended that the same corporate monopolists they battled at home were dragging the United States into perpetual intervention overseas. Activists in women's organizations bemoaned the "present intoxication with the hashish of conquest" as they urged "women's values" on a male government so as to rein in the "champing steeds" of American militarism and expansion.[28]

Roosevelt vigorously debated his critics. Exuberant and calculating, he centralized foreign-policy decision making, frequently bypassed Congress, and believed "the people" so ignorant about foreign affairs that they should not direct an informed president like himself. At the same time, he kept favorite journalists and other "intelligent observers sufficiently enlightened to prevent their going wrong."[29] Seeking world stability, Roosevelt advocated "minimizing the chances of war among civilized people" and "multiplying the methods and chances of honorably avoiding war in the event of controversy."[30] Indeed, he won the Nobel Peace Prize in 1906 for his mediation of the Russo-Japanese War at the Portsmouth Conference (see pages 253). The robust Roosevelt relished debate with those he considered his intellectual equals, and he invited favored foreign diplomats to be members of his boisterous Tennis Cabinet. "The biggest matters," this progenitor of the imperial presidency later wrote, "I managed without consultation with anyone; for when a matter is of capital importance, it is well to have it handled by one man only."[31]

Roosevelt and other shapers of American foreign policy before World War I were members of an American quasi-aristocracy who moved comfortably in the affluent, cosmopolitan, upper-class society of the Atlantic seaboard. Roosevelt, a graduate of Harvard College and prolific author, had served as assistant secretary of the navy and governor of New York. His successor, Ohioan William Howard Taft, a graduate of Yale, had served as a federal circuit court judge, governor general of the Philippines (1901–1904), and secretary of war (1904–1908). Woodrow Wilson earned a Ph.D. from Johns Hopkins, wrote books on government and history, and

Jules Jusserand (1855–1932). This distinguished scholar and diplomat served capably as France's ambassador to the United States from 1903 to 1924. An old friend of Theodore Roosevelt, he often joined the president in his celebrated "scrambles" through Washington's Rock Creek Park. TR's motto on such excursions was "over, under, or through, but never around," which meant jumping, wading, or swimming across any watery obstacle. On one occasion, as Roosevelt's entourage stripped to plunge into a pond, the president noticed that the ambassador had removed all clothes except his lavender gloves. "It would be embarrassing if we should meet ladies," Jusserand explained. His diplomatic memoir *What Me Befell* (1933) remains a classic. (Library of Congress)

was president of Princeton and governor of New Jersey before entering the White House. Each president believed that "we owe to our less fortunate [international] neighbors" the same "neighborly feeling and aid that a successful man in a community owes to his less fortunate fellow citizens."[32]

Their secretaries of state, with one exception, belonged to the same elite. John Hay, secretary from 1898 to 1905, was educated at Brown University. A poet, novelist, biographer, and editor of the *New York Tribune,* the wealthy Hay had served as Lincoln's personal secretary during the Civil War and much later as McKinley's ambassador to Great Britain, becoming a chief architect of the Anglo-American rapprochement. His successor, Elihu Root (1905–1909), graduated from Hamilton College, took a law degree at New York University, and became one of America's most successful corporation lawyers. As secretary of war from 1899 to 1904, Root created mechanisms, such as the Platt Amendment for Cuba, for managing the

American empire. Like TR, he believed that the "main object of diplomacy is to keep the country out of trouble" and maintain order abroad.[33] Philander C. Knox (1909–1913) followed Root. A corporation lawyer, Knox served as attorney general and U.S. senator before entering the State Department. He liked to play golf at Chevy Chase, spend summers with his trotters at his Valley Forge Farms estate, vacation in Florida in the winter, and delegate departmental work to subordinates. He advocated "dollar diplomacy" as a means of creating order in revolution-prone areas—that is, using private financiers and business leaders to promote foreign policy, and using diplomacy to promote American commerce and investment abroad. As his *second* secretary of state, President Wilson named New Yorker Robert Lansing (1915–1920), a graduate of Amherst College, son-in-law of a former secretary of state, and practitioner of international law. Reserved and conservative, Lansing also abhorred disorder in the U.S. sphere of Latin America.

William Jennings Bryan, Wilson's *first* appointment (1913–1915), lacked such conservative elite status. The "boy orator" of Nebraska could mesmerize crowds by decrying the "cross of gold" on which eastern capitalists were crucifying western and southern farmers, but he could not win a presidential election (he ran in 1896, 1900, and 1908). The "Great Commoner" languished for years as the most prominent has-been of the Democratic party until Wilson named him secretary of state as a reward for support at the convention of 1912. The president let Bryan appoint "deserving Democrats" to diplomatic posts and indulge his fascination with "cooling off" treaties, but Wilson bypassed him in most important diplomatic decisions, even to the point of composing overseas cables on his own White House typewriter.

The conservative managers of American foreign policy believed that a major component of national power was a prosperous, expanding economy invigorated by a healthy foreign trade. The principle of the "Open Door"—to keep open trade and investment opportunities—became a governing tenet voiced globally, if often tarnished in application. In 1900 the United States exported goods valued at $1.5 billion. By 1914 that figure stood at $2.5 billion. Exports to Latin America increased markedly, from $132 million at the turn of the century to $309 million in 1914. Investments there in sugar, transportation, and banking shot up. By 1913 the United Fruit Company, the banana empire, had some 130,000 acres in cultivation in Central America, a fleet of freighters, and substantial political influence as well. By 1914 U.S. entrepreneurs dominated nickel mining in Canada and sugar production in Cuba, and total American investments abroad stood at $3.5 billion.

But those statistics meant more than fat pocketbooks for the corporate elite. Americans believed that economic expansion also carried abroad positive values of industriousness, honesty, morality, and private initiative. Thus Yale University-in-China and the Young Men's Christian Association (YMCA) joined Standard Oil Company and Singer Sewing in China as advance agents of civilization. Taft said about the Chinese: "The more civilized they become the more active their industries, the wealthier they become, and the better market they will become for us."[34] President Wilson, adding missionary paternalism to the quest for order, said simply that he would "teach the South American Republics to elect good men."[35] Not all foreigners viewed Americans as benevolent. One Venezuelan writer characterized "Yanquis" as "rough and obtuse Calibans, swollen by brutal appetites, the enemies of idealism, furiously enamored of the dollar," whiskey-soaked sots, "overwhelming, fierce, [and] clownish."[36] The Russian novelist Fyodor Dostoevsky depicted the United States as "a geographic outlaw, a place where his fictional protagonists fled never to return."[37] Whatever Americans' intentions, their compulsion to shape the lives of other peoples while denying any selfish desire to dominate showed a persistent and often glaring disjunction between the practices and professed ideals of U.S. foreign policy.

Cuba's Limited Independence Under the Platt Amendment

In December 1898, President McKinley promised a "free and independent" status for Cuba once the U.S. occupation had established "complete tranquility" and a "stable government."[38] To accelerate Cuban democracy and stability, he appointed General Leonard Wood as the military governor of the island. A Harvard graduate with a degree in medicine, Wood favored outright annexation of Cuba, but he loyally carried out the administration's policy of patrician tutelage. During his tenure as military governor (1899–1902), he worked to eradicate yellow fever, Americanize education, construct highways, and formulate an electoral law. He even added "before" and "after" photographs of public toilets in his reports. The general defined his objectives narrowly: "When money can

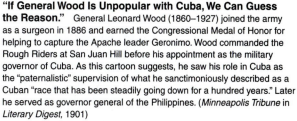

"If General Wood Is Unpopular with Cuba, We Can Guess the Reason." General Leonard Wood (1860–1927) joined the army as a surgeon in 1886 and earned the Congressional Medal of Honor for helping to capture the Apache leader Geronimo. Wood commanded the Rough Riders at San Juan Hill before his appointment as the military governor of Cuba. As this cartoon suggests, he saw his role in Cuba as the "paternalistic" supervision of what he sanctimoniously described as a Cuban "race that has been steadily going down for a hundred years." Later he served as governor general of the Philippines. (*Minneapolis Tribune* in *Literary Digest*, 1901)

be borrowed at a reasonable rate of interest and when capital is willing to invest in the Island, a condition of stability will have been reached."[39] Only the North Americans had the resources to reconstruct war-ravaged Cuba. Those Cuban elites who spoke English and knew American ways could serve as local managers, traders, agents, and advisers. The occupation stressed English in public schools because "the Cuban people will never understand the people of the United States until they appreciate our institutions."[40]

Secretary of War Elihu Root sought a Cuban-American political relationship that would weather the storms of independence. Working closely with Senator Orville Platt, Root fashioned the Platt Amendment to the Army Appropriation Bill of 1901. By the amendment's terms, Cuba could not make a treaty with any nation that might impair its independence. Should Cuban independence ever be threatened, or should Cuba fail to protect "life, property, and individual liberty," the United States had the right to intervene. For these purposes, Cuba would cede to the United States "lands necessary for coaling or naval stations."[41]

Cubans protested. On Good Friday 1901, the front page of Havana's *La Discusión* carried a cartoon of "The Cuban Calvary" depicting the Cuban people as Christ and Senator Platt as a Roman soldier. Root piously denied any "intermeddling or interference with the affairs of a Cuban government," but Wood privately conceded that "little or no independence [was] left Cuba under the Platt Amendment."[42] A reluctant Cuban convention adopted the measure as an amendment to the new constitution on June 12, 1901, and the two governments signed a treaty embodying the Platt Amendment on May 22, 1903. That same year the U.S. Navy constructed a naval base at Guantánamo Bay; "Gitmo," as the marines christened it, was leased to the United States in perpetuity for a small annual fee. With North American investments pouring into capital-starved Cuba, extending control over sugar, tobacco, mining, transportation, utilities, and cattle ranching, the Reciprocity Treaty of 1902 permitted Cuban products to enter the United States at specially reduced tariff rates, thereby further interlocking the two economies.

The first president of the Republic of Cuba, Tomás Estrada Palma, acted "more plattish than Platt himself" until discontented Cuban nationalists rebelled.[43] In September 1906, the U.S. consul general in Havana reported Estrada Palma's inability to "protect life and property."[44] "I am so angry with that infernal little Cuban republic," exploded Roosevelt, "that I would like to wipe its people off the face of the earth." All he wanted was for the Cubans to "behave themselves."[45]

Into this turmoil stepped the portly Secretary of War William Howard Taft, sent by TR to mediate between the warring factions. Estrada Palma resigned, permitting Taft to establish a new government with himself as governor. Likening Cuban efforts at self-rule to "making bricks without straw," Taft concluded that Cubans woefully lacked a "mercantile spirit," a "desire to make money, to found great enterprises."[46] He returned home in mid-October, leaving behind a government headed by an American civilian, administered by U.S. Army officers, and backed by 5,000 American soldiers. For twenty-eight months Governor Charles E. Magoon attempted to reinstate Leonard Wood's electoral and humanitarian reforms, while Roosevelt worried that "those ridiculous dagoes would flare up over some totally unexpected trouble and start to cutting one another's throats."[47]

Under his successor, Taft, and under Taft's successor, Woodrow Wilson, U.S. policy toward Cuba reflexively supported existing governments, by force if necessary. Order took precedence over democracy; no serious effort was made to expand participatory politics or to empower historically disenfranchised poor, black, and mixed-race populations. The United States instead used "dollar diplomacy" to foster stability in Cuban politics and security for investments and commerce, particularly in sugar. The $50 million invested by Americans in 1896 jumped to $220 million in 1913. By 1920 American-owned mills produced about half of Cuba's sugar. Annual Cuban exports to the United States in 1900 equaled $31 million, by 1914 $131 million, and by 1920 $722 million, thus confirming José Martí's dictum that *"el pueblo que compra, manda"* ("the country which buys, commands").[48] U.S. entrepreneurs helped establish missionary schools (such as the Candler school in Havana, named after the founder of Coca-Cola) that, in effect, trained Cubans for employment in North American companies. When revolution threatened these interests, as in May 1912 and February 1917, marines went ashore. After Havana followed Washington's lead and declared war against Germany in April 1917, some 2,500 U.S. troops occupied the island, ostensibly to protect the sugar plantations that helped feed the Allied armies.

The Constable of the Caribbean: The Roosevelt Corollary, Venezuela, and the Dominican Republic

In his first annual message, on December 3, 1901, President Roosevelt called the Monroe Doctrine "a guarantee of the commercial independence of the Americas." The United States, however, as protector of that independence, would "not guarantee any state against punishment if it misconducts itself, provided that punishment does not take the form of the acquisition of territory by any non-American power."[49] If a Western Hemispheric country misbehaved toward a European nation, Roosevelt promised to "let the European country spank it."[50]

The president was thinking principally of Germany and Venezuela. The flamboyant Venezuelan dictator Cipriano Castro had perpetually deferred payment on $12.5 million in bonds held by European investors, once showing olfactory contempt during negotiations by "breaking wind" against indignant German diplomats.[51] In December 1902, after clearing the way with Washington, Germany and Britain delivered an ultimatum demanding immediate settlement of their claims, seized several Venezuelan vessels, bombarded two forts, and blockaded all ports. To all of this Roosevelt initially acquiesced, despite the doctrine of Argentina's Foreign Minister Luis M. Drago that "physical force cannot be used to compel the collection of public debt under any circumstances."[52]

In mid-January 1903, the German navy bombarded two more forts. This time Roosevelt delivered a quiet warning to desist. He also sent Admiral George Dewey on naval maneuvers in the Caribbean, which were intended, Dewey later boasted, as "an object lesson to the Kaiser."[53] TR worried that the "fuss-cat" kaiser might spark war through his "incessant hysterical vacillations."[54] Impressed by the U.S. reaction, the kaiser replaced his ill-informed ambassador with Hermann Speck von Sternburg, an old friend of Roosevelt. The president urged on him a quick settlement. Thereupon, Britain and Germany in February lifted the blockade and submitted the dispute to the Permanent Court of Arbitration at The Hague. Speck von Sternburg averred that the kaiser "would no more think of violating that [Monroe] doctrine than he would of colonizing the moon."[55] When the Hague arbiters found in favor of Germany and England in early 1904, a State Department official complained that this decision put "a premium on violence" and made likely similar European interventions in the future.[56]

TR also fretted about the Dominican Republic, revolution-torn since 1899 and seemingly vulnerable to German interests. "I have about the same desire to annex it," Roosevelt confessed privately, "as a gorged boa constrictor might have to swallow a porcupine wrong-end to."[57] An American firm claimed damages of several million dollars, and European creditors demanded action by their governments. The president prayed that the Dominicans "would behave so that I would not have to act in any way." By spring 1904 he thought he might have to do "what a policeman has to do."[58] If he said "'Hands off' to the powers of Europe, then sooner or later we must keep order ourselves," he told Root.[59]

On December 6, 1904, Roosevelt described to Congress his conception of the United States as hemispheric policeman. "Chronic wrongdoing, or an impotence which results in a general loosening of the ties of civilized society," he proclaimed, "may in America, as elsewhere, ultimately require intervention by some civilized nation, and in the Western Hemisphere the adherence of the United States to the Monroe Doctrine may force the United States, however reluctantly, in flagrant cases of such wrongdoing or impotence, to the exercise of an international police power."[60] James Monroe "certainly would no longer recognize" his own doctrine because TR had transformed the ban on European meddling into a brash assertion of U.S. military and political hegemony over the Americas.[61]

The Rough Rider soon donned his constable's badge. He appointed a U.S. collector of Dominican customs. "The Constitution," Roosevelt later explained, "did not explicitly give me the power to bring about the necessary agreement with Santo Domingo. But the Constitution did not forbid me."[62] Yet "policing" and "civilizing" the Dominican Republic by presidential order provoked nationalist resentment, as Dominicans soon quieted "their children with the threat 'There comes an American. Keep quiet or he will kill you.'"[63] Taft's secretary of state, Philander C. Knox, applauded the customs receivership in the Dominican Republic for curing "century-old evils" and halting corruption.[64] The assassination of the Dominican president in November 1911 suggested that Knox spoke prematurely. And in 1912 revolutionaries operating from contiguous Haiti marauded throughout the Dominican Republic, forcing the closure of several customs houses. To restore order, Taft in September 1912 sent a commission backed by 750 marines. The commissioners redefined the Haitian-Dominican border, forced the corrupt Dominican president to resign, and avoided direct interference in a new election.

His denunciation of "dollar diplomacy" notwithstanding, Woodrow Wilson's search for stability in Latin America retraced familiar steps. When, in September 1913, revolution again threatened the Dominican government, Secretary of State

Bryan promised "every legitimate means to assist in the restoration of order and the prevention of further insurrections."[65] When Wilson ordered naval intervention after further Dominican disorders in May 1916, he said: "If a man will not listen to you quietly in a seat, sit on his neck and make him listen."[66] As the 400 marines of Admiral William Caperton's landing force entered the city of Santo Domingo at dawn on May 15, they found empty streets, bolted doors, shuttered windows, and Dominican flags festooned with black crepe. A new treaty was imposed giving the United States full control over Dominican finances. In November, as U.S. participation in the European war became increasingly probable, Wilson proclaimed the formal military occupation of the Dominican Republic, ostensibly to suppress revolutionaries suspected of a pro-German bias. The U.S. Navy formally governed the country until 1922. The main legacy of the occupation, in the historian Bruce Calder's understated judgment, was "a strong anti-U.S. feeling" among the Dominican people.[67]

Ordering Haiti and Nicaragua

The Dominican Republic shares the island of Hispaniola with Haiti, where revolution became an increasingly popular mode of changing governments in the early twentieth century. American investments in Haiti were limited to ownership of a small railroad and a one-third share in the Haitian National Bank. Nationals of France and Germany controlled the bank, and disorder thus could give either European nation a pretext for intervention. After the outbreak of World War I, the Wilson administration worried about "the ever present danger of German control" of Haiti and its deepwater harbor of Môle Saint Nicolas.[68] The Navy Department, content with bases in Cuba and Puerto Rico, nonetheless remembered the German gunboat *Panther*'s sinking a Haitian gunboat in 1902. The State Department sought to buy the Môle "to take it out of the market."[69] Wilson also pressed for an American customs receivership on the Dominican model.

The Haitians resisted successfully until July 1915, when the regime of Guillaume Sam fell in an orgy of grisly political murders. Wilson ordered the navy to "amicably take charge" of the "dusky little republic."[70] After 2,000 troops imposed martial law and seized the customshouses, the African American activist-historian W. E. B. Du Bois admonished: "SHAME ON AMERICA!" because "murder in Port-au-Prince is no worse than … lynching in Georgia."[71] Subsequent fighting between occupiers and native guerrillas, which critics perceived as "a racial war of extermination," killed more than 2,250 Haitians compared to 16 marine casualties.[72] Until the marines finally departed in 1934, U.S. officials observed "the intense feeling … practically everywhere against the American occupation."[73]

The United States also intervened, virtually at will, in Nicaragua. In 1907 Roosevelt and Mexico's president jointly proposed a peace conference to end the incessant warfare among Central American states. As Secretary of State Root explained, their conduct mattered because the Panama Canal put them "in the front yard of the United States."[74] When President José Santos Zelaya solicited funds to build a second interoceanic canal, especially from Germany (whose capital investments were three times greater than U.S. properties in Nicaragua), Washington turned against a leader whom some Nicaraguans had compared to Roosevelt

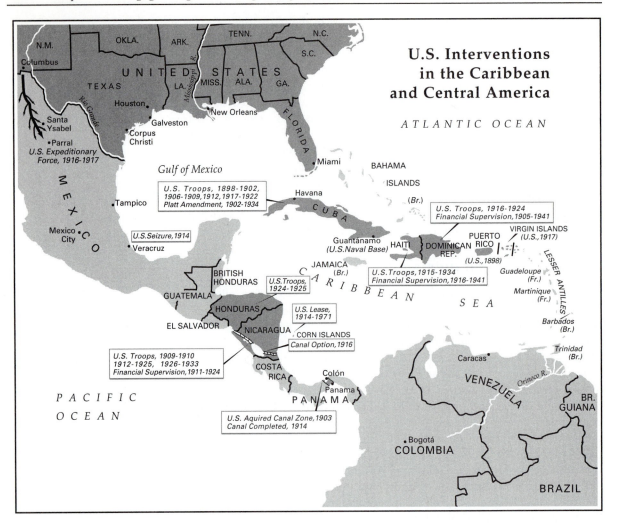

U.S. Interventions in the Caribbean and Central America

himself. For Zelaya's crime of seeking a "better economic position for Nicaragua outside the U.S. economic subsystem," Secretary of State Knox called his regime "a blot upon the history of Nicaragua" and President Taft said he would no longer deal with "such a medieval despot."[75]

After Zelaya executed two Americans for aiding rebels, Washington broke diplomatic relations in November 1909, sent a battleship for "moral effect," forced Zelaya into exile, and threatened to "knock heads together until they should maintain peace."[76] Secretary Knox then negotiated a treaty with the victorious conservatives led by Adolfo Díaz, providing for U.S. control of the customs service and an American loan. Instead of gratitude, "the natural sentiment of an overwhelming majority of Nicaraguans is antagonistic to the United States," the U.S. envoy reported.[77] Rebuffed by the U.S. Senate, Knox and a group of bankers simply went ahead without a treaty. In September 1912, the administration sent 354 marines into battle on behalf of the Díaz regime, which the State Department deemed representative of "the ablest people of the country."[78] After routing the newest revolutionary army, the leathernecks returned home, leaving one hundred behind as a legation guard in Managua. The marines could prevent a coup d'état, but "*keeping* a surrogate in power in Central America was often as problematical as *putting* him in power."[79]

The Wilson administration did much the same. In the spring of 1913 Secretary Bryan dusted off a shelved draft treaty granting the United States a canal option in Nicaragua in exchange for $3 million. The secretary also added a clause similar to the Platt Amendment before sending the Bryan-Chamorro Treaty to the Senate. When the upper house balked, Bryan deleted the U.S. right of intervention. Ratification in February 1916 did help Nicaragua's finances. The treaty also effectively excluded European powers from naval bases in the Gulf of Fonseca, and to make that point stick, Wilson ordered U.S. warships to cruise offshore during the 1916 Nicaraguan presidential campaign. Although nominally independent, Nicaragua remained a U.S. protectorate until 1933.

Resisting Revolution in Mexico

Revolution in Mexico posed major problems for Washington. In 1911 Francisco I. Madero toppled Porfirio Díaz, the aged dictator who had maintained order, personal power, and a healthy environment for North American investments since the late 1870s. U.S. citizens owned more than 40 percent of Mexico's property, and Mexico had become the world's third largest oil producer, thanks to the Standard Oil Company, Texas Oil Company (Texaco), and other firms. The revolution thus inevitably took on an anti-Yankee tinge. Despite the threat to American lives and property, Taft determined to "sit tight on the lid and it will take a good deal to pry me off."[80] One of Taft's diplomats, however, soon reversed the president's policy of nonintervention. In February 1913, Ambassador Henry Lane Wilson encouraged one of Madero's trusted generals, Victoriano Huerta, to overthrow the revolutionary nationalist. Indeed, Huerta had Madero shot and then set about to consolidate his own power. The German ambassador called these events "the usual American policy of replacing hostile regimes with pliable ones through revolutions without taking official responsibility for it."[81] But one of the state governors, Venustiano Carranza, organized the "Constitutionalist" revolt on February 26, igniting a period of vicious internal conflict. When American residents became caught in the crossfire, the departing Taft administration refused recognition until Huerta punished the "murderers of American citizens" and ended "discriminations against American interests."[82]

Appalled by Madero's murder, President Woodrow Wilson vowed not to recognize a "government of butchers."[83] He privately described his purpose as that of a benevolent neighbor who would help Mexico "adjust her unruly household."[84] Seemingly unconcerned about private American properties in Mexico worth some $1.5 billion, Wilson refused to act as "the servant of those who wish to enhance the value of their Mexican investments."[85] When Ambassador Wilson continued to urge recognition of Huerta to protect those U.S. interests, the president recalled him in July 1913 for "treason, perfidy, and assassination in an assault on constitutional government."[86] The president thereafter treated with Mexico through special emissaries, only one of whom spoke fluent Spanish.

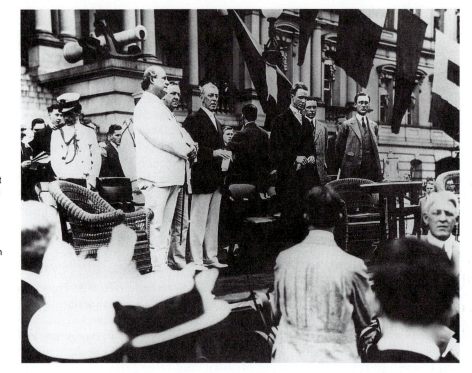

William Jennings Bryan (1860–1925), Woodrow Wilson (1856–1924), and Franklin D. Roosevelt (1882–1945), 1913. President Wilson, in white trousers and dark jacket, speaks while Secretary of State Bryan, to the president's right, and Assistant Secretary of the Navy Roosevelt, at the far right of the picture, look on. Wilson spoke proudly of his "missionary diplomacy," for he believed that "every nation needs to be drawn into the tutelage of America." To achieve this goal, Wilson sent more U.S. warships into more Caribbean harbors than did any other president. (Franklin D. Roosevelt Library)

In August one such representative, John Lind, arrived in Mexico City. A former governor of Minnesota without diplomatic experience, Lind delivered Wilson's proposal for an armistice between Huerta's federalist troops and all revolutionary groups, "an early and free election," and Huerta's promise not to run for president. In exchange, the United States pledged recognition and aid to "the administration chosen and set up … in the way and on the conditions suggested." With sublime arrogance, Woodrow Wilson wondered: "Can Mexico give the civilized world a satisfactory reason for rejecting our good offices?"[87] "Where in the hell does he get the right to say who shall or shall not be President of Mexico," wrote one Mexican after Wilson's "counsels" were rebuffed.[88] After this snub, Woodrow Wilson announced a restrained policy of "watchful waiting."[89]

Undeterred, Huerta in October held a special election, which returned an entirely submissive congress ready to extend his presidency indefinitely. Wilson then turned to Carranza in northern Mexico, but the latter contemptuously refused Wilsonian mediation and rejected any solution short of his own triumph. Wilson informed the other powers in November of his renewed policy "to isolate General Huerta entirely … and so to force him out."[90]

Most European powers, especially Germany, had recognized Huerta in defiance of Wilson. "Good. Finally unity against the Yankee," the kaiser had noted in July 1913.[91] The British, however, their capital investments in Mexico ranking second only to those of the United States and their navy relying on Mexican oil, did not want to antagonize Wilson, with tensions mounting in Europe. The British

Foreign Office therefore notified Huerta that it would not support him against the United States, and urged him to resign—all the while viewing Wilson's policies as "most impractical and unreasonable."[92]

With British compliance assured, Wilson lifted the U.S. arms embargo in February 1914 and permitted large quantities of arms to flow to both factions, although mostly to Carranza. As the latter's resupplied forces pushed south, the president sent U.S. naval vessels to the oil-producing town of Tampico on the Gulf of Mexico. On April 9, at Tampico, Huerta's troops arrested several American sailors loading gasoline onto a whaleboat docked provocatively near a Mexican military installation. The Mexican colonel in charge quickly freed the sailors and apologized orally. The hotheaded U.S. squadron commander, Rear Admiral Henry T. Mayo, demanded a formal twenty-one-gun salute because Mexico had insulted the flag. When Huerta refused, the president on April 20 requested congressional approval to use armed force to obtain "the fullest recognition of the rights and dignity of the United States."[93] Without waiting for congressional authorization, Wilson then ordered U.S. warships to the port of Veracruz to stop a German arms shipment intended for Huerta.

On April 21, 1914, 800 American sailors and marines landed. Huerta's troops withdrew but cadets from the naval academy, joined by prisoners liberated from jails and other irregulars, put up a bloody resistance. Nineteen Americans and several hundred Mexicans died. An anguished Wilson bemoaned that "it was I who ordered those young men to their deaths."[94] Despite his intent to undermine Huerta, the capture of Veracruz temporarily rallied Mexicans behind the dictator. Rejecting advice from his military advisers, who wanted to march to Mexico City, Wilson accepted mediation when proposed by Argentina, Brazil, and Chile (the ABC powers) on April 25. These mediation talks, held on the Canadian side of Niagara Falls that summer, accomplished little, but in mid-July Huerta fled to Europe, and on August 20 a triumphant Carranza paraded before enthusiastic throngs in Mexico City.

The Constitutionalist triumph did not last. One of Carranza's northern generals, Francisco (Pancho) Villa, soon broke from the ranks, marched south, and in December occupied Mexico City. Wilson saw Villa as "the only instrument of civilization in Mexico" whose "firm authority allows him to create order and to educate the turbulent masses of peons so prone to pillage."[95] Because Villa had not criticized the U.S. assault on Veracruz, the president facilitated arms exports to him and refused to recognize Carranza. To prevent a military clash with any Mexican faction, all American troops withdrew from Veracruz on November 23, 1914. Once again, Wilson watched and waited.

U.S. relations with Mexico remained tense during early 1915. Carranza's forces gradually drove Villa north, but in the process Mexico City became a no-man's-land, with bread riots and starvation threatening its inhabitants, including 2,500 Americans and 23,000 other foreign residents. Further complications arose along the Mexico-U.S. borderland, especially in southern Texas, where the massive influx of refugees and revolutionaries exacerbated local tensions between Anglos and *Tejanos*. The Plan of San Diego, an anarchist manifesto broadcast in early 1915, demanded return of all lands "robbed in a most perfidious manner," execution of every North American "over sixteen years of age," restoration of Indian lands, and sovereign territory for blacks.[96] The ensuing raids and counterraids turned south Texas into a war zone as vigilantes and Texas rangers killed at least 150 Mexicans. A new verb—"rangered"—described summary treatment of suspects by Texas authorities.[97] Preoccupied by the *Lusitania* crisis with Germany after May 1915 (see page 271), Wilson reluctantly concluded that "Carranza will somehow have to be digested."[98] With American oil fields under Carranza's protection, Wilson extended de facto recognition to the Constitutionalist regime in June 1915, permitted arms exports (while banning them to opponents), and beefed up the U.S. military presence along the border.

Francisco (Pancho) Villa (1878–1923). The intelligent, dedicated revolutionary nationalist bedeviled both Mexico and the United States. His daring raid on an American border town was calculated to outrage President Wilson, whom he mocked as "an evangelizing professor of philosophy who is destroying the independence of a friendly people." This photograph was taken in 1908. (Library of Congress)

Egged on by German agents who envisaged a Mexican-American war as "a noose … to tie the United States to the American continent," Villa denounced *Carranzistas* as "vassals" of the United States.[99] In the predawn hours of March 9, 1916, Villa led a band of *Villistas* across the border into Columbus, New Mexico, initiating a battle that left seventeen Americans and more than a hundred Mexicans dead. Within hours of the attack, Wilson unleashed the Punitive Expedition of 7,000 soldiers, commanded by General John J. Pershing, which soon penetrated 350 miles into Mexico in a vain search for Villa. Nonetheless, a clash with *Carranzista* troops occurred at Carrizal in June 1916. Wilson resisted demands to withdraw Pershing's forces until February 1917. Later that month, the secret Zimmermann telegram, proposing an anti-American alliance between Germany and Mexico, came into the hands of the State Department, courtesy of British intelligence. This German threat prompted the United States to extend de jure recognition of the Carranza government on August 31, 1917, in order to ensure Mexican neutrality during the fight against Germany. After four futile years, Wilson had finally given up trying to tutor the Mexicans.

Japan, China, and Dollar Diplomacy in Asia

Managing Asian affairs proved even more difficult after 1900. Secretary of State John Hay's Open Door notes did not prevent the further humiliation of China. During the Boxer Rebellion Russia stationed 175,000 troops in Manchuria and demanded exclusive rights from China, including a commercial monopoly. Roosevelt and Hay disingenuously acquiesced because the Open Door had "always recognized the exceptional position of Russia" in Manchuria and had merely sought the commercial freedom "guaranteed to us by … the whole civilized world."[100] Thinking it folly "to play the role of an Asian power without military power," Roosevelt retreated because the American people would not fight for nebulous principles of Chinese integrity in Manchuria.[101] His successors in the White House did not always follow his example.

Japan viewed the question quite differently. Russia blocked Japanese economic expansion into Manchuria, posed a potential naval menace, and endangered the Japanese position in Korea. Tokyo covered its flanks with an Anglo-Japanese Alliance in 1902 and prepared for war. On February 8, 1904, the Japanese navy destroyed Russia's Asian fleet and naval base in a surprise attack at Port Arthur. At first Roosevelt cheered privately, "for Japan is playing our game," but he worried about "the creation of either a yellow peril or a Slav peril."[102] By spring 1905, Japanese soldiers had taken Mukden, where Russia lost 97,000 men. Revolutionary stirrings had hit St. Petersburg, and Admiral Heihachiro Togo had sunk the Russian Baltic fleet at Tsushima Strait (between Japan and Korea). On May 31, Japanese envoy Kogoro Takahira requested Roosevelt "to invite the two belligerents to come together" for direct peace negotiations.[103]

Hoping to balance the belligerents "so that each may have a moderative action on the other" and thus protect U.S. access to the Pacific and Asia, Roosevelt assembled Japanese and Russian diplomats at Portsmouth, New Hampshire, in August 1905.[104] Japan demanded Russia's leasehold on the Liaodong Peninsula and the railroad running from Harbin to Port Arthur, evacuation of Russian

"Spread-eagleism" in China. The missionary teacher Grace Roberts teaches a Bible class in 1903 in Manchuria. Americanism and religious work, flag and mission, became partners. The missionary force was thus feminized—the majority of missionaries were women. (By permission of the Houghton Library, Harvard University, ACB 78.1)

troops from Manchuria, and recognition of Japan's control of Korea. The Russians quickly conceded these points but rejected demands for an indemnity and cession of the island of Sakhalin. Roosevelt broke the deadlock by proposing a division of Sakhalin and agreement "in principle" on an indemnity. Tsar Nicholas II agreed to partition but "not a kopeck of compensation."[105] Japan yielded and in late August signed a peace treaty. Roosevelt had earned the Nobel Peace Prize.

The president's search for equipoise in East Asia did not end at Portsmouth. As early as March 1904, the president had conceded to Japan a relationship with Korea "just like we have with Cuba."[106] Secretary of War Taft reaffirmed the concession with Prime Minister Taro Katsura on July 27, 1905. In the Taft-Katsura "agreed memorandum of conversation," Japan denied any designs on the Philippines, and Taft thereby put an American "seal on the death warrant of an independent Korea."[107] A year later the Japanese reopened southern Manchuria to foreign and American trade but discouraged foreign capital investments. Japan formally annexed Korea in 1910.

A domestic dispute in California soon soured Japanese-American amity. On October 11, 1906, the San Francisco School Board created a special "Oriental Public

School" for all Japanese, Chinese, and Korean children. Japan immediately protested, and TR denounced the "infernal fools in California" whose exclusion of Japanese from all other public schools was "as foolish as if conceived by the mind of a Hottentot."[108] Given existing federal-state jurisdictions, however, he could do little more than rail against the recalcitrant school board, apply political pressure to the governor and California legislature to prevent statewide discriminatory measures, and propose federal legislation to naturalize Japanese residing permanently in the United States. Defending segregation, the *San Francisco Examiner* editorialized: "Californians do not want their growing daughters to be intimate in daily school contact with Japanese young men. Is this remarkable?"[109] Always the political realist, Roosevelt accepted what he personally disliked and sought accommodation with Japan. In February 1907, he reached a "Gentlemen's Agreement" with Tokyo, sharply restricting Japanese immigration on a voluntary basis.

Because "the Japanese jingoes are ... about as bad as ours," the president shrewdly pressed for more battleships and fortification of Hawai'i and the vulnerable Philippines, now America's "heel of Achilles," so that the United States would "be ready for anything that comes."[110] He also dramatized the importance of a strong navy to Congress and to Japan by ordering the battle fleet to the Pacific and around the world. An armada of sixteen battleships steamed out of Hampton Roads, Virginia, in December 1907, not to return until February 1909. Germany's kaiser predicted that U.S. warships in the Pacific "will upset all British and Japanese calculations."[111] Just after the "Great White Fleet" visited Tokyo in October 1908, Japan's ambassador received instructions to reach an agreement with the United States recognizing the Pacific Ocean as an open avenue of trade, pledging the integrity of Japanese and American insular possessions in the Pacific, and promising equal opportunity in China. The ensuing Root-Takahira declaration of November 30, 1908, seemed to restore Japanese-American harmony.

The promising new epoch was spoiled by conflicting Japanese-American goals toward China. Despite the Open Door notes, American commerce with China stalled during the Roosevelt era, in part because of resurgent nationalism. When Congress barred Chinese immigration in 1904, the Chinese staged a short-lived boycott of American goods. A protest song against "American Flour-Made Mooncakes" became popular in Chinese cities.[112] In addition, prostitution flourished in China's treaty ports. This illegitimate China trade ("deeply corrupt, overtly predatory, transnational, transracial, conducted without regard to a 'national interest'") undercut the gains of legitimate American commerce in China.[113] Because Roosevelt viewed the Chinese as passive and effete, "sunk in Oriental stagnation and corruption," he placed strategic interests first and refused to antagonize Japan over China.[114]

Roosevelt's successor thought otherwise. Instead of a decrepit China in decay, President Taft envisioned expanded trade with a "young China, rousing from a centuries-old slumber and rubbing the sand of its past from its eyes."[115] During a 1905 trip to East Asia, Taft had met the intensely anti-Japanese American consul general in Mukden, Willard Straight. Two years later, after calling the Root-Takahira agreement "a terrible diplomatic blunder" because it accepted Japan's exploitation of Manchuria, Straight proposed the creation of a Manchurian bank, to be financed by the American railroad magnate E. H. Harriman.[116] Under Taft, Straight and the

Elihu Root (1845–1937).
Root served as secretary of
state (1905–1909). He helped
devise methods for managing
the American empire. (Library of
Congress)

State Department quickly inspired several New York banks to form a combination, headed by J. P. Morgan, to serve as the official agency of American railroad investment in China. As acting chief of the department's new Far Eastern Division, Straight demanded admission of the American bankers into a European banking consortium undertaking construction of the Huguang Railway linking Beijing and Guangzhou (Canton). Straight then resigned from the State Department to become the Morgan group's roving representative.

In November 1909, Washington had proposed to Britain the neutralization of Manchurian railroads through extending a large international loan to China for the purchase of the lines. Britain, however, joined both Japan and Russia to reject the proposal. Instead of an open door in Manchuria, Secretary of State Knox had "nailed that door closed with himself on the outside."[117] In the fall of 1910, an agreement expanded the Huguang Railway consortium to include American bankers, but the Chinese Revolution broke out in May 1911 against the Manchu dynasty and foreign interests and delaying railroad construction until 1913. "Dollar diplomacy," Straight ruefully admitted, "made no friends" in the Huguang matter.[118]

Hoping to reap tangible benefits by dissociating the United States from the other powers, President Wilson and Secretary Bryan repudiated American participation in the international consortium on March 18, 1913—to do otherwise would have cost the United States "the proud position ... secured when Secretary Hay stood for the Open Door in China after the Boxer Uprising." Wilson extended formal diplomatic recognition to the Chinese Republic in May.[119] He had thereby renewed America's commitment to the political integrity of China, a goal pragmatically abandoned by Roosevelt, unsuccessfully resuscitated by Taft, and consistently opposed by Japan.

Wilson's Asian policy started out tentatively, but events at home and abroad eventually caused it to resemble Taft's more than Roosevelt's. In April 1913, Democratic and Progressive politicians placed before the California legislature a bill denying residents "ineligible to citizenship" the right to own land. The measure struck directly at the 50,000 Japanese living in California. Racist passions erupted, with one farmer recoiling from the prospect of racial intermarriage: "What is that baby? It isn't a Japanese. It isn't white."[120] Basically sharing the Californians' anti-Japanese prejudices and sensitive to states' rights, Wilson nonetheless sent Bryan to Sacramento to beg for a milder statute. But the California legislature passed the offensive bill on May 3, 1913. When Japan protested the "unfair and intentionally racially discriminatory" measure, Wilson and Bryan lamely argued that one state's legislation did not constitute a "national discriminatory policy."[121]

Wilson's antipathy toward Japan reappeared in fall 1914 when Japan declared war on Germany, seized the German Pacific islands north of the equator, and swept across China's Shandong Peninsula to capture the German leasehold of Jiaozhou. "When there is a fire in a jeweller's shop," a Japanese diplomat arrogantly theorized, "the neighbours cannot be expected to refrain from helping themselves."[122] Tokyo immediately followed with the Twenty-One Demands of January 18, 1915, asserting extensive political and economic rights in Shandong, southern Manchuria, and Mongolia. Preoccupied with Mexico and the *Lusitania* crisis, the Wilson administration refused to recognize Japan's gains, which amounted to a repudiation of the Open Door policy.

Wilson's nonrecognition policy ran counter to secret treaties in which the European Allies promised to support Japan's conquests at the peace conference after World War I. Washington soon compromised. In an agreement with Viscount Kikujiro Ishii, signed November 2, 1917, Secretary Lansing admitted that "territorial propinquity creates special relationships between countries, and consequently ... Japan has special interests in China," while Ishii reiterated his nation's dedication to the Open Door and integrity of China.[123] The Wilson administration also revived the international banking consortium as the only way to check further unilateral Japanese economic penetration of China proper. The wheel had turned full circle for Wilson. Like Taft before him, Wilson failed to protect China's fragile sovereignty because he could neither conciliate nor deter Japan.

Anglo-American Rapprochement and Empire Building

American policies toward Asia and Latin America often fell short of their proclaimed goals because of the pseudoscientific thinking about race characteristic of the early twentieth century. Americans viewed Asians as "inscrutable and somnolent," depicted Latin Americans as black children or alluring maidens, imagined Africa as the "dark continent" of "savage beasts and beastly savages," and referred to Filipinos as "our little brown brothers." These biased stereotypes inevitably aroused resentment from Bogotá to Beijing, from Managua to Manila.[124] Yet such Darwinist racial attitudes also facilitated much closer relations between the United States and Great Britain. Because victory "in the international competition among the races ... might not go to the refined and peaceful peoples but rather to the amoral, the cunning, the fecund, and the power hungry," England and the United States sought to "cultivate a sense of solidarity and a capacity for cooperation."[125] "Buffalo Bill" Cody certainly thought the "hatchet" had been "buried" when Queen Victoria attended his Wild West Show and "bowed" before the American flag.[126] So too did the British, as shown by their willingness to accept exclusive U.S. control of a canal in Panama. Also prompted by Britain's search for allies against Germany (evidenced in the Anglo-Japanese Alliance of 1902 and the Entente Cordiale with France in 1904), London's pursuit of "the most cordial and constant cooperation" with the United States led to a celebrated "great rapprochement."[127]

The tenuous new Anglo-American affinity nearly dissolved in 1903 over the Alaska boundary controversy, which stemmed from Canadian claims to large areas of the Alaskan panhandle. As the power responsible for the Dominion's foreign relations (Canada did not establish a foreign office until 1909), Britain found itself backing Ottawa's dubious contention that much of the panhandle's coastline actually belonged to Canada. Expostulating that Canada had less claim "than the United States did to Cornwall or Kent," President Roosevelt refused arbitration and sent 800 soldiers to Alaska to awe his opponents, both foreign and domestic.[128] London finally agreed in January 1903 to an American proposal for a mixed boundary commission composed of six jurists, three from each side. Taking no chances, Roosevelt appointed Senator Henry Cabot Lodge and Secretary Root, hardly disinterested judges, to the commission. He informally warned London he would demarcate the line himself if the

John Bull in Need of Friends.
Battered by criticism over its war against the Boers in South Africa and challenged by a rising Germany, Great Britain found a new friend in the United States. Not all Britons embraced Anglo-American affinity. "Only 1/4 of the population of the United States are what you might call natives," wrote a British admiral in 1901. "The rest are Germans, Irish, Italians, and the scum of the earth! all of them hating the English like poison." (*Des Moines Leader* in *Literary Digest*, 1901)

commissioners failed to agree. One British commissioner sided with the Americans, and on October 20, 1903, by a vote of 4 to 2, the commission panel officially decided for the United States. The British "made the inevitable choice to please a power ten times the size of Canada and with more than ten times the wealth."[129]

Canadian-American relations did improve with the Migratory Bird Treaty of 1916. Conservationists and scientists, alarmed by a decline in North American birds caused by reckless sport and commercial hunting, pressed for this agreement under the principle of "common property resources." The death of the last passenger pigeon, in the Cincinnati Zoo in 1914, symbolized the crisis. Because the treaty restricted hunting, especially during the mating season, it sparked some opposition in the United States. Representative John Tillman, a Democrat from Arkansas who defended duck hunting in gendered terms, cried that the accord "should be bedecked with skirts" because it "would feminize our boys."[130] The bird population increased, and similar wildlife protection, evident in the Inland Fisheries Treaty (1908) and the North Pacific Fur Seal Convention (1911), became landmarks in international environmental history.

Entente also characterized the Anglo-American settlement of the North Atlantic fisheries dispute. Since 1782, American fishermen had insisted on retaining their pre-Revolutionary privileges off Canada's Newfoundland. Indeed, "a gilded wooden cod" still hung from the ceiling of the Massachusetts State House.[131] The modus vivendi of 1888, under which they had fished for several years, collapsed in 1905 when Newfoundland placed restrictions on American fishing vessels. Senator Lodge cried for warships to protect his constituents' livelihood. Instead, Roosevelt proposed, and London accepted, arbitration at The Hague Tribunal. In 1910 the arbiters ruled that Britain could oversee fishing off Newfoundland if it established reasonable regulations, that a fisheries commission would hear cases, and that Americans could fish in large bays if they remained three miles from shore. This compromise defused the oldest dispute in American foreign relations and symbolized London's political withdrawal from the Western Hemisphere.

The naval retreat had occurred earlier, when the Admiralty abolished the North Atlantic station based at Jamaica. After 1902 the Royal Navy patrolled the Caribbean only with an annual visit by a token squadron of cruisers. Admiral Sir John Fisher wanted to concentrate his heavy ships in the English Channel and North Sea as monitors of the growing German navy. He regarded the United States as "a kindred state with whom we shall never have a parricidal war."[132]

Even the aggressive hemispheric diplomacy of Taft and Wilson did not undermine the Anglo-American rapprochement. Britain criticized both dollar diplomacy in Latin America and Wilson's quixotic efforts to dislodge Huerta. But Foreign Secretary Sir Edward Grey tersely laid to rest all talk of a challenge: "His Majesty's Government cannot with any prospect of success embark upon an active counterpolicy to that of the United States, or constitute themselves the champions of Mexico or any of these republics against the United States."[133] In reciprocation, Wilson protected British oil interests in Mexico and made it a "point of honor" to eliminate the one potentially dangerous British grievance inherited from his predecessor.[134] Late in the Taft administration, Congress had exempted American intercoastal shippers from payment of Panama Canal tolls. British opinion condemned this shifting of canal maintenance costs to other users. Because it unfairly discriminated against foreign shipping, Wilson persuaded Congress to revoke the law in June 1914.

In the end, rapprochement meant mutual respect for each other's empires. In addition to having the "Great White Fleet" visit "white man's country" in New Zealand and Australia, Roosevelt encouraged London to frustrate native aspirations for independence in India, while the British accepted the American suppression of the Filipinos and U.S. hegemony in Latin America.[135] American leaders usually spoke favorably of independence for colonial peoples—but independence only after long-term tutelage to make them "civilized" enough to govern. In 1910 in Egypt, a country that the ex-president considered "years, even generations" away from self-government, he lectured Muslim nationalists about Christian respect for womanhood.[136] In chronically unstable Liberia, where the United States in 1912 instituted a financial receivership in the African nation resembling that in the Dominican Republic, the British encouraged Washington to use a strong hand in what London called America's "protectorate."[137]

While building an empire, U.S. policymakers largely adhered to the tradition of aloofness from continental European political and military affairs. Even Roosevelt overtly tampered only once with Europe's balance of power. In 1904 France acquiesced in British control of Egypt in exchange for primacy in Morocco. A year later, Germany decided to test the solidity of the new Anglo-French entente by challenging France's claims in Morocco. The kaiser belligerently demanded a German political role in Morocco, which France at once refused. After a brief European war scare, in which Britain stood by its ally, Germany asked Roosevelt to induce France and England to convene a conference to settle Morocco's future. Worried about Kaiser Wilhelm's "violent and often wholly irrational zigzags," Roosevelt accepted the personal invitation only after assuring Paris that his "sympathies … at bottom [were] with France."[138] During the conference, held in early 1906 at Algeciras, Spain, Roosevelt devised a pro-French compromise and persuaded the kaiser to accept it. This political intervention isolated Germany and reinforced the Anglo-French entente, but it generated criticism at home. Roosevelt's successors made sure they did not violate the American policy of nonentanglement with Europe during the more ominous second Moroccan and Balkan crises preceding the First World War.

Nonentanglement also doomed the sweeping arbitration treaties that Secretary Hay negotiated with several world powers. When the Senate attached crippling amendments, Roosevelt withdrew the treaties because they did "not in the smallest degree facilitate settlements by arbitration."[139] After 1905 Secretary Root persuaded Roosevelt to accept watered-down bilateral arbitration treaties, and Secretary Bryan later negotiated a series of supplementary "cooling-off" treaties by which nations pledged to refrain from war during international investigations of serious disputes. None of these arrangements, however, effectively bound signatories, and like the Permanent Court of Arbitration at The Hague, they represented a backwater in international diplomacy. Ambassador Whitelaw Reid compared U.S. participation in the Hague Peace Conference of 1907 to a farmer taking his hog to market: "That hog didn't weigh as much as I expected he would, and I always knew he wouldn't."[140]

The mainstream of American foreign policy between 1900 and 1914 flowed through the Panama Canal, a momentous political, military, and technological achievement. The United States became the unchallenged policeman of the Caribbean region, empowering Washington, in Taft's words, "to prevent revolutions" so that "we'll have no more."[141] Although German authorities thought that the canal would shift American priorities to Asia and "today's Atlantic fleet will become the Pacific fleet," the United States still lacked the power to challenge Japan or Britain.[142] As Roosevelt understood, the Open

Naval Arms Race. The international naval competition in the early twentieth century was foreboding. Disarmament talks at The Hague Conferences in 1899 and 1907 and arbitration treaties did not curb the arms buildup. Roosevelt's decision to send the "Great White Fleet" around the world in 1907–1908 may have encouraged both Japan and Germany to speed up their naval programs. (*Detroit News* in *Literary Digest,* 1904)

Door "completely disappears as soon as a powerful nation determines to disregard it."[143] One military officer told Congress in 1910: "We have grown from a little frontier army to one spread all over the world—in America, Puerto Rico, Hawai'i, Alaska, the Philippines, and sometimes in Cuba—and we have not got the officers and men to do it."[144]

American insensitivity to the nationalism and distinct cultural identities of other peoples became another imperial legacy. Filipino resistance to American domination, Cuban anger at the Platt Amendment, Colombian outrage over Panama, and Mexican rejection of Wilsonian intervention bore witness to the depth of nationalistic sentiments and to resentment at U.S. efforts to control. Like the European powers who were carving up Asia, Africa, and the Middle East, the United States developed its empire by subjugating peoples and compromising their sovereignty in Latin America and the Pacific. As a Panamanian diplomat later explained: "When you hit a rock with an egg, the egg breaks. Or when you hit an egg with a rock, the egg breaks. The United States is the rock. Panama is the egg. In either case, the egg breaks."[145] With the exception of the Virgin Islands, purchased from Denmark for $25 million in 1917 to forestall any wartime German seizure, the empire grew little from outright territorial gains. It was, instead, an informal empire administered by troops, financial advisers, and reformers who frequently ran roughshod over the culture, politics, and economies of the peoples they dominated. The U.S. governor of Guam captured the prevailing outlook when he depicted the indigenous Chamorros as children, "easily controlled and readily influenced by example, good or bad."[146]

Puerto Rico thus seemed the "good" territorial possession, and political cartoons portrayed the populace as a "polite schoolchild, sometimes female, in contrast to ruffian boys" in Cuba and the Philippines.[147] Under the Foraker Act (1900), Puerto Rico and its naval base on Culebra became a "new constitutional animal"—an "unincorporated territory" subject to the will of the U.S. Congress and governed by the War Department (until 1934).[148] In a series of decisions called the Insular Cases (1901–1904), the Supreme Court upheld the Foraker Act, providing Washington with a means to govern people it did not wish to organize as a state. In March 1917, Congress granted Puerto Ricans U.S. citizenship just in time for them to be drafted into the U.S. armed forces in the war against Germany. "Increasingly tied to the United States and insistently defined as not part of it," Puerto Rico still remains a colony, or "commonwealth," and Puerto Ricans remain divided in their views about statehood, independence, and commonwealth status.[149]

The adventurous nature of American foreign relations under an imperial ideology and the male ethos in the years 1900–1914 attracted many capable, well-educated young men to diplomatic service. "It was TR's call to youth which lured me to Washington," the diplomat William Phillips later recalled.[150] Career ambassador Joseph C. Grew first gained presidential favor by shooting a tiger in China. Several of these young foreign-service career officers, virtually all graduates of Ivy League colleges, including Phillips, Grew, Willard Straight, former Rough Rider Henry P. Fletcher, and soldier-diplomat Frank R. McCoy, lived in an exclusive bachelors' townhouse at 1718 H Street during their Washington service. Known among themselves as "the Family," these youthful professionals blended camaraderie with careers and "became the elite or legendary 'inner circle' of the State Department" for the next forty years.[151] The New York attorney Henry L. Stimson, himself a protégé of Elihu Root, served as secretary of war under Taft (1911–1913) and continued this tradition of recruiting some of the brightest public servants to a succession of high-level posts through the end of World War II.

The American empire burgeoned culturally, as well as militarily and economically, during these years. Just as Buffalo Bill Cody's Wild West Show had "hyped" American cultural myths abroad since the 1890s, Wilbur Wright's airplane tour of Europe in 1908 set records, thrilled crowds, and impressed military strategists.[152] The cruise of the "Great White Fleet" provided as much pageantry as statecraft— "a feast, a frolic, or a fight," as Admiral Robley D. Evans put it.[153] Colonial subjects became popular on college campuses, as anthropologists and ethnographers offered courses on "Savage Childhood" and "Peoples of the Philippines."[154] When academic exchanges with European universities expanded after 1900, Harvard University commemorated its new Germanic Museum by bestowing an honorary doctorate on Prince Henry of Prussia, the kaiser's brother—"a simple, natural person who got used in a day to our troublesome democratic ways."[155]

Hundreds of thousands of U.S. tourists ("the world's wanderers") traveled abroad clutching their Baedeker guidebooks, spending American dollars, and sometimes acquiring foreign titles through marriage, as in the case of Jennie Jerome and Lord Randolph Churchill, whose son Winston valued Anglo-American partnership.[156] A French humorist commented that for American women "the freedom to flirt is as sacred and inalienable … as the immortal principles of 1789 are in our country."[157] Civic leaders took pride in hosting the Olympic Games in St. Louis in 1904, hailed an American victory in the 1908 Round-the-World Automobile race, became weekend frontiersmen after organizing the Boy Scouts of America in 1910, and cheered the gold medals won by Native American Jim Thorpe at the Stockholm Olympics in 1912. Just as they seemed to take up the great game of empire from Great Britain, so too did Americans become proficient in that most diplomatic of athletic competitions, the royal and ancient Scottish sport of golf. For some Americans, true Anglo-American entente did not occur until young Francis Ouimet bested British champions Harry Vardon and Ted Ray in the U.S. Open at Brookline, Massachusetts, in 1913.

Yet beneath the glitter lurked danger. Winston Churchill later wrote of living in two different worlds: "the actual, visual world with its peaceful activities" and "a hypothetical world 'beneath the threshold'"—"a world at one moment utterly fantastic, at the next seeming to leap into reality—a world of monstrous shadows moving in convulsive combination through vistas of fathomless catastrophe."[158] Once the world started spinning around the catastrophic assassination in Sarajevo, Bosnia, it became difficult for the growing American empire to escape the maelstrom of world war.

What if … *manliness and civilization had not become linked in the minds of American leaders in the period 1900–1917?*

Without the heavy emphasis on virility and civilization as a rationale for U.S. empire after 1898, certain features of that imperial experience might have been different. Had imperialists such as Theodore Roosevelt, William Howard Taft, and Gen. Leonard Wood not regarded Filipinos and Cubans as racial inferiors, as weak women and children who needed American tutelage, Americans might have opted to negotiate with them—a process that implies equal partnership—instead of using coercion, including the "water cure" and forcing the Platt Amendment upon Cuba. By treating peoples of Asia and Latin America as equals rather than subordinates, U.S. leaders might have appeared less self-righteous and aroused less anti-Americanism in the long term. The United States, in short, might have secured its interests in the area without violating its own best principles of fair play and self-determination. It is also improbable that a president of less blatant *machismo* than Theodore Roosevelt would have crudely impugned the masculinity of anti-imperialists by calling them mollycoddles and "nice old women of both sexes." Such gender-based language mattered because it undermined legitimate criticism, exalted the presidency over Congress in the checks-and-balance U.S. system, and stifled debate—the very stuff of the democratic process. A less conspicuously virile Roosevelt might not have imagined his own manhood challenged by Colombian "dagoes" and might have renegotiated a canal treaty with Bogotá instead of "taking" Panama.

For masculinity not to have mattered, though, would have required the undoing of gendered and race-based attitudes and practices that had been refined and affirmed through centuries of slavery, Indian removal, and institutionalized female inequality. In both rhetoric and practice, gendered language helped shape and give meaning to an official American worldview that envisaged conflict and competition as consistent with democracy and capitalism, and that assumed a natural hierarchy of power and order in the world where white males of European descent asserted supremacy over all others.

Nonetheless, we should be careful not to attribute too much weight to the masculinity factor alone. True, Roosevelt's nemesis Woodrow Wilson—whose commitment to the strenuous life consisted largely of throwing out baseballs on opening day and ineffectual attempts at golf—rejected Roosevelt's straightforward strategic rationale of policing the Caribbean to forestall European intervention, favoring instead the less bellicose alternative of missionary diplomacy (wherein Wilson would presumably teach Latin Americans to elect better men). Yet Wilson also sent more U.S. marines into more foreign ports than TR ever did. Even as he demonstrated modest anti-imperialist credentials by supporting the Jones Acts of 1916 and 1917 (which promised eventual Philippines independence and granted citizenship to Puerto Ricans), Wilson subscribed to notions of masculine honor that sanctioned the use of military force. When Mexican authorities refused to salute the U.S. flag at Tampico in April 1914, Wilson sent marines ashore at Veracruz, resulting in more resistance and more deaths than the shocked president expected. Although Wilson spoke about a nation being too proud to fight in rejecting war with Germany after the *Lusitania* sinking in 1915, he demanded "pledges" from Berlin that Germans would adhere to "civilized" rules of warfare. When Germany violated these pledges in 1917, the president whom Roosevelt called a college sissy led the country into a crusade to make civilization safe for democracy. Core values of manliness and civilization thus proved flexible in application. While their presence was ubiquitous, their manifestation varied in accordance with leadership and historical context.

FURTHER READING FOR THE PERIOD 1900–1914

See studies listed in the last two chapters and Michael C. C. Adams, *The Great Adventure* (1990); A. J. Bacevich, *Diplomat in Khaki* (1989) (General Frank McCoy); William H. Becker, *The Dynamics of Business-Government Relations* (1982); Gail Bederman, *Manliness & Civilization* (1995); Frances A. Boyle, *Foundations of World Order* (1999); Lester H. Brune, *The Origins of American Security Policy* (1981); Richard D. Challener, *Admirals, Generals, and American Foreign Policy, 1898–1914* (1973); Kendrick A. Clements, *William Jennings Bryan* (1982); Kurkpatrick Dorsey, *The Dawn of Conservation Diplomacy* (1999); Lloyd C. Gardner, *Safe for Democracy* (1984); Frank H. Goday, *Face of Empire* (2004); Robert E. Hannigan, *The New World Power* (2002); Robert C. Hilderbrand, *Power and the People* (1981); Kevin Murphy, *Political Manhood* (2008); David Traxel, *Crusader Nation* (2006); Cyrus Veeser, *A World Safe for Capitalism* (2002); Richard H. Werking, *The Master Architects* (1977) (foreign service); William C. Widenor, *Henry Cabot Lodge and the Search for an American Foreign Policy* (1980); and Mira Wilkins, *The Emergence of Multinational Enterprise* (1970).

Theodore Roosevelt is the subject of Howard K. Beale, *Theodore Roosevelt and the Rise of America to World Power* (1956); H. W. Brands, *T.R.* (1997); Richard H. Collin, *Theodore Roosevelt* (1985); John M. Cooper, Jr., *The Warrior and the Priest* (1983); Kathleen Dalton, *Theodore Roosevelt* (2002); Thomas G. Dyer, *Theodore Roosevelt and the Idea of Race* (1980); Raymond A. Esthus, *Theodore Roosevelt and the International Rivalries* (1970); Lewis L. Gould, *The Presidency of Theodore Roosevelt* (1991); Jonathan Hawley, *Theodore Roosevelt* (2008); Henry J. Hendrix, *Theodore Roosevelt's Naval Diplomacy* (2009); James R. Holmes, *Theodore Roosevelt and World Order* (2006); Frederick W. Marks, *Velvet on Iron* (1979); Edmund Morris, *Theodore Rex* (2001); Natalie A. Naylor et al., eds., *Theodore Roosevelt* (1992); and William N. Tilchin, *Theodore Roosevelt and the British Empire* (1997).

For the Taft administration, see David H. Burton, *William Howard Taft* (2004); Paolo E. Coletta, *The Presidency of William Howard Taft* (1973); Ralph E. Minger, *William Howard Taft and American Foreign Policy* (1975); and Walter V. Scholes and Marie V. Scholes, *The Foreign Policies of the Taft Administration* (1970).

For Wilson policies, see the next chapter and Frederick S. Calhoun, *Power and Principle* (1986) and *Uses of Force and Wilsonian Foreign Policy* (1993); Kendrick A. Clements, *The Presidency of Woodrow Wilson* (1990); and Edward S. Kaplan, *U.S. Imperialism in Latin America* (1997) (on Bryan's policies).

U.S. relations with Latin America are examined in Laura Briggs, *Reproducing Empire* (2002) (Puerto Rico); José A. Cabranes, *Citizenship and the American Empire* (1979) (Puerto Rico); Bruce J. Calder, *The Impact of Intervention* (1984) (Dominican Republic); Raymond A. Carr, *Puerto Rico* (1984); Arturo M. Carrión, *Puerto Rico* (1983); Mark T. Gilderhus, *Pan American Visions* (1986) (Wilson); David Healy, *Drive to Hegemony* (1989) and *Gunboat Diplomacy in the Wilson Era* (1976) (Haiti); Warren G. Kneer, *Great Britain and the Caribbean, 1901–1913* (1975); Walter LaFeber, *Inevitable Revolutions* (1993) (Central America); Lester D. Langley, *Struggle for the American Mediterranean* (1976), *The United States and the Caribbean, 1900–1970* (1980), and *The Banana Wars* (2002); Lester D. Langley and Thomas Schoonover, *The Banana Men* (1995); Nancy Mitchell, *The Danger of Dreams* (1999); Dana Munro, *Intervention and Dollar Diplomacy* (1964); Thomas F. O'Brien, *The Revolutionary Mission* (1996); Fredrick B. Pike, *The United States and Latin America* (1992); Brenda G. Plummer, *Haiti and the United States* (1992) and *Haiti and the Great Powers, 1902–1915* (1988); Mary Renda, *Taking Haiti* (2001); Emily Rosenberg, *Financial Missionaries to the World* (1999) (dollar diplomacy); Hans Schmidt, *The United States Occupation of Haiti, 1915–1934* (1971); Thomas D. Schoonover, *The United States in Central America, 1860–1911* (1991); David Sheinin, *Searching for Authority* (1998) (Argentina) and *Beyond the Ideal* (2000) (Pan Americanism); Lars Schoultz, *Beneath the United States* (1998); and Richard P. Tucker, *Insatiable Appetite* (2000).

For the Panama Canal, see Richard H. Collin, *Theodore Roosevelt's Caribbean* (1990); Michael L. Conniff, *Panama and the United States* (1992); and *Panama and the United States* (2001); James Howe, *The People Who Would Not Kneel* (1998); Richard L. Lael, *Arrogant Diplomacy* (1987); Walter LaFeber, *The Panama Canal* (1989); John Lindsay-Poland, *Emperors in the Jungle* (2003); John Major, *Prize Possession* (1993); David McCullough, *The Path Between the Seas* (1977); Matthew Parker, *Panama Fever* (2008); and Stephen J. Randall, *Colombia and the United States* (1992).

U.S. hegemony in Cuba is discussed in David Healy, *The United States in Cuba, 1898–1902* (1963); José M. Hernández, *Cuba and the United States* (1993); James H. Hitchman, *Leonard Wood and Cuban Independence, 1898–1902* (1971); Allan R. Millett, *The Politics of Intervention* (1968); and Louis A. Pérez, Jr., *Cuba and the United States* (2003), *On Becoming Cuban* (1999), and *Cuba Under the Platt Amendment, 1902–1934* (1986).

Relations with Mexico are treated in Jonathan C. Brown, *Oil and Revolution in Mexico* (1993); Jules Davids, *American Political and Economic Penetration of Mexico, 1877–1920* (1976); Jorge Domínguez and Rafael Fernandez de Castro, *United States and Mexico* (2001); Joseph M. Gilbert, *Revolution from Without* (1982); Mark T. Gilderhus, *Diplomacy and Revolution* (1977); John M. Hart, *Revolutionary Mexico* (1988) and *Empire and Revolution* (2002); Friedrich Katz, *The Life and Times of Pancho Villa* (1998) and *The Secret War in Mexico* (1981); Alan Knight, *U.S.–Mexican Relations, 1910–1940* (1987); Daniel Nugent, ed., *Rural Revolt in Mexico and U.S. Intervention* (1988); Ramón E. Ruíz, *The Great Rebellion* (1980); Karl M. Schmitt, *Mexico and the United States, 1821–1973* (1974); Joseph A. Stout, Jr., *Border Conflict* (1999); Paul J. Vanderwood and Frank N. Samponaro, *Border Fury* (1988); and Josefina Vázquez and Lorenzo Meyer, *The United States and Mexico* (1985).

For America's interactions with Asia and China, see William R. Braisted, *The United States Navy in the Pacific, 1897–1909* (1958) and *1909–1922* (1971); Jongsuk Chay, *Diplomacy of Asymmetry* (1990) (Korea);

Warren I. Cohen, *America's Response to China* (2000); Daniel M. Crane and Thomas A. Breslin, *An Ordinary Relationship* (1986); Jose D. Fermin, *1904 World's Fair* (2004); Jonathan Goldstein et al., eds., *America Views China* (1991); Michael H. Hunt, *The Making of a Special Relationship* (1983); Akira Iriye, *Across the Pacific* (1967); Delber L. McKee, *Chinese Exclusion Versus the Open Door Policy, 1900–1906* (1976); Dennis L. Noble, *The Eagle and the Dragon* (1990); Noel H. Pugach, *Paul S. Reinsch* (1979); Eileen Scully, *Bargaining with the State from Afar* (2001) (Extraterritoriality); and Guanhua Wang, *In Search of Justice* (2002).

Japanese-American relations are studied in Burton F. Beers, *Vain Endeavor: Robert Lansing's Attempt to End the American-Japanese Rivalry* (1962); Raymond A. Esthus, *Double Eagle and Rising Sun* (1988) (Portsmouth) and *Theodore Roosevelt and Japan* (1966); Akira Iriye, *Pacific Estrangement* (1972); Walter LaFeber, *The Clash* (1997); Charles E. Neu, *An Uncertain Friendship* (1967) and *The Troubled Encounter* (1975); and E. P. Trani, *The Treaty of Portsmouth* (1969).

American missionaries, especially in Asia, are covered in Kenton J. Clymer, *Protestant Missionaries in the Philippines, 1898–1916* (1986); Gael Graham, *Gender, Culture, and Christianity* (1995); Patricia R. Hill, *The World Their Household* (1985) (women); Jane Hunter, *The Gospel of Gentility* (1984) (women in China); Xi Lian, *The Conversion of Missionaries* (1997); and James Reed, *The Missionary Mind and American East Asia Policy, 1911–1915* (1983).

U.S. relations with Europe and Great Britain, and rivalry with Germany, are discussed in Stuart Anderson, *Race and Rapprochement* (1981); A. E. Campbell, *Great Britain and the United States, 1895–1903* (1960); Charles S. Campbell, *Anglo-American Understanding, 1898–1903* (1957); David Dimbleby and David Reynolds, *An Ocean Apart* (1989); Holger H. Herwig, *Politics of Frustration* (1976); Manfred Jonas, *The United States and Germany* (1984); B. J. C. McKercher and Lawrence Aronson, eds., *The North Atlantic Triangle in a Changing World* (1996); Bradford Perkins, *The Great Rapprochement* (1968); Hans-Jürgen Schröder, ed., *Confrontation and Cooperation* (1993) (Germany); and Frederick F. Travis, *George Kennan and the Russian-American Relationship, 1865–1924* (1990).

The peace movement and the role of The Hague are discussed in Peter Brock, *Pacifism in the United States* (1968); Charles Chatfield, *The American Peace Movement* (1992); Calvin Davis, *The United States and the First Hague Conference* (1962) and *The United States and the Second Hague Peace Conference* (1975); Charles DeBenedetti, *The Peace Reform in American History* (1980); Sondra R. Herman, *Eleven Against War* (1969); Charles F. Howlett and Glen Zeitzer, *The American Peace Movement* (1985); C. Roland Marchand, *The American Peace Movement and Social Reform, 1898–1918* (1973); and David S. Patterson, *Toward a Warless World* (1976).

See also the General Bibliography, the following notes, and Robert L. Beisner, ed., *Guide to American Foreign Relations Since 1600* (2003).

NOTES TO CHAPTER 7

1. All quotations from U.S. Congress, *Diplomatic History of the Panama Canal,* Senate Doc. 474 (1914), pp. 345–363.
2. Quoted in John Major, *Prize Possession* (New York: Cambridge University Press, 1993), p. 45.
3. Elting E. Morison, ed., *The Letters of Theodore Roosevelt* (Cambridge: Harvard University Press, 1951–1954; 8 vols.), II, 1185–1187.
4. James A. Froude quoted in John Lindsay-Poland, *Emperors in the Jungle* (Durham: Duke University Press, 2003), p. 5.
5. *Diplomatic History of the Canal,* p. 261.
6. Quoted in Dwight C. Miner, *The Fight for the Panama Route* (New York: Columbia University Press, 1940), p. 275.
7. Quoted in Henry F. Pringle, *Theodore Roosevelt* (New York: Harcourt, Brace, 1931), p. 311.

8. Quoted in Howard K. Beale, *Theodore Roosevelt and the Rise of America to World Power* (Baltimore: Johns Hopkins Press, 1956), p. 33.
9. *New York World,* June 14, 1903.
10. Quoted in Lars Schoultz, *Beneath the United States* (Cambridge: Harvard University Press, 1998), p. 164.
11. Quoted in Thomas Schoonover, "Max Farrand's Memorandum on the U.S. Role in the Panamanian Revolution of 1903," *Diplomatic History, XII* (Fall 1988), 505.
12. Quoted in Stephen J. Randall, *Colombia and the United States* (Athens: University of Georgia Press, 1992), p. 88.
13. Quoted in Serge Ricard, "The Roosevelt Corollary," *Presidential Studies Quarterly, XXXVI* (March 2006), 20.

14. C. F. Adams to Moorfield Story, December 9, 1903, Moorfield Story Papers, Massachusetts Historical Society, Boston; Roosevelt quoted in H. W. Brands, *T.R.* (New York: BasicBooks, 1997), p. 487.

15. Quoted in Walter LaFeber, *The Panama Canal* (New York: Oxford University Press, 1989; updated ed.), pp. 225–226.

16. *New York Times,* March 25, 1911.

17. Lord Bryce quoted in Michael Adas, *Dominance by Design* (Cambridge: Harvard University Press, 2006), p. 186.

18. Quoted *ibid,* p. 198.

19. Quoted in Robert E. Hannigan, *The New World Power* (Philadelphia: University of Pennsylvania Press, 2002), p. 46.

20. Quoted in Wayne A. Wiegand, *Patrician in the Progressive Era* (New York: Garland, 1988), p. 120.

21. Quoted in Stephen R. Rock, *Why Peace Breaks Out* (Chapel Hill: University of North Carolina Press, 1989), p. 132.

22. Ronald H. Spector, *Professors of War* (Newport, R.I.: Naval War College Press, 1977).

23. John Milton Cooper, Jr., "Progressivism and American Foreign Policy," *Mid-America, LI* (October 1969), 261.

24. Quoted in John Morton Blum, *The Republican Roosevelt* (New York: Atheneum [1954], 1973), p. 127.

25. Quoted in Beale, *Theodore Roosevelt,* p. 77; G. Wallace Chessman, *Theodore Roosevelt and the Politics of Power* (Boston: Little, Brown, 1969), p. 70.

26. Quoted in Frank Ninkovich, *Modernity and Power* (Chicago: University of Chicago Press, 1994), p. 6.

27. Quoted in Beale, *Theodore Roosevelt,* p. 140.

28. Quoted in Judith Papachristou, "American Women and Foreign Policy, 1896–1905," *Diplomatic History, XIV* (Fall 1990), 499, 501, 509.

29. Quoted in Frederick F. Travis, *George Kennan and the Russian-American Relationship, 1865–1924* (Athens: Ohio University Press, 1990), p. 266.

30. Quoted in Ninkovich, *Modernity,* p. 13.

31. Quoted in John Milton Cooper, Jr., *The Warrior and the Priest* (Cambridge: Harvard University Press, 1983), p. 75.

32. Taft quoted in Hannigan, *New World Power,* p. 282.

33. Quoted in Richard W. Leopold, *Elihu Root and the Conservative Tradition* (Boston: Little, Brown, 1954), p. 50.

34. Quoted in Ralph E. Minger, *William Howard Taft and United States Foreign Policy* (Urbana: University of Illinois Press, 1975), p. 179.

35. Quoted in Ray S. Baker, *Woodrow Wilson* (Garden City, N.Y.: Doubleday, Doran, 1927–1939; 8 vols.), *IV,* 289.

36. Jesus Samprun quoted in David M. Pletcher, *The Diplomacy of Trade and Investment* (Columbia: University of Missouri Press, 1998), p. 393.

37. Jessica C. E. Gienow-Hecht, "Always Blame the Americans," *American Historical Review, CXI* (October 2006), 1074.

38. William Shafter quoted in Louis A. Pérez, Jr., *The War of 1898* (Chapel Hill: University of North Carolina Press, 1898), p. 29; *Foreign Relations, 1898* (Washington, D.C.: Government Printing Office, 1901), pp. lvi–lvii.

39. Quoted in David F. Healy, *The United States in Cuba, 1898–1902* (Madison: University of Wisconsin Press, 1963), p. 133.

40. U.S. Commissioner Robert P. Porter quoted in Louis A. Pérez, Jr., *Cuba and the United States* (Athens: University of Georgia Press, 1997, 2nd ed.), p. 127.

41. *Congressional Record, XXXIV* (February 26, 1901), 3036.

42. Quoted in H. Hagedorn, *Leonard Wood* (New York: Harper, 1931; 2 vols.), *I,* 362; Healy, *United States in Cuba,* p. 178.

43. Quoted in R. H. Fitzgibbon, *Cuba and the United States, 1900–1935* (New York: Russell & Russell, 1964), p. 112.

44. Quoted in Allan R. Millett, *The Politics of Intervention* (Columbus: Ohio State University Press, 1968), p. 72.

45. Quoted in David H. Burton, *Theodore Roosevelt* (Philadelphia: University of Pennsylvania Press, 1968), p. 106.

46. James D. Richardson, ed., *A Compilation of the Messages and Papers of the Presidents, 1789–1897* (Washington, D. C.: Government Printing Office, 1896–1899; 10 vols.), *X,* 7436–7437; quoted in David H. Burton, *William Howard Taft* (Philadelphia: St. Joseph's University Press, 2004), p. 44.

47. Quoted in Schoultz, *Beneath,* p. 201.

48. Quoted in Alistair Hennessy, "The Origins of the Cuban Revolt," in Angel Smith and Emma Davila-Cox, eds., *The Crisis of 1898* (New York: St. Martin's, 1999), p. 85.

49. Fred L. Israel, ed., *The State of the Union Messages* (New York: Chelsea House, 1967; 3 vols.), *II,* 2038.

50. Morison, *Letters of Roosevelt, III,* 116.

51. William Haggard quoted in Nancy Mitchell, *The Danger of Dreams* (Chapel Hill: University of North Carolina Press, 1999), p. 69.

52. Francis Anthony Boyle, *Foundations of World Order* (Durham: Duke University Press, 1999), p. 81.

53. Quoted in John G. Clifford, "Admiral Dewey and the Germans, 1903," *Mid–America, XLIX* (July 1967), 218.

54. Quoted in Kathleen Dalton, *Theodore Roosevelt* (New York: Knopf, 2002), p. 238.

55. Quoted in Manfred Jonas, *The United States and Germany* (Ithaca: Cornell University Press, 1985), p. 73.

56. Quoted *ibid.,* p. 420.

57. Quoted in Brands, *T.R.,* p. 524.

58. Quoted in Dexter Perkins, *The Monroe Doctrine, 1867–1907* (Baltimore: Johns Hopkins Press, 1937), p. 420.

59. Quoted in Warren G. Kneer, *Great Britain and the Caribbean, 1901–1913* (East Lansing: Michigan State University Press, 1975), p. 103.

60. Quoted in Ricard, "Roosevelt Corrollary," p. 23.

61. Jules Jusserand, quoted in Cyrus Veeser, "Inventing Dollar Diplomacy," *Diplomatic History, XXVII* (June 2003), 320.

62. Theodore Roosevelt, *An Autobiography* (New York: Charles Scribner's Sons, 1926), p. 511.

63. Quoted in Richard D. Challener, *Admirals, Generals, and American Foreign Policy, 1898–1914* (Princeton: Princeton University Press, 1973), p. 142.

64. *Foreign Relations, 1912* (Washington, D.C.: Government Printing Office, 1919), p. 1091.

65. *Foreign Relations, 1913* (Washington, D.C.: Government Printing Office, 1920), p. 426.

66. Quoted in Frederick S. Calhoun, *Uses of Force and Wilsonian Foreign Policy* (Kent, Ohio: Kent State University Press, 1993), p. 53.

67. Bruce Calder, *The Impact of Intervention* (Austin: University of Texas Press, 1984), p. 250.

68. Quoted in Dana G. Munro, *Intervention and Dollar Diplomacy in the Caribbean* (Princeton: Princeton University Press, 1964), p. 336.

69. Quoted in Brenda G. Plummer, *Haiti and the Great Powers, 1902–1915* (Baton Rouge: Louisiana State University Press, 1988), p. 188.

70. Quoted in Hannigan, *New World Power,* p. 49.

71. Quoted in Alan McPherson, "Americanism against American Empire," in Michael Kazin and Joseph A. McCartin, eds., *Americanism* (Chapel Hill: University of North Carolina Press, 2006), p. 181.

72. Alexander DeConde, *Ethnicity, Race, and American Foreign Policy* (Boston: Northeastern University Press, 1993), pp. 79–80.

73. Victor Hoiser quoted in Mary Renda, *Taking Haiti* (Chapel Hill: University of North Carolina Press, 2001), p. 34.

74. Quoted in Munro, *Intervention*, p. 155.

75. Thomas D. Schoonover, *The United States in Central America, 1860–1911* (Durham: Duke University Press, 1991), p. 130; Knox quoted in Michel Gobat, *Confronting the American Dream* (Durham: Duke University Press, 2005), p. 70; Taft quoted in Stephen Kinzer, *Overthrow* (New York: Times Books, 2006), p. 66.

76. Zelaya quoted in Lester D. Langley and Thomas D. Schoonover, *The Banana Men* (Lexington: University Press of Kentucky, 1995), p. 89; quoted in Emily S. Rosenberg, *Financial Missionaries to the World* (Cambridge: Harvard University Press, 1999), p. 67; Taft quoted in Burton, *William Howard Taft*, p. 66.

77. Elliott Northcott quoted in Walter LaFeber, *The American Search for Opportunity, 1865–1913* (New York: Cambridge University Press, 1993), p. 219.

78. Quoted in John E. Findling, *Close Neighbors, Distant Friends* (Westport, Conn.: Greenwood, 1987), p. 61.

79. Langley and Schoonover, *Banana Men*, p. 114.

80. Quoted in Paolo E. Coletta, *The Presidency of William Howard Taft* (Lawrence: University Press of Kansas, 1973), p. 176.

81. Quoted in Friedrich Katz, *The Secret War in Mexico* (Chicago: University of Chicago Press, 1981), p. 113.

82. *Foreign Relations, 1912*, p. 846.

83. Quoted in David Traxel, *Crusader Nation* (New York: Knopf, 2006), p. 86.

84. Quoted in Michael H. Hunt, *The American Ascendancy* (Chapel Hill: University of North Carolina Press, 2007), p. 57.

85. Quoted in Arthur S. Link, *Wilson: Confusions and Crises, 1915–1916* (Princeton: Princeton University Press, 1964), p. 317.

86. William Bayard Hale quoted in Schoultz, *Beneath*, p. 240.

87. Quoted in Arthur S. Link, *Wilson: The New Freedom* (Princeton: Princeton University Press, 1956) p. 358.

88. Quoted in Elizabeth McKillen, "Wilsonian Internationalism Reconsidered," *Diplomatic History, XXV* (Fall 2001), 567.

89. Quoted in Kenneth J. Grieb, *The United States and Huerta* (Lincoln: University of Nebraska Press, 1969), p. 137.

90. Quoted in Link, *Wilson: New Freedom*, pp. 386–387.

91. Quoted in Katz, *Secret War*, p. 216.

92. Quoted in Grieb, *United States and Huerta*, p. 135.

93. Quoted in Mark T. Gilderhus, *Diplomacy and Revolution* (Tucson: University of Arizona Press, 1977), p. 11.

94. Quoted in Cary T. Grayson, *Woodrow Wilson* (New York: Holt, Rinehart and Winston, 1960), p. 30.

95. Wilson quoted in Hannigan, *New World Power*, p. 177.

96. Quoted in Douglas Monroy, "Fence Cutters, *Sedicioso*, and First Class Citizens," in Paul Buhle and Dan Georgakis, eds., *The Immigrant Left in the United States* (Albany: State University of New York Press, 1996), pp. 21–22.

97. Quoted in James A. Sandos, *Rebellion in the Borderlands* (Norman: University of Oklahoma Press, 1992), p. 92.

98. Quoted in Arthur S. Link, *Wilson: The Struggle for Neutrality, 1914–1915* (Princeton: Princeton University Press, 1960), p. 491.

99. Katz, *Secret War*, p. 560; Villa quoted in Friedrich Katz, "Pancho Villa and the Attack on Columbus, New Mexico," *American Historical Review, LXXXIII* (February 1978), 111, 114.

100. Morison, *Letters of Roosevelt, III*, 497–498.

101. Akira Iriye, *The Cold War in Asia* (Englewood Cliffs, N.J: Prentice Hall, 1974), p. 35.

102. Morison, *Letters of Roosevelt, IV*, 724, 761.

103. Quoted in Raymond A. Esthus, *Double Eagle and Rising Sun* (Durham: Duke University Press, 1988), p. 39.

104. Quoted in Brands, *T.R.*, p. 534.

105. Quoted in Norman Saul, *Concord and Conflict* (Lawrence: University Press of Kansas, 1996), p. 504.

106. Quoted in Raymond A. Esthus, *Theodore Roosevelt and Japan* (Seattle: University of Washington Press, 1966), p. 101.

107. John Edward Wilz, "Did the United States Betray Korea in 1905?" *Pacific Historical Review, LIV* (August 1985), 252.

108. Quoted in Akira Iriye, *Across the Pacific* (New York: Harcourt, Brace & World, 1967), p. 107.

109. Quoted in Ian Mugridge, *The View from Xanadu* (Montreal: McGill–Queen's University Press, 1995), p. 51.

110. Quoted in Walter A. McDougall, *Let the Sea Make a Noise* (New York: BasicBooks, 1993), p. 479; Morison, *Letters of Roosevelt, V*, 729–730, 761–762.

111. Quoted in Ute Mehnert, "German *Weltpolitik* and the American Two Front Dilemma," *Journal of American History, LXXXII* (March 1996), 1458.

112. Quoted in Guanhua Wang, *In Search of Justice* (Cambridge: Harvard University Press, 2001), p. 90.

113. Quoted in Eileen P. Scully, "Taking the Low Road" *Journal of American History, LXXXII* (June 1995), 63–64.

114. Anders Stephanson, *Manifest Destiny* (New York: Hill & Wang, 1995), p. 97.

115. Ninkovich, *Modernity*, p. 25.

116. Quoted in Herbert Croly, *Willard Straight* (New York: Macmillan, 1925), p. 276.

117. A. Whitney Griswold, *The Far Eastern Policy of the United States* (New Haven: Yale University Press, 1938), p. 157.

118. Quoted in Croly, *Straight*, pp. 392–393.

119. Quoted in Daniel M. Crane and Thomas A. Breslin, *An Ordinary Relationship* (Miami: Florida International University Press, 1986), p. 122.

120. Quoted in Roger Daniels, *The Politics of Prejudice* (New York: Atheneum, [1962], 1968), p. 59.

121. Quoted in Link, *Wilson: New Freedom*, pp. 300–301.

122. Quoted in George C. Herring, *From Colony to Superpower* (New York: Oxford University Press, 2008), p. 384.

123. *Foreign Relations, 1922* (Washington, D.C.: Government Printing Office, 1938; 2 vols.), *II*, 591.

124. Quoted in Michael H. Hunt, *Ideology and U.S. Foreign Policy* (New Haven: Yale University Press, 1987), pp. 69, 71, 79, 81.

125. *Ibid.*, p. 79.

126. Cody quoted in Robert W. Rydell and Rob Kroes, *Buffalo Bill in Bologna* (Chicago: University of Chicago Press, 2005), p. 108.

127. Herbert Asquith quoted in Rock, *Why Peace*, p. 51; Bradford Perkins, *The Great Rapprochement* (New York: Atheneum, 1968).

128. Roosevelt quoted in Frederick W. Marks, *Velvet on Iron* (Lincoln: University of Nebraska Press, 1979), p. 168.

129. Robert Bothwell, *Canada and the United States* (New York: Twayne, 1992), p. 8.

130. Quoted in Kurk Dorsey, "Scientists, Citizens, and Statesmen," *Diplomatic History, XIX* (Summer 1995), 426.

131. Mark Kurlansky, *Cod* (New York: Walker, 1997), p. 79.

132. Quoted in Arthur Marder, *From the Dreadnought to Scapa Flow* (London: Oxford University Press, 1961–1970; 5 vols.), *I*, 125.

133. Quoted *ibid.*, p. 201.

134. Quoted in Link, *Wilson: New Freedom*, p. 308.

135. Quoted in Lisle A. Rose, *Power at Sea: The Age of Navalism, 1890–1918* (Columbia: University of Missouri Press, 2007), p. 145.

136. Quoted in Michael B. Oren, *Power, Faith, and Fantasy* (New York: Norton, 2007), p. 318.

137. Quoted in Emily S. Rosenberg, "The Invisible Protectorate," *Diplomatic History, IX* (Summer 1985), 194, 198.

138. Quoted in Tilchin, *Theodore Roosevelt*, p. 67; quoted in Hannigan, *New World Power*, p. 204.

139. Morison, *Letters of Roosevelt, IV*, 1119.

140. Quoted in Calvin Davis, *The United States and the Second Hague Peace Conference* (Durham: Duke University Press, 1975), p. 296.

141. Quoted in Minger, *William Howard Taft*, p. 106.

142. Quoted in Mehnert, "German *Weltpolitik*," p. 1461.

143. Quoted in Jerry Israel, *Progressivism and the Open Door* (Pittsburgh: University of Pittsburgh Press, 1971), p. 96.

144. General William Carter quoted in Brian Linn, *Guardians of Empire* (Chapel Hill: University of North Carolina Press, 1997), p. 62.

145. Quoted in Michael L. Conniff, *Panama and the United States* (Athens: University of Georgia Press, 1992), p. 3.

146. G. L. Dyer quoted in Julian Go, "Modes of Rule in America's Overseas Empire," in Sanford Levinson and Bartholomew H. Sparrow, eds., *Louisiana Purchase and American Expansion, 1803–1898* (New York: Rowman & Littlefield, 2005), p. 278.

147. Laura Briggs, *Reproducing Empire* (Berkeley: University of California Press, 2002), p. 2.

148. Raymond Carr, *Puerto Rico* (New York: Vintage, 1984), p. 36.

149. Cesar J. Ayala and Rafael Bernabe, *Puerto Rico in the American Century* (Chapel Hill: University of North Carolina Press, 2007), p. 28.

150. William Phillips, *Ventures in Diplomacy* (Boston: Beacon Press, 1952), p. 6.

151. Quoted in A. J. Bacevich, *Diplomat in Khaki* (Lawrence: University Press of Kansas, 1989), p. 48.

152. Emily S. Rosenberg, *Spreading the American Dream* (New York: Hill & Wang, 1982), p. 35.

153. Quoted in Robert A. Hart, *The Great White Fleet* (Boston: Little, Brown, 1965), p. 45.

154. Quoted in Franklin Ng, "Knowledge for Empire," in Robert David Johnson, ed., *On Cultural Ground* (Chicago: Imprint Publications, 1994), p. 135.

155. Charles W. Eliot quoted in Frank Trommler, "Inventing the Enemy," in Hans-Jürgen Schröder, *Confrontation and Cooperation* (Providence, R.I.: Berg, 1993), p. 101.

156. Quoted in Christopher Endy, "Travel and World Power," *Diplomatic History, XXII* (Fall 1998), 574.

157. Crosnier de Varigny quoted in Philippe Roger, *The American Enemy* (Chicago: University of Chicago Press, 2005), p. 186.

158. Winston S. Churchill, *The World Crisis* (New York: Charles Scribner's Sons, 1927; 6 vols.), *I*, 18.

CHAPTER 8

War, Peace, and Revolution in the Time of Wilson, 1914–1920

Mass Grave of* Lusitania *Victims. *In Cork, Ireland, a large burial ground holds more than a hundred victims of the* Lusitania *disaster of 1915, which rudely brought World War I to American consciousness. It did not, however, lead to an immediate declaration of war. (U.S. War Department, National Archives)*

DIPLOMATIC CROSSROAD

❖ *The Sinking of the* Lusitania, *1915*

"PERFECTLY SAFE; SAFER than the trolley cars in New York City," claimed a British Cunard Line official the morning of May 1, 1915.[1] More than twice as long as an American football field, the majestic *Lusitania,* with its watertight compartments and swiftness, seemed invulnerable. The British Admiralty had stipulated that the 30,396-ton vessel could be armed if necessary, but "Lucy's" priority was pleasure, not war. Resplendent with tapestries and carpets, the luxurious floating palace dazzled. One American found the ship "more beautiful than Solomon's Temple— and big enough to hold all his wives."[2]

A crew of 702 attended the 1,257 travelers who departed from New York's Pier 54 on May Day. Deep in the *Lusitania's* storage area rested a cargo of foodstuffs and contraband (4.2 million rounds of ammunition for Remington rifles, 1,250 cases of empty shrapnel shells, and eighteen cases of nonexplosive fuses). The Cunarder thus carried, said a U.S. State Department official, both "babies and bullets."[3]

In the morning newspapers of May 1 a rather unusual announcement, placed by the German Embassy, appeared beside the Cunard Line advertisement. The German "Notice" warned passengers that the waters around the British Isles constituted a war zone wherein British vessels were subject to destruction. Only a handful of passengers transferred to the *New York,* ready to sail under the American flag that same day. The *New York* was slow and for the American "smart set" socially unacceptable. The State Department did not warn the 197 American passengers away from the *Lusitania.* Most Americans accepted the Cunard Line statement: "She is too fast for any submarine. No German war vessel can get her or near her."[4]

Captained by William T. Turner, the *Lusitania* steamed into the Atlantic at half past noon on May 1. Manned by an ill-trained crew (the best men now on war duty), "Lucy" enjoyed a smooth crossing in calm water. Despite lifesaving drills, complacency about the submarine danger lulled captain, crew, and passengers alike. Passengers joked about torpedoes, played cards, consumed liquor, and listened to concerts on deck. On May 6, as the *Lusitania* neared Ireland, Turner received a warning from the Naval Centre at Queenstown: "Submarines active off south coast of Ireland."[5] The captain posted lookouts but took no other precautions, despite follow-up warnings. He had standing orders from the Admiralty to take a zigzag path, to steer a mid-channel course, and to steam at full speed to keep lurking German submarines from zeroing in on their prey. But Turner steered straight ahead.

Unusually good visibility, recorded Lieutenant Walter Schwieger in his log on May 7. The young German commander was piloting his *U-20* submarine along the southern Irish coast. That morning it had submerged because British ships capable of ramming the fragile, slender craft were passing nearby. He surfaced at 1:45 P.M. and soon spotted a four-funneled ship in the distance. Schwieger quickly submerged and set a course toward the *Lusitania.* At 700 meters the *U-20* released a torpedo. The deadly missile plunged through the water tailed by bubbles. A watchman on the starboard

The *Lusitania* and *U-20*.
The majestic passenger liner was sunk by the German submarine *U-20* off the coast of Ireland on May 7, 1915. "Suppose they should sink the *Lusitania* with American passengers on board," King George V had mused to Colonel Edward M. House on that fateful morning. (The Lusitania Courtesy of the Peabody Essex Museum, Salem, MA)

bow of the *Lusitania* cried out one minute before the torpedo struck, but Captain Turner did not hear the megaphone. Had he heeded the warning, the ship *might* have veered sharply and avoided danger. Turner felt the explosion as it ripped into the *Lusitania*. Panic swept the passengers as they stumbled about the listing decks or groped in the darkness below. Steam whistled from punctured boilers. Less than half the lifeboats were lowered; some capsized or cast off only partially loaded. Within eighteen minutes the "Queen of the Atlantic" sank, killing 1,198—128 of them Americans. A survivor recalled that the *Lusitania* went down with "a terrible moan."[6]

Captain William T. Turner (1856–1933). His command of the *Lusitania* led to disaster. (U.S. War Department)

Lieutenant Walter Schwieger (1885–1917). His *U–20* sank the *Lusitania*. (Bundesarchiv)

President Woodrow Wilson had just ended a cabinet meeting when he learned of the disaster. His special assistant, Colonel M. Edward House, then in London, predicted: "We shall be at war with Germany within a month."[7] Fearing war, Secretary of State William Jennings Bryan advised the president that "ships carrying contraband should be prohibited from carrying passengers. ... [I]t would be like putting women and children in front of an army."[8] Ex-president Theodore Roosevelt bellowed that "this represents ... piracy on a vaster scale of murder than old-time pirates ever practiced."[9] American after American voiced horror, but few wanted war. Wilson secluded himself to ponder a response to the ghastly event. Just months before, he had said he would hold Berlin strictly accountable for any American ships or lives lost due to submarine warfare. Thereafter, Wilson found himself trying to fulfill America's "double wish"—"to maintain a firm front ... [toward] Germany and yet do nothing that might by any possibility involve us in war."[10]

Wilson spoke in Philadelphia on May 10. His words, much misunderstood, suggested he had no backbone: "There is such a thing as a man being too proud to fight. There is such a thing as a nation being so right that it does not need to convince others by force that it is right."[11] He quickly regretted his impromptu remarks. Preoccupied by his intense courtship of his future second wife, Wilson did "not know just what I said in Philadelphia ... because my heart was in such a whirl."[12] The next morning he told the cabinet that he would send a note to Berlin insisting that Americans had a right to travel on the high seas and demanding a German disavowal of the inhumane acts of its submarine commanders. Secretary Bryan, long troubled about an apparent American double standard in protesting more against German than British violations of American neutral rights, pleaded for a simultaneous protest to London. But only one note went out on May 13—to

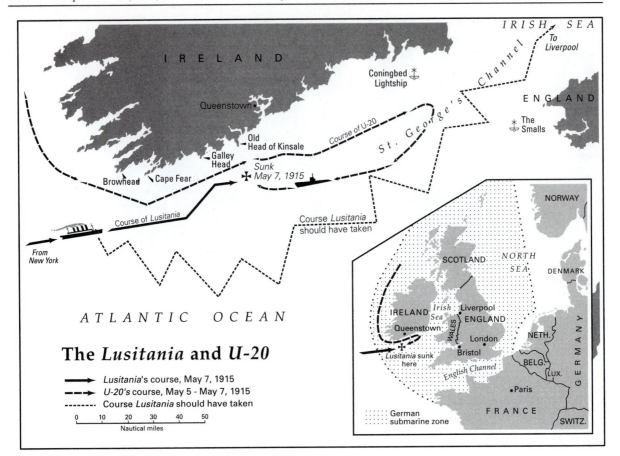

The *Lusitania* and *U-20*

→ *Lusitania*'s course, May 7, 1915
--→ *U-20*'s course, May 5 - May 7, 1915
------ Course *Lusitania* should have taken

0 10 20 30 40 50
Nautical miles

Berlin: "The Imperial Government will not expect the United States to omit any word or any act necessary to the performance of its sacred duty of maintaining the rights of the United States and its citizens and of safeguarding their free exercise and enjoyment."[13] In short, end submarine warfare, or else.

The German government took no pleasure in the destruction of the *Lusitania*. Chancellor Theobold von Bethmann-Hollweg had more than once chastised the navy for inviting war with the United States through submarine attacks on neutral or Allied merchant vessels. On May 28 he sent an evasive reply to Wilson's note. The *Lusitania* case could not be settled until they clarified certain questions. The German note claimed that the ship was armed, carried munitions, and had orders to ram submarines. Germany asked Washington to investigate. That same day, in a secret meeting with German Ambassador Johann von Bernstorff, Wilson proposed that if Germany would settle the *Lusitania* crisis favorably, he would press the British to suspend their blockade and then call a conference of neutrals to mediate an end to the war on the following basis: "1. The status quo in Europe; 2. Freedom of the seas. ... 3. Adjustments concerning colonial possessions."[14]

Wilson convened his cabinet on June 1. One member recommended a strong note demanding observance of American rights, while another suggested a note to England to protest British interference with American commerce. Debate grew heated. A majority rejected simultaneous notes. When the U.S. ambassador in Berlin reported that the Germans wanted to keep the issue "'jollied' along until the American papers get excited by baseball or a new scandal and forget," Wilson sent a second "*Lusitania* note" that vigorously demanded an end to warfare by submarines.[15] He rejected Bryan's plea for a warning to passengers and a protest note to England. The secretary of state then quietly resigned in protest on June 8, and Wilson went to the golf links to free himself from the blinding headaches of the past several days. "He is absolutely *sincere,*" the president said of Bryan. "That is what makes him dangerous."[16]

More correspondence on the *Lusitania* followed. The United States insisted that Germany must admit it had committed an illegal act; but Germany, unwilling to abandon one of its few effective weapons against British mastery of the ocean, refused and asked for arbitration. "Utterly impertinent," sniffed Kaiser Wilhelm II, who preferred victory to Wilson's mediation.[17] Eventually Germany sought compromise. On February 4 it expressed regret over the American deaths and offered an indemnity (ultimately paid in the early 1920s). Wilson accepted the German concession.

The horrible deaths from the *Lusitania* remained etched in American memories. For Germany, the torpedoing of the magnificent Cunarder marked a "naval victory worse than a defeat," as Britons and Americans alike depicted the "Huns" as depraved.[18] The sinking also hardened Wilson's opinion against Germany. After Germany spurned his secret mediation offer, Wilson no longer made diplomatic life easier for the Germans by simultaneously protesting British infractions. The British were violating property rights, he held, but the Germans violated rights of life and liberty. Wilson stubbornly refused to warn Americans away from belligerent ships. In short, if a U-boat attacked a British ship with Americans aboard, Germany would have to take the consequences. Wilson did not spell out those consequences, but the logical implication was war—just what Bryan feared. His successor, pro-Allied Robert Lansing, expected "that we would ultimately become an ally of Great Britain."[19] The sinking of the *Lusitania* exposed, for all to see, the complexities, contradictions, and uncertainties inherent in American neutrality during the European phase of the First World War, 1914–1917. Such complications had been apparent prior to the War of 1812, and they would reemerge between 1939 and 1941.

The Travails of Neutrality

Woodrow Wilson acted virtually as his own secretary of state during the First World War. "Wilson makes confidant of no one. No one gets his whole mind," an aide wrote.[20] British Prime Minister Lloyd George put it less kindly: Wilson "believed in mankind but ... distrusted all men."[21] The president encapsulated an approach to American foreign policy—what historians call "Wilsonianism"—that anticipated major themes of twentieth-century U.S. diplomacy. Above all else, Wilson promoted an *open* world unencumbered by imperialism, war, or revolution. Barriers to trade and democracy had to come down, and secret diplomacy and alliances—like those that had triggered world war—had to give way to public negotiations. The right of self-determination (national self-rule) would force the collapse of empires. Constitutional procedures would replace revolution. A free-market, humanized capitalism would ensure economic, as well as political democracy. Disarmament would restrict weapons. The Open Door of equal trade and investment would harness the economic competition that led to war. Wilson, like so many Americans, saw the United States as exceptional—its mission was "to redeem the world and make it fit for free men like ourselves to live in."[22] His "semi-divine power to select the right" incongruously blended with realism.[23] The president calculated the nation's economic and strategic needs and devised a foreign policy to protect them. Yet many Americans feared that his world-reforming efforts might invite war, dissipate American resources, and undermine reform at home. Wilson led a divided nation.

Few Americans, Wilson included, desired war. Most watched in shock as the European nations savagely slashed at one another in 1914. The conviction that civilization had advanced too far for such bloodletting was ruthlessly challenged. Before 1914 the new machine guns, howitzers, submarines, and dreadnoughts seemed too awesome for leaders to launch them. The outbreak of World War I smashed illusions and tested innocence. Progressive-era Americans nonetheless exuded optimism, and the crusading Wilson sought to retrieve a happier past by assuming the role of civilized instructor: America would help Europe come to its senses by teaching it the rules of humane conduct. The war's carnage justified the mission. In 1915 alone France suffered 1.3 million casualties, including 330,000 deaths. Germany suffered 848,000 casualties, 170,000 of them deaths. Britain followed with 313,000 casualties, and 73,000 deaths. By war's end 12 million soldiers had died—"half the seed of Europe," in poet Wilfred Owen's mournful phrase.[24]

Americans had reason, then, to believe that Europe needed help in cleaning its own house. The outbreak of the war seemed so senseless. By June 1914, the great powers had constructed two blocs, the Triple Alliance (Germany, Austria-Hungary, and Italy) and the Triple Entente (France, Russia, and Great Britain). Some called this division of Europe a balance of power, but an assassin's bullet unbalanced it. Between Austria and Serbia lay Bosnia, a tiny province in the Austro-Hungarian Empire. Slavic nationalists sought to build a greater Serbia—an independent Slavic state—by annexing Bosnia, which the Austro-Hungarian Empire had absorbed in 1909. A Slavic terrorist group, the Black Hand, decided to force the issue. On June 28 the

Makers of American Foreign Relations, 1914–1920

President	Secretaries of State
Woodrow Wilson, 1913–1921	William Jennings Bryan, 1913–1915
	Robert Lansing, 1915–1920
	Bainbridge Colby, 1920–1921

heir to the Hapsburg Crown of Austria-Hungary, Archduke Franz Ferdinand, visited Sarajevo, the capital of Bosnia. As his car moved through the streets of the city, a Black Hand assassin gunned him down.

Austria-Hungary sent impossibly harsh demands to Serbia. The Serbs rejected them. Austria-Hungary had already received encouragement from Germany, and Serbia had a pledge of support from Russia, which in turn received backing from France. A chain reaction followed. On July 28 Austria-Hungary declared war on Serbia; on August 1 Germany declared "preventive" war on Russia and two days later on France; on August 4 Germany invaded Belgium, and Great Britain declared war on Germany. In a few weeks Japan joined the Allies (Triple Entente) and Turkey the Central Powers (Triple Alliance), and Italy entered on the Allied side the next year. Wilson's friend Colonel House, visiting Europe that May, had reported "jingoism run stark mad … there is some day to be an awful cataclysm."[25]

Wilson issued a Proclamation of Neutrality on August 4, followed days later by an appeal to Americans to be neutral in thought, speech, and action. Laced with patriotic utterances, the decree sought to cool the passions of immigrant groups who identified with the belligerents. America must demonstrate to a troubled world that it was "fit beyond others to exhibit the fine poise of undisturbed judgment, the dignity of self-control, the efficiency of dispassionate action."[26] It was a lofty call for restraint, an expression of America as the beacon of common sense in a world gone mad, a plea for unity at home—but altogether difficult to achieve.

Few Americans proved capable of neutral thoughts. Loyalties to fatherlands and motherlands did not abate. German Americans identified with the Central Powers. Many Irish Americans, nourishing their traditional Anglophobia at a time when Ireland chafed under British rule and readied itself for rebellion, wished catastrophe on Britain. But Anglo-American traditions and cultural ties, as well as slogans such as "Remember Lafayette," pulled most Americans toward a pro-Allied position. Since the 1890s, Anglophobia had weakened in the face of the calming Anglo-American rapprochement. Woodrow Wilson himself harbored pro-British sentiment, telling the British ambassador that a German victory "would be the crowning calamity."[27] Wilson's advisers, House and Lansing, were ardently pro-British. The U.S. ambassador to England, Walter Hines Page, even wanted Americans "to hang our Irish agitators and shoot our hyphenates and bring up our children with reverence for English history."[28]

German war actions, exaggerated by British propaganda, also undermined neutrality. To Americans, the Germans, led by arrogant Kaiser Wilhelm II (who later boasted to the U.S. ambassador that "there was no longer any international law"), became symbols of the dreaded militarism and conscription of the Old World.[29] Germany seemed an upstart nation, an aggressive latecomer to the scramble for imperialist prizes, and a noisy intruder in the Caribbean where the British had already acknowledged U.S. hegemony. Eager to grasp world power and encouraging Austria-Hungary to war, Berlin certainly had little claim on virtue. The European powers had guaranteed Belgium its neutrality by treaty, but Bethmann-Hollweg dismissed it as a "scrap of paper."[30] On August 4, 1914, hoping to outflank the French, the Germans attacked Belgium and, angered that the Belgians resisted, ruthlessly razed villages, unleashed firing squads against townspeople, and deported young workers

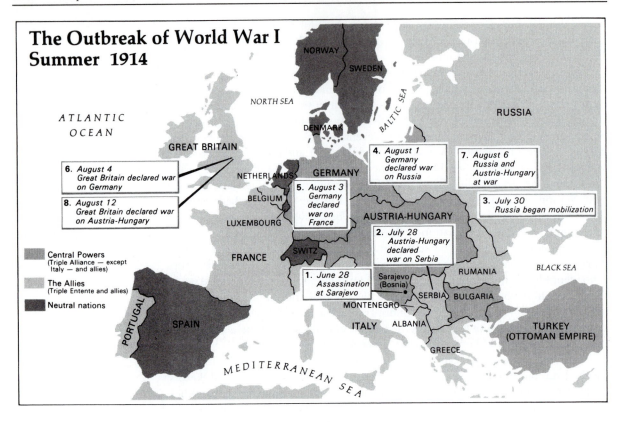

The Outbreak of World War I Summer 1914

6. *August 4 Great Britain declared war on Germany*

8. *August 12 Great Britain declared war on Austria-Hungary*

4. *August 1 Germany declared war on Russia*

7. *August 6 Russia and Austria-Hungary at war*

5. *August 3 Germany declared war on France*

3. *July 30 Russia began mobilization*

2. *July 28 Austria-Hungary declared war on Serbia*

1. *June 28 Assassination at Sarajevo*

Central Powers
(Triple Alliance — except
Italy — and allies)

The Allies
(Triple Entente and allies)

Neutral nations

to Germany. One magazine called Belgium "a martyr to civilization, sister to all who love liberty, or law; assailed, polluted, trampled in the mire, heel-marked in her breast, tattered, homeless."[31] American hearts and hands went out in the form of a major relief mission headed by a young, wealthy, and courageous mining engineer, Herbert Hoover.

American economic links with the Allies also undermined neutrality. England had always been America's best customer, and wartime conditions simply intensified the relationship. The Allies needed both war matériel and consumer goods. Americans, inspired by huge profits and a chance to pull out of a recession, obliged. In 1914 U.S. exports to England and France equaled $754 million; in 1915 the figure shot up to $1.28 billion; and in 1916 the amount more than doubled to $2.75 billion. Comparable statistics for Germany reveal why Berlin believed the United States was taking sides. In 1914 U.S. exports to Germany totaled $345 million; in 1915 they plummeted to $29 million; and in 1916 they fell to $2 million. In 1914–1917 New York's banking house of J. P. Morgan Company served as an agent for England and France and arranged for the shipment of more than $3 billion worth of goods. By April 1917, British purchasing missions were spending $83 million a week for American copper, steel, wheat, oil, and munitions.

Britain and France sold many of their American securities and liquidated investments to pay for these goods. This netted them several billion dollars. In appeals to prominent American bankers and State Department officials, they also sought loans. In 1914 Bryan discouraged private American loans to the belligerents, observing that "money is the worst of all contrabands because it commands everything else."[32] After Bryan's resignation, Robert Lansing argued that loans to the Allies would prevent "restriction of output, industrial depression, idle capital, idle labor, numerous failures, financial demoralization, and general unrest and suffering among the laboring classes."[33] Because U.S. industries "will burst their jackets if they cannot find a free outlet to the markets of the world," Wilson approved $2.3 billion in loans to the Allies during 1914–1917—a sharp contrast to loans of only $27 million to Germany.[34] Once it joined the war as a belligerent, the American economic powerhouse became even more the dispenser of munitions, food, and money to the Allies.

Berlin, of course, protested such "unneutral" economic ties. Yet curbing trade with Britain, which ruled the seas, would have constituted unneutral behavior in favor of the Germans, for under international law a belligerent could buy, at its own risk, contraband and noncontraband goods from a neutral. Neutral or not, the United States had become the arsenal of the Allied war effort.

Submarines, Neutral Rights, and Mediation Efforts

To strangle Germany, the British invoked legal doctrines of retaliation and contraband without ever technically declaring a blockade. They mined the North Sea, expanded the contraband list to include foodstuffs and cotton, forced American ships into port for inspection, seized "contraband" from neutral vessels, halted American trade with Germany's neutral neighbors Denmark and Holland, armed British merchant ships, used decoy ships to lure U-boats into traps, flew neutral (often American) flags on their merchant vessels, and rammed whenever possible any U-boats that complied with international law by surfacing to warn a British merchant vessel of an imminent attack. The Wilson administration issued protests, some mild, some tough, against these illegalities. The Foreign Office usually paid appropriate verbal deference to international law and went right on with its restrictive behavior. Britain sometimes compensated U.S. businesses for damages and purchased large quantities of goods at inflated prices. Americans thus came to tolerate the indignities of British economic warfare. By these measures, Britain managed brilliantly to sever American economic lines to the Central Powers without rupturing Anglo-American relations.

Germans protested vehemently against American acquiescence in the British "hunger" blockade. To continue the war, Germany had to have imports and had to curb the flourishing Anglo-American trade that fueled the Allied war machine. The German surface fleet, bottled up in ports, seemed inadequate for the task, so German leaders hesitantly turned to a relatively new experimental weapon of limited maneuverability: the submarine. At the start they possessed just 21 U-boats, and at peak strength in October 1917 they had but 127. Only a third of this fleet operated at sea at any one time. On February 4, 1915, Berlin announced that it was retaliating against British strangulation by declaring a war zone around Britain. All *enemy* ships

William Jennings Bryan (1860–1925). The great agrarian reformer went to Congress in 1890 as a Democrat from Nebraska. After several unsuccessful runs for the presidency, Bryan endorsed Wilson in the 1912 election and became secretary of state the following year. He favored the arbitration of international disputes, and he perpetuated U.S. interventionist policy in Latin America. Believing that Wilson was tilting toward the British after the *Lusitania* disaster of 1915, Bryan resigned in protest. A colleague called him "too good a Christian to run a naughty world." (Library of Congress)

in the area would be destroyed. Germany warned neutral ships to *stay out* of the zone because of possible mistaken identity. Passengers from neutral countries were urged, moreover, to *stay off* enemy passenger vessels. Six days later Wilson held Germany to strict accountability for the loss of American life and property.

The British continued to arm their merchant vessels, which thereby became warships and theoretically ineligible to take on arms or munitions in neutral ports. But Washington invoked a fine distinction between offensive and defensive armaments and permitted such "defensively" armed British craft to carry war supplies from American ports. Crying foul, the Germans also argued that old international law, which Wilson invoked, did not fit the submarine. Rules adopted during the era of sailing ships held that an attacking cruiser about to sink or capture enemy merchant vessels had to give adequate warning so as to ensure the safety of passengers and crew. Yet if a submarine surfaced in its sluggish fashion, the merchant ship's crew might sink it with a deck gun. This was the problem bewildering Schwieger of *U-20* when he spotted the *Lusitania*. Had he surfaced to warn the ship, the *Lusitania* probably would have attempted to ram *U-20* or flee and would have sent distress signals to British warships in the vicinity. Even if the *Lusitania* had submitted to the warning, it might have taken an hour for passengers to get into lifeboats before Schwieger could torpedo the *Lusitania,* by which time British warships might have closed in. In short, from the German point of view, to comply with an international law that failed to anticipate the submarine was not possible. Wilson retorted that differences over international law could be "adjusted after the war," whereas Germany's "sheer acts of piracy on the high seas … might easily lead to actual hostilities."[35]

Secretary Bryan tried diplomacy in early 1915, asking Germany to give up use of unannounced submarine attacks in exchange for a British promise to disarm its merchant carriers and permit food to flow to Germany. The Germans seemed interested, but London refused. In March 1915, Wilson did send Colonel House to Europe to sound out possibilities for mediation, but to no avail. Nonetheless, Wilson failed to adjust or shelve traditional international law, which had no provision for the submarine. He accepted British modifications but not German ones, for both economic and humanitarian reasons.

Between February and May 1915, marauding submarines sank ninety ships in the war zone. One American citizen, on the British passenger ship *Falaba,* died in the sinking of that vessel on March 28. Then came the *Lusitania* in May with 128 American deaths. Through Wilson's many protest notes, a U.S. posture took shape: uneasy tolerance of British violations of property rights and rejection of German violations of what later generations would call human rights. Despite secret German orders to submarine commanders to avoid a repetition of the *Lusitania* incident, on August 19 the *Arabic,* another British liner, was torpedoed with the loss of two American lives. A worried Ambassador Bernstorff publicly pledged that U-boats would now spare passenger ships.

In early 1916, calling the United States ideally suited to be the "mediating nation of the world," Wilson tried to bring the warring parties to the conference table.[36] Colonel House talked with British officials in London but departed with no promises for peace. He journeyed next to Berlin, where German leaders gave no assurances. Both sides would fight on. "Hell will break loose in Europe this spring and summer as never before," House informed Wilson.[37] House then traveled to Paris, where he rashly informed his skeptical French hosts: "If the Allies obtain a small success this spring or summer, the U.S. will intervene to promote a peaceful settlement, but if the Allies have a setback, the United States will intervene militarily and will take part in the war against Germany."[38] House did not report his prediction to the president.

House returned to London to press Sir Edward Grey, the British foreign secretary, to heed Wilson's call for a peace conference. The American envoy recorded their agreements in the House-Grey Memorandum of February 22, 1916, a document loaded with "ifs." The first paragraph read: "Colonel House told me that President Wilson was ready, on hearing from France and England that the moment was opportune, to propose that a Conference should be summoned to put an end to the war. Should the Allies accept the proposal, and should Germany refuse it, the United States would probably enter the war against Germany." The record of conversation also reported that House had said that the peace conference would secure terms "not unfavourable to the Allies" and should the conference failed to achieve peace, "the United States would leave the Conference as a belligerent on the side of the Allies, if Germany was unreasonable."[39] Wilson pronounced the memorandum a diplomatic triumph, but he clouded its uncertain meaning all the more by inserting a "probably" before the word "leave" in the sentence quoted above. He took the document much more seriously than did the British or French, who shelved it, snubbed American mediation, and vowed victory over Germany.

As House moved among European capitals, Lansing informed the Allied governments that the United States sought a modus vivendi to defuse naval crises: The Allies would disarm merchant vessels, and the Germans would follow international law by warning enemy merchant ships. This suggestion revealed that Wilson understood the German argument that armed merchant vessels actually operated as offensive craft—that is, warships. The British and Colonel House protested when they received this news from Washington. The Germans seemed to endorse the proposal by declaring on February 10 that submarines would henceforth attack only *armed* merchant ships without warning. Suddenly Wilson reversed policy. He abruptly abandoned the modus vivendi in order to restore his standing with the British and sustain House's mediation efforts in London. Lansing announced, furthermore, that the United States would not ban its citizens from traveling on "defensively" armed merchant ships.

Edward M. House (1858–1938). This Texas "colonel" served as Wilson's trusted emissary abroad. In the House-Grey Memorandum of 1916 he showed signs of the deviousness that led to his break with the president after the Versailles conference of 1919. President Wilson once identified House as "my second personality. He is my independent self. If I were in his place I would do just as he suggested." An opponent called House "an intimate man … even when he was cutting your throat." (National Portrait Gallery, Smithsonian Institution/Art Resource, N.Y.)

Wilson's Choices Bring America into World War

Why let one American passenger and a trigger-happy U-boat captain start a war? Why not keep Americans off belligerent ships and require them instead to sail on American vessels? From August 1914 to mid-March 1917 only three Americans (on the oil tanker *Gulflight,* May 1, 1915) had lost their lives on an American-flagged ship torpedoed by a U-boat. In contrast, about 190 Americans, including the *Lusitania*'s 128, died on belligerent-owned ships. After the *Falaba* was sunk, Bryan had acknowledged the right of neutrals to travel on belligerent vessels, but he wanted Wilson to forgo that right. Americans on belligerent ships seemed no different than

**Woodrow Wilson
(1856–1924).** Scholar,
professor, president of Princeton
University, and Democratic
governor of New Jersey, Woodrow
Wilson was usually cocksure
once he made a decision. "I would
rather fail in a cause that will
ultimately triumph than triumph in
a cause that will ultimately fail," he
once said. (*Cartoons,* 1912)

"those who by remaining in a belligerent country assume risk of injury."[40] Wilson had, after all, urged Americans to leave war-torn Mexico. Ambassador James W. Gerard in Berlin also wondered: "Why should we enter a great war because some American wants to cross on a ship where he can have a private bathroom?"[41]

In January 1916, Congressman Jeff McLemore of Texas, a Democrat, introduced a resolution to prohibit Americans from traveling on armed belligerent vessels. In February Senator Thomas P. Gore of Oklahoma, another Democrat, submitted a similar resolution in his chamber. Wilson bristled at this challenge from Congress. He unleashed cabinet members with patronage muscle on timid legislators, suggesting that Gore-McLemore was a pro-German ploy. To halt American passage on belligerent ships, Wilson declared, would be to accept national humiliation and destruction of the "whole fine fabric of international law."[42] In short, he stuck with rigid, archaic concepts, refusing to adjust to the new factor of the submarine or to appreciate the impact on Germany of the obvious British violations of the same law. In early March, the Gore-McLemore resolution lost 68 to 14 in the Senate and 276 to 142 in the House. The resolution had asked America to give up very little. Wilson's message to Berlin rang loud and clear: Do not use your submarines.

In March 1916, another passenger ship, another U-boat, another torpedo, more American injuries: The French ship *Sussex,* moving across the English Channel, took a hit but did not sink. Aboard was a young American scholar, Samuel Flagg Bemis, later a renowned historian of foreign relations but then fresh from archival research on Jay's Treaty. Bemis glimpsed the swirling wake of a torpedo. "The entire bow was blown off and with it the people who were in the dining room," he recalled.[43] Four Americans sustained injuries, but Bemis escaped serious harm by jumping overboard while holding on to his research notes.

The *Sussex* attack violated the "*Arabic* pledge," even though the U-boat commander mistook the ship for a minelayer. Wilson delivered an ultimatum warning the Germans on April 18 that he would sever relations if they did not halt their submarine warfare against passenger and merchant vessels. With the unsuccessful German offensive at Verdun costing more than half a million lives, Berlin did not want war with the United States. With the "*Sussex* Pledge" in early May, Germany promised that submarines would not attack passenger or merchant ships without prior warning. The Germans also nagged Washington to stop British infractions of international law.

The British clamped down even harder on trade with the Central Powers. In July London issued a "blacklist" of more than eighty American companies that had traded with the Central Powers. Even Wilson now fumed that he was "about at the end of my patience with Great Britain and the Allies."[44] He contemplated a ban on loans and exports to them, but he did little. Many Americans also condemned the brutal British smashing of the Irish Easter Rebellion in April 1916.

Shortly after his reelection in 1916, under the slogan "He Kept Us Out of War," the president boldly asked the belligerents to state their war aims. Neither side, still seeking military victory, welcomed Wilson's mediation. Germany coveted Poland, Lithuania, Belgium, and the Belgian Congo; Britain sought German colonies; France wanted Alsace-Lorraine. On January 22, 1917, however, Wilson instead called for a "peace without victory" because only through a peace founded on the "equality of nations" could a lasting world order be achieved. He regarded victory as "an intoxicant that fires the national brain and leaves a craving for more."[45] The French novelist Anatole France responded cynically: "Peace without victory is bread without yeast …, love without quarrels, a camel without humps, night without moon, roof without smoke, town without brothel."[46]

In early 1917, crises mounted quickly. On January 31, Berlin announced that German submarines would attack without warning and sink all vessels, enemy and neutral, found near British waters. This declaration of unrestricted submarine warfare expressed Germany's calculated risk that it could defeat England and France before the United States could mobilize and send soldiers overseas. The supremely arrogant German naval minister remarked: "From a military standpoint, America's entrance is as nothing."[47] German naval officers persuaded the kaiser that the U-boats, now numbering about one hundred, could knock Britain out of the war in six months. Army officers, bogged down in trench warfare, hoped to end their costly immobility through a bold stroke.

On February 3, Washington severed diplomatic relations with Berlin. According to Lansing, Wilson became "more and more impressed with the idea that 'white civilization' and its domination over the world rested largely on our ability to keep this country intact, as we would have to build up the nations ravaged by the war."[48] Yet Wilson had also committed himself to stand firmly against unrestricted submarine warfare. Allied ships carrying war supplies soon suffered increasing losses, and the few American vessels carrying contraband languished in port or shifted to trade outside the European war zones. The U.S. economy seemed imperiled.

Next came an apparent challenge to U.S. security. Washington had already endured espionage and sabotage by German agents, most notably the explosions at the Black Tom munitions factories across from the Statue of Liberty in July 1916. In late February the British passed to Ambassador Walter Hines Page an intercepted telegram dated January 16 and sent to Mexico by German foreign minister Arthur Zimmermann. The message proposed that Mexico and Germany "make war together, make peace together," and then Berlin would help Mexico "to reconquer the lost territories in Texas, New Mexico, and Arizona."[49] Although the skeptical Mexican government never took up the German offer, Wilson now saw Germany as a "madman that should be curbed."[50]

Wilson now asked Congress for authority to arm American merchant vessels. On March 1, to create a favorable public opinion for the request, he released the Zimmermann telegram to the press. But antiwar senators Robert La Follette and George Norris led a filibuster—a "little group of willful men," Wilson snarled—that killed the armed ship legislation.[51] Stubbornly ignoring the Senate, Wilson ordered the arming anyway. To no avail: during March 16–18 alone, U-boats sunk the American ships *City of Memphis, Illinois,* and *Vigilancia.* Buttressed by the unanimous support of his cabinet, the president decided for war.

After several intense days writing his own speech with help from Colonel House, Wilson addressed a special joint session of Congress on the evening of April 2. He asked for a declaration of war against Germany—a war that Berlin had "thrust" on the United States. The "unmanly business" of using submarines, he asserted, constituted "warfare against mankind." Freedom of the seas, commerce, American lives, human

Jeannette Rankin (1880–1973). A native of Montana, Rankin, in 1916, became the first woman to be elected to the House of Representatives. A lifelong pacifist, she voted against war in 1917, only to lose her seat the following year. In the interwar period she lobbied for peace and was again elected to Congress in 1940. This time she cast the only vote against war in 1941. She later marched against the Vietnam War. Rankin took pride in being "the first woman who was ever asked what she thought about war [and] said 'NO.'" (Library of Congress)

rights—the "outlaw" U-boats challenged all. Economic self-interest, morality, and national honor compelled Americans to fight. He characterized the German government as a monster tearing at the "very roots of human life." The "Prussian autocracy" stirred up trouble through spies and the Zimmermann telegram. He also hailed the Russian Revolution of March, which created a democratic government and made Russia "a fit partner for a league of honor" in a crusade against autocracy. Then came the potent and unforgettable words: "The world must be made safe for democracy."[52]

Although the oration simplified issues and promised too much from American intervention, the moment evoked patriotic fervor. "It is [Kaiser] Bill against Woodrow, Germany against America, Hell against Heaven," proclaimed the evangelist Billy Sunday, as he demonized the "wolfish Huns, whose fangs drip with blood."[53] By votes of 82 to 6 in the Senate on April 4 and 373 to 50 in the House on April 6, Congress endorsed Wilson's call for a war for peace.

Submarine warfare precipitated the American decision to enter the war. Had no submarine menaced American lives, property, and the U.S. definition of international law, no American soldiers would have gone to France. Critics have argued, however, that from the German perspective, the submarine became necessary because of the long list of unfriendly American acts: acquiescence in the British blockade, which was part of a general pro-British bias; huge munitions shipments to the Allies; large loans; an interpretation of neutral rights that insisted that American passengers could sail anywhere on any ship, even into a war zone. Take away those acts, which the Germans considered unneutral, and they might not have unleashed the U-boats. To dissenters it seemed wrong that American ideals and interests could depend so perilously on armed ships carrying contraband, heading for Britain, and steaming through a war zone. Yet Wilson and his advisers had so defined the problem.

Permeating Wilson's policies was the traditional American belief that others must conform to U.S. prescriptions and that America's ideals served as a beacon for the world. "We created this Nation," the president once proclaimed, "not to serve ourselves, but to serve mankind."[54] When the Germans defied America's rules, ideals, and property, and threatened its security through a proposed alliance with Mexico, they had to be punished. Here was an opportunity to protect both humane principles and commercial interests. When Wilson spoke passionately of the right of a neutral to freedom of the seas, he demonstrated the perceived interconnections among American moral, economic, and strategic interests. Wilson sought the role of peacemaker and promised to remake the world in the American image—a world order in which barriers to political democracy and the Open Door came down, in which revolution and aggression no longer threatened. The war coincided with the Progressive Era of energetic social and political reformism in the nation's history—a "plastic juncture," in the philosopher John Dewey's words, that rendered Americans particularly receptive to the idea of fighting to reshape the world according to democratic principles.[55]

The Debate over Preparedness

Berlin's assumption that massive numbers of U.S. soldiers could not reach France fast enough to reverse an expected German victory proved a gross misjudgment. American military muscle and economic power decisively tipped the balance against

Germany. Given the information available in early 1917, however, the German calculation did not seem so unrealistic. In April the United States had no capacity to send a major expedition to the western front. At that date the Regular Army counted only 130,000 officers and men, backed by 180,000 national guardsmen. Although some officers had been seasoned by interventions in Cuba, the Philippines, and Mexico, many soldiers lacked adequate training. Arsenals had meager supplies of such modern weapons as the machine gun. The "Air Service," then part of the army, did not have an airplane of modern design with a machine gun, and some warships had never fired a gun.

An American "preparedness movement" had been underway for months, encouraged by prominent Americans such as General Leonard Wood, who argued that America's military weakness invited attack. After 1914, Wood, Theodore Roosevelt, the National Security League, the Army League, and the Navy League lobbied for bigger military appropriations with the argument that "preparedness" offered insurance against war. When the hit pacifist song "I Didn't Raise My Boy to Be a Soldier" became "an icon of popular antiwar sentiment" in 1915, preparedness proponents countered with "I Didn't Raise My Boy to Be a Coward."[56] One propaganda film, *The Battle Cry of Peace* (1916), depicted spike-helmeted soldiers rampaging through New York City. That same year a U.S. admiral claimed that a single hostile dreadnought could "knock down all the buildings in New York …, smash all the cars, break down all the bridges, and sink all the shipping."[57]

Convinced that "a great standing army" was "antidemocratic," Wilson belatedly sought moderate preparedness.[58] He asked for a half-billion-dollar naval expansion program in late 1915, including ten battleships. The new force would surpass Britain as "incomparably the greatest navy in the world."[59] He also urged that land forces be enlarged and reorganized.

Senator La Follette, Representative Claude Kitchin, and prominent reformers such as William Jennings Bryan, Lillian Wald, and Oswald Garrison Villard spurred a movement against these measures. These peace advocates, especially the Women's Peace Party (representing "the mother half of humanity"), prophetically argued that war would interrupt reform at home, benefit big business, and curtail civil liberties.[60] Several peace leaders also joined the auto manufacturer Henry Ford in December 1915 as he sailed to Europe on his peace ship, *Oscar II,* to establish a Neutral Conference for Continuous Mediation—a quixotic attempt to end the war and get "the boys out of the trenches by Christmas."[61] The American Union Against Militarism agitated against preparedness with its papier-mâché dinosaur, "Jingo," whose collar read "ALL ARMOR PLATE—NO BRAINS."[62] Because his support of mediation, disarmament, and a postwar association of nations appealed to antiwar liberals and socialists ("progressive internationalists"), Wilson hoped that moderate preparedness would not alienate them. Chicago's famed social reformer Jane Addams remembered "moments of uneasiness," but she and others endorsed Wilson in the 1916 presidential campaign, for it seemed "at last that peace was assured and the future safe in the hands of an executive who had received an unequivocal mandate from the people 'to keep us out of war.'"[63]

In January 1916, Wilson set out on a two-month speaking tour, often criticizing members of his own party for their opposition to a military buildup. U-boat sinkings aided the president's message. In May 1916, Congress passed the National Defense Act, increasing the Regular Army to some 200,000 men and 11,000 officers, and the National Guard to 440,000 men and 17,000 officers. The act also authorized summer training camps, modeled after one held in Plattsburg, New York, in 1915 for the social and economic elite. Despite Jane Addams's query, "Why spend $45,000,000 for warships, when they will only be reduced to scrap heap after this war?" the naval appropriations bill passed in August 1916.[64] Theodore Roosevelt thought the measures inadequate, but the anarchist Emma Goldman saw no difference between Roosevelt, "the born bully who uses a club," and Wilson, "the history professor who uses the smooth polished mask."[65] TR denounced pacifists as "active agents of the devil."[66]

Once in the war, after learning what the Allies "want and need is men, whether trained or not," Wilson relied on the Selective Service Act of May 1917.[67] National military service, proponents believed, would not only prepare the nation for battle but also instill respect for order, democracy, and sacrifice. Under the selective service system, 24,340,000 men eventually registered for the draft. Some 3,764,000 men received draft notices, and 2,820,000 were inducted. Over all, 4,744,000 soldiers, sailors, and marines served. "The Jews, the Wops, and the Dutch and the Irish cops,/ They're all in the Army now!" went a popular tune.[68] The typical serviceman was a white, single, poorly educated draftee between twenty-one and twenty-three years of age. Officer training camps turned out "ninety-day wonders," thousands of

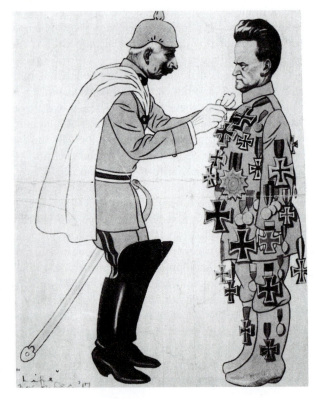

Senator Robert M. La Follette (1855–1925). This *Life* magazine cartoon depicted the antiwar, progressive reformer as a traitor. La Follette wanted a referendum on the war, certain that the American people would vote no. Some Americans thought that he should be expelled from the Senate. Others claimed that he took orders from the German kaiser, here shown pinning medals on the Wisconsin senator. La Follette withstood the intolerance of dissent and continued to speak against organized power and for the powerless, who, he said, were the people destined to do the fighting and dying abroad. (State Historical Society of Wisconsin)

commissioned officers drawn largely from people of elite background. Although excluded from military combat, women became navy clerks, telephone operators in the Army Signal Corps, and nurses and physical therapists to the wounded and battle-shock cases (the term then used for post-traumatic stress syndrome).

With the Allies begging for soldiers, General John J. "Black Jack" Pershing, now head of the American Expeditionary Forces to Europe, soon sent a "show the flag" contingent to France to boost Allied morale. Neither Wilson nor Pershing, however, would accept the European recommendation that U.S. troops be inserted in Allied units. American units would cooperate in joint maneuvers with other forces, but the U.S. Army would remain separate and independent. National pride dictated this decision, but so did the realization that Allied commanders had for years wasted the lives of hundreds of thousands in trench warfare. For more than two years officers had been ordering their men to charge out of the trenches, cross a "no man's land" of barbed wire and shell holes, and attack defenders off enemy trenches. Too often the assaulters were mowed down by machine gun fire, blown apart by artillery, or asphyxiated by chlorine gas, first used by Germany in 1915. Nor did Wilson endorse exploitative Allied war aims. Thus did the United States call itself an "associated" rather than an "allied" power in the war.

The Doughboys Make the Difference in Europe

On July 4, 1917, General Pershing reviewed the first battalion to arrive in France, as nearly a million Parisians tossed flowers, hugged the "doughboys" (apparently so-called because their buttons resembled dumplings made of dough), and cheered wildly. *"Lafayette, nous sommes ici!"* ("we are here!") shouted Pershing's aide.[69]

To the dismay of American leaders, taverns and brothels quickly surrounded military camps in the United States, even as alcohol and prostitution, remained taboo during the Progressive era. "Fit to Fight" became the government's slogan, as it moved to close "red-light districts," designated "sin-free zones" around camps, and banned the sale of liquor to men in uniform. Super patriots condemned those "treacherous Germans: Pabst, Schlitz, Blatz, and Miller."[70] The YMCA and the Jewish Welfare Board sent song leaders to camps. Movies, athletic programs, and well-stocked stores sought to keep soldiers on the base by making them feel "at home."

Success against venereal disease in the United States contrasted with a major flu epidemic, which first struck camps in spring 1918. The extremely contagious flu virus cut across race, gender, and class lines. At Camp Sherman, Ohio, one of the bases hit hardest, 1,101 people died between September 27 and October 13. Whereas about 51,000 soldiers died in battle during the war, some 62,000 soldiers died from diseases. Doughboys infected with the virus carried the flu with them to the European war, where it ignored national boundaries and turned into a global pandemic that killed more than 21 million people by spring 1919.

The approximately 400,000 African-American troops suffered racism and discrimination during this war "to make the world safe for democracy." Military camps were segregated and "white only" signs posted. In 1917 in Houston, Texas, whites provoked blacks into a riot that left seventeen whites and two blacks dead. In the army, three out of every four black soldiers served in labor units, where they wielded a shovel, not a gun, or where they cooked or unloaded supplies. African Americans endured second-class citizenship and the glaring contradiction between America's war-time rhetoric and reality. A statistic revealed the problem: 382 black Americans were lynched in the period 1914–1920. Segregation nonetheless did score one diplomatic success when the polyrhythms of the 169th Infantry's Harlem Hellcats marching band "touched off France's passion for jazz."[71]

The first official American combat death in Europe came only ten days after Congress declared war—that of Edmund Charles Clinton Genet, the great-great-grandson of French Revolutionary diplomat Citizen Genet and member of the famed American volunteer air squadron, the Lafayette Escadrille. Despite Allied impatience, General Pershing hesitated to commit his green soldiers to full-scale battle. As it was, great numbers of troops shipped over in British vessels and had to borrow French weapons. Disease continued to stalk U.S. forces. American reformers hoped soldiers had enough social armor not to be tempted by "sin" overseas, but the venereal-disease rate spiraled up. French premier Georges Clemenceau offered licensed—health-inspected—prostitutes. When Secretary of War Newton Baker

Red Cross Postcard. Women served in many roles in the war. They became workers in weapons factories. They sold Liberty Bonds and publicized government mobilization programs as members of the Women's Committee of the Council of National Defense. In France, women nurses and canteen workers became envoys of the U.S. home front, representing the mothers, wives, and sisters left behind. As the historian Susan Zeiger has written, the government's sponsorship of these wartime roles for women cleverly blunted the feminist-pacifist claim that women were "inherently more peaceful than men and would oppose war out of love for their children." (Library of Congress)

received the Gallic proposal, he exclaimed: "For God's sake ... don't show this to the President or he'll stop the war."[72] Prevention programs and the threat of court-martial eventually reduced the "VD" problem.

By early 1918, the Allies had become mired in a murderous strategy of throwing ground forces directly at enemy ground forces. German troops were mauling Italian forces, and the French army was still suffering from mutinies of the year before. In March, after Germany swallowed large chunks of European Russia through the Brest-Litovsk Treaty, Wilson warned of a German "empire of force" out to "dominate the world itself" and urged Americans to "arm and prepare themselves to contest the mastery of the world."[73] In April he called for the national exertion of "Force, Force to the utmost, Force without stint or limit."[74] U.S. forces soon trooped into battle.

In March the German armies, swollen by forty divisions from the Russian front, launched a great offensive. Allied forces retreated, and by late May the kaiser's soldiers encamped near the Marne River, less than fifty miles from Paris. Saint-Mihiel, Belleau Wood, Cantigny, Château-Thierry—French sites where U.S. soldiers shed their blood—soon became household words for Americans. In June at Château-Thierry the doughboys dramatically stopped a German advance. From May through September 1918 more than 1 million American troops went to France—2 million by the November armistice. In mid-July the Allies launched a counteroffensive; nine American divisions fought fiercely near Château-Thierry, helping to lift the German threat from Paris. In the Meuse-Argonne offensive (begun in late September), more than 1 million doughboys joined French and British units in a six-week struggle that

First Division Troops Encounter German Gas Warfare, 1918.   Near Soissons, France, U.S. soldiers attacked German lines through air contaminated with poisonous gas. The soldier in the foreground, wounded by fire, tore off his gas mask. Before U.S. intervention, President Wilson had deplored "this vast, gruesome contest of systematized destruction" and denied any "glory commensurate with the sacrifice of millions of men." The last surviving U.S. combat veteran of World War I, Corporal Harold V. Ramsay, died in 2008 at age 108. (Library of Congress)

cost 26,277 American deaths and 95,786 wounded—the "deadliest battle in all of American history."[75] "The American infantry in the Argonne won the war," German Marshal Paul von Hindenburg later commented, perhaps with overstatement.[76] Not only was the German army in retreat, but the U-boats had been defeated at sea and the Atlantic had become an uninterrupted highway for the reinforcement of men and war supplies from the United States. The logistical avalanche would soon bury Germany, so Berlin sought peace.

On October 4, the German chancellor asked Wilson for an armistice. German troops had mutinied; revolution and riots plagued German cities; Bulgaria had left the war in September. Then Turkey dropped out in late October, and Austria-Hungary surrendered on November 3. Germany had no choice but to seek terms. The kaiser fled to Holland. On November 11, in a railroad car in the Compiègne Forest, German representatives capitulated.

The Fourteen Points and a Contentious Peace Conference

During the combat, President Wilson had begun to explain his plans for the peace. He trumpeted his vision most dramatically in his "Fourteen Points" speech before Congress on January 8, 1918. The first five points promised an "open" world after the war, a world distinguished by "open covenants, openly arrived at," freedom of navigation on the seas, equal trade opportunity and the removal of tariffs, reduction of armaments, and an end to colonialism. Points six through thirteen called for self-determination for national minorities in Europe. Point fourteen stood paramount: a "general association of nations" to ensure "political independence and territorial integrity to great and small states alike."[77] His Fourteen Points signaled a generous, nonpunitive postwar settlement. They served, too, as effective American propaganda against revenge-fueled Allied aims and Russian Bolshevik appeals for European revolution.

Despite secret treaties that promised German colonies and other territorial gains, Allied leaders feared that Wilson would deny them the spoils of war. Nor did they appreciate his promises to slay the "dragons of reaction" in Europe.[78] In view of the comparative wartime losses, Europeans believed that Wilson "had bought his seat at the peace table at a discount."[79] When, in September and October 1918, Wilson exchanged notes with Germany and Austria-Hungary about an armistice, the Allied powers expressed strong reservations about the Fourteen Points. Wilson hinted at a separate peace with the Central Powers and even threatened to publicize the exploitative Allied war aims. Facing possible reduced American shipments to Europe, London, Paris, and Rome reluctantly accepted, in the armistice of November, peace negotiations on the basis of the Fourteen Points.

Wilson relished his opportunity. The United States could now claim a major role in deciding future international relations. The pictures of dying men dangling from barbed-wire fences and the battle-shock victims who staggered home persuaded many Americans of the need to prevent another conflagration. Wilson's call for a just peace commanded the backing of countless foreigners as well. Italians hoisted banners reading *Dio di Pace* ("God of Peace") and *Redentore dell' Humanità* ("Redeemer of Humanity") to welcome Wilson to Europe.

Yet the president weakened his position even before the peace conference. Congressional leaders wanted him to stay home to handle domestic problems. Lansing feared that Wilson would have only one vote in the day-to-day conference bickering, whereas from Washington he could symbolically marshal the votes of humankind. Wilson retorted that "England and France have not the same views with regard to peace that we have," so he had to attend personally to defend the Fourteen Points.[80]

Domestic politics soon set Wilson back. In October 1918, Wilson "hurled a brick into a beehive" by asking Americans to return a Democratic Congress loyal to him.[81] Partisan Republicans proceeded to capture the November election and majorities in both houses of Congress; they would sit in ultimate judgment of Wilson's peacemaking. The president also made the political mistake of appointing neither an important Republican nor a senator to the American Peace Commission. Wilson, House, and Lansing sat on it; so did Henry White, a seasoned diplomat and nominal Republican. Some concessions to his political opposition, and to senatorial prerogatives in foreign affairs, might have smoothed the path later for his peace treaty.

On December 4, with great fanfare, Wilson departed from New York aboard the *George Washington*. He settled into a quiet voyage, surrounded by advisers and nearly 2,000 reports produced by "The Inquiry," a group of scholars who had studied issues likely to arise at the peace conference. Confident that "we can force" the Allies "to our way of thinking" because they will be "financially in our hands," the president had made few concrete plans.[82] After reaching France on December 15, Wilson basked in the admiration of enthusiastic Parisian crowds. Later, thousands in Italy and England cheered him with near religious fervor. Wilson assumed that this generous outpouring meant that *his* peace aims were universally popular and that Americans "would be the only disinterested people" at Versailles.[83] Such "man-in-the-street" opinion did not impress David Lloyd George, prime minister of Britain, French Premier Georges Clemenceau, or Italian Prime Minister Vittorio Orlando, Wilson's antagonists at the peace conference.

With Germany and Bolshevik Russia (see page 300) excluded from the Versailles conference, thirty-two nations sent delegations, which essentially followed the lead of the "Big Four." Most sessions worked in secrecy, hardly befitting Wilson's first "point." Clemenceau resented Wilson's "sermonettes" and preferred to work with the more compliant Colonel House. "The old tiger [Clemenceau] wants the grizzly bear [Wilson] back in the Rocky Mountains before he starts tearing up the German Hog," commented Lloyd George, who sought to build a strong France and to ensure German purchases of British exports.[84] A fervent Italian nationalist, Orlando concerned himself primarily with enlarging Italian territory. These leaders sought a vengeful peace. Lloyd George complained of a chameleonlike Wilson—"the noble visionary, the implacable and unscrupulous partisan, the exalted idealist and the man of rather petty personal rancour."[85] Wilson, in turn, thought the Europeans "too weatherwise to see the weather."[86]

Much wrangling occurred over the disposition of colonies and the creation of new countries. "Tell me what's right and I'll fight for it," said Wilson as he appealed

David Lloyd George (1863–1945). "America," said the British prime minister, referring to the League of Nations, "had been offered the leadership of the world, but the Senate had tossed the sceptre into the sea." (Library of Congress)

for self-determination.[87] After hard negotiating, the conferees mandated former German and Turkish colonies to the countries that had conquered them, to be loosely supervised under League of Nations auspices. Under the mandate system—a compromise between outright annexation and complete independence—France (with Syria and Lebanon) and Britain (with Iraq, Trans-Jordan, and Palestine) received parts of the Middle East. Wilson voiced support for Britain's Balfour Declaration that promised "a national home for the Jewish people" in Palestine, and he briefly considered an American mandate for Armenia (where the Turks had committed genocidal atrocities during the war) but rejected it because he could "think of nothing that the people of the United States would be less inclined to accept than military responsibility in Asia."[88] Japan acquired China's Shandong Province and some of Germany's Pacific islands. After Wilson's reluctant acceptance of the Shandong arrangement, the president deemed it "the best that could be accomplished out of a 'dirty past'" and expected the League of Nations to "decide the matter later."[89] Outraged Chinese students in Beijing protested by launching the May Fourth Movement, claiming that "we could no longer depend upon the principle of any so-called great leader like Woodrow Wilson."[90]

With his rhetoric combining the "text of modern liberalism with the subtext of racism," Wilson conspicuously ignored a petition calling for self-determination in French Indochina and signed by, among others, Nguyen Al Quoc—later famous under the name Ho Chi Minh.[91] France gained the demilitarization of the German

Wilson in Dover, England, 1919. Wilson received flowers from English schoolchildren. The biographer Louis Auchincloss has written that "the ringing shouts in the streets and squares of the Old World must have made him [Wilson] feel like a messiah endowed with the vision to understand that the multitude was on the side of the merciful angels of a fair and lasting peace and that only a minority of stubborn old men wanted to crush the enemy to dust. He never learned that the only leader who can take advantage of the momentary enthusiasm of the common man is a dictator who can use its force to blast his way to power; a democrat must abide by the decision of those whom the common man has elected to represent him." (U.S. Signal Corps, National Archives)

Rhineland and a stake in the coal-rich Saar Basin. Italy annexed South Tyrol and Trieste from the collapsed Austro-Hungarian Empire. Some 1,132,000 square miles changed hands. Newly independent countries also emerged from the defunct Austro-Hungarian Empire: Austria, Czechoslovakia, Hungary, Romania, and Yugoslavia. The Allies further exploited nationalism to recognize a ring of hostile states already established around Bolshevik Russia: Finland, Poland, Estonia, Latvia, and Lithuania, all formerly part of the Russian empire (see map on page 295). The mandate system smacked of imperialism, in violation of the Fourteen Points, but the new states in Europe fulfilled Wilson's self-determination pledge. To assuage French fears of a revived Germany, Britain and the United States signed a security pact with France guaranteeing its borders, but Wilson never submitted it for Senate approval.

Reparations proved a knotty issue. The United States wanted a limited indemnity for Germany to avoid a harsh peace that might arouse long-term German resentment or debilitate the German economy and politics. "Excessive demands," Wilson predicted, "would most certainly sow the seeds of war."[92] To cripple Germany, France pushed for a large bill of reparations. The conferees composed a "war guilt clause," which held Germany responsible for all of the war's damages. Rationalizing that the League would ameliorate any excesses, Wilson gave in on both reparations and war guilt. It was a major mistake. The Reparations Commission in 1921 presented a hobbled Germany with a huge reparations bill of $33 billion, thereby helping to destabilize international economic relations for more than a decade.

The Allies played to Wilson's priorities: "Give him the League of Nations and he will give us all the rest."[93] Drafted largely by Wilson, the League's covenant provided for an influential council of five big powers (permanent) and representatives from smaller nations (by election) and an assembly of all nations for discussion. Wilson saw the heart of the covenant as Article 10, a provision designed to curb aggression and war: "The Members of the League undertake to respect and preserve as against external aggression the territorial integrity and existing political independence of all Members of the League." In case of aggression or threat, "the Council shall advise upon the means by which this obligation shall be fulfilled."[94] Wilson persuaded the conferees to merge the League covenant and the peace terms in a package, with the charter constituting the first 26 articles of a 440-article Treaty of Paris. Wilson deemed the League covenant the noblest part of all—"It is practical, and yet it is intended to purify, to rectify, to elevate."[95]

The Germans, without having previously participated in the deliberations, signed sullenly on June 28 in the elegant Hall of Mirrors at Versailles. By stripping Germany of 13 percent of its territory, 10 percent of its population, and all of its colonies, and by demanding reparations, the treaty humiliated the Germans without crushing them. In one historian's words, the treaty contained "a witches' brew" with "too little Wilsonianism to appease, too little of Clemenceau to deter; enough of Wilson to provoke contempt, enough of Clemenceau to inspire hatred."[96] When Wilson died on February 3, 1924, the Weimar Republic in Berlin refrained from issuing an official condolence, and the German Embassy in Washington broke custom by not lowering its flag to half-mast.

Principle, Personality, Health, and Partisanship: The League Fight

Wilson spent almost six months in Europe negotiating the postwar peace. From February 24 to March 14, 1919, however, he returned to the United States for executive business. On arrival, he asserted that any U.S. failure to back the League "would break the heart of the world."[97] In Washington, Republicans peppered Wilson with questions about the degree to which the covenant limited American sovereignty. When Wilson spoke vaguely, Senator Frank Brandegee of Connecticut said he felt as if he had been "wandering with Alice in Wonderland and had tea with the Mad Hatter."[98] In early March, Republican Senator Henry Cabot Lodge of Massachusetts engineered a "Round Robin," a statement by thirty-nine senators (enough to deny the treaty a two-thirds vote) that questioned the League covenant and requested that the peace treaty and the covenant be acted on separately. Many of Lodge's signers feared that the League would limit U.S. freedom to act independently in international affairs.

A defiant Wilson sailed again for France, determined that "little Americans," full of "watchful jealousies [and] of rabid antagonisms," would not destroy his beloved League.[99] Still, he was politician enough to seek changes in Paris. He amended the covenant so that League members could refuse mandates, League jurisdiction over purely domestic issues was precluded, and the Monroe Doctrine was safeguarded against League interference. But he would not alter Article 10. When he returned to the United States in July, Wilson submitted the long Treaty of Versailles to the Senate on July 10, with an address that resembled an evangelical sermon: "The stage is set, the destiny disclosed. It has come about by no plan of our conceiving, but by the hand of God, who led us into this way."[100] Asked if he would accept senatorial "reservations" to the treaty, Wilson snapped: "Anyone who opposes me in that, I'll crush."[101] "If it won't work," he said of the League, "it must be made to work."[102]

Wilson, against strong odds in Paris, gained a good percentage of his goals as outlined in the Fourteen Points. Self-determination for nationalities was advanced as never before in Europe, and the League ranked as a notable achievement. But Wilson did compromise, especially with Clemenceau. Both Italy and Japan had threatened to walk out unless they realized some territorial goals. Still, Wilson had so built up a case for an unselfish peace that when the conquerors' hard bargaining and harsh terms dominated the conference, observers could only conclude that the president had failed badly to live up to his millennial rhetoric. Critics said that Wilson should have left Paris in protest, refusing to sign, or that he might have threatened the Allies with U.S. economic pressure. Believing desperately that the League, with Article 10, would rectify all, Wilson warned Congress that without it, "the United States and every other country will have to arm to the teeth."[103]

He would not compromise at home, however. And he seldom provided systematic, technical analysis to treaty clauses. He simply expected the Senate dutifully to ratify his masterwork. Yet his earlier bypassing of that body and his own partisan speeches and self-righteousness ensured debate, if not defeat. Progressive internationalists protested that "the capitalists wanted the League as a superstate to protect their exploitative concessions in underdeveloped countries."[104] Henry Cabot Lodge

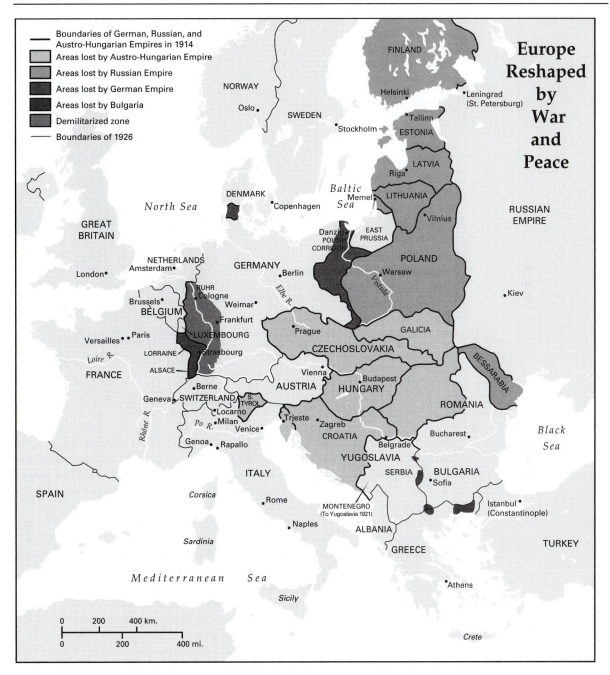

Europe
Reshaped
by
War
and
Peace

Boundaries of German, Russian, and
Austro-Hungarian Empires in 1914
Areas lost by Austro-Hungarian Empire
Areas lost by Russian Empire
Areas lost by German Empire
Areas lost by Bulgaria
Demilitarized zone
Boundaries of 1926

FINLAND
Helsinki
Leningrad
(St. Petersburg)
NORWAY
Oslo
SWEDEN
Stockholm
Tallinn
ESTONIA
LATVIA
Riga
*Baltic
Sea*
Memel
LITHUANIA
Vilnius
RUSSIAN
EMPIRE
DENMARK
Copenhagen
North Sea
Danzig
POLISH
CORRIDOR
EAST
PRUSSIA
GREAT
BRITAIN
POLAND
Warsaw
NETHERLANDS
Amsterdam
GERMANY
Berlin
Vistula
Kiev
London
RUHR
Cologne
Brussels
BELGIUM
Weimar
Frankfurt
LUXEMBOURG
Prague
GALICIA
Versailles
Paris
LORRAINE
Strasbourg
CZECHOSLOVAKIA
Loire R.
ALSACE
FRANCE
Vienna
Budapest
BESSARABIA
Berne
AUSTRIA
HUNGARY
Geneva
SWITZERLAND
S.
TYROL
Locarno
Trieste
ROMANIA
Rhône R.
Po R.
Milan
Venice
Zagreb
Bucharest
*Black
Sea*
Genoa
Rapallo
CROATIA
Belgrade
ITALY
YUGOSLAVIA
SPAIN
Corsica
Rome
SERBIA
BULGARIA
Sofia
MONTENEGRO
(To Yugoslavia 1921)
Istanbul
(Constantinople)
Naples
ALBANIA
TURKEY
Sardinia
GREECE
Mediterranean   Sea
Athens
Sicily
0   200   400 km.
0   200   400 mi.
Crete

Georges Clemenceau (1841–1929).
Auguste Rodin's bronze aptly conveys the
formidable stature of "The Tiger" from France, eager
for revenge against Germany. "I had a wife, she
abandoned me," he once growled. "I had children,
they turned against me; I had friends, they betrayed
me. I have only my claws, and I use them." (The
Rodin Museum, Philadelphia: Bequest of Jules E.
Mastbaum, 1929)

asked a key question: "Are you willing to put your soldiers and your sailors at the disposition of other nations?"[105] Senator James Reed of Missouri feared racial peril from a League initially comprising fifteen white nations and seventeen nations of "black, brown, yellow, and red races," which, he claimed, ranked low in "civilization" and high in "barbarism."[106]

Article 10 seemed to rattle everybody. The article did not require member states to use force, but it implied they should. Senator William Borah complained that "I may be willing to help my neighbor …, but I do not want him … [to] decide for me when and how I shall act or to what extent I shall make sacrifice."[107] Because of its apparent commitment to territorial integrity, Senator Hiram Johnson of California claimed that Article 10 would "freeze the world into immutability and put it in a straightjacket," keeping "subject peoples … subject until the crack of doom."[108] The article seemed too open-ended to most opponents.

Henry Cabot Lodge towered as Wilson's chief legislative obstacle. Chair of the Senate Foreign Relations Committee, nationalist-imperialist, author, Republican partisan, like Wilson a scholar in politics, Lodge packed his committee with anti-League senators, dragged out hearings for weeks, kept most Republicans together on treaty votes, and nurtured a personal animosity toward Wilson matched only by Wilson's detestation for Lodge. He attacked obliquely by proposing "reservations" to the League covenant. Although in retrospect these reservations, intended to guard

American sovereignty, do not appear to have been death blows to the League, at the time they stirred impassioned debate. They addressed the central question of American national interest—the degree to which the United States would limit its freedom of action, the degree to which the United States should engage in collective security. In fact, many of the fourteen reservations stated the obvious—that Congress would retain its constitutional role in foreign policy. Another denied the League jurisdiction over American domestic legislation. The reservation on Article 10 disclaimed any obligation to preserve the territorial integrity or political independence of another country unless authorized by Congress. For Wilson this meant "nullification of the treaty."[109] He was wrong.

The Senate divided into four groups. Wilson counted on about forty loyal Democrats called the Non-Reservationists. Another group, the Mild-Reservationists, led by Frank B. Kellogg, numbered about thirteen Republicans. The third faction, managed by Lodge, stood together as the Strong-Reservationists—some twenty Republicans and a few Democrats. The fourth group, consisting of sixteen Irreconcilables, ardently opposed the treaty with or without reservations. Most of them were Republicans, including Borah, La Follette, George Norris of Nebraska, and Hiram Johnson of California. "If the Savior of mankind would revisit the earth and declared for a League," vowed Borah, "I would be opposed to it."[110]

Wilson met individually with some twenty-three senators over two weeks, but he suffered a minor stroke on July 19, 1919. He thereafter rigidly refused to accept any reservations. He argued that a treaty ratified with reservations would have to go back to another conference for acceptance and every nation would then rush in with its pet reservations. The British punctured this hollow claim by announcing that they would accept American reservations. In September 1919, Wilson set off on a 10,000-mile train trip across the United States. Growing more exhausted with each day, suffering severe headaches and nighttime coughing spells, Wilson pounded the podium in forty speeches. He blasted his traducers as "absolute, contemptible quitters."[111] He confused his audiences when he stated that Article 10 meant that the United States had a moral, not a legal, obligation to use armed force, and that Congress was "absolutely free to put its own interpretation on it."[112] Failure to join the League, he prophesied "with absolute certainty" meant that "within another generation there will be another world war."[113] On September 26, after an impassioned speech in Pueblo, Colorado, he awoke to nausea and uncontrollable facial twitching. When his doctor ordered him to cancel the rest of his trip, Wilson wept.

After Wilson returned to Washington, a massive stroke paralyzed his left side. He lay flat in bed for six weeks and saw virtually no one except his wife and Dr. Cary Grayson. For months Edith Bolling Galt Wilson ran her husband's political affairs, screening messages and banishing House and Lansing, among others, from presidential favor. The president should have resigned, as Dr. Grayson advised him to do in early 1919. As it was, his concentration diminished and his stubbornness accentuated by the stroke, Wilson adamantly refused to change his all-or-nothing position.

In November 1919, the Senate balloted on the complete treaty *with* reservations and rejected it, 39 to 55 (Irreconcilables and Non-Reservationists in the

Henry Cabot Lodge (1850–1924). Wilson's partisan rival observed of the League Covenant that "it might get by at Princeton," Wilson's alma mater, "but certainly not at Harvard," where Lodge had earned a Ph.D. Lodge's opposition to Wilson's League, was motivated in part by his belief that the United States should control the Americas and act cautiously in European political and military affairs. He was a long-time expansionist who had declared in 1895: "From the Rio Grande to the Arctic Ocean there would be but one flag and one country." (Library of Congress)

Woodrow Wilson After His Stroke. Recent scholarly assessments of medical evidence reveal that Wilson had a long history of cerebrovascular disease. Wilson remained in the White House after his massive stroke in October 1919, while his wife and doctor tried to keep secret the severity of his physical incapacity. Dr. Edwin A. Weinstein, who has studied the effects of Wilson's health and personality on his decision making, has noted that the president after his stroke could not maintain his train of thought and was prone to bursts of temper. An increasingly paranoid president broke with such close advisers as Colonel House and Secretary Lansing for alleged slights and betrayals. (Library of Congress)

negative). Then it voted on the treaty *without* reservations and also rejected it, 38 to 53 (Irreconcilables and Reservationists in the negative). The president had instructed loyal Democrats not to accept any "reserved" treaty. In March 1920, another tally saw some Democrats vote in favor of reservations. Not enough, the treaty failed, 49 to 35, several votes short of the two-thirds majority required for approval. When his wife urged him to accept reservations, Wilson admonished: "Little girl, don't you desert me. That I cannot stand."[114] Still a fighter, the president claimed that the election of 1920 would be a "solemn referendum" on the treaty. Other questions actually blurred the League issue in that campaign, and Republican Warren G. Harding, who as a senator had supported reservations, promptly condemned the League after his election as president. In July 1921, Congress officially terminated the war, and in August, by treaty with Germany, the United States claimed as valid for itself the terms of the treaty of Versailles—exclusive of the League articles.

The memorable League fight had ended. The tragic dénouement occurred because of political partisanship, personal animosities, senatorial resentments, the president's failing health, popular adherence to traditional unilateralism, and disinterest and confusion in the public mind. Progressive internationalists, many of them harassed by wartime restrictions on civil liberties and disappointed by Wilson's compromises with the imperial powers, no longer backed a president they thought reactionary. Then, of course, there was Wilson himself—stubborn, pontificating, combative, and increasingly ill. He might have conceded that the peace had imperfections. He might have provided more careful analysis of a long, complicated document. He might, further, have admitted that his opponents held a respectable intellectual position. Instead, he often chose shrill rhetoric and rigid self-righteousness. Most importantly, he saw the difference between himself and his critics as fundamental: whether it was in America's national interest to participate in collective security or seek safety unilaterally. As one critic put it, Wilson sought "collective security without forming an alliance." He wanted the "omelet" without "cracking the eggs."[115]

Although the League came into being without the United States as a member, none of the great powers wished to bestow significant authority on the new organization. Japan's foreign minister called it "nothing but a great hypocritical monster under the cloak of justice and humanity."[116] Even if Washington had joined, the United States most likely would have acted outside the League's auspices, especially regarding its own empire in Latin America. No international association at that time could have outlawed war, dismantled empires, or scuttled navies. Wilson overshot reality in thinking that he could reform world politics through a new international body. The League represented a commendable restraint against war, but hardly a panacea for world peace.

What if ... *the president had accepted Senate reservations and the United States had joined the League of Nations in 1919–1920?*

Had Woodrow Wilson resigned following his stroke in October 1919, as his personal physician Dr. Cary Grayson urged him to do, the Senate and Vice President Thomas Marshall almost certainly would have reached some agreement on admission to the League, probably with reservations to Article 10 of the Covenant. Similar to the veto in the United Nations since 1945, the United States could have decided if and when it would follow League recommendations. Contemporary observers would not have misinterpreted the divisive presidential election of 1920 as a solemn referendum for or against League membership, even though Republicans most likely would have won because of public disenchantment with Wilsonian rhetoric, the Red Scare, wartime inflation, postwar recession, and failed promises. The Senate might also have ratified the Anglo-American treaty of guarantee of France, which Wilson had refused to submit until the Senate approved the League. As Senator Henry Cabot Lodge actually preferred, a de facto alliance among the United States, France, and Britain might have continued into the 1920s. As with the Locarno Treaty of 1925, such a treaty would have guaranteed Germany's western boundaries with France and Belgium but not its eastern boundaries with Poland and Czechoslovakia. Washington could probably have joined the World Court with minimum controversy, albeit with little practical effect.

Would U.S. membership in the League have altered the history of the interwar period? Washington's hegemony within the Western Hemisphere would surely not have changed. Participation by U.S. experts in the League's Reparations Commission in 1920–1921 might have resulted in a total bill of much less than $33 billion and an easier schedule of payments for Weimar Germany. If so, Germany's default by inflation, the Franco-Belgian occupation of the Ruhr in 1923, and readjustment of reparations payments and private U.S. bank loans to Germany under the Dawes Plan of 1924 need not have occurred. Nonetheless, without Washington's willingness to lower its tariff walls, to grant generous reconstruction aid to Europe, or to write off wartime debts to the allies, the jerry-rigged recycling of loans, reparations, and debts would still have left the international economy vulnerable to the stock market crash and depression after 1929. Notwithstanding U.S. participation in multiple League-sponsored forums culminating in the London Economic Conference of 1933, cooperative efforts offered no effective solutions to the Great Depression. Similarly, it is difficult to imagine that direct U.S. participation would have bolstered the League's tepid response to the Manchurian Crisis of 1931 or to the Italian invasion of Ethiopia in 1935. In fact, some American diplomats viewed League membership as an excuse for such countries as Britain and France not to act more forcefully. In any event, the peace lobby, continued public disillusionment with World War I, and New Deal domestic priorities would still have constrained President Franklin D. Roosevelt from multilateral initiatives to deter German and Japanese expansion until later in the decade.

When "independent internationalism" failed to prevent a second world war (see next chapter), Americans readily grasped a second chance to rectify the apparent mistakes of 1919–1920 by embracing a new version of the League. Spurred on by a resurgence of Wilsonianism, including the lavish Hollywood film *Wilson* (1944), the Roosevelt administration sought bipartisan support from Republicans and successfully persuaded Americans to join a modified collective security organization known as the United Nations. American participation and leadership, it was hoped, would ensure a peaceful international order. The checkered history of the United Nations since 1945, however, suggests that earlier membership would have made little difference. Despite Wilson's messianic vision, the League was never more than the sum of its collective parts.

Red Scare at Home and Abroad: Bolshevism and Intervention in Russia

"Paris cannot be understood without Moscow [Russia]," wrote Wilson's press secretary Ray Stannard Baker.[117] As he traveled to France aboard the *George Washington,* President Wilson depicted Bolshevism as "the poison of disorder, the poison of revolt, the poison of chaos."[118] Revolutionary and anticapitalist, the Bolsheviks, or Communists, threw fright into the leaders of Europe and America. At home and abroad the peacemakers battled the radical left. In the United States the Wilson administration trampled on civil liberties during an exaggerated "Red Scare," which sent innocent people to jail or deported them. Wilson himself seemed to think that "the only way to kill Bolshevism is … to open all the doors to commerce."[119] Only belatedly, after authorizing secret aid and espionage against the "Reds," did the president openly "cast in his lot" with the other powers in a futile attempt to destroy the new revolutionary regime.[120]

Most Americans applauded the Russian Revolution of March 1917, which toppled Tsar Nicholas II. Wilson himself viewed it as a thrust against autocracy, war, and imperialism. But when the moderate Provisional government under Alexander Kerensky fell to the radical Bolsheviks in October, Americans responded first with irritation and then anger. Their disapproval became acute in March 1918 after the Bolsheviks signed the Brest-Litovsk Treaty with Germany and ceded Ukraine and Finland, among other territories—a total of 1,267,000 square miles, 62 million people, and one-third of Russia's best agricultural land. A necessary peace for a devastated Russia from the Bolshevik perspective, the treaty seemed a stab in the back for the Allies, a decisive victory for Berlin. Because German authorities had allowed Vladimir I. Lenin to travel to Russia via Germany in 1917, some irate American officials even considered Bolsheviks pro-German. Others recoiled after Ambassador David Francis's testimony that Bolsheviks had "nationalized women."[121]

Lenin actually treated the United States as a special, favored case, and he consistently sought accommodation with Washington. Soviet representatives held a series of cordial conversations from December 1917 to May 1918 with Red Cross official Raymond Robins, a de facto U.S. representative, and reached agreements on food relief, purchase of strategic materials, and exemption of American corporations from

Тов. Ленин ОЧИЩАЕТ
землю от нечисти.

"Comrade Lenin Sweeps the Globe Clean." Vladimir Ilyich Lenin (1870–1924) is shown in this Bolshevik art as a revolutionary ridding the world of monarchs and capitalists. But Lenin also craved Western trade and investment to spur his nation's economic reconstruction. As he said in 1919: "We are decidedly for an economic understanding with America—with all countries, but especially with America." (By Mikhail Cheremnykh and Victor Deni in Mikhail Guerman, comp., *Art of the October Revolution,* Leningrad: Aurora Art Publishers, 1979)

Bolshevik nationalization decrees. Prior to Brest-Litovsk, Robins urged prompt recognition of the Bolshevik government to keep Russia in the war, but President Wilson paid more heed to Francis's prediction that the Bolshevik regime would soon collapse.

Although American officials in Russia engaged in propaganda and espionage and cooperated with Allied and "White" agents in anti-Bolshevik activities after November 1917, Wilson knew only broad outlines of this "secret war" when he sent U.S. troops to Archangel in northern Russia in August 1918. Ordered to avoid military action in the Russian civil war, they inevitably cooperated with British and French forces in attempts to roll back Bolshevik influence. Wilson said publicly that he authorized the expedition only to prevent German seizure of military supplies and a railroad, but he quickly approved $50 million in secret payments to White armies fighting the Bolsheviks. Wilson's motives were thus "simultaneously anti-German and anti-Bolshevik."[122] Some 5,000 American troops suffered through a bitter winter of fifty-below-zero temperatures. Their morale sagged; mutiny threatened. In December 1918, Senator Hiram Johnson introduced a resolution to withdraw them from Russia. It failed by one vote. U.S. soldiers did not leave Russia until June 1919. Two hundred twenty-two American soldiers died in what critics dubbed "Mr. Wilson's little war with Russia."[123]

A. Mitchell Palmer (1872– 1936). When U.S. troops were intervening in Bolshevik Russia, Wilson's attorney general, A. Mitchell Palmer, was chasing suspected radicals at home. An architect of the "Red Scare," Palmer believed that the "blaze of revolution" was "eating its way into the homes of the American workmen, its sharp tongues of revolutionary heat … licking the altars of the churches, leaping into the belfry of the school bell, crawling into the sacred corners of American homes, burning up the foundations of society." After jailing and deporting thousands with little or no due process, Palmer claimed that the government could not "stand idly by and wait for the actual throwing of bombs or the actual use of arms in military operations before it can defend itself." (Library of Congress)

Wilson claimed to be "sweating blood over the question of what is right and feasible … in Russia. It goes to pieces like quicksilver under my touch."[124] Pressure from the deeply anticommunist French and British and expansionist Japanese and his own anti-Bolshevism inclined him to send another expedition, this time to Siberia, where many envisioned the growth of a non-Bolshevik Russian bastion. In July 1918, he approved the expedition, later officially explaining to the American people that he was sending the troops (eventually numbering 10,000) to rescue a group of 70,000 Czechs stranded in Russia. Organized earlier as part of the tsarist Russian army to fight for a Czech homeland in Austria-Hungary, the Czech legion was battling Bolsheviks along the Trans-Siberian Railroad in an effort to reach Vladivostok and possible transportation to the western front. Wilson's avowed purpose of evacuating the Czech legion derived also from his "friendly feelings" for Professor Thomas Masaryk and Czechoslovakia's independence, which Wilson soon recognized in October.[125]

Despite his disingenuous official explanation, Wilson believed that "a limited, indirect intervention to help the Russian people overcome domination by Bolsheviks and Germans would not contradict, but rather [would] facilitate self-determination."[126] Yet intervention in Siberia became openly anti-Bolshevik because the Czechs were fighting Lenin's forces. Once Wilson found it impossible to evacuate the Czechs in time for them to fight in Europe, he reluctantly bowed to Allied pressure and gave support to the anti-Bolshevik White Russian leader Admiral A. V. Kolchak in the hope that he could form a pro-Western constitutional government. Despite money and supplies from the Allies, Kolchak faltered and his armies were routed before they could reach Moscow in June 1919. U.S. troops finally withdrew from Siberia in 1920, with one departing soldier noting that Vladivostok looked better in photographs because "the 'smell' ain't in the pictures or it m't be 'good night' when you opened the letter that contained them."[127]

At the Paris peace conference, the victors tried to isolate what they considered revolutionary contagion. The organization of the Third International in Moscow in early 1919 alarmed postwar leaders, as did communist Bela Kun's successful revolution in Hungary in March 1919, which lasted only until August. Accordingly, the conferees granted territory to Russia's neighbors (Poland, Romania, and Czechoslovakia) and recognized the nations of Finland, Estonia, Latvia, and Lithuania as a ring of states unfriendly to Russia. During the conference, besides the military interventions, the Allies imposed a strict economic blockade on Russia, sent aid to the White forces, and extended relief assistance to Austria and Hungary to stem political unrest.

Even though Wilson perceived the Soviets as the "negation of everything that is American," he never settled on a definitive, workable policy to co-opt or smash Bolshevism.[128] By not leading decisively, the president allowed subordinates and circumstances to determine U.S. policy toward Russia. His growing estrangement at Versailles from Colonel House, a conduit for pro-Soviet liberals, meant that the interventionist Allies and the rabidly anti-Bolshevik Secretary Lansing exerted greater influence.

Wilson's one serious effort to end the civil war in Russia through diplomacy came in January 1919 when he invited the warring groups to meet on Prinkipo

Island off the Turkish coast. The Bolsheviks cautiously accepted the invitation, but the anti-Bolsheviks rejected any meeting. Next, in February, House helped arrange a trip by William C. Bullitt, a member of the U.S. delegation at Versailles, and Lincoln Steffens, the radical muckraking journalist, to Russia. Wilson envisioned only a fact-finding mission. The ambitious Bullitt nonetheless negotiated a proposal whereby the Allies would withdraw their troops, suspend military aid to White forces, and lift the economic blockade; in return the Soviets promised a cease-fire in which their opponents would hold the territories they occupied. Bullitt and Steffens returned to Paris convinced that their agreement would satisfy all parties. Lloyd George opposed it; Wilson ignored it. Bullitt resigned in protest.

The Allied counterrevolution proved costly. "It intensified the civil war and sent thousands of Russians to their deaths," the British official Bruce Lockhart later wrote. "Its direct effect was to provide the Bolsheviks with a cheap victory, … and to galvanize them into a strong and ruthless organism."[129] Kremlin leaders also nurtured long memories. "Never have any of our soldiers been on American soil," Premier Nikita S. Khrushchev lectured Americans as late as 1959, "but your soldiers were on Russian soil."[130] Participation by such young men as Allen and John Foster Dulles in Wilson's "secret war" against the Bolsheviks provided "the formative experiences that inclined [them] to rely on propaganda and covert action" when they later directed U.S. policies during the Cold War.[131] Such tactics ultimately backfired, as Wilson recognized before his death. "Bolshevism is a mistake," Wilson said. "If left alone it will destroy itself. It cannot survive because it is wrong."[132]

The Whispering Gallery of Global Disorder

More than 116,000 American soldiers died in World War I, which cost the U.S. government more than $30 billion. A third of the figure was paid through taxes; the other two-thirds represented borrowed money, which postwar generations would have to pay back. If one counts the long-term expense of veterans' benefits, the cost to the United States probably equaled three times the immediate direct costs. What President Dwight D. Eisenhower would later call the "military-industrial complex" had its origins in a high degree of government-business cooperation during the war; economic decision making for the nation became centralized as never before; and the increased application of efficient methods in manufacturing contributed to U.S. economic power. The era of World War I witnessed other domestic events that impinged on foreign affairs: racial conflict, evidenced by twenty-five race riots in 1919; suppression of civil liberties under the Espionage and Sedition Acts, by which people who dissented from the war were silenced; the stunting of radical commentary (Socialist leader Eugene Debs and the pacifist Alice Paul, among others, went to jail for opposing the war) and hence the imposition of coercive consensus; and the withering of the reform impulse.

In foreign affairs, the White House assumed more authority in initiating policy and controlling its execution. The State Department read diplomatic messages that Wilson had typed on his own machine. Wilson bypassed Congress on a number of occasions, failing to consult that body about the Fourteen Points, the goals at Paris,

The Cambridge American Cemetery and Memorial. The American Doughboy-poet John McCrae famously wrote: "In Flanders Field the poppies blow / Between the crosses row on row." England's Cambridge University donated thirty acres that contain the graves of 3,812 American war dead. Even though these concentric circles of white gravestones evoke an atmosphere of serenity and repose, the wartime ambulance driver Ernest Hemingway later wrote: "I had seen nothing sacred, and the things that were glorious had no glory and the sacrifices were like the stockyards at Chicago." (Courtesy American Battle Monuments Commission)

and the intervention in Russia. He acted "like a divine-right monarch in the conduct of foreign relations."[133] The Senate finally rebelled by rejecting the League of Nations, but that negative decision did not reverse the trend of growing presidential power over foreign policy.

World War I took the lives of some 14,663,400 people—8 million soldiers and 6.6 million civilians, not including victims of the influenza pandemic. Russia led with 3.7 million dead; Germany followed with 2.6 million; then came France with 1.4 million, Austria-Hungary with 950,000, and Britain with 939,000. One out of every two French males who would have been between the ages of twenty and thirty-two in 1914 died during the war. It had been a total war, involving whole societies, not merely their armies. Never before had a war left the belligerents so exhausted, so battered. New destructive weapons made their debut—tanks, airplanes, poison gas, and submarines—"a preview of the Pandora's box of evils that the linkage of science with industry in the service of war was to mean."[134] The war reinforced American desires to avoid foreign entanglement. Captain of Artillery Harry S. Truman of Missouri claimed that most soldiers "don't give a whoop (to put it mildly) whether Russia has a Red Government or no government and if the King of the Lollipops wants to slaughter his subjects or his Prime Minister it's all the same to us."[135] Disillusioned clergy regretted their participation in the "shrieking and hysterical patriotism."[136] The war had ended "the artificial glow of past American idealism," wrote the novelist Ellen Glasgow.[137]

World War I stacked the cards for the future by bequeathing "time bombs" of political instability.[138] "Empires cannot be shattered and new states raised upon their ruins without disturbance," noted Colonel House.[139] The Europe-oriented international order of the turn of the century fragmented and left, in Thomas Masaryk's words, "a laboratory atop a vast cemetery" that included several new states in central and eastern Europe.[140] In what the historian Erez Manela has called the "Wilsonian Moment," anticolonial nationalists in Egypt, India, Korea, Indochina, and elsewhere capitalized on Wilson's rhetoric of self-determination to set goals of "full-fledged" autonomous nationhood based in part on Wilson's ideal of self-determination.[141] "Wilson's proposals, once set forth, could not be recalled," said Sun Zhongshan (Sun Yat-Sen) in 1924 as his China battled imperialist domination.[142] In Latin America, prewar economic ties with Europe withered, inviting the United States to expand its interests there, even though nationalists resented the greater North American presence. The rise of Bolshevism in Russia and the hostility it aroused around the world made an already fluid international system even more so. Because of fear of a revived Germany, European leaders tried to strip it of power, creating bitter resentments among the German people. Facing reconstruction problems at home, the victors tagged Germany with a huge reparations bill that would disorient the world economy. Nobody seemed happy with the postwar settlement; many would attempt to recapture lost opportunities or to redefine the terms. Yet to blame World War II on Wilson's failures, as the historian Margaret MacMillan has noted, "is to ignore the actions of everyone—political leaders, diplomats, soldiers, ordinary voters—for twenty years between 1919 and 1939."[143]

World War I made the United States the world's leading economic power. Wilson confidently predicted: "The financial leadership will be ours. The industrial primacy will be ours. The commercial advantage will be ours."[144] During the war years, to meet the need for raw materials, American companies expanded operations in developing nations. Goodyear went into the Dutch East Indies for rubber, Swift and Armour reached into South America, tin interests tapped Bolivia, copper companies penetrated Chile, and oil firms sank new wells in Latin America and gained new concessions in the Middle East. Washington encouraged this economic expansion by building up the merchant marine, which by 1919 had grown 60 percent larger than its prewar size. By 1920 the United States produced about 40 percent of the world's coal and 50 percent of its pig iron.

Because the U.S. government and American citizens loaned heavily to the Allies during the war, the nation shifted from a debtor to a creditor, with New York replacing London as the world's financial center. Whereas before the war Americans owed foreigners some $3 billion, after the conflict foreigners owed Americans and the U.S. government about $13 billion ($10 billion of which represented other governments' debts). Americans had devised plans to seize the apparent economic opportunities given them by the war—the Edge Act to permit the establishment of foreign branch banks, and the Webb-Pomerene Act to allow trade associations to continue to combine for export trading without fear of antitrust action, for example—but a key question remained: How could Europeans liquidate their enormous indebtedness to the United States? The answer lay somewhere in a complicated tangle of loans, reparations, tariffs, and world trade.

Economic disorder and political instability thus became the twin legacies of global war. "The world is all now one single whispering gallery," Wilson asserted in September 1919. "All the impulses … reach to the ends of the earth; … with the tongue of the wireless and the tongue of the telegraph, all the suggestions of disorder are spread." More than most Americans, Woodrow Wilson understood that global interdependence exposed America to "disorder and discontent and dissolution throughout the world."[145] And, he admitted with supreme regret, "democracy has not yet made the world safe against irrational revolution."[146]

FURTHER READING FOR THE PERIOD 1914–1920

Many of the works listed in the last chapter also explore the themes, events, and personalities in the era of World War I. See also Anthony Boyle, *Foundations of World Order* (1999); John W. Chambers, *The Tyranny of Change* (1992); Alan Dawley, *Changing the World* (2003); Robert E. Hannigan, *The New World Power* (2002); Ellis W. Hawley, *The Great War and the Search for a Modern Order* (1992); Clayton D. James and Anne Sharp Wells, *America and the Great War* (1998); Bernadotte E. Schmitt and Harold C. Vedeler, *The World in the Crucible, 1914–1919* (1984); Tony Smith, *America's Mission* (1994); David Stevenson, *Cataclysm* (2004); and Spencer C. Tucker, *The Great War* (1998).

For Woodrow Wilson and his foreign-policy views, consult Lloyd E. Ambrosius, *Wilsonianism* (2002); Louis Auchincloss, *Woodrow Wilson* (2000); H. W. Brands, *Woodrow Wilson* (2003); Kendrick A. Clements, *The Presidency of Woodrow Wilson* (1990) and *Woodrow Wilson* (1987); John Milton Cooper, Jr., *The Warrior and the Priest* (1983); Ross Kennedy, *The Will to Believe* (2008); Thomas J. Knock, *To End All Wars* (1992); Phyllis Lee Levin, *Edith and Woodrow* (2001); Arthur S. Link, *Wilson* (1960–1965) and *Woodrow Wilson* (1979); Barksdale Maynard, *Woodrow Wilson* (2008); Frank Ninkovich, *The Wilsonian Century* (1999); Jan Willem Schulte Nordholt, *Woodrow Wilson* (1991); and John A. Thompson, *Woodrow Wilson* (2001).

Wilson's health problems and their relationship to decision making are examined in Robert H. Ferrell, *Ill-Advised* (1992), and Edwin A. Weinstein, *Woodrow Wilson: A Medical and Psychological Biography* (1981). See also the essays by Dr. Bert E. Park in volumes of Arthur S. Link et al., eds., *The Papers of Woodrow Wilson,* and Park's *Ailing, Aging, and Addicted* (1993) and *The Impact of Illness on World Leaders* (1986).

Central actors in the period's drama are presented in LeRoy Ashby, *William Jennings Bryan* (1987); Kendrick A. Clements, *William Jennings Bryan* (1982); Paolo Coletta, *William Jennings Bryan* (1956–1969); John Milton Cooper, Jr., *Walter Hines Page* (1977); Ross Gregory, *Walter Hines Page* (1970); Geoffrey Hodgson, *Woodrow Wilson's Right Hand* (2006) (Edward House); Jim Lacey, *Pershing* (2008); Gerald Leinwand, *William Jennings Bryan* (2007); George H. Nash, *The Life of Herbert Hoover* (1996); Ronald Steel, *Walter Lippmann and the American Century* (1981); David P. Thelen, *Robert M. La Follette and the Insurgent Spirit* (1976); and William C. Widenor, *Henry Cabot Lodge and the Search for an American Foreign Policy* (1980).

For European questions and the neutrality issue on the U.S. road to World War I, see Thomas A. Bailey and Paul B. Ryan, *The Lusitania Disaster* (1975); Henry Blumenthal, *Illusion and Reality in Franco-American Diplomacy, 1914–1945* (1986); John W. Coogan, *The End of Neutrality* (1981); David M. Esposito, *The Legacy of Woodrow Wilson* (1996); Robert H. Ferrell, *Woodrow Wilson and World War I* (1985); Richard M. Gamble, *The War for Righteousness* (2003); Ross Gregory, *The Origins of American Intervention in the First World War* (1971); Ernest R. May, *The World War and American Isolation, 1914–1917* (1959); Diana Preston, *Lusitania* (2002); David Ramsey, *Lusitania* (2002); Hew Strachan, *The First World War* (2003); and Robert W. Tucker, *Woodrow Wilson and the Great War* (2007).

The German-American relationship is spotlighted in Reinhard R. Doerries, *Imperial Challenge* (1989); Manfred Jonas, *The United States and Germany* (1984); Hans-Jürgen Schröder, ed., *Confrontation and Cooperation* (1993); and Barbara Tuchman, *The Zimmermann Telegram* (1958).

The Anglo-American relationship is featured in Kathleen Burk, *Britain, America, and the Sinews of War, 1914–1918* (1985); G. R. Conyne, *Woodrow Wilson: British Perspectives, 1912–21* (1992); and Joyce G. Williams, *Colonel House and Sir Edward Grey* (1984).

For the peace movement, see works cited in the previous chapter and Charles DeBenedetti, ed., *Peace Heroes in Twentieth-Century America* (1986); Allen F. Davis, *American Heroine* (1974) (Addams); Frances H. Early, *A World Without War* (1997); Barbara S. Kraft, *The Peace Ship* (1978); Kathleen Kennedy, *Subversive Mothers and Scurrilous Citizens* (1999); Erika A. Kuhlman, *Petticoats and White Feathers* (1997); Ernest A. McKay, *Against Wilson and War* (1996); David S. Patterson, *The Search for a Negotiated Peace* (2008); and Allison L. Sneider, *Suffragettes in an Imperial Age* (2008).

America's preparedness and warmaking experiences are discussed in Robert B. Bruce, *A Fraternity of Arms: America & France in the Great War* (2003); John W. Chambers, *To Raise an Army* (1987); J. Garry Clifford, *The Citizen Soldiers* (1972); Wesley K. Clark, *Pershing* (2008); Edward M. Coffman, *The War to End All Wars* (1968); Byron Farrell, *Over There* (1999); Robert H. Ferrell, *America's Deadliest Battle* (2007); Kenneth J. Hagan, *This People's Navy* (2008); Jennifer D. Keene, *The Doughboys, the Great War, and the Remaking of America* (2002); Thomas C. Leonard, *Above the Battle* (1978); Bullitt Lowry, *Armistice, 1918* (1997); William N. Still, *The Crisis at Sea* (2007); David F. Trask, *The AEF and Coalition Warmaking* (1993), *Captains & Cabinets: Anglo-American Naval Relations, 1917–1918* (1980), and *The United States in the Supreme War Council* (1961); Jonathan Reed Winkler, *Nexus* (2008) (strategic communications); David R. Woodward, *Trial by Friendship: Anglo-American Relations, 1917–1918* (1993); Susan Zeiger, *In Uncle Sam's Service* (1999) (women); and Robert H. Zieger, *America's Great War* (2001).

For the wartime home front, civil-liberties issues, and propaganda, see Allan M. Brandt, *No Magic Bullet* (1985) (venereal disease); Alfred W. Crosby, *America's Forgotten Pandemic* (1989); Leslie Midkiff DeBauche, *Reel Patriotism* (1997); Mark Ellis, *Race, War, and Surveillance* (2002); David M. Kennedy, *Over Here* (1980); Elizabeth McKillen, *Chicago Labor and the Quest for a Democratic Diplomacy* (1995); Joseph A. McCartin, *Labor's Great War* (1998); Paul L. Murphy, *World War I and the Origin of Civil Liberties* (1979); Richard Polenberg, *Fighting Faiths* (1987); Ronald Schaffer, *America in the Great War* (1991); John A. Thompson, *Reformers and War* (1986); and Stephen Vaughn, *Hold Fast the Inner Lines* (1980) (Committee on Public Information).

The Versailles peacemaking and League debate are discussed in Lloyd E. Ambrosius, *Wilsonian Statecraft* (1991) and *Woodrow Wilson and the American Diplomatic Tradition* (1987); Manfred F. Boeneke et al., eds., *The Treaty of Versailles* (1998); John M. Cooper, Jr., *Breaking the Heart of the World* (2002); Inga Floto, *Colonel House in Paris* (1973); Lawrence E. Gelfand, *The Inquiry* (1963); Derek Heater, *National Self-Determination* (1994); Warren F. Kuehl, *Seeking World Order* (1969); Warren F. Kuehl and Lynne K. Dunne, *Keeping the Covenant* (1997); Antony Lentin, *Lloyd George, Woodrow Wilson, and the Guilt of Germany* (1985); Margaret MacMillan, *Paris 1919* (2002); Erez Manela, *The Wilsonian Moment* (2007); Herbert F. Margulies, *The Mild Reservationists* (1989); Daniela Rossini, *Woodrow Wilson and the American Myth in Italy* (2007); Klaus Schwabe, *Woodrow Wilson, Revolutionary Germany, and Peacemaking* (1985); Alan Sharp, *The Versailles Settlement* (1991); Ralph A. Stone, *The Irreconcilables* (1970); Marc Trachenberg, *Reparations in World Politics* (1986); and Arthur Walworth, *America's Moment, 1918* (1977) and *Wilson and His Peacemakers* (1986).

The U.S. response to Bolshevism, intervention in Russia, and the Red Scare are investigated in Kenneth D. Acherman, *Young J. Edgar* (2007); Leo Bacino, *Reconstructing Russia* (1999); Donald E. Davis and Eugene P. Trani, *The First Cold War* (2000); Victor M. Fic, *The Collapse of American Policy in Russia and Siberia, 1918* (1995); David S. Foglesong, *America's Secret War Against Bolshevism* (1995); Lloyd Gardner, *Safe for Democracy* (1984); George F. Kennan, *Russia Leaves the War* (1956) and *The Decision to Intervene* (1958); Linda Killen, *The Russian Bureau* (1983); N. Gordon Levin, Jr., *Woodrow Wilson and World Politics* (1968); Arthur S. Link, ed., *Woodrow Wilson and a Revolutionary World, 1913–1921* (1982); Arno Mayer, *Politics and Diplomacy of Peacemaking* (1967); David W. McFadden, *Alternative Paths* (1993); William Pencak, *For God and Country* (1989) (American Legion); Benjamin D. Rhodes, *The Anglo-American Winter War with Russia, 1918–1919* (1988); Neil V. Salzman, *Reform and Revolution* (1991) (Robins); Norman Saul, *War and Revolution* (2001); Ilya Somin, *Stillborn Crusade* (1996); John Thompson, *Russia, Bolshevism, and the Versailles Peace* (1966); and Betty Miller Unterberger, *America's Siberian Expedition* (1956) and *The United States, Revolutionary Russia, and the Rise of Czechoslovakia* (1989).

U.S. economic expansion abroad during the war is studied in Burton I. Kaufman, *Efficiency and Expansion* (1974); Emily S. Rosenberg, *World War I and the Growth of United States Predominance in Latin America* (1987); and Jeffrey J. Safford, *Wilsonian Maritime Diplomacy, 1913–1921* (1978).

Also see the General Bibliography, the following notes, and Robert L. Beisner, ed., *Guide to American Foreign Relations Since 1600* (2003).

NOTES TO CHAPTER 8

1. Quoted in Thomas Bailey and Paul Ryan, *The* Lusitania *Disaster* (New York: Free Press, 1975), p. 81.
2. Quoted in Edward Ellis, *Echoes of Distant Thunder* (New York: Coward, McCann & Geoghegan, 1975), p. 195.
3. Quoted in Bailey and Ryan, Lusitania *Disaster,* p. 94.
4. Quoted *ibid.,* p. 82.
5. Quoted *ibid.,* p. 133.
6. Quoted in C. L. Droste and W. H. Tantum, eds., *The* Lusitania *Case* (Riverside, Conn.: 7 C's Press, 1972), p. 172.
7. Quoted in Burton J. Hendrick, *Life and Letters of Walter Hines Page* (Garden City, N.Y.: Doubleday, Page, 1922–1925; 3 vols.), *II,* 2.
8. William Jennings Bryan and Mary B. Bryan, *Memoirs* (Chicago: Winston, 1925), pp. 398–399.
9. Quoted in William Harbaugh, *The Life and Times of Theodore Roosevelt* (New York: Oxford University Press, 1975), p. 448.
10. John Milton Cooper, Jr., *The Warrior and the Priest* (Cambridge: Harvard University Press, 1983), p. 288.
11. R. S. Baker and W. E. Dodd, eds., *Public Papers of Woodrow Wilson* (New York: Harper & Brothers, 1926; 2 vols.), *I,* 321.
12. Quoted in August Hecksher, *Woodrow Wilson* (New York: Charles Scribner's Sons, 1991), p. 365.
13. *Foreign Relations, 1915, Supplement* (Washington, D.C.: Government Printing Office, 1928), p. 396.
14. Quoted in Richard R. Doerries, *Imperial Challenge* (Chapel Hill: University of North Carolina Press, 1989), p. 105.
15. Robert W. Tucker, *Woodrow Wilson and the Great War* (Charlottesville: University of Virginia Press, 2007), p. 110.
16. Quoted in LeRoy Ashby, *William Jennings Bryan* (Boston: Twayne, 1987), p. 161.
17. Quoted in Doerries, *Imperial Challenge,* p. 111.
18. Bailey and Ryan, Lusitania *Disaster,* p. 340.
19. Robert Lansing, *War Memoirs* (Indianapolis: Bobbs-Merrill, 1935), p. 128.
20. Ray S. Baker quoted in Arthur S. Link et al., eds., *The Papers of Woodrow Wilson* (Princeton: Princeton University Press, 1989), *LXI,* 383.
21. Quoted in Rohan Butler, "The Peace Settlement of Versailles, 1918–1933," in C. L. Mowat, ed., *The New Cambridge Modern History,* vol. *XII* (Cambridge, Eng.: Cambridge University Press, 1968), p. 214.
22. Quoted in Zara Steiner, *The Lights That Failed: European International History, 1919-1933* (New York: Oxford University Press, 2005), p. 35.
23. Lansing quoted in Margaret MacMillan, *Paris 1919* (New York: Random House, 2002), p. 10.
24. Quoted in C. D. Lewis, ed., *The Collected Poems of Wilfred Owen* (New York: New Directions, 1965), p. 42.
25. Quoted in Robert E. Hannigan, *The New World Power* (Philadelphia: University of Pennsylvania Press, 2002), p. 228.
26. Baker and Dodd, *Public Papers, I,* 157–159.
27. Wilson quoted in Michael H. Hunt, *The American Ascendancy* (Chapel Hill: University of North Carolina Press, 2007), p. 59.
28. Quoted in Alexander DeConde, *Ethnicity, Race, and American Foreign Policy* (Boston: Northeastern University Press, 1992), p. 86.
29. Quoted in Alan Kramer, *Dynamic of Destruction* (New York: Oxford University Press, 2007), p. 46.
30. Quoted in Barbara Tuchman, *The Guns of August* (New York: Dell [1962], 1963), p. 153.
31. *Life* quoted in Mark Sullivan, *Our Times* (New York: Charles Scribner's Sons, 1926–1937; 6 vols.), *V,* 59.
32. Quoted in Ray Stannard Baker, *Woodrow Wilson* (New York: Doubleday, Doran, 1927–1939; 8 vols.), *V,* 175.
33. Quoted in Elisabeth Glaser, "J. P. Morgan & Company and Aid for the Allies, 1914–1916," in Elisabeth Glaser and Hermann Wellenreuther, eds., *Bridging the Atlantic* (New York: Cambridge University Press, 2002), p. 230.
34. Quoted in Ross A. Kennedy, "Woodrow Wilson, World War I, and an American Conception of National Security," *Diplomatic History, XXV* (Winter 2001), 23.
35. Frederick Dixon quoting Wilson in G. R. Conyne, *Woodrow Wilson* (New York: St. Martin's, 1992), p. 51.
36. Quoted in Frederick S. Calhoun, *Uses of Force and Wilsonian Foreign Policy* (Kent, Ohio: Kent State University Press, 1993), p. 100.
37. Quoted in Arthur S. Link, *Woodrow Wilson and the Progressive Era, 1910–1917* (New York: Harper and Row, 1954), p. 203.
38. French report quoted in Joyce G. Williams, *Colonel House and Sir Edward Grey* (Lanham, Md.: University Press of America, 1984), p. 83.
39. Quoted in Arthur S. Link, *Wilson: Confusions and Crises, 1915–1916* (Princeton: Princeton University Press, 1964), pp. 134–135.
40. Bryan and Bryan, *Memoirs,* p. 397.
41. *Foreign Relations, 1915, Supplement,* p. 461.
42. Link, *Papers of Wilson, XXXVI* (1981), 213–214.
43. Samuel Flagg Bemis, "A Worcester County Student in Wartime London and Paris (via Harvard): 1915–1916," *New England Galaxy, XI* (Spring 1970), 20.
44. Quoted in Patrick Devlin, *Too Proud to Fight* (New York: Oxford University Press, 1975), p. 517.
45. Quoted in Frank Ninkovich, *Modernity and Power* (Chicago: University of Chicago Press, 1994), p. 50.
46. Quoted in Arthur S. Link, *Wilson: Campaigns for Progressivism and Peace, 1916–1917* (Princeton: Princeton University Press, 1965), p. 274.
47. Quoted *ibid.,* p. 289.
48. Lansing, *War Memoirs,* p. 212.
49. Quoted in Fred Anderson and Andrew Cayton, *The Dominion of War* (New York: Viking, 2005), p. 347.
50. Quoted in Manfred F. Boeneke, "Woodrow Wilson's Image of Germany," in Manfred F. Boeneke, Gerald D. Feldman, and Elisabeth Glaser, eds., *The Treaty of Versailles* (New York: Cambridge University Press, 1998), p. 610.
51. Quoted in Thomas W. Ryley, *A Little Group of Willful Men* (Port Washington, N.Y.: Kennikat Press, 1975), p. 2.
52. Link, *Papers of Wilson, XLI* (1983), 519–527.
53. Quoted in Alan Dawley, *Changing the World* (Princeton: Princeton University Press, 2003), pp. 145–146.
54. Quoted in Robert E. Osgood, *Ideals and Self-Interest in American Foreign Relations* (Chicago: University of Chicago Press, 1953), p. 177.
55. Quoted in Michael S. Sherry, *In the Shadow of War* (New Haven: Yale University Press, 1995), p. 8.
56. Susan Zeiger, "She Didn't Raise Her Boy to Be a Slacker," *Feminist Studies, XXII* (Spring 1996), 11–12.

57. Bradley Fiske quoted in Kenneth J. Hagan, ed., *In Peace and War* (3d. ed., Westport, Conn.: Praeger, 2008), p. 146.

58. Quoted in Kennedy, "Conception of National Security," p. 4.

59. Quoted in Kenneth J. Hagan, *The People's Navy* (New York: Free Press, 1991), p. 252.

60. Quoted in Dawley, *Changing the World,* p. 94.

61. Quoted in Barbara S. Kraft, *The Peace Ship* (New York: Macmillan, 1978), p. 1.

62. Quoted in Thomas J. Knock, *To End All Wars* (New York: Oxford University Press, 1992), p. 63.

63. Jane Addams, *Peace and Bread in Time of War* (New York: King's Crown Press, 1945), p. 58.

64. Erika Kuhlman, *Petticoats and White Feathers* (Westport, Conn.: Greenwood, 1997), p. 56.

65. Quoted in J. Garry Clifford, *The Citizen Soldiers* (Lexington: University Press of Kentucky, 1972), p. 123.

66. Quoted in Clifford Putney, *Muscular Christianity* (Cambridge: Harvard University Press, 2001), p. 172.

67. General Tasker Bliss quoted in Calhoun, *Uses of Force,* p. 114.

68. Quoted in David Traxel, *Crusader Nation* (New York: Knopf, 2006), p. 296.

69. Colonel Charles Stanton quoted in Robert B. Bruce, *A Fraternity of Arms* (Lawrence: University Press of Kansas, 2003), p. 94.

70. James A. Marone, *Hellfire Nation* (New Haven: Yale University Press, 2003), p. 313.

71. Richard T. Arndt, *The First Resort of Kings* (Washington: Potomac Books, 2006), p. 25.

72. Quoted in Allen F. Davis, "Welfare, Reform, and World War I," *American Quarterly, XIX* (Fall 1967), 531.

73. Quoted in Ninkovich, *Modernity and Power,* p. 52.

74. Link, *Papers of Wilson, XLVII* (1984), 270.

75. Robert H. Ferrell, *America's Deadliest Battle* (Lawrence: University Press of Kansas, 2007), p. xi.

76. Quoted in Donald Smythe, *Pershing* (Bloomington: Indiana University Press, 1986), p. 237.

77. Link, *Papers of Wilson, XLV* (1984), 529.

78. Quoted in Selig Adler, *The Isolationist Impulse* (New York: Collier Books, [1957], 1961), pp. 60–61.

79. H. G. Nicholas essay in *Wilson's Diplomacy* (Cambridge: Schenkman, 1973), p. 81.

80. Quoted in James D. Startt, "American Propaganda in Britain During World War I," *Prologue, XXVIII* (Spring 1996), 20.

81. Knock, *To End All Wars,* p. 180.

82. Quoted in Inbal Rose, *Conservatism and Foreign Policy During the Lloyd George Coalition 1918–1922* (London: Frank Cass, 1999), p. 121.

83. Quoted in William C. Widenor, "The Structure of the American Interpretation: The Pro-Treaty Version," in Boeneke, *Treaty of Versailles,* p. 550.

84. Quoted in David W. McFadden, *Alternative Paths* (New York: Oxford University Press, 1993), p. 209.

85. Quoted in Herbert Hoover, *The Ordeal of Woodrow Wilson* (New York: McGraw-Hill, 1958), p. 254.

86. Quoted in Walter A. McDougall, *Promised Land, Crusader State* (Boston: Houghton Mifflin, 1997), p. 139.

87. Quoted in Neil Smith, *American Empire* (Berkeley: University of California Press, 2003), p. 169.

88. Quoted in Michael B. Oren, *Power, Faith, and Fantasy* (New York: Norton, 2007), pp. 365, 382.

89. Quoted in John Milton Cooper, Jr., *Breaking the Heart of the World* (New York: Cambridge University Press, 2001), p. 85; quoted in Noriko Kawamura, *Turbulence in the Pacific* (Westport, Conn.: Praeger, 2000), p. 148.

90. Quoted in Erez Manela, "Imagining Woodrow Wilson in Asia: Dreams of East-West Harmony and the Revolt against Empire in 1919," *American Historical Review, CXI* (December 2006), 1349.

91. Quoted in Mark Philip Bradley, *Imagining Vietnam and America* (Chapel Hill: University of North Carolina Press, 2000), p. 10.

92. Quoted in Lawrence E. Gelfand, "Where Ideals Confront Self-Interest," *Diplomatic History, XVIII* (Winter 1994), 133.

93. Billy Hughes quoted in David Reynolds, *Britannia Overruled* (New York: Longman, 2000), p. 110.

94. U.S. Congress, Senate, *Treaties,* Senate Doc. 348 (Washington, D.C.: Government Printing Office, 1923), pp. 3336–3345.

95. Link, *Papers of Wilson, LV* (1985), 177.

96. Antony Lentin, *Lloyd George, Woodrow Wilson, and the Guilt of Germany* (Baton Rouge: Louisiana State University Press, 1984), p. 132.

97. Wilson quoted in Cooper, *Breaking the Heart,* p. 62.

98. Quoted in D. F. Fleming, *The United States and the League of Nations, 1918–1920* (New York: Russell & Russell, 1968), p. 134.

99. Quoted in Beth McKillen, "The Corporatist Model, World War I, and the Debate over the League of Nations," *Diplomatic History, XV* (Spring 1991), 174.

100. Link, *Papers of Wilson, LXI* (1989), 436.

101. Quoted in Louis Auchincloss, *Woodrow Wilson* (New York: Viking, 2000), p. 112.

102. Quoted in Michael Lind, *The American Way of Strategy* (New York: Oxford University Press, 2006), p. 97.

103. Quoted in Kennedy, "Conception of National Security," p. 30.

104. Robert David Johnson, *The Peace Progressives and American Foreign Relations* (Cambridge: Harvard University Press, 1995), p. 102.

105. Quoted in William C. Widenor, "The United States and the Versailles Peace Settlement," in John M. Carroll and George C. Herring, Jr., eds., *Modern American Diplomacy* (Wilmington, Del.: Scholarly Resources, 1986), p. 49.

106. Quoted in Lloyd E. Ambrosius, *Woodrow Wilson and the American Diplomatic Tradition* (New York: Cambridge University Press, 1987), p. 139.

107. Quoted in Osgood, *Ideals and Self-Interest,* p. 286.

108. Johnson, *Peace Progressives,* p. 96.

109. Wilson quoted in Frank Ninkovich, *The Wilsonian Century* (Chicago: University of Chicago Press, 1999), p. 74.

110. Quoted in David Mayers, *Dissenting Voices in America's Rise to Power* (New York: Cambridge University Press, 2007), p. 247.

111. Link, *Papers of Wilson, LXIII* (1990), 35.

112. Quoted in Lloyd E. Ambrosius, "Woodrow Wilson, Alliances, and the League of Nations," *Journal of the Gilded Age and Progressive Era, V* (April 2006), 9.

113. Quoted in Stephen C. Schlesinger, *Act of Creation* (Boulder, Col: Westview Press, 2003), p. 25.

114. Quoted in Auchincloss, *Wilson,* p. 118.

115. Walter Lippmann quoted in Walter LaFeber, "Age of American Unilateralism," in R. Laurence Moore and Maurizio Vaudagna, eds., *The American Century in Europe* (Ithaca: Cornell University Press, 2003), p. 34.

116. Goto Shimpei quoted in Sadao Asada, "Between the Old Diplomacy and the New, 1918-1922," *Diplomatic History, XXX* (April 2006), 213.

117. Quoted in John M. Thompson, *Russia, Bolshevism, and the Versailles Peace* (Princeton: Princeton University Press, 1966), pp. 3–4.

118. Quoted in David S. Foglesong, *America's Secret War Against Bolshevism* (Chapel Hill: University of North Carolina Press, 1995), p. 25.
119. Quoted in McFadden, *Alternative Paths*, p. 247.
120. Winston Churchill quoting Wilson in Lloyd C. Gardner, *Safe for Democracy* (New York: Oxford University Press, 1984), p. 239.
121. Quoted in Foglesong, *Secret War*, p. 43.
122. *Ibid.*, p. 77.
123. Quoted in Alexander DeConde, *Presidential Machismo* (Boston: Northeastern University Press, 2000), p. 106.
124. Quoted in Leo J. Bacino, *Reconstructing Russia* (Kent, Ohio: Kent State University Press, 1999), p. 76.
125. Betty Miller Unterberger, "Woodrow Wilson and the Russian Revolution," in Arthur S. Link, ed., *Woodrow Wilson and a Revolutionary World, 1913–1921* (Chapel Hill: University of North Carolina Press, 1982), p. 70.
126. Foglesong, *Secret War*, p. 190.
127. Verne Bright quoted in Norman Saul, *War and Revolution* (Lawrence: University Press of Kansas, 2001), p. 329.
128. Quoted in David S. Foglesong, *The American Mission and the "Evil Empire"* (New York: Cambridge University Press, 2007), p. 51.
129. Quoted in McFadden, *Alternative Paths*, p. 154.
130. Quoted in Benjamin D. Rhodes, *The Anglo-American War with Russia, 1918–1919* (Westport, Conn.: Greenwood, 1988), p. 123.
131. Foglesong, *Secret War*, p. 296.
132. Quoted *ibid.*, p. 291.
133. Arthur S. Link, *The Higher Realism of Woodrow Wilson* (Nashville: Vanderbilt University Press, 1971), p. 83.
134. Quoted in Gordon A. Craig, "The Revolution in War and Diplomacy," in Jack J. Roth, ed., *World War I* (New York: Knopf, 1967), p. 12.
135. Quoted in Robert H. Ferrell, *Woodrow Wilson and World War I* (New York: Harper and Row, 1985), p. 180.
136. Ozora Davis quoted in Putney, *Muscular Christianity*, p. 192.
137. Quoted in Lloyd E. Ambrosius, *Wilsonianism* (New York: Palgrave, 2002), p. 6.
138. David Stevenson, *Cataclysm* (New York: 2004), p. 477.
139. Quoted in Patrick O. Cohrs, *The Unfinished Peace after World War I* (New York: Cambridge University Press, 2006), p. 24.
140. Quoted in Tony Smith, *America's Mission* (Princeton: Princeton University Press, 1994), p. 102.
141. Erez Manela, *The Wilsonian Moment: Self-Determination and the Origins of Anticolonial Nationalism* (New York: Oxford University Press, 2007), p. 224.
142. Quoted in Hans Schmidt, "Democracy in China," *Diplomatic History, XXII* (Winter 1998), 28.
143. MacMillan, *Paris 1919*, p. 493.
144. Link, *Papers of Wilson, LXII* (1990), 47.
145. Quoted in Foglesong, *Secret War*, p. 1.
146. Quoted in Donald E. Davis and Eugene P. Trani, *The First Cold War* (Columbia: University of Missouri Press, 2002), p. 201.

APPENDIX

Makers of American Foreign Relations

Presidents	Secretaries of State	Chairs of the Senate Foreign Relations Committee
George Washington (1789–1797)	Thomas Jefferson (1790–1793) Edmund Randolph (1794–1795) Timothy Pickering (1795–1797)	
John Adams (1797–1801)	Timothy Pickering (1797–1800) John Marshall (1800–1801)	
Thomas Jefferson (1801–1809)	James Madison (1801–1809)	
James Madison (1809–1817)	Robert Smith (1809–1811) James Monroe (1811–1817)	James Barbour (1816–1817)
James Monroe (1817–1825)	John Quincy Adams (1817–1825)	James Barbour (1817–1818) Nathaniel Macon (1818–1819) James Brown (1819–1820) James Barbour (1820–1821) Rufus King (1821–1822) James Barbour (1822–1825)
John Quincy Adams (1825–1829)	Henry Clay (1825–1829)	Nathaniel Macon (1825–1826) Nathan Sanford (1826–1827) Nathaniel Macon (1827–1828) Littleton W. Tazewell (1828–1829)
Andrew Jackson (1829–1837)	Martin Van Buren (1829–1831) Edward Livingston (1831–1833) Louis McLane (1833–1834) John Forsyth (1834–1837)	Littleton W. Tazewell (1829–1832) John Forsyth (1832–1833) William Wilkins (1833–1834) Henry Clay (1834–1836) James Buchanan (1836–1837)
Martin Van Buren (1837–1841)	John Forsyth (1837–1841)	James Buchanan (1837–1841)
William H. Harrison (1841)	Daniel Webster (1841)	William C. Rives (1841)

Makers of American Foreign Relations *(continued)*

Presidents	Secretaries of State	Chairs of the Senate Foreign Relations Committee
John Tyler (1841–1845)	Daniel Webster (1841–1843) Abel P. Upshur (1843–1844) John C. Calhoun (1844–1845)	William C. Rives (1841–1842) William S. Archer (1842–1845)
James K. Polk (1845–1849)	James Buchanan (1845–1849)	William Allen (1845–1846) Ambrose H. Sevier (1846–1848) Edward A. Hannegan (1848–1849) Thomas H. Benton (1849)
Zachary Taylor (1849–1850)	John M. Clayton (1849–1850)	William R. King (1849–1850)
Millard Fillmore (1850–1853)	Daniel Webster (1850–1852) Edward Everett (1852–1853)	Henry S. Foote (1850–1851) James M. Mason (1851–1853)
Franklin Pierce (1853–1857)	William L. Marcy (1853–1857)	James M. Mason (1853–1857)
James Buchanan (1857–1861)	Lewis Cass (1857–1860) Jeremiah S. Black (1860–1861)	James M. Mason (1857–1861)
Abraham Lincoln (1861–1865)	William H. Seward (1861–1865)	Charles Sumner (1861–1865)
Andrew Johnson (1865–1869)	William H. Seward (1865–1869)	Charles Sumner (1865–1869)
Ulysses S. Grant (1869–1877)	Elihu B. Washburne (1869) Hamilton Fish (1869–1877)	Charles Sumner (1869–1871) Simon Cameron (1871–1877)
Rutherford B. Hayes (1877–1881)	William M. Evarts (1877–1881)	Hannibal Hamlin (1877–1879) William W. Eaton (1879–1881)
James A. Garfield (1881)	James G. Blaine (1881)	Ambrose E. Burnside (1881) George F. Edmunds (1881)
Chester A. Arthur (1881–1885)	Frederick T. Frelinghuysen (1881–1885)	William Windon (1881–1883) John F. Miller (1883–1885)
Grover Cleveland (1885–1889)	Thomas F. Bayard (1885–1889)	John F. Miller (1885–1887) John Sherman (1887–1889)
Benjamin Harrison (1889–1893)	James G. Blaine (1889–1892) John W. Foster (1892–1893)	John Sherman (1889–1893)
Grover Cleveland (1893–1897)	Walter Q. Gresham (1893–1895) Richard Olney (1895–1897)	John T. Morgan (1893–1895) John Sherman (1895–1897)
William McKinley (1897–1901)	John Sherman (1897–1898) William R. Day (1898) John Hay (1898–1901)	William P. Frye (1897) Cushman K. Davis (1897–1901)
Theodore Roosevelt (1901–1909)	John Hay (1901–1905) Elihu Root (1905–1909) Robert Bacon (1909)	William P. Frye (1901) Shelby M. Cullom (1901–1909)

Makers of American Foreign Relations *(continued)*

Presidents	Secretaries of State	Chairs of the Senate Foreign Relations Committee
William Howard Taft (1909–1913)	Philander C. Knox (1909–1913)	Shelby M. Cullom (1909–1913)
Woodrow Wilson (1913–1921)	William Jennings Bryan (1913–1915)	Augustus O. Bacon (1913–1915)
	Robert Lansing (1915–1920)	William J. Stone (1915–1919)
	Bainbridge Colby (1920–1921)	Henry Cabot Lodge (1919–1921)
Warren G. Harding (1921–1923)	Charles E. Hughes (1921–1923)	Henry Cabot Lodge (1921–1923)
Calvin Coolidge (1923–1929)	Charles E. Hughes (1923–1925)	Henry Cabot Lodge (1923–1924)
	Frank B. Kellogg (1925–1929)	William E. Borah (1925–1929)
Herbert C. Hoover (1929–1933)	Henry L. Stimson (1929–1933)	William E. Borah (1929–1933)
Franklin D. Roosevelt (1933–1945)	Cordell Hull (1933–1944)	Key Pittman (1933–1940)
	Edward R. Stettinius, Jr. (1944–1945)	Walter F. George (1940–1941)
		Tom Connally (1941–1945)

Presidents	Secretaries of State	Chairs of the Senate Foreign Relations Committee	Secretaries of Defense	Assistants to the President for National Security Affairs
Harry S. Truman (1945–1953)	Edward R. Stettinius, Jr. (1945)	Tom Connally (1945–1947)	James V. Forrestal (1947–1949)	
	James F. Byrnes (1945–1947)	Arthur H. Vandenberg (1947–1949)	Louis A. Johnson (1949–1950)	
	George C. Marshall (1947–1949)	Tom Connally (1949–1953)	George C. Marshall (1950–1951)	
	Dean G. Acheson (1949–1953)		Robert A. Lovett (1951–1953)	
Dwight D. Eisenhower (1953–1961)	John F. Dulles (1953–1959)	Alexander Wiley (1953–1955)	Charles E. Wilson (1953–1957)	Robert Cutler (1953–1955 & 1957–1958)
	Christian A. Herter (1959–1961)	Walter F. George (1955–1957)	Neil H. McElroy (1957–1959)	Dillon Anderson (1955–1956)
		Theodore F. Green (1957–1959)	Thomas S. Gates, Jr. (1959–1961)	William H. Jackson (1956)
		J. William Fulbright (1959–1961)		Gordon Gray (1958–1961)
John F. Kennedy (1961–1963)	Dean Rusk (1961–1963)	J. William Fulbright (1961–1963)	Robert S. McNamara (1961–1963)	McGeorge Bundy (1961–1963)
Lyndon B. Johnson (1963–1969)	Dean Rusk (1963–1969)	J. William Fulbright (1963–1969)	Robert S. McNamara (1963–1968)	McGeorge Bundy (1963–1966)
			Clark M. Clifford (1968–1969)	Walt W. Rostow (1966–1969)

Makers of American Foreign Relations *(continued)*

Presidents	Secretaries of State	Chairs of the Senate Foreign Relations Committee	Secretaries of Defense	Assistants to the President for National Security Affairs
Richard M. Nixon (1969–1974)	William P. Rogers (1969–1973) Henry A. Kissinger (1973–1974)	J. William Fulbright (1969–1974)	Melvin R. Laird (1969–1973) Elliot L. Richardson (1973) James R. Schlesinger (1973–1974)	Henry A. Kissinger (1969–1974)
Gerald R. Ford (1974–1977)	Henry A. Kissinger (1974–1977)	J. William Fulbright (1974–1975) John Sparkman (1975–1977)	James R. Schlesinger (1974–1976) Donald Rumsfeld (1976–1977)	Henry A. Kissinger (1974–1975) Brent Scowcroft (1975–1977)
James E. Carter (1977–1981)	Cyrus R. Vance (1977–1980) Edmund Muskie (1980–1981)	John Sparkman (1977–1979) Frank Church (1979–1981)	Harold Brown (1977–1981)	Zbigniew Brzezinski (1977–1981)
Ronald W. Reagan (1981–1989)	Alexander M. Haig, Jr. (1981–1982) George P. Shultz (1982–1989)	Charles Percy (1981–1985) Richard G. Lugar (1985–1987) Claiborne Pell (1987–1989)	Caspar Weinberger (1981–1987) Frank C. Carlucci (1987–1989)	Richard Alien (1981) William P. Clark, Jr. (1981–1983) Robert C. McFarlane (1983–1985) John M. Poindexter (1985–1986) Frank C. Carlucci (1986–1987) Colin L. Powell (1987–1989)
George H. W. Bush (1989–1993)	James A. Baker III (1989–1992) Lawrence Eagleburger (1992–1993)	Claiborne Pell (1989–1993)	Richard B. Cheney (1989–1993)	Brent Scowcroft (1989–1993)
William J. Clinton (1993–2001)	Warren M. Christopher (1993–1997) Madeleine K. Albright (1997–2001)	Claiborne Pell (1993–1995) Jesse Helms (1995–2001)	Les Aspin (1993–1994) William J. Perry (1994–1997) William S. Cohen (1997–2001)	Anthony Lake (1993–1996) Samuel R. Berger (1996–2001)
George W. Bush (2001–2009)	Colin L. Powell (2001–2005) Condoleezza Rice (2005–2009)	Joseph R. Biden, Jr. (2001–2003) Richard G. Lugar (2003–2007) Joseph R. Biden, Jr. (2007–2009)	Donald Rumsfeld (2001–2006) Robert Gates (2006–2009)	Condoleezza Rice (2001–2005) Stephen Hadley (2005–2009)
Barack H. Obama (2009–)	Hillary R. Clinton (2009–)	John F. Kerry (2009–)	Robert Gates (2009–)	James L. Jones, Jr. (2009–)

General Bibliography

General Reference Works

See also "Overviews of Relations with Countries, Regions, and Other Places of the World" and "Overviews of Subjects," both below, and your library's computer-based sources. Comprehensive bibliographies also appear in Robert L. Beisner, ed., *Guide to American Foreign Relations Since 1600* (2003) and Bruce W. Jentleson and Thomas G. Paterson, eds., *Encyclopedia of U.S. Foreign Relations* (1997).

Annual Surveys: *Environmental Resource Handbook* (2001–); *Facts on File* (1941–); *Human Development Report* (1990–); *Keesing's Record of World Events* (also titled *Keesing's Contemporary Archives*) (1931–); London Institute of World Affairs, *The Yearbook of World Affairs* (1947–); Alan F. Pater and Jason R. Pater, eds., *What They Said In ...: The Yearbook of World Opinion* (1971–); *Political Handbook of the World* (1928–); *The Statesmen's Year-Book World Gazetteer* (1864–); United Nations, *Demographic Yearbook* (1948–); *The World Bank Atlas* (1967–); *World Development Report* (1978–). See also "Statistics."

Atlases and Gazetteers: Ewan W. Anderson and Don Shewan, *An Atlas of World Political Flashpoints* (1993); Andrew Boyd, *An Atlas of World Affairs* (1998); Saul B. Cohen, *Columbia Gazetteer of the World* (1998); Rodger Doyle, *Atlas of Contemporary America* (1994); Robert Ferrell and Richard Natkiel, *Atlas of American History* (1987); *Hammond Atlas of the World* (1992); Derek Hayes, *The Historical Atlas of the United States* (2007); Eric Homberger, *The Penguin Historical Atlas of North America* (1995); Michael Kidron and Ronald Segal, *The State of the World Atlas* (1995); Catherine Mattson and Mark T. Mattson, *Contemporary Atlas of the United States* (1998); David Munro, ed., *Chambers World Gazetteer* (1988); *National Geographic Atlas of the World* (1992); Stuart Murray, *Atlas of American Military History* (2005); Richard Natkiel et al., eds., *Atlas of the Twentieth Century* (1982); *The New York Times Atlas of the World* (1992); *Oxford Atlas of the World* (2000); Rand McNally, *Today's World* (1996); Dan Smith, *The State of War and Peace Atlas* (1997); Dean Smith and Michael Kidron, *The State of the World Atlas* (1999); U.S. Military Academy, *West Point Atlas of American Wars* (1997).

Bibliographies: Samuel Flagg Bemis and Grace Gardner Griffin, *Guide to the Diplomatic History of the United States, 1775–1921* (1935); Richard Dean Burns, ed., *A Guide to American Foreign Relations Since 1700* (1982); Congressional Information Service, *American Foreign Policy Index* (1994–); Council on Foreign Relations, *Foreign Affairs Bibliography* (1933–1972); Byron Dexter, ed., *The Foreign Affairs 50-Year Bibliography* (1972); Frank Freidel, ed., *Harvard Guide to American History* (1974); Mary Beth Norton, ed., *Guide to Historical Literature* (1995); Francis P. Prucha, *Handbook for Research in American History* (1987). The journal *Diplomatic History* regularly publishes articles that review the historiography of major topics and periods and provide extensive bibliographical guidance. The *Journal of American History* regularly lists recent publications. Journals such as *Foreign Affairs* and *Political Science Quarterly* regularly publish reviews of recent books.

Biographical Aids: John S. Bowman, *The Cambridge Dictionary of American Biography* (1995); Asa Briggs, *A Dictionary of Twentieth Century World Biography* (1990); Mari Jo Buhle et al., eds., *The American Radical* (1994); David Crystal, ed., *The Cambridge Biographical Encyclopedia* (1994); *Current Biography* (1940–); *Dictionary of American Biography* (1928–); *Encyclopedia of World Biography* (1998); John A. Garraty and Mark C. Carnes, eds., *American National Biography* (1999); John Garraty and Jerome L. Sternstein, eds., *The Encyclopedia of American Biography* (1996); *International Who's Who* (1935–); Bernard K. Johnpoll and Harvey Klehr, eds., *Biographical Dictionary of the American Left* (1986); Warren F. Kuehl, ed., *Biographical Dictionary of Internationalists* (1983); *National Cyclopedia of American Biography* (1898–); Alan Palmer, *Who's Who in Modern History* (1980); Philip Rees, *Biographical Dictionary of the Extreme Right Since 1890* (1991); Frank W. Thackery and John E. Findling, eds., *Statesmen Who Changed the World* (1993); U.S. Department of State, *Biographic Register* (1860–1974) and *Foreign Service List* (1929–); *Who Was Who in America* (1963–); *Who's Who in America* (1899–); *Who's Who in the World* (1971–).

Chronologies: Lester H. Brune, *Chronological History of U.S. Foreign Relations* (2002); Gorton Carruth, *The Encyclopedia of American Facts and Dates* (1993) and *The Encyclopedia of World Facts and Dates* (1993); Council on Foreign Relations, *Foreign Affairs Chronology, 1978–1989* (1990) and *The United States in World Affairs* (1932–1972);

Robert H. Ferrell and John S. Bowman, eds., *The Twentieth Century* (1984); Bernard Grun, *The Timetables of History* (1991); John E. Jessup, *A Chronology of Conflict and Resolution, 1945–1985* (1989); Royal Institute of International Affairs, *Survey of International Affairs, 1920–1963* (1972–1977); Laurence Urdang, ed., *The Timetables of American History* (1996). See also "Annual Surveys."

Documentary Collections and Series: Martin P. Claussen, ed., *The National State Papers of the United States: Texts of Documents (1789–1817)* (1980–); Council on Foreign Relations, *Documents on American Foreign Relations, 1938/1939–1970* (1939–1973); Jussi M. Hanhimäki and Odd Arne Westad, eds., *The Cold War* (2004); Royal Institute of International Affairs, *Documents on International Affairs, 1928–1963* (1929–1973); Arthur M. Schlesinger, Jr., ed., *The Dynamics of World Power: A Documentary History of U.S. Foreign Policy, 1945–1973* (1973); U.S. Congress, *American State Papers* (1852–1859); U.S. Department of State, *A Decade of American Foreign Policy: Basic Documents, 1941–1949* (1985), *American Foreign Policy: Basic Documents, 1950–1955* (1957), *American Foreign Policy: Basic Documents, 1977–1980* (1983–1986), *American Foreign Policy: Current Documents, 1956–1967* (1956–1967), *American Foreign Policy: Current Documents, 1981–* (1984–), *Bulletin* (1938–), *Dispatch* (1990–), *Foreign Relations of United States 1861–* (1862–), and *Press Conferences of the Secretaries of State, 1922–1974* (n.d.); *Vital Speeches of the Day* (1934–).

Encyclopedias and Dictionaries: John Whiteclay Chambers, ed., *Oxford Companion to American Military History* (1999); Alexander DeConde et al., eds., *Encyclopedia of American Foreign Policy* (2002); *Encyclopedia of the World's Nations* (2002); John Drexel, ed., *The Facts on File Encyclopedia of the 20th Century* (1991); Graham Evans and Jeffrey Newnham, *The Penguin Dictionary of International Relations* (1999); John M. Farragher, ed., *The American Heritage Encyclopedia of American History* (1998); John E. Findling, *Dictionary of American Diplomatic History* (1989); Paul Finkelman and Joseph C. Miller, eds., *MacMillan Encyclopedia of World Slavery* (1998); Charles W. Freeman, Jr., *The Diplomat's Dictionary* (1997); Kenneth L. Hill, *Encyclopedia of Conflicts Since World War II* (1998); Bruce W. Jentleson and Thomas G. Paterson, eds., *Encyclopedia of U.S. Foreign Relations* (1997); Stanley I. Kutler, ed., *Encyclopedia of the United States in the Twentieth Century* (1995); Jeffrey A. Larson and James M. Smith, eds., *Historical Dictionary of Arms Control and Disarmament* (2005); Leonard Levy and Louis Fisher, eds., *Encyclopedia of American Presidents* (1994); Robert A. Meyers, ed., *The Encyclopedia of Environmental Analysis and Remediation* (1998); Richard B. Morris et al., *Encyclopedia of American History* (1996); Immanuel Ness, *The Encyclopedia of Global Population and Demographics* (1999); Cathal J. Nolan, *The Greenwood Encyclopedia of International Relations* (2002); Bruce Norton, *Encyclopedia of American War Heroes* (2002); James H. Olson, *Historical Dictionary of the Great Depression* (2001); Norman Polmar and

Thomas B. Allen, *Spybook: The Encyclopedia of Espionage* (2004); David Robertson, *A Dictionary on Human Rights* (2004); Jerry K. Sweeney et al., *America and the World, 1776–1998* (2000); Ruud van Dijk et al, eds., *Encyclopedia of the Cold War* (2008); Thomas G. Weiss and Sam Davis, eds., *The Oxford Handbook on the United Nations* (2007).

Statistics: Erik W. Austin and Jerome C. Clubb, *Political Facts of the United States Since 1789* (1986); International Monetary Fund, *International Financial Statistics* (1948–); George T. Kurian, ed., *The Illustrated Book of World Rankings* (1996); Robert D. Schulzinger, ed., *A Companion to American Foreign Relations* (2003); Victor Showers, *World Facts and Figures* (1989); Ruth L. Sivard, *World Military and Social Expenditures* (1974–); Charles L. Taylor and David A. Jodice, *World Handbook of Political and Social Indicators* (1983); United Nations, *Demographic Yearbook* (1948–), *Report on the World Social Situation* (1952–), and *Statistical Yearbook* (1948–); U.S. Agency for International Development, *United States Overseas Loans and Grants and Assistance from International Organizations, July 1, 1945–Sept. 30, 1980* (1981); U.S. Bureau of the Census, *Historical Statistics of the United States* (1975) and *Statistical Abstract of the United States* (1878–); U.S. Central Intelligence Agency, *Handbook of International Economic Statistics* (1971–) and *The World Factbook* (1981–); World Bank, *World Tables* (1974–); World Resources Institute, *World Resources* (1990–). See also "Annual Surveys."

Overviews of Relations with Countries, Regions, and Other Places of the World, Including Atlases and Gazetteers (A), Annual Surveys and Chronologies (AS), Bibliographies (B), Biographical Aids (BA), Chronologies (C), Encyclopedias and Dictionaries (E), and Statistics (S)

Afghanistan: Larry Goodson, *Afghanistan's Endless War* (2001); M. Hassar Kakar, *Afghanistan: The Soviet Invasion and the Afghan Response* (1995); William Maley, ed., *Fundamentalism Reborn* (2002); Nancy P. Newell and Richard S. Newell, *The Struggle for Afghanistan* (1981); Leon B. Poullada, *The Kingdom of Afghanistan and the United States, 1828–1973* (1995); Ahmed Rashid, *Taliban* (2001) and *Descent into Chaos* (2008); Jeffrey J. Roberts, *The Origins of the Conflict in Afghanistan* (2002); Barnet Rubin, *The Fragmentation of Afghanistan* (2002).

Africa: Thomas Borstelmann, *Cold War and the Color Line* (2001); Chris Cook and David Killinway, *African Political Facts Since 1945* (1991) (E); Howard F. French, *Continent for the Taking* (2004); Peter Duignan and Lewis H. Gann, *The United States and Africa* (1987); David F. Gordon et al., *The United States and Africa* (1998); Piero Gleijeses, *Conflicting Missions* (2001); Dennis Hickey and Kenneth White, *An*

Enchanting Darkness (1993); Lawrence C. Howard, *American Involvement in Africa South of the Sahara, 1800–1860* (1988); Henry F. Jackson, *From the Congo to Soweto* (1982); Zaki Laidi, *The Superpowers and Africa* (1990); Colin Legum, ed., *Africa Contemporary Record* (1968–) (AS); Michael McCarthy, *Dark Continent* (1983); Lysle E. Meyer, *The Farther Frontier* (1992); Thomas Noer, *Cold War and Black Liberation* (1985); Anthony G. Pazzanita and Tony Hodges, *Historical Dictionary of Western Sahara* (1994) (E); Peter J. Schraeder, *United States Foreign Policy Toward Africa* (1994); Elliot P. Skinner, *African-Americans and U.S. Policy Toward Africa, 1850–1924* (1992); George White, *Holding the Line* (2005); U.S. Library of Congress, *The United States and Sub-Saharan Africa* (1984) (B); Robert Anthony Waters, Jr., *Historical Dictionary of United State-Africa Relations* (2009) (E). See also countries.

Alaska: Paul S. Holbo, *Tarnished Expansion* (1983); Ronald J. Jensen, *The Alaska Purchase* (1975); Walter A. McDougall, *Let the Sea Make a Noise* (1993). See also Kushner and Saul in "Russia and the Soviet Union."

Albania: William B. Bland, *Albania* (1988) (B); Nicholas J. Costa, *Shattered Illusions* (1998).

Algeria: Charles-Robert Ageron, *Modern Algeria* (1992); Matthew Connelly, *A Diplomatic Revolution* (2002); R. Cameron Hume, *Mission to Algiers* (2007); Martin Stone, *The Agony of Algeria* (1997); Irwin W. Wall, *France, the United States, and the Algerian War* (2001). See also "North Africa."

Angola: Richard Black, *Angola* (1992) (B); Susan H. Broadhead, *Historical Dictionary of Angola* (1992) (E); Chester A. Crocker, *U.S. and Angola* (1986); Thomas Collelo, ed., *Angola* (1990); Fernando A. Guimãres, *The Origins of the Angolan Civil War* (1998); Lawrence W. Henderson, *Angola* (1979); John A. Marcum, *The Angolan Revolution* (1969, 1978); Kenneth Mokoena and Nicole Gaymon, eds., *The Angola Crises* (1991); Inge Tvedten, *Angola* (1997); George Wright, *Destruction of a Nation* (1997). See also "Africa."

Antarctica: Peter J. Beck, *The International Politics of Antarctica* (1986); Robert Headland, *Chronological List of Antarctic Expeditions* (1989) (E and C); Christopher C. Joyner and Ethel R. Theis, *Eagle over the Ice* (1997); Frank G. Klotz, *America on the Ice* (1990); Jeffrey D. Myhre, *The Antarctic Treaty System* (1986); John Stewart, *Antarctica* (1990) (E); Gilligan D. Triggs, ed., *The Antarctic Treaty Regime* (1987).

Arab World: See "Israel, Palestine, and Arab-Israeli Conflict" and "Middle East."

Arctic: Elizabeth B. Elliot-Meisel, *Arctic Diplomacy: Canada and the United States in the Northwest Passage* (1998); Clive Holland, *Arctic Exploration and Development* (1993) (E). See also "Canada."

Argentina: Alan Biggs, *Argentina* (1991) (B); Glen Dorn, *Peronistas and New Dealers* (2005); Deborah Norden and Robert Guillermo Russell, *Argentina and the United States* (2002); Harold F. Peterson, *Argentina and the United States* (1964); David Rock, *Argentina* (1985); David Sheinin, *Searching for Authority* (1998) and *United States and Argentina* (2006); Joseph Tulchin, *Argentina and the United States* (1990); Arthur P. Whitaker, *The United States and the Southern Cone* (1976). See also "Latin America."

Armenia: James B. Gidney, *A Mandate for Armenia* (1967); Vrej Nerses Neressian, *Armenia* (1993) (B).

Asia and Pacific Islands: Alexander Besher, *The Pacific Rim Almanac* (1991) (E); Jessica S. Brown et al., eds., *The United States in East Asia* (1985) (B); Frederica M. Bunge and Melinda W. Cooke, eds., *Oceania* (1985); I. C. Campbell, *A History of the Pacific Islands* (1989); Warren I. Cohen, *The Asian American Century* (2002); Donald Denoon and Stewart Firth, eds., *The Cambridge History of the Pacific Islanders* (1997); John C. Dorance, *The United States and the Pacific Islands* (1992); Norman Douglas and Ngaire Douglas, eds., *Pacific Islands Yearbook* (1932–) (AS); Arthur P. Dudden, *The American Pacific* (1992); Ainslie T. Embree, *Encyclopedia of Asian History* (1988) (E); John R. Eperjesi, *Imperialist Imaginary* (2005); Gerald Fry, *Pacific Basin and Oceania* (1987) (B); Roger W. Gale, *The Americanization of Micronesia* (1979); Marc Gallichio, *The Scramble for Asia* (2008); Arrell M. Gibson, *Yankees in Paradise* (1993); David Hanlon, *Remaking Micronesia* (1998); Donald D. Johnson, *The United States in the Pacific* (1995); Christina Klein, *Cold War Orientalism* (2003); James I. Matray, *Encyclopedia of U.S.–East Asian Relations* (2002) (E); John C. Perry, *Facing West* (1994); Priscilla Roberts, *Behind the Bamboo Curtain* (2006); Deryck Scarr, *The History of the Pacific Islands* (1990); Gerald Segal, *Rethinking the Pacific* (1990); David Shavit, *The United States in Asia* (1990) (E); Roger C. Thompson, *The Pacific Rim Since 1945* (1994); Howard Willens and Deanne C. Seimar, *National Security and Self-determination* (2000) (Micronesia). See also countries and "Vietnam and Southeast Asia."

Australia: Glen St. John Barclay, *Friends in High Places* (1985); Philip Bell, *Implicated* (1993); Norman Harper, *A Great and Powerful Friend* (1987); E. C. Paul, *Little America* (2006); Joseph Siracusa and Yeong-Han Cheong, *America's Australia, Australia's America* (1997).

Austria: Günter Bischof and Anton Pelinka, *The Americanization/Westernization of Austria* (2003); James Jay Carafano, *Waltzing into the Cold War* (2002); Audrey K. Cronin, *Great Power Politics and the Struggle over Austria, 1945–1955* (1986); Barbara Jelavich, *Modern Austria* (1988); Mellany A. Sully, *A Contemporary History of Austria* (1990); Reinhold Wagnleitner, *Coca-Colonization and the Cold War* (1994). See also "Europe."

Azerbaijan: Ian Bremmer and Ray Taras, eds., *Nations and Politics in the Soviet Successor States* (1993) Edmund Herzog, *The New Caucasus* (1999). See also "Russia and the Soviet Union."

Baltic States: Walter C. Clemens, Jr., *Baltic Independence and Russian Empire* (1991); David Flint, *The Baltic States* (1992); Kristian Gerner, *The Baltic States and the End of the Soviet Empire* (1993); Walter R. Iwaskiw, ed., *Estonia, Latvia, and Lithuania* (1996); Anatol Lieven, *The Baltic Revolution* (1993); Inese A. Smith and Marita V. Grunts, *The Baltic States* (1993).

Belarus: Helen Fedor, *Belarus and Moldova* (1995).

Belgium: Jonathan E. Helmreich, *United States Relations with Belgium and the Congo* (1998); Frank E. Hugget, *Modern Belgium* (1969). See also "Europe."

Bolivia: Rex A. Hudson and Dennis M. Haggerty, eds., *Bolivia* (1991); Kenneth D. Lehman, *Bolivia and the United States* (1999); Waltraud Q. Morales, *Bolivia* (1992).

Bosnia-Herzegovina: Ivo Daalder, *Getting to Dayton* (2000); Noel Malcolm, *Bosnia* (1994).

Brazil: Jan Black, *United States Penetration of Brazil* (1977); Elizabeth A. Cobbs, *The Rich Neighbor Policy* (1992); John Dickenson, ed., *Brazil* (1997) (B); Gerald K. Haines, *The Americanization of Brazil* (1989); Stanley Hilton, *Brazil and the Great Powers* (1975); Rex A. Hudson, ed., *Brazil* (1998); Frank McCann, *The Brazilian-American Alliance, 1937–1945* (1973); Micol Siegel, *Uneven Encounters* (2009); Joseph Smith, *Unequal Giants* (1991); Steven C. Topik, *Trade and Gunboats* (1996); W. Michael Weis, *Cold Warriors and Coups d'État* (1993).

Bulgaria: Glenn A. Curtis, ed., *Bulgaria* (1993).

Cambodia: MacAlister Brown and Joseph J. Zasloff, *Cambodia Confronts the Peacemakers, 1979–1998* (1998); David P. Chandler, *The Tragedy of Cambodian History* (1991); Kenton J. Clymer, *Troubled Relations* (2007); Michael Haas, *Cambodia, Pol Pot, and the United States* (1991); Henry Kamm, *Cambodia* (1998); Ben Kiernan, *How Pol Pot Came to Power* (1985) and *The Pol Pot Regime* (1996); Russell R. Ross, ed., *Cambodia* (1990); William Shawcross, *The Quality of Mercy* (1984) and *Sideshow* (1979).

Cameroon: Julius A. Amin, *The Peace Corps in Cameroon* (1992); Mark DeLancey, *Cameroon* (1986) (B); Mark DeLancey and H. Mbella Mokeba, *Historical Dictionary of Cameroon* (1990) (E). See also "Africa."

Canada: David J. Bercuson and J. L. Granatstein, *The Collins Dictionary of Canadian History* (1988) (E); Robert Bothwell, *Canada and the United States* (1992); Stephen Clarkson, *Uncle Sam and Us* (2003); Charles Doran, *Forgotten Partnership* (1984); John Findlay and Ken S. Coates, eds., *Parallel Destinies* (2002); J. L. Granatstein and Robert Bothwell, *Pirouette* (1990); J. L. Granatstein and Norman Hillmer, *For Better or For Worse* (1992); Lansing Lamont and Duncan Edmonds, eds., *Friends So Different* (1989); Seymour Martin Lipset, *Continental Divide* (1990); Lawrence Martin, *The Presidents and the Prime Ministers* (1982); Graeme S. Mount, *Invisible and Inaudible in Washington* (1999); Denis Smith, *Diplomacy of Fear* (1988); Reginald C. Stuart, *United States Expansionism and British North America 1775–1871* (1988); John H. Thompson and Stephen J. Randall, *Canada and the United States* (1998). See also "Great Britain."

Caribbean: Charles D. Ameringer, *The Caribbean Legion* (1974); David Healy, *Drive to Hegemony* (1988); Roger Hughes, *The Caribbean* (1987) (B); Lester D. Langley, *The United States and the Caribbean, 1900–1970* (1980) and *The United States and the Caribbean in the Twentieth Century* (1989); Sandra W. Meditz and Dennis M. Hanratty, eds., *Islands of the Commonwealth Caribbean* (1989); Harvey Neptune, *Caliban and the Yankees* (2008) (Trinidad); Robert F. Smith, *The Caribbean World and the United States* (1994).

Central African Republic: Pierre Kalck, *Historical Dictionary of the Central African Republic* (1992) (E).

Central America: Tom Barry, *Central America Inside Out* (1991) (C and E); Leslie Bethel, ed., *Central America Since Independence* (1991); Morris J. Blachman et al., eds., *Confronting Revolution* (1986); John Booth and Thomas Walker, *Understanding Central America* (1993); John Coatsworth, *Central America and the United States* (1994); Kenneth M. Coleman and George C. Herring, eds., *Understanding the Central American Crisis* (1991); John E. Findling, *Close Neighbors, Distant Friends* (1987); Kenneth J. Grieb, *Central America in the Nineteenth and Twentieth Centuries* (1988) (B); Walter LaFeber, *Inevitable Revolutions* (1993); Thomas M. Leonard, *Central America and the United States* (1991) and *Central America and U.S. Policies, 1820s–1980s* (1985) (B); Mark B. Rosenberg and Luis G. Solis, *United States and Central America* (2007); Thomas D. Schoonover, *The United States in Central America, 1860–1911* (1991); Ralph L. Woodward, *Central America* (1985).

Chad: Mario J. Azevedo, *Roots of Violence* (1998); Thomas Collelo, ed., *Chad* (1990); Samuel Decalo, *Historical Dictionary of Chad* (1987) (E).

Chile: Lubna Z. Qureshi, *Nixon, Kissinger, and Allende* (2009); Michael Francis, *The Limits of Hegemony* (1977); David Mares and

Francisco Rosas Arevena, *United States and Chile* (2001); Michael Monteon, *Chile in the Nitrate Era* (1982); Heraldo Munoz and Carlos Portales, *Elusive Friendship* (1991); William F. Sater, *Chile and the United States* (1990); Paul E. Sigmund, *The United States and Democracy in Chile* (1993).

China (and Taiwan): Gordon Chang, *Friends and Enemies* (1990); Warren I. Cohen, *America's Response to China* (2000); Jacques Downs, *The Golden Ghetto* (1997); Jonathan Fenby, *Modern China* (2008); Rosemary Foot, *The Practice of Power* (1995); Jonathan Goldstein et al., eds., *America Views China* (1991); Harry Harding, *A Fragile Relationship* (1992); Michael H. Hunt, *The Making of a Special Relationship* (1983); Chen Jian, *Mao's China and the Cold War* (2001); Arnold Xiangze Jiang, *The United States and China* (1988); Noam Kochavi, *A Conflict Perpetuated* (2002); David M. Lampton, *Same Bed Different Dreams* (2000); Wei-chin Lee, *Taiwan* (1990) (B); Ernest R. May and John K. Fairbank, eds., *America's China Trade in Historical Perspective* (1986); Thomas D. Lutze, *China's Inevitable Revolution* (2007); James Peck, *Washington's China* (2006); Simei Qing, *From Allies to Enemies* (2007); Robert S. Ross, *Negotiating Cooperation* (1995); Michael Schaller, *The United States and China* (2002); Robert Suettinger, *Beyond Tiananmen* (2003); David Shambaugh, *Beautiful Imperialist* (1991); Nancy B. Tucker, *Taiwan, Hong Kong, and the United States* (1994) and *Dangerous Strait* (2005); Qiang Zhai, *China and the Vietnam Wars* (2000); Shu Guang Zhang, *Deterrence and Strategic Culture* (1992).

Colombia: Marcelo Bucheli, *Bananas and Business* (2005); David Bushnell, *The Making of Modern Colombia* (1993); Bradley Lynn Coleman, *Colombia and the United States* (2008); Robert H. Davis, *Colombia* (1990) (B); Dennis M. Hanratty and Sandra W. Meditz, eds., *Colombia* (1990); Richard L. Lael, *Arrogant Diplomacy* (1987); Stephen J. Randall, *Colombia and the United States* (1992) and *The Diplomacy of Modernization* (1977); Bert Ruiz, *Colombia's Civil War* (2002).

Congo (Kinshasa): David N. Gibbs, *The Political Economy of Third World Intervention* (1991); Madeline G. Kalb, *The Congo Cables* (1982); Sean Kelly, *America's Tyrant: The CIA and Mobutu of Zaire* (1993); Sandra W. Meditz and Tim Merrill, eds., *Zaire* (1994); Michael G. Schatzberg, *Mobutu or Chaos* (1991); Crawford Young and Thomas Turner, *The Rise and Decline of the Zairian State* (1985).

Costa Rica: Theodore S. Creedman, *Historical Dictionary of Costa Rica* (1991) (E); Martha Honey, *Hostile Acts* (1994); Kyle Longley, *The Sparrow and Hawk* (1997); Charles L. Stansifer, *Costa Rica* (1991) (B).

Cuba: James G. Blight and Philip Brenner, *Sad and Luminous Days* (2002); James G. Blight et al., *Cuba on the Brink* (2002); Ronald H. Chilcote and Sheryl Lutjens, eds., *Cuba, 1953–1978* (1986) (B); Juan del Aguilar, *Cuba* (1988); Esteban Morales Dominguez and Gary Prevost, *United States-Cuban Relations* (2008); Jorge Domínguez, *To Make the World Safe for Revolution* (1989); Jesse J. Dossick, ed., *Cuba, Cubans, and Cuban-Americans, 1902–1991* (1992) (B); José M. Hernández, *Cuba and the United States* (1993); Howard Jones, *Bay of Pigs* (2008); Morris H. Morley, *Imperial State and Revolution* (1987); Morris Morley and Christopher McGillon, *Unfinished Business* (2002) and *Cuba, the United States, and the Post-Cold War World* (2005); Thomas G. Paterson, *Contesting Castro* (1994); Louis A. Pérez, Jr., *Cuba* (1995), *Cuba* (1988) (B), *Cuba and the United States* (2003), and *Cuba in the American Imagination* (2008); Lars Schoultz, *That Infernal Little Cuban Republic* (2008); Sheldon M. Stern, *Averting the "Final Failure"* (2003); Jaime Suchlicki, *Historical Dictionary of Cuba* (1988) (E); Victor Anders Triay, *Fleeing Castro* (1998).

Cyprus: Tozun Bahcheli, *Greek-Turkish Relations Since 1955* (1990); Henry A. Richter, *Greece and Cyprus Since 1920* (1991) (B); Eric Solsten, ed., *Cyprus* (1991).

Czech Republic (and Czechoslovakia): David Short, *Czechoslovakia* (1986) (B); Gordon Skilling, *Czechoslovakia* (1991); Walter Ullmann, *The United States in Prague, 1945–1948* (1978); Betty Miller Unterberger, *The United States, Revolutionary Russia, and the Rise of Czechoslovakia* (1989).

Dominican Republic: G. Pope Atkins and Larman C. Wilson, *The Dominican Republic and the United States* (1998) and *The United States and the Trujillo Regime* (1972); Ian Bell, *The Dominican Republic* (1981); Bruce J. Calder, *The Impact of Intervention* (1984); Lauren Derby, *The Dictator's Seduction* (2009); Eric Thomas Chester, *Rag-Tags, Scum, Riff-Raff, and Commies* (2001); Piero Gleijeses, *The Dominican Crisis* (1978); Richard A. Haggerty, ed., *Dominican Republic and Haiti* (1991); Eric P. Roorda, *The Dictator Next Door* (1998); Kai Schoenhals, *Dominican Republic* (1990) (B); Howard J. Wiarda, *The Dominican Republic* (1992).

Eastern Europe: Robert F. Byrnes, *U.S. Policy Toward Eastern Europe and the Soviet Union* (1989); Stephen A. Garrett, *From Potsdam to Poland* (1986); Bennett Kovrig, *Of Walls and Bridges* (1991); Geoffrey Swain and Nigel Swain, *Eastern Europe Since 1945* (1993).

Ecuador: David Corkill, *Ecuador* (1989) (B); Dennis M. Hanratty, ed., *Ecuador* (1991); Ronn Pineo, *Ecuador and the United States* (2007); David W. Schodt, *Ecuador* (1987).

Egypt: Gregory L. Aftandilian, *Egypt's Bid for Arab Leadership* (1993); Geoffrey Aronson, *From Sideshow to Center Stage* (1986); William J. Burns, *Economic Aid and American Policy Toward Egypt, 1955–1981*

(1985); Peter L. Hahn, *The United States, Great Britain, and Egypt, 1945–1956* (1991); Matthew F. Holland, *America and Egypt* (1996); Ragai N. Makar, *Egypt* (1988) (B); Helen C. Metz, ed., *Egypt* (1991); Gail E. Meyer, *Egypt and the United States* (1980); William B. Quandt, *The United States and Egypt* (1990).

El Salvador: America's Watch, *El Salvador's Decade of Terror* (1991); Cynthia Arnson, *El Salvador* (1982); Enrique A. Baloyra, *El Salvador in Transition* (1982); Martin Diskin and Kenneth Sharpe, *The Impact of U.S. Policy in El Salvador, 1979–1986* (1986); Richard A. Haggerty, ed., *El Salvador* (1990); T. S. Montgomery, *Revolution in El Salvador* (1982); Ralph Lee Woodward, *El Salvador* (1988) (B).

Estonia: Toivo U. Raun, *Estonia and the Estonians* (1991).

Ethiopia: David A. Korn, *Ethiopia, the United States, and the Soviet Union* (1986); Jeffrey S. Lefebvre, *Arms for the Horn* (1991); Harold G. Marcus, *Ethiopia, Great Britain, and the United States, 1941–1974* (1983); Thomas P. Ofcansky, ed., *Ethiopia* (1993); Chris Prouty and Eugene Rosenfeld, *Historical Dictionary of Ethiopia* (1994) (E).

Europe: Peter Coffey, *The EC and the United States* (1993); Carol Fink and Frank Hadler, *1956* (2006); Victoria de Grazia, *Irresistible Empire* (2005); Jeffrey Glen Giauque, *Grand Designs and Visions of Unity* (2002); John L. Harper, *American Visions of Europe* (1994); William I. Hitchcock, *The Struggle for Europe* (2003); Robert Kagan, *Of Paradise and Power* (2003); Ethan B. Kapstein, *The Insecure Alliance* (1990); John Killick, *The United States and European Integration, 1945–1960* (1998); Deborah Kisatsky, *The United States and the European Right, 1945–1955* (2005); Geir Lundestad, *"Empire" by Integration* (1998) and *United States and Western Europe Since 1945* (2003); Elizabeth Pond, *Friendly Fire* (2004); Kevin Ruane, *The Rise and Fall of the European Defense Community* (2000); Thomas A. Schwartz, *Lyndon Johnson and Europe* (2003); William Shawcross, *Allies* (2004); Marc Trachtenberg, ed., *Between Empire and Alliance* (2003) and *A Constructed Peace* (1999); Pascaline Winand, *Eisenhower, Kennedy, and the United States of Europe* (1993).

Finland: Jussi M. Hanhimäki, *Containing Coexistence* (1997); Robert Rinehart, ed., *Finland and the United States* (1993); Eric Solsten and Sandra W. Meditz, *Finland* (1990).

France: Henry Blumenthal, *A Reappraisal of Franco-American Relations, 1830–1871* (1959), *France and the United States* (1970), and *Illusion and Reality in Franco-American Diplomacy, 1914–1945* (1986); Charles Cogan, *Oldest Allies, Guarded Friends* (1994); Frank Costigliola, *The Cold Alliance* (1992); Michael Creswell, *Question of Balance* (2006); William Hitchcock, *France Restored* (2001); Brian McKenzie,

Remaking France (2005); Robert O. Paxton and Nicholas Wahl, eds., *De Gaulle and the United States, 1930–1970* (1994); Jacques Portes, *Fascination and Misgiving* (2000); Irwin M. Wall, *The United States and the Making of Postwar France* (1991); Marvin Zahniser, *Uncertain Friendship* (1975) and *Then Came Disaster* (2002).

Gabon: David E. Gardinier, *Historical Dictionary of Gabon* (1994) (E).

Germany and Berlin: David E. Barclay and Elisabeth Glaser-Schmidt, eds., *Transatlantic Image and Perceptions* (1997); Steven Casey, *Cautious Crusade* (2001); Hans W. Gatzke, *Germany and the United States* (1980); Petra Goedde, *GIs and Germans* (2003); William Glenn Gray, *Germany's Cold War* (2003); Wolfram F. Hanrieder, *Germany, America, Europe* (1989); Maria Hohn, *GIs and Fräuleins* (2002); Patrick Thaddeus Jackson, *Civilizing the Enemy* (2006); Manfred Jonas, *The United States and Germany* (1984); Margrit Krewson, *German-American Relations* (1995) (B); James McAlister, *No Exit* (2002); Frank Ninkovich, *Germany and the United States* (1995); M. E. Sarotte, *Dealing with the Devil* (2001); Timothy Schroer, *Recasting Race after World War II* (2007); Hans-Jürgen Schröder, ed., *Confrontation and Cooperation* (1993); Thomas A. Schwartz, *America's Germany* (1991); Eric Solsten, ed., *Germany* (1996); W. R. Smyser, *Kennedy and the Berlin Wall* (2009); Stephen F. Szabo, *Parting Ways* (2004); Ian Wallace, *Berlin* (1993) (B); Peter Wyden, *Wall* (1989).

Ghana: LaVerde Berry, ed., *Ghana* (1995); Kevin Kelly Gaines, *American Africans in Ghana* (2006); Daniel McFarland, *Historical Dictionary of Ghana* (1985).

Great Britain: C. J. Bartlett, *"The Special Relationship"* (1992); David Dimbleby and David Reynolds, *An Ocean Apart* (1989); Alan P. Dobson, *Anglo-American Relations in the Twentieth Century* (1995); John Dumbrell, *Special Relationship* (2006); Sylvia Ellis, *Historical Dictionary of Anglo-American Relations* (2009) (E); Robert M. Hathaway, *Great Britain and the United States* (1990); David A. Lincove and Gary R. Treadway, eds., *The Anglo-American Relationship* (1988) (B); William Roger Louis and Hedley Bull, eds., *The Special Relationship* (1986); Jonathan Hollowell, ed., *Twentieth Century Anglo-American Relations* (2001); B. J. C. McKercher, *Transition of Power* (1999); John Moser, *Twisting the Lion's Tail* (1999); Anne Orde, *The Eclipse of Great Britain* (1996); Richie Ovendale *Anglo-American Relations in the Twentieth Century* (1998); David Reynolds, *Britannia Overruled* (2000); Andrew Roberts, *A History of the English-Speaking Peoples Since 1900* (2008); Mark Stoler, *Allies at War* (2005).

Greece: Louis Cassimatis, *American Influence in Greece, 1917–1929* (1988); Theodore A. Couloumbis, *The United States, Greece, and Turkey* (1983); Theodore A. Couloumbis and John O. Iatrides, eds.,

Greek-American Relations (1980); Glenn E. Curtis, ed., *Greece* (1995); John O. Iatrides, ed., *Ambassador MacVeagh Reports* (1980); Jon V. Kofas, *Intervention and Underdevelopment* (1989); Monteagle Stearns, *Entangled Allies* (1991); Lawrence S. Wittner, *American Intervention in Greece, 1943–1949* (1982).

Grenada: Peter M. Dunn and Bruce W. Watson, eds., *American Intervention in Grenada* (1985); Gordon K. Lewis, *Grenada* (1987); Kai P. Schoenhals and Richard A. Melanson, eds., *Revolution and Intervention in Grenada* (1985); Gary Williams, *U.S.-Grenada Relations* (2007).

Guam: Timothy P. Maga, *Defending Paradise* (1988); Earl S. Pomeroy, *Pacific Outpost* (1951); Robert F. Rogers, *Destiny's Landfall* (1995).

Guatemala: Nick Cullather, *Secret History* (1999); Paul J. Dosal, *Doing Business with the Dictators* (1993); Piero Gleijeses, *Shattered Hope* (1991); Jim Handy, *Gift of the Devil* (1985); Richard Immerman, *The CIA in Guatemala* (1982); Stephen M. Streeter, *Managing the Counterrevolution* (2001).

Guyana: Tim Merrill, ed., *Guyana and Belize* (1993); Stephen G. Rabe, *U.S. Intervention in British Guiana* (2005).

Haiti: Gordon S. Brown, *Toussaint's Clause* (2005); Frances Chambers, *Haiti* (1983) (B); Tim Matthewson, *Proslavery Foreign Policy* (2003); David Nicholls, *From Dessalines to Duvalier* (1979); Brenda Gayle Plummer, *Haiti and the United States* (1992); Ralph Pezzullo, *Plunging into Haiti* (2006); Mary Renda, *Taking Haiti* (2001); Robert I. Rotberg, *Haiti* (1971).

Hawai'i: Helena G. Allen, *The Betrayal of Queen Lilioukalani* (1982); Stephen Kinzer, *Overthrow* (2006); Ralph S. Kuykendall, *The Hawaiian Kingdom* (1938–1967); Nancy Morris and Love Dean, *Hawai'i* (1992) (B); Gary Okihiro, *Island World* (2008); Noenoe K. Silva, *Aloha Betrayed* (2004).

Honduras: Alison Acker, *Honduras* (1988); Pamela F. Howard-Reguindin, *Honduras* (1992) (B); Harvey Meyer and Jessie Meyer, *Historical Dictionary of Honduras* (1994) (E).

Hungary: László Borhi, *Hungary in the Cold War, 1945–1956* (2004); Stephan R. Burant, ed., *Hungary* (1990); Charles Gati, *Failed Illusions* (2006); Johanna C. Granville, *The First Domino* (2004).

India: William J. Barnds, *India, Pakistan, and the Great Powers* (1972); H. W. Brands, *India and the United States* (1990); W. Norman Brown, *The United States and India, Pakistan, and Bangladesh* (1972); Srinivas M. Chary, *The Eagle and the Peacock* (1994); Kenton J. Clymer, *Quest for Freedom* (1995); James Heitzman and Robert L. Worden, eds., *India* (1996); Dennis Kux, *India and the United States* (1992); Robert J. McMahon, *The Cold War on the Periphery* (1994); Dennis Merrill, *Bread and the Ballot* (1990); Norman D. Palmer, *The United States and India* (1984); Andrew Rotter, *Comrades at Odds* (2000); Santosh C. Saha, *Indo-U.S. Relations, 1947–1988* (1990) (B); Strobe Talbott, *Engaging India* (2004).

Indian Ocean: Helen C. Metz, ed., *Indian Ocean: Five Island Countries* (1995).

Indonesia: Theodore Friend, *Indonesian Destinies* (2003); Paul F. Gardner, *Shared Hopes, Separate Fears* (1997); Frances Gouda, *American Visions of the Netherlands East Indies/Indonesia* (2002); Michael Leifer, *Indonesia's Foreign Policy* (1983); Robert J. McMahon, *Colonialism and Cold War* (1981); Andrew Roadnight, *United States Policy Toward Indonesia in the Truman and Eisenhower Years* (2002); Robert L. Worden, ed., *Indonesia* (1993).

Iran: Gholam Reza Afkhami, *The Life and Times of the Shah* (2008); Ali M. Ansari, *Confronting Iran* (2006); James A. Bill, *The Eagle and the Lion* (1988); Richard W. Cottam, *Iran and the United States* (1988); Mark J. Gasiorowski, *U.S. Foreign Policy and the Shah* (1991); Sīrūs Ghanī, *Iran and the West* (1987) (B); James F. Goode, *The United States and Iran, 1946–51* (1989); Nikki R. Keddie and Mark J. Gasiorowski, eds., *Neither East nor West* (1990); Mark H. Lytle, *The Origins of the Iranian-American Alliance, 1941–1953* (1987); Rouhollah K. Ramazani, *The United States and Iran* (1982); Barry Rubin, *Paved with Good Intentions* (1980); Kuross A. Samii, *Involvement by Invitation* (1987); Abraham Yeselson, *United States–Persian Diplomatic Relations, 1883–1921* (1956).

Iraq: Rick Atkinson, *Crusade* (1993); Robert Brigham, *Is Iraq Vietnam?* (2006); Lawrence Freedman and Efraim Karsh, *The Gulf Conflict, 1990–1991* (1993); Kenneth J. Campbell, *A Tale of Two Quagmires* (2007); Bruce Jentleson, *With Friends like These* (1994); Barry Lando, *Web of Deceit* (2007); Sandra Mackey, *The Reckoning* (2002); Helen C. Metz, ed., *Iraq* (1990); Morris M. Mottale, *The Origins of the Gulf Wars* (2001); Geoff Simons, *Targeting Iraq* (2002); William Stivers, *Supremacy and Oil* (1982).

Ireland: Thomas N. Brown, *Irish-American Nationalism, 1870–1890* (1966); Francis M. Carroll, *American Opinion and the Irish Question, 1910–1923* (1978) and *The American Presence in Ulster: A Diplomatic History, 1796–1996* (2005); Sean Cronin, *Washington's Irish Policy, 1916–1986* (1987); Troy D. Davis, *Dublin's American Policy* (1998).

Israel, Palestine, and Arab-Israeli Conflict: George W. Ball and Douglas B. Ball, *The Passionate Attachment* (1992); Abraham Ben-Zvi,

The United States and Israel (1994); Ian J. Bickerton and Carla L. Klausner, *A Concise History of the Arab-Israeli Conflict* (1998); Herbert Druks, *The Uncertain Friendship* (2001); William Roger Louis and Robert W. Stookey, eds., *The End of the Palestine Mandate* (1986); Michael I. Karpin, *The Bomb in the Basement* (2006); Camille Mansour, *Beyond Alliance* (1994); Michelle Mart, *Eye on Israel* (2006); John J. Mearsheimer and Stephen M. Walt, *Israel Lobby and U.S. Foreign Policy* (2007); Donald Neff, *Fallen Pillars: U.S. Policy Towards Palestine and Israel Since 1945* (1995); Ilan Pappe, *The Israel/Palestine Question* (1999); William B. Quandt, *Peace Process* (1993); John Quigley, *Palestine and Israel* (1990); Bernard Reich, ed., *An Encyclopedia of the Arab-Israeli Conflict* (1996) (E) and *The United States and Israel* (1984); Cheryl Rubenberg, *Israel and the American National Interest* (1986); David Schoenbaum, *The United States and the State of Israel* (1993); Charles D. Smith, *Palestine and the Arab-Israeli Conflict* (1992); Steven Spiegel, *The Other Arab-Israeli Conflict* (1985); Michael W. Suleiman, ed., *U.S. Policy on Palestine* (1995); Mark Tessler, *A History of the Israeli-Palestinian Conflict* (1994); Edward Tivnan, *The Lobby* (1987).

Italy: Alessandro Brogi, *A Question of Self-esteem* (2002); Alexander DeConde, *Half-Bitter, Half-Sweet* (1971); H. Stuart Hughes, *The United States and Italy* (1979); James E. Miller, *The United States and Italy, 1940–1950* (1986); David F. Schmitz, *The United States and Fascist Italy, 1922–1940* (1988); Leo J. Wollemborg, *Stars, Stripes, and Italian Tricolor* (1990).

Japan: Sadao Asada, *Japan and the World* (1989) (B); Michael A. Barnhart, *Japan and the World Since 1868* (1995); John H. Boyle, *Modern Japan* (1993); Roger Buckley, *US-Japan Alliance Diplomacy, 1945–1990* (1992); Donald E. Dolan and Robert L. Worden, eds., *Japan* (1992); Tsuyoshi Hasegawa, *Racing the Enemy* (2005); Akira Iriye and Robert A. Wampler, eds., *Partnership* (2001); Walter LaFeber, *The Clash* (1997); Takeshi Matsuda, *Soft Power and Its Perils* (2007); Gavan McCormack, *Client State* (2007); Rita E. Neri, *U.S. and Japan Foreign Trade* (1988) (B); Charles E. Neu, *The Troubled Encounter* (1975); Ian Nish, *Japanese Foreign Policy in the Interwar Period* (2002); Michael Schaller, *Altered States* (1997) and *The American Occupation of Japan* (1985); Sayuri Shimizu, *Creating People of Plenty* (2001); Naoko Shibusawa, *America's Geisha Ally* (2006); John Swenson-Wright, *Unequal Allies?* (2005); and John Van Sant et al., *Historical Dictionary of United States-Japan Relations* (2007) (E).

Jordan: Madiha Rashid al-Madfai, *Jordan, the United States, and the Middle East Peace Process* (1993); Miriam Joyce, *Anglo-American Support for Jordan* (2008); Helen C. Metz, ed., *Jordan* (1991).

Kazakhstan: Glenn E. Curtis, *Kazakhstan, Kyrgyzstan, Tajikistan, Turkmenistan, and Uzbekistan* (1997); Michael Mandelbaum, ed., *Central Asia and the World* (1994).

Korea and Korean War: Greg Brazinsky, *Nation Building in South Korea* (2007); Jongsuk Chay, *Diplomacy of Asymmetry* (1990); Bruce Cumings, *Korea's Place in the Sun* (1997) and *The Origins of the Korean War* (1981, 1990); Paul M. Edwards, *The Korean War* (1998) (B); David Halberstam, *Coldest Winter* (2007); Burton I. Kaufman, *The Korean War* (1997); Chae-Jin Lee, *Troubled Peace* (2006); Yun-Bok Lee and Wayne Patterson, eds., *Korean-American Relations, 1866–1997* (1998); Mitchell B. Lerner, *The "Pueblo" Incident* (2002); Peter Lowe, *The Korean War* (2000); Donald S. Macdonald, *U.S.-Korean Relations* (1992); James I. Matray, ed., *Historical Dictionary of the Korean War* (1991) (E); Keith McFarland, *The Korean War* (1986) (B); Katherine H. S. Moon, *Sex Among Allies* (1997); Andrew C. Nahm, *Historical Dictionary of the Republic of Korea* (1993) (E); Stanley Sandler, *The Korean War* (1995) (E); Andrea M. Savada, ed., *North Korea* (1994) and *South Korea* (1992); Andre Schmid, *Korea Between Empires* (2002); Leon V. Sigal, *Disarming Strangers* (1998); William Stueck, *The Korean War* (1995), *Rethinking the Korean War* (2002), and *The Korean War in World History* (2004); Harry G. Summers, Jr., *Korean War Almanac* (1990) (C and E); Spencer Tucker, *Encyclopedia of the Korean War* (E) (2000).

Kuwait: Abdul-Reda Assiri, *Kuwaiti Foreign Policy* (1990); Jill Crystal, *Kuwait* (1992) and *Oil and Politics in the Gulf* (1995).

Laos: Timothy N. Castle, *At War in the Shadow of Vietnam* (1993); Helen Cordell, *Laos* (1993) (B); Arthur J. Dommen, *Laos* (1985); Jane Hamilton-Merritt, *Tragic Mountains* (1993); Andrea M. Savada, ed., *Laos* (1995); Charles A. Stevenson, *The End of Nowhere* (1972).

Latin America: G. Pope Atkins, *Encyclopedia of the Inter-American System* (1997) (E) and *Latin America in the International System* (1995); John A. Britton, *The United States and Latin America* (1997) (B); Peter Calvert, *The International Politics of Latin America* (1994); David W. Dent, *U.S.–Latin American Policymaking* (1995) (B); Mark T. Gilderhus, *The Second Century* (2000); Greg Grandin, *The Last Colonial Massacre* (2004); Jack W. Hopkins, ed., *Latin America and Caribbean Contemporary Record* (1983–) (AS); John J. Johnson, *A Hemisphere Apart* (1990); Gilbert Joseph and Daniela Spenser, *In From the Cold* (2007); Lester D. Langley, *America and the Americas* (1989); William M. LeoGrande, *Our Own Backyard* (1998); Thomas M. Leonard, ed., *United States–Latin American Relations, 1850–1903* (1999); Kyle Longley, *In the Eagle's Shadow* (2002); Abraham F. Lowenthal, ed., *Exporting Democracy* (1991); Alan McPherson, *Yankee No!* (2003) and *Intimate Ties, Bitter Struggles* (2006); Nancy Mitchell, *The Danger of Dreams* (1999); Fredrick B. Pike, *The United States and Latin America* (1992); David M. Pletcher, *The Diplomacy of Trade and Investment* (1998); Henry Raymont, *Troubled Neighbors* (2005); Fred Rosen, *Empire and Dissent* (2008); Lars Schoultz, *Beneath the United States* (1998); David Shavit, *The United States in Latin America* (1992) (E); David Sheinin, ed., *Beyond the Ideal*

(2000); Joseph Smith, *United States and Latin America* (2005); Peter H. Smith, *Talons of the Eagle* (1996).

Lebanon: C. H. Bleaney, *Lebanon* (1991) (B); Thomas L. Friedman, *From Beirut to Jerusalem* (1989); Irene Gendzier, *Notes from the Minefield* (1997); Dilip Hiro, *Lebanon* (1993); Itamar Rabinovich, *The War for Lebanon, 1970–1985* (1986).

Liberia: D. Elwood Dunn, *The Foreign Policy of Liberia During the Tubman Era, 1944–1971* (1979); Katherine Harris, *The United States and Liberia* (1985); Richard Moose, *U.S. Policy Toward Liberia* (1980); Hassan B. Sisay, *Big Powers and Small Nations* (1985); Charles M. Wilson, *Liberia* (1985).

Libya: Scott L. Bills, *The Libyan Arena* (1995); Mahmoud G. El Warfally, *Imagery and Ideology in U.S. Policy Toward Libya, 1969–1982* (1988); P. Edward Haley, *Qaddafi and the United States Since 1969* (1984); Ronald Bruce St. John, *Two Centuries of Strife* (2002); Dirk Wandewalle, ed., *Qadhafi's Libya* (1995).

Lithuania: Saulius Sužiedelis, *Historical Dictionary of Lithuania* (1997) (E); Robert A. Vitas, *United States and Lithuania* (1990).

Mauritania: Robert E. Handloff, ed., *Mauritania* (1990).

Mauritius: Larry Bowman, *Mauritius* (1991).

Mexico: Peter Andreas, *Border Games* (2000); Leslie Bethel, ed., *Mexico Since Independence* (1991); Jorge Domínguez and Rafael Fernandez de Castro, *United States and Mexico* (2001); John D. Dwyer, *The Agrarian Dispute* (2008); Donald S. Frazier, ed., *The United States and Mexico at War* (1998) (E); John M. Hart, *Empire and Revolution* (2002); Lester D. Langley, *Mexico and the United States* (1991); Krystina M. Libura et al, *Echoes of the Mexican American War* (2004); David E. Lorey, ed., *United States–Mexico Border Statistics Since 1900* (1990) (S) and *The U.S.–Mexican Border in the Twentieth Century* (2000); Jacqueline Mazza, *Don't Disturb the Neighbors* (2001); Robert A. Pastor and Jorge G. Castañeda, *Limits to Friendship* (1988); George D. C. Philip, *Mexico* (1993) (B); W. Dirk Raat, *Mexico and the United States* (1997); Clint E. Smith, *Inevitable Partnership* (2000); Daniela Spenser, *The Impossible Triangle* (1999).

Middle East: Robert J. Allison, *The Crescent Observed* (1995); Warren Bass, *Support Any Friend* (2003); Martin Gilbert, *Atlas of the Arab-Israeli Conflict* (1993) (A); Peter Hahn, *Caught in the Middle East* (2006) and *Historical Dictionary of United States-Middle East Relations* (2007) (E); Gregory Harms, *The Palestine Israel Conflict* (2008); Burton I. Kaufman, *The Arab Middle East and the United States* (1996); Colin Legum et al., eds.,

Middle East Contemporary Survey (1978–) (AS); George Lenczowski, *American Presidents and the Middle East* (1989); David Lesch, *The Arab-Israeli Conflict* (2008); Douglas Little, *American Orientalism* (2008); Melani McAllister, *Epic Encounters* (2001); Marc J. O'Reilly, *Unexceptional* (2008); Michael B. Oren, Power, *Faith, and Fantasy: America in the Middle East* (2007); Reeva S. Simon et al., eds., *The Encyclopedia of the Modern Middle East* (1996) (E); Kenneth Stein, *Heroic Diplomacy* (1999); Alan R. Taylor, *The Superpowers and the Middle East* (1991).

Mongolia: Robert C. Worden and Andrea M. Savada, eds., *Mongolia* (1991).

Morocco: Leon B. Blair, *Western Window in the Arab World* (1970); Luella J. Hall, *The United States and Morocco, 1776–1956* (1961).

Mozambique: Mario Azevedo, *Historical Dictionary of Mozambique* (1991) (E); Chester A. Crocker, *U.S. Policy Toward Mozambique* (1987); Margaret Hall and Tom Young, *Confronting Leviathan* (1997); Malyn Newitt, *A History of Mozambique* (1995).

Myanmar: John F. Cady, *The United States and Burma* (1976); Patricia M. Herbert, *Burma* (1991) (B).

Namibia: John J. Grotpeter, *Historical Dictionary of Namibia* (1994) (E).

Nepal: Andrea M. Savada, ed., *Nepal and Bhutan* (1993).

Netherlands: Doeko Bosscher et al., eds., *American Culture in the Netherlands* (1996); Hans Loeber, ed., *Dutch-American Relations, 1945–1969* (1992); J. W. Schulte Nordholt and Robert P. Swierenga, eds., *A Bilateral Centennial: A History of Dutch-American Relations, 1783–1982* (1982); Gertrude Reichenbach-Consten and Abraham Noordergraaf, eds., *Two Hundred Years of Netherlands-American Interaction* (1985); Cornelius van Minnen, *American Diplomats in the Netherlands, 1815–50* (1993).

Nicaragua: Karl Berman, *Under the Big Stick* (1986); E. Bradford Burns, *Patriarch and Folk* (1991); Paul C. Clark, Jr., *The United States and Somoza* (1992); Michael D. Gambone, *Eisenhower, Somoza, and the Cold War in Nicaragua* (1997); Michel Gobat, *Confronting the American Dream* (2005); Peter Kornbluh, *Nicaragua* (1987); Tim L. Merrill, ed., *Nicaragua* (1994); Morris H. Morley, *Washington, Somoza, and the Sandinistas* (1994); Neil Narr, *Sandinista Nicaragua* (1990) (B); Robert Pastor, *Condemned to Repetition* (1987); Mauricio Salaún, *U.S. Intervention and Regime Change in Nicaragua* (2005); Thomas W. Walker, *Nicaragua* (1991), ed., *Reagan Versus the Sandinistas* (1987), and ed., *Revolution and Counterrevolution in Nicaragua* (1991); Knut Walter, *The Regime of Anastasio Somoza* (1993); Ralph Lee Woodward, *Nicaragua* (1994) (B).

Nigeria: Bassey E. Ate, *Decolonization and Dependence* (1987); Helen C. Metz, ed., *Nigeria* (1992); Robert B. Shepard, *Nigeria, Africa, and the United States* (1991); Joseph E. Thompson, *American Policy and African Famine* (1990).

North Africa: Charles F. Gallagher, *The United States and North Africa* (1963); Richard S. Parker, *North Africa* (1984).

Norway: Mats Berdal, *The United States, Norway, and the Cold War* (1997); Wayne S. Cole, *Norway and the United States* (1989); Ronald C. Popperwell, *Norway* (1972); Sigmund Skard, *The United States in Norwegian History* (1976); Rolf Tamnes, *The United States and the Cold War in the High North* (1991).

Oman: Joseph A. Kechichian, *Oman and the World* (1995).

Pakistan: David Armstrong and Joseph Trento, *America and the Islamic Bomb* (2007); Peter R. Blood, ed., *Pakistan* (1995); Dennis Kux, *The United States and Pakistan, 1947–2000* (2001); Adrian Levy, *Deception* (2007); Iftikhar Malik, *U.S.–South Asian Relations, 1940–1947* (1991); Shirin Tahir-kheli, *The United States and Pakistan* (1982); David D. Taylor, *Pakistan* (1990) (B); M. S. Venkataramani, *The American Role in Pakistan, 1947–1958* (1982).

Panama (and Panama Canal): Michael L. Conniff, *Panama and the United States* (1992); David N. Farnsworth and James W. McKenney, *U.S.-Panama Relations, 1903–1978* (1983); Walter LaFeber, *The Panama Canal* (1990); Thomas M. Leonard, *Panama, the Canal, and the United States* (1993) (B); John Lindsay-Poland, *Emperors in the Jungle* (2003); John Major, *Prize Possession* (1993); David McCullough, *The Path Between the Seas* (1977); Aims McGuiness, *Path of Empire* (2007); Matthew Parker, *Panama Fever* (2008).

Paraguay: Anibal Miranda, *United States–Paraguay Relations* (1990); Frank O. Mora and Jerry W. Cooney, *Paraguay and the United States* (2007); Riordan Roett and Richard S. Sacks, *Paraguay* (1991).

Persian Gulf: Bruce R. Kuniholm, *The Persian Gulf and United States Policy* (1984) (B); Charles A. Kupchan, *The Persian Gulf and the West* (1987); Helen C. Metz, ed., *Persian Gulf States* (1993); Marc O'Reilly, *Unexceptional* (2008); Michael A. Palmer, *Guardians of the Gulf* (1992).

Peru: Lawrence A. Clayton, *Peru and the United States* (1999); Rex A. Hudson, ed., *Peru* (1993); Cynthia McClintock and Fabian Vallas, *The United States and Peru* (2003); Fredrick B. Pike, *The United States and the Andean Republics* (1977); Ronald B. St. John, *The Foreign Policy of Peru* (1992).

Philippines: David H. Bain, *Sitting in Darkness* (1984); H. W. Brands, *Bound to Empire* (1992); Nick Cullather, *Illusions of Influence* (1994); Ronald E. Dolan, ed., *Philippines* (1993); Julian Go and Anne L. Foster, eds., *The American Colonial State in the Philippines* (2003); Stanley Karnow, *In Our Image* (1989); Paul A. Kramer, *Blood of Government* (2006); Brian M. Linn, *The Philippine War* (2000); Glenn A. May, *Battle for Batangas* (1991); Jim Richardson, *Philippines* (1989) (B).

Poland: Debra J. Allen, *The Oder-Neisse Line* (2003); Glenn E. Curtis, ed., *Poland* (1994); Richard Lukacs, *Bitter Legacy* (1982); Helene Sjursen, *The United States, Western Europe, and the Polish Crisis* (2003); Anthony Kemp-Welch, *Poland Under Communism* (2008).

Portugal: Scott B. MacDonald, *European Destiny, Atlantic Transformations* (1993); Kenneth Maxwell and Michael H. Haltzel, eds., *Portugal* (1990); Eric Solsten, ed., *Portugal* (1994).

Puerto Rico: Rafael Bernabe, *Puerto Rico in the American Century* (2007); Laura Briggs, *Reproducing Empire* (2002); Raymond Carr, *Puerto Rico* (1984); Arturo Morales Carrión, *Puerto Rico* (1984); Elena E. Cevallos, *Puerto Rico* (1985) (B); Truman B. Clark, *Puerto Rico and the United States, 1917–1933* (1975); Ronald Fernandez, *The Disenchanted Island* (1996); A. W. Maldonado, *Teodora Moscoso and Puerto Rico's Operation Bootstrap* (1997); José Trías Monge, *Puerto Rico* (1997).

Romania: Ronald D. Bachman, ed., *Romania* (1990); Joseph F. Harrington and Bruce J. Courtney, *Tweaking the Nose of the Russians* (1991); Elizabeth W. Hazard, *Cold War Crucible* (1996).

Russia and the Soviet Union: N. N. Bolkhovitinov and J. Dane Hartgrove, *Russia and the United States* (1987) (B); Peter G. Boyle, *American-Soviet Relations* (1993); Archie Brown et al., eds., *The Cambridge Encyclopedia of Russia and the Soviet Union* (1994) (E); Donald Davis and Eugene P. Trani, *The First Cold War* (2000); Philip J. Funigiello, *American-Soviet Trade in the Cold War* (1988); A. A. Fursenko and Timothy J. Naftali, *Khrushchev's Cold War* (2006); John Lewis Gaddis, *Russia, the Soviet Union, and the United States* (1990); Raymond L. Garthoff, *Détente and Confrontation* (1985) and *The Great Transition* (1994); Yoram Gorlizki and O.V. Khlevniuk, *Cold Peace* (2004); Hope M. Harrison, *Driving the Soviets up the Wall* (2003); Walter LaFeber, *America, Russia, and the Cold War* (2002); James K. Libbey, *American-Russian Economic Relations* (1989) (B); J. D. Parks, *Culture, Conflict, and Coexistence* (1983); Norman E. Saul, *Concord and Conflict* (1996), *The United States and Russia, 1763–1867* (1991), *War and Revolution* (2002), and *Historical Dictionary of United States-Russian/Soviet Relations* (2009) (E); David Shavit, *United States Relations with Russia and the Soviet Union* (1993) (E); V. M. Zubok, *A Failed Empire* (2007).

Rwanda: Jared Cohen, *One Hundred Days of Silence* (2007); Learthen Dorsey, *Historical Dictionary of Rwanda* (1994) (E).

Samoa (American): J. A. C. Gray, *Amerika Samoa* (1960); Paul Kennedy, *The Samoan Tangle* (1974); George H. Ryden, *The Foreign Policy of the United States in Relation to Samoa* (1933).

Saudi Arabia: Irvine H. Anderson, *Aramco, the United States, and Saudi Arabia* (1981); Rachel Bronson, *Thicker Than Oil* (2006); Nathan J. Citino, *From Arab Nationalism to OPEC* (2002); Parker T. Hart, *Saudi Arabia and the United States* (1999); Helen C. Metz, ed., *Saudia Arabia* (1993); Aaron D. Miller, *Search for Security* (1980); Nadav Safran, *Saudi Arabia* (1986); Craig Unger, *House of Bush, House of Saud* (2004); Robert Vitalis, *America's Kingdom* (2007).

Scandinavia: Jussi M. Hanhimäki, *Scandinavia and the United States* (1997); Geir Lundestad, *America, Scandinavia, and the Cold War* (1980); Franklin D. Scott, *Scandinavia* (1975) and *The United States and Scandinavia* (1950).

Senegal: R. M. Dilley and J. S. Eades, *Senegal* (1994) (B).

Somalia: John L. Hirsch and Whert B. Oakley, *Somalia and Operation Restore Hope* (1995); Helen C. Metz, ed., *Somalia* (1993).

South Africa: James Barber and John Barratt, *South Africa's Foreign Policy* (1990); Thomas Borstelmann, *Apartheid's Reluctant Uncle* (1993); Rita M. Byrnes, ed., *South Africa* (1997); Christopher Coker, *The United States and South Africa, 1968–1985* (1986); Jeffrey V. Davis, *South Africa* (1994) (B); Terrell D. Hale, *United States Sanctions and South Africa* (1993) (B); Richard W. Hull, *American Enterprise in South Africa* (1990); C. T. Keto, *American–South African Relations, 1784–1980* (1985) (B); Y. G. M. Lulat, *U.S. Relations with South Africa* (1991) (B); Princeton N. Lyman, *Partner to History* (2002); Robert K. Massie, *Loosing the Bonds* (1997); William Minter, *King Soloman's Mines Revisited* (1986); Francis N. Nesbitt, *Race for Sanctions* (2004); Thomas J. Noer, *Briton, Boer, and Yankee* (1978) and *Cold War and Black Liberation* (1985).

Spain: Michael Alpert, *A New International History of the Spanish Civil War* (1998); Rodrigo Botero, *Ambivalent Embrace* (2001); Thomas Chavez, *Spain and the Independence of the United States* (2002); James W. Cortada, *Two Nations over Time* (1978) and ed., *Spain in the Twentieth-Century World* (1980); Robert W. Kern, *Historical Dictionary of Modern Spain* (1990) (E); Boris N. Liedtke, *Embracing a Dictatorship* (1998).

Sudan: Carolyn Fkuehr-Lobban et al., *Historical Dictionary of Sudan* (1992) (E); Julie Flint and Alex deWaal, *Darfur* (2008); Helen C. Metz, ed., *Sudan* (1992); Peter Woodward, *Sudan* (1989).

Sweden: Sture Kindmark and Tore Tallroth, eds., *Swedes Looking West* (1983).

Switzerland: Heinze K. Meier, *Friendship Under Stress* (1970) and *The United States and Switzerland in the Nineteenth Century* (1963).

Syria: David W. Lesch, *Syria and the United States* (1992); Moshe Ma'oz, *Syria and Israel* (1995); Andrew Rathwell, *Secret War in the Middle East* (1995); Bonnie Saunders, *The United States and Arab Nationalism* (1996); Eyal Zisser, *Assad's Legacy* (2002).

Thailand: Richard Aldrich, *The Key to the South* (1993); Daniel Fineman, *Special Relationship* (1997); Barbara L. LePoer, ed., *Thailand* (1989); Robert J. Muscat, *Thailand and the United States* (1990).

Trieste: Bogdan C. Novak, *Trieste, 1941–1954* (1970); Roberto Rabel, *Between East and West* (1988).

Turkey: David J. Alvarez, *Bureaucracy and Cold War Ideology* (1980); William Hale, *Turkey, the U.S., and Iraq* (2007); George S. Harris, *Troubled Alliance* (1972); Harry H. Howard, *Turkey, the Straits, and U.S. Policy* (1974); Helen C. Metz, ed., *Turkey* (1996); Nasa Uslu, *Turkish-American Relationship between 1947 and 2003* (2003).

Uganda: Rita M. Byrnes, ed., *Uganda* (1992).

Ukraine: Lubomyr A. Hajda, ed., *Ukraine in the World* (1998); Steven Woehrel, *Ukraine* (1994).

Uruguay: Kitty L. Drummond, *Relations Between Uruguay and the United States* (1936); Rex A. Hudson and Sandra W. Meditz, eds., *Uruguay* (1992); Martin Weinstein, *Uruguay* (1987).

Venezuela: Judith Ewell, *Venezuela and the United States* (1996); Eva Golinger, *Bush Versus Chávez* (2008); Janet Kelley and Carlos A. Romero, *United States and Venezuela* (2001); Sheldon B. Liss, *Diplomacy and Independence* (1978); Stephen G. Rabe, *The Road to OPEC* (1982); Darlene Rivas, *Missionary Capitalist* (2002); Miguel Tinker Salas, *The Enduring Legacy* (2009).

Vietnam and Southeast Asia: David L. Anderson, ed., *Shadow on the White House* (1993); David Anderson, *The Columbia Guide to the Vietnam War* (2002) (E); Pierre Asselin, *A Bitter Peace* (2002); Larry Berman, *No Peace, No Honor* (2001); James G. Blight, janet M. Lang, and David A. Welch, *Vietnam If Kennedy Had Lived* (2009); John S. Bowman, ed., *The Vietnam War* (1986) (C); Mark Philip Bradley, *Making Sense of the Vietnam Wars* (2008); Robert Brigham, *Guerrilla Diplomacy* (1998); Lester H. Brune and Richard Dean Burns, eds., *America and* *the Indochina Wars, 1945–1990* (1991) (B); Peter Busch, *All the Way with JFK* (2003); Robert Buzzanco and Marilyn Young, eds., *A Companion to the Vietnam War* (2002) (E); Philip E. Catton, *Diem's Final Failure* (2002); William J. Duiker, *Historical Dictionary of Vietnam* (1989) (E); H. Bruce Franklin, *Vietnam and Other American Fantasies* (2002); Joseph A. Fry, *Debating Vietnam* (2008); Lloyd C. Gardner, *Approaching Vietnam* (1988); George C. Herring, *America's Longest War* (2000); Gary R. Hess, *Vietnam and the United States* (1998) and *Vietnam* (2009); George McT. Kahin, *Intervention* (1986); David Kaiser, *American Tragedy* (2000); Gabriel Kolko, *Anatomy of a War* (1985); Stanley I. Kutler, ed., *Encyclopedia of the Vietnam War* (1995) (E); Frederik Logevall, *Choosing War* (1999); Robert J. McMahon, *The Limits of Empire* (1999); Edwin F. Moise, *Historical Dictionary of the Vietnam War* (2001) (E); Mark Moyar, *Triumph Forsaken* (2006); Charles E. Neu, *After Vietnam* (2000); James S. Olson, *Dictionary of the Vietnam War* (1988) (E) and *The Vietnam War* (1993) (B); Andrew J. Rotter, *The Path to Vietnam* (1987); Robert D. Schulzinger, *A Time for War* (1997); Harry G. Summers, Jr., *Vietnam War Almanac* (1985) (C); Spencer C. Tucker, ed., *Encyclopedia of the Vietnam War* (1998) (E); Donald E. Weatherbee, *Historical Dictionary of United States–Southeast Asia Relations* (2008) (E); Randall B. Woods, ed., *Vietnam and the American Political Tradition* (2003); Marilyn Young, *The Vietnam Wars* (1991).

Virgin Islands and West Indies: William W. Boyer, *America's Virgin Islands* (1983); Cary Fraser, *Ambivalent Anti-Colonialism* (1994); Verna P. Moll, *Virgin Islands* (1991) (B); Andrew Jackson O'Shaughnessy, *An Empire Divided* (2000); Stephen J. Randall and Graeme Malent, *The Caribbean Basin* (1998); Charlie Witham, *Bitter Rehearsal* (2002).

Yemen: Ahmed Nomen Al-Madhaqi, *Yemen and the USA* (1994); Fred Halliday, *Revolution and Foreign Policy* (1989).

Yugoslavia: Leonard Cohen, *Broken Bonds* (1993); Misha Glenny, *The Balkans* (2000); Lorraine M. Lees, *Keeping Tito Afloat* (1997); Miron Rezan, *Europe's Nightmare* (2001); Ivo Tasovic, *American Policy and Yugoslavia, 1939–1941* (1999); Susan Woodward, *Balkan Tragedy* (1995).

Zimbabwe: Andrew DeRoche, *Black, White, and Chrome* (2001); Gerald Horne, *From the Barrel of a Gun* (2001); R. Kent Rasmussen, *Historical Dictionary of Zimbabwe* (1990) (E).

Overviews of Subjects, Including Atlases (A), Annual Surveys (AS), Bibliographies (B), Biographical Aids (BA), Chronologies (C), Encyclopedias (E), and Statistics (S)

African Americans: Carol Anderson, *Eyes Off the Prize* (2003); Thomas Borstelmann, *The Cold War and the Color Line* (2001); Chris Dixon, *African America and Haiti* (2000); Mary Dudziak, *Cold War Civil Rights* (2000); Robert Gallicho, *The African American Encounter with Japan and China* (2001); Gerald Horne, *Black and Red* (1986); Michael L. Krenn, *Black Diplomacy* (1998); Azza Salema Layton, *International Relations and Civil Rights* (2000); James H. Meriwether, *Proudly We Can Be Africans* (2002); Kenneth O'Reilly, *Nixon's Piano* (1995); Brenda Gayle Plummer, *Rising Wind* (1996); "Symposium: African Americans and U.S. Foreign Relations," *Diplomatic History, XX* (Fall 1996); Jonathan Rosenberg, *How Far the Promised Land?* (2006); Lamin Sanneh, *Abolitionists Abroad* (2000); Timothy Schroer, *Recasting Race after World War II* (2007) (Germany); Penny Von Eschen, *Race Against Empire* (1997).

AIDS Pandemic: Jonathan Engel, *Epidemic: A Global History of AIDS* (2006); J. Mann, Daniel Tarantola, and T. Netter, eds., *AIDS in the World* (1992, 1996); Matthew Smallman-Raynor et al., *Atlas of AIDS* (1992) (A).

Air Force and Air Power: Charles D. Bright, ed., *Historical Dictionary of the U.S. Air Force* (1992) (E); Alan P. Dobson, *Peaceful Air Warfare* (1991); Richard P. Hallion, *The Literature of Aeronautics, Astronautics, and Air Power* (1984) (B); John B. Rae, *Climb to Greatness* (1968); Michael S. Sherry, *The Rise of American Air Power* (1987); Jeffrey S. Underwood, *The Wings of Democracy* (1991); Bruce W. Watson and Susan W. Watson, *The United States Air Force* (1992) (E).

Alliance for Progress: Jerome Levinson and Juan de Onís, *The Alliance That Lost Its Way* (1970); L. Ronald Scheman, ed., *The Alliance for Progress* (1988); Jeffrey F. Taffet, *Foreign Aid as Foreign Policy* (2007).

American Revolution: Richard Blanco, ed., *The American Revolution* (1993) (E); Mark M. Boatner III, *Encyclopedia of the American Revolution* (1974) (E); Lester J. Cappon, ed., *Atlas of Early American History: The Revolutionary Era, 1760–1790* (1976) (A); John M. Faragher, ed., *The Encyclopedia of Colonial and Revolutionary America* (1990) (E); Jack P. Greene and J. R. Pole, eds., *The Blackwell Encyclopedia of the American Revolution* (1991) (E); John W. Raimo, ed., *Biographical Directory of American Colonial and Revolutionary Governors, 1607–1789* (1980) (BA).

Anti-Americanism: Seth D. Armas, *French Anti-Americanism (1930–1948)* (2007); Dan Diner, *German Anti-Americanism* (1995); Peter J. Katzenstein and Robert O. Keohane, *Anti-Americanisms in World Politics* (2007); Rob Kroes and Maarten van Rossem, eds., *Anti-Americanism in Europe* (1986); Denis Lacorne et al., eds., *The Rise and Fall of Anti-Americanism* (1990); Andrei Markovits, *Uncouth Nation* (2007); Richard Pells, *Not Like Us* (1997); Philip Roger, *The American Enemy* (2005); Alvin Z. Rubenstein and Donald E. Smith, eds., *Anti-Americanism in the Third World* (1985); Andrew Ross and Kristin

Ross, *Anti-Americanism* (2004); Barry Rubin and Judith Colp Rubin, *Hating America* (2006).

Anticommunism and McCarthyism: Jeff Broadwater, *Eisenhower and the Anti-Communist Crusades* (1992); Peter H. Buckingham, *America Sees Red* (1987) (B); Thomas P. Doherty, *Cold War, Cool Medium* (2003); Richard M. Fried, *Nightmare in Red* (1990); Robert Griffith, *The Politics of Fear* (1987); Joel Kovel, *Red Hunting in the Promised Land* (1994); Stanley I. Kutler, *The American Inquisition* (1982); David K. Johnson, *The Lavender Scare* (2003); Ted Morgan, *Reds* (2003); Richard G. Powers, *Not Without Honor* (1995); Athan Theoharis, *Chasing Spies* (2002); Stephen J.Whitfield, *The Culture of the Cold War* (1996); Michael J.Ybarra, *Washington Gone Crazy* (2004).

Arms Sales and Trade: Michael Broszka and Thomas Ohlson, *Arms Transfers to the Third World* (1987); Michael T. Klare, *American Arms Supermarket* (1984); Edward J. Laurence, *The International Arms Trade* (1992); Andrew J. Pierre, *The Global Politics of Arms Sales* (1982).

Biological and Chemical Warfare: G. M. Burck and Charles C. Flowerree, *International Handbook on Chemical Weapons Proliferation* (1991) (E); Anthony H. Cordesman, *Weapons of Mass Destruction in the Middle East* (1991); Arthur J. Dommen et al., *The United States and Biological Warfare* (1999); Stephen Endicott and Edward Hagerman, *The United States and Biological Warfare* (1999); Sheldon H. Harris, *Factories of Death* (1994); John Norris and Will Fowler, *NBC: Nuclear, Biological, and Chemical Warfare on the Modern Battlefield* (1998) (E); Amy E. Simpson, ed., *The Chemical Weapons Convention Handbook* (1993).

Civil Defense: Laura McEnany, *Civil Defense Begins at Home* (2000); Kenneth D. Rose, *One Nation Underground* (2001).

Civil War (American): Mark M. Boatner III, *The Civil War Dictionary* (1988) (E); D. P. Crook, *The North, the South, and the Powers* (1974); Richard N. Current, ed., *Encyclopedia of the Confederacy* (1993) (E); David S. Heidler et al., *Encyclopedia of the American Civil War* (2000) (E); John T. Hubbell and James W. Geary, eds., *Biographical Dictionary of the Union* (1995) (BA); David C. Roller and Robert W. Twyman, eds., *The Encyclopedia of Southern History* (1979) (E); Jon L. Wakelyn, ed., *Biographical Dictionary of the Confederacy* (1977) (BA); Steven E. Woodworth, ed., *The American Civil War* (1996) (B).

Coast Guard, U.S.: Irving H. King, *The Coast Guard Expands* (1996), *The Coast Guard Under Sail* (1989), and *George Washington's Coast Guard* (1978); Robert E. Johnson, *Blood Stained Sea* (2004) and *Guardians of the Sea* (1987).

Cold War: Thomas S. Arms, *Encyclopedia of the Cold War* (1994) (E); H. W. Brands, *The Devil We Knew* (1993); John Lewis Gaddis, *We Now Know* (1997) and *The Cold War* (2005); Michael H. Hunt, *The World Transformed* (2004); Michael Kort, *The Columbia Guide to the Cold War* (2001) (E); Walter LaFeber, *America, Russia, and the Cold War* (2001); Tom Lansfors, *Historical Dictionary of the Cold War* (2007) (E); Melvyn P. Leffler, *For the Soul of Mankind* (2007); Ralph B. Levering, *The Cold War* (2005); Ralph B. Levering et al., *Debating the Origins of the Cold War* (2002); Wilford Loth, *Overcoming the Cold War* (2002); Thomas J. McCormick, *America's Half-Century* (1995); Robert J. McMahon, *The Cold War* (2003); Wilson D. Miscamble, *From Roosevelt to Truman* (2007); Richard Schwartz, *Cold War Culture* (E) (1998); Joseph Smith and Simon Davis, *Historical Dictionary of the Cold War* (E) (2000); Thomas G. Paterson, *Meeting the Communist Threat* (1988) and *On Every Front* (1992); Odd Arne Westad, *The Global Cold War* (2008); Vladislav M. Zubok, *A Failed Empire* (2007). See also "Disarmament and Arms Control," "Nuclear Arms," "Russia and the Soviet Union," and "Threat Perception and Calculation."

Communications: James L. Baughman, *The Republic of Mass Culture* (1992); Menahem Blondheim, *New Over the Wires* (1994); David H. Culbert, *News for Everyman* (1976) (radio); Wilson Dizard, Jr., *Digital Diplomacy* (2001); Paul R. Edwards, *The Closed World* (1996) (computers); Howard H. Frederick, *Global Communications and International Relations* (1992); Bradley S. Greenberg, ed., *Communication and Terrorism* (2001); Julian Hale, *Radio Power* (1975); Elizabeth C. Hanson, *The Information Revolution and World Politics* (2008); Daniel R. Headrick, *The Invisible Weapon* (1991); David Paull Nickles, *Under the Wire* (2003); James G. Savage, *The Politics of International Telecommunications Regulation* (1989); James Schwoch, *The American Radio Industry and Its Latin American Activities* (1990); Philip M. Taylor, *Global Communications* (1997).

Congress (House and Senate): Betty Austin, *J. William Fulbright* (1995) (B); David M. Barrett, *The CIA and Congress* (2005); Stephen G. Christianson, *Facts About the Congress* (1996); Congressional Quarterly, *Biographical Directory of the American Congress* (1997) (BA) and *Congress and the Nation, 1945–1984* (1965–1985) (E); Robert U. Goehlert and John R. Sayre, *The United States Congress* (1981) (B); Lewis L. Gould, *The Most Exclusive Club* (2005) (Senate); Ronald L. Hatzenbeuhler and Robert L. Ivie, *Congress Declares War* (1983); Barbara Hinckley, *Less Than Meets the Eye* (1994); Robert David Johnson, *Congress and the Cold War* (2006); James M. Lindsey, *Congress and the Politics of U.S. Foreign Policy* (1994); Goran Rystad, ed., *Congress and American Foreign Policy* (1982); U.S. Congress, *Biographical Directory of the United States Congress, 1774–1989* (1989) (BA); Gerald F. Warburg, *Conflict and Consensus* (1989); Stephen R. Weissman, *A Culture of Deference* (1995).

Constitution and Constitutional Interpretation: David G.Adler and Larry N. George, eds., *The Constitution and American Foreign Policy*

(1996); Henry B. Cox, *War, Foreign Affairs, and Constitutional Power, 1829–1901* (1984); Louis Fischer, *Constitutional Conflicts Between the President and Congress* (1985); Thomas M. Franck and Michael J. Glennon, *Foreign Relations and National Security Law* (1993); Louis Henkin, *Constitutionalism, Democracy, and Foreign Affairs* (1990) and *Foreign Affairs and the United States Constitution* (1996); Harold Honggju Koh, *The National Security Constitution* (1990); Leonard W. Levy et al., eds., *Encyclopedia of the American Constitution* (1986) (E); Gordon Silberstein, *Imbalance of Powers* (1997); Joan E. Smith, *The Constitution and American Foreign Policy* (1989); Abraham Sofaer, *War, Foreign Affairs, and Constitutional Power* (1976).

Containment: Terry L. Deibel and John Lewis Gaddis, eds., *Containment* (1986); John Lewis Gaddis, *Strategies of Containment* (2005); Charles Gati, ed., *Caging the Bear* (1974); Deborah Larson, *Origins of Containment* (1985).

Counterinsurgency: Benjamin R. Beede, *Intervention and Counterinsurgency* (1984) (B); Douglas S. Blaufarb, *The Counterinsurgency Era* (1977); Larry E. Cable, *Conflict of Myths* (1986); Anthony James Joes, *America and Guerrilla Warfare* (2000); Gil Merom, *How Democracies Lose Small Wars* (2003); Michael T. Klare and Peter Kornbluh, eds., *Low-Intensity Warfare* (1988); Michael McClintock, *Instruments of Statecraft* (1992); D. Michael Shafer, *Deadly Paradigms* (1988).

Credibility: Robert J. McMahon, "Credibility and World Power," *Diplomatic History, XV* (Fall 1991), 455–471; Jonathan Mercer, *Reputation and International Politics* (1996).

Cultural Relations: Christian G. Appy, ed., *Cold War Constructions* (2000); Jongsuk Chay, ed., *Culture and International Relations* (1990); Heidi Fehrenbach and Uta G. Poiger, eds., *Transactions, Transgressions, and Transformations* (2000); Jessica C. E. Gienow-Hecht, *Transmission Impossible* (1999); Petra Goedde, *GIs and Germans* (2003); Gilbert G. Gonzales, *Culture of Empire* (2004); Akira Iriye, *Cultural Internationalism and World Order* (1997); Robert D. Johnson, ed., *On Cultural Ground* (1994); Gilbert M. Joseph et al., eds., *Close Encounters of Empire* (1998); Amy Kaplan and Donald E. Pease, eds., *Cultures of United States Imperialism* (1993); Michael Krenn, *Fall-out Shelters for the Human Spirit* (2005); Rob Kroes, *If You've Seen One You've Seen the Mall* (1996); Peter J. Kuznick and James Gilbert, eds., *Rethinking Cold War Culture* (2001); Naima Prevots, *Dance for Export* (1998); Uta G. Poiger, *Jazz, Rock, and Rebels* (2000); Yale Richmond, *Cultural Exchange and the Cold War* (2003); Emily Rosenberg, *Spreading the American Dream* (1982); Frances Sauders, *The Cultural Cold War* (1999); Leonard Sussman, *The Culture of Freedom* (1992); Penny Von Eschen, *Satchmo Blows Up the World* (2004); Reinhold Wagnleitner and Elaine T. May, eds., *"Here, There, and Everywhere": The Foreign Politics of American Popular Culture* (2000).

Decolonization: Franz Ansprenger, *The Dissolution of Colonial Empires* (1989); Prosser Gifford and William Roger Louis, eds., *Decolonization and African Independence* (1988); D. A. Low, *Eclipse of Empire* (1991); David P. Newsom, *Imperial Mantle* (2001); David Ryan and Victor Pugong, eds., *The United States and Decolonization* (2000); Hendrik Spruyt, *Ending Empire* (2005); Brian Urquhart, *Decolonization and World Peace* (1989).

Department of State, Foreign Service, and Diplomatic Practice: Robert Dean, *Imperial Brotherhood* (2001); Robert U. Goehlert and Elizabeth Hoffmeister, *The Department of State and American Diplomacy* (1986) (B); Charles S. Kennedy, *The American Consul* (1990); Henry E. Mattox, *The Twilight of Amateur Diplomacy* (1989); Edward S. Mihalkanin, *American Statesmen* (2004); Robert H. Miller et al., *Inside an Embassy* (1992); Cathal Nolan, ed., *Notable U.S. Ambassadors Since 1775* (1998); Elmer Plischke, *United States Diplomats and Their Mission* (1979) and *U.S. Department of State* (1999); Martin Weil, *A Pretty Good Club* (1978); Richard H. Werking, *The Master Architects* (1977).

Dependency: Fernando Henrique Cardoso and Enzo Faletto, *Dependency and Development in Latin America* (1979); Andre Gunder Frank, *Capitalism and Underdevelopment in Latin America* (1967); Vincent A. Mahler, Dependency Approaches to International Political Economy (1980); Robert A. Packenham, *The Dependency Movement* (1992); Richard Peet, *Theories of Development* (1999).

Deterrence: Alexander L. George and Richard Smoke, *Deterrence in American Foreign Policy* (1974); Ted Hopf, *Peripheral Visions* (1994); Robert Jervis et al., *Psychology and Deterrence* (1985); Derek Smith, *Deterring America* (2006).

Dictatorships: H. E. Chehabi and Juan J. Linz, *Sultanistic Regimes* (1998); Ernest R. May, et al., *Dealing With Dictators* (2006); David F. Schmitz, *Thank God They're on Our Side* (1999) and *The United States and Right-Wing Dictatorships, 1965–1989* (2006).

Diplomatic Immunity: Linda S. Frey and Marsha L. Frey, *The History of Diplomatic Immunity* (1999); Grant V. McClanahan, *Diplomatic Immunity* (1989).

Disarmament and Arms Control: Sheikh Rustum Aki, *The Peace and Nuclear War Dictionary* (1989) (E); Stephen E. Atkins, *Arms Control and Disarmament* (1989) (B); Richard Dean Burns, ed., *Encyclopedia of Arms Control and Disarmament* (1993) (E); Jeffrey M. Elliot and Robert Reginald, *The Arms Control, Disarmament, and Military Security Dictionary* (1989) (E); Milton S. Katz, *Ban the Bomb* (1986); Jeffrey A. Larson and James M. Smith, eds., *Historical Dictionary of Arms Control and Disarmament* (2005) (D); Kendrick Oliver, *Kennedy, MacMillan, and the*

Nuclear Test Ban Treaty, 1961–63 (1998); Henry D. Sokoloski, *Best of Intentions* (2001); Stockholm International Peace Research Institute, *SIPRI Yearbook: International Armaments and Disarmament* (1969–) (AS and S); David Tal, *The American Nuclear Disarmament Dilemma, 1945–1963* (2008) United Nations, *Disarmament Yearbook* (1976–) (AS); Lawrence S. Wittner, *The Struggle Against the Bomb* (1993–2003).

Dollar Diplomacy: Emily S. Rosenberg, *Missionaries to the World* (1999); Cyrus Veeser, *A World Safe for Capitalism* (2002).

Drug Trafficking: Bruce M. Bagley, ed., *Drug Trafficking Research in the Americas* (1997) (B); Ted Galen Carpenter, *Bad Neighbor Policy* (2003); Richard Crandall, *Driven by Drugs* (2002); Jurg Gerber and Eric L. Benson, *Drug War, American Style* (2001); Donald J. Mabry, ed., *The Latin American Narcotics Trade and U.S. National Security* (1989); Scott B. MacDonald and Bruce Zagaris, eds., *International Handbook on Drug Control* (1992) (E); Alfred W. McCoy, *The Politics of Heroin* (2003) and *War on Drugs* (1992); Katherine Meyer and Terry Parssinen, *Webs of Smoke* (2002); Peter Dale Scott, *Drugs, Oil, and War* (2002); Arnold H. Taylor, *American Diplomacy and the Narcotics Traffic, 1900–1931* (1969); William O. Walker III, *Drug Control in the Americas* (1981), ed., *Drugs in the Western Hemisphere* (1996), and *Opium and Foreign Policy* (1991).

Economic Relations and Business: William H. Becker and Samuel F. Wells, eds., *Economics and World Power* (1984); Alfred E. Eckes, Jr., *Opening America's Market* (1995); Niall Ferguson, *The Ascent of Money* (2008); Dana Frank, *Buy American* (1999); Michael J. Freeman, *Atlas of the World Economy* (1991) (A); Francis J. Gavin, *Gold, Dollars, and Power* (2003); Carolyn Gibson, *The McGraw-Hill Dictionary of International Trade* (1994) (E); Robert Gilpin, *Global Political Economy* (2002); Judith Goldstein, *Ideas, Interests, and American Trade Policy* (1993); Bernard Hoekman and Michel Kostecki, *The Political Economy of the World Trading System* (1996); John N. Ingham, *Biographical Dictionary of American Business Leaders* (1983) (BA); John N. Ingham and Lyness B. Feldman, *Contemporary American Business Leaders* (1990) (BA); Edward S. Kaplan and Thomas W. Ryley, *Prelude to Trade Wars* (1994); Diane Kunz, *Butter and Guns* (1997); Thelma Liesner, *One Hundred Years of Economic Statistics* (1989) (S); Charles R. Morris, *The Trillion Dollar Meltdown* (2008); Wahib Nasrallah, *United States Corporation Histories* (1991) (B); Timothy O'Donnell et al., eds., *World Economic Data* (1991) (S); James S. Olsen, *Dictionary of American Economic History* (1992) (E); Robert Soloman, *Money on the Move* (1999); Joan E. Spero and Jeffrey A. Hart, *The Politics of International Economic Relations* (1997); Amy Staples, *The Birth of Development* (2007); United Nations, *International Trade Statistics Yearbook* (1985– (AS and S), *World Economic Survey* (1955–) (AS and S), and *Yearbook of International Trade Statistics* (1950–1982) (AS and S); Malcolm Warner, ed., *International Encyclopedia of Business and Management* (1996) (E); Mira Wilkins, *The Emergence of Multinational Enterprise* (1970) and *The Maturing of Multinational Enterprise* (1975); Thomas W. Zeiler, *Free Trade, Free World* (1999).

Economic Sanctions and Export Controls: Alan P. Dobson, *U.S. Economic Statecraft for Survival, 1933-1999* (2002); Gary C. Hufbauer and Jeffrey J. Schott, *Economic Sanctions Reconsidered* (1990); William J. Long, *U.S. Export Control Policy* (1989); Donald Losman, *International Economic Sanctions* (1979); Homer E. Moyer, Jr., and Linda L. Mabry, *Export Controls as Instruments of Foreign Policy* (1988); R. T. Naylor, *Economic Warfare* (2001); Meghan O'Sullivan, *Shrewd Sanctions* (2003); Thomas G. Weiss, *Political Gain and Civilian Pain* (1998); Ka Zeng, *Trade Threats, Trade Wars* (2004).

Environment: Scott Barrett, *Environment and Statecraft* (2003); Lee-Anne Broadhead, *International Environmental Politics* (2002); Robert Broadman, *International Organization and the Conservation of Nature* (1981); Lester R. Brown et al., *State of the World* (1984–) (AS); Lynton K. Caldwell, *International Environmental Policy* (1990); André R. Cooper, Sr., ed., *Cooper's Comprehensive Environmental Desk Reference* (1996) (E); Kurkpatrick Dorsey, *The Dawn of Conservation Diplomacy* (1999); Thomas Friedman, *Hot, Flat, and Crowded* (2008); Michael T. Klare, *Rising Powers, Shrinking Planet* (2008); Fridtjof Nansen Institute (Norway), *Green Globe Yearbook* (1992–) (AS); John McCormick, *The Global Environment* (1995) and *Reclaiming Paradise: The Global Environmental Movement* (1989); Organisation for Economic Co-operation and Development, *The State of the Environment* (1991) (E and S); Robert Paehlke, ed., *Conservation and Environmentalism* (1995) (E); Kirkpatrick Sale, *The Green Revolution* (1993); Philip Shabecoff, *Earth Rising* (2000); Richard P. Tucker, *Insatiable Appetite* (2007); World Resources Institute, *Environmental Almanac* (1992) (E); World Resources Institute (or International Institute for Environment and Development), *World Resources* (1976–); Ernest Zedillo, ed., *Global Warming* (2008).

Ethics: Gerald Elfstrom, *Ethics for a Shrinking World* (1990); J. E. Hare and Carey B. Joynt, *Ethics and International Affairs* (1982); Dorothy V. Jones, *Code of Peace* (1991); Kenneth W. Thompson, ed., *Ethics and International Relations* (1985) and *Moral Dimensions of American Foreign Policy* (1984).

Ethnic Conflict: David Callahan, *Unwinnable Wars* (1997); Human Rights Watch, *Slaughter Among Neighbors* (1995); David A. Lake and Donald Rothchild, eds., *The International Spread of Ethnic Conflict* (1998); Robin M. Williams, Jr., *Wars Within* (2003); Stefan Wolff, *Ethnic Conflict* (2006).

Ethnic Groups and Immigration: Gerald Chaliand and Jean-Pierre Rageau, *The Penguin Atlas of Diasporas* (1995) (A); Francesco Cordasco, ed., *Dictionary of American Immigration History* (1990) (E);

Alexander DeConde, *Ethnicity, Race, and American Foreign Policy* (1992); Izumi Hirobe, *Japanese Pride, American Prejudice* (2001); R. Kent Rasmussen, ed., *Immigration in U.S. History* (2006); David M. Reimers, *Still the Golden Door* (1992); Abdul Aziz Said, ed., *Ethnicity and U.S. Foreign Policy* (1977); Tony Smith, *Foreign Attachments* (2000); Stephen Thernstrom, ed., *Harvard Encyclopedia of American Ethnic Groups* (1980) (E); Robert W. Tucker et al., eds., *Immigration and U.S. Foreign Policy* (1990).

Expansion: See "Imperialism," "Manifest Destiny and Imperialism," and "West (U.S) and Frontier."

Export-Import Bank: Frederick C. Adams, *Economic Diplomacy* (1976); William H. Becker, *The Market, the State, and the Export-Import Bank of the United States, 1934–2000* (2003); Richard E. Feinberg, *Subsidizing Success* (1982); Rita M. Rodriquez, ed., *The Export-Import Bank at Fifty* (1987).

Extraterritoriality: Wesley R. Fishel, *The End of Extraterritoriality* (1952); Dietr Lange and Gary Born, eds., *The Extraterritorial Application of National Laws* (1987); Elaine Scully, *Bargaining with the State from Afar* (2001).

Films, Television, and Cultural Expansion: Royce J. Ammon, *Global Television and the Shaping of World Politics* (1999); Robert Burgoyne, *Film Nation* (1997); David A. Cook, *Lost Illusions* (2000); Thomas Doherty, *Cold War, Cool Medium* (2003) and *Projections of War* (1999); Susan Jeffords, *Hard Bodies* (1993); James F. Larson, *Global Television and Foreign Policy* (1988); Thomas J. Saunders, *Hollywood in Berlin* (1994); Robert Brent Toplin, *Reel History* (2002).

Food Diplomacy and Relief: Kristin L. Ahlberg, *Transplanting the Great Society* (2008); Nicole Ball, ed., *World Hunger* (1981) (B); Raymond F. Hopkins and Donald J. Puchala, *Global Food Interdependence* (1980); Don Paarlberg, *Toward a Well-Fed World* (1988); Vernon W. Ruttan, ed., *Why Food Aid?* (1993); Hans W. Sinder et al., *Food Aid* (1987); Claire Stanford, ed., *World Hunger* (2007); Ross B. Talbott, *The Four World Food Agencies in Rome* (1990).

Foreign Aid: David H. Lumsdaine, *Moral Vision in International Politics* (1993); Robert A. Packenham, *Liberal America and the Third World* (1973); Roger Riddell, *Foreign Aid Reconsidered* (1987); Vernon W. Ruttan, *United States Development Assistance Policy* (1995).

Foreign Investment in the United States: Mira Wilkins, *The History of Foreign Investment in the United States to 1914* (1989).

French and Indian War: Fred Anderson, *Crucible of War* (2001); Frank W. Brecher, *Losing a Continent* (1998); Ronald J. Dale, *The Fall* of New France (2004); Jonathan Dull, *The French Navy and the Seven Years' War* (2005); Frank McLynn, *1759* (2004); Matt Schumann and Karl W. Schweizer, *The Seven Years' War* (2008); Seymour I. Schwartz, *The French and Indian War, 1754–1763* (1995) (E); Franz A.J. Szabo, *The Seven Years' War in Europe, 1756–1763* (2008).

Genocide: Patrick Brantlinger, *Dark Vanishings* (2003); Israel Charney, ed., *Genocide* (1988) (B) and *Encyclopedia of Genocide* (1999) (E); Ben Kiernan, *Blood and Soil* (2007); Leo Kuper, *Genocide* (1981); Lawrence J. LeBlanc, *The United States and the Genocide Convention* (1991); Samantha Power, *The Problem from Hell* (2002); Charles B. Stroozier and Michael Flynn, eds., *Genocide, War, and Human Survival* (1996); Benjamin A. Valentino, *Final Solutions* (2004). See also "Holocaust," "Humanitarian Relief and Intervention," and "War Crimes and Trials."

Good Neighbor Policy: Irwin Gellman, *Good Neighbor Diplomacy* (1979); David Green, *The Containment of Latin America* (1971); Fredrick B. Pike, *FDR's Good Neighbor Policy* (1995); Bryce Wood, *The Dismantling of the Good Neighbor Policy* (1985).

Health and Medical History of Leaders: Kenneth R. Crispell and Carlos F. Gomez, *Hidden Illness in the White House* (1988); Robert H. Ferrell, *Ill-Advised* (1992); Robert E. Gilbert, *The Mortal Presidency* (1992); Bert E. Park, *Ailing, Aged, Addicted* (1993) and *The Impact of Illness on World Leaders* (1986).

Health Organizations: Kelly Lee, *Historical Dictionary of the World Health Organization* (1998) (E); Javid Siddiqi, *World Health and World Politics* (1994); Paul Weindling, ed., *International Health Organizations and Movements* (1995).

Holocaust: Yehudi Bauer, *Rethinking the Holocaust* (2001); Richard Breitman, *Official Secrets* (1998); Richard Breitman and Alan M. Kraut, *American Refugee Policy and European Jewry* (1987); Henry L. Feingold, *Bearing Witness* (1995); Saul Friedlander, *The Years of Extermination* (2007); Martin Gilbert, *Auschwitz and the Allies* (1981); Israel Gutman, ed., *Encyclopedia of the Holocaust* (1990) (E); Deborah E. Lipstadt, *Beyond Belief* (1993); Michael R. Marrus, *The Holocaust in History* (1987); David Wyman, *The Abandonment of the Jews* (1984) and *Paper Walls* (1968).

Hostage–Taking: Russell D. Buhite, *Lives at Risk* (1995); David R. Farber, *Taken Hostage* (2005); David P. Houghton, *U.S. Foreign Policy and the Iran Hostage Crisis* (2001); Russell Lee Moses, *Freeing the Hostages* (1996).

Humanitarian Relief and Intervention: Gary J. Best, *Freedom's Battle* (2008); Robert C. DiPrizo, *Armed Humanitarians* (2002); David

Kennedy, *The Dark Side of Virtue* (2004); Larry Minear and Thomas G. Weiss, *Humanitarian Politics* (1995); David Rieff, *Bed for the Night* (2002); Robert I. Rotberg and Thomas G. Weiss, eds., *From Massacres to Genocide* (1996).

Human Rights: Amnesty International, *The Amnesty International Report* (1977–) (AS); Elizabeth Borgwardt, *A New Deal for the World* (2007); Peter R. Baehr, *The Role of Human Rights in Foreign Policy* (1994); Jack Donnelly and Rhoda E. Howard, eds., *International Handbook of Human Rights* (1987) (E); Carole Fink, *Defending the Rights of Others* (2007); Charles Humana, *World Human Rights Guide* (1992); Human Rights Watch, *World Report* (1983–) (AS); Michael Ignatieff, *American Exceptionalism and Human Rights* (2005); Natalie Kaufman, *Human Rights Treaties and the Senate* (1990); William Korey, *The Promises We Keep* (1993); Edward Lawson, *Encyclopedia of Human Rights* (1991) (E); A. Glenn Mower, *Human Rights and American Foreign Policy* (1987) and *The United States, the United Nations, and Human Rights* (1979); A. H. Robertson and J. G. Merrills, *Human Rights in the World* (1997) (B); Roger Normand and Sarah Zaidi, *Human Rights at the UN* (2008); David Robertson, *A Dictionary on Human Rights* (2004) (E); Lars Schoultz, *Human Rights and United States Policy Toward Latin America* (1981); Kathryn Sikkink, *Mixed Signals* (2004).

Ideology: Richard J. Barnet, *Roots of War* (1972); David C. Engerman, *Staging Growth* (2003); John Fousek, *To Lead the Free World* (2002); Joan Hoff, *A Faustian Foreign Policy* (2008); Richard T. Hughes, *Myths America Lives By* (2003); Michael H. Hunt, *Ideology and U.S. Foreign Policy* (1987); Jacob Heilbrun, *They Knew They Were Right* (2008) (neoconservatives); Christina Klein, *Cold War Orientalism* (2003); Michael E. Latham, *Modernization as Ideology* (2000); Ron Robin, *The Making of the Cold War Enemy* (2001); William A. Williams, *The Tragedy of American Diplomacy* (1962); Nicholas Xenos, *Cloaked in Virtue* (2008).

Imperialism: Michael B. Brown, *The Economics of Imperialism* (1974); Philip Darby, *Three Faces of Imperialism* (1987); Michael Doyle, *Empires* (1986); Niall Ferguson, *Empire* (2003) and *Colossus* (2006); Peter L. Hahn and Mary Ann Heiss, eds., *Empire and Revolution* (2001); Eric Hinderaker, *Elusive Empires* (1997); Amy Kaplan, *The Anarchy of Empire in the Making of U.S. Culture* (2002); Gabriel Kolko, *The Roots of American Foreign Policy* (1969); Frank Ninkovich, *The United States and Imperialism* (2001); Marc J. O'Reilly, *Unexceptional* (2008); Tony Smith, *The Pattern of Imperialism* (1981).

Indians (Native Americans): Brian W. Dippie, *The Vanishing American* (1982); Michael Green, *The Politics of Indian Removal* (1982); Barry Klein, ed., *Reference Encyclopedia of the American Indian* (1993) (E); Calvin Martin, ed., *The American Indian and the Problem of History* (1986); Jane T. Merritt, *At the Crossroads* (2003);

Francis Paul Prucha, *Atlas of American Indian Affairs* (1990) (A) and *The Indian in American Society* (1985); Jayme Sokolow, *The Great Encounter* (2002); Paul Stuart, *Nation Within a Nation* (1987) (S); Carl Waldman, *Atlas of the North American Indian* (1985) (A); Anthony F. C. Wallace, *Jefferson and the Indians* (2001); Philip Weeks, *"They Made Us Many Promises"* (2002).

Intelligence, CIA, and Covert Action: David Alvarez, *Secret Messages* (2000); Christopher Andrew, *For the President's Eyes Only* (1995); Christopher Andrew and Vasili Mitrokhin, *The World Was Going Our Way* (2005); T. H. Bagley, *Spy Wars* (2007); James Bamford, *Body of Secrets* (2001) and *The Shadow Factory* (2008); Richard Breitman, *U.S. Intelligence and the Nazis* (2005); Marjorie W. Cline et al., *Scholar's Guide to Intelligence Literature* (1983) (B); Steve Coll, *Ghost Wars* (2004); George C. Constantinides, *Intelligence & Espionage* (1983) (B); Arthur B. Darling, *The Central Intelligence Agency* (1990); John Diamond, *The CIA and the Culture of Failure* (2008); William J. Daugherty, *Executive Secrets* (2004); Melvin A. Goodman, *The Failure of Intelligence* (2008); Kristian Gustafson, *Hostile Intent* (2007); John Earl Haynes, *Early Cold War Spies* (2006); Rhodri Jeffreys-Jones, *The CIA and American Democracy* (2003) and *Cloak and Dollar* (2002); Rhodri Jeffreys-Jones and Andrew Lownie, eds., *North American Spies* (1991); Loch K. Johnson, *Secret Agencies* (1996) and *Bombs, Bugs, Drugs, and Thugs* (2000); Loch Johnson and James Wirtz, eds., *Intelligence and National Security* (2007); Stephen Kinzer, *Overthrow* (2006); Stephen F. Knott, *Secret and Sanctioned* (1996); Mark Lowenthal, *U.S. Intelligence* (1992); Thomas Mahnken, *Uncovering the Ways of War* (2002); Ernest R. May, ed., *Knowing One's Enemies* (1985); Ernest R. May et al., *Dealing with Dictators* (2006); Alfred W. McCoy, *A Question of Torture* (2006); Elizabeth McIntosh, *Sisterhood of Spies* (2009); Gregory Mitrovich, *Undermining the Kremlin* (2000); John Jacob Nutter, *CIA's Black Ops* (2008); Norman Polmar and Thomas B. Allen, *Spy Book* (2004); Neal H. Petersen, *American Intelligence, 1775–1990* (1992) (B); Walter Pforzheimer, *Bibliography of Intelligence Literature* (1985) (B); Thomas Powers, *Intelligence Wars* (2003); John Prados, *The Presidents' Secret Wars* (1986) and *Safe for Democracy* (2006); John Ranelagh, *The Agency* (1986); James Risen, *State of War* (2006); Jeffrey T. Richelson, *A Century of Spies* (1995), *Spying on the Bomb* (2006), and *The U.S. Intelligence Community* (1995); Frank J. Smist, Jr., *Congress Oversees the United States Intelligence Community* (1994); Bradley F. Smith, *The Shadow Warriors* (1983); Michael J. Sullivan, *American Adventurism Abroad* (2008); William Taubman, *Secret Empire* (2003); Athan Theoharis, *The Quest for Absolute Security* (2007); Evan Thomas, *The Very Best Men* (1995); Gregory F. Treverton, *Covert Action* (1987); David Tucker and Christopher Lamb, *United States Special Operations* (2008); Nigel West, *Historical Dictionary of Cold War Counterintelligence* (2007) (E); Hugh Wilford, *The Mighty Wurlitzer* (2007); Robin W. Winks, *Clock & Gown* (1987).

International Law and Hague Conferences: Robert L. Bledsoe and Boleslaw A. Boczek, *The International Law Dictionary* (1987) (E); Calvin D. Davis, *The United States and the First Hague Conference* (1962) and *The United States and the Second Hague Conference* (1976); Ingrid Delupis, ed., *Bibliography of International Law* (1975) (B); Richard Falk et al., eds., *International Law* (1985); James Fox, *Dictionary of International and Comparative Law* (1991) (E); Daniel P. Moynihan, *The Law of Nations* (1990).

International Monetary Fund and System: Michael N. Barnett, *Rules for the World* (2004); Barry Eichengreen, *Globalizing Capital* (1996); Harold James, *International Monetary Cooperation Since Bretton Woods* (1996); Mary E. Johnson, *The International Monetary Fund* (1993) (B); Robert Soloman, *Money on the Move* (1999); Jean Tirole, *Financial Crises, Liquidity, and the International Monetary Fund System* (2002); Ngaire Woods, *The Globalizers* (2006).

International Organizations: Sheikh Ali, *The International Organization and World Order Dictionary* (1992) (E); John Boli and George M. Thomas, eds., *Constructing World Culture* (1999); George W. Baer, ed., *International Organizations, 1918–1945* (1981) (B); Akira Iriye, *Global Community* (2002); Edward C. Luck, *Mixed Messages* (1999); Edward J. Osmanczyk, *The Encyclopedia of the United States and International Organizations* (1990) (E); Hans-Albrecht Schraepler, *Directory of International Organizations* (1996); Union of International Associations, *Yearbook of International Organizations* (1948–) (AS).

Isolationism: Wayne S. Cole, *Roosevelt and the Isolationists* (1983); Justus D. Doenecke, *Anti-Intervention* (1987) (B), *The Battle Against Intervention, 1939–1941* (1997), and *Storm on the Horizon* (2001); Thomas N. Guinsburg, *The Pursuit of Isolationism in the United States Senate* (1982); Manfred Jonas, *Isolationism in America, 1935–1941* (1966).

Journalism and Media: James L. Baughman, *Henry R. Luce and the Rise of the American News Media* (1988); Robert Herzstein, *Henry R. Luce* (1994) and *Henry R. Luce, Time, and the American Crusade in Asia* (2005); Gerd Horten, *Radio Goes to War* (2002); Joseph P. McKerns, ed., *Biographical Dictionary of American Journalism* (1989) (BA); Brigitte Lebens Nacos, *The Press, Presidents, and Crises* (1990); Johanna Neuman, *Lights, Camera, War* (1995); David D. Permutter, *Photojournalism and Foreign Policy* (1998); Arch Puddington, *Broadcasting Freedom* (2000); Michael Schudson, *The Power of News* (1995); Simon Serfaty, *The Media and Foreign Policy* (1990); Michael S. Sweeney, *Secrets of Victory* (2000); William H. Taft, ed., *Encyclopedia of Twentieth-Century Journalists* (1986) (BA); John Tebbel and Sarah Miles Watts, *The Press and the Presidency* (1985).

Labor: Robert W. Cherny and William Issel, *American Labor and the Cold War* (2004); Philip S. Foner, *U.S. Labor Movement and Latin America* (1988); Ronald Radosh, *American Labor and United States Foreign Policy* (1969); Federico Romero, *The United States and the European Trade Union Movement, 1944–1951* (1992); Shelton Stromquist, ed., *Labor's Cold War* (2008); Edmund F. Wehrle, *Between a River and a Mountain* (2005).

Law of the Sea: Jack N. Barkenbus, *Deep Seabed Resources* (1979); Ann L. Hollick, *U.S. Foreign Policy and the Law of the Sea* (1981); Ralph B. Levering and Miriam L. Levering, *Citizen Action for Global Change* (2002); D. P. O'Connell, *The International Law of the Sea* (1982); Clyde Sanger, *Ordering the Oceans* (1987); United Nations, *The Law of the Sea* (1991) (B); Harry N. Scheiber, ed., *The Law of the Sea* (2000).

League of Nations: John Milton Cooper, *Breaking the Heart of the World* (2001); Warren F. Kuehl, *Seeking World Order* (1969); F. S. Northedge, *The League of Nations* (1986).

Manifest Destiny and Expansion: Laura E. Gomez, *Manifest Destinies* (2007); Amy S. Greenberg, *Manifest Manhood and the Antebellum American Empire* (2005); Thomas R. Hietala, *Manifest Design* (2003); Reginald Horsman, *Race and Manifest Destiny* (1981); Linda S. Hudson, *Mistress of Manifest Destiny* (2001); Robert W. Johannsen, ed., *Manifest Destiny* (1998); Robert E. May, *Manifest Destiny's Underworld* (2002); Christopher Morris and Sam W. Haynes, eds., *Manifest Destiny and Empire* (1998); Ivan Musicant, *Empire by Default* (1998); Frank Ninkovich, *The United States and Imperialism* (2001); Walter Nugent, *Habits of Empire* (2008); Anders Stephanson, *Manifest Destiny* (1995); Albert K. Weinberg, *Manifest Destiny* (1935).

Marshall Plan: John Bledsoe Bonds, *Bipartisan Strategy* (2002); Michael J. Hogan, *The Marshall Plan* (1987); Brian McKenzie, *Remaking France* (2005); Alan S. Milward, *The Reconstruction of Western Europe, 1945–51* (1984); Martin A. Schain, ed., *The Marshall Plan* (2001); Imanuel Wexler, *The Marshall Plan Revisited* (1983).

Marine Corps, U.S.: Joseph H. Alexander et al., *A Fellowship of Valor* (1997); Allan R. Millett, *Semper Fidelis* (1980).

Merchant Marine: John A. Butler, *Sailing on Friday* (1997); Rene De La Pedraja, *A Historical Dictionary of the U.S. Merchant Marine and Shipping Industry* (1994) (E).

Military, U.S. Army, and Wars: William M. Arkin et al., *Encyclopedia of the U.S. Military* (1990) (E); Andrew Bacevich, *The Limits of Power* (2008); Benjamin R. Beede, *Military and Strategic Policy* (1990) (B); Susan Brewer, *Why America Fights* (2009); John W. Chambers, *To Raise an Army* (1987) and *Oxford Companion to American Military History* (1999) (E); Edward M. Coffman, *The Regulars* (2005);

E. Ernest Dupuy and Trevor N. Dupuy, *The Harper Encyclopedia of Military History* (1993) (E); John C. Fredriksen, *Shield of the Republic/Sword of Empire* (1990) (B); Kenneth J. Hagan and William R. Roberts, eds., *Against All Enemies* (1986); Christopher Layne, *The Peace of Illusions* (2006); Robin Higham and Donald J. Mrozek, eds., *A Guide to the Sources of United States Military History* (1975–) (B); International Institute for Strategic Studies, *Strategic Survey* (1966–) (AS) and *The Military Balance* (1959/1960–) (AS); *International Military and Defense Encyclopedia* (1993) (E); John E. Jessup and Louise B. Ketz, eds., *Encyclopedia of the American Military* (1994) (E); Michael Lind, *The American Way of Strategy* (2008); Brian M. Linn, *The Echo of Battle* (2008); Allan R. Millett and Peter Maslowski, *For the Common Defense* (1994); Jay M. Shafritz et al., eds., *Dictionary of Military Science* (1989); Roger J. Spiller and Joseph G. Dawson III, eds., *Dictionary of American Military Biography* (1984) (BA); Jerry K. Sweeney, ed., *A Handbook of American Military History* (1996) (E); Herbert K. Tillema, *International Armed Conflict Since 1945* (1991) (B); Peter G. Tsouras et al., *The United States Army* (1991) (E); Cynthia Watson, *U.S. National Security Policy Groups* (1990) (E); Russell F. Weigley, *History of the United States Army* (1984).

Minerals: Alfred E. Eckes, *The United States and the Global Struggle for Minerals* (1979); Jordan E. Helmreich, *Gathering Rare Ores* (1986); David Hollett, *More Precious Than Gold* (2008); Mark Kurlansky, *Salt: A World History* (2002); Ronnie Lipschutz, *When Nations Clash* (1989).

Missionaries: Henry Bowden, *Dictionary of American Religious Biography* (1993) (BA); John K. Fairbank, ed., *The Missionary Enterprise in China and America* (1974); Gael Graham, *Gender, Culture, and Christianity* (1995); Patricia Hill, *The World Their Household* (1985); Jane Hunter, *The Gospel of Gentility* (1984); William R. Hutchison, *Errand to the World* (1987); Paul A. Varg, *Missionaries, Chinese, and Diplomats* (1958).

Monroe Doctrine: James E. Lewis, Jr., *The American Union and the Problem of Neighborhood* (1998); Ernest R. May, *The Making of the Monroe Doctrine* (1975); Gretchen Murphy, *Hemispheric Imaginings* (2004); Gaddis Smith, *The Last Years of the Monroe Doctrine* (1994).

Nation-Building: James Dobbins et al., *America's Role in Nation-Building* (2003); Cynthia Watson, *Nation-building* (2004).

National Security Council: Gerry Andrianopoulos, *Kissinger and Brzezinski* (1991); John Prados, *Keepers of the Keys* (1991); David Rothkopf, *Running the World* (2005); Andrew Preston, *War Council* (2006); Douglas Stuart, *Creating the National Security State* (2008); Bromley K. Smith, *Organizational History of the National Security Council During the Kennedy and Johnson Administrations* (1988).

Navy, U.S., and Sea Power: George W. Baer, *One Hundred Years of Sea Power* (1994); James C. Bradford, *Admirals of the New Steel Navy* (1990), *Captains of the Old Steam Navy* (1986), and *Command Under Sail* (1985); William B. Cogan, *Dictionary of Admirals of the United States Navy* (1989) (BA); Paolo E. Coletta, *A Selected and Annotated Bibliography of American Naval History* (1988) (B); Paolo E. Coletta et al., eds., *American Secretaries of the Navy* (1980) (BA); Michael J. Crawford and Christine F. Hughes, *The Reestablishment of the Navy, 1787–1801* (1995) (B); Kenneth J. Hagan, ed., *In Peace and War* (2008) and *This People's Navy* (1991); John B. Hattendorf and Lynn C. Hattendorf, *A Bibliography of the Works of Alfred Thayer Mahan* (1986) (B); David F. Long, *Gold Braid and Foreign Relations* (1988); Barbara A. Lynch and John E. Vajda, *United States Naval History* (1993) (B); Franklin D. Margiotta, ed., *Brassey's Encyclopedia of Naval Forces and Warfare* (1996) (E); Nathaniel Philbrick, *Sea of Glory* (2003); Jack Sweetman, ed., *American Naval History* (1984) (C); Bruce W. Watson and Susan M. Watson, *The United States Navy* (1991) (E).

Neutralism and Nonalignment: H. W. Brands, *The Specter of Neutralism* (1989); K. C. Chaudhary, *Non-aligned Summitry* (1988); Steven R. David, *Choosing Sides* (1991); Richard L. Jackson, *The Non-aligned, the UN, and the Superpowers* (1983); Lawrence W. Martin, ed., *Neutralism and Nonalignment* (1962).

Nobel Peace Prize: Irwin Abrams, *The Nobel Peace Prize and the Laureates* (1988); Oaula McGuire, ed., *Nobel Prize Winners Supplement* (1992); Judith Stiehm, *Champions for Peace* (2006); Tyler Wasson, ed., *Nobel Prize Winners* (1987).

North American Free Trade Agreement (NAFTA): Maxwell A. Cameron and Brian W. Tomlin, *The Making of NAFTA* (2001); Allan Metz, *A NAFTA Bibliography* (1996) (B); John R. Macarthur, *The Selling of "Free Trade"* (2002); John S. Odell, ed., *Negotiating Trade* (2006); William A. Orme, Jr., *Understanding NAFTA* (1996); Maryse Robert, *Negotiating NAFTA* (2002); Jerry M. Rosenberg, *Encyclopedia of the North American Free Trade Agreement* (1984) (E).

North Atlantic Treaty Organization (NATO): Ronald A. Asmus, *Opening NATO's Door* (2002); Timothy Ireland, *Creating the Entangling Alliance* (1981); Robert S. Jordan, Jr., ed., *Generals in International Politics* (1987); Lawrence S. Kaplan, *NATO 1948* (2007), *NATO United, NATO Divided* (2004), and *The Long Entanglement* (1999); Augustus R. Norton et al., *NATO* (1985) (B); S. V. Papacosma et al., *NATO After Fifty Years* (2001); S. V. Papacosma and Mary Ann Heiss, *NATO and the Warsaw Pact* (2008); Joseph Smith, ed., *The Origins of NATO* (1990).

Nuclear Arms: Timothy Botti, *Ace in the Hole* (1996); Paul Boyer, *By the Bomb's Early Light* (1985); McGeorge Bundy, *Danger and*

Survival (1990); Joseph Cirincione, *Bomb Scare* (2008); Campbell Craig, *Destroying the Village* (1998); Gerard J. De Groot, *The Bomb: A Life* (2005); Robert A. Divine, *The Sputnik Challenge* (1993); Lawrence Freedman, *The Evolution of Nuclear Strategy* (1989); Gregg Herken, *Counsels of War* (1985); David Holloway, *The Soviet Union and the Arms Race* (1984); Robert S. Morris, *Racing for the Bomb* (2002); John Newhouse, *War and Peace in the Nuclear Age* (1989); Septimus Paul, *Nuclear Rivals* (2000); William G. M. Pearson, *The Nuclear Arms Race* (1989) (E); Ronald E. Powaski, *March to Armageddon* (1987) and *Return to Armageddon* (2000); Richard Rhodes, *Arsenals of Folly* (2007); Scott D. Sagan, *The Limits of Safety* (1993); Stephen I. Schwartz, ed., *Atomic Audit* (1998); S. S. Schweber, *In the Shadow of the Bomb* (2000); Richard Smoke, *National Security and the Nuclear Dilemma* (1987); Spencer R. Weart, *Nuclear Fear* (1988); Allan M. Winkler, *Life Under a Cloud* (1993).

Oil: M. A. Adelman, *The Genie out of the Bottle* (1995); Jeremy Leggett, *Carbon War* (2002); Michael T. Klare, *Blood and Oil* (2005); David S. Painter, *Oil and the American Century* (1986); Stephen J. Randall, *United States Foreign Oil Policy, 1919–1984* (1985); Anthony Sampson, *The Seven Sisters* (1991); Fiona Venn, *Oil Diplomacy in the Twentieth Century* (1986); Daniel Yergin, *The Prize* (1991).

Olympics: Allen Guttmann, *The Games Must Go On* (1984) and *The Olympics* (1992); Christopher R. Hill, *Olympic Politics* (1996); Kristine Toohey, *Olympic Games* (2000); David Wallechinsky, *The Complete Book of the Summer Olympics* (1996) (E) and *The Complete Book of the Winter Olympics* (1993) (E).

Organization of American States (OAS): David Sheinin, *The Organization of American States* (1996) (B).

Organization of Petroleum Exporting Countries (OPEC): M. E. Ahrari, *OPEC* (1986); Albert L. Danielson, *The Evolution of OPEC* (1982); Ian Skeet, *OPEC* (1988).

Peace Corps: Fritz Fischer, *Making Them Like Us* (1998); Elizabeth Cobbs Hoffman, *All You Need Is Love* (1998); T. Zane Reeves, *The Politics of the Peace Corps & Vista* (1988); Gerald T. Rice, *Bold Experiment* (1985); Robert Ridinger, *The Peace Corps* (1989) (B): D. David Searles, *The Peace Corps Experience* (1997).

Peacekeeping: Jane Boulden, *Peace Enforcement* (2002); Paul F. Diehl, *International Peacekeeping* (1993); William J. Durch, ed., *The Evolution of UN Peacekeeping* (1993); Frederick H. Fleitz, Jr., *Peacekeeping Fiascoes of the 1990s* (2002); Rachel Gisselquist, *To Rid the Scourge of War* (2003); Alan James, *Peacekeeping in International Politics* (1990); Zisk Martin, *Enforcing the Peace* (2003). William G. O'Neill, *New Challenge for Peacekeepers* (2004).

Peace Movements: Harriet Hyman Alonso, *Peace as a Women's Issue* (1993); Scott H. Bennett, *Radical Pacifism* (2003); Peter Brock, *Pacifism in the United States from the Colonial Era to the First World War* (1968); Peter Brock and Nigel Young, *Pacifism in the Twentieth Century* (1999); Charles Chatfield, *The American Peace Movement* (1992); Charles DeBenedetti, ed., *Peace Heroes in Twentieth Century America* (1986) and *The Peace Reform in American History* (1980); Matthew Evangelista, *Unarmed Forces* (1999); Michael S. Foley, *Confronting the War Machine* (2003); Catherine Foster, *Women for All Seasons* (1989); Charles F. Howlett, *The American Peace Movement* (1990) (B); Rhodri Jeffreys-Jones, *Peace Now!* (1999); Harold Josephson et al., eds., *Biographical Dictionary of Modern Peace Leaders* (1985) (BA); Robert Kleidman, *Organizing for Peace: Neutrality, the Test Ban, and the Freeze* (1993); Elvin Laszlo and Jong Youl Yoo, eds., *World Encyclopedia of Peace* (1986) (E); Robert S. Meyer, *Peace Organizations Past and Present* (1988) (E); David S. Patterson, *Toward a Warless World* (1976); Nancy L. Roberts, *American Peace Writers, Editors, and Periodicals* (1991) (BA); Lawrence S. Wittner, *Rebels Against War* (1984) and *The Struggle Against the Bomb* (1993–2003); Valarie H. Ziegler, *The Advocates of Peace in Antebellum America* (1992).

Pearl Harbor, 1941: Stanley L. Falk, "Pearl Harbor," *Naval History* (1988) (B); Richard F. Hill, *Hitler Attacks Pearl Harbor* (2002); Robert W. Love, Jr., ed., *Pearl Harbor Reexamined* (1990); Martin V. Melosi, *The Shadow of Pearl Harbor* (1977); Frank P. Mintz, *Revisionism and the Origins of Pearl Harbor* (1985); James W. Morley, ed., *The First Confrontation* (1995); Gordon W. Prange, *Pearl Harbor* (1986); Emily Rosenberg, *A Date Which Will Live* (2003); Myron J. Smith, Jr., *Pearl Harbor* (1991) (B).

Philanthropy and Foundations: Robert Arnove, *Philanthropy and Cultural Imperialism* (1980); Edward H. Berman, *The Influence of the Carnegie, Ford, and Rockefeller Foundations on American Foreign Policy* (1983); Marcos Cueto, ed., *Missionaries of Science: The Rockefeller Foundation and Latin America* (1994); Robert L. Daniel, *American Philanthropy in the Near East, 1820–1960* (1970); Raymond Fosdick, *The Story of the Rockefeller Foundation* (1989); Helen Laville, *Cold War Women* (2002).

Population: *The Encyclopedia of Global Population and Demographics* (1998) (E); Matthew Connelly, *Fatal Misconception* (2008); William Peterson and Renee Peterson, *Dictionary of Demography* (1986) (E).

President (General): Eric Alterman, *When Presidents Lie* (2004); James Barber, *The Presidential Character* (1992); Michael R. Beschloss, *Presidential Courage* (2007); Meena Bose, *Shaping and Signaling Presidential Policy* (1998); J. Garry Clifford and Theodore A. Wilson, eds., *Presidents, Diplomats, and Other Mortals* (2007); Alexander DeConde,

Presidential Machismo (2000); Robert U. Goehlert and Fenton S. Martin, *The Presidency* (1985) (B); Louis Gould, *The Modern American Presidency* (2003); Stephen Graubard, *Command of Office* (2004); Mark Grossman, *Encyclopedia of the United States Cabinet* (E) (2000); Dale R. Herspring, *The Pentagon and the Presidency* (2005); Gary Hess, *Presidential Decisions for War* (2001); George T. Kurian, *A Historical Guide to the U.S. Government* (1997) (E); Leonard W. Levy and Louis Fisher, eds., *Encyclopedia of the American Presidency* (1993) (E); Theodore Lowi, *The Personal President* (1985); John E. Mueller, *War, Presidents, and Public Opinion* (1973); Anna K. Nelson, ed., *The Policy Makers* (2009); Richard E. Neustadt, *Presidential Power and the Modern Presidents* (1990); Richard M. Pious, *Why Presidents Fail* (2008); Arthur M. Schlesinger, Jr., *The Imperial Presidency* (1973) and *War and the American Presidency* (2004); Robert Sobel, ed., *Biographical Directory of the United States Executive Branch, 1774–1977* (1977) (BA).

Privateering: Donald B. Chidsey, *The American Privateers* (1962); Reuben E. Stivers, *Privateers and Volunteers* (1975); Carl E. Swanson, *Predators and Prizes* (1991).

Propaganda and Public Diplomacy: Laura A. Belmonte, *Selling the American Way* (2008); Lori Lyn Bogle, *The Pentagon's Battle for the American Mind* (2004); Nicholas Cull, *Selling War* (1995); Robert Cole, *The Encyclopedia of Propaganda* (1997) (E); Andrew Defty, *Britain, America, and Anti-Communist Propaganda, 1945–1953* (2004); Walter Hixson, *Parting the Curtain* (1997); David F. Krugler, *The Voice of America and the Domestic Propaganda Battles, 1945–1953* (2000); Alexandre Lauien, *The Voice of America* (1988); Clayton D. Laurie, *The Propaganda Warriors* (1996); Gifford Malone, *Political Advocacy and Cultural Communication* (1988); Jarol B. Manheim, *Strategic Public Diplomacy and American Foreign Policy* (1994); Sig Mickelson, *America's Other Voice* (1983); Michael Nelson, *War of the Black Heavens* (1997); Caroline Page, *Propaganda and Foreign Policy in the 20th Century* (2007); Shawn J. Parry-Giles, *The Rhetorical Presidency, Propaganda, and the Cold War, 1945–1955* (2002); Holly C. Shulman, *The Voice of America* (1990); Chris Tudda, *The Truth is Our Weapon* (2006); Allen M. Winkler, *The Politics of Propaganda* (1978).

Public Opinion: Eric Alterman, *Who Speaks for America* (1998); Richard J. Barnet, *The Rockets' Red Glare* (1990); H. Schuyler Foster, *Activism Replaces Isolationism: U.S. Public Attitudes, 1940–1975* (1983); George Gallup, *The Gallup Poll: Public Opinion* (1972–) (AS and S); Ole R. Holsti, *Public Opinion and American Foreign Policy* (1996); David D. Newsom, *The Public Dimension of Foreign Policy* (1996); Melvin Small, *Democracy and Diplomacy* (1996). Robert Sobel, *The Impact of Public Opinion on U.S Foreign Policy Since Vietnam* (2001).

Race and Racism: Kate A. Baldwin, *Beyond the Color Line and Iron Curtain* (2002); Gerald Horne, *Race War* (2004); Michael L. Krenn,

ed., *Race and U.S. Foreign Policy* (1998); Yukiko Koshiro, *Transpacific Racisms* (1999); Paul Gordon Lauren, *Power and Prejudice* (1988); Eric L. Love, *Race over Empire* (2004); Hazel M. McFerson, *The Racial Dimension of American Overseas Colonial Policy* (1997); Jason C. Parker, *Brother's Keeper* (2008); Brenda Gayle Plummer, ed., *Window on Freedom* (2003); Cheryl Russell, ed., *Racial and Ethnic Diversity* (2002); George E. Shepherd, ed., *Racial Influence on American Foreign Policy* (1971); Jay A. Sigler, ed., *International Handbook on Race and Race Relations* (1987) (E); Megan Weinberg, *World Racism and Related Inhumanities* (1992); George White, *Holding the Line* (2005).

Red Cross: Nicholas O. Berry, *War and the Red Cross* (1997); Pierre Bossier, *From Solferino to Tsushima* (1985); John F. Hutchinson, *Champions of Charity* (1996).

Refugees: Anna Bramwell, ed., *Refugees in the Age of Total War* (1988); Gil Loescher, *Beyond Charity* (1993); Gil Loescher and John A. Scalan, *Calculated Kindness* (1986); J. Bruce Nichols, *The Uneasy Alliance: Religion, Refugee Work, and U.S. Foreign Policy* (1988); Michael S. Teitelbaum and Myron Weiner, eds., *Threatened Peoples, Threatened Borders* (1995); U.S. Committee on Refugees, *World Refugee Survey* (1980–) (AS).

Scientists and Science: Michael Adas, *Dominance by Design* (2006); Greta Jones, *Science, Politics and the Cold War* (1988); Clarence Lasby, *Operation Paperclip* (1971); Joseph Rotblat, ed., *Scientists, the Arms Race, and Disarmament* (1982).

Slave Trade and Slavery: David Brion Davis, *Inhuman Bondage* (2006); William Dusinberre, *Slavemaster President* (2003); Don E. Fehrenbacher, *The Slaveholding Republic* (2001); Randall Miller and John Smith, eds., *Dictionary of Afro-American Slavery* (1988) (E); Junius P. Rodriguez, ed., *The Historical Encyclopedia of World Slavery* (1997) (E).

The South (U.S.): Joseph A. Fry, *Dixie Looks Abroad* (2002); Alfred Hero, *The Southerner and World Affairs* (1965); Charles O. Lerche, *The Uncertain South* (1964); Tim Mathewson, *A Proslavery Foreign Policy* (2003); Tennant S. McWilliams, *The New South Faces the World* (1988); Peter Trubowitz, *Defining the National Interest* (1998).

Space and Satellites: William E. Burrows, *Deep Black* (1986); Walter A. McDougall, *The Heavens and the Earth* (1985); Jeffrey T. Richelson, *America's Secret Eyes in Space* (1990); Paul B. Stares, *The Militarization of Space* (1985).

Spanish-American-Cuban-Filipino War: Benjamin R. Beede, ed., *The War of 1898 and U.S. Interventions, 1899–1934* (1994) (B); James C. Bradford, ed., *Crucible of Empire* (1993); Kristin Hoganson,

Fighting for American Manhood (1998); Jerry Keenan, ed., *Encyclopedia of the Spanish-American and Philippine-American War* (E) (2001); Louis A. Peréz, Jr., *The War of 1898* (1998); Anne C. Venzon, *The Spanish-American War* (1990) (B).

Sports: David Goldblatt, *The Ball Is Round* (2008) (soccer); Allen Guttmann, *Games and Empires* (1994); Barbara Keys, *Globalizing Sports* (2006); Walter LaFeber, *Michael Jordan and the New Global Capitalism* (2002); Thomas W. Zeiler, *Ambassadors in Pinstripes* (2006).

Summit Conferences: Elmer Plischke, *Diplomat in Chief* (1986) and *Summit Diplomacy* (1958); Robert D. Putnam and Nicholas Bayne, *Hanging Together: The Seven-Power Summits* (1984); Gordon R. Weihmiller and Dusko Doder, *U.S.-Soviet Summits* (1986).

Tariffs and Protectionism: David A. Lake, *Power, Protection, and Free Trade* (1988); James M. Lutz, *Protectionism* (1988) (B); Paul Wolman, *Most Favored Nation* (1992); Thomas Zeiler, *American Trade and Power in the 1960s* (1992).

Terrorism: Susan K. Anderson et al., *Historical Dictionary of Terrorism* (2002) (E); Stephen Brill, *After* (2003); Richard J. Chasdi, *Tapestry of Terror* (2002); Anthony H. Cordesman, *Terrorism, Asymmetric Light Warfare, and Weapons of Mass Destruction* (2001); Martha Crenshaw and John Pimlott, eds., *Encyclopedia of World Terrorism* (1996) (E); Richard Crockett, *American Embattled* (2003); Christopher Dobson and Ronald Payne, *The Never Ending War* (1987); Norman Friedman, *Terrorism, Afghanistan, and America's New Way of War* (2003); Rohan Gunaratna, *Inside Al Qaeda* (2002); Dilip Hiro, *War Without End* (2002); Giles Kepel, *Jihad* (2002); Robert Kumamoto, *International Terrorism and American Foreign Relations, 1945–1976* (1999); Walter Laqueur, *The Age of Terrorism* (1987); Cecilia Menjívar and Néstor Rodriguez, *When States Kill* (2005); Edward F. Mickolus et al., *International Terrorism in the 1980s* (1989) (C), *Terrorism, 1988–1991* (1993) (C), and *Transnational Terrorism, 1968–1979* (1980) (C); Suzanne R. Ontiveros, *Global Terrorism* (1986) (B); Ahmed Rashid, *Jihad* (2002; Barry Rubin, ed., *The Politics of Terrorism* (1990); Mark Selden and Alvin Y. So, *War and State Terrorism* (2004); Jeffrey D. Simon, *The Terrorist Trap* (1994); Jessica Stern, *The Ultimate Terrorists* (1999); John R. Thackrah, *Encyclopedia of Terrorism and Political Violence* (1987) (E); Lawrence Wright, *The Looming Tower* (2006).

Threat Perception and Calculation: Noel E. Firth and James H. Noren, *Soviet Defense Spending: A History of CIA Estimates, 1950–1990* (1998); Robert H. Johnson, *Improbable Dangers* (1994).

Think Tanks: Donald E. Abelson, *American Think-Tanks and Their Role in US Foreign Policy, 1976–88* (1996); Peter Grose, *Continuing the*

Inquiry (1996); David M. Ricci, *The Transformation of American Politics* (1993); Robert D. Schulzinger, *The Wise Men of Foreign Affairs* (1984); Christopher Simpson, ed., *Universities and Empire* (1999); Bruce L. R. Smith, *The Rand Corporation* (1966); James A. Smith, *The Idea Brokers* (1991); Michael Wala, *The Council on Foreign Relations and American Foreign Policy in the Early Cold War* (1994).

Tourism and Travel: James Clifford, *Routes* (1997); Christopher Endy, *Cold War Holidays* (2004) (France); Cynthia Enloe, *Bananas, Beaches, and Bases* (1990); Maxine Fieffer, *Tourism in History* (1985); Marie-Franáoise Lanfant et al., *International Tourism* (1995); Sara Mills, *Discourses of Difference* (1991); Margaritte S. Shaffer, *See America First* (2001); David Spurr, *The Rhetoric of Empire* (1993); John Urry, *The Tourist Gaze* (1990).

United Nations: Carol Anderson, *Eyes Off the Prize* (2003); Joseph P. Baratta, *Strengthening the United Nations* (1987) (B); Seymour M. Finger, *American Ambassadors at the United Nations* (1987); Thomas M. Frank, *Nation Against Nation* (1985); Robert F. Gorman, *Great Debates at the United Nations* (2001); Max Harrelson, *Fires All Around the Horizon* (1989); Robert C. Hilderbrand, *Dumbarton Oaks* (1990); Evan Luard and Derek Herter, *The United Nations* (1993); Kumiko Matsuura et al., *Chronology and Fact Book of the United Nations, 1941–1991* (1992) (C); Edmund Jan Osmanczyk, *The Encyclopedia of the United Nations and International Relations* (1990) (E); Gary B. Ostrower, *The United States and the United Nations* (1998); William Preston, Jr., et al., *Hope and Folly* (1989) (UNESCO); Caroline Pruden, *Conditional Partners* (1998); Stephen Schlesinger, *Act of Creation* (2003).

War Crimes and Trials: Omar Bartov et al., eds., *Crimes of War* (2002); Gary Jonathan Bass, *Stay the Hand of Vengeance* (2002); Norman Cigar and Paul Williams, *Indictment at the Hague* (2002); Richard L. Lael, *The Yamashita Precedent* (1982); John R. Lewis, *Uncertain Judgment* (1979) (B); Timothy Maga, *Judgment at Tokyo* (2002); Philip R. Piccigallo, *The Japanese on Trial* (1979); Telford Taylor, *Nuremberg and Vietnam* (1970); Norman E. Tutorow, ed., *War Crimes, War Criminals, and War Crimes Trials* (1986) (B).

War of 1812: John C. Fredriksen, *Free Trade and Sailors' Rights* (1985) (B); John Latimer, *1812* (2007); Dwight L. Smith, *The War of 1812* (1985) (B).

War Powers: Louis Fischer, *Presidential War Power* (1995); Christopher N. May, *In the Name of War* (1989); Gary M. Stein and Morton H. Halperin, eds., *The U.S. Constitution and the Power to Go to War* (1994); John H. Sullivan, *The War Powers Resolution* (1982); Francis D. Wormuth and Edwin B. Firmage, *To Chain the Dog of War* (1989).

West (U.S.) and Frontier: William A. Beck and Ynez D. Haase, *Historical Atlas of the American West* (1989) (A); William Goetzmann and Glyndwr Williams, *The Atlas of North American Exploration* (1992) (A); J. Norman Heard, *Handbook of the American Frontier* (1987) (E); Adrian Johnson, *America Explored* (1974) (E); Howard R. Lamar, ed., *The New Encyclopedia of the American West* (1998) (E); Patricia Nelson Limerick et al., eds., *Trials* (1991); Clyde A. Milner III et al., eds., *The Oxford History of the American West* (1994) (E); Charles Phillips and Alan Axelrod, eds., *Encyclopedia of the American West* (1996) (E); Dan L. Thrapp, *The Encyclopedia of Frontier Biography* (1988–) (BA).

Women and Gender Issues: Homer L. Calkin, *Women in the Department of State* (1978); Kyle A. Courdileone, *Manhood and American Political Culture in the Cold War* (2005); Edward P. Crapol, ed., *Women and American Foreign Policy* (1992); Rebecca Grant and Kathleen Newland, eds., *Gender and International Relations* (1991); Human Rights Watch, *Global Report on Women's Human Rights* (1995); Susan Jeffords, *The Remasculinization of America* (1989); Rhodri Jeffreys-Jones, *Changing Differences* (1995); Nancy W. McGlen and Meredith Reid Sarkes, *Women in Foreign Policy* (1993); Linda Schott, *Reconstructing Women's Thoughts* (1997); Mari Yoshihara, *Embracing the East: White Women and American Orientalism* (2003).

World Court: Michael Dunne, *The United States and the World Court, 1920–1935* (1988); D. F. Fleming, *The United States and the World Court* (1945); Shabtai Rosenne, *The World Court* (1989) (E).

World's Fairs: John E. Findling, ed., *Historical Dictionary of World's Fairs and Expositions* (1990); Robert H. Haddow, *Pavilions of Plenty* (1997); Robert W. Rydell, *All the World's a Fair* (1987) and *World of Fairs* (1993); Robert W. Rydell and Nancy Gwinn, eds., *Fair Representations* (1994).

World-System Analysis: Thomas J. McCormick, *America's Half-Century* (1995); Immanuel Wallerstein, *Geopolitics and Geoculture* (1991), *The Modern World-System* (1974), *Politics of the World-Economy* (1984), and *World Inequality* (1975).

World War I: Arthur Banks, *A Military History Atlas of the First World War* (1975) (A); Martin Gilbert, *Atlas of World War I* (1994) (A); Holger H. Herwig and Neil M. Heyman, *Biographical Dictionary of World War I* (1982) (BA); George T. Kurian, *Encyclopedia of the First World War* (1990) (E); Stephen Pope and Elizabeth-Anne Wheal, *The Dictionary of the First World War* (1995) (E); Anne C. Venzon, ed., *The United States and the First World War* (1995) (B).

World War II: Marcel Baudot et al., eds., *The Historical Encyclopedia of World War II* (1980) (E); I. C. B. Dear and M. R. D. Foot, eds., *The Oxford Companion to World War II* (1995) (E); John Keegan, ed., *The Times Atlas of the Second World War* (1989) (A) and *World War II* (2000) (E); Williamson Murray and Allen Millet, *A War to Be Won* (2000); Norman Polmar and Thomas B. Allen, *World War II* (1991) (E); John J. Sbrega, *The War Against Japan* (1989) (B); U.S. Military Academy, *Campaign Atlas to the Second World War* (1980) (A); Peter Young, ed., *Atlas of the Second World War* (1973) (A); Gerhard Weinberg, *A World at Arms* (1995); David T. Zabecki, *World War II in Europe* (1997) (E).

Index

Italic page numbers indicate maps, photos, illustrations, or captions.